# ADVANCE PRAISE FOR

## *The Maryland Campaign of 1862*
## *Vol. 1: South Mountain*

"Ezra Carman's long-unpublished history of the 1862 Maryland Campaign is an essential source on the operations that produced the bloodiest day in American military history and largest surrender of U.S. troops before World War II and there is no one better qualified than Thomas Clemens to bring it to print. Not only does this volume make Carman's study broadly accessible to students of the war, but Clemens's many years studying the events of September 1862 and unmatched knowledge of Carman and his work enable him to skillfully and authoritatively explain and scrutinize Carman's take on events. In addition to being a magnificent contribution to literature on the Civil War, this outstanding book will also advance the process of securing Clemens a place alongside Carman and Harsh in the pantheon of Maryland Campaign scholars. I cannot recommend it highly enough."

— Ethan S. Rafuse, author of *McClellan's War: The Failure of Moderation in the Struggle for the Union* and *Antietam, South Mountain, and Harpers Ferry: A Battlefield Guide*

"The word 'indispensable' comes to mind whenever I think of the Carman manuscript, which I have used extensively in my own research. Carman's work is unparalleled, a rich balance of history and firsthand accounts of one of the most significant campaigns of the Civil War. Tom Clemens has done a masterful job editing and annotating this manuscript, and his footnotes alone are worth the price of admission. Researchers and students of the war will be forever in his debt."

— Bradley M. Gottfried, author of *The Maps of Gettysburg*, and a forthcoming atlas on the Maryland Campaign of 1862

"Tom Clemens has spent many long years poring over both the Carman manuscript and related letters and documents from other holdings to provide Civil War students with the most up-to-date version of Carman's Maryland Campaign epic. The past few decades have witnessed the publication of thousands of books on the Civil War. Only a slim handful stand the test of time. I can confidently conclude that this volume will remain one of the most important of the genre ever to be published."

— Ted Alexander, Historian, Antietam National Battlefield

# The
# Maryland Campaign
# of September 1862

## Vol. 1: South Mountain

### by Ezra Carman

Edited and annotated by

## Thomas G. Clemens

Savas Beatie
New York and California

© 2010 by Thomas G. Clemens

Cataloging-in-Publication Data is available from the Library of Congress.

ISBN 978-1-932714-81-4

05 04 03 02 01   5 4 3 2 1
First edition, first printing

SB

Published by
Savas Beatie LLC
521 Fifth Avenue, Suite 1700
New York, NY 10175

Editorial Offices:

Savas Beatie LLC
P.O. Box 4527
El Dorado Hills, CA 95762
Phone: 916-941-6896
(E-mail) editorial@savasbeatie.com

Savas Beatie titles are available at special discounts for bulk purchases in the United States by corporations, institutions, and other organizations. For more details, please contact Special Sales, P.O. Box 4527, El Dorado Hills, CA 95762, or you may e-mail us at sales@savasbeatie.com, or visit our website at www.savasbeatie.com for additional information.

To Ezra Ayres Carman, a soldier and historian who in the tradition of Thuycidides became an objective chronicler of his own war.

Also to those brave men North and South who, as the Maryland monument so aptly states, "offered their lives in maintenance of their principles."

May God bless them all.

This A.R. Waud woodcut is taken from the Oct. 25, 1862 issue of *Harpers Weekly* and depicts a fanciful version of the Union attack at Crampton's Gap being met with a strong Confederate defensive line. *Harpers Weekly*

# Contents

Contents (continued)

*Maps and Illustrations*

A gallery of photos and original maps by Gene Thorp
begins after page xx

# Foreword

"

Ezra Carman, a veteran of the battle and a member of the Antietam Battlefield Board, spent most of the 1890s composing 'The Maryland Campaign of 1862,'" wrote historian Joseph Harsh in the introduction to his seminal work *Taken at the Flood: Robert E. Lee and Confederate Strategy in the Maryland Campaign of 1862*. "His history is perhaps the best study produced by any participant of the war." Dr. Harsh went on to write that Carman's 1,800-page manuscript is "an invaluable source of anecdotes and insights that historians have barely begun to utilize."

Indeed, Carman's work is the bible on Antietam and one of the most detailed studies of any major Civil War campaign. Carman was both a participant in the Battle of Antietam and its principal scholar. He spent a lifetime studying America's bloodiest day, starting immediately after the battle by interviewing wounded soldiers in field hospitals from both sides, as well as local civilians. Carman's work has often been compared to that of John Bachelder. Like Carman, Bachelder also devoted much of his life to studying one battle (Gettysburg) and interviewing hundreds of participants. Unlike Carman, however, Bachelder never saw combat during the Civil War (and did not witness Gettysburg like Carman witnessed Antietam). In addition, modern scholars have questioned some of Bachelder's information and conclusions, particularly regarding troop positions at Gettysburg.

Scholarly use of Carman's work has been an evolutionary process. While Gettysburg scholars have had ready access to the Bachelder papers for years, Carman's papers remain scattered between five major repositories, with individual letters popping up frequently in other holdings. The late James Murfin listed the Carman manuscript in the bibliography of his groundbreaking study *The Gleam of Bayonets: The Battle of Antietam and Robert E. Lee's Maryland Campaign, September 1862*. A close perusal of his endnotes, though, reveals very few actual citations to that work. And then along came Stephen W. Sears with his critically acclaimed book *Landscape Turned Red: The Battle of Antietam.* Sears took the Carman research a bit further by referring to the several collections in the National Archives, the Carman letters at Dartmouth, and the manuscript housed at the Library of Congress.

Other historians have followed suit by tapping the rich holdings of Carman's papers. Popular author John Michael Priest utilized both the Carman manuscript at the Library of Congress and the so-called "Antietam Studies" at the National Archives for his books on the battles of South Mountain and Antietam. To date, the most extensive use of the Carman collections has been the three-volume study by the aforementioned Joseph Harsh. In 2008, Joseph Pierro, one of Harsh's graduate students at George Mason University, edited the Carman manuscript for Routledge Press. Pierro did a credible job providing annotated footnotes that both corrected errors in the text and explained more about events and individuals mentioned in the narrative.

Enter Thomas Clemens—a professor of history at Hagerstown Community College, a lifetime student of the Civil War and the Battle of Antietam, and another graduate student of Professor Harsh. Besides his classroom duties, Tom has spent more than three decades as a volunteer at Antietam National Battlefield. Here, he has done everything from delivering lectures to giving costumed interpretive talks on artillery, assisting in the park library, and working weekends with fellow preservationists to clear brush on the battlefield. Tom is also a founder and current President of SHAF: Save Historic Antietam Foundation. With his depth of knowledge and total immersion into the subject for the past decades, Tom could easily carry the nickname "Mr. Antietam."

Tom has spent many long years poring over both the Carman manuscript and related letters from other holdings to provide Civil War students with the most up-to-date version of Carman's Maryland Campaign story. With the Savas Beatie publication of *The Maryland Campaign of September 1862,* we have the convergence of two experts. Ezra Carman, the leading authority on the Maryland Campaign and Antietam, and Tom Clemens, who is easily this country's foremost authority on Ezra Carman.

The past few decades have witnessed the publication of thousands of books on the Civil War. Only a slim handful stands the test of time. I can confidently conclude that Tom Clemens' editing of the Carman manuscript will remain one of the most important of the genre ever to be published.

Ted Alexander
Historian, Antietam National Battlefield

# Ezra Carman and the
# Maryland Campaign of 1862

Ezra Ayres Carman, a Civil War veteran and self-taught historian, produced the most detailed and accurate narrative study of the Antietam Campaign. His work has guided all subsequent studies of the Maryland operations, provides the most accurate maps of the troop movements in the battle, and is still the basis for the current interpretive plan of Antietam National Battlefield. Although several treatments of Carman's manuscript have been circulated recently, none have sought to "deconstruct" his effort. Like any work of history, Carman's manuscript is only as good as his sources. One of the primary intents of this book is to discover, as far as possible, the sources Carman relied upon, how they influenced his writing, and the soundness of his conclusions.

The Antietam Battlefield Board, which Carman headed for many years, received nearly 2,000 letters from veterans of the campaign. Carman's friend and fellow historian John M. Gould of Maine gave him access to the more than 1,000 additional letters Gould received in his quest to resolve the controversy surrounding General Joseph Mansfield's death of September 17 at Antietam. Add to this wealth of information the published *Official Records of the Union and Confederate Armies in the War of the Rebellion*, articles by various commanders in the *Battles and Leaders* series that appeared in *Century Magazine*, and the memoirs and regimental histories that appeared before his death, and it is clear that Carman had access to a staggering amount of firsthand material. While I have not been completely successful in discovering every source Carman utilized, I have been able to identify and evaluate most of them and, by doing so, arrived at a much deeper understanding of why Carman wrote what he did. Before discussing the strengths and weaknesses of Carman's work, it is appropriate to discuss the man himself, and how he came to write this fascinating and vital document.

Ezra Ayres Carman was born February 27, 1834, in Oak Tree, a small town in Middlesex County, New Jersey. He was educated at Western Military Academy, Drenanon Springs, Kentucky, graduating as valedictorian of the class of 1855. That same year the school moved to Tennessee and eventually became the University of Tennessee. Carman moved with it and was appointed Assistant Professor of Mathematics for the term 1855-6. He also married that year but his wife, the former Louisa Salmon, died in childbirth. In 1858, Carman received his Master's degree from the University of Tennessee and with his newborn son, moved back to New Jersey to become a bookkeeper for T. A. Howell's Leather Manufacturing Company. There, he married Louisa's younger sister Ada and eventually had three children with her. This happiness was tempered by the death of their son John in 1860. It was also in New Jersey that Carman continued his interest in history and helped found the New Jersey Historical Society in Newark.[1]

In the election of 1860 Carman supported Lincoln and the Republican party. When war broke out, Carman considered applying his military training to New Jersey's service. He turned down an appointment as a captain in the 2nd New Jersey, a three-year regiment offered by New Jersey's Governor Charles S. Olden, due to ill health and his family responsibilities, including a newborn son. While visiting the 2nd New Jersey he witnessed the battle of Bull Run on July 21, 1861, and the panicked retreat of the Union forces. This incident ended Carman's reluctance to serve, and he was soon appointed by Governor Olden as lieutenant colonel of the 7th New Jersey Infantry. The colonel of the regiment was Joseph Revere, a grandson of Paul Revere. Carman evidently respected Revere in some traits, but later complained that Revere left him to do much of the training of the regiment.[2]

The 7th New Jersey was assigned in March of 1862 to Brigadier General Joseph Hooker's Division, Brigadier General Samuel Heintzelmen's Third Corps,

---

1   Solid information about Carman's early life is difficult to discover. His diary, Document M 1003 (hereafter referred to as Carman *Diary*), is part of the *Carman Papers* (Manuscript Group Series No. MG-1761) of the New Jersey Historical Society, Newark, New Jersey (hereinafter referred to as "*Carman Papers*, NJHS"), with later notes, contains some information about his early life. There is a short biography of Carman in the *Carman Papers*, NJHS, written by Eva Bilkes, which was evidently annotated by Carman's son Louis. This will be cited as "Bilkes Biography, NJHS." Carman's Pension Records File (RG-15, National Archives, Washington D.C.), has useful information about his life. This file will be cited as "*Pension Records*, NA."

2   Bilkes Biography, NJHS; *Pension Records*, NA; Carman, "Battle of Williamsburg," *Carman Papers*, NJHS; Stewart Sifakis, *Who Was Who in the Union* (New York: Facts on File, 1988), p. 330.

in Major General George B. McClellan's Army of the Potomac. This was the beginning of a lifelong friendship between Hooker and Carman. The regiment participated in the siege of Yorktown, with its first battle occurring on May 5, 1862, near Williamsburg, Virginia. Carman was in command of the regiment there (Revere being absent) and was wounded in the right arm shortly after it began. His brigade commander, Brigadier General Francis E. Patterson, complimented Carman's performance and lamented his loss. The wound, which eventually secured a pension for him after the war and helped him obtain government jobs, was serious but did not incapacitate him for further service.[3]

In July of 1862 while on furlough because of his wound and a recurrent case of dysentery, Carman met Governor Olden at Trenton. Olden appointed Carman as colonel of the newly-recruited 13th New Jersey Infantry. His service at the head of this regiment continued throughout the war and ended with a promotion to brevet brigadier general.[4]

The 13th regiment was mustered into Federal service on August 25, 1862, and on August 30 received orders to report to Washington, D.C. Many new regiments, including the 13th, were ordered to Washington in late August as Confederate General Robert E. Lee's Army of Northern Virginia threatened the nation's capital. Several of these regiments, including Carman's, participated in the Maryland Campaign.[5]

The 13th New Jersey was used to replenish the diminished numbers of Colonel George H. Gordon's Third Brigade, Brigadier General Alpheus Williams' Second Division, Second Corps, in the Army of Virginia, soon to be designated the Twelfth Corps of the Army of the Potomac. The regiment first saw action on September 17 in the battle of Antietam. Carman later said he taught the regiment how to deploy into line of battle by forming them along a fence line in the East Woods. The regiment later moved into the famous Cornfield fighting. The New Jersey men

3  Frederick H. Dyer, *A Compendium of the War of the Rebellion* (Dayton, OH: Morningside Press, 1978 reprint of 1908 edition), p. 1359, hereinafter cited as "Dyer's *Compendium*"); *Pension Records*, NA; *War of the Rebellion: The Official Records of the Union and Confederate Armies*, 70 vols., 128 parts, (Washington, DC: GPO, 1884), Series I, vol. 11 pt. 1, p. 488, hereinafter cited as *OR* with volume and part cited as follows: *OR* 11, pt. 1, p. 488. All citations are from Series 1 unless otherwise noted.

4  Carman *Diary*, NJHS; "Sketch of the Early History of the Thirteenth New Jersey," *Carman Papers*, NJHS; *Pension Records*, NA.

5  Dyer's *Compendium*, p. 1362. Lincoln's call for troops is found in Roy P. Basler's *Collected Works of Lincoln*, vol. 5, pp. 296-7. For the military events providing the backdrop for the Thirteenth's movements, see James M. McPherson's *Ordeal By Fire*, chapters 15 and 17.

xii        *The Maryland Campaign of 1862: South Mountain*

were flanked there and driven back, but not routed. Carman's report makes it clear that his regiment performed well in its first combat.[6]

As a harbinger of his later career, Carman toured the Antietam battlefield in November of 1862, collecting information about the fighting and talking to civilians in and around the town. While there, he confided to his diary that he was making a map and writing an account of the battle. Little did he know it would become the most important work of his long life.[7]

Carman and the 13th New Jersey served throughout the war in the Twelfth Corps. He and his regiment had a limited role in the Chancellorsville campaign, where Carman was injured and sick. At Gettysburg, the 13th was in position on the Union right and was not extensively engaged.

In April of 1864, the Eleventh and Twelfth Corps were combined into the Twentieth Corps, sent west, and participated in General William T. Sherman's campaigns to Atlanta and then east to Savannah and the sea. Carman's hearing was damaged at Kennesaw Mountain in Georgia that June when a shell struck a tree and exploded near where he and General Hooker were standing. Carman served as a brigade commander on Sherman's famous "March to the Sea." After the war he claimed his brigade could have prevented Confederate General Hardee's men from escaping the city of Savannah, and blamed Sherman for fumbling the opportunity.[8]

After the war Carman was initially unsuccessful in gaining employment with the government and returned to private business in New Jersey. He won election as a reading clerk for the state legislature and served as Comptroller for Jersey City. In 1877, he was appointed by President Rutherford B. Hays as Chief Clerk of the U.S. Department of Agriculture, where he worked for eight years. He lost his job in 1885 when a Democratic administration cleaned house and returned to private life, but throughout these years his interest in gathering materials on the war never ceased. Carman was active in veteran's groups and communicated with former comrades on a regular basis. He also served on various veterans' commissions to locate troop

---

6   Organization records are found in OR 19.1:179; Carman's description of combat is from his unpublished manuscript *History of the Maryland Campaign*, part of *Papers of Ezra Carman*, Manuscript Division, Library of Congress, chapter 16, p. 133. Hereinafter this will be referred to as *Carman Manuscript*. His report is in OR 11, pt. 1, p. 488.

7   Carman *Diary*, and *Carman Papers*, NJHS. It is interesting that in his official report of the battle Carman made an error of referring to the Dunkard Church as a "schoolhouse." His report was written on September 24, 1862, before he had time to realize his error. Although it was a common mistake in Union reports, given his attention to detail as a historian, it probably embarrassed him. See OR 11, pt. 1, p. 488.

8   Dyer's *Compendium*, p. 178; Carman *Diary*, and *Carman Papers*, NJHS.

positions at Chickamauga and Chattanooga, served as secretary of the Newark Library, and on the Board of the New Jersey Historical Society.[9]

Carman spent a lot of time writing and gathering material on other campaigns. He began—but did not finish—manuscripts on the history of the war in West Virginia, the Twentieth Corps, and an entire history of the war. Many of these items are located in the New York Public Library, where Carman's son Louis deposited them.[10]

His first official duty related to Antietam was serving on the Executive Committee of the Board of Trustees for the National Cemetery, where he remained for many years. On August 30, 1890, President Benjamin Harrison signed legislation to create the Antietam National Battlefield Site. From 1891 to 1894, the appointed Battlefield Board sought information about the battle. Carman applied to be on the Board in 1891 but was not appointed until 1894 when John Stearns resigned due to ill health. On October 8, 1894, he was given the title of Historical Expert with a salary of $200 a month. Along with other members of the Board, Carman began to plan and mark the battlefield as we know it today. His assigned task was to create a map showing the terrain and troop positions during the battle, which would be verified by surviving veterans; to mark points of general interest; and to create a report that "will result in a pamphlet" to guide future policy. Carman's "pamphlet" became an 1,800-page manuscript history of the entire Maryland Campaign (the Carman Manuscript) and occupied much of his attention for the next several years.[11]

The funding for the Battlefield Board ran out sporadically and the Board was reduced to Carman alone by the late 1890s. He declared the base map finished in 1898, then submitted a request for an additional $1,000 to complete the sequential maps and have them bound and distributed. By this time Carman was working on the maps in his spare time, as he was again a clerk working in the War Records Office. Carman continued to refine the maps and correspond with veterans

9  Bilkes Biography, NJHS; *Carman Papers*, NJHS.

10 Hereinafter referred to *"Carman Papers*, NYPL." His papers in all repositories—Newark, New York Public Library, National Archives, and Library of Congress—have letters and uncompleted papers on a wide range of Civil War topics.

11 Charles W. Snell and Sharon A. Brown, *Antietam National Battlefield and National Cemetery: An Administrative History* (Washington, DC: Dept. of the Interior/National Park Service, 1986), pp. 85-6, hereinafter referred to as "Snell, *Administrative History*"; Oct. 8, 1894 letter from Secretary of War Daniel S. Lamont, *Antietam Battlefield Board Papers*, Series 706, RG 92, NA, hereinafter referred to as *"Battlefield Board Papers*, NA."

through 1906. The original edition of the maps was printed in 1904, but comments from veterans and corrections led to a revised version in 1908.[12]

Carman's interest in the battle of Antietam continued after his official appointment ended and the maps were completed. He tried to acquire the appointment as Superintendent of the battlefield, but the job went to another man. In 1903, President Theodore Roosevelt dedicated a monument at Antietam to Carman's regiment. Carman attended the ceremony, and must have taken great pride in it. In 1905, Carman was appointed as a commissioner of Chickamauga–Chattanooga Park Commission in Tennessee. He was Chairman of that board by 1908, but the following year contracted pneumonia and died on Christmas Day, 1909. He is buried in Arlington National Cemetery, a testament to his long service on behalf of the nation's military history.[13]

## Origin and Importance of the Manuscript

The major portion of the work mandated by Congress fell to Carman. His correspondence and interviews were invaluable, and his efforts to judge, analyze, interpret, and adjudicate various accounts are evident in many of the letters in the various archives. He stated in several letters that he wanted his manuscript to be the most correct narration of the battle.

Carman was a good man for the job. He managed (for the most part) to keep his objectivity and win the support and confidence of men from both sides of the Mason Dixon line. Letters attesting to his ability are found throughout the collections. Some veterans even encouraged their comrades to write to Carman by publishing favorable comments about him. An example from a Virginia artilleryman taken from the *Richmond Times* dated April 21, 1895, reads: "I found General Carman one of the most affable and civil gentleman that I have met on any occasion, and shall long remember his kindness and consideration shown me on this occasion. He is an officer and a gentleman in the right place."[14]

In his years at Antietam Carman produced three major bodies of work. The first is the 238 cast iron War Department plaques seen today on the battlefield and at several related sites including Harpers Ferry, South Mountain, and Shepherdstown. Carman created the text of these markers from official records reports, interviews with and letters from survivors of the battle, and in some cases

---

12 Snell, *Administrative History*.

13 Bilkes Biography, NJHS.

14 Clipping found in the Carman Papers, MS473, New York Public Library.

simply his best estimate of what happened. While the plaques were in progress, Carman, working with the other members of the Battlefield Board, was also producing a series of sequential maps (fourteen in all) that are the best record of what happened in the battle. Their creation is a testament to Carman's research.[15]

It is his mammoth handwritten text narrating events from the secession movement in Maryland to the removal of General McClellan from command on November 7, 1862, however, that remains his greatest work. The maps show troop movement but serve better as a supplement to his 1,800-page narrative. His manuscript cites sources as recent as 1900, but there is evidence of work on it after that year. He kept little record of when or how he wrote it, but in creating this manuscript Carman left a treasure trove of information for future historians. Many of the veteran accounts do not exist in any other form, and Carman clearly used them in his manuscript to tell the story of the Maryland Campaign with the best sources available at that time.[16]

His efforts have withstood the test of time. His maps and manuscript remain the foundation for studying the campaign. Every subsequent book about this aspect of the war incorporates the fruits of Carman's labor, and his works are still regarded as the best source of information about the specific details of the September 17 battle along Antietam Creek. This singular attribute alone makes Carman's manuscript an indispensable source.

## Carman's Process

Even before Ezra Carman joined the Battlefield Board, previous members were canvassing veterans to share their memories. Advertisements appeared in both Confederate and Union veteran's magazines and newspapers.

Carman's handwritten manuscript offers a challenge because of its immense size and the problems of documentation and reliability. His correspondence and his research may seem primitive by today's standards, but for his time Carman was very thorough. His most frequent citations come from the regimental histories, individual soldiers' letters, the *Official Records*, *Battles and Leaders*, and regimental histories. He understood the difference between primary and secondary source material, favoring primary sources whenever he could obtain them. For example,

---

15 "Report of Major George W. Davis to Secretary of War, October 15, 1897," *Battlefield Board Papers*, NA. See also George Large and Joe Swisher's misleadingly titled *Battle of Antietam: The Official History by the Battlefield Board* (Shippensburg, PA: Burd Street Press, 1998). This book does include the text of the tablets, but not any references to the manuscript.

16 *Carman Papers*, NJHS; *Battlefield Board Papers*, NA; *Carman Manuscript*.

several times he cited muster rolls of Confederate units to get accurate figures of the number of men present.

Carman also recognized and realized the problems faced by historians in dealing with intangibles such as participants' faulty memory of events, as well as the possible bias and lack of objectivity of sources. He also often quoted or excerpted portions of books or articles without attribution. In editing his manuscript, I have endeavored to properly cite these quotations or paraphrases, although not always successfully. It should be noted that Carman was not much different from other nineteenth century historians, most of whom did not cite sources as often as modern researchers and writers are trained to do.

The strength of Carman's work comes from the many letters he received from veterans of the battle, and the conversations he had with them when they visited the battlefield. The process of gathering soldier's accounts began prior to Carman's appointment to the Battlefield Board. A form letter was sent to veterans asking about their location on the battlefield and the troops near them in battle. He also kept memoranda of interviews with important participants, thus creating more primary source material. The replies Carman received provided a rich, varied, and sometimes conflicting, source of primary information. Using these interviews and accounts, the after-action reports in the *Official Records*, and available printed sources, Carman wrote the manuscript history in addition to the text of the cast iron plaques marking the battlefield, and the fourteen sequential maps tracing the movements of the troops in the battle.

Carman's manuscript is not entirely free from bias, and he demonstrates his own prejudices and lack of objectivity. His savagely critical comments about General Henry W. Halleck in Chapter 6 are a good example of this. What is remarkable is his lack of animosity toward the Confederates. Considering that Carman himself was a veteran, and that he was writing fewer than forty years after the war, his treatment of Confederate leaders and their cause is very balanced. While the government used the pejorative term "War of the Rebellion" in compiling reports and correspondence, Carman avoided terms that might cause hostility and seemed to be on good terms with his former enemies. The Confederate accounts in Carman's papers indicate that they respected Carman and appreciated his task.[17]

In like fashion, I intend to respect the words of the veterans who contributed to Carman's and our understanding of one of the most significant and bloodiest campaigns in America's history. This is not to say all memoirs and letters will be

---

17  The source for this general statement is the author's study of various letters to Carman from Confederate participants.

taken at face value, but as with Carman, they will be weighed against the material that has surfaced in the past 100 years. The intent of this edition of Carman's manuscript is to provide the most thorough and detailed investigation of his study of the Maryland Campaign of 1862 to date. By recognizing the strengths and weaknesses of Carman's manuscript and identifying and assessing its sources, it is my hope that this book will be the most accurate and detailed first-person account ever published of this pivotal campaign of the Civil War.

Acknowledgments

Since I believe in thanking those first who have made the greatest contribution to the project, Dr. Joseph L. Harsh of George Mason University must lead this list of distinguished people. It was he who first mentioned the importance of editing Carman's manuscript to me, and then suggested I take it on when the exigencies of time did not permit him to do so. His scholarship and intellect inspire me, yet my efforts pale in comparison to his abilities. His friendship is numbered amongst my most valued treasures.

Following closely in importance is my wife Angela, who provided the correct mis of encouragement, patience, nudging, and love to make this work possible. are Also my children, Sarah and Joseph, endured countless hours of being slighted in favor of this project, and yet recognized how important Ezra Carman's manuscript was to me and have managed to love me anyway. I owe a great debt to all three.

Of inestimable assistance was Steve Stotelmyer, the guru of Turner's Gap and Fox's Gap. Steve shared his maps, sources, knowledge, and friendship, probably in reverse order. Gene Thorp, *cartographer extraordinaire*, whose depth of knowledge of the Maryland Campaign and skills at portraying the arcane aspects of the movements of both armies are unmatched, cannot be thanked enough for his help.

My brother Lawrence Clemens, a reference librarian at Nimitz Library, U.S. Naval Academy in Annapolis, Maryland, provided his usual superb help tracking down obscure texts and arcane references, to say nothing of his patience in accommodating my innumerable other requests. Much assistance, guidance, and help came from the staff at Antietam National Battlefield, especially historian Ted Alexander. Ted's help in gathering Carman material has been inestimable. The comments provided by John Hoptak and Brian Baracz were of great help in refining the notes and comments. Keith Snyder, Mannie Gentile, and Allan Schmidt contributed their keen thoughts, comments, and encouragement. Keith also used his technical wizardry to provide photographs of Lee, McClellan, and Carman.

I have also received tremendous help from the faculty and administration at the Hagerstown Community College, including Dr. Guy Altieri, Dr. Judy Oleks,

Dr. Michael Parsons, Dr. Dave Warner, and Professors Joan Johnson and Marge Nikpourfard, who made my sabbaticals possible and encouraged me at every step, as well as the staff of the Library and Reprographic Services. Karen Giannoumis provided inter-library loans that aided immensely in this effort.

Others who have provided valuable information and assistance include Allan Tischler, Marshall Krolick, Nicholas Picerno, Patricia Stepanek, Maurice D'Aoust, Vince Armstrong, Steve Recker, Scott Hann, Steve Bockmiller, John Frye at the Washington County Public Library's Western Maryland Room, Scott Hartwig at Gettyburg National Military Park, and Todd Bolton at Harpers Ferry National Historical Park. My sincere thanks to all of these people cannot be properly expressed here, but know is deeply felt.

I would be remiss not to mention my too-numerous-to-name friends and compatriots of the Civil War Discussion Group and the Talk Antietam group, hosted by a great Antietam scholar named Brian Downey. The many favors done and many thought-provoking points made have aided and guided my thinking. Brian also was invaluable in setting up my blog and social networking sites.

Ethan Rafuse, a steadfast friend and constant supporter, was kind enough to read the drafts. His insightful comments have strengthened the analysis of Carman's work, yet the weaknesses are mine alone. Mark Snell shared several insights and letters related to General William Franklin, and his encouragement is deeply appreciated.

Dr. Victoria Salmon and Dr. Jane Turner Censer of George Mason University provided steadfast encouragement and support which greatly benefitted this entire project.

Certainly without Theodore P. Savas and the helpful staff at Savas Beatie, my publisher, this book would not exist. Ted has been uniformly helpful and supportive as he guided me through a plethora of entanglements. Marketing Director Sarah Keeney has done a splendid job developing a marketing plan for the book and has assisted me in innumerable other ways. Others at Savas Beatie who labored long and patiently include Kim Rouse and Veronica Kane. I thank them all for their help.

No doubt there are others I have overlooked, and I ask their forgiveness for it. I am grateful to everyone who over the years have encouraged and prodded me to get this finished. You know who you are, and I thank you from the bottom of my heart.

Thomas G. Clemens
Keedysville, Maryland

# Note on the Carman Manuscript

The handwritten pages of Carman's manuscript contain a number of problems for transcribers. A few words about the transcription process are in order.

Carman's handwriting is cramped and occasionally illegible, and the pages are stained, ink-spotted, and deteriorating. Throughout this version of the manuscript, I have endeavored to reproduce Carman's work in its *original* version. This includes, where legible, cross-outs and Carman's reference citations, which he placed in the body of the text set off by lines from the rest of the text.

Carman used uppercase letters freely, as was the custom of his era. To enhance readability the capitalization has been made consistent. Very infrequently Carman misspelled a word; these misspellings and corrections are noted in the text.

Carman frequently constructed interminable sentences that combine multiple thoughts. I have usually resisted the temptation to edit his sentences too heavily, leaving them as written. He frequently misused punctuation marks, particularly commas. The confusion of ink spots and other material on the original manuscript occasionally make it unclear which punctuation mark was used, or where he intended to end sentences and begin new ones. I have endeavored to follow his work as much as possible.

Carman often made notes within the text. To simplify these, I have moved them to the footnotes, separating Carman's notes from my own. Many of his quotations in the body of the text are not provided with a source, and sometimes he failed to identify the author. As noted in the Introduction, the documentation standards of his time were different than those of today. As much as possible these unattributed quotes are identified in the footnotes.

Given the lapse of time since the manuscript was written in 1894 to c. 1900, and the lack of bibliographic references by Carman, it is virtually impossible to compile a complete identification of source material. I have made every effort to use sources available to Carman, and especially those that he cited. When no citation is given, I tried to use contemporary source material that Carman might have used. Failing in that, I simply provided documentation of where the information can be found today. A Carman bibliography at the end of the second volume will provide full publication details for the sources Carman cited.

Carman created several maps to accompany the chapters of his manuscript covering the advances of both armies to Sharpsburg, although they are probably unfinished drafts. These maps, drawn by H. W. Mattern and found in the Library of Congress, have never been published. They are keyed to specific pages in his manuscript and obviously were intended to go with it. Because of their size and crude markings, the publisher and I decided to instead use modern cartography based upon Carman's maps, thus fulfilling Carman's desire to illustrate the marches of the early portion of the campaign.

Carman in Uniform

Ezra Ayres Carman, born February 27, 1834, in Middlesex County, New Jersey.
He is shown here as colonel of the 13th New Jersey Infantry. This regiment was
mustered in on August 25, 1862, and a little more than three weeks later fought at
Antietam. Carman held this rank until he mustered out June 8, 1865, dating this
photograph within those three years. *Courtesy of Antietam National Battlefield*

Carman as Civilian (Postwar)

After the war Carman (shown here as a middle-aged wounded veteran with a pension) held several governmental positions in New Jersey. He was appointed Chief Clerk of the U.S. Department of Agriculture in 1877 by his friend, President Rutherford B. Hayes. Carman left this position in 1885. This photo was likely taken during this time period. *Courtesy of Antietam National Battlefield*

Carman Near the Turn of the Century

After serving on the Board of Trustees for Antietam National Cemetery for many years, Carman was appointed to the Antietam National Battlefield Board in 1894. He served on this board until 1905, when he was transferred to the Chickamauga Battlefield Board. This undated photograph was probably taken during his days on the Antietam board. *Courtesy of Antietam National Battlefield*

General Robert E. Lee

General Lee had only been in command of the Army of Northern Virginia for
three months by September of 1862. He was 55 years old and riding a tide of
successes that began with his bold defense of Richmond in June and continued as
he carried the war northward. Although his battered army was small in number
and poorly equipped, Lee hoped to achieve Southern independence in a campaign
north of the Potomac River. *Courtesy of Antietam National Battlefield*

Major General George B. McClellan

The 35-year old McClellan led a hastily organized conglomerate of forces from Washington D.C., in an effort to thwart Lee's northern offensive. Having failed to capture Richmond, and at odds with radical Republicans in the Congress, it is ironic that McClellan's success in the Maryland Campaign would prove to be the catalyst for the Emancipation Proclamation and a radicalizing of the war effort.

*Courtesy of Antietam National Battlefield*

Wise's cabin as it appeared in 1895 looking southwest from Wise's North Field. This image has been mislabeled as the Hagerstown Road at Sharpsburg.

*Bushrod W. James, Echoes of Battle (1895)*

The Rudy house on Main Street in Middletown, Maryland, where future president Rutherford B. Hayes was treated after he was wounded at Fox's Gap.

*Steve Bockmiller*

This postwar view was taken from the Ridge Road looking south. The Wise cabin and surrounding stone wall are visible.

*U.S. Military History Institute, Carlisle, PA*

Uberto Adelbert Burnham, a veteran of Co. D, 76th New York Volunteer Infantry, stands in Wise's South Field in 1922 in a photograph by Fred Cross. Wise's North Field and the Reno monument are visible in the background.

*Fred Wilder Cross Collection, Courtesy of Doug Bast, Boonsborough Museum of History*

Wise's South Field in the foreground with the Reno monument along the Old Sharpsburg Road. Wise's North Field is visible in the background. *Courtesy of Doug Bast, Boonsborough Museum of History*

This postwar photo depicts the attack field of Slocum's division at Crampton's Gap. The stone wall along the Mountain Church Road is visible in the middle ground, with the gap behind it. The area is overgrown today, which makes this view essential for understanding the terrain. *An unmounted and unspecified page in the Ezra Carman Papers, New York Public Library*

## LEGEND

### Campaign maps

| Confederate States | | United States |
|:---:|:---:|:---:|
| | | |
| | Infantry division*/brigade | |
| | Cavalry brigade/detachment | |
| | Artillery | |
| | Infantry movement | |
| | Cavalry movement | |
| | Retreat | |

\* Also represents at least five new
unassigned regiments

### Tactical maps

| Confederate States | | United States |
|:---:|:---:|:---:|
| | | |
| | Infantry brigade/regiment | |
| | Cavalry brigade/detachment | |
| | Artillery | |
| | Skirmish line | |
| | Infantry movement | |
| | Cavalry movement | |
| | Retreat | |

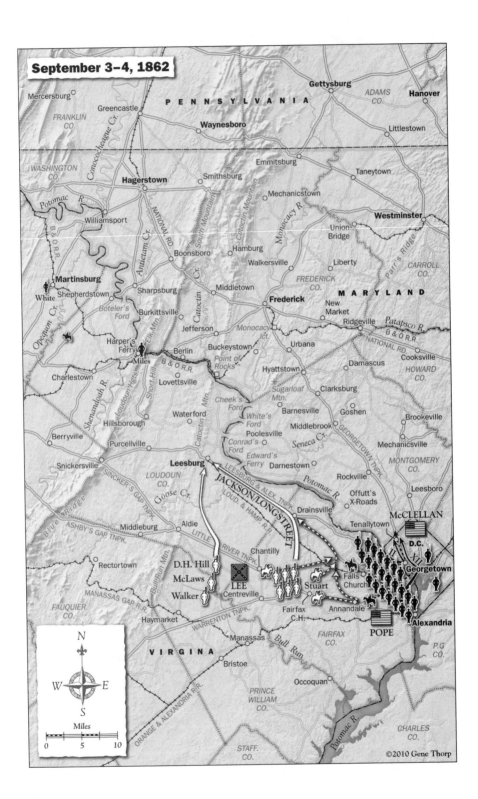

September 3–4, 1862

PENNSYLVANIA

Mercersburg
Greencastle
Waynesboro
ADAMS CO.
Gettysburg
Hanover
Littlestown

FRANKLIN CO.

Conococheague Cr.

WASHINGTON CO.
Hagerstown
Smithsburg
Emmitsburg
Taneytown
Westminster

Potomac R.
Williamsport
B & O R.R.

Martinsburg
White
Shepherdstown
Sharpsburg
Boonsboro
Hamburg
Walkersville
Liberty
Union Bridge

CARROLL CO.

Parr's Ridge

FREDERICK CO.

MARYLAND

NATIONAL RD.

Antietam Cr.

South Mountain

Catoctin Mountain

Monocacy R.

Middletown
Frederick
New Market
Ridgeville
Patapsco R.
B & O R.R.
Cooksville

Boteler's Ford
Burkittsville
Catoctin Cr.
Jefferson
Monocacy Jct.
Urbana
NATIONAL RD.
Damascus
HOWARD CO.

Opequon Cr.
Harper's Ferry
Miles
Berlin
B & O R.R.
Point of Rocks
Buckeystown
Hyattstown
Clarksburg
Goshen
Brookeville

Charlestown

Shenandoah R.

ELK Mtn.

Short Hill

Loudoun Hgts.

Catoctin Mtn.

Cheek's Ford
Sugarloaf Mtn.
Barnesville
Middlebrook
Mechanicsville

Hillsborough
Waterford
White's Ford
Poolesville
Seneca Cr.
GEORGETOWN TNPK.
MONTGOMERY CO.

Berryville
Purcellville
Conrad's Ford
Edward's Ferry
Darnestown
Rockville
Leesboro

Snickersville
Leesburg
LEESBURG & ALEX. TNPK.
Potomac R.
Offutt's X-Roads
Leesboro

SNICKER'S GAP TNPK.
LOUDOUN CO.
Goose Cr.
LOUD. & HAMP. R.R.
Drainsville
McCLELLAN

JACKSON/LONGSTREET

Blue Ridge
ASHBY'S GAP TNPK.
Middleburg
Aldie
LITTLE RIVER TNPK.
Chantilly
Tenallytown
D.C.
XII
Georgetown

Rectortown
BULL RUN MTN.
D.H. Hill
McLaws
Walker
LEE
Centreville
Stuart
Falls Church

MANASSAS GAP R.R.
FAUQUIER CO.
Haymarket
WARRENTON TNPK.
Fairfax C.H.
Annandale
Alexandria

VIRGINIA
Manassas
Bull Run
FAIRFAX CO.
POPE
P.G. CO.

Bristoe
Occoquan
PRINCE WILLIAM CO.

ORANGE & ALEXANDRIA R.R.
Potomac R.
CHARLES CO.

STAFF. CO.

N
W   E
S

Miles
0      5      10

©2010 Gene Thorp

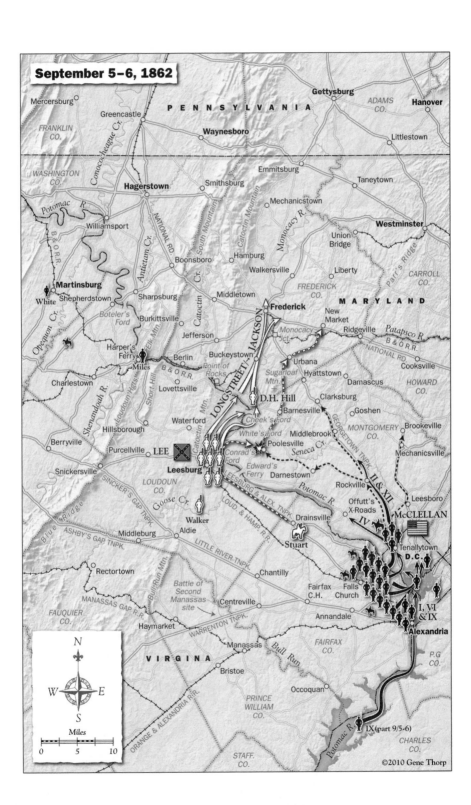

September 5–6, 1862

PENNSYLVANIA

Mercersburg
Greencastle
Waynesboro
Gettysburg
ADAMS CO.
Hanover
Littlestown

FRANKLIN CO.

WASHINGTON CO.
Hagerstown
Smithsburg
Emmitsburg
Taneytown
Westminster

Williamsport
Mechanicstown
Union Bridge
CARROLL CO.

Boonsboro
Hamburg
Walkersville
Liberty
Parr's Ridge

Martinsburg
Middletown
FREDERICK CO.
MARYLAND

White
Shepherdstown
Sharpsburg
Frederick
New Market
Ridgeville
Patapsco R.

Boteler's Ford
Burkittsville
Monocacy Jct.
Cooksville
HOWARD CO.

Harper's Ferry
Berlin
Buckeystown
Urbana
Damascus

Charlestown
Point of Rocks
Sugarloaf Mtn.
Hyattstown
Clarksburg
Goshen
Brookeville

Hillsborough
Waterford
Barnesville
Middlebrook
MONTGOMERY CO.
Mechanicsville

Berryville
Purcellville
LEE
Leesburg
Poolesville
Seneca Cr.
Leesboro

Snickersville
LOUDOUN CO.
Edward's Ferry
Darnestown
Rockville
Offutt's X-Roads
McCLELLAN

Middleburg
Walker
Drainesville
Tenallytown
D.C.

Rectortown
Stuart
Fairfax C.H.
Falls Church
I, VI & IX

Battle of Second Manassas site
Centreville
Annandale
Alexandria

Haymarket
Manassas
Bull Run
FAIRFAX CO.
P.G CO.

VIRGINIA
Bristoe
PRINCE WILLIAM CO.
Occoquan
IX (part 9/5-6)
CHARLES CO.

N
W E
S

Miles
0   5   10

STAFF. CO.

©2010 Gene Thorp

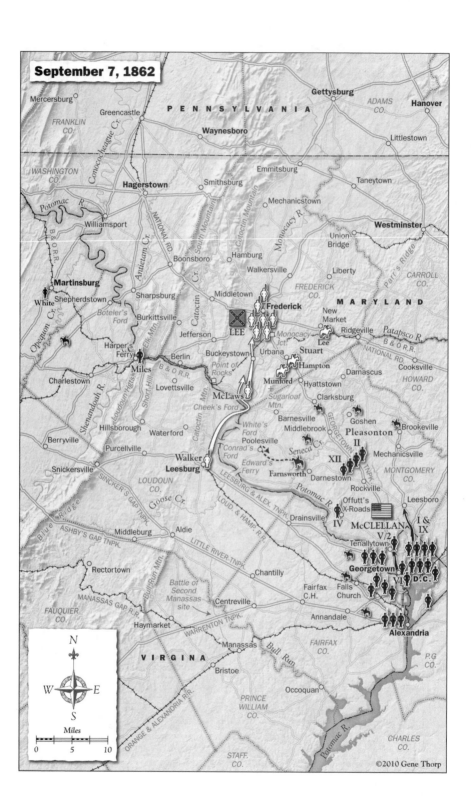

September 7, 1862

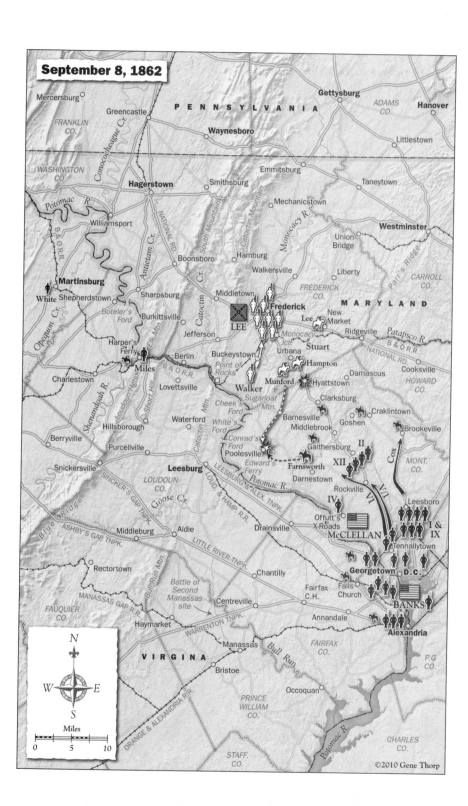

September 8, 1862

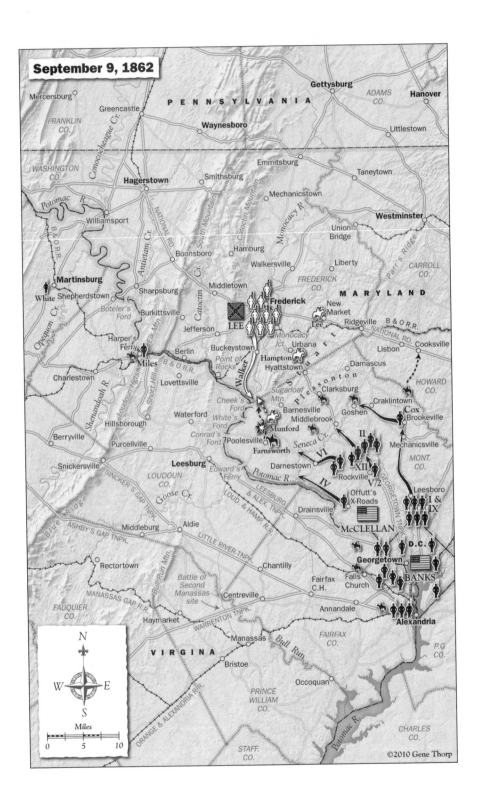

September 9, 1862

PENNSYLVANIA

Mercersburg
Greencastle
Waynesboro
FRANKLIN CO.
Conococheague Cr.

Gettysburg
ADAMS CO.
Hanover
Littlestown

Emmitsburg
Taneytown
WASHINGTON CO.

Hagerstown
Smithsburg
Mechanicstown

Westminster

Williamsport
Potomac R.
B. & O.R.R.
Boonsboro
Hamburg
Walkersville
Union Bridge
Liberty

Martinsburg
White
Shepherdstown
Sharpsburg
Antietam Cr.
Middletown
Catoctin Mountain
South Mountain
Monocacy R.
FREDERICK CO.
MARYLAND
CARROLL CO.
Parr's Ridge

Boteler's Ford
Burkittsville
Frederick
New Market
Ridgeville
B. & O.R.R.
Opequon Cr.
Charlestown
Harper's Ferry
Miles
Jefferson
LEE
Lee
Cooksville
Lisbon
NATIONAL RD.
HOWARD CO.

Berlin
Buckeystown
Point of Rocks
Monocacy Jct.
Urbana
Damascus
Craklintown
Cox
Brookeville

Short Hill
Lovettsville
B. & O.R.R.
Hampton
Hyattstown
Clarksburg
Goshen
Mechanicsville

Loudoun Heights
Cheek's Ford
Sugarloaf Mtn.
Barnesville
Middlebrook
Walker
Stuart
Pleasonton
Waterford
White's Ford
Munford
Conrad's Ford
Poolesville
Seneca Cr.
II
Hillsborough
Berryville
Purcellville
Snickersville
Leesburg
Farnsworth
Darnestown
VI
XII
V72
Rockville
MONT. CO.
GEORGETOWN TNPK.
Leesboro
I & IX

LOUDOUN CO.
Edward's Ferry
Goose Cr.
Potomac R.
IV
Offutt's X-Roads
Drainsville
McCLELLAN

SNICKER'S GAP TNPK.
ASHBY'S GAP TNPK.
Middleburg
Aldie
LEESBURG & ALEX. TNPK.
LOUD. & HAMP. R.R.
LITTLE RIVER TNPK.
Chantilly
Fairfax C.H.
Falls Church
Georgetown
D.C.
BANKS

Blue Ridge
Bull Run Mtn.
Rectortown
MANASSAS GAP R.R.
Battle of Second Manassas site
Centreville
Annandale

FAUQUIER CO.
Haymarket
WARRENTON TNPK.
Manassas
FAIRFAX CO.
Alexandria
P.G. CO.

VIRGINIA
Bristoe
Bull Run
Occoquan
PRINCE WILLIAM CO.
Potomac R.
CHARLES CO.

N
W E
S
Miles
0    5    10

ORANGE & ALEXANDRIA R.R.
STAFF. CO.

©2010 Gene Thorp

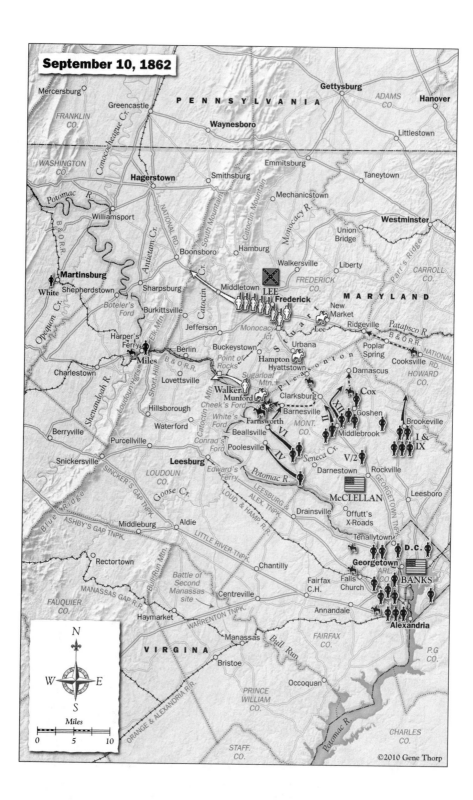

September 10, 1862

PENNSYLVANIA

Mercersburg    Greencastle    Gettysburg    ADAMS    Hanover
                                            CO.
FRANKLIN                      Waynesboro              Littlestown
CO.

WASHINGTON                         Emmitsburg
CO.            Smithsburg                      Taneytown
        Hagerstown
                                Mechanicstown
Potomac R.
    Williamsport                              Westminster
                                    Union
                                    Bridge
                  Boonsboro     Hamburg
            Walkersville    Liberty    CARROLL
Martinsburg                                      CO.
                        Middletown    Walkersville
White  Shepherdstown         LEE   Frederick   MARYLAND
        Sharpsburg                   New
    Boteler's  Burkittsville              Lee   Market   Ridgeville
    Ford                          Monocacy              Poplar    NATIONAL
            Jefferson      Jct.        Urbana      Spring   RD.
    Harper's                Buckeystown                 Cooksville   HOWARD
    Ferry    Berlin    Point of   Hampton              Damascus    CO.
Miles                   Rocks    Hyattstown
Charlestown    Lovettsville   Sugarloaf            Cox
                    Mtn.   Clarksburg        Goshen    Brookeville
        Hillsborough   Walker                XIII              I &
                    Munford   Barnesville              IX
        Waterford    Cheek's Ford          Middlebrook
Berryville         White's   Farnsworth   MONT.
            Ford    VI    CO.
    Purcellville   Conrad's   Beallsville
            Ford    Poolesville          Rockville
Snickersville         IV    Seneca Cr.   V/2   Leesboro
        Leesburg         Darnestown
        LOUDOUN   Edward's
        CO.    Ferry         Potomac R.   McCLELLAN
    Goose Cr.              Drainsville   Offutt's
                        X-Roads
    Middleburg   Aldie              Tenallytown
Rectortown                           D.C.
        Chantilly         Georgetown
        Battle of    Fairfax   Falls        BANKS
        Second    C.H.   Church   ARL.
MANASSAS GAP R.R.  Manassas         CO.
FAUQUIER    site   Centreville         Annandale
CO.                              Alexandria
    Haymarket    WARRENTON TNPK.
            Manassas    FAIRFAX   P.G
VIRGINIA         CO.    CO.
        Bristoe
            Bull Run
                Occoquan
            PRINCE
            WILLIAM
N           CO.
W   E                      CHARLES
    S                      CO.
Miles
0    5    10    ©2010 Gene Thorp

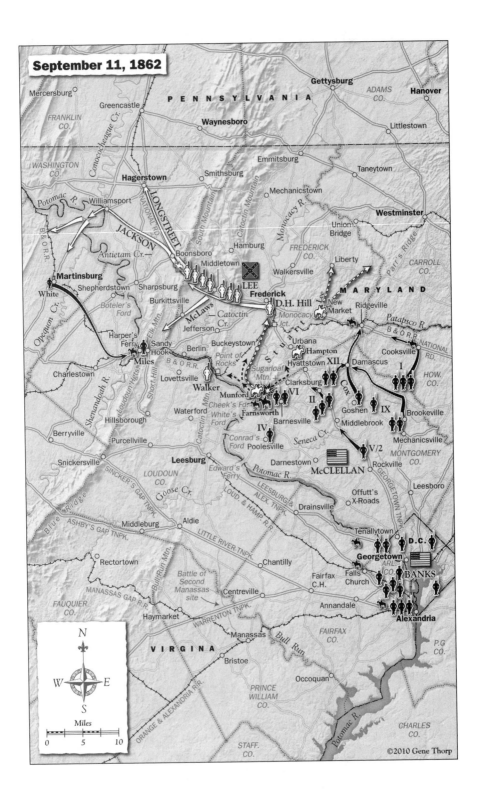

September 11, 1862

©2010 Gene Thorp

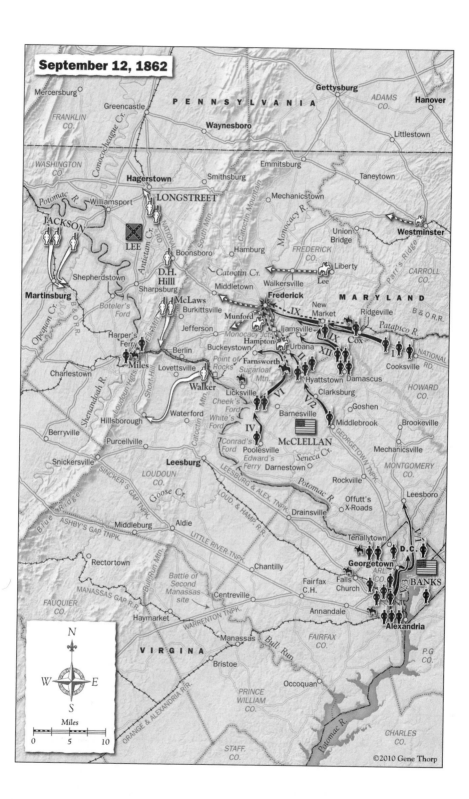

September 12, 1862

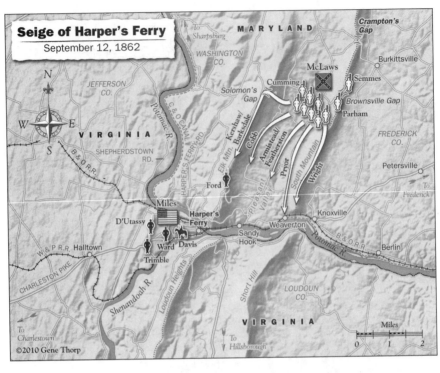

**Seige of Harper's Ferry**
September 12, 1862

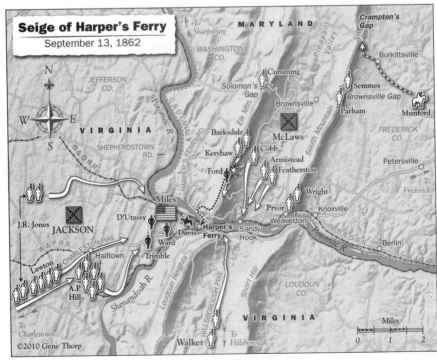

**Seige of Harper's Ferry**
September 13, 1862

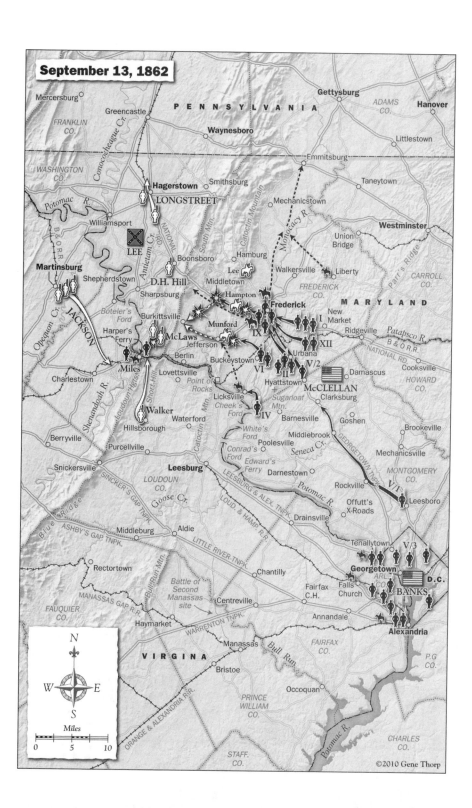

September 13, 1862

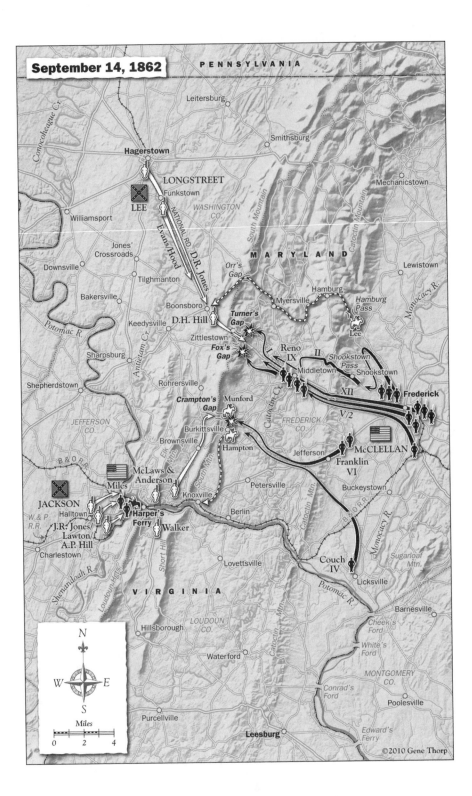

**September 14, 1862**

PENNSYLVANIA

Leitersburg
Smithsburg
Hagerstown
LONGSTREET
Funkstown
Mechanicstown
LEE
WASHINGTON CO.
Williamsport
Jones' Crossroads
Downsville
MARYLAND
Lewistown
Bakersville
Tilghmanton
Orr's Gap
Myersville
Hamburg
Hamburg Pass
Lee
Keedysville
Boonsboro
D.H. Hill
Turner's Gap
Sharpsburg
Zittlestown
Fox's Gap
Reno
IX
II
Shookstown Pass
Shookstown
Shepherdstown
Rohrersville
Middletown
XII
Frederick
Crampton's Gap
Munford
V/2
JEFFERSON CO.
Burkittsville
Brownsville
FREDERICK CO.
Hampton
Jefferson
McCLELLAN
Petersville
Franklin VI
Buckeystown
McLaws & Anderson
Miles
Knoxville
Berlin
JACKSON
Halltown
Harper's Ferry
Walker
J.R. Jones/ Lawton/ A.P. Hill
Charlestown
Lovettsville
Couch IV
VIRGINIA
Sugarloaf Mtn.
Licksville
Hillsborough
LOUDOUN CO.
Barnesville
Cheek's Ford
White's Ford
Waterford
MONTGOMERY CO.
Conrad's Ford
Purcellville
Poolesville
Edward's Ferry
Leesburg

N
W E
S
Miles
0 2 4

©2010 Gene Thorp

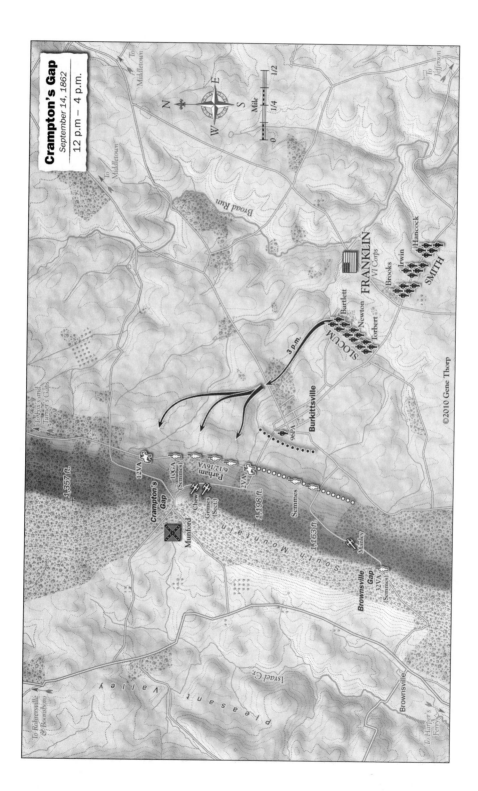

Crampton's Gap
*September 14, 1862*
12 p.m. – 4 p.m.

N E S W

Mile
0    1/4    1/2

©2010 Gene Thorp

To Middletown

To Middletown

Broad Run

To Fox's and Turner's Gaps

1,357 ft.

Crampton's Gap

Munford

Chew

Grimes (Sect.)

12 VA

10 GA (Semmes)

Parham 6/12/16 VA

4,498 ft.

Semmes

2 VA

96 PA

Burkittsville

South Mountain

4,463 ft.

Manley

Brownsville Gap

32 VA (Semmes)

Brownsville

To Harper's Ferry

Israel Cr.

Pleasant Valley

To Rohrersville & Boonsboro

3 p.m.

SLOCUM

Bartlett

Newton

Torbert

FRANKLIN

VI Corps

Brooks

Irwin

Hancock

SMITH

To Jefferson

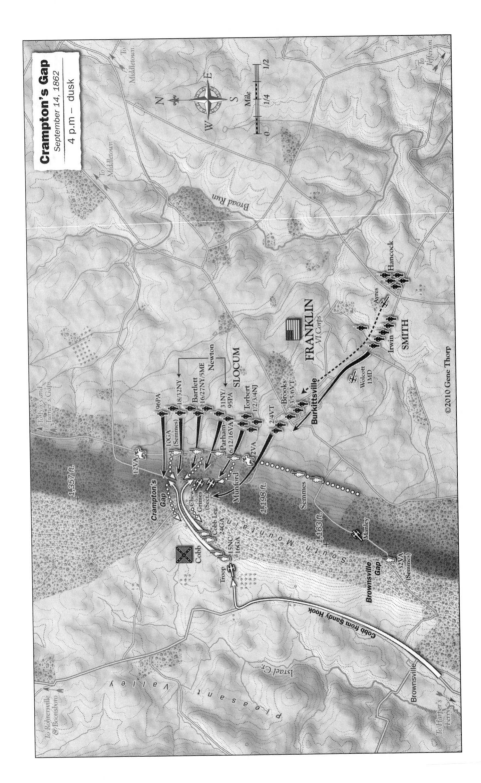

**Crampton's Gap**
*September 14, 1862*
4 p.m – dusk

©2010 Gene Thorp

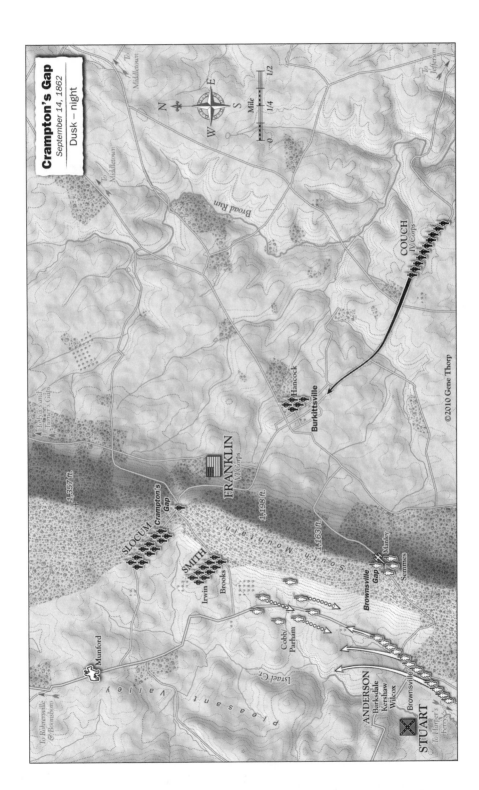

**Crampton's Gap**
*September 14, 1862*
Dusk – night

©2010 Gene Thorp

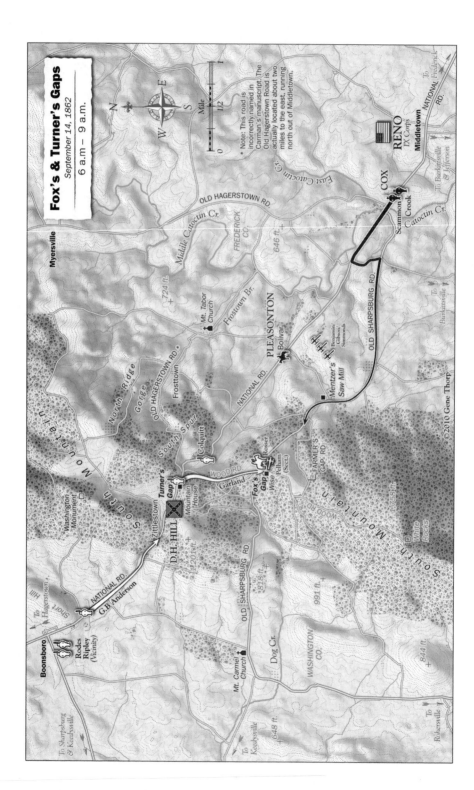

# Fox's & Turner's Gaps
### September 14, 1862
### 6 a.m – 9 a.m.

N
E
S
W

Mile
0    1/2

\* Note: This road is
incorrectly named in
Carman's manuscript. The
Old Hagerstown Road is
actually located about two
miles to the east, running
north out of Middletown.

Myersville

OLD HAGERSTOWN RD.

Middle Catoctin Cr.

East Catoctin Cr.

FREDERICK
CO.

646 ft.

724 ft.

Mt. Tabor
Church

Frostown Br.

PLEASONTON

Bolivar

Benjamin
Gibson
Simmonds

Mentzer's
Saw Mill

OLD SHARPSBURG RD.

COX

Scammon
Crook

Catoctin Cr.

RENO
IX Corps

Middletown

NATIONAL RD.

To Frederick

To Burkittsville
& Jefferson

To Barkersville

©2010 Gene Thorp

North Ridge
Gorge

OLD HAGERSTOWN RD.

Frosttown

NATIONAL RD.

South Spur

Colquitt

1500 ft.

Turner's
Gap

Mountain
House

WOOD RD.

Garland

Rosser

Wise

Pelham
(Sect.)

Fox's
Gap

FARMER'S
GAP RD.

WOOD RD.

875 ft.

South Mountain

South Mountain

Wite
Rocks

991 ft.

844 ft.

To
Richersville

Washington
Monument

D.H. HILL

Zittlestown

1420 ft.

OLD SHARPSBURG RD.

816 ft.

WASHINGTON
CO.

Dog Cr.

Mt. Carmel
Church

648 ft.

To
Keedysville

To
Keedysville

Boonsboro

Rodes
Ripley
(Vicinity)

Short Hill

To
Hagerstown

NATIONAL RD.

G.B. Anderson

To Sharpsburg
& Keedysville

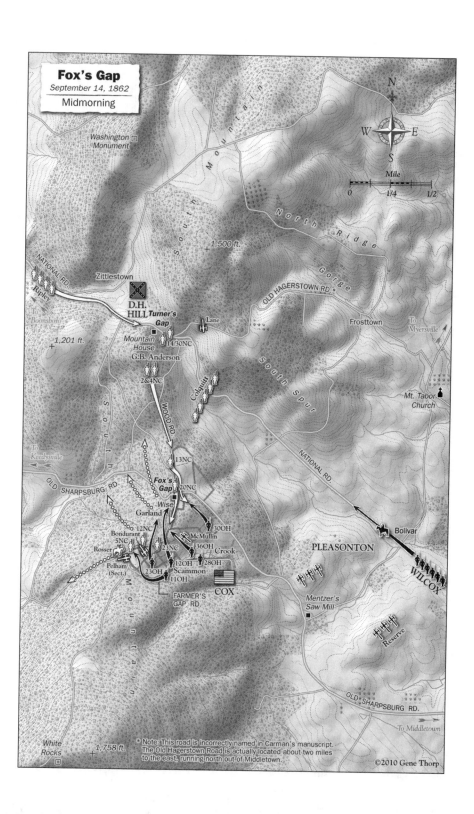

**Fox's Gap**
*September 14, 1862*
Midmorning

N
W E
S

Mile
0    1/4    1/2

Washington
Monument

South Mountain

North Ridge

Gorge

1,500 ft.

NATIONAL RD.

Ripley

Zittlestown

To Boonsboro

D.H. HILL

Turner's Gap

Lane

Old Hagerstown Rd.

Frosttown

To Myersville

Mountain House

1,201 ft.

G.B. Anderson

14/30NC

2&4NC

Colquitt

South Spur

Mt. Tabor Church

WOOD RD.

OLD SHARPSBURG RD.

To Keedysville

13NC

Fox's Gap

20NC

NATIONAL RD.

Bolivar

12NC

Wise

Garland

30OH

Bondurant

McMullin

PLEASONTON

5NC

23NC

36OH

Crook

WILCOX

Rosser

12OH

28OH

Pelham (Sect.)

23OH

Scammon

11OH

COX

FARMER'S GAP RD.

Mentzer's Saw Mill

Reserve

OLD SHARPSBURG RD.

To Middletown

White Rocks

1,758 ft.

Note: This road is incorrectly named in Carman's manuscript.
The Old Hagerstown Road is actually located about two miles
to the east, running north out of Middletown.

©2010 Gene Thorp

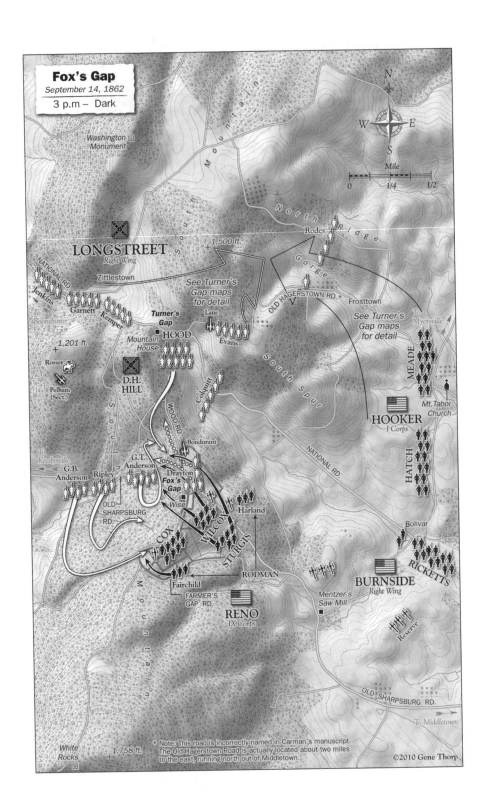

**Fox's Gap**
*September 14, 1862*

3 p.m – Dark

Washington Monument

N

W E

S

Mile
0      1/4      1/2

South Mountain

North Ridge

Rodes

LONGSTREET
*Right Wing*

Gorge

1,500 ft.

NATIONAL RD.
Jenkins

Zittlestown

See Turner's Gap maps for detail

OLD HAGERSTOWN RD. *

Frosttown

To Boonsboro

Garnett
Kemper

Turner's Gap

Lane

See Turner's Gap maps for detail

To Myersville

1,201 ft.

Mountain House

HOOD

Evans

MEADE

Rosser

South Spur

Pelham (Sect.)

D.H. HILL

Colquitt

HOOKER
*I Corps*

Mt. Tabor Church

WOOD RD.

Bondurant

HATCH

To Keedysville

G.B. Anderson

Ripley

G.T. Anderson

Drayton

NATIONAL RD.

Fox's Gap

Wise

Harland

Bolivar

OLD SHARPSBURG RD.

COX

WILCOX

STURGIS

RICKETTS

Fairchild

RODMAN

BURNSIDE
*Right Wing*

FARMER'S GAP RD.

Mentzer's Saw Mill

RENO
*IX Corps*

South Mountain

Reserve

OLD SHARPSBURG RD.

To Middletown

White Rocks

1,758 ft.

* Note: This road is incorrectly named in Carman's manuscript. The Old Hagerstown Road is actually located about two miles to the east, running north out of Middletown.

©2010 Gene Thorp

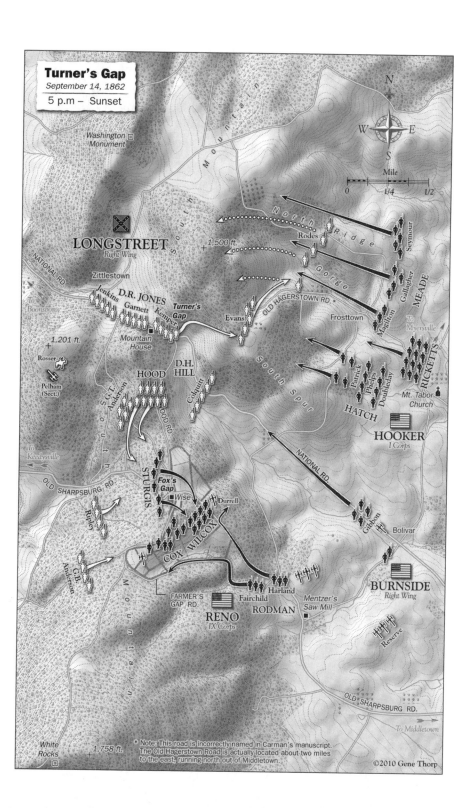

**Turner's Gap**
*September 14, 1862*

5 p.m – Sunset

N
W E
S

Mile
0    1/4    1/2

Washington
Monument

South Mountain

North Ridge

Gorge

LONGSTREET
*Right Wing*

1,500 ft.

Rodes

Seymour

Gallagher

MEADE

NATIONAL RD.

Zittlestown

To
Boonsboro

Jenkins
Garnett

D.R. JONES

Kemper

Turner's
Gap

Evans

OLD HAGERSTOWN RD. *

Frosttown

Magilton

To
Myersville

1,201 ft.

Mountain
House

RICKETTS

Rosser

S.G.T. Anderson

D.H.
HILL

Colquitt

South Spur

Patrick
Phelps
Doubleday

Mt. Tabor
Church

Pelham
(Sect.)

HOOD

HATCH

To
Keedysville

WOOD RD.

HOOKER
*I Corps*

OLD SHARPSBURG RD.

STURGIS

Fox's
Gap

Wise

Durrell

NATIONAL RD.

Ripley

COX

WILCOX

Gibbon

Bolivar

G.B.
Anderson

Harland

BURNSIDE
*Right Wing*

FARMER'S
GAP RD.

Fairchild

RODMAN

Mentzer's
Saw Mill

RENO
*IX Corps*

Reserve

Mountain

OLD SHARPSBURG RD.

White
Rocks

1,758 ft.

To Middletown

* Note: This road is incorrectly named in Carman's manuscript.
The Old Hagerstown Road is actually located about two miles
to the east, running north out of Middletown.

©2010 Gene Thorp

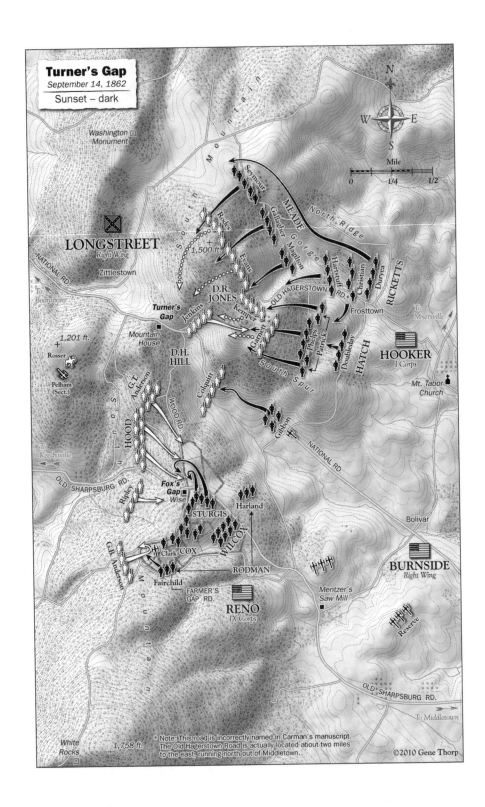

**Turner's Gap**
*September 14, 1862*
Sunset – dark

N
W E
S

Mile
0    1/4    1/2

Washington
Monument

South Mountain

North Ridge

MEADE

Seymour

Rodes

1,500 ft.

Gallagher Magilton

Hartsuff Hartsuff RD.

Christian

Duryea

RICKETT'S

LONGSTREET
*Right Wing*

NATIONAL RD.

Zittlestown

To
Boonsboro

D.R.
JONES

Evans

OLD HAGERSTOWN

Frosttown

To
Myersville

1,201 ft.

Mountain
House

Jenkins

Kemper

Garnett

Phelps

Patrick

HOOKER
*I Corps*

Rosser

**Turner's
Gap**

D.H.
HILL

South Spur

Doubleday

HATCH

Mt. Tabor
Church

Pelham
(Sect.)

G.T.
Anderson

WOOD RD.

Colquitt

HOOD

South Mountain

To
Keedysville

OLD SHARPSBURG RD.

Ripley

**Fox's
Gap**
Wise

Harland

Gibbon

NATIONAL RD.

STURGIS

Bolivar

G.B. Anderson

Clark COX

WILCOX

BURNSIDE
*Right Wing*

Fairchild

RODMAN

FARMER'S
GAP RD.

Mentzer's
Saw Mill

RENO
*IX Corps*

Reserve

OLD SHARPSBURG RD.

To Middletown

White
Rocks

1,758 ft.

* Note: This road is incorrectly named in Carman's manuscript.
The Old Hagerstown Road is actually located about two miles
to the east, running north out of Middletown.

©2010 Gene Thorp

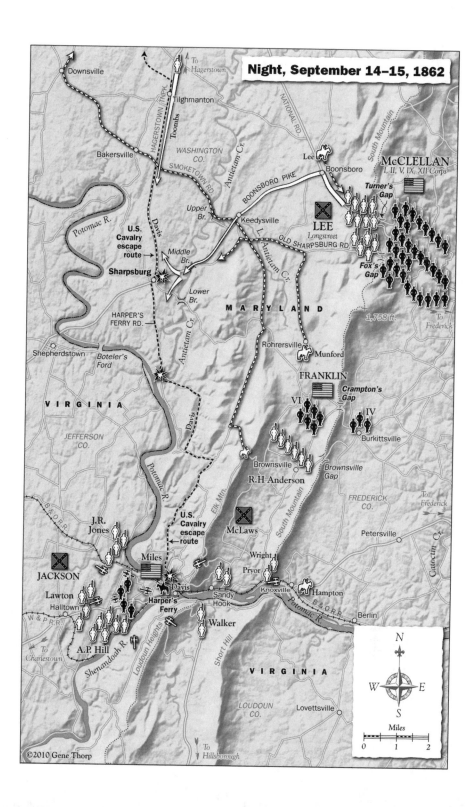

**Night, September 14–15, 1862**

Downsville

To Hagerstown

Tilghmanton

HAGERSTOWN TNPK.

Toombs

NATIONAL RD.

Bakersville

WASHINGTON CO.

Antietam Cr.

SMOKETOWN RD.

Lee

Boonsboro

South Mountain

McCLELLAN
I, II, V, IX, XII Corps

Turner's Gap

BOONSBORO PIKE

Upper Br.

Keedysville

LEE
Longstreet

OLD SHARPSBURG RD.

Fox's Gap

Davis

U.S. Cavalry escape route

Middle Br.

L. Antietam Cr.

Potomac R.

Sharpsburg

Lower Br.

M A R Y L A N D

HARPER'S FERRY RD.

1,758 ft.

To Frederick

Shepherdstown

Boteler's Ford

Antietam Cr.

Rohrersville

Munford

FRANKLIN

Crampton's Gap

VI

IV

V I R G I N I A

Davis

JEFFERSON CO.

Burkittsville

Brownsville

Brownsville Gap

R.H Anderson

FREDERICK CO.

To Frederick

Elk Mtn.

South Mountain

McLaws

Petersville

Potomac R.

B. & O. R.R.

J.R. Jones

U.S. Cavalry escape route

Miles

Wright

Pryor

Catoctin Cr.

JACKSON

Davis

Knoxville

Hampton

Lawton

Halltown

Harper's Ferry

Sandy Hook

Potomac R.

B. & O. R.R.

Berlin

W. & P. R.R.

A.P. Hill

Walker

Short Hill

Loudoun Heights

Shenandoah R.

To Charlestown

V I R G I N I A

N
W   E
S

Miles

LOUDOUN CO.

Lovettsville

To Hillsborough

0    1    2

©2010 Gene Thorp

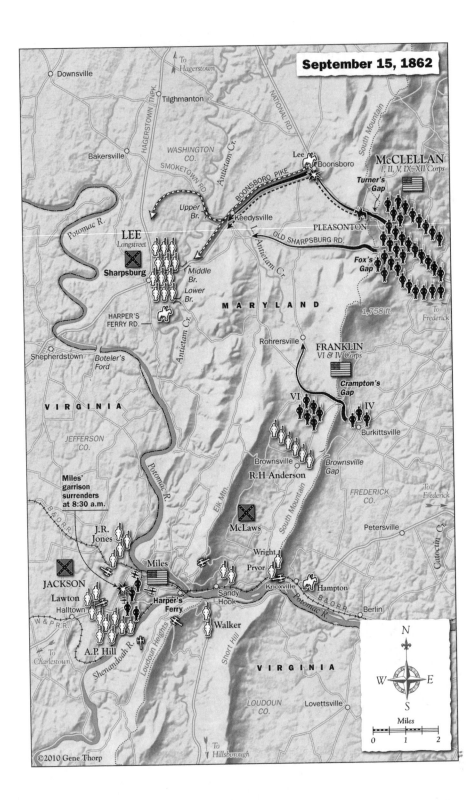

**September 15, 1862**

Downsville

To Hagerstown

Tilghmanton

HAGERSTOWN TNPK.

NATIONAL RD.

South Mountain

Bakersville

WASHINGTON CO.

SMOKETOWN RD.

Antietam Cr.

Lee

Boonsboro

BOONSBORO PIKE

**McCLELLAN**
*I, II, V, IX~XII Corps*

*Turner's Gap*

Potomac R.

Upper Br.

Keedysville

PLEASONTON

**LEE**
Longstreet

Middle Br.

OLD SHARPSBURG RD.

L. Antietam Cr.

*Fox's Gap*

**Sharpsburg**

Lower Br.

**M A R Y L A N D**

*1,758 ft.*

To Frederick

HARPER'S FERRY RD.

Antietam Cr.

Shepherdstown

Boteler's Ford

Rohrersville

**FRANKLIN**
*VI & IV Corps*

*Crampton's Gap*

**V I R G I N I A**

VI

IV

*JEFFERSON CO.*

Burkittsville

Miles' garrison surrenders at 8:30 a.m.

Potomac R.

Brownsville

Brownsville Gap

**R.H Anderson**

*FREDERICK CO.*

To Frederick

B.&O.R.R.

J.R. Jones

Elk Mtn.

**McLaws**

Petersville

Catoctin Cr.

Miles

Wright

South Mountain

**JACKSON**

Pryor

Lawton

Knoxville

Hampton

Berlin

Halltown

**Harper's Ferry**

Sandy Hook

Potomac R.

B.&O.R.R.

W.&P.R.R.

**A.P. Hill**

Shenandoah R.

Loudoun Heights

**Walker**

Short Hill

**V I R G I N I A**

To Charlestown

To Hillsborough

*LOUDOUN CO.*

Lovettsville

N

W E

S

*Miles*

0  1  2

©2010 Gene Thorp

# Chapter 1

# Maryland

I n the early days of the War of the Rebellion, Maryland was represented by the Southern People as a weeping maiden, bound and fettered, seeking relief from the cruel fate that had deprived her of liberty and forced her to an unholy and unnatural alliance with the North. Southern orators and writers dilated largely and eloquently on her wrongs, sentiment and song were invoked to save her, and General Lee records that one of the objects of his campaign of September 1862, was by military succor, to aid her in any efforts she might be disposed to make to recover her liberties.[1] It is well, therefore, before entering upon the narrative of this military campaign, to consider the condition of the state and see which liberties had been taken from her and wherein she had been suppressed.

Maryland was at heart a loyal state, although she had much sympathy with her Southern sisters. Her position was a peculiar one. Bounded on her entire southern

---

1   U.S. War Department, *War of the Rebellion: Official Records of the Union and Confederate Armies*, (Washington: GPO, 1889, 70 volumes in 128 parts), Series 1, vol. 19, pt. 1, p. 144; pt. 2, pp. 293-4, hereafter *OR*). All references are to Series 1 unless otherwise noted. Carman cited the *Official Records* often, but referred to them as the "War Records," abbreviated in his text as W.R. I have left it that way when Carman cited it, but will use *OR* for my own citations.

border by Virginia; having the same interests in slavery; closely connected with her by business interests and family ties, she watched the course of that state with great anxiety. Slavery was the source of much of her wealth, and she had a greater financial interest at stake in the preservation or the Union, with slavery, than any other southern state. It is estimated that the value of the slaves in the state, in 1861, was fully $50,000,000 and her proximity to free territory made them a very precarious kind of property. The largest slaveholding counties were those adjacent to Washington and in the southern part of the state. Like Virginia, a part of her territory was bordered by free states and the free state of Pennsylvania had the same effect on Maryland that free Ohio had on western Virginia.[2]

After the secession of the cotton states many, believing the Union hopelessly divided, favored a grand middle confederacy, stretching from the Atlantic to the Pacific, leaving out the seceded states and New England. The best men of Baltimore and of the state opposed secession; they as strongly opposed coercion. They desired to be strictly neutral. Many were ready to make common cause with the seceded states should North Carolina, Kentucky, Tennessee and Virginia take a position of resistance to the government. Like the other Border States and states North and West, a majority of her people could not and did not appreciate the impending crisis and fondly hoped that the Union might be preserved. The state had been faithful in the observance of all its constitutional obligations, was conciliatory in all its actions, and had kept aloof from the extreme schemes or the Southern leaders. It was as little disposed to take political lessons from South Carolina as from Massachusetts, and it is safe to say that four fifths of her people regarded the action of South Carolina and other cotton states, as rash and uncalled for. But they were almost unanimous against coercion.[3]

2   *The American Annual Cyclopedia and Register of Important Events*, 14 vols. (New York: D. Appleton, 1862-1875), p. 442. Carman's projection of $50,000,000 as the 1860 value of slaves in Maryland is probably conservative. This amount is mentioned in Benson Lossing, *A Pictorial History of the Civil War in America*, 2 vols. (Philadelphia: George W. Childs, 1866), 1, p. 196. According to the Census of 1860, there were 117,189 slaves in the state (U.S. Bureau of the Census, 8th Census, vol. 2, p. 247). Carman's estimate would allow an average value of only $573.47 per slave, about half the market price. In 1868, Prince Georges County—immediately north and east of Washington—had the largest number of slaves (12,479), while Charles County—immediately southeast—had the highest percentage of slaves in its population (58.4%). Baltimore had the largest number of slaveholders (1,296), but most slave owners owned fewer than two slaves (average 1.7 per owner). *Ibid.*, p. 231.

3   The turmoil in Maryland continued, as Carman points out, for some time after the secession of South Carolina. For general works detailing the situation in Maryland, and especially Baltimore, see William J. Evitts' *A Matter of Allegiances: Maryland From 1850-1861* (Baltimore: Johns Hopkins University Press, 1974), p. 165; George William Brown's *Baltimore and the 19th of*

Immediately after the election of Mr. Lincoln, Governor Hicks was solicited to call an extra session of the Legislature, to consider the condition of the country and determine what course should be taken. The secessionists had made a careful canvass and found that a majority of that body were in full sympathy with them and would act according to their dictation, could they be convened. Their intention was to have a convention similar to those by which South Carolina and other states had been declared out of the Union. Governor Hicks well knew the designs of these men and refused to convene the Legislature, again and again refusing, when repeatedly urged and threatened.

It was urged upon him, by those who honestly believed that Maryland, by a wise and conservative course, could control events, that she had influence with the North and South, and that this influence could be exercised to promote harmony. But the greatest pressure came from those who desired an expression of sympathy with the South, those who would have the state follow the example of South Carolina.

On the 27th of November, Governor Hicks, in a letter to ex-Governor Pratt and others, replied to those urgent appeals, declining to convene the Legislature, for reasons that he fully set forth. He did not consider the election of Abraham Lincoln, who was fairly and constitutionally chosen a sufficient cause for the secession of any state, and he proposed to give his administration a proper support. He knew from personal observation that an immense majority of all parties were opposed to the assemblage of the Legislature. He would at least wait until Virginia acted. He would await the action of the National Executive, whose duty it was to look, not to Maryland alone, but to the entire Union. He believed that to convene the Legislature would have the effect to increase and revive the excitement pervading the country, then, apparently on the decline.[4]

---

*April, 1861* (Baltimore, MD: Johns Hopkins University, 1887); George L. Radcliffe's *Governor Thomas H. Hicks of Maryland and the Civil War* (Baltimore, MD: Johns Hopkins Press, 1901); Scott Sheads and Daniel Toomey, *Baltimore During the Civil War* (Baltimore, MD: Toomey Press, 1997); Lawrence M. Denton, *A Southern Star for Maryland* (Baltimore, MD: Publishing Concepts, 1995). Although Brown's was the only one of these sources available to Carman, he also seems to have used a source he quotes in later chapters compiled by Clement Evans, a former Confederate officer, who assembled and edited a multi-volume work entitled *Confederate Military History* (Atlanta: Confederate Publishing Co., 1899), hereafter *CMH*. Bradley Johnson, mentioned in this chapter frequently, wrote the Maryland portion. *CMH* is a biased, but contemporary, source. Like George Brown, Johnson was a player in the events he wrote about.

4   For Hicks's response to Pratt and others, see Radcliffe, *Governor Thomas H. Hicks*, p. 22, and Horace Greeley, *American Conflict: A History of the Great Rebellion in the United States*, 2 Vols. (Hartford, CT: O. D. Case and Co., 1864-1866), 1, pp. 349-50.

A large and influential body of the people believed in the Governor and confided in his judgment. He was born and lived in a slaveholding county of the state, was himself a slaveholder, and had always identified himself with the extreme southern wing of the Whig party. In hearty sympathy with those who were defending Southern rights, he was opposed to the policy of secession and distrusted those who were leading in that direction. With some apparent inconsistencies he was, however, a Union man, and in his persistent refusal to call an extra session of the Legislature, at that time, doubtless prevented the secession of Maryland and performed an inestimable service to the Union and to the cause of humanity.

In the appointment of commissioners by the seceding states, Maryland was especially remembered. The commissioner from Mississippi, Mr. A. H. Handy addressed the citizens of Baltimore, December 19, 1860, on the objects and purposes of the secessionists. Upon his arrival in Maryland, he asked the Governor to convene the Legislature for the purpose of counseling with the constituted authorities of Mississippi, as represented by himself.[5] The very day he was addressing the citizens of Baltimore, on the peculiar designs of the secessionists, Governor Hicks was writing him that "the state though unquestionably identified with the Southern States in feeling, is conservative, and above all things devoted to the Union of those states under the Constitution. The people intend to uphold the Union and I cannot consent, by any precipitate or revolutionary action, to aid in its dismemberment."[6]

Mr. Handy was a native of Maryland and his speech to the people of Baltimore, on the 19th made a deep impression, of which those in sympathy with the South took quick advantage. They called a meeting for December 22nd at the Universalist Church to "take some action in regard to convening the Legislature."[7] The meeting

---

5  "Mississippi to Maryland" *Baltimore Sun*, December 19, 1860, "Mississippi to Maryland: Meeting at the Maryland Institute Hall," *Baltimore Sun*, December 20, 1860, and Frank Moore, ed., *The Rebellion Record: A Diary of American Events, With Documents, Narratives, Illustrative Incidents, Poetry, etc.*, 12 Vols. (New York: G. P. Putnam, 1861-1863, Van Nostrand, 1864-1868 ), 3, Diary of Events. Carman likely used Moore as the source.

6  Hicks to Handy, December 19, 1860, was published in the Baltimore newspapers and is quoted in Moore, *The Rebellion Record*, 1, Doc., p. 1. Information on emissaries from Southern states to Maryland, and other border states, can be found in Charles Dew, *Apostles of Disunion: Southern Secession Commissioners and the Causes of the Civil War* (Charlottesville, VA: University Press of Virginia, 2001).

7  The Maryland Southerner's call (quoted) for meeting December 22, and a report of that meeting, are found in "The Baltimore Riots," by Frederick Emory, *Philadelphia Weekly Times*, as reprinted in Alexander McClure's *Annals of the War* (Philadelphia, PA: Weekly Times, 1878), p. 778. Carman used that article for this quote. See also *Baltimore Sun*, December 24, 1860; Radcliffe, *Governor Thomas H. Hicks*, pp. 28-9.

was fully attended and a free interchange of opinions resulted in the appointment of a committee to wait upon the Governor.

The committee discharged this duty on Christmas Eve and urged him to convene the Legislature. They used taunts and threatened him. They intimated fears for his personal safety, should he decline their request, said that blood would be shed and Mr. Lincoln not be permitted to be inaugurated. To which the Governor responded that he was a Southern man, but could not see the necessity for shedding blood or convening the Legislature.

Following this there were meetings in Anne Arundel, Prince Georges, Queen Anne, St. Mary's, Charles and other counties of the state, with resolutions demanding an extra session. Public meetings and strong resolutions were supplemented by personal appeals and social blandishments, but all to no purpose, the Governor would not yield.[8] From Alabama came as commissioner, J. L. M. Curry, a minister formerly a member or Congress, a man of character and ability. Governor Hicks was absent from the Capital, but Mr. Curry, under date of December 28, 1860, informed him that as a commissioner from the Sovereign State of Alabama, to the Sovereign State of Maryland, he came to advise and consult with the Governor and Legislature, as to what was to be done to protect the rights, interests and honor of the slaveholding states, to secure concert and effectual cooperation between Maryland and Alabama; to secure a mutual league, united thought and counsels, between those whose hopes and hazards were alike joined in the enterprise of accomplishing deliverance from abolition domination, to oppose that "anti-slavery fanaticism that sentiment of the sinfulness of slavery embedded in the Northern conscience, that infidel theory corrupting the Northern heart." "To unite with the seceding states," said the sanguine commissioner, "is to be their peers as confederates and have an identity of interests, protection of property and superior advantages in the contests for the Markets, a monopoly of which has been enjoyed by the North. To refuse union with the Seceding States is to accept inferiority, to be deprived of an outlet for surplus slaves and to remain in a hostile Government in a hopeless minority and remediless dependency."[9]

On the 6th day of January, 1861, the Governor appealed to the people in these words:

8  The report of various county meetings to pressure Governor Hicks can be found in Moore, *The Rebellion Record*, 1, Diary, p. 9, quoted from the *Baltimore American.*

9  Carman quotes from correspondence between Curry and Hicks on 12/28/1860. OR Series 4, 1, pp. 38-42. For Hicks' reply, see Moore, *The Rebellion Record*, 1, Diary, p. 12.

I firmly believe that a division of this Government would inevitably produce civil war. We are told by the leading spirits of the South Carolina Convention that neither the election of Mr. Lincoln, nor the non-execution of the Fugitive slave law, nor both combined constitute their grievances. They state that the real cause of their discontent dates as far back as 1833. Maryland and every other state in the Union with a united voice, then declared the cause insufficient to justify the course of South Carolina. Can it be that these people, who then unanimously supported the cause of General [Andrew] Jackson, will now yield their opinions at the bidding of modern secessionists.

That Maryland is a conservative Southern State all know who know anything of her people or her history. The business and agricultural classes, planters, merchants, mechanics and laboring men; those who have a real stake in the community, who would be forced to pay the taxes and do the fighting are the persons to be heard in preference to excited politicians, many of whom have nothing to lose from the destruction of the Government but hope to derive some gain from the ruin of the State. Such men will naturally urge you to pull down the pillars of this 'accursed Union,' which their allies in the North have denominated a 'covenant with hell.' The people of Maryland, if left to themselves, would decide, with scarcely an exception, that there is nothing in the present causes of complaint to justify immediate secession; and yet against our judgment and solemn convictions of duty, we are to be precipitated into this revolution, because South Carolina thinks differently. Are we not equals? Or shall her opinions control our actions? After we have solemnly declared for ourselves as every man must do, are we to be forced to yield our opinions to those of another State, and thus in effect obey her mandates? She refuses to wait for our counsels. Are we bound to obey her commands? The men who have embarked on this scheme to convene the Legislature will spare no pains to carry their point. The whole plan of operation, in the event of assembling the Legislature, is, as I have been informed, already marked out, the list of ambassadors who are to visit the other States have been agreed upon, and the resolutions which they hope will be passed by the Legislature, fully committing this State to secession, are said to be already prepared. In the course of nature, I cannot have long to live, and I fervently trust to be allowed to end my days a citizen of this glorious Union. But should I be compelled to witness the downfall of the Government inherited from our fathers, established as it were by the special favor of God, I will at least have the consolation, at my dying hour, that I neither by word nor deed assisted in hastening its disruption.[10]

10  Hicks' address to the citizens of Maryland is in *Annual Cyclopedia, 1861*, p. 443, and Moore, *The Rebellion Record*, 1, Doc., pp. 17-18, taken from Baltimore newspapers. As was Carman's custom, he copied snippets of Hicks' speech and used them to continue the thought, usually without attribution.

The Governor had a powerful supporter in the person of Henry Winter Davis, a representative in Congress from the City of Baltimore. On the 2nd of January, Mr. Davis issued a strong appeal to the voters of his district, taking ground against the calling of the Legislature or the assembling of a "Border State" Convention. He denied that Maryland had been wronged by the General Government; and asserted that her interests were indissolubly connected with the integrity of the United States. She had not an interest that would survive the government under the Constitution. "Peaceful secession is a delusion," said Mr. Davis,

> and if you yield to the arts now employed to delude you, the soil of Maryland will be trampled by armies struggling for the National capital. If the present Government be destroyed, Maryland slaveholders lose the only guarantee for the return of their slaves. Every commercial line of communication is severed. Custom-house barriers arrest her merchants at every frontier. Her commerce on the ocean is the prey of every pirate, or the sport of every maritime power. Her great railroad loses every connection which makes it valuable. . . . Free trade would open every port, and cotton and woolen factories and the iron and machine works of Maryland would be prostrate before European competition.

The hope held out to them by the secessionists that Baltimore would be the emporium of a Southern Republic was a delusion too ridiculous to need refutation, nothing ever intended for the South would ever pass Norfolk. Davis opposed the calling of the Legislature because the halls of legislation would immediately become the focus of revolutionary conspiracy. "Under specious pretexts, the people will be implicated, by consultations with other States, by concerted plans, by inadmissible demands, by extreme and extensive pretensions, in a deeply-laid scheme of simultaneous revolt, in the event of the failure to impose on the Free States the Ultimatum of the Slave States. Maryland will find herself severed from more than half of the States, plunged in anarchy, and wrapped in the flames of civil war, waged by her against the Government in which we now glory." In the face of such circumstances he contended there were no justifications, no excuse, for convening the Legislature. Within its constitutional powers it could do nothing, and there was nothing for it to do.

As to the meeting of the Border States, Mr. Davis was utterly opposed to it, the Constitution forbid any agreement between Maryland and any other States for any purpose. He warned his constituents against the agitation of subjects in which they had no earthly interest, which was of no practical importance to them:

> If by common consent any change can be made which will silence clamor, or soothe the sensibilities, or satisfy the jealousies excited by the recent contest, let the changes

be made. But that is the only interest you have in any change; and if none can be obtained of that character, it is our policy to let that question alone. . . . The firm attitude of Maryland is now the chief hope of peace. If you firmly hold to the United States against all enemies, resolved to obey the Constitution and see it obeyed, your example will arrest the spirit of revolution, and greatly aid the Government in restoring without bloodshed, its authority. If Maryland yields to this revolutionary clamor, she will be overcome in a few months in the struggle for the National capital; and her young men, torn from the pursuits of peace, excluded from the work-shop and counting—house, must shoulder the musket to guard their homes at the cost of fraternal blood.[11]

Much in the same vein wrote another of her patriotic sons:

Maryland has no future out of the Union. It is impossible, in the event of a separation, that she should go with the South or the North. As a member of the Southern Confederacy, she would be a slave State without a single slave within her borders, and a Southern State on the wrong side of the division line. As a member of the Northern Confederacy, her fellowship would be far away from her sympathies. It is indeed by no means certain that her territory would not be split in two, and the parts go off in opposite directions. Baltimore would be a provincial town, with the grass growing in her streets, and the fox looking out of the window . . . Maryland has in her keeping the capital of the nation. It was confided to her by George Washington. To the great duty of its safe keeping she has been consecrated by an authority but, one remove a little lower than the Divine. Like the sons of Aaron and the tribe of Levi, she has the charge of the tabernacle and the holy things of the temple; and let the storm come, let the earthquake come, and they will find her faithful and true to her charge."[12]

The progress of affairs in Maryland was watched with the keenest interest in the North and Governor Hicks was urged by many its prominent men to resist every attempt of those who were seeking to have the Legislature convened; among others was Governor Charles S. Olden of New Jersey, who wrote early in January, imploring him not to yield to the demands of the "secessionists" and expressing the

---

11  Henry Winter Davis' Address to Voters in the Fourth Congressional District, January 2, 1861, in Henry W. Davis, *Speeches and Addresses Delivered in the Congress of the United States and Other Occasions* (New York: Harper & Brothers, 1867), pp. 196-8. Similar quotations are in Bernard Steiner, *Life of Henry Winter Davis* (Baltimore, MD: John Murphy Co., 1916), pp. 171-7.

12  The source for this quotation has not been determined.

belief, shared by many others, that "the peaceful inauguration of Mr. Lincoln depends on the firmness of your excellency."[13]

The secession element grew stronger and the leaders more and more impatient at the Governor's refusal to convoke the Legislature. They insisted that their representatives should, in body assembled, give expression to the will of the State. "They insisted that their representatives should meet, so as to act for them as occasion might require. If Virginia seceded, then to join Maryland and Virginia in one common destiny, weal or for woe. If the Middle States submitted, then to place Maryland side by side with them in protecting the Gulf States from war."[14]

It was anticipated, however, by these men that any expression would be that of full sympathy with the South and a call for a State convention. As the Governor was immovable some of the most ardent friends of the South hit upon the plan of holding, what they pleased to term, a sovereign convention. St. Mary's, Prince George and Charles Counties, the three strongest slave counties in the State, elected delegates to a convention to be held in January. Citizens of Frederick County, led by some of the young men, prominent, among whom was Bradley T. Johnson, held a meeting on January 8th, issued an address to the people; called a convention for February 22nd, and elected delegates to it.[15]

Meanwhile the Union men of the State were not inactive. They held Union meetings in country, town and city and 5,000 citizens of Baltimore, united in a letter to Governor Hicks approving his course in declining to convene the Legislature. On the evening of January 10th, an immense union meeting was held at the Maryland Institute, which was addressed by Reverdy Johnson, A. W. Bradford, W. H. Collins and others. Resolutions were adopted expressive of Maryland's love for the Union, of her hopes of peace by concession and compromise, and in support of the position assumed by Governor Hicks. This meeting, the most imposing as to

---

13 Governor Olden to Hicks, January 1861. The letter is cited in Radcliffe, *Governor Thomas H. Hicks*, p. 43, from a manuscript copy in Hicks's papers.

14 Quotation is from Bradley T. Johnson, "Memoirs of the First Maryland Campaign," *Southern Historical Society Papers*, 52 Vols. (Southern Historical Society, Richmond, 1876-1959), vol. 9, July - August, 1881, p. 346, hereafter cited as *SHSP*. This invaluable set was published in magazine format from 1876 to 1959. Citations are from the Guild Press CD-Rom edition (Carmel, IN: Guild Press, n.d.).

15 Details of the pro-Southern meetings are also from Johnson "Memoirs," *SHSP*, p. 346. The committee from the pro-Southern conference included prominent members of the legislature. Their lack of success on their visit to Annapolis to persuade Hicks to call a convention was written up in several Baltimore newspapers, from which Carman evidently quoted. See Radcliffe, *Governor Thomas H. Hicks*, pp. 31-3, and notes.

numbers and respectability that had ever assembled in Baltimore, quickened the Union sentiment.[16]

On the same day that this imposing Union meeting was held, a conference took place in the "Law Building" relative to the threatening condition of public affairs. All parts of the State were represented and after a conference of two days, the Crittenden Compromise measures were approved and a committee appointed to wait on the Governor, and solicit him to issue a proclamation calling on the people to vote, whether a convention should, or should not, be called.[17] The committee went to Annapolis on the 12th, where they had a long interview with the Governor, and urged his immediate action on this request. They were sure that the position of Maryland was misunderstood, both at the South and at the North, that the failure of the people to declare themselves, was construed at the South as a determination to make no further struggle against the advance of abolitionism, while at the North it was construed as an admission of the justice of republicanism and an acquiescence in its teachings. They magnified the importance of their State by suggesting that through the in fluence of Maryland, "the extremists of the South might be persuaded to be more moderate, and the fanatics of the North compelled to be more just." But the Governor turned a deaf ear to their entreaty, he declined to issue the proclamation. Meanwhile prominent men took sides, openly declaring for and against secession, and again on the 30th of January, the Governor was appealed to, to convene the Legislature, in response to public meetings. The request came from the President of the Senate and the Speaker of the House of Delegates, but was refused.[18]

As we have seen, much of the pressure for the secession of Maryland came from outside the State. The revolutionary spirits at the National capital, seeking to control events, advanced and maintained the idea that if Maryland should secede the District of Columbia would revert to the State, by which it had been ceded to

---

16 The January 10th pro-Union meeting, attended by more than 5,000 people, featured these addresses in support of Hicks. Baltimore *Sun*, January 10 and 11, 1861, reprinted in *Annals of the War*, pp. 775-6.

17 The pro-Southern conference at the law building met on January 11-12, and was discussed in the *Baltimore Sun* January 11 and 12, 1861. See also Radcliffe, *Governor Thomas H. Hicks*, pp. 31-2. The Crittenden Compromise, mentioned by Carman, refers to Kentucky Senator John Crittenden's proposal to extend the Missouri Compromise line across the new territories added from the treaty with Mexico. It was rejected by both Lincoln and the Southern leaders.

18 On January 30, the President of Senate (John B. Brooke) and Speaker of House (E. G. Kilbourn) appealed for the convening of the legislature. Governor Hicks refused. See *Baltimore Sun*, January 4, 1861, as quoted in Evitts, *A Matter of Allegiances*, p. 165. See also an interview with Governor Hicks, *Baltimore Sun*, January 15, 1861.

the General Government. That the secession of Maryland was confidently relied upon, by them is well-known, and it was hoped that Washington could be seized before the inauguration of Mr. Lincoln. So, at this time, increased pressure was brought to bear by outside parties.

At a large and enthusiastic meeting at Maryland Institute Hall on the evening of February 1st, called by the citizens of Baltimore who were "in favor of restoring the Constitution of the Union of the States, and who desire the position of Maryland in the existing crisis to he ascertained by a convention of the people;"[19] resolutions were passed denouncing Governor Hicks and calling a "Sovereign Convention;" and Robert M. McLane declared "by the living God, if the administration shall dare to bring its Black Republican cohorts to the banks of the Susquehanna, to coerce the South, the river shall run red with blood before the first man shall cross it. I for one pledge here my life and means to march with you to the banks of the Susquehanna to forbid the passage of those invaders." Although a graduate of West Point, the speaker did not enter the military service of either side during the war.[20]

Ex-Governor Lowe insisted that Maryland should link her destiny with Virginia, and at the proper time take possession of the District of Columbia. If the Governor refused the demands for the assembling of the Legislature and a convention of the people, he would raise the banner of revolt. He said, "If after Virginia and Tennessee have spoken and the loyal men of Maryland have spoken, he refuses, we will gibbet him."[21]

Pursuant to the action of this meeting, a convention was held by the States-Rights men, in the Universalist Church at Baltimore, on the 18th of February, to take advisory action on the state of the country. All the counties of the State were represented by able and influential men. The sense of the convention as expressed in resolutions offered by Robert M. McLane and adopted, was that, "the secession of several slaveholding States from the Union was induced by the aggression of the non-slaveholding States, in violation of the Constitution of the United States," and the moral and the geographical position of the State demand that it should act with Virginia in the crisis, co-operating with that State "in all honorable efforts to maintain and defend the Constitutional rights of its citizens in the Union, and failing in that, to associate with her in confederation with our sister

19 *Speeches of Severn Teakle Wallis Esq. as Delivered at the Maryland Institute on Friday Evening, February 1, 1861* (Baltimore: Murphy & Co., 1861), p. 1.

20 The meeting at Institute Hall on February 1, 1861, is discussed in Radcliffe, *Governor Thomas H. Hicks*, pp. 40-1. The McLane and Lowe quotations are not included, but several other speakers are mentioned. Carman combined these two sources to maker one quotation.

21 The source for this quotation has not been found.

States of the Union." It further resolved that the honor of the State required that it should not permit its soil to be made a highway for Federal troops, sent to make war upon sister States of the South, and it was the expressed opinion of the convention that an attempt on the part of the Federal Government to coerce the States which had seceded, would necessarily result in civil war and the destruction of the Government itself.[22] After a session of two days the convention adjourned to reassemble on March 12th, unless meanwhile Virginia should take decided action; in that event the Convention was to reassemble as soon as possible.

While this conference was in session in Baltimore, a meeting was held in Howard County, which was addressed by the Speaker of the House of Delegates, and a resolution was adopted that "immediate steps ought to be taken for the establishment of a Southern Confederacy, by consultation and co-operation with such other Southern and slave States as may be ready therefor."[23]

Mr. A. W. Wright, commissioner from Georgia, arrived at Baltimore, February 18th, and one week thereafter, after two failures, succeeded in obtaining an interview with the Governor and left for his consideration a long and able communication, stating that he came to Maryland to urge upon her people the policy of secession from the power known as the United States, and co-operation with the State of Georgia and other independent Southern States in the formation of a new confederation. In language that reads like a parody on the Declaration of Independence, he laid at the door of the Republican party every political crime known to modern times, and warned the Governor and people of Maryland that "the irrepressible conflict with them is just begun. Their mission is to annihilate slavery from the American Continent." Referring to the presence of United States troops in and around Washington and the adjoining States of Maryland and Virginia, he said, "These are the overtures for peace extended to us now by the Northern Federal Government, Scott and scorpions, cannon and cartridge." The North, these Northern people: "By what bonds can such a people be held? They ignore the Bible, violate oaths, nullify the laws, and Pharisaically call upon Jehovah

---

22 The Pro-Southern meeting was at Universalist Church on February 18. The resolutions by McLane were adopted, but only called for a convention, but did not declare one. The quotation is from *OR* Series 4, 1, pp. 151-152. The original address was published in Baltimore but Carman used a version from the *Official Records*, suggesting that he did not use newspaper archives for his research. Evitts also discusses these two meetings, but mistakenly put the former on February 2 in his *A Matter of Allegiances*, p. 166.

23 At the Howard County meeting, Speaker of House E. G. Kilbourn was quoted, from Edward McPherson, *The Political History of the United States of America, During the Great Rebellion, Including a Classified Summary of the Legislation of the Second Session of the Thirty-Sixth Congress* . . . (Washington, DC: Philp and Solomons, 1865), p. 9.

to guide and support them in their infamous course. To redress and resist the wrongs committed by these people Georgia offers to make common cause with Maryland. She is not unmindful of the past history of your noble State. The wealth, population and commercial importance of her great metropolis, Baltimore, point out that city as the great commercial and financial centre of the Southern Republic." In glowing sentences he depicted the future of Baltimore, that with her natural advantages, no less than from her varied and extended commercial relations with the civilized world, "she will become the great importing agent for the entire South; whilst her facilities for, and her great proficiency in the art of ship building, will make her the carrier of our immense production of rice, grain, cotton and sugar." He hoped that the descendants of Chase, Carroll and McHenry, would no longer be deterred by a consultation with their fears. "Georgia warns Maryland against any patched up adjustment of existing difficulties."[24]

The ambassador from Georgia was not more successful than were those from Mississippi and Alabama, and was obliged to report to his Governor, that though he had received no written reply to his communication, for which he long waited, he regretted to inform him that as the result of a personal interview he found Governor Hicks not only opposed to the secession of Maryland from the Federal Union, but that if she should withdraw from the Union, he would advise and urge her to confederate with the Middle States, in the formation of a new confederacy, and that he had already in his official capacity entered into a correspondence with the Governors of those States including New York, Pennsylvania, New Jersey, Delaware, Virginia, Missouri and Ohio, with a view, in the ultimate disruption of the Federal Union, to the establishment of such a Central Confederacy. He would interpose no objection to the march of troops through the State to coerce the Southern States, nor would he convene the Legislature to take action in the matter. The Governor went so far as to declare that the seceded States were attempting to coerce Maryland. But, from those with whom he associated the ambassador was led to believe that the gallant, patriotic, and brave people of Maryland were "true to the memories of the past," and should Virginia withdraw from the Union they would, in the shortest possible period of time, assume the responsibility, assemble in

---

24 Ambrose R. Wright was misidentified by Carman as A. W. Wright. Ezra Warner, *Generals in Gray* (Baton Rouge: Louisiana State University, 1959), p. 345. Wright's letter to Hicks (dated Feb. 25) is quoted. It is also in *OR* Series 4, vol. 1, pp. 153-60, though Carman cited selected portions to create this section. Wright's appeal to the memory of Chase, Carroll, and McHenry refers to three leading Maryland men who played prominent roles in the early history of the nation.

spontaneous convention and unite their destinies with the Confederate States of the South.[25]

Meanwhile a recruiting office was opened in Baltimore and enlisted men sent to join the forces besieging Fort Sumter in Charleston Harbor. The office was in charge of Texas Senator Louis T. Wigfall, and was authorized by Jefferson Davis, to whom Wigfall reported that he believed he would meet with great success.[26]

From the day of Mr. Lincoln's arrival in Washington until the day of his inauguration, on the 4th day of March 1861, Baltimore was a quiet city and Maryland a peaceful State. Rumor, it is true, peopled her borders with banded conspirators who threatened to seize the public buildings and archives of the Government, proclaim the Southern Confederacy at Washington, and prevent the inauguration of Mr. Lincoln, but, in truth, such things were seriously thought of by only a few, and then only in case Maryland should first secede. Many who sympathized with the South, particularly those without family, left the State and entered the service of the Southern Confederacy. There was a pause on all sides, an anxious waiting to see what was to come next, a suspense that hung on the tone of the President's inaugural address. It was hoped that through his conservative nature a peaceful solution of difficulties would be reached. His promised peace gave strength to the Union sentiment of the State. His appointment of Montgomery Blair, a citizen of her State, to a seat in his cabinet, cleared the political atmosphere and soothed the apprehensions of all parties.

On March 12th, the State Conference Convention reassembled at Baltimore. As Virginia had not yet seceded, an event, that on the 18th of February was hoped for, it again adjourned, not, however, before appointing a committee of influential gentlemen to visit the Richmond Convention and urge that body to recommend a convention of the Border States. This duty the committee performed by laying before that body a communication inviting such action "to secure, as far as may be done, a full, fair, and accurate impression of the popular will, in such form as to leave no doubt either of its character, or of the authority of those who may he selected as its agents and representatives." Virginia was not then prepared to act in

---

25 Wright's report to Georgia's former governor and the leader of the seccession convention George W. Crawford on March 13 includes this interview with Hicks. See OR Series 4, 1, pp. 151-53.

26 The story of Wigfall's recruiting efforts in Baltimore can be followed in *OR* 1, pp. 276, 278, 279, 281, 284. He was aided by Capt. W. Dorsey Pender, later a Confederate general.

this direction and the committee returned, without any success in the accomplishment of its mission.[27]

The younger members of the committee were not satisfied with this conservative action. They were

> convinced that Virginia would eventually be forced into the war; insisted upon preparing the people, organizing minutemen, collecting and distributing arms and ammunition, and placing affairs in such a train that the blow once struck in Maryland would rouse the neighboring states and involve them in one common cause. The older and more cautious portion were opposed to this and only suggested waiting for Virginia. They had no other plan. They were told that Virginia might linger until Maryland was overpowered, and then it would be too late, but they were unable to perceive the crisis, and refused to co-operate. But the more ardent spirits threw their energies into the work. They organized companies, formed bands of minute-men and prepared for action as quickly and rapidly as possible.[28]

The unmistakable hostile intentions of the secessionists, the knowledge that recruiting for the armies of the Southern Confederacy was being carried out under the auspices of a United States Senator, backed by the financial aid of the wealthiest businessmen of Baltimore, the fact that these bodies of men were nightly drilling in out of the way halls and rooms, impressed Governor Hicks that he should prepare for the worst, and, March 18th, he asked the Secretary of War, if, in case of necessity, he could be furnished arms for 2,000 men. "I am," says the Governor, "strongly inclined to believe that a spirit of insubordination is increasing and that any unfortunate movement on the part of the Virginia Convention, may cause an outbreak in Maryland." Secretary Cameron assured the Governor that his requisition, should the emergency arise, would be complied with.[29]

The attack upon and fall of Fort Sumter caused great excitement in Baltimore and throughout the State of Maryland, which was intensified by the President's call for troops. Opinion was sharply divided and Union men and secessionists gave

27 Maryland's state conference reassembled on the date mentioned. It adjourned with no real progress, but appointed committees. Carman quoted part of several resolutions. See *Annual Cyclopedia, 1861*, p. 444, which does not include the quotations but covered the general business of the session. The specific quotations, which Carman may have used because Confederate records were stored in Washington, can be found in the *Journals and Papers of the Virginia State Convention 1861* (Richmond: Virginia State Library, 1966), 3, document #15.

28 Johnson, "Memoirs," *SHSP*, p. 347.

29 Hicks's letter was to General Winfield Scott, March 18, 1861, with Scott's endorsement of March 20, and Cameron's response to Hicks on March 20, *OR* 51, pt. 1, pp. 317-318.

expression to their views. Breaches of the peace were frequent and angry threats were heard on all sides. Peaceful men armed themselves and the lawless became defiant. But over all there was a strong Union feeling. The thoughtful and influential saw for Maryland no place but in the Union, and men sharing that view sustained Governor Hicks.

Excitement increased on the morning of the 18th, when reports came from Harrisburg that Pennsylvanians were on the way to Washington and would arrive in Baltimore early in the afternoon. Crowds assembled on the streets and threats were freely made that no "Yankee" troops should pass through Baltimore to coerce the South. Thanks to the efficiency of the Baltimore police the Pennsylvanians passed safely through the city and reached Washington in the morning.[30]

The news that Virginia had seceded, the passage of the troops through Baltimore, collisions in the streets, and two secession meetings held during the day, in which armed resistance to the Government was advised, increased the excitement in the city to a fever heat. Business was entirely suspended; the streets were crowded until late at night and, under the stress of circumstances, Unionism was nearly crushed out. Opposition to the passage of Northern troops through Baltimore was unanimous. "The staidest and soberest citizens were infected by it. Men, who all along had been opposed to secession, now openly advocated armed resistance, and it was declared, over and over again, in the most public manner, that no Northern troops should be permitted to enter Baltimore, or if they did enter, to leave the city alive."[31]

Moved by the events of the day Governor Hicks issued an address to the people of Maryland, counseling moderation of speech and invoking them to obey the laws and aid the constituted authorities in preserving the peace. He promised them that no troops should be sent from Maryland, unless for the defense of the National Capital, and assured them of an opportunity "in a special election for

---

30 Several of the Pennsylvanians were injured by bricks thrown by an angry crowd. Sheads and Toomey, *Baltimore During the Civil War*, p. 13.

31 Referring to April 18, an unidentified quotation on the determination to prevent passage of troops through Baltimore was repeated by Carman. Although Carman does not include this quotation, the *Baltimore Sun* referred to a meeting on April 18. *Baltimore Sun*, April 19, 1861. Radcliffe, *Governor Thomas H. Hicks*, p. 64, referred to this as the "States Rights and Southern Rights Convention." The quotation may come from another newspaper. It is not in any of the printed works about the "Pratt Street Riots." The passage of the Pennsylvania troops is not as well known as the attack on the 6th Massachusetts, but is included in most modern works.

members of the Congress of the United States, to express their devotion to the Union, or their desire to see it broken up."[32]

Mayor Brown of Baltimore followed the Governor in issuing a proclamation to the people of the city, concerning the Governor's determination to preserve the peace and maintain inviolate the honor and integrity of Maryland, and expressing satisfaction at his resolution that no troops were to be sent from the State to the soil of any other State.[33]

On the morning of the 19th feeling was intensified by news from Harper's Ferry that the Virginians had driven from that place the small United States garrison and seized the government property. Quick upon the heels of this came the 6th Massachusetts Regiment, its march through the city, rioting and bloodshed in the streets. The story has been so often told that it is too well known to require repetition.[34]

Immediately after the riot Governor Hicks and Mayor Brown united in advising that all troops, en route to Washington, be sent back to the Maryland line, and President Lincoln was appealed to, to send no troops through the city. Early on the morning of the 20th, the bridges on the railroads running north from Baltimore were burned.[35]

When, on the 15th, President Lincoln called for Maryland's quota of troops, four regiments, for the defense of the capital, Governor Hicks called upon the Secretary of War and General Scott, to have an explicit understanding where those troops were to be used "for the defense of the United States Government, the maintenance of the Federal authority and the protection of the Federal Capital," and whether their services would be required out of the State. Two days later he asked that the President reduce the agreement to writing, and the Secretary of War replied, "The troops called for from Maryland are destined for the protection of the Federal capital and the public property of the United States within the limits of the State of Maryland, and it is not intended to remove them beyond those limits except

---

32 The text of Hicks's address of April 18, Moore, *The Rebellion Record*, 1, pp. 76-77, and *Annual Cyclopedia*, 1861, p. 444.

33 For Brown's proclamation, including quotations, see Greeley, *American Conflict*, 1, p. 461.

34 For more about the 6th Massachusetts and the attack in Baltimore, see Brown, *Baltimore and the 19th of April, 1861.*

35 For Brown to Lincoln and Hicks to Lincoln, both April 19, see OR 2, p. 12. The militia officer who carried out the bridge burning, John Merryman, was arrested and became the subject of the famous *habeas corpus* Supreme Court case entitle *Ex-parte Merryman.*

for the defense of the District."[36] Three days later, on the 20th, while his militia was under arms in the city of Baltimore, to prevent troops from other States going through that city to the defense of the Nation's capital, and, while he, in person, at the capital of his state, was vainly beseeching General B. F. Butler not to land Massachusetts men in Annapolis, to reach Washington by going around Baltimore, he wrote to Secretary Cameron declining, for the present, to furnish the four regiments of infantry. He had passed under the influence of the mob.[37]

Governor Hicks was not the only Union man that bent before the storm. It seemed best that, for the time being, the lovers of the Union should acquiesce in the preparations to resist the passage of Northern troops. It was thought better to go with the current than endeavor to stem it. The leading Union papers appealed to the people to sustain Governor Hicks and Mayor Brown in their determination that no Northern troops should pass through Baltimore, nor "unharmed through the State of Maryland for the purpose of subjugating the South." Reverdy Johnson visited President Lincoln and requested him to bring no more troops through Maryland; that, if he did so, all Union sentiment would be annihilated. Other Union men gave the same counsel, and at the moment, it appeared that all Union sentiment was crushed.[38]

There was yielding, too, on the part of the National Government. Sincerely desirous of avoiding any pretext for a collision President Lincoln and General Scott assured the Baltimore authorities that no more troops should be passed through that city and those en route were turned back to Pennsylvania. This concession emboldened a suggestion and then a demand that no more troops should be

36  Lincoln's call for militia, which assigned a quota for regiments from all non-seceding states, is found in OR Series 3, 1, pp. 67-68. For Hicks to Lincoln, including interview, and Cameron's reply, both of April 17, see 3 OR Series 3, vol. 1, pp. 79-80. For Hicks to Cameron, April 20, see OR Series 2, vol. 1, p. 565.

37  Carman's criticism of Hicks "passing under influence of the mob" is generally today judged unfair. What Carman referred to here is the mass meeting in Monument Square in Baltimore that afternoon where Hicks pledged that he would oppose further troop passage through Baltimore and seemed to denounce coercion. Radcliffe, *Governor Thomas H. Hicks*, pp. 54-5. It was, however, that same night, April 19, that Hicks supposedly gave orders to burn the bridges on the railroads leading to Baltimore. He later denied giving the order, *ibid.*, pp. 56-7. Hicks's loyalty was not questioned and he was perceived as acting in the best interest of his state by many people. *Ibid.*, pp. 60-1, 72, Evitts, *A Matter of Allegiances*, pp. 186-7, and OR 2, p. 581.

38  J. Thomas Scharf, *The Chronicles of Baltimore* . . . (Baltimore: Turnbull Brothers, 1874), p. 598. For Reverdy Johnson's visit to Lincoln, and Lincoln's reply to him, see Roy Basler, *The Collected Works of Abraham Lincoln*, 8 Vols. (New Brunswick, NJ: Rutgers University, 1953), 4, pp. 342-3.

brought through Maryland, but to this the President would not consent. He must have troops for the defense of the Capital.[39]

Immediately following the rioting in the streets of Baltimore volunteer companies of infantry and cavalry came from various parts of the State and, on the afternoon of April 21st, General George H. Steuart, in command of the troops in the city, sent special messengers to Colonel Robert E. Lee, informing him that "the people of Baltimore and, indeed, the citizens of Maryland generally, are united in one thing at least, that troops volunteering for Federal service against Virginia and other sister Southern States shall not, if they can help it, pass over the soil of Maryland."[40] Colonel Isaac R. Trimble, who had but recently resigned from the United States army, was looked to as the leader of all military movements, a military dictator in fact. He allowed no boat, vehicle or person to leave the city without his permission. It was well for Baltimore that his rule was absolute. The unruly and vicious element began to show itself. Theft was common and the law abiding became timid. The militia which had been called out on the 19th, and the volunteer companies paraded the streets, under the State flag of Maryland, repressed disorder and turbulence as fully as they could, but, still there was an element which was let loose in those hot hours, which was more feared by the thoughtful than the march of all Massachusetts through Baltimore.[41]

The weakness of the secession cause in Baltimore was soon made evident. A special election was held, April 24th, to choose members of the Legislature. To the dismay of the secessionists and the great joy of the Union men, out of 30,000 votes in Baltimore, but 9,244 were cast. They represented the full strength of rebellion in the city. From that day the Union element asserted itself; the secessionists lost heart. The showing was too plain to be disputed. The next day the Police Board directed all officers and others in the employ of the Board, and all other parties whatsoever, to offer no obstruction to the running of the trains to Washington, the railroad and telegraph lines were repaired, and vessels allowed to leave port.[42]

39 Lincoln's April 20 assurances to Hicks and Brown are in Basler, *Lincoln*, 4, p. 340.

40 Steuart's letter to Lee has not been found, but see Steuart to Letcher, April 25, OR 51, pt. 2, pp. 14-35. See also Bayne and Chancellor to Lee, April 22, which was the cover letter for the message from Steuart, in *ibid.*, Series 2, p. 774. The quotation by Carman is from this source.

41 *Ibid.*, P. 740. Evans, *CMH*, 2, p. 23. Trimble commanded 15,000 men in the vicinity of Baltimore and controlled the city briefly. Brown, *Baltimore and the 19th of April, 1861*, p. 63.

42 The April 24 election was a special election to fill Baltimore's vacant seats in the legislature because of fraud during the 1860 election. The slate was unopposed, making the supposed unanimity somewhat suspect. Evitts, *A Matter of Allegiances*, p. 188, and Brown, *Baltimore and the 19th of April, 1861*, pp. 79-80. The results are in Evans, *CMH*, 2, p. 25.

Meanwhile stirring events were taking place in the State, outside the city of Baltimore. Prevented from coming through Baltimore, troops, en route for Washington, went by way of Annapolis, and the credit of opening that route belongs to General B. F. Butler and the 8th Massachusetts Regiment. Butler, who reached Perryville, on the Susquehanna, by rail on the 20th, embarked on the steamer *Maryland*, and arrived at Annapolis, early on the morning of the 21st. Governor Hicks advised him not to land his men, on account of the great excitement, and informed him that he had telegraphed to that effect to the Secretary of War. But the most surprising act of the Governor was to request the President to order the troops elsewhere and ask Lord Lyons, the British Minister, to act as mediator between the North and South. After some sharp correspondence between General Butler and Governor Hicks, the troops were landed without opposition, and two or three days later arrived in Washington. Many regiments followed by the same route.[43]

Horace Greeley, and many in the North agreed with him, insisted that, practically, on the morning of April, 20th, Maryland was a member of the Southern Confederacy, and that Governor Hicks was in full sympathy and confidence of the secessionists leaders. To this charge Mayor Brown replied:

> It is true that the city then, and for some days afterwards, was in an anomalous condition, which may be best described as one of 'armed neutrality'; but it is not true that in any sense it was, on the 20th of April, or at any other time, a member of the Southern Confederacy. On the contrary, while many, especially among the young and reckless, were doing their utmost to place it in that position, regardless of consequences, and would, if they could, have forced the hands of the city authorities, it was their conduct which prevented such a catastrophe. Temporizing and delay were necessary. As soon as passions had time to cool, a strong reaction set in and the people rapidly divided into two parties—one on the side of the North, and the other on the side of the South; but whatever might be their personal or political sympathies, it was clear to all who had not lost their reason that Maryland, which lay open from the North by both land and sea, would be left in the Union for the sake of the National Capital, even if it required the united power of the nation to accomplish it.[44]

The riot in Baltimore, and enforced isolation of Washington from the North and West, gave great encouragement to secessionists elsewhere, and fostered the

---

43  The letter from Hicks to Butler, April 21, advising him not to land troops, is found in OR 2, pp. 586-7. Hicks to Lincoln concerning Lord Lyons is in Basler, 4, p. 341n.

44  The quotation is by Mayor George Brown, *Baltimore and the 19th of April, 1861*, p. 77.

belief and hope that Maryland would secede and demand Washington, as South Carolina had demanded Fort Sumter. The secessionists in Maryland were urged to persevere in the work they had undertaken; arms and ammunition were promised, some of the former reaching Baltimore from Harper's Ferry on the 23rd. Everywhere in the South the great importance of Baltimore was recognized, but vigorous action did not follow.

Prominent among many Southern men, whom Secretary Seward had taken into his confidence, was John A. Campbell of Alabama, an Associate Justice of the Supreme Court of the United States. Judge Campbell had acted as intermediary between the Government and the Commissioners of the Southern Confederacy, during the negotiations regarding Fort Sumter and, although from the South, was regarded as a Union man and so trusted. He remained at Washington, drawing his pay from the United States Treasury and acting as an advisor to the Southern Confederacy. He gave his opinion of the importance of Baltimore to the Confederates, in these words to Jefferson Davis, written at Washington, April 23, 1861:

> Maryland is the object of chief anxiety with the North and the Administration. Their fondest hopes will be to command the Chesapeake and relieve the Capital. Their pride and their fanaticism would be sadly depressed by a contrary issue. This will be the greatest point in all negotiations I am inclined to think that they are prepared to abandon the south of the Potomac. But not beyond. Maryland is weak. She has no military man of talents, and I did hear that Colonel Huger was offered command and declined it—however his resignation had not been accepted. Huger is plainly not competent for such a purpose. Lee is in Virginia. Think of the condition of Baltimore and provide for it, for there is the place of danger. The events in Baltimore have placed a new aspect upon everything at the North. There is a perfect storm there. While it has to be met, no unnecessary addition should he made to increase it.[45]

The *Richmond Examiner* was especially pleased. In its issue of April 23rd, it said:

> The glorious conduct of Maryland decides the contest at hand. With a generous bravery, worthy of her ancient renown, she has thrown herself into the pathway of the enemy, and made of her body a shield for the South. She stands forth in our day the

---

45 Carman's source for the Campbell letter is John G. Nicolay and John Hay, *Abraham Lincoln: A History*, 10 Vols. (New York: Century Co. 1890), 4, pp. 148-9. It is an incorrect transcription of the original, printed in vol. 7, Haskell M. Monroe, James T. McIntosh, and Lynda Lasswell Crist, eds., *The Papers of Jefferson Davis* (LSU Press: Baton Rouge, 1996 - 2009), 7, pp. 117-20. I have followed the Davis Papers editors' reading of Huger/Hughes, rather than Carman's reading of Huger/Huger.

leader of the Southern cause. The heart of all Maryland responds to the action of Baltimore, and that nursery of fine regiments, rather than becoming the camping ground of the enemy, preparing to rush on the South, will speedily become the camping ground of the South, preparing to cross the line of Mason and Dixon. It is impossible to estimate the moral effect of the action of Maryland. To have gained Maryland is to have gained a host. It insures Washington City and the ignominious expulsion of Lincoln from the White House. It makes good the words of Secretary Walker at Montgomery, in regard to the Federal metropolis. It transfers the line of battle from the Potomac to the Pennsylvania border. It proclaims to the North that, except abolitionized Delaware, the South is a unit against them. . . . It gives us the entire waters of the Chesapeake. It rounds out the fairest domain on the globe for the Southern Confederacy. . . . Maryland is the Louisiana of the East. Baltimore and Richmond will be the New York and Philadelphia of the South, and Norfolk her Boston and Portland combined. The South could not have spared Maryland. Her territory, her waters, her slaves, her people, her soldiers, her ship-builders, her machinists, her wealth, enterprise and bravery were all essential to us.[46]

The *Richmond Enquirer*, April 25th, called upon Virginia to disregard state lines and hold both sides of the Potomac. "The Marylanders must not be left without instant and efficient aid. We must not allow them to be crushed by the powerful army which is coming upon them. We must rush to their aid. We must send them men and arms, and we must do it at once. Maryland is ours by ties of blood, by the memories of the past, by the deeds of her past, by a common and indissoluble interest. Washington is Southern soil, and we must have it."[47]

Jefferson Davis, Governor Letcher and other Southern officials and leaders urged instant relief and assistance to Baltimore, the whole Southern forces re-echoed the cry. But no action was taken.

The grave events transpiring in Baltimore and the excitement throughout the State impelled the Governor to summon the Legislature. The immediate cause of this action was the issuance of a call by a single senator, Coleman Yellott, for that body to meet at Baltimore. Knowing that such a meeting in that city, filled with secessionists, would lead inevitably to the secession of the State and more

46 *Richmond Examiner*, April 23, 1861. Carman may have used this newspaper account or a source not found, but a different quotation from the same issue is in Greeley, *American Conflict*, 1, p. 470, note 13.

47 *Richmond Enquirer* of April 25, 1861. This is not in Moore, *Rebellion Record*, so it may be an original paper in Carman's files or the Confederate Archives. The last sentence is not part of the article. Carman either conflated it from another source or, less likely, invented it.

bloodshed in its streets and on the soil of Maryland, the Governor forestalled such action, by convening it at Frederick, in a loyal part of the State.

The Legislature assembled in Frederick, at noon, April 26th, and received the Governor's message. After revisiting the steps taken to maintain order in Baltimore, to prevent the passage of troops through Maryland, and his unsuccessful effort to have Lord Lyons act as mediator between the loyal and the seceded States, Governor Hicks said that events satisfied him that the War Department had concluded to make Annapolis the point for landing troops, and had rushed to open and maintain communication between that place and Washington. His convictions were that the only safety of Maryland was in forging a neutral position between the people of the North and South. Maryland had violated no rights of either section. She had been loyal to the Union. He commended Maryland to take no side against the General Government, until it should commit outrages which justify resistance to its authority. He was for Union and Peace; this was the sole groundwork of his policy.[48]

On the 27th the Senate, by a unanimous vote, issued an address to the people of Maryland soliciting their confidence in the fidelity with which they proposed to discharge their duties and disclaiming all idea, intention or authority to pass any ordinance of secession.

Two, at least, of the Senators, who by their votes thus assured the people of Maryland that all fears of secession were without foundation, were, on that same day, carrying on an intrigue with the Confederate General Ruggles, looking to co-operation with Virginia troops, on Maryland soil, for the capture of Fort Washington and a dash on the National capital.[49]

Every shade of opinion was represented by the resolutions proposed as to Maryland's duty. They were all referred, as were those proposing the organization of the militia, to the committee on Federal Relations in both houses. On the 9th of May, the committee of the House of Delegates presented an exceedingly able and

48  For the calling of the Maryland legislature for Frederick on April 26 and Hicks's message to that body, see *Annual Cyclopedia*, 1861, pp. 444-6, and Greeley, *American Conflict*, 1, pp. 470-1. Moore, *The Rebellion Record*, pp. 159-61, has a copy from a New York newspaper. Denton, *A Southern Star for Maryland*, pp. 75-116, provides a useful summary of this legislative session, as does Radcliffe, *Governor Thomas H. Hicks*, Chapters 7 and 8. Coleman Yellott was a Know-Nothing state senator known to be of secessionist leanings. *Ibid.*, pp. 71-3 for Yellott and the address. The full text of the address, which Carman mentioned, is found in the *Maryland General Assembly's Maryland Senate Journal*, April 27, 1861, p. 8.

49  The source of the story of two Maryland state senators conspiring with Confederate Daniel Ruggles for the capture of Fort Washington and a dash on the capital has not been found. This may be from a newspaper or another source. Ruggles, not yet a Confederate general, was in command of Virginia troops in the district along the Potomac River. *OR* 2, p. 775.

elaborate report drawn by S. Teakle Wallis, reviewing all the constitutional points in the question of secession and the "coercion of sovereign States" denouncing President Lincoln for what they considered his illegal act in calling out the militia to wage war against the Southern Confederacy, and criticizing Governor Hicks for the stand he had taken, regretting that in acknowledging the President's call for troops "the response of his Excellency, the Governor, should have fallen so far short, in this regard, of the manly and patriotic spirit with which the Governors of Virginia, North Carolina, Tennessee, Kentucky and Missouri threw back the insulting proposition of the Administration."[50]

The spirit of the Legislature is shown in the above quotation. The majority of the members would gladly have voted for immediate secession, but they feared the consequences. They argued up to the point of resistance, but they did not resist. They protested, but, under all the circumstances, reached the conclusion that the only possible attitude of the State towards the Federal Government was of submission "voluntary and cheerful submission on the part of those who can persuade themselves that the Constitution remains inviolate and the Union unbroken, or that the Union can survive the Constitution—unwilling and galling submission on the part of those who think and feel differently; but still, peaceful submission on both sides." As to calling a sovereign convention and arming the militia, they favored both, but these things could not be done when the State was prostrate and the Constitution silenced by Federal bayonets.

Following this report the committee prepared the adoption of resolutions protesting against the war which the Federal Government had declared upon the Confederate States and the State of Virginia; asking the Federal Government in the name of God and humanity, to cease the unholy and unprofitable strife; demanding the peaceful and immediate recognition of the Confederate States; denouncing the military occupation of Maryland, and calling on all good citizens to abstain from violent and unlawful interference, with the troops in transit through or quartered in the State.[51]

These resolutions passed the House of Delegates on May 10th by a vote of 45 to 12. The Senate added a resolution providing for the appointment of four

---

50 The quotation is from the *Report of Committee of Federal Relations*, written by Severn Teakle Wallis. A full text of the resolutions coming from the legislature can be found in *Maryland General Assembly*, House and Senate Documents, 1861, Document "F." The resolution also appears in Evans, *CMH*, 2, pp. 30-2, which Carman more likely used.

51 Carman treats this report by Wallis as a separate resolution, but they were all approved as a group; the vote count in the next paragraph is correct. See Evitts, *A Matter of Allegiances*, p. 188, and Evans, *CMH*, 2, pp. 30-2.

members of each house, four of whom should wait upon the President of the United States and four upon the President of the Southern Confederacy, to obtain, if possible, a cessation of hostilities, with a view to an adjustment of existing troubles by means of negotiations, rather than the sword.[52]

Among the measures proposed and one which caused much discussion in the Senate and great uneasiness throughout the State, was a bill presented by Mr. Yellott, Senator from Baltimore, entitled: "An Act to provide for the safety and people of Maryland." This bill provided for a board, to be appointed by the Legislature, vested with extraordinary powers and had for its object the transfer of the executive power from the Governor to a body of men of well known secessionist sympathies. It authorized the expenditure of $5,000,000 for the defense of the State and gave the entire control of the military into the hands of the board, including the appointment and removal of commissioned officers. As soon as the features of the bill became generally known, from every part of the State came vigorous protests against its passage. It was denounced as unconstitutional, despotic, and fatal to the interests of Maryland. Some petitions favored its passage, but sentiment was so overwhelmingly against it, that its friends became alarmed and abandoned it. Bradley T. Johnson, who was constant and ardent in pressing the measure, says, "The plan of the projections of the Committee of Safety was to arm the militia. They expected to equip 40,000 men as promptly as the Northern States had armed and equipped their volunteers, and they knew that Maryland volunteers would take arms as quickly as those of Massachusetts and Ohio. They did not propose to carry the State out of the Union, but they intended to arm their young men and command the peace in the State. When that failed, as fail they knew it would, the State would be represented by 40,000 armed and equipped volunteers, who would carry her flag in the front line and would make her one of the Confederate States in fact, if not in name."[53]

When Johnson saw that the bill could not be carried through the Legislature he arranged with Captain James Ashby, then at Point of Rocks, to dash into Frederick, seize Governor Hicks and carry him into Virginia, and then break up the State

---

52 The Senate's call for committees to visit both Lincoln and Davis is mentioned in Radcliffe, *Governor Thomas H. Hicks*, p. 105, and also is in the Maryland Senate Journal, May 13, 1861, p. 140. It is not in Evans, *CMH*, or other contemporary works, but Carman may have picked it up from the newspapers.

53 Yellott's bill intended to strip Governor Hicks of his power by calling for a "board" to decide issues dealing with the defense for the state, including control of the militia. Yellott had hand-picked secessionists to pack the board and overrule the governor. See Denton, *A Southern Star for Maryland*, p. 107; Greeley, *American Conflict*, 1, p. 471; McPherson, *Political History*, p. 9; Johnson's quotation on the Board of Safety comes from Evans, *CMH*, 2, p. 36.

Government and throw it into the hands of the Legislature, that would be obliged to take charge during the interregnum. When notice of this intention was given to leaders in the Legislature, they promptly demanded that Johnson desist from the enterprise, and Johnson dropped the matter.[54]

On the 14th of May the Legislature adjourned until the 4th of June. When it assembled on the 2lth of April it was ripe for secession. Three-fourths of its members were ready to call a "sovereign convention," as secession bodies were then termed, vote the State out of the Union, and form an alliance with Virginia. But events moved too rapidly. Annapolis was held by a strong Union force. Washington was secured. Pennsylvania threatened the northern border of the State, the North demanded a thoroughfare to the National capital, and the cry of commercial distress came up from Baltimore.[55]

Nor was Virginia all powerful. The secessionists had looked to her action with much interest. From the secession of South Carolina down to the meeting of the Maryland Legislature they had squared their actions with those of Virginia. She was looked upon as an exemplar and a guide. Above all things an alliance with her was most popular. It will be remembered that a committee, that visited Richmond about the middle of March, did not find the Virginians prepared for a decided step, but, after the secession of the State, the Virginians became very active in bringing influence to bear upon the deliberations of the Maryland Legislature. Many self constituted agents came across the border to instill lessons of statesmanship into the heads of the Maryland legislature, and Governor Letcher sent, as special commissioner, Ex-Senator James M. Mason to assure the Legislature of the sympathy of Virginia and to say that should they think proper "to commit the power and authority of the State of Maryland, in co-operation with Virginia and the Confederate States, in resistance to the Government in Washington, then and in that case Virginia will afford all practicable facilities for the furtherance of such object, and will place such arms at the disposal of the Maryland authorities as she may have it in her power to give."[56]

At first, Mr. Mason was greatly encouraged and reported that the Legislature was probably for secession, but he soon ascertained that he could not enter into a

---

54 The story of the plan to kidnap Hicks comes from Johnson in Evans, *CMH*, 2, pp. 36-7. Carman wrote James Ashby, but obviously meant Capt. Turner Ashby.

55 Carman's assessment of the Maryland legislature follows Johnson's account in Evans, *ibid.*, Chapter 2.

56 Mason served as an unofficial commissioner to Maryland from Virginia. The quotation comes from *OR* 2, p. 774, and his appointment is in *ibid.*, p. 772; *ibid.*, 51, pt. 2, p. 519. Mason's report to Jefferson Davis is in Davis, *Papers*, 7, pp. 148-52.

compact committing Maryland to secession and an alliance with Virginia. The time had passed. The sober, second thought of the people had asserted itself, and the United States Government had quartered 40,000 soldiers on her soil and overlooking it. She was securely moored to the Union.

On the night of May 13th, General Butler marched into Baltimore and camped on Federal Hill, completely controlling the city. Next morning he issued a proclamation in which he promised protection to all law abiding citizens and gave notice that all traitorous acts must cease. From the 19th of April to the 14th of May a great change had taken place in the attitude of the city toward the General Government. In spite of the activity and energy of the secessionists it was apparent that the Union men were largely in the majority. Many causes contributed to this result.[57]

Encouraged by the growth of the Union feeling in Baltimore and throughout the State, and strengthened by the arms of the National Government, Governor Hicks thought of complying with the requisition of the Secretary of War for four regiments, but was deterred by the menacing attitude of the Legislature. But, immediately upon the adjournment of this body, on May 14th, he issued his proclamation, calling for four regiments of infantry to serve within the limits of the State, or for the defense of the capital of the United States.

This proclamation and the occupation of Baltimore, by General Butler, on the same day, dates the death of secession in Maryland and the complete ascendancy of the National Government.[58]

Meanwhile there were those who, doubting the loyalty of Governor Hicks or despairing of prompt and decided action on his part, made direct overtures to the National authorities to volunteer for the defense of the National capital. Of these was James Cooper, a native of the State, but a resident of Pennsylvania, who, April 10th, asked if the Secretary of War of the United States Government had authority to commission the officers of a brigade or regiment, raised in Maryland independent of the State authority and, whether, possessing the authority, it could be relied upon to do so. The response was favorable. Cooper was appointed by the President a brigadier-general of volunteers, assigned to duty in Maryland and authorized to accept volunteers, under the call of May 2nd, for three years or during

---

57 Butler's report of operations, including his proclamation, may be found in *OR* 2, pp. 29-32. See Denton, *A Southern Star for Maryland*, Chapter 5, and Evans, *CMH*, Chapter 3, for a summary of activity in Maryland during this time.

58 Hicks's May 14 proclamation calling for four regiments is in Greeley, *American Conflict*, 1, p. 412.

the war, and by the middle of May reported that he had filled Maryland's quota and awaited muster into service.[59]

Under the circumstances the Secretary of War did not need the services of the four regiments, for three months service, and so advised the Governor, and also of the fact that General Cooper had been authorized to accept Maryland's quota under the call of May 2nd. The 1st Regiment, raised primarily in Baltimore, was mustered into the United States service before the end of May, recruiting for the 2nd began in June and for the 3rd in July.[60]

Maryland's contribution to the army of the Union was large. From the beginning of the war to its close she furnished twenty regiments and one independent company of infantry; four regiments, one battalion and one independent company of cavalry, and six batteries of light artillery. The records of the War and Navy Departments show that, from 1861 to 1865, she furnished 50,316 white troops, 8,718 colored troops, and 3,925 sailors and marines, or a grand total of 62,959 men, nearly one-tenth of the entire population, or over 15 per cent of the male population, and more than one half of her available military population—good men and true.[61]

Maryland contributed liberally to the Southern cause, also, and many of her sons attained high rank and made brilliant records in the Confederate army. When it became apparent that Maryland would not join her fortunes with the South, many of her younger sons thought they had but one honorable course, and that was to carry the flag of Maryland with the Southern army and rally around it such Maryland men as could he collected. First to move in this direction was Bradley T. Johnson of Frederick. He was an ardent secessionist, and one or the first to lead a company into Baltimore after the riots of April 19th. When the Legislature convened, he intently watched its movement and essayed to direct them. He looked with contempt upon conservative action, within the forms of the law, and advocated revolutionary methods. When he saw that Maryland would not act, he applied to Mr. Mason, the commissioner from Virginia, and procured from him authority to raise troops for the Southern army and proceeded to Harper's Ferry to obtain Colonel Thomas J.

---

59  For James Cooper's activities, see *OR* Series 3, vol. 1, pp. 138, 210, 618, 931.

60  *Ibid.*, p. 210

61  The figures for Maryland's contribution to the Union army and navy are given in William F. Fox, *Regimental Losses in the Civil War* (Morningside, Dayton Ohio, 1985), pp. 532, 534. Carman's figures do not match the official numbers cited in Fox for the number of white army volunteers. Both Fox and Dyer's *Compendium*—and most modern sources—agree that it was 33,995. All other figures agree. Carman mistakenly added a group of men who paid the commutation fee but did not serve. *OR* Series 3, 4, p. 1,269.

Jackson's permission to rendezvous and ration his men at Point of Rocks, the most available point for that section of Maryland. On the 8th of May, Johnson marched his company out of Frederick and crossed over to Virginia, at Point of Rocks, and reported to Captain Turner Ashby. Some sons of Maryland preceded Bradley T. Johnson, many more followed him and, from the secession of Virginia until the surrender of Appomattox, it is estimated that more than 15,000 of them served the Confederate cause, and they served it bravely.[62]

It is known to the student of the history of the time under consideration that slavery had but little share in determining Maryland's position at the outbreak of the rebellion. Political lines of separation did not run between opposing opinions on that subject, nor were the advocates of freedom confined to one party. Many of the heaviest slaveholders in the State were uncompromising Union men and most of the secessionists had no pecuniary interest in slavery. In fact, slavery was not an appreciable factor in Maryland politics. In Baltimore and in the northern part of the State there were but few slaveholders and slavery was of a nominal character. All state legislation had been in the direction of improved condition for the slave.[63]

The Maryland Legislature resumed its sitting on June 4th and Mr. Goldsborough, from the committee to intercede with the Federal Government, reported that the purposes of the committee were defeated by the movement of Federal troops in Virginia and an active commencement of hostilities, and that they had not felt authorized on the part of the sovereign State of Maryland in presenting a request which had been in advance repudiated. The dignity of the State and the self respect of the committee demanded this course.[64]

The committee appointed at the preceding session to visit Montgomery, Alabama, laid before the Senate and House a letter of Jefferson Davis, in which he expressed the hope "that at no distant day, a State whose people, habits, and institutions are so clearly related and assimilated with theirs, will seek to unite their fate and fortunes with those of the Confederacy," but as to a cessation of all hostilities, that depended on the action of the Federal Government, as to the

62 Johnson, "Memoirs," *SHSP*, pp. 349-53; Carman's estimate of 15,000 Marylanders in the Confederate Army may be on the low side. Other estimates put the number at 20,000 to 25,000. For a discussion of Maryland Confederates, see Dan Hartzler's *Maryland in the Confederacy* (Silver Spring MD: Family Line Publications, 1986), pp. 1-3, and Denton, *A Southern Star for Maryland*, Chapter 6.

63 The source for Carman's statement is unknown, and may be his opinion. The general thrust of his argument is borne out in Evitts, *A Matter of Allegiances*, p. 136-7, and Robert J. Brugger, *Maryland: A Middle Temperament 1634-1980* (Baltimore: Johns Hopkins University Press, 1988) pp. 262-3, 270.

64 Goldsborough's committee is reported in *Annual Cyclopedia, 1861*, p. 447.

Confederacy, "Its policy cannot be but peace—peace with all nations and people."[65]

Petitions poured in from all parts of the State demanding the immediate adjournment of the Legislature *sine die*, that the public welfare would be promoted thereby, that they could do no good for the people, whose sentiments they failed to represent. They expressed alarm at the propositions before the Legislature and declared their fixed purpose to resist, by force, if necessary, any attempt to drag Maryland into collision with the General Government. They solemnly protested against the appointment by the Legislature of ambassadors and demanded that the delegates chosen under the reign of terror in Baltimore City should at once retire permanently from the positions they held. They protested against the so-called "Bill of Ratification" of outrages in Baltimore and against the call of a convention to determine whether the people of Maryland should remain citizens of the United States.[66]

Notwithstanding the angry protests of the people from all parts of the State, the Legislature proceeded with its hostility to the Union cause. The Senate, June 5th, asked the Governor why he had taken the arms from certain military companies in Baltimore and deposited them for safe keeping in Fort McHenry and what security he had for their return. The Governor promptly replied that he did so because he was satisfied that many of them had been carried beyond the limits of the State, and more of them were likely to be used for disloyal purposes. He had ordered them deposited in Fort McHenry because other arms belonging to the State had previously been taken from the depository selected in Baltimore, and he did not deem it prudent to again incur a similar risk. The security he had for them was the honor of the United States Government, and of its loyal officers; he deemed it absurd and insulting to ask for more.[67]

On June 11th, S. Teakle Wallis, chairman of the committee on Federal Relations of the House of Delegates, made a report on the "arbitrary proceedings of the United States authorities." The Governor was charged with neglect of duty in not protecting John Merryman "a prisoner at Fort McHenry, a victim of military

---

65 Davis to Maryland Commissioners is not in Davis, *Papers*, but is in Dunbar Rowland, ed., *Jefferson Davis, Constitutionalist: His Letters, Papers and Speeches*, 10 Vols. (Jackson, MS: Mississippi Department of Archives and History, 1923), 5, pp. 100-1. Editors of the Davis, *Papers* cite it from *OR* Series 2, vol. 1, p. 680, but it is not there, and is not in the other volumes of the *OR*.

66 Journal of Proceedings of the Senate, pp. 140-3.

67 On the June 5 request of the Senate concerning arms taken from local militias, and Hicks's reply, see Radcliffe, *Governor Thomas H. Hicks*, pp. 103-7 and Denton, *A Southern Star for Maryland*, pp. 140-1. The full text of the order is in Radcliffe, *Governor Thomas H. Hicks*, p. 97.

lawlessness and arbitrary power," and Ross Winans, a venerable and prominent citizen, a useful and respected member of the House, "arrested by military force, without color of lawful authority, and hurried into illegal imprisonment within the walls of a Federal fortress." The committee offered for consideration resolutions declaring their "earnest and unqualified protest against the oppressive and tyrannical assertion and exercise of military jurisdiction, within the limits of Maryland, over the persons and property of her citizens, by the Government of the United States, and do solemnly declare the same to be subversive of the most sacred guarantees of the Constitution and in flagrant violation of the fundamental and most cherished principles of American free government." These resolutions, passed on the 22nd, were sent to the Senators from Maryland, in the Senate of the United States, with the request that they "present the same to the Senate, to be recorded among its proceedings, in vindication of the right, and in perpetual memory of the solemn remonstrance of this State against the manifold usurpations and oppressions of the Federal Government."[68]

On the same day the Senate concurred in resolutions, passed by the House, protesting against the acts of the United States Government in quartering large standing armies upon the soil of Maryland, in seizing and using her railroads and telegraphs, in depriving her citizens of arms and subjecting them to arrest, declaring that "the right of separation from the Federal Union is a right neither arising under nor prohibited by the Constitution, but a sovereign right, independent of the Constitution to be exercised by the several states upon their own responsibility." They demanded that the war should cease and that the Southern Confederacy be recognized, and viewed with the utmost alarm and indignation the exercise of the despotic power that dared to suspend the writ of Habeas Corpus and held John Merryman within the walls of Fort McHenry.[69]

On June 25th, the Legislature adjourned until July 30th. The whole session had been marked by hostility to the National Government and an intense dislike of Governor Hicks, who stood as a bulwark against its disunion schemes and who, after it adjourned, continued the work, in which he had been some time engaged, of disarming the disloyal militia.

68 Wallis's report on June 11 demands the release of Merryman. The resolutions were passed June 22 and sent to Anthony Kennedy and James A. Pearce, Maryland's two U.S. senators. *OR* Series 2, vol. 1, pp. 586-7.

69 On June 22, the Maryland Senate passed resolutions condemning U.S. repression and asking recognition of Confederacy. Brown, Baltimore and the 19th *of April, 1861*, p. 98, and Radcliffe, *Governor Thomas H. Hicks*, p. 106. Carman's interpretation—that the legislature was more secessionist than Governor Hicks—coincides with most modern interpretations, as found in Evitts, *A Matter of Allegiances*, and Denton, *A Southern Star for Maryland*.

While the Legislature was in session secessionists in the State and beyond its borders looked for assistance from the Confederate troops at Harper's Ferry, and both President Davis and General Lee were appealed to, to take position in Maryland. It was hoped that Confederate occupation would counteract the effect of National possession and revive the waning secession feeling. Particularly was it desired to lay strong hold on Western Maryland. On the day that the Legislature assembled, June 4, I. R. Trimble, a native of Maryland, an officer in the Confederate service, then at Norfolk, Virginia, addressed an elaborate communication to General Lee suggesting a strong movement to Hagerstown, Maryland, it being a better point to defend Virginia than Harper's Ferry. He was particularly anxious that, before the election in Maryland, this movement should be made and he urged a simultaneous movement on Baltimore, which would revolutionize the State of Maryland and bring 6000 armed men into the Confederate ranks and probably have the effect of driving Lincoln out of Washington and down the Potomac.[70]

Plans were prepared for organizing secretly a military force for the liberation of the State. Companies, regiments and brigades were to be recruited at different parts of the State and sworn into the Confederate service, rendezvous to be designated for each, and certain trustworthy persons in Maryland were to be appointed to organize this force and arm it with shotguns, rifles, pistols and anything else calculated to destroy the enemy, and strike for Baltimore or Washington as should be determined by the authorities at Richmond. The great advantage of the proposed plan was that "when Maryland does turn upon her oppressors she will have a regular organized force, and not a mere rabble without organization."[71]

On the 10th of June, General N. P. Banks was appointed to command of the Department of Annapolis, with headquarters at Baltimore. On the 27th, he arrested Marshal Kane, committed him to Fort McHenry, and suspended the Commissioner of Police. Four days later he arrested and imprisoned the Police Commissioner and revolutionized the entire city government. The removal of the municipal authorities and the substitution of military rule was excused on the plea of military necessity. Baltimore had sinned on the 19th of April, it might sin again, and the risk was too great of having a barrier placed on one of the principal routes

---

70 Trimble's letter to Lee dated June 4, 1861, is in OR 51, pt. 2, pp. 129-30. Carman calls Trimble a native of Maryland, but he was born in Culpeper, Virginia. See Appendix 1, Biographical Dictionary, for more information about Trimble.

71 The plan for organizing secret Confederate forces in Maryland was proposed by Severn T. Wallis to James D. McCabe. McCabe passed it on the Leroy Pope Walker, Confederate Secretary of War. The full letter, which Carman quoted, is in OR 51, pt. 2, pp. 155-7. Wallis refers to the letter being written in cipher and requests an answer in the same manner.

connecting the Capital of the Nation with the North. In a lesser degree the whole State was under suspicion and it was the mailed hand that was offered her.[72]

The Legislature, which re-assembled on the 30th of July, continued in session until the 7th of August. It spent its days in talking and resolving, and after adopting a vigorous protest against the "unconstitutional and illegal acts of President Lincoln" adjourned to meet on the 17th of September.[73]

As the time approached for the adjourned meeting there were apprehensions that the passage of an ordinance of secession was contemplated and, September 11th, the Secretary of War instructed General Banks, then in command of troops at Darnestown, Maryland, that such action must be prevented and, if necessary to that end, all or any number of the members should be arrested. On the 12th, General [George] McClellan advised General Banks that the seizure of the members would be made on the 17th, and instructed him to "have everything prepared to arrest the whole party, and be sure that none escape." If successfully carried out McClellan thought it would "go far toward breaking the back bone of the rebellion."[74]

Preliminary to the arrest of the legislature, Mayor Brown and several prominent citizens of Baltimore were quietly arrested and committed to Fort McHenry. Among them were the members of the Legislature from that city.

Both houses of the Legislature were called at noon, on the 17th, as no quorum appeared an adjournment was effected until the next day. Meanwhile the military surrounded the city and permitted none to leave it. On the 18th several officers and members of the Senate and House of Delegates were arrested and the Legislature broken up.

It was stoutly maintained by the National authorities that the Legislature intended passing an ordinance of secession; it was quite as earnestly denied by those who had means of knowing. Mayor George W. Brown says: "The apprehension that the Legislature intended to pass an act of secession, as intimated by Secretary Cameron, was, in view of the position in which the State was placed, and the whole condition of affairs, so absurd that it is difficult to believe that he seriously

---

72 Banks' arrest orders for Kane and others are in *ibid.*, 2, pp. 138-56. The arrests are summarized in Brown, *Baltimore and the 19th of April, 1861*, pp. 97-9, and are mentioned in Moore, ed., *The Rebellion Record*, 2, Diary, pp. 8-9.

73 The quotation from the August 7th resolution is similar to language in Brown, *Baltimore and the 19th of April, 1861*, p. 100.

74 McClellan's letter to Banks is printed in full in Stephen Sears, ed., *The Civil War Papers of George McClellan* (New York: Ticknor Fields, 1989), p. 99. For more information on the arrests, and Cameron's letter to Banks, see *OR* 5, pp. 193-7. How Carman knew of this letter from McClellan is unknown, although a reference to the arrests is in George B. McClellan, *McClellan's Own Story* (Charles L. Webster and Company, New York, 1887), p. 146.

entertained it. The blow was no doubt, however, intended to strike with terror the opponents of the war, and was one of the effective means resorted to by the Government to obtain, as it soon did, entire control of the State."[75]

The action met the approval of Governor Hicks, who, two days later, congratulated General Banks; said he concurred in all that he had done; that the good fruit produced by the arrests was already apparent, and that there be no longer any mincing matters with "these desperate people."[76]

For five months the Legislature, sustained and encouraged by less than one fifth of the people, had kept the State in a turmoil and filled the National authorities with grave apprehensions. It was well known that it did not reflect or represent the wishes or intents of the State and, when finally broken up, there was much relief and great satisfaction to all who had at heart the true interests of the State. A large majority of her people had the good sense to see that the welfare of the State was inseparably blended with the Union but such had been the fraudulent and violent spirit and course of the secessionists that they were overawed. The dispersal of the legislature and the determination of the National Government that no more should that body stir up strife in the State and Baltimore threaten the security of Washington, gave encouragement to Union men everywhere and strengthened the growth of Union expression in Maryland. Volunteering became brisk and confidence grew that the Union men could take care of the State.

On November 6th a state election was held resulting in the choice of A. W. Bradford, the candidate of the Union party, for governor, by a majority of 31,438, and a Legislature largely Union. Ten days thereafter, November 16th, Governor Hicks called the newly elected Legislature in extra session, December 3rd, "to consider and determine the steps necessary to be taken to enable the State of Maryland to take her place with the other loyal States, in defense of the Constitution and the Union."[77]

It is beyond our purpose to pursue the subject further. The struggle of the Union majority for supremacy had been bitter, and agitated the State from Mountains to the sea, but with the National and State authorities in accord peace was assured and tranquility restored. Many secessionists and the turbulent left the State and those, only, who essayed to provoke disorder or encourage revolution felt

---

75 The quotation from Mayor Brown is from Brown, *Baltimore and the 19th of April, 1861,* p. 103. See also the series of letters in *OR* 5, pp. 193-7.

76 The quote is from Hicks letter to Banks, *ibid.,* p. 197.

77 For details of the November election and Hicks's call for loyalty to the Union, see *Annual Cyclopedia, 1861,* p. 448, except for number of votes, see *New York Tribune Almanac, 1862* (New York: Tribune Publishing Co., 1863), p. 59.

the "despot's heel" or complained of oppression. Those who walked and lived within the law were in the full enjoyment of their rights and liberties.[78]

*The despot's heel is on thy shore,*
*Maryland!*
*His torch is at thy temple door,*
*Maryland!*
*Avenge the patriotic gore*
*That flecked the streets of Baltimore,*
*And be the battle queen of yore,*
*Maryland, My Maryland!*

*Hark to an exiled son's appeal,*
*Maryland*
*My mother State to thee I kneel*
*Maryland!*
*For life or death, for woe or weal,*
*Thy peerless chivalry reveal,*
*And gird thy beauteous limbs with steel,*
*Maryland, My Maryland!*

*Thy wilt not cower in the dust,*
*Maryland!*
*Thy beaming sword shall never rust,*
*Maryland!*
*Remember Carroll's sacred trust,*
*Remember Howard's warlike thrust,*
*And all that slumber with the dust,*
*Maryland, My Maryland!*
*Come! 'Tis the red dawn of the day,*
*Maryland!*
*Come with the panoplied array,*
*Maryland!*
*With Ringgold's spirit for the fray,*
*With Watson's blood at Monterey,*

---

78 Carman summed up his feeling about the secession movement and demonstrates his Union proclivities by stressing the mild occupation of the state. Given his background, his attitude is not surprising. Why Carman chose to include James Ryder Randall's poetic appeal for Maryland to secede is a mystery.

*With Fearless Lowe and dashing May,*
*Maryland, My Maryland!*

*Dear Mother, burst the tyrants' chain,*
*Maryland!*
*Virginia should not call in vain,*
*Maryland!*
*She meets her sisters on the plain,*
*"Sic Semper!" 'tis the proud refrain*
*That baffles minions back amain,*
*Maryland!*
*Arise in majesty again,*
*Maryland, My Maryland!*

*Come! for thy shield is bright and strong,*
*Maryland!*
*Come! for thy dalliance does thee wrong,*
*Maryland!*
*Come to thine own heroic strong,*
*Stalking with liberty along,*
*And chant thy dauntless slogan-song*
*Maryland, My Maryland!*

*I see the blush upon thy cheek,*
*Maryland!*
*But thou was ever bravely meek,*
*Maryland!*
*But Lo! There surges forth a shriek,*
*from hill to hill, from creek to creek,*
*Potomac calls to Chesapeake,*
*Maryland, My Maryland!*

*Thou wilt not yield the Vandal toil,*
*Maryland!*
*Thou wilt not crook to his control,*
*Maryland!*
*Better the fire upon thee roll,*
*Better the shot, the blade, the bowl,*
*Than crucifixion of the soul,*
*Maryland, My Maryland!*

*I hear the distant thunder-hum,*
*Maryland!*
*The "Old Line's" bugle, fife and drum,*
*Maryland!*
*She is not dead, nor deaf, nor dumb;*
*Huzza! she spurns the Northern scum.*
*She breathes, she burns! she'll come!*
*Maryland, My Maryland!*

The author of this popular song is James R. Randall, who at the time of writing was professor of English Literature at Poydras College, in Louisiana. On April 26, 1861, he read in a New Orleans paper an account of the attack on the 6th Massachusetts Regiment, as it passed through Baltimore. Mr. Randall says: "This account excited me greatly. I had been long been absent from my native city, and the startling event there inflamed my mind that night. I could not sleep, for my nerves were all unstrung and I could not dismiss what I had read in the paper from my mind. About midnight I arose, lit a candle, and went to my desk. Some powerful spirit appeared to possess me, and almost immediately I proceeded to write the song of My Maryland. I remember that the idea appeared to take shape first as music in the brain—some wild air that I cannot not now recall. The whole poem of nine stanzas, as originally written was dashed off rapidly when once begun."

The manner in which the words were wedded to music is told by Miss Hattie Carey, of Baltimore, afterwards the wife of Professor H. N. Martin, of Johns Hopkins University:

The Glee Club was to hold its meeting in our parlor one evening early in June, and my sister Jennie, being the only musical member of the family, had charge of the program on the occasion. With a schoolgirl's eagerness to score a success, she resolved to secure some new and ardent expression of feelings that were by this time wrought up to the point of explosion. In vain she searched through her stock of songs and airs—nothing seemed intense enough to suit her. Aroused by her tone of despair, I came to the rescue with the suggestion that she should adopt the words of 'Maryland, My Maryland,' which had been continually on my lips since the appearance of the lyric a few days before in the South. I produced the paper and began disclaiming the verses. "Lauriger Horitis," she exclaimed, and in a flash the immortal song found a voice in the stirring air so perfectly adapted to it. That night when her contralto voice rang out the stanzas, the refrain rolled forth from every throat without pause or preparation; and the enthusiasm communicated itself with such effect to the crowd assembled beneath our windows as to endanger seriously the liberties of the party.[79]

---

79  Louis A. Banks, *Immortal Songs of Camp and Field* (Clevelan: Burrows Bros., 1898). The story of James R. Randall and his poem "Maryland" is properly cited, *ibid.*, pp. 205-7.

# The Confederate
# Invasion of Maryland

I n the preceding chapter we have noted the effort of prominent individuals, mass meetings, city and county conventions and the Legislature to ally Maryland with the Southern Confederacy. We have noted, also, the great desire of the South for such an alliance to round out the fair proportions of the new Confederacy. There were some proposed military movements, also, to that end, but these were to be made in connection with legislative action and, measurably, to influence it.

When the Confederate army began to gather in front of Washington more specific measures were canvassed and proposed. On July 18, 1861, General Beauregard, commanding the Confederate Army of the Potomac, sent Colonel James Chesnut, Jr., of his staff, to Richmond, with a suggestion to Jefferson Davis that General Johnston's Army of the Shenandoah, then at Winchester, and the Army of the Potomac, under his command, be united at Manassas, advance upon and crush General McDowell in the vicinity of Fairfax Court House, then turn upon and defeat General Patterson near Winchester. General Garnett was to be re-enforced sufficiently to defeat McClellan in West Virginia, and then join

Johnston at Winchester; "who was forthwith to cross the Potomac into Maryland with his whole force, arouse the people as he advanced, to the recovery of their political rights and the defense of their homes and families from an offensive invader, and then march to the investment of Washington in the rear," while he (Beauregard) assumed the offensive in front. The complicated plan was not seriously considered and Beauregard's official report, in which the subject is mentioned, bears the endorsement of Mr. Davis that the plan "was based on the improbable and inadmissible supposition that the enemy was to await [everywhere], isolated and motionless, until our forces could effect junction to attack them in detail.[1]

There was much disappointment in the South at the failures of Generals Johnston and Beauregard to follow up the defeat of General McDowell, at Manassas, July 21, 1861, by an advance on Washington and into Maryland. A few weeks later both Johnston and Beauregard, joined by General Gustavus W. Smith, commanding Johnston's old corps, favored an immediate offensive campaign beyond the Potomac, provided an adequate force could be concentrated for that purpose. These three senior generals of the Confederate army, threatening Washington, were satisfied that the number of men "present for duty," in the army, about 40,000, was not sufficient for making an active campaign of invasion, and thought if President Davis would come to headquarters, of the army, away from the interruption caused by disturbing elements in Richmond he, too, would be satisfied that the best policy, at this time, would be to concentrate, in that vicinity, as rapidly as possible, all the available forces of the Southern Confederacy, cross the Potomac with the army thus re-enforced, and, by pressing the fighting in the enemy's country, make a determined effort, in the autumn of 1861, to compel the Northern States to recognize Confederate independence. The campaign to be sharp and, if possible, decisive, before active operations would have to be suspended because of approaching winter.[2]

In furtherance of this idea Beauregard wrote Davis, September 6th, suggesting an advance of the army beyond the Potomac and argued the good results of such a movement, in relieving the pressure upon other points. Mr. Davis replied on the 8th: "It is true that a successful advance across the Potomac would relieve other

---

1  For Beauregard's offensive plans, see Chesnut to Beauregard, July 16, 1861, OR 2, pp. 506-7, and Johnson's report of First Manassas, *ibid.*, pp. 484-5. Davis' reply is *ibid.*, pp. 504-5.

2  Gustavus Smith, *Confederate War Papers, Fairfax Court House New Orleans, Seven Pines, Richmond and North Carolina* (New York: Atlantic Engraving and Publishing Co., 1884), p. 22. For a discussion of Johnston's and Beauregard's plans and their larger strategic context, see Joseph L. Harsh's *Confederate Tide Rising* (Kent, OH: Kent State University Press, 1998), pp. 27-30.

places, but if not successful ruin would befall us." He regretted that he had not arms to place in the hands of the volunteers, necessary to the purpose, besides which, Missouri and Kentucky demanded his attention and the Southern coast needed additional defense.[3]

On September 26th, Johnston reported to the Secretary of War that he had made preparations "to remove the troops from the unhealthy atmosphere of the valley of Bull Run and to be ready to turn the enemy's position and advance into Maryland, when the strength of the army would justify it." He followed with the suggestion that the President be induced to visit the army, or send a representative, to confer upon the matter of an advance. The letter was sent by Captain Preston, of his staff, who was instructed to make a statement to the Secretary and answer such questions as should come up. Benjamin replied, on the 29th: "It is extremely difficult, even with the aid of such information as Captain Preston has been able to give us orally, as suggested by you, to determine whether or not we can furnish you the further means you may deem necessary to assume the offensive."[4]

A few days thereafter Mr. Davis arrived at Fairfax Court House, and a conference was held, in which were present, Davis, Johnston, Beauregard and G. W. Smith. It was the unanimous opinion that the military force of the Confederacy was at the highest point it could attain without arms from abroad; that the army grouped around Fairfax was in the finest fighting condition; that if kept inactive it must retrograde immensely in every respect during the winter, the effect of which was foreseen by all. On the other hand, the enemy was daily increasing in numbers, arms, discipline, and efficiency; and a sad state of things was anticipated at the opening of the spring campaign.

Mr. Davis was asked: "Is it not possible to increase the effective strength of this army and put us in condition to cross the Potomac and carry the war into the enemy's country? Can you not by stripping other points to the least they will bear, and, even risking defeat at all other places, put us in condition to move forward?" The generals sought to impress upon Mr. Davis that success, at that time, would save everything, defeat would lose all. General Smith says:

> In explanation and as an indication of this, the unqualified opinion was advanced,
> that, if for want of adequate strength on our part in Kentucky, the Federal forces
> should take military possession of that whole State, and enter and occupy a

3  Davis' reply to Beauregard is in *OR* 5, pp. 833-4. The correspondence and quotations preceding the October Fairfax Council are in *ibid.*, pp. 881-3; Smith, *Confederate War Papers*, pp. 29, 32.

4  Benjamin to Johnston, *OR* 5, p. 883.

portion of Tennessee, a victory gained by this army, beyond the Potomac, would, by threatening the heart of the Northern States, compel their armies to fall back, free Kentucky and give us the line of the Ohio, within ten days thereafter. On the other hand should our forces in Tennessee and Southern Kentucky be strengthened so as to enable us to take, and to hold, the Ohio River as boundary, a disastrous defeat of this army would at once be followed by an overwhelming wave of Northern invasion, which would sweep over Kentucky and Tennessee, extending to the northern part of the Cotton States, if not to New Orleans. Similar views were expressed in regard to ultimate results in North Western Virginia, being dependent upon the success or failure of this army, and various other special illustrations were afforded. Showing, in short, that success here was success everywhere defeat here, defeat everywhere, and that this was the point upon which all the available forces of the Confederate States should be concentrated.[5]

It was acknowledged by all, that the army at Fairfax Court House was not strong enough to carry a campaign beyond the Potomac, that 10,000 to 20,000 additional men were required, seasoned men; these Mr. Davis could not spare from other points, nor had he arms to put into the hands of recruits; the whole country was demanding protection at his hands, and praying for arms and troops for defense. Want of arms was the great difficulty, without these from abroad, he could not re-enforce the army.

Mr. Davis then proposed some operations of a partisan character, especially an expedition, by a detachment, against Hooker's Division, in Lower Maryland, opposite Evansport. Johnston objected to this proposition, because he had no means of transporting a sufficient body of men to the Maryland shore quickly; and the Potomac being controlled by Federal vessels-of-war, such a body, if thrown into Maryland, would inevitably be captured or destroyed in attempting to return, even if successful against the land forces. Upon Johnston declining such an enterprise, the conference terminated.[6]

---

5   Smith, *Confederate War Papers*, p. 17. The question to Davis was asked by Smith, and is found with the reply in *OR* 5, p. 885. Carman seemed to lean on the first chapter of Smith's *Confederate War Papers* for his account of the formation of Confederate offensive strategy during the early days of the war. The other two participants, Beauregard and Johnston, both died as Carman began his writing. Beauregard's first biographer completed his study in 1884, and Johnston's chosen biographer had just begun his work. This may explain Carman's reliance on Smith's memoirs.

6   Joseph E. Johnston, *Narrative of Military Operations, Directed, During the Late War Between the States* (New York: D. Appleton & Co., 1874), p. 77.

On the 8th of October, Gustavus W. Smith again called the attention of Mr. Davis to the necessity of an offensive movement and that the morale of the army was suffering because of its enforced idleness; to which Davis replied on the 10th:

> Your remarks about the moral effect of repressing the hope of the volunteers for an advance are in accordance with the painful impression made on me, when in our council it was revealed to me that the Army of the Potomac had been reduced to about one-half of the legalized strength, and that the arms to restore the number were not in depot. As I there suggested, though you may not be able to advance into Maryland and expel the enemy, it may be possible to keep up the spirits of your troops by expeditions, such as that particularly spoken of against Sickles' brigade, on the Lower Potomac, or Banks', above, by destroying the canal, and making other rapid movements whenever opportunity presents to beat detachments or to destroy lines of communication.[7]

Three days later Secretary Benjamin wrote to Johnston: "I had hoped almost against hope that the condition of the army would justify you in coming to the conclusion that some forward movement could be made, and that the roofs to shelter the troops, during the approaching winter, would be found on the other side of the Potomac; but our destitute condition so far as arms are concerned renders it impossible to increase your strength."[8]

A few weeks after the Fairfax Court House conference, General T. J. Jackson proposed that the Confederates should invade the North in two columns, winter at Harrisburg and, in the spring of 1862, advance directly upon Philadelphia. As preliminary to this he would move into northwestern Virginia with 10,000 men, reclaim that country from Federal sway, and summon the inhabitants to his standard. Of those he thought he could recruit 15,000 to 20,000 which would place his command to at least 25,000. He would then rapidly move his entire force across the Monongahela, into Monongalia County, march upon Pittsburgh, seize that place and destroy the arsenal there, and then, in co-operation with a column crossing the Potomac, near Leesburg, and forming a junction with his own column,

---

7   The discussion is a summary by Davis to Smith of the Fairfax Council, *OR* 5, pp. 884-7. The long quotation from Davis is an excerpt from *ibid.*, P. 894. Carman pasted this typed clipping into his handwritten manuscript. See also Smith, *Confederate War Papers*, p. 20, Jefferson Davis, *The Rise and Fall of the Confederate Government*, 2 Vols. (New York: D. Appleton, 1881), 1, pp. 450-58.

8   Judah Benjamin to Johnston, *OR* 5, p. 896.

advance upon Harrisburg and occupy it. From Harrisburg he proposed that the united column should advance, in the spring, upon Philadelphia.

Gustavus W. Smith gives the argument presented by Jackson:

> McClellan with his army of recruits will not attempt to come out against us this autumn. If we remain inactive they will have greatly the advantage over us next spring. Their raw recruits will have then become an organized army, vastly superior in numbers to our own. We are ready at the present moment for active operations in the field, while they are not. We ought to invade their country now, and not wait for them to make the necessary preparations to invade ours. If the President would re-enforce this army by taking troops from other points not threatened, and let us make an active campaign of invasion before winter sets in, McClellan's raw recruits could not stand against us in the field. Crossing the upper Potomac, occupying Baltimore, and taking possession of Maryland, we could cut off the communications of Washington, force the Federal Government to abandon the capital, beat McClellan's army if it comes out against us in the open country, destroy industrial establishments wherever we found them, break up the lines of interior commercial intercourse, close the coal mines, seize and, if necessary, destroy the manufactories and commerce of Philadelphia, and of other large cities within our reach; take and hold the narrow neck of land between Pittsburg and Lake Erie; subsist mainly on the country we traverse, and, making unremitting war amidst their homes, force the people of the North to understand what it will cost them to hold the South in the Union at the bayonet's point.

Jackson, at this time, commanded a brigade in Smith's corps, and, in presenting his plan and the argument for it, urged Smith to use his influence with Johnston and Beauregard and with the authorities at Richmond to have it approved. When informed by Smith of the substance of the Fairfax Court House conference Jackson was sorely disappointed and dropped the matter.[9]

Considering the circumstances it is not so certain that the Confederates would have achieved such success as to compel the North to recognize their independence before winter set in. Indeed, the probabilities are to the contrary. The fighting quality of Northern troops was underestimated and their quick recovery

---

9   Smith's quote is from Lt. Col. G. F. R. Henderson, *Stonewall Jackson and the American Civil War*, 2 Vols. (New York: Grossett and Dunlap, American edition, 1898), 1, p. 213. Carman used Smith, *Confederate War Papers*, pp. 30-1, as well as Henderson's quote of a letter from Smith citing Jackson's early desire for a northern offensive. The direct quote from Henderson, *Stonewall Jackson*, pp. 132-3, suggests Carman used a different edition. The South could not have supplied such an extended campaign.

from defeat not appreciated. Nor was it taken into account that the patriotism of the people of the North was not to be quenched by a temporary reverse, and that they had come to the determination, cost what it would, to preserve the Government. Mr. Davis knew all this and appreciated it at its worth; he saw, too, the political reasons against the step; conditions of the South which he could not disregard in weighing the subject and coming to a conclusion. As he says: "The whole country was demanding protection at his hands, and praying for arms and troops for defense."[10] The opinion is a correct one that "he could not have consolidated his people for the long struggle which was to come, if he had denied defense to all, for the sole purpose of an invasion from Virginia."[11]

There might have been temporary success, but not such measure of success as would have held Maryland; discouraged the North, or compelled the recognition of Confederate independence. However far the military arm fell short of consummating the hopes of the secessionists of Maryland and the people of the Southern Confederacy, the Confederate Congress was quick to express itself in favor of "speedy and efficient exertion" for the relief of the people of Maryland. On December 21st 1861, it passed these resolutions:

> Whereas, The State of Maryland has suffered the same wrongs which impelled these Confederate States to withdraw from the United States and is intimately associated with those states by geographical situation, by mutual interest, by similarity of institutions and by enduring sentiments of reciprocal amity and esteem, and whereas, it is believed that a large majority of the good people of Maryland earnestly desire to unite their State with the Confederate States, a desire which is proved to exist even by the violent, extraordinary and tyrannical measures employed by our enemy to restrain the expression thereof; and whereas the Government of the United States, by imprisoning members of the Legislature of Maryland, by establishing powerful armies of foreigners within that State and along her borders, and by suppressing, with armed force, the freedom of speech and election, has prevented the people and their representatives from adopting the political connection which they prefer, and, in revenge of their preference, has inflicted upon them many outrages, and established over them a foreign despotism, and whereas the ascension of Maryland to the Confederation will be mutually beneficial and is essential to the integrity and security of the Confederate Union be it known therefore:

---

10 Here Smith is quoting Davis, *War Papers*, p. 18.

11 No source for this quote has been found.

First. Resolved by the Congress of the Confederate States of America, that the suffering of the good people of Maryland, under the oppression of our enemy, excite our profound sympathy, and entitle them to speedy and efficient exertion on our part for their relief.

Second. That it is the desire of this government, by appropriate measures to facilitate the accession of Maryland, with the free consent of her people, to the Confederate States.

Third. That no peace ought to be concluded with the United States, which does not insure to Maryland the opportunity of forming a part of the Confederacy.[12]

This idea was constantly kept in view by the Confederate Executive, when it was thought that the Confederate Government was about to be recognized by Britain and France and intervention resorted to, to end the war. Mr. Davis was prompt to inform his representatives abroad that there were certain conditions that would be insisted upon by the Confederate Government and these were expressed in a communication prepared by the Confederate Secretary of State. After dilating upon the great advantages that would accrue to Great Britain and France by the recognition of the Southern Confederacy and its establishment as one of the powers of the world, which the signs of the times indicated were near at hand, he laid down conditions upon which intervention would not be deprecated:

No treaty of peace can be accepted which does not secure the independence of the Confederate States, including Maryland, Virginia, Kentucky, Missouri, the States south of them, and the territories of New Mexico and Arizona.

The Union of the States of Maryland, Kentucky and Missouri with the Southern Confederacy might be contingent upon a fair vote of the citizens of these States to be uninfluenced by force or the presence of the troops either of the Confederate or the United States."[13]

He set forth the inducement to such an arrangement and the great interest Great Britain and France had in the increase of the supply of cotton and sugar and the

12 The December 21, 1861, resolutions are found in *OR* Series 4, 1, pp. 805-6.

13 Davis's terms of peace are found in the U.S. Navy Department's *The War of the Rebellion: Official Records of the Union and Confederate Navies* (Washington, DC: Gov't Printing Office, 1894-1927), 30 vols., hereafter referred to as *ORN*, series 2, 3, pp. 333-4. Because the naval official records were published after Carman's death, he must have worked with the captured original letterbooks and documents.

enlargement of markets, in which and for which they could exchange their manufactures upon convenient and easy terms. For this purpose the Southern Confederacy ought to be so constituted as to enable the States growing cotton and sugar to devote their labor almost exclusively to those objects, and to draw their provisions from other States better suited to the production of such supplies. He held that:

> The Union of North Carolina, Virginia, Maryland, Kentucky and Missouri with the cotton growing States south of them is essential to constitute a Confederacy. By such a union we shall enlarge the area in which agriculture would be the principal employment, and increase greatly the number of customers who would design to purchase British manufactures at as low a rate of duty as would be consistent with their revenue wants. The value of this market would be enhanced, too, from the fact that it would include in the circle of its exchange not only cotton, sugar and rice, but tobacco, naval stores, timber and provisions, the articles most sought after by Great Britain in her foreign trade. Such a Confederacy would be independent, of its Northern neighbors in all respects. Its people would find within themselves the means of supplying all their wants, except those of manufactures and of transportation by sea, which they would seek abroad. Such a Confederacy, too, would be able to take care of itself, and protect its own independence and interests against all assaults from neighbors. But if Maryland, Kentucky and Missouri should be united in the Northern Confederacy, all hope of a balance of power between the two would be gone, and the Southern Confederacy would be in constant danger of aggression from its Northern neighbors. A temptation would then be held out to the formation of a party for reconstruction of the old political union, not only for the purpose of peace, but to secure the trade of the border slave states, which is so advantageous if not indispensable to them. At least they would probably seek to restore the old connection in trade by means of treaties which might favor their Northern neighbors beyond all foreign nations. Such an arrangement of boundaries would either lead to this state of things or else to frequent wars; and the intervening parties would find that they had given not a peace, but a hollow truce. This state of things would prove a constant state of expense, trouble and turmoil to all concerned. The simple and natural plan of uniting all the slaveholding States would avoid all these difficulties. Although nominally inferior to the United States, it is easy to see from their position on the map, and a comparison of their resources, that there would be no uneven balance between them. In this connection it may be proper to show the immense importance of the Chesapeake Bay to the Confederate States. In the new Confederacy by means of railroads and water lines its streams of commerce will flow from sources far west of the Mississippi and range in their northern and southern boundaries from St. Louis to

New Orleans. By the concentration of so much commerce at such a point the European shipping is saved the tedious and sometimes dangerous circumnavigation of the Southern Atlantic coast and of the Gulf of Mexico.[14]

The Secretary then went on to say that when the union of all the slaveholding States, save Delaware, was once established, its commercial and industrial development would be unparalleled in the past, but a union of all the slaveholding States, save Delaware, was necessary for this purpose. Without such a union, constant wars must arise from the efforts of those States to get together again. There was no other road to a solid and permanent peace which the highest interests of mankind seemed to demand.[15]

At the same time it was declared that intervention was not sought, and that the government had no doubt of its ability to achieve independence and drive the invader from its soil. It might require time and sacrifices, blood and money, but effort should not cease until it was accomplished.

In his inaugural address to the Confederate Congress, February 22, 1862, Mr. Davis said: "Maryland, already united to us by hallowed memories and material interests, will, I believe, when enabled to speak with unstifled voice, connect her destiny with the South."[16] But there were those who would not wait on the voice of the people of Maryland and no sooner had the Congress assembled than there arose a hot clamor for an immediate movement into Maryland, to redeem Baltimore and Annapolis and cut off railroad connection with the North. Not into Maryland, only, did they demand an advance, they insisted upon a movement farther North, to compel the men and wealth of New York, Philadelphia, Boston and other cities, to pay the South for the losses she had sustained. But these visionary schemes were not shared by the majority, which was held to a strict defensive by the personal influence of Mr. Davis.

---

14 Carman uses "He" to continue Davis' instructions to the commissioners in Europe. This long quotation is in *ORN* Series 2, 3, pp. 333-6, although Carman simply identifies it as Hunter to the Commissioners. See also "Hunter to Commissioners, July 29, 1861," *ibid.*, pp. 227-9.

15 R. M. T. Hunter to James M. Mason, February 8, 1862. These instructions provide an insight into the strategic thinking of Confederate leaders early in the war. Two important points emerge: that a Confederacy of all slave-holding states (save Delaware) was of primary concern, and that an alliance with England and France was considered critical to the success of the Confederacy. Carman emphasized mentions of Maryland here and in Davis' inaugural remarks (see following note) to make this topic germane to the strategy of the Maryland campaign.

16 Davis' inaugural address, February 22, 1862, in Davis, *Rise and Fall*, 1, pp. 484-5, and Moore, *Rebellion Record*, 4, p. 201. Both sources were available to Carman.

On the contrary, there were some extremists who did want Maryland as a member of the Southern Confederacy, upon any consideration; they had not welcomed Virginia, because she had a habit of absorbing all the offices; their ideal was a Confederacy of cotton-growing States. Mr. Benjamin, Confederate Secretary of War, assured Reuben Davis of Mississippi, early in March 1862, that there was no doubt of the recognition of the Southern Confederacy by England within ninety days and that would end the war. When questioned what measures, meanwhile, would be taken to drive the Union forces from Tennessee, Mr. Benjamin replied that such measures were not necessary; that the South would hold from the Memphis and Charleston Railroad south, and the Northern States could ["can have" in original] what was north of that line.[17]

The great majority, however, would not listen to any proposition that did not embrace Maryland as one of the Confederate States, and unceasing efforts were exerted to impress upon civil and military authorities the high and solemn duty of liberating her. These efforts were seconded by many prominent men and women of Maryland, who, leaving their State, crossed the Potomac and journeyed to Richmond, where, like exiled Stuarts, they held court, thronged the official residences, mingled in the gayeties of the Capital, and poured their sorrows into the sympathetic ears of the influential. Expressions of sympathy for them and for their State were manifest at all times and on all occasions, were shared by the highest and the lowest, and "Maryland, My Maryland" was the popular air of the day, and was heard everywhere.[18]

When it was known that McClellan had transferred the Army of the Potomac from the front of Washington to the York Peninsula, General Johnston was assigned to command the army for the defense of Richmond and he advised that it be concentrated behind defensive works around that place. There was a difference of opinion among the Confederate chiefs as to the advisability of this plan and, about the middle of April 1862, a conference was held at which were present Jefferson Davis, Generals R. E. Lee, Joseph E. Johnston, G. W. Smith and James Longstreet. Among the propositions brought forward was one offered by Smith, which was to garrison Richmond, occupy McClellan in besieging that place, move the larger part of the Confederate army rapidly across the border and make an active, offensive campaign beyond the Potomac, striking Baltimore and Washington, if not Philadelphia and New York, before McClellan could take the

---

17 Reuben Davis, *Recollections of Mississippi* (Cambridge; Houghton Mifflin and Co., 1889), p. 432.

18 The paragraph including the reference to "exiled Stuarts" sounds like a quotation (not yet identified), but may simply be Carman's term.

works around Richmond. Both Davis and Lee opposed this plan as well as that of Johnston, to hold the army in the defenses of Richmond, and the result of the conference was an order to Johnston to occupy the line selected by Magruder on the Peninsula, the Warwick River and Yorktown line.[19]

McClellan set himself down before this line and made elaborate preparations to break it. Johnston saw the impossibility of preventing this or successfully resisting the march of the Army of the Potomac, up the Peninsula, to the gates of Richmond, and April 29th, wrote Lee, "The fight for Yorktown, as I said in Richmond, must be one of artillery, in which we cannot win. The result is certain; the time only doubtful. . . . We must abandon the Peninsula now." As two or three days, more or less, would signify little, Johnston considered it best for the sake of the capital, to abandon Yorktown and put his army into position to defend Richmond, and notified Lee of his intentions do so, as soon as it could be done conveniently. On the next day he renewed the suggestion made by Smith two weeks before. The suggestion was in a letter to Lee, under date of April 30:

> We are engaged in a species of warfare at which we can never win. It is plain that General McClellan will adhere to the system adopted by him last summer, and depend for success upon his artillery and engineering. We can compete with him in neither. We must, therefore, change our course, take the offensive, collect all the troops we have in the East and cross the Potomac with them, while Beauregard, with all we have in the West, invades Ohio. Our troops have always wished for the offensive, and so does the country. Please submit this suggestion to the President. We can have no success while McClellan is allowed, as he is by our defensive, to choose his mode of warfare.[20]

General Lee replied on May 1st:

> The feasibility of the proposition has been the subject of consideration with him (the President) some time, so far as advancing a column to the Potomac with all the troops that can be made available. The proposed invasion of Ohio by General Beauregard, however desirable, it is feared at this time is impracticable, though it

---

19 Carman's description of the Richmond conference of April 1862 is likely taken from Smith, *Confederate War Papers*, pp. 41-44, Davis, *Rise and Fall*, and one of Gen. James Longstreet's various accounts. All of these men wrote about the meeting, and Carman used their works in other places. This conference is mentioned in James Kegel, *North With Lee and Jackson* (Mechanicsburg, PA: Stackpole Books, 1996), p. 90. A fuller discussion of this conference is in Harsh, *Confederate Tide Rising*, pp. 36-8. Johnston's quotation is in *OR* 11, pt. 3, p. 473.

20 Johnston's quotation is in *ibid.*, p. 473, and his other letter is *ibid.*, p. 477.

will also be considered. He concurs in your views as to the benefits to be obtained by taking the offensive, and is very desirous of being able to carry it into effect."[21]

Johnston abandoned Yorktown and McClellan advanced up the Peninsula and fronted Richmond. Meanwhile, Stonewall Jackson was conducting that brilliant campaign in the Shenandoah Valley, resulting in the defeat of Banks, Frémont and Shields. As he saw Banks' troops retreating across the Potomac, above Harper's Ferry, his thoughts again turned to an invasion of the North and, at Halltown, May 30th, he instructed a member of his staff to proceed to Richmond and tell the authorities that, if his army could be increased to 40,000 men, a movement might be made beyond the Potomac which would raise the siege of Richmond and transfer the campaign from the banks of the James to those of the Susquehanna. Jackson's staff officer was delayed in reaching Richmond; meanwhile Frémont was disposed of at Cross Keys, June 8, and Shields at Port Republic, June 9th, and Jackson took position at Brown's Gap, from which he again he sent his staff officer to Richmond to make formal application to the government to increase his command to 40,000 men in order that he might carry into effect the movement he had proposed at Halltown on the 30th of May. "By that means," he said, "Richmond can be relieved and the campaign can be transferred to Pennsylvania." In making the proposed counter-movement northward he would advance toward the Potomac along the eastern side of the Blue Ridge, masking his march as much as possible, and by rapidly crossing the mountain at the most available gap he could, by getting in the rear of Banks, who had returned to Winchester, quickly dispose of him, and thereby open up the road to Western Maryland and Pennsylvania by way of Williamsport and Hagerstown.[22]

Jackson's messenger arrived at Richmond on the 14th of June and laid his message before the Secretary of War, who referred him to Mr. Davis, who, in turn, referred him to General Lee. Lee listened attentively as Jackson's plans were unfolded, inquired as to the condition of his army, the crop prospects of the valley, and finally expressed the opinion that it would be better for Jackson to come down to Richmond and help drive McClellan's troublesome people away from it. Two days later he said the movement proposed by Jackson "will have to be postponed"

21 Lee's reply is *ibid.*, p. 485.

22 Jackson's dispatching of Congressmen Alexander Boteler to persuade Davis and Lee to approve his plan is in *SHSP* (1915), 40, pp. 164-73, which was published too late for Carman to have used. It also appeared in the *Philadelphia Weekly Times*, February 11,1862, and was later included in *Annals of the War* (1879), p. 651.

and the reasons were the necessity for the use of his command in giving a crushing blow to McClellan.[23]

Jackson moved down to Richmond and joined Lee, McClellan was attacked and driven to Harrison's Landing, on James River, where his impregnable position forbade farther Confederate action in that quarter. Jackson was for aggressive action; he would give the North no time to reorganize his armies or to drill the new levies flooding to its camps. He would give not a day's respite, but would strike heavy blows at every favoring opportunity, above all he would invade the North.

According to Robert Lewis Dabney:

> While the army lay near Westover, resting from its toils, General Jackson called his friend, the Hon. Mr. Boteler (the staff officer who had carried his propositions to Mr. Davis in June) to his tent, to communicate his views of the future conduct of the war, and to beg that on his next visit to Richmond, he would impress them upon the Government. He said that it was manifest by every sign, that McClellan's was a thoroughly beaten army, and was no longer capable of anything, until it was reorganized and reinforced. There was danger, he foresaw, of repeating the error of Manassas Junction (July 21, 1861); where the season of victory was let slip by an ill-timed inaction, and the enemy was allowed full leisure to repair his strength. Now, since it was determined not to attempt the destruction of McClellan where he lay, the Confederate army should at once leave the malarious district, move northward, and carry the horrors of invasion from their own borders, to those of the guilty assailants. This, he said, was the way to bring them to their senses, and to end the war. And it was within the power of the Confederate Government to make a successful invasion, if their resources were rightly concentrated. Sixty thousand men could march into Maryland, and threaten Washington City, producing most valuable results. But, he added, while he wished these views to be laid before the President, he would disclaim earnestly the charge of self-seeking, in advocating them. He wished to follow, and not to lead, in this glorious enterprise; he was willing to follow anybody: General Lee, or the gallant Ewell. 'Why do you not at once urge these things,' asked Mr. Boteler, 'on General Lee himself.' 'I have done so,' replied Jackson. 'And what,' asked Mr. Boteler, 'does he say to them?' General

---

23 Carman either describes only one visit, or conflates two visits into one, but it is clear from other sources that there were two separate trips made to Richmond. See James I. Robertson, Jr., *Stonewall Jackson: The Man, The Soldier, The Legend* (New York: Simon and Schuster, 1997), pp. 416, 454. Lee to Jackson, June 16, 1862, in OR 11, pt. 3, p. 602, seems to be a reply to this letter from Jackson, but does not contain the exact words "will have to be postponed" that Carman used here. Boteler, in "Stonewall Jackson in the Campaign of 1862," *SHSP*, 42 (September 1917), includes this phrase, but it was published after Carman was dead.

Jackson answered, 'He says nothing.' But he added: 'Do not understand that I complain of this silence; it is proper that General Lee should observe it. He is a sagacious and prudent man; he feels that he hears a fearful responsibility. He is right in declining a hasty expression of his purpose, to a subordinate like me.' The advice of Jackson was laid before the President."[24]

Mr. Davis had looked with disfavor upon all projects for an invasion of the North and Jackson's suggestions, were, apparently unnoticed but that the offensive policy had been considered was evident from the fact that on July 5, 1862, Jefferson Davis, in an address to the army, after reciting the great deeds it had accomplished, in expelling McClellan from the front of Richmond, said: "Let it be your pride to relax in nothing which can promote your future efficiency; your one great object being to drive the invader from your soil, and carry your standards beyond the outer borders ["boundaries" in original] of the Confederacy, to wring from an unscrupulous foe the recognition of your birthright, community, independence." Thus was publicly announced[25] the project of an aggressive campaign and two weeks later, July 19th, Mr. Benjamin, Confederate Secretary of State, wrote John Slidell, at Paris: "This government and people are straining every nerve to continue the campaign with renewed energy before the North can recover from the shock of their bitter disappointment, and if human exertion can compel it, our banners will be unfurled beyond the Potomac in a very short time."[26]

The policy of concentration forced upon the administration by General Lee, and the sweeping conscription law, that "robbed the cradle and the grave," gave the Southern Confederacy two powerful armies to accomplish the object; the Army of Northern Virginia, under General Lee, and the Army of Tennessee, under General Bragg. Lee was to clear Virginia of Union troops and advance beyond the Potomac; Bragg was to recover Tennessee and Kentucky, redeem Missouri, and invade Ohio. These things accomplished it was fondly hoped that the United States Government, as well as England and France, would acknowledge the independence of the Southern Confederacy.

---

24 In addition to the series of quotations from Robert Lewis Dabney's *Life and Campaigns of Lieut. Gen. Thomas J. Jackson* (New York: Blelock and Co., 1866), pp. 486-7, see Davis, *Rise and Fall*, 2, p. 150, for Jackson's desire to follow up McClellan's retreat.

25 Carman cited this as *War Records*, Vol. XI, pt. III, p. 690. He was, as noted earlier, referencing the *Official Records*.

26 Confederate Archives Mss. As discussed earlier, the naval *Official Records (ORN)* were not yet published. They and diplomatic correspondence, however, were available in Washington D.C. where Carman did much of his work. This letter is found in *ORN* Series 2, vol. 3, p. 466.

It has been noted that the Southern leaders were extremely anxious for the accession of Maryland to the Southern Confederacy, and they taught themselves to believe that the majority of the people of that State were loyal to the cause of the South and would welcome the armies of the Confederacy. The same delusion prevailed as to Kentucky; it was believed, especially by the Government at Richmond, where the belief was a mania, that the people of that State, as well as those of Maryland, stood ready to receive them with open arms, feed them with their substance, and rally to their standard to throw off Union domination and assist in conquering a peace beyond the Ohio.[27]

The advance of the Union armies on Chattanooga and Knoxville, in June and July 1862, was a serious menace to the South; Chattanooga and Knoxville were reinforced and General Bragg, commanding the Western Department, was authorized by Jefferson Davis to make a counter move into Middle Tennessee and Kentucky. The time for the movement seemed ripe; McClellan had been driven from Richmond and the Confederate Government had passed from its defensive policy and listened to the voice of its people that the war should be carried into the enemy's country.

Bragg was then at Tupelo, Mississippi, whither the Confederate army had retreated from Corinth, May 29 1862, and General E. Kirby Smith was in command of the department embracing Chattanooga and Knoxville. These two officers had a conference at Chattanooga, July 31st, and arrived at an understanding to cooperate in freeing Tennessee and Kentucky from Union domination. Information led them to believe that, if properly armed, the people would rise and assist them. At the same time Generals Earl Van Dorn and Sterling Price were to make a simultaneous advance from Mississippi into West Tennessee, and Bragg trusted that all would unite in Ohio. Isham G. Harris, the refugee Governor of Tennessee, was to accompany the army and Bragg assured him that he would carry him into Nashville before the last of August. Bragg, who had begun the movement of his army from Tupelo, on the 21st of July, took a very rosy view of the situation and wrote: "Everything is ripe for success, the country is aroused and expecting us."[28] The Kentucky delegation in the Confederate Congress were sanguine that the

---

27 Carman is identifying long-range strategy of the Confederacy, something not widely discussed in his day. For a fuller discussion of Confederate war aims, see Harsh, *Confederate Tide Rising*, pp. 11-20. The reference to the Confederacy having "robbed the cradle and the grave" refers to the first Conscription Act (a wartime draft) in American history. Enacted by the Confederacy on April 16, 1862, the ages called up were initially 18 to 35, but by the end of the war included men 17 to 50 years old.

28 Bragg to Kirby Smith, August 15, 1862, *OR* 16, pt. 2, p. 759.

movement would result in the overthrow of the Union State Government of Kentucky "and give the people an opportunity of establishing such a government as they desired." On the 25th of August General Bragg issued orders at Chattanooga for the forward movement, closing with these words: "Soldiers, the enemy is before you and your banners are free. It is for you to decide whether our brothers and sisters of Tennessee and Kentucky shall remain bondsmen and bondswomen of the Abolition tyrant or be restored to the freedom inherited from their fathers."[29]

Meanwhile Kirby Smith had left Knoxville and marched through Big Creek and Roger's Gap into Kentucky, to carry out his part of the programme in co-operating with Bragg in the movement to the Ohio. He routed the Union forces at Richmond, Kentucky on August 30th and advanced to Lexington September 2nd, from which place General Henry Heth, with about 6,000 men, was sent to threaten Cincinnati, Smith remaining at Lexington to collect supplies, gather in recruits, and await Bragg's movements. He informed Bragg that he could add 25,000 Kentuckians to his army in a few days, and reported to Richmond that "the heart of Kentucky is with the South," and that the people were rallying to his ranks, and urged upon the government the importance of supporting the movement into Kentucky by sending all the men and arms that could be spared. A few days dispelled the dreams indulged in by Smith and, September 18th, he reported to Bragg, "the Kentuckians are slow and backward in rallying to our standards. Their hearts are evidently with us, but their blue- grass and fat grasses are against us."[30]

General Bragg crossed the Tennessee River near Chattanooga and, August 18th, his column took up its march over the Cumberland Mountains and threatened Nashville, upon which Buell, who was advancing on Chattanooga, fell back to cover Nashville and his communications with Louisville. Finding that Buell had covered Nashville, Bragg crossed the Kentucky line and reached Glasgow, September 13th, thus throwing his army between Buell and Kirby Smith, and between Buell and Louisville. Munfordsville [sic] surrendered to Bragg's forces on September 17th, while McClellan and Lee were in deadly struggle at Antietam, and Bragg issued an order of congratulation at the crowning success of the campaign, and upon the redemption of Tennessee and Kentucky.[31]

---

29  Bragg's order of August 25,1862, in *ibid.*, p. 779.

30  The optimistic quotation from Bragg is from *ibid.*, pt. 1 pp. 932, 933, and his less enthusiastic assessment is from *ibid.*, pt. 2, p. 848.

31  The movements and aims of Bragg, Smith, and Buell can be traced in *ibid.*, pt. 1, and also in Kenneth Hafendorfer, *Perryville: Battle for Kentucky* (Louisville, KY: KH Press, 1991), and Kenneth Noe, *Perryville: This Grand Havoc of Battle* (Lexington: University of Kentucky Press,

Bragg took up a strong position, barring the road to Louisville; Buell, advancing from Bowling Green, made dispositions for attack, when it was discovered that Bragg had withdrawn. Bragg had found it impossible to remain in a country destitute of supplies and turned his head of column where he expected to find them. He ordered Kirby Smith to march from Lexington to Shelbyville, that their combined operations might be immediately undertaken against Louisville, and marched his own column to Bardstown. This left the way open to Buell, the proposed junction of Bragg and Kirby Smith was not promptly made; Buell reached Louisville and proceeded to organize an army that marched out on October [sic] and on the 8th fought Bragg at Perryville, and on the 13th Bragg began his retreat from the State he had sought to redeem, to find shelter in East Tennessee. The day preceding the beginning of his retreat through Cumberland Gap, Bragg wrote to the Adjutant General of the Confederate army:

> The campaign here was predicated on the belief and the most positive assurance that the people of the country would rise in mass to assert their independence. No people ever had so favorable an opportunity, but I am distressed to add there is little or no disposition to avail of it. Willing perhaps to accept their independence, they are neither disposed nor willing to risk their lives or their property in its achievement. With ample means to arm 20,000 men and a force with that to fully redeem the State, we have not yet issued half the arms left us by casualties incident to the campaign.

Bragg entered Kentucky with high hopes of marching through the State to and beyond the Ohio River, and of occupying the cities of Louisville and Cincinnati. He was to redeem the State and establish a Confederate state government. He retreated sadly disappointed and thoroughly disgusted. He had won barren victories at Richmond and Munfordsville [sic], otherwise he had been outgeneraled. He had taken neither Louisville, nor Cincinnati, nor had he caught a distant glimpse of the Ohio. The "blue-grass and fat grass" Kentuckians did not rally to his colors, and the Governor he had inaugurated at Frankfort was a fugitive before the ceremonies had been fully completed.[32] His campaign in Kentucky was paralleled by that of Lee in Maryland, to which we now turn.

---

2001). Carman left out the date (October 1, 1862) when Buell's army left Louisville. Bragg's congratulatory order of September 17, 1862 is in *OR* 16, pt. 2, p. 843.

32 The quotation from Bragg about the disappointing results of the Kentucky campaign is from *ibid.*, pt. 1, p. 1,088. Carman precedes many historians in linking the summer campaigns in Maryland and Kentucky as parallel in many ways. See James Murfin, *Gleam of Bayonets: The Battle*

General Lee had not utterly destroyed McClellan's army on the Peninsula as he hoped and expected to do and, as he asserts, under ordinary circumstances should have been done, but he had saved Richmond and paralyzed McClellan. On the 8th of July he fell back to Richmond; on the 19th Jackson, on the march to meet Pope, reached Gordonsville. On the 9th of August Jackson defeated Banks at Cedar Mountain, but was obliged to fall back behind the Rappahannock [Rapidan] and await reinforcements, which could not be immediately given, in view of the uncertain intentions of McClellan's army on the banks of the James and the report that he was being reinforced to resume the offensive. As soon as it was known that McClellan was being withdrawn from the Peninsula to reinforce Pope, Lee put his army in motion to overthrow Pope, before McClellan's force could reach him. His point of concentration was Gordonsville. On the 15th of August Jackson, with his division and those of Ewell and A. P. Hill of the infantry and Stuart of the cavalry, led the advance, crossed the Rapidan on the 20th, and the Rappahannock on the 24th. Then followed the battles of Groveton, Second Manassas and Chantilly and the resultant defeat of Pope's army and its retreat to Washington.[33]

The proximity of the fortifications around Alexandria and Washington, thanks to McClellan's foresight, rendered further pursuit useless and Lee's army rested on the 2nd near Chantilly, Pope being followed only by the cavalry, which continued to harass him until he reached the defensive lines near the Potomac.

When Lee was acting in an advisory capacity to President Davis he united with his chief in opposing the suggestion of Johnston, G. W. Smith and Longstreet to defend Richmond by an advance of the main Confederate army into the North, but, when the fortunes of war, by the wounding of Joseph E. Johnston, placed him in command he formed and steadfastly held the opinion, till the close of his military career, that the proper defense of Richmond and the Confederacy lay in the transfer of the Confederate army to the vicinity of Washington and, preferably, to an entrance into Maryland. This idea he pressed on Mr. Davis; so, when McClellan was driven back to the James River, his thoughts instantly turned to dislodging him from that position and from the entire Peninsula by an advance northward to

of Antietam and Robert E. Lee's Maryland Campaign (New York: Thomas Yoseloff, 1965), pp. 68-70; Stephen Sears, Landscape Turned Red: The Battle of Antietam (New Haven, CT: Ticknor Fields, 1983), pp. 65-9.

33 Regarding Lee's disappointment at not destroying McClellan's army, see OR 11, pt. 2, p. 497. Carman quoted some of the words directly from Lee's report. Widely regarded as a great Confederate victory, which in a strategic sense it was, the Seven Days fighting, as Carman shows through Lee's words, was a lost opportunity for the Confederacy. After failing to destroy McClellan's army, Lee spent much of July and August of 1862 guarding Richmond against another thrust by McClellan. See Harsh, Confederate Tide Rising, Chapter 4.

overthrow Pope and menace Washington, with the result known to history. Lee was not averse to bearing heavy burdens and in his plans embraced other fields than the one in which he was operating and over which he had command. He aimed not only to relieve the pressure on Richmond and the Peninsula but upon the whole of Virginia and upon other parts of the Confederacy. When prisoners were taken on the Rappahannock from Burnside's men from North Carolina and Cox's from West Virginia, showing that troops had been drawn from these points, he pointed to the fact as proof of the correctness of his theory, or, rather, of the success of his plan. Failing to demolish Pope between the Rapidan and the Rappahannock, as he had planned to do, and which it is contended he might have done but for the failure of Fitzhugh Lee's cavalry, Lee then pursued Pope with the determination to cut him off from Washington or drive him into it. This would open the way to another campaign, which, from the necessities of the case must be conducted outside of Virginia. He did not cut Pope off from Washington but he fought him back to its defenses.

The condition of affairs was now favorable for an invasion of the North, and Lee saw the way clear to carry out the understanding between Mr. Davis and himself that, when opportunity presented, the Confederate army should enter Maryland and demand recognition of Confederate independence.[34]

There were those who agreed with Lee, as the conditions were then presented, that he had no great risk to face in the prosecution of a campaign beyond the Potomac and as far north as Pennsylvania, and that the time and opportunity had come to strike a blow in the enemy's country, that would go far toward securing the independence of the South. Many victories in Virginia had raised the spirit of the army to the highest point, and it felt equal to any task. It could be relied upon to put forth its greatest efforts; that done, the results were not doubted; and it was reasonably considered that such a grievous stroke as had been given Pope in Virginia, would have been well nigh fatal had it been administered in Maryland, within easy reach of Washington, or in Pennsylvania, near the pulse of manufacture and trade. To crown their brilliant victories in Virginia, the colors of the Southern Confederacy must be carried to the banks of the Susquehanna, in Pennsylvania,

---

34 Lee's plans and the formation of strategy to defeat Pope's Army of Virginia before it could unite with McClellan's Army of the Potomac is best covered in *ibid.*, Chapters 4 and 5. Some of Carman's wording came from Lee's letters, and Lee's intent can be divined by reading his correspondence in vols. 11 and 12 of the *OR*.

and, fortune favoring, displayed in Independence Square, Philadelphia. Dreams of this kind were indulged in in those early September days.[35]

Beyond considerations of a purely military nature, there were those of a political character, domestic and foreign, that called for an invasion, at this time, of Northern territory. One of the delusions of the South was an abiding faith in the words and promises of many of the leaders of the Democratic party of the North. That party has produced many of the great names of American History, names that will live as long as patriotism is recognized as a virtue, and loyalty to American principles, as laid down in the Declaration of Independence, is regarded as a to duty to humanity. But, in the few years preceding the outbreak of Rebellion, the party of Thomas Jefferson and Andrew Jackson had sadly degenerated and its broad principles of early days narrowed to the single idea of the perpetuation and extension of human slavery. Everything else was secondary and subordinate to this. That the Southern man should contend for this was, considering his environment, very natural, but the pity of it is that many Democrats of the North, followed blindly the leaders of the extremists of the South. They yielded to the views of these extremists in the construction of political platforms and, by their votes, supported slave legislation in Congress. Their whole course led the South to believe that it would receive their support and that of their followers, in any course it chose to pursue and, on more than one occasion, Northern members of Congress asserted, on the floor of the House of Representatives, that should the incoming administration of Abraham Lincoln undertake to coerce the South, it would first have to deal with the Democracy of the North and, after the beginning of hostilities, there were some parties in Massachusetts, Connecticut, Illinois, Indiana and elsewhere, who offered volunteer companies to Jefferson Davis to fight in the ranks of the Confederate army.[36]

As early as January 6, 1860, Franklin Pierce of New Hampshire, Ex-President of the United States, wrote to Jefferson Davis, complaining that in the debate in Congress full justice had not been done to the Democracy of the North. He said:

35 Carman's description of the spirit of the army and the strategic situation at the close of the Second Manassas campaign sound suspiciously like a quotation. No source for it has been found, but it could also simply be Carman's summation of various sources.

36 For a summary of political affairs in the North during the first two years of the war, and more detail on affairs within the Northern Democratic Party, see James McPherson, *Ordeal By Fire: The Civil War and Reconstruction* (New York: McGraw Hill, 1992), Chapter 16. Carman displayed his Republican sentiments by ascribing some fairly extreme motives and positions on slavery and rebellion to the Northern Democrats. These accusations were part of the contemporary political rhetoric, but this is a rare example of Carman's political bias overtaking his historical objectivity.

Without discussing the question of right, of abstract power to secede, I have never believed that actual disruption of the Union can occur without blood; and if through the madness of Northern abolitionism that dire calamity must come, the fighting will not be along Mason's and Dixon's line merely. It will be within our own borders, in our own streets, between the two classes of citizens to whom I have referred. Those who defy law and scoff constitutional obligations will, if we ever reach the arbitrament of arms, find occupation enough at home.[37]

Is it strange that after such an expression from high Democratic authority, Laurence M. Keitt, speaking at Charleston, South Carolina, in November 1860, said: "Let me tell you, there are a million of Democrats [sic] in the North, who, when the Black Republicans attempt to march upon the South, will be found [sic] a wall of fire in the front." In the South Carolina Secession Convention, December 1860, Mr. Dargan said: "It is not true in point of fact, that all the Northern people are hostile to the rights of the South. We have a Spartan band in every Northern State."[38]

That these secessionists correctly gauged the attitude of their Democratic brethren of the North, we have evidence from the Democratic party of Ohio, at a State convention held January 8, 1861, the anniversary of the battle of New Orleans. General J. D. Cox says:

On the 8th of January the usual Democratic convention and celebration of the battle of New Orleans had taken place, and a series of resolutions had been passed, in which, professing to speak in the name of 200,000 Democrats of Ohio the convention had very significantly intimated that this vast organization of men would be found in the way of any attempt to put down secession until the demands of the South in respect to slavery were complied with. A few days afterward I was returning to Columbus from my home in Trumbull County, and meeting upon the railway train with David Tod, then an active Democratic politician, but afterward one of our loyal 'war governors,' the conversation turned on the action of the convention which had just adjourned. Mr. Tod and I were personal friends and neighbors, and I freely expressed my surprise that the

37  The letter from Pierce is in Rowland, ed., *Jefferson Davis, Constitutionalist*, vol. 4. Carman used a version printed in John A. Logan, *The Great Conspiracy: Its Origins and History* (New York: A.R. Hart & Co. 1886), p. 261. Its flaws in transcription when compared to the Rowland text match Logan's book and also make the letter more damning to Northern Democrats than its author intended.

38  These bombastic quotes from two South Carolinians are found in Henry Wilson, *History of the Rise and Fall of the Slave Power in America* (Boston: James R. Osgood & Co. 1877), p. 69.

convention should have committed itself to what must be interpreted as a threat of insurrection in the North, if the administration should, in opposing secession by force, follow the example of Andrew Jackson, in whose honor they had assembled. He rather vehemently asserted the substance of the resolution, saying that us Republicans would find the 200,000 Ohio Democrats in front of us, if we attempted to cross the Ohio River.[39]

On the 9th of January 1861, Fernando Wood, the Democratic mayor of New York City, sent a message to the common council, suggesting that New York should he made a "free city" and the proposition met with much favor among his followers. The idea was advanced that when secession of the South became a fixed fact, that not only the city but the States of New York, New Jersey and other Middle States would withdraw from the Union and unite with the insurgent South.[40]

Following in the footsteps of Wood was Rodman M. Price, formerly a Democratic governor of New Jersey, who published a letter urging his State to "go with the South from every wise, prudential and patriotic reason." In public speech and private conversation he denounced the idea of coercion and advocated armed resistance to it. The action of Wood and Price was undisguised treason, but they truly represented the feeling of a great majority of their party in 1860-1861, who, opposed to coercion and favorable to an abject surrender to the South, encouraged the South in its course.

Henry Wilson truly says: "If the South had not found auxiliaries out of the North ready to lend them aid, they would never have entered in the rash experiment."[41]

There was encouragement to secession in the tone of the *New York Tribune*, the leading Republican paper of the country, edited by Horace Greeley. On November 9, 1860, the Tribune said: "If the Cotton States consider the value of the Union debatable, we maintain their perfect right to discuss it; nay, we hold with Jefferson, to the inalienable right of communities to alter or abolish forms of government that have become offensive or injurious, and if the Cotton States decide that they can do better out of the Union than in it, we insist on letting them go in peace. The right to

39  The quotation cited by Carman is from Robert U. Johnson and Clarence Buell, eds., *Battles and Leaders of the Civil War*, 4 vols. (New York: Century Magazine, 1884-1887), vol. 2, p. 86. All subsequent citations are to vol. 2. Cox was an avid Republican, which influenced his views.

40  Wood's proposal, which was severely criticized, is found in "Mayor's Message," *New York Journal of Commerce*, January 18,1861, and a response in the *New York Herald*, January 17,1861. The actual date was January 6, not January 9 as Carman has it.

41  These quotations from Price and Wilson are found in Greeley, *American Conflict*, 1, p. 439, although Carman changed the wording slightly.

secede may be a revolutionary one, but it exists nevertheless, and we do not see how one party have [sic] a right to do what another party has a right to prevent."[42] On December 17, 1860, just three days before the secession of South Carolina, Mr. Greeley again said in the *Tribune*: "If it (the Declaration of Independence) justified the secession from the British Empire of 3,000,000 colonists in 1776, we do not see why it would not justify the secession of 5,000,000 of [sic] Southerners from the Federal Union in 1861. If we are mistaken on this point, why does not someone attempt to show wherein and why?" Again, February 23, 1861, five days after the inauguration of Jefferson Davis, at Montgomery, Mr. Greeley said: "We have repeatedly said, and we once more insist, that the great principle embodied by Jefferson in the Declaration of American Independence, that governments derive their just powers from the consent of the governed, is sound and just, and that if the Slave States, the Cotton States or the Gulf States only, choose to form an independent nation, they have a clear moral right to do so."[43]

Although Mr. Greeley did not correctly represent the sentiment of the great body of the Republican party of the North it must he admitted that many of that party, without conceding the right of secession, looked with complacency upon a peaceful separation of the States; and General Scott, the veteran commander of the army of the United States, advised that the "wayward sisters" be permitted to "depart in peace."[44]

The *New York Herald*, an independent Democratic paper, editorialized on November 9, 1860, that "Each State is organized as a complete government,

42 The first quotation from Greeley's newspaper, titled "The Right of Secession," December 17, 1860, is also in Davis, *Rise and Fall*, 1, p. 252, although Carman's quotation includes sentences that Davis's does not. Carman likely used the accounts in Greeley. Carman built a case here for Northern opposition to coercion, which was a subtle but important distinction from opposition to secession. Greeley's editorial stand was not uncommon among Northern conservatives, many of whom opposed secession but also denied the power of coercion to hold states in the Union. The most well-known man who held this view was President James Buchanan. See James Richardson, *Compilation of the Messages and Papers of the Presidents, 1787-1897* 20 Vols. (Washington DC, 1897-1913), 5, pp. 626-42. Carman offers further examples of Northern reluctance to coercion in the next few pages.

43 *New York Tribune*, "Self Government," February 23, 1861.

44 This misrepresentation of Greeley's position and Scott's recommendation is a common one. The confusion stems from a list of options Scott wrote to Secretary of State Seward on March 3, 1861. Scott never specifically endorsed this option; he simply listed it among other possible responses to Seward. Newspapers at the time missed this distinction. See David Mearns, *The Lincoln Papers: The Story of the Collection, With Selections to July 4, 1861*, 2 Vols. (Garden City, NY: Doubleday, 1948), 2, pp. 456-7. For more on the relations between Scott and Lincoln, see Ethan Rafuse, "Former Whigs in Conflict, Winfield Scott, Abraham Lincoln and the Secession Crisis Revisited," Lincoln Herald, No. 103 (Spring 2001), pp. 8-22.

holding the purse and wielding the sword; possessing the right to break the tie of the confederation as a nation might break a treaty, and to repel coercion as a nation might repel invasion. . . . Coercion, if it were possible, is out of the question." While conceding the right of secession and deprecating coercion the *Herald* did not go so far as to countenance an alliance with the secession leaders for a possible opposition to the course of the Government, but the acknowledged leaders of the Democratic party gave no uncertain indication of their designs.[45]

On January 31, 1861 a Democratic State Convention was held in Tweddle Hall at Albany, New York. The convention was large in numbers, a representative one, and embraced the talent of the party. Reuben H. Walworth made a speech in which he asserted that "it would be as brutal to send men to butcher our own brothers of the Southern States as it would be to massacre them in the Northern States." He was followed by James S. Thayer who said:

> The public mind will bear the avowal, and let us make it, that if a revolution of force is to begin, it shall be inaugurated at home. And if the incoming administration shall attempt to carry out the line of policy that has been foreshadowed, we announce that, when the hand of Black Republicanism turns to blood red, and seeks from the fragment of the Constitution to construct a scaffolding for coercion, another name for execution, we will reverse the order of the French Revolution and save the blood of the people by making those who would inaugurate a reign of terror the first victims of a national guillotine.

The sentiment of the speaker was greeted with enthusiastic and long continued applause. He had fairly expressed the views of the Democratic leaders of New York.[46]

The action of this convention, a declaration against coercion and a demand for concession to the South, was hailed by the secession leaders, and those who sympathized with them, South and North, as evidence that: "If the President should

---

45 "The Effect in the South of the Election of Lincoln—Manifest Duty of the President Elect," *New York Herald*, November 9, 1860. It is unclear where Carman found this article.

46 The convention in Albany, New York, was the Peace Convention. The two quotations are in Davis, *Papers*, vol. 7, pp. 254-5, but he mistakenly says it was "a great meeting and in New York City." See Greeley, *American Conflict*, 1, pp. 388-96, and Wilson, *Rise and Fall of the Slave Power in America*, p. 64, for the source of the quoted material. Both of these men were Republicans, and may be presenting their bias in reporting these Democratic speeches. Tweddle Hall was a "renowned Albany theatre" that burned January 16, 1883. See Sawchuk, Brown and Associates, www.sawchukbrown.com/albany/d1hisb.htm. The source for the comments by Thayer and Walworth is Davis, *Rise and Fall*, 1, pp. 254-5. This section of Davis' book contains numerous references to Northern Democratic opposition to coercion.

attempt coercion he will encounter more opposition at the North than he can overcome."[47] All through the South were repeated the expressions of Dargan and Keitt "that a Spartan band in every Northern State" was true to their interests and that "a million Democrats in the North" would stand like a wall of fire to beat back the Black Republicans should they attempt to march upon the South." It was published widely that the action of the Democratic conventions of Ohio and New York showed that the party of human slavery and secession had loyal and devoted followers in the North, those who would see that no Union troops crossed to the south bank of the Ohio, or left the limits of New York without becoming the "victims of a national guillotine." It was a firm reliance upon the division of the North and an active alliance of the Democracy that impelled a Senator in the Confederate Congress to boast that he would soon quaff wine from golden goblets in the palaces of New York, and that caused the boast of Robert Toombs that he would call the roll of his slaves at the foot of Bunker Hill Monument.[48]

On February 2, 1861, the *Detroit Free Press* said, "If troops shall be raised in the North to march against the people of the South, a fire in the rear will be opened upon such troops, which will either stop their march altogether, or wonderfully accelerate it. In other words, if, in the present posture of the Republican party toward the National difficulties, war shall waged, that war will be fought in the North. We warn it that the conflict, which it is precipitating will not be with the South, but with tens of thousands of people in the North. When Civil War shall come, it will be here in Michigan, here in Detroit, and in every Northern State."[49]

When Mr. Lincoln was inaugurated he recognized the fact that the seed of treason had been so broadly sown in the North and that any immediate attempt to apply force against the people of the South would be followed by riots and civil war in some of the Northern cities, therefore, he hesitated to reinforce Fort Sumter and reunite the divided North.

In his *History of the Rise and Fall of the Confederate Government*, Jefferson Davis reviews the condition of affairs at the North in 1860-1861, as shown in the

---

47 Greely, *American Conflict*, 1, p. 396.

48 The source for Toombs's boast has not been found. Alexander H. Stephens, in his book *A Constitutional View of the Late War Between the States: Its Causes, Character, Conduct and Results Presented in a Series of Colloquies at Liberty Hall* (Philadelphia: National Publishing Co., 1868-1890), p. 217, claims Toombs never said this, although he acknowledged that it had appeared in print in several books. This statement was also refuted by Pleasant A. Stovall, *Robert Toombs: Statesman, Speaker, Soldier, Sage* (Cassell Publishing Co., New York, 1892).

49 A portion of this Detroit newspaper quotation also appears in Davis, *Rise and Fall*, 1, p. 256, but Carman probably took it from a later reprint of the original article, which was included in Moore, *Rebellion Record*.

utterances of public men and the press, of devotion to the South and a fixed determination to oppose by force any attempt by the administration to enforce the laws, then he says: "And here the ingenuous reader may very naturally ask, What became of all this feeling? How was it that, in the course of a few weeks, it had disappeared like a morning mist? Where was the host of men who had declared that an army marching to invade the Southern States should first pass over their dead bodies?"

The answer is to be found in the order of Mr. Davis and cabinet to open fire upon a United States fort and the flag of the Union. The attack upon Fort Sumter caused a rude awakening. It united the North, party lines were obliterated and the great party upon which the South depended for moral and physical support, was found true to the principles of its fathers and loyal to the Union. Leading men were prompt to declare themselves; many entered the Union service and rose to high position and enduring fame; and the masses, who were expected to form mobs and resist authority in the North, crowded the recruiting offices and, later, left their patriotic blood, in generous measure, on every battlefield of the war.[50]

There were some Southern men who correctly measured the effect of opening fire upon Fort Sumter. Among them was Robert Toombs, the Confederate Secretary of State. Although he boasted he would call the roll of his slaves at the foot of Bunker Hill Monument, when the cabinet met to consider the propriety of firing on Fort Sumter, he said: "Mr. President, at this time it is suicide, murder, and will lose us many friends at the North. You will wantonly strike a hornets' nest which extends from mountain to ocean, and legions now quiet will swarm out and sting us to death. It is unnecessary, it puts us in the wrong."[51]

Early to recognize the true state of affairs was John A. Campbell, a Justice of the Supreme Court of the United States. Although a Southern man he had not resigned from office and, April 28th, wrote from Washington to Mr. Davis: "The Northern States are in the wildest condition of excitement. Some of the truest friends of the South have given in their adhesion to the policy of 'defending the capital.' General Pierce, General Cushing, and Mr. Dickinson will occur to you at once as men not likely to yield to a slight storm.... We cannot get along at all by

---

50 Quotation is from Davis, *Rise and Fall*, 1, p. 257.

51 For the impact of the firing on Fort Sumter and the Southern opposition opinion to it, see Robert Hendrickson, *Sumter: The First Day of the Civil War* (New York: Promontory Press, 1990), and W. A. Swanburg, *First Blood: The Story of Fort Sumter* (New York: Scribner's, 1957). It is worth noting that Carman chose Toombs among all Confederate leaders to illustrate his point about the firing on Fort Sumter. He may have been foreshadowing his later chapters, where Toombs plays a significant role. The quote is from Stovall, *Robert Toombs*, p. 226.

looking only at our side of the question, or the emanations of our own people... New York, Boston and Philadelphia will pour out capital, even for subjugation. The impression that we had firm, stanch friends North who would fight for us was a delusion. Oh! I pray you do not act upon it."[52]

Mr. Davis was not convinced that the Southern cause had lost all its friends in the North, indeed, he knew to the contrary, and with many who still adhered to it and who opposed the National Administration, he kept up constant communication during the entire war. He was kept well informed of the temper of the North and the discussions of the people. He was advised that the reverses of the Union army, before Richmond and elsewhere, were having a dispiriting effect upon some sections of the North and upon the great money and commercial centers, and that the element demanding peace was growing in strength. Nor was it necessary that he should depend upon this source of information, the papers of the great cities, in their news columns and on their editorial pages, told him of the increasing discontent; of faction in the party of the administration; of the great unpopularity of the draft; of the difficulties in recruiting for the army, and of the growing desire for peace: "Peace for the North and independence for the South." Nor were these indications confined to Democratic politicians and the Democratic press; they were shown in carping criticism and wanton attacks by prominent Republican journals upon the Administration and its policy. That the summer of 1862 was a gloomy one for loyal men of the country is well known, and Horace Greeley has put on record this opinion:

> It is highly possible that had a public election been held at any time during the year following the 4th of July 1862, on the question of continuing the war, or arresting it on the best attainable terms, a majority would have voted for peace; while it is highly probable that a still larger majority would have voted against emancipation.[53]

Mr. Davis knew all this and recognized the fact that the appearance of the Confederate army in Maryland and Pennsylvania would go far to intensify the peace

---

52 The letter from Judge Campbell was cited in Nicolay and Hay, *Abraham Lincoln: A History*. The people he refers to are Franklin Pierce, Caleb Cushing, and Daniel S. Dickinson.

53 See Greeley, *American Conflict*, 2, p. 254, for a summary of Davis' views as Carman states them. See also Davis, *Rise and Fall*, Chapter 9. See Harsh, *Confederate Tide Rising*, pp. 185-90, for a brief discussion of Davis's assessment of the political climate and how Lee's strategy included a goal to diminish Northern morale. Carman used the Greeley quotation, *supra*, pp. 254-5 to reinforce his views on Northern support for the war.

feeling at the North, strengthening the opponents of the National Administration, and have a signal effect upon the elections to be held in many Northern States, in October, for members of Congress. This idea was partially shared by General Lee and runs through his correspondence.

There were urgent reasons, beyond those of a purely military character and effect upon sentiment at the North, that impelled the Confederate Government to pass from the defensive and assume the offensive, with the intention of winning more victories and securing Maryland, Kentucky and Missouri to the Southern Confederacy; these have a direct bearing upon the campaign, now under consideration, and must be noted.

For over a year the Confederate leaders had been anxiously awaiting the recognition of the Confederacy by foreign powers, and their intervention to raise the blockade and give its cause moral and physical support, and for more than a year they had been told that recognition would follow their decided successes in the field. They had looked to no war as the outcome of secession and had from the first had no doubt of a speedy recognition by the European Powers; any hesitation in that direction was expected to be overcome by King Cotton. "We can live, if need be, without commerce," said Senator Iverson of Georgia in United States Senate, January 28, 1861. "But when you shut out our cotton from the looms of Europe we shall see whether other nations will not have something to do on that subject. Cotton is King and it will find means to raise your blockade and disperse your ships." In the campaign in West Virginia, July 1861, the colors of a Georgia regiment were captured. Under the representation of the State arms was the inscription, in letters of gold, Cotton is King.[54]

The Confederate leaders reasoned that the cotton-spinning powers of Europe must have cotton or a famine, and as they could not have cotton without slavery they would swallow slavery and find some pretext for intervention, and were firm "in the conviction that cotton was King in England as well as in the United States, and that an interruption of its supply would be so serious in its consequences that a new republic, where cotton was to be King and slavery its corner-stone, would be

---

54 Senator Alfred Iverson was the father of Confederate Col. (and later Gen.) Alfred Iverson, Jr. The flag was captured from the Southern Guards, Company D, 1st Georgia Infantry in the Rich Mountain campaign during General Robert Garnett's retreat from Rich Mountain. *OR* 3, pp. 993-4. The *Columbus Georgia Daily Sun*, February 7, 1861, describes the flag as "white silk . . . arms of Georgia painted on it. Upon the right is added the figure of a Negro seated on a cotton bale. The familiar words COTTON IS KING in gilt letters are within the arch." It is unclear why Carman used this rather than the famous James Henry Hammond quote that spawned the "Cotton is King" phrase. Carman may have known about this quote from government records, Northern newspaper accounts, or more likely in his research from the West Virginia campaigns.

welcomed into the family of nations as the surest possible guaranty against the occurrence of such a disaster."[55]

It was argued that, in any event, Great Britain must have American cotton to keep her spindles moving, and it was expected that in exchange for this the South would be supplied with such manufactured goods as she had been in the habit of purchasing in Northern markets. To secure recognition and commercial advantages were the first objects of Confederate diplomacy, and this diplomacy rested entirely upon cotton. Many opposed the policy of endeavoring to force recognition by cotton; among these were Vice President Alexander H. Stephens, who said it was a very serious mistake at the beginning of the war to consider cotton as a political instead of a commercial power.

As early as February 13, 1861, the Confederate Congress authorized President Davis to appoint three persons to Great Britain, France and the other European Powers. William L. Yancey, P. A. Rost, and A. Dudley Mann were named and directed to visit London and seek an audience with Queen Victoria's Secretary of State for Foreign Affairs. They were instructed to inform the Secretary of the secession of several States and the formation of an independent, government, which presented itself for admission to the family of independent nations and asked for their acknowledgment and friendly recognition "due to every people capable of self government, and possessed of the power to maintain their independence."[56] They were to assure the Secretary that under no condition would they consent to a re-union with their late associates, that they had a well organized government, capable of taking care of itself, even to the taking up of arms if necessary, which they did not anticipate, as the United States was in no condition to make war upon them. They were instructed to inform the Secretary that the high protective tariff, forced upon them by the North, was the prime cause of secession, and they were empowered to negotiate a treaty of friendship, commerce and navigation and impress upon the British mind that wise maxim of political economy: "Buy where you can buy cheapest and sell where you can sell dearest."

55 The reference to "cotton is to be King and slavery its corner-stone" combines Hammond's quotation and Alexander H. Stephens's equally famous speech. This quote appears in its entirety in John Bigelow, *Retrospectives of an Active Life*, 5 Vols. (New York: Baker & Taylor Co. 1909), 1, p. 527, published the same year as Carman's death.

56 Carman included these instructions by the Confederate Secretary of State Robert Toombs to their European representatives. The quoted portion is from *ORN* Series 2, 3, pp. 191-3,. 221, 223, 238-46, 248. Part of these instructions are also in Moore, *Rebellion Record*, 1, Supplement, pp. 460-4, but not exactly this text.

Then the subject of cotton was to be presented. Mr. Davis rested the foreign policy of the Confederacy on the absolute supremacy of cotton and upon this point, the instructions to the commissioners read:

> The Confederate States produced nearly nineteenth-twentieths of all the cotton grown in the States which recently constituted the United States. There is no extravagance in the assertion that the gross amount of the annual yield of the manufactures of Great Britain, from the cotton of the Confederate States reaches nearly $600,000,000. The British ministry will comprehend fully the condition to which the British realm would be reduced if the supply of our staple should suddenly fail or even be considerably diminished. A delicate allusion to the probability of such an occurrence might not be unkindly received by the Minister of Foreign Affairs, an occurrence, I will add, that is inevitable, if this country shall be involved in protracted hostilities with the North."[57]

During the month of May, 1861, the Confederate Commissioners had two conferences with Lord John Russell, from whom they received the impression that the British Ministry had no settled policy on the recognition of the Southern Confederacy; that they would adhere to the declaration of neutrality, but would postpone a decision as to recognition as long as possible "at least until some decided advantage is obtained by the Confederate States in the field, or the necessity of having cotton becomes pressing." They were sanguine of success "when the cotton crop is ready for market," but were doubtful of recognition before cotton was picked and a favorable military event was announced. Such a military success they thought had been achieved at Bull Run, July 21st, and they addressed a communication to Lord John Russell in which they discussed the causes leading to secession; went into a labored argument of States' Rights and sovereignty; called attention to the resources of the South, especially in cotton and tobacco; criticized the English stand of neutrality, and pointed to the fact that they had achieved a signal victory over the forces of the United States; were able to maintain their independence and "possessed all the elements of a great and powerful nation, capable of clothing, feeding and defending themselves and of clothing all the nations of Europe under the benign influence of peace and free trade," and asking for recognition. The morality of slavery they would not discuss, but they called attention to the fact that the "cotton picking season" had commenced and that an average crop would be placed, as usual, on the wharves at Southern ports, "when there shall be a prospect of the blockade being raised and

---

57 *ORN* Series 2, vol. 3, pp. 191-193. Also see ibid., 221, 223, 238-46, 248.

not before." The reply to this communication was that the English government would not acknowledge the independence of the seceding states until the fortune of arms or the more peaceful mode of negotiation should have more clearly determined the respective position of the two belligerents.

The summer had passed away when the Confederate Congress came to the conclusion to send abroad commissioners of greater reputation, though of less ability. James M. Mason, of Virginia, being named for England, and John Slidell, of Louisiana, for France. The instructions to each (September 23rd) were similar to those under which Yancey, Rost, and Mann were acting, and the key-note was cotton and free-trade.[58]

The English masses, the plain people; those who earned their living by the sweat of their faces, and those of modest trade, were friendly to the North and free institutions. They saw that the cause of the North was the cause of Democracy in their own land. On the other hand the governing class, the aristocracy, the commercial class, and the great body of the established church were favorable to the slave Confederacy. Their views can be stated in two quotations. Lord Palmerston said to August Belmont, of New York, July 1861: "We do not like slavery, but we want cotton, and we dislike very much your Morrill tariff."[59] The *London Times* said: "It is for their trade that the South are resolved to fight. They dissolved the Union to create more slave states, that is, to make more cotton. They undertook the war for the very object we have most at heart."[60]

The religious middle class, those one would naturally suppose to be strong in support of human liberty and free institutions, sympathized with a government whose corner-stone was African slavery, and lent influence to perpetuate and extend it. They had departed from the humane and lofty teachings of Clarkson and Wilberforce and others prominent in English history. The governing class, the

---

58 The sources for Carman's discussion of the Confederate Commissioners and Lord Russell, along with the excerpted quotations, are found in Moore, *Rebellion Record*, 1, Supplement, pp. 460-4, "Russell to the Commissioners, August 14, 1861." Carman offered his own view of the various commissioners, closely following the assessment rendered in Charles Francis Adams Jr., *Charles Francis Adams, By His Son* (Cambridge, MA: Houghton Mifflin and Co., 1900), Chapter 14. Carman used this book for the next several quotations and summaries before mentioning "his biographer writes . . . ," indicating his use of this book.

59 The Palmerston to Belmont quotation is found in James Ford Rhodes, *History of the United States from the Compromise of 1850* (New York: Harper & Brothers Publishers 1899), p. 433. Representative Justin Morrill is perhaps better known for the Land Grant College Act of 1862, but his tariff bill doubled the rate on imports, harming England's export businesses.

60 "Evils Often Diminish in Magnitude as We Approach," *London Times*, May 2, 1861. Carman's version is different in a few places, suggesting he used a different source.

aristocracy, the sordid commercial class, the established church and the religious middle class agreed in opinion that the South was entitled to, and was certain to achieve its independence, and the sooner the fact was acknowledged the better for all.[61]

From early in March the French minister at Washington had been advising his government of the complete disintegration of the Union and suggesting the recognition of the Southern Confederacy. He dwelt somewhat on the necessity of raising the blockade to supply cotton for the French manufacturers, for its scarcity was producing much distress. The French government was favorable and approached Lord Russell on the subject, who, October 17th, wrote Lord Palmerston: "It will not do for England and France to break a blockade for the sake of getting cotton." But Russell proposed to offer fair and equitable terms of pacification, and, if either belligerent rejected them, harsh measures were to be resorted to. Palmerston thought that the time had not yet come to act and replied to Russell's note: "Our best and true policy is to go on as we have begun and to keep quite clear of the conflict." About this time, a Liverpool paper declared that the supply of cotton was the greatest question of the civilized world.[62]

The Emperor of France was awaiting, with some impatience, the action of the English government, and, at the same time, maturing his Mexican schemes, and the failure of Lord Palmerston to respond favorably to his proposition was a keen disappointment. He could not act alone because he was bound by an agreement to act jointly with Great Britain. The Confederate commissioners were duly informed of the agreement between France and England, and the attitude of the English ministry, and advised that the temper of both North and South was such that action was not politic, but that "important military success might determine the period of their action."[63]

<hr/>

61 For a view of relations between England and the U.S. see Moore, *Rebellion Record*, 1, Supplement, pp. 14-19. Carman's assessment of the social and economic divisions in England as they pertain to the support for Confederate recognition is similar to that of McPherson, *Ordeal By Fire*, pp. 217-9. McPherson does not define a religious middle class as did Carman, but the other groups are similarly identified. Carman may have been influenced about the religious beliefs by Adams, *Charles Francis Adams*, pp. 272-3. Clarkson and Wilberforce were two well-known British advocates of abolition of slavery.

62 The quotations are in Spencer Walpole, *Life of Lord John Russell* (London, Longmans, Green, and Co., 1889), 2, p. 394, and Evelyn Ashley's *The Life of Henry John Temple, Viscount Palmerston: 1846-1865, With Selections from his Speeches and Correspondence*, 5 Vols. (London: R. Bentley and Son, 1876), 2, pp. 218-9.

63 Confederate Commissioners to Hunter, *ORN* 3, pp. 287-8.

Mr. Charles Francis Adams, the American Minister to England, was kept quite in the dark as to those exchanges of diplomatic opinion, but from the utterances of public men; the hostile tone of the press, and other indications, came to the conclusion that recognition was imminent and so advised his government; his biographer writes: "It is safe to say that between May and November 1861, the chances in Europe were as ten to one, in favor of the Southern Confederacy and against the Union." The seizure of the *Trent* and the capture of Mason and Slidell increased the chances against the Union.[64]

Taking advantage of the intense feeling in England, the commissioners promptly lodged with Lord Russell, November 27th, a protest against such "an infamous act" and, two days later, under express directions from Mr. Davis, presented Lord Russell evidence to show that the blockade was ineffectual, and that the further observance of neutrality was an injustice to parties "who are so deeply interested in a ready and easy access to the cheapest and most abundant sources of cotton supply." The feeling against the United States was now so intensely bitter that the commissioners were sanguine of a favorable response and early recognition of the Confederacy, but, to their great surprise, Lord Russell replied to their notes of November 27th and 29th that, in the present state of affairs, he "must decline to enter into official communications with them."[65]

Thanks to the great common sense of Abraham Lincoln peaceful relations were preserved between the United States and England, but the incident and the hostile feeling it engendered was a distinct gain to the Southern Confederacy.

James M. Mason, upon being given up by the United States, made his way to London, where he arrived January 29, 1862, and was not favorably impressed with the aspect of affairs.

The *London Times*, January 11, said: "They (Mason and Slidell) are here for their own interests and . . . rather disappointed perhaps that their detention has not provoked a new war. . . . They must not suppose, because we have gone to the very verge of a great war that they are precious in our eyes. We should have done just as much to rescue two of their own negroes. . . . Let the commissioners come up

---

64 See Adams, *Charles Francis Adams*, pp. 265-72, for a full discussion of the relations between Great Britain and the U.S. The quotation about the chances of Confederate recognition is found in *ibid.*, p. 148. See pp. 196-9 for relations with the French, and the note on p. 261 for quotation about military success. The British steamer *Trent* was unlawfully stopped on the high seas by a U.S. warship, an event that brought America and England closer to open hostilities.

65 The protest lodged by the commissioners to Lord Russell, November 27, 1861, is in *ORN* Series 1, 1, pp. 152-4. Carman has the date wrong for the second quotation (it was "three days later.") The unattributed quotation concerning the attitude of the British ministry is taken from a copy of a note found in *ibid.*, Series 2, 3, 310.

quietly to town and have their say with anyone who may have time to listen to them. For our part, we cannot see how anything they may have to tell can turn the scale of British duty and deliberation."[66]

He was coldly received and found the ministry averse to raising the blockade of the Southern ports, or recognizing the Confederacy, and apparently anxious to avoid any further broil with the United States. John Slidell, at Paris, found the sentiment quite as strong as it was in England and the French Minister for Foreign Affairs refused to discuss the subject of recognition.

On February 8, 1862, Mr. Hunter, Confederate Secretary of State, instructed Mason that no terms of agreement would be entered into, as the result of English intervention, that did not concede Maryland, Kentucky, and Missouri to the South.[67]

The Union victories of Mill Springs, Roanoke Island and Fort Donelson clouded Confederate prospects and produced a feeling throughout England that the South would fail, unless sustained by outside help, and the Richmond authorities were notified that, if these reverses were not counterbalanced by success elsewhere, the South "must bid adieu to all hopes of recognition." A little later Lord Russell's prediction of an early termination of the war, by the establishment within three months of two mighty republics in the territory of the late United States, heightened the prospects of speedy recognition, and the Confederate government was so advised; it was, however, cautioned not to place too much reliance upon Lord Russell's words, but to work out its own salvation by winning victories in the field. Upon this situation came the fall of New Orleans. Confederate sympathizers minimized the reverse and Mason and Slidell hastened to inform the powers that it would in no degree change the determination of the South to carry on the war.[68]

England gave no official sign but Slidell was given to understand that France was becoming dissatisfied with the tortuous course pursued by England; but that there was a seeming change in the tone of the English ministry; that if New Orleans had not fallen, Confederate recognition could not have been much longer delayed, but that, even after that disaster, if the Confederates obtained decided successes in Virginia and Tennessee, or could hold the enemy at bay, for a month or two, the same result would follow. At the same time the Emperor of France was reported to have said that he "would at once dispatch a formidable fleet to the mouth of the

---

66  *London Times*, January 11, 1861.

67  Hunter's instructions are in *ORN* Series 2, 3, pp. 333-6

68  Slidell to Hunter, March 10, 1862, *ibid.*, p. 356. Although Carman does not call it such, the prediction is from Russell's famous "three months" speech, which was delivered in the House of Lords in February of 1862. See Adams, *Charles Francis Adams*, p. 272 and note.

Mississippi" and that England would send an equal force, and that they would demand free egress and ingress for their merchant men, with their cargoes and supplies of cotton, which were essential to the world.[69]

The fall of New Orleans and other Confederate reverses were soon followed by Confederate successes and the tide of hope turned. The brilliant campaign of Stonewall Jackson, in the Shenandoah Valley, and the initial victories of Lee, in front of Richmond, intensified the determination of the government to put forth new efforts and work out the salvation of the cause by military success, and Benjamin, the Confederate Secretary of State, wrote both Mason and Slidell (July 19, 1862) that the government was to take the offensive and cross the Potomac. He concluded his letter in a confident strain:

> Our sky is at last bright and is daily becoming more resplendent. We expect (we can scarcely hope the contrary possible) that this series of triumphs will have at least satisfied the most skeptical of foreign cabinets that we are an independent nation, and have a right to be so considered and treated. A refusal by foreign nations now to recognize us would surely be far less than simple justice requires and would indicate rather settled aversion than impartial neutrality. On this theme however, I think it hardly necessary to say more than to assure you of the entire reliance felt by the President and the Department that you will spare no effort to avail yourself of the favorable opportunity presented by our recent successes in urging our right to recognition. We ask for no mediation, no intervention, no aid. We simply insist on the acknowledgment of a fact patent to mankind. Of the value of recognition as a means of putting an end to the war I have spoken in a former dispatch. In our finances at home its effect would be magical, and its collateral advantages would be innumerable. It is not to be concealed that a feeling of impatience and even of resentment is beginning to pervade our people, who feel that in the refusal of this legitimate demand the nations of Europe are in point of fact rendering active assistance to our enemies and are far from keeping the promise of strict neutrality which they held out to us at the beginning of the war."[70]

This communication, conveying the declaration of the intention of the Confederacy to recover lost ground and move into Maryland, was sent by special

---

69 For views of French activities and the Emperor's quotation, see *ORN* Series 2, 3, pp. 393-5. Johnson, "Memoirs,"*SHSP*, cites the sentiment in France as a factor in the Maryland Campaign.

70 Judah Benjamin, Secretary of State, to Mason and Slidell, *ORN* Series 2,, 3, p. 467.

messenger, who was instructed to inform Mason and Slidell that Kentucky, Tennessee and Missouri were to be redeemed, McClellan destroyed or captured, Pope overthrown, and the North invaded. Close upon these expected successes, the envoys were to demand immediate recognition.

France was becoming still more anxious to intervene but was restrained by its understanding with England. The French Emperor was encouraging the South with the view of neutralizing the power of the United States. On July 3, 1862, he wrote to General Ferry: "In the present state of the civilization of the world, the prosperity of America is not a matter of Indifference to Europe, for it is the country which feeds our manufactures and gives an impulse to our commerce. We have an interest in the Republic being powerful and prosperous, but not that she should take possession of the whole of the Gulf of Mexico, thence commanding the Antilles as well as South America, and being the only dispenser of the products of the New World."[71]

> At this period the French government discarding all the traditions of national policy, had openly extended its sympathies to the enemies of the American Union, and under the name, sometimes of recognition, sometimes of mediation, it had already been several times anxious to intervene in their favor. The wisdom of the English government which refused to participate in these measures, had prevented France from pursuing so fatal a policy. But the numerous friends of the Confederacy did not despair of dragging England into the cause, and thus securing them the support of these two great European powers. In order to accomplish this, they only asked of their client some success which could be adroitly turned to advantage; a victory achieved beyond the Potomac would have enabled them to maintain that the North, beaten on her own soil, would never he able to conquer those vast states which had rebelled against her laws.[72]

The cotton famine now made itself felt, none could be had; the mills were closed, and thousands were thrown out of employment, and obliged to seek municipal relief. In France the situation was about the same; in one district alone "no less than 130,000 persons, aggregating, with those dependent upon them, a

---

71 Carman once again mangled a quotation. Napoleon wrote this letter to Elie Frederic Forey, not General Ferry, on July 2, 1862. It was reprinted in the *New York Times* on February 20 and August 31, 1863.

72 Comte de Paris, *History of the Civil War in America*, 4 Vols. (Philadelphia: Porter & Coates, 1876), 2, p. 309.

total, of some 300,000 souls, were absolutely destitute, all because of the cotton famine."[73]

The starvation of the English workingmen did not appeal so strongly to the sympathy of the English government as did the losses of the commercial and manufacturing classes, and from these came strong pressures for recognition and the raising of the blockade, and members of the Ministry began to give serious thought to the propriety and necessity for such action. These thoughts were strengthened by the successes of the Confederates in the field. The defeat of McClellan's army on the Peninsula and the reverses of Pope's army, in front of Washington, intensified the pressure, and close upon the disaster of the Second Manassas, both France and England took measures for intervention, which were checked by the failure of Lee's Maryland campaign. We have made this digression in our narrative to bring before the reader the momentous importance of the campaign under consideration and to show the imminence of the crisis, when Lee, after defeating Pope in front of Washington, turned his victorious columns toward the Potomac.

In the Confederate camps for more than a year, events in Europe had been watched with the keenest interest, and in all ranks, from the general to the private, there was an abiding faith in the intervention of England and France. This was strengthened as the army approached the Potomac; and as it neared the boundary line of the Confederacy, they were confident that the time had come and doubted not, that the entrance into Maryland would bring the matter to a speedy and favorable issue. This was believed, not only by the army, but throughout the Confederacy, and there was good reason for the belief.

Therefore, when Lee concluded to cross the Potomac, he was playing for a great stake and thought he held a winning hand. As said by Bradley T. Johnson, Lee "had the possibility of ending the war and achieving the independence of his people by one short and brilliant stroke of genius, endurance and courage."[74]

Lee's orders were issued on September 2nd, and the movement began the next morning. He had been joined by the troops ordered up from Richmond ten days before, the infantry divisions of D. H. Hill, Lafayette McLaws, Hampton's brigade of cavalry and a number of batteries. These commands had numbered at Richmond about 19,000 men, but they had been diminished by the severity of the march to join Lee.

---

73 The quotation about cotton famine in France is found in Adams, pp. 265-71.

74 Johnson, "Memoirs," *SHSP*, pp. 10-12, addressed the international situation in a brief fashion, but the fact that Carman quoted it immediately after the previous paragraph suggests he might have used this source.

Putting his columns in motion towards the Potomac, to gain a footing in Maryland before the Union army could recover from its defeat and reorganize to meet him, Lee paused at the end of the first day's march to write this letter to Jefferson Davis:

HEADQUARTERS ALEXANDRIA AND LEESBURG ROAD,
Near Dranesville, September 3, 1862.

His Excellency President DAVIS,
Richmond, Va.:

Mr. PRESIDENT: The present seems to be the most propitious time since the commencement of the war for the Confederate Army to enter Maryland. The two grand armies of the United States that have been operating in Virginia, though now united, are much weakened and demoralized. Their new levies, of which I understand 60,000 men have already been posted in Washington, are not yet organized, and will take some time to prepare for the field. If it is ever desired to give material aid to Maryland and afford her an opportunity of throwing off the oppression to which she is now subject, this would seem the most favorable.

After the enemy had disappeared from the vicinity of Fairfax Court-House, and taken the road to Alexandria and Washington, I did not think it would be advantageous to follow him farther. I had no intention of attacking him in his fortifications, and am not prepared to invest them. If I possessed the necessary munitions, I should be unable to supply provisions for the troops. I therefore determined, while threatening the approaches to Washington, to draw the troops into Loudoun, where forage and some provisions can be obtained, menace their possession of the Shenandoah Valley, and, if found practicable, to cross into Maryland. The purpose, if discovered, will have the effect of carrying the enemy north of the Potomac, and, if prevented, will not result in much evil.

The army is not properly equipped for an invasion of an enemy's territory. It lacks much of the material of war, is feeble in transportation, the animals being much reduced, and the men are poorly provided with clothes, and in thousands of instances are destitute of shoes. Still, we cannot afford to be idle, and though weaker than our opponents in men and military equipments, must endeavor to harass if we cannot destroy them. I am aware that the movement is attended with much risk, yet I do not consider success impossible, and shall endeavor to guard it from loss. As long as the army of the enemy are employed on this frontier I have no fears for the safety of Richmond, yet I earnestly recommend that advantage be taken of this period of comparative safety to place its defense, both by land and water, in the most perfect condition. A respectable force can be collected to defend its approaches by land, and the steamer Richmond, I hope, is now ready to clear the river of hostile vessels.

Should General Bragg find it impracticable to operate to advantage on his present frontier, his army, after leaving sufficient garrisons, could be advantageously employed in opposing the overwhelming numbers which it seems to be the intention of the enemy now to concentrate in Virginia.

I have already been told by prisoners that some of Buell's cavalry have been joined to General Pope's army, and have reason to believe that the whole of McClellan's, the larger portion of Burnside's and Cox's, and a portion of Hunter's, are united to it.

What occasions me most concern is the fear of getting out of ammunition. I beg you will instruct the Ordnance Department to spare no pains in manufacturing a sufficient amount of the best kind, and to be particular, in preparing that for the artillery, to provide three times as much of the long-range ammunition as of that for smooth-bore or short-range guns. The points to which I desire the ammunition to be forwarded will be made known to the Department in time. If the Quartermaster's Department can furnish any shoes, it would be the greatest relief. We have entered upon September, and the nights are becoming cool.

I have the honor to be, with high respect, your obedient servant,

R. E. LEE,
General.[75]

Again on the following day, he wrote:

HEADQUARTERS,
Leesburg, Va., September 4, 1862
His Excellency President DAVIS,
Richmond, Va.

Mr. PRESIDENT: I am extremely indebted to Your Excellency for your letter of the 30th ultimo, and the letter from Washington, which you inclosed to me. You

---

75 From here to the end of the chapter, Carman pasted in a series of clippings from the *OR* and *B&L*. The analysis in between the clips evidently was Carman's own. He begins with *OR* 19, pt. 2, pp. 590-1, the famous letter from Lee to Davis dated September 3, 1862, wherein Lee announced the beginning of the Maryland campaign. After much elaboration of Maryland's political and social climate in the early days of the war, Carman chooses this point to begin the military story of the Maryland Campaign of 1862.

will already have learned all that I have ascertained subsequently of the movements of McClellan's army, a large part, if not the whole, of which participated in the battle of Saturday last, as I have good reason to believe.

Since my last communication to you, with reference to the movements which I propose to make with this army, I am more fully persuaded of the benefit that will result from an expedition into Maryland, and I shall proceed to make the movement at once, unless you should signify your disapprobation. The only two subjects that give me any uneasiness are my supplies of ammunition and subsistence. Of the former, I have enough for present use, and must await results before deciding to what point I will have additional supplies forwarded. Of subsistence, I am taking measures to obtain all that this region will afford; but to be able to obtain supplies to advantage in Maryland, I think it important to have the services of some one known to, and acquainted with, the resources of the country. I wish, therefore, that if ex-Governor Lowe can make it convenient, he will come to me at once, as I have already requested by telegram. As I contemplate entering a part of the State with which Governor Lowe is well acquainted, I think he could be of much service to me in many ways. Should the results of the expedition justify it, I propose to enter Pennsylvania, unless you should deem it unadvisable upon political or other grounds. As to the movements of the enemy, my latest intelligence shows that the army of Pope is concentrating around Washington and Alexandria in their fortifications. Citizens of this county report that Winchester has been evacuated, which is confirmed by the Baltimore Sun of this morning, containing extracts from the Washington Star of yesterday. This will still further relieve our country and, I think, leaves the valley entirely free. They will concentrate behind the Potomac.

I have the honor to be, with high respect, your obedient servant,

R. E. LEE,
General[76]

These two communications reveal Lee's intentions at the beginning of his Maryland campaign. He proposed to free Virginia of Federal troops, gather for himself the rich supplies of the Shenandoah Valley and, should it not be inadvisable upon political or other grounds, enter Pennsylvania. His reasons are more fully set forth in his official report here quoted:

76 The next excerpt is Lee's letter to Davis dated September 4, 1862, *ibid.*, pp. 591-2, in which he continues his reasoning for crossing the Potomac River.

The enemy having retired to the protection of the fortifications around Washington and Alexandria, the army marched on September 3 toward Leesburg. The armies of Generals McClellan and Pope had now been brought back to the point from which they set out on the campaigns of the spring and summer. The objects of those campaigns had been frustrated and the designs of the enemy on the coast of North Carolina and in Western Virginia thwarted by the withdrawal of the main body of his forces from those regions. Northeastern Virginia was freed from the presence of Federal soldiers up to the intrenchments of Washington, and soon after the arrival of the army at Leesburg information was received that the troops which had occupied Winchester had retired to Harper's Ferry and Martinsburg. The war was thus transferred from the interior to the frontier, and the supplies of rich and productive districts made accessible to our army. To prolong a state of affairs in every way desirable, and not to permit the season for active operations to pass without endeavoring to inflict further injury upon the enemy, the best course appeared to be the transfer of the army into Maryland. Although not properly equipped for invasion, lacking much of the material of war, and feeble in transportation, the troops poorly provided with clothing, and thousands of them destitute of shoes, it was yet believed to be strong enough to detain the enemy upon the northern frontier until the approach of winter should render his advance into Virginia difficult, if not impracticable. The condition of Maryland encouraged the belief that the presence of our army, however inferior to that of the enemy, would induce the Washington Government to retain all its available force to provide against contingencies, which its course toward the people of that State gave it reason to apprehend. At the same time it was hoped that military success might afford us an opportunity to aid the citizens of Maryland in any efforts they might be disposed to make to recover their liberties. The difficulties that surrounded them were fully appreciated, and we expected to derive more assistance in the attainment of our object from the just fears of the Washington Government than from any active demonstration on the part of the people, unless success should enable us to give them assurance of continued protection.

Influenced by these considerations, the army was put in motion, D. H. Hill's division, which had joined us on the 2d, being in advance, and between September 4 and 7 crossed the Potomac at the fords near Leesburg, and encamped in the vicinity of Fredericktown.

It was decided to cross the Potomac east of the Blue Ridge, in order, by threatening Washington and Baltimore, to cause the enemy to withdraw from the south bank, where his presence endangered our communications and the safety of those engaged in the removal of our wounded and the captured property from the late battlefields. Having accomplished this result, it was proposed to move the army into Western Maryland, establish our communications with Richmond through the Valley of the Shenandoah, and, by threatening Pennsylvania, induce the enemy to follow, and thus draw him from his base of supplies.[77]

When the Second Bull Run campaign closed we had the most brilliant prospects the Confederates ever had. We then possessed an army which, had it been kept together, the Federals would never have dared to attack. With such a splendid victory behind us and such bright prospects ahead, the question arose as to whether or not we should go into Maryland. General Lee, on account of our short supplies, hesitated a little, but I reminded him of my experience in Mexico where sometimes we were obliged to live two or three days on green corn. I told him we could not starve at that season of the year so long as the fields were loaded with "roasting ears." Finally, he determined to go on, and accordingly crossed the river and went to Frederick.[78]

On September 8th, after reaching Frederick, Maryland, General Lee said to General John G. Walker, one of his division commanders: "In ten days from now, if the military situation is then what I confidently expect it to be after the capture of Harper's Ferry, I shall concentrate the army at Hagerstown, effectually destroy the Baltimore and Ohio road and march to this point," placing his finger at Harrisburg, Pennsylvania. "That is the objective point of the campaign. You remember, no doubt, the long bridge of the Pennsylvania railroad over the Susquehanna, a few miles west of Harrisburg. Well, I wish effectually to destroy that bridge, which will disable the Pennsylvania railroad for a long time. With the Baltimore and Ohio in our possession, and the Pennsylvania railroad broken up, there will remain to the enemy but one route of communication with the West, and that very circuitous by way of the Lakes. After that I can turn my attention to Philadelphia, Baltimore or Washington, as may seem best for our interests. . . . You doubtless regard it hazardous to leave McClellan practically on my line of communication, and to march into the heart of the enemy's country?"

Walker acknowledged that he did regard the movement as hazardous, upon which Lee continued: "He (McClellan) is an able general but a very cautious one. . . . His army is in a very disorganized and chaotic condition, and will not be prepared

77 Carman pasted three paragraphs from Lee's report, *ibid.*, pt. 1, pp. 144-145.

78 The quotation following the clipping from the *OR* (the opening ten lines) is from Longstreet, *B&L*, p. 663. As usual with Longstreet's memoirs, he magnifies his influence and importance. The previous letters from Lee to Davis provide several reasons for invasion, and he expresses no concern about provisioning his army in Maryland and beyond. For a detailed analysis of Lee's intentions in the Maryland Campaign, see Joseph L. Harsh, *Taken at the Flood* (Kent OH: Kent State University Press, 1999), Chapters 1 and 2.

for offensive operations, or he will not think it so, for three or four weeks. Before that time I hope to be on the Susquehanna."[79]

Jackson moved from Chantilly on the morning of the 3rd, crossed the Loudoun and Hampshire Railroad at Vienna and Hunter's Mill, struck the Leesburg and Alexandria Turnpike, and followed it through Dranesville in the direction of Leesburg, camping that night on Sugar Land Run, not far from Dranesville. On the 4th he passed through Leesburg and went into camp near Big Spring, nearly two miles from town.

Longstreet followed Jackson. He left Chantilly on the 3rd, the divisions of R. H. Anderson and D. R. Jones marching by way of Dranesville, while McLaws took the Gum Spring road, the three divisions being concentrated at Leesburg on the night; of the 4th, where they remained until the morning of the 6th.

Hood's Division and Evans' Brigade, both unassigned to a corps, followed Longstreet from Chantilly and arrived at Leesburg on the evening of the 4th.

Longstreet says, "As our columns approached Leesburg 'Maryland, My Maryland' was in the air, and on the lips of every man from General Lee down to the youngest drummer. Our chief could have safely ordered the ranks to break in Virginia and assemble at Fredericktown."[80]

Lee's army was made up of Longstreet's command, the four divisions of Lafayette McLaws; Richard H. Anderson, D. R. Jones and John G. Walker; divisions of R. S. Ewell, A. P. Hill and John R. Jones; containing fourteen brigades; of D. H. Hill's Division of five brigades; of John B. Hood's Division of two brigades; and the unassigned brigade of N. G. Evans; in all forty brigades of

---

79 Carman quotes from General John G. Walker, *B&L*, p. 605, who offered an account of Lee's plans. Walker's memoir, quoted by Carman, contradicted much of his contemporary report in the *OR*. In his after-action report, Walker had little to offer about Lee's intentions and plans, but after a lapse of more than twenty years he became almost prescient. Walker's *B&L* account has been largely discredited by Harsh, *Taken at the Flood*, pp. 134-45, who points out that many veterans did not use Walker's account, but Carman seemed to be unaware of Walker's probable fabrications.

80 Lee's army movements to Frederick are traced here. See Harsh, *Taken at the Flood*, Chapters 2 and 3, for a detailed account of these marches. Carman uses the term "corps," which the Confederacy had not yet adopted. Carman was correct, however, in pointing out the independent status of Brig. Gen. John B. Hood's division and Brig. Gen. Nathan "Shanks" Evans' brigade. These two generals had a dispute that convinced Lee to divide the former division and put Hood under arrest. See John B. Hood, *Advance and Retreat* (New Orleans: for the Hood Orphans Memorial Fund, 1880), pp. 38-40. Many historians have struggled in trying to divide Lee's army in Maryland into two "wings" or "corps." See Harsh, *Sounding the Shallows* (Kent, OH: Kent State University Press, 2000), Chapter 2, for the best discussion of this topic. The quotation is from James Longstreet, *From Manassas to Appomattox: Gen. James Longstreet* (Bloomington, IN: Indiana University Press, 1960), p. 199.

infantry; Stuart's cavalry division of three brigades, and seventy-three batteries of artillery, aggregating three hundred and eighteen guns.

The strength of the army is disputed. Longstreet says that it numbered "60,000 men encouraged, matured, and disciplined by victory." Southern writers do not admit this number; it is safe to say that, including D. H. Hill's and John G. Walker's divisions, was not far from 48,000 men; 48,000 men whose superiors could not be found on the planet, whose spirits were raised to the highest pitch by the victories they had achieved and by the prospect of a successful invasion of the North.[81]

Lee states that he was not properly equipped for an invasion, lacking much of the materiel of war, feeble in transportation and thousands of his men destitute of shoes. He knew, however, that the country north of the Potomac was rich in horses and supplies for his men, and "that his army was equal to any service to which he thought to call it, and ripe for the adventure, that he could march into Maryland and remain until the season for the enemy's return into Virginia for another campaign had passed, improve transportation supplies and the clothing of his army, and do that, if not more, for the relief of Southern fields and limited means, besides giving his army and cause a moral influence of great effect at home and abroad.[82]

The invasion of Maryland being determined on the army was stripped of all encumbrances, and transportation reduced to a mere sufficiency to carry cooking utensils and the absolute necessaries of a regiment. Surplus artillery was turned in and all animals, not actually employed for artillery, cavalry or draught purposes, were left to be recruited. Batteries were to select the best horses for use, turning over all others. As the army was about to engage in most important operations, where any excess committed would exasperate the people, lead to disastrous results, and enlist the populace on the side of the Union forces, quartermasters and commissaries were directed to all arrangements for the purchase of supplies needed for the army, thereby removing all excuse for depredations upon a people whose friendship was desired. A provost guard was organized to follow in rear of the army, arrest stragglers, and punish summarily all depradators and keep the men with their commands. Stringent orders were issued against straggling and plundering, orders

81  The strength and organization of Lee's army, a most confusing matter, is outlined in a later chapter by Carman. The quoted portion is from Longstreet, *Manassas to Appomattox*, p. 279. See also Harsh, *Sounding the Shallows*, Chapter 2.

82  This description of the deficiencies of Lee's army is in Longstreet, *Manassas to Appomattox*, pp. 200-01, and lifted from the previously cited Lee to Davis, September 3, 1862, OR 19, pt. 2, pp. 590-1.

which were strictly enforced throughout the campaign, "but it was found impossible to prevent the straggling of half sick and barefooted men."[83]

"Many thousands of the men were ill clad and barefooted. The shoes, captured or supplied, had been altogether insufficient to keep the army shod and now they were about to march through a stony country and over turnpike roads. In addition to this, the effect of the insufficient food and the green corn diet of the past week or two were telling in the large number men weakened by diarrhea and other similar complaints, whom a day's march would turn into stragglers."

At Leesburg Lee learned that General Julius White, commanding a brigade of Union troops at Winchester, had abandoned the place, whereupon he gave orders to secure the town as a depot of supplies for his army; crippled and feeble soldiers, wending their way to the army, were directed to march through the valley and join him in Maryland, and he suggested to the Confederate Secretary of War that conscripts and deserters be gathered from the counties of Virginia, wrested from Federal occupation, and sent to Richmond to swell the garrison for the defense of that place. Another suggestion was, that General W. W. Loring, then operating in the Kanawha Valley, should make short work with the Union forces in that quarter and then should move to the lower Shenandoah Valley, about Martinsburg, and guard approaches in that direction, but Loring found full employment on the Kanawha and Lee's flank and rear in the great valley were entrusted to a few squadrons of Virginia cavalry detached from Stuart's cavalry division.[84]

On the eve of crossing the Potomac Lee again addressed Mr. Davis:

HEADQUARTERS ARMY OF NORTHERN VIRGINIA,
Leesburg, Va., September 5, 1862.
Richmond, Va.:

---

83 The provost guard quotation is from William Allan, *The Army of Northern Virginia in 1862* (Boston: Houghton Mifflin and Co., 1892), p. 325. It preceded the quote from Allan Carman used below, "introducing" a new source, as was his habit. For documentation about the stripped-down condition of Lee's army during this campaign, see General Order #102, OR 19, pt. 2, p. 592.

84 This quotation is from Allan, *The Army of Northern Virginia in 1862*, p. 324. The establishment of a base in Winchester demonstrates that Lee's movement was not a short-term foray. He intended to spend some time north of the Potomac and needed a depot to forward reinforcements and supplies. See OR 19, pt. 1, p. 140. The route through Manassas Junction was no longer usable due to the proximity of Union troops in Washington, D. C., And the destruction of the bridges on the railroads. Lee's thoughts on the coordinated use of General Loring are found in *ibid.*, pt. 2, pp. 593-4, which is part of the following letter to Davis. Also see *ibid*, pp. 589-90.

His Excellency President Davis,

Mr. PRESIDENT: As I have already had the honor to inform you, this army is about entering Maryland, with a view of affording the people of that State an opportunity of liberating themselves. Whatever success may attend that effort, I hope, at any rate, to annoy and harass the enemy. The army being transferred to this section, the road to Richmond, through Warrenton, has been abandoned as far back as Culpeper Court-House, and all trains are directed to proceed by way of Luray and Front Royal from Culpeper Court House to Winchester. I desire that everything coming from Richmond may take that route, or any nearer one turning off before reaching Culpeper Court House. Notwithstanding the abandonment of the line, as above mentioned, I deem it important that as soon as the bridge over the Rapidan shall be completed, that over the Rappahannock should be constructed as soon as possible, and I have requested the president of the road to have timber prepared for that purpose. My reason for desiring that this bridge shall be repaired is, that in the event of falling back it is my intention to take a position about Warrenton, where, should the enemy attempt an advance on Richmond, I should be on his flank; or, should he attack me, I should have a favorable country to operate in, and, bridges being repaired, should be in full communication with Richmond.

I have had all the arms taken in the late battles collected as far as possible, and am informed that about 10,000 are now at Gainesville. All empty trains returning to Rapidan are ordered to take in arms at Gainesville to transport to Rapidan. They should be sent at once to Richmond to be put in order, as arms may be needed in Maryland. I desire that Colonel Gorgas will send some one to take charge of these arms at once, as the cavalry regiments now on duty in the vicinity of Gainesville will have to be withdrawn.

We shall supply ourselves with provisions and forage in the country in which we operate, but ammunition must be sent from Richmond. I hope that the Secretary of War will see that the Ordnance Department provides ample supplies of all kinds. In forwarding the ammunition it can be sent in the way above designated for the other trains, or it can be sent to Staunton, and thence by the Valley road to Winchester, which will be my depot. It is not yet certain that the enemy have evacuated the valley, but there are reports to that effect, and I have no doubt that they will leave that section as soon as they learn of the movement across the Potomac. Any officer, however, proceeding toward Winchester with a train will, of course, not move without first ascertaining that the way is clear. I am now more desirous that my suggestion as to General Loring's movements shall be carried into effect as soon as possible, so that with the least delay he may move to the lower end of the valley, about Martinsburg, and guard the approach in that direction. He should first drive the enemy from the Kanawha Valley, if he can, and afterward, or if he finds he cannot accomplish that result, I wish him to move by way of Romney toward Martinsburg and take position in that vicinity.

I have the honor to be, with high respect, your obedient servant,

R. E. LEE,
General.[85]

The movement into Maryland was covered by a threatened advance on Washington. This was confided to General J. E. B. Stuart's Cavalry Division. The battle of Chantilly or Ox Hill was fought on the evening of September 1st. On the next day General Fitzhugh Lee's Brigade occupied Fairfax Court House, where on the same day, it was joined by General Wade Hampton's Brigade, just arrived from Richmond, where it had been on duty, guarding the retirement of the army and its march north from that place. During the day the 2nd Virginia Cavalry, Colonel T. T. Munford, of General B. H. Robertson's Brigade, advanced to Leesburg, drove from the town Captain S. C. Means and his company of cavalry and pursued to Waterford, a distance of seven miles. On the same day Wade Hampton made a reconnaissance and came upon a rearguard of Sumner's Union Corps at Flint Hill. After some firing of sharpshooters and artillery, Sumner's rearguard retired, followed by Hampton and his entire brigade, with two pieces of artillery, in charge of Captain John Pelham. Sumner's men were soon overtaken and Pelham opened on them with one of his rifled guns, creating some confusion. It was now growing dark, the pursuit was slow and cautious, and Hampton was finally checked by artillery and infantry commanding the road on which he was advancing, upon which he withdrew.[86]

On the morning of the 3rd Fitzhugh Lee, with his brigade and some horse artillery, made a demonstration toward Alexandria, while Hampton, moving by way of Hunter's Mill to the Leesburg Turnpike, below Dranesville, encamped near that place; General B. H. Robertson's Brigade, at Chantilly since the 1st, crossing over from the Little River Turnpike and camping near Wade Hampton. Demonstrations were kept up toward Groveton and the Chain Bridge. These demonstrations did not impose on Halleck, who cautioned McClellan, on the 3rd, that there was every probability that the Confederates would cross the Potomac and make a raid into

---

85  At this point Carman pasted in *OR* 19, pt. 2, pp. 593-4, Lee to Davis, September 5, 1862. Lee refined his plans with emphasis on supply and communication.

86  These cavalry actions were intended to screen the movement of Lee's army toward Leesburg. For a better description of the purposes and successes of the cavalry actions of September 2-4, 1862, see Harsh, *Taken at the Flood*, pp. 17-19, 56-7, and 67.

Maryland and Pennsylvania, and Pleasonton, who was at the front, came to the same conclusion, that "the enemy is only making a show of force to conceal his movements on the upper Potomac."

On the morning of the 4th, Robertson, moving in the direction of Falls Church, encountered Pleasonton's cavalry pickets, between Vienna and Lewinsville, and drove them in. Posting a part of his command and one gun of Chew's Battery near Lewinsville, to prevent surprise, Robertson opened fire with two guns from the hill overlooking the church, to the right of the main road, where, in a conspicuous position he had drawn up his cavalry.

Pleasonton replied with two guns and the firing was kept up until nearly sundown, when, perceiving Pleasonton about to advance on him in force, Robertson retired in the direction of Leesburg, near which place Stuart was concentrating his division, covering the rear of Lee's main army, now crossing the Potomac.[87]

---

87 Pleasonton's caution is a direct quotation from OR 19, pt. 2, p. 169. The quotation Carman cited from Halleck is *ibid.*, p. 178. After establishing the Confederate screening movement in the previous paragraph, Carman illustrated that it did not fool Pleasonton or Halleck.

# Chapter 3

# The Confederate Army Crosses the Potomac

he Confederate advance into Maryland was led by General D. H. Hill's Division, which had left Petersburg on the 21st of August and joined Lee at Chantilly on the 2d of September. On the morning of the 3rd it marched up Pleasant Valley in the direction of Dranesville, to strike the turnpike at that place, or between it and Leesburg, and reached the vicinity of Leesburg the same day, whence on the morning of the 4th, General Geo. B. Anderson's Brigade was pushed to the Potomac, opposite Point of Rocks, to demonstrate on the Baltimore and Ohio Railroad, interrupt communications with Baltimore and Washington, and divert attention from the fords below. While Anderson was engaged in this duty and amusing Colonel H. B. Banning, who, with the 87th Ohio, some Maryland troops, and two guns of Captain J. H. Graham's battery of New York Artillery, had been sent from Harper's Ferry to guard the crossings of the river at and below Point of Rocks, D. H. Hill, with two brigades, brushing away a detachment of thirty men of the 1st Regiment Potomac Home Brigade, under command of Lieutenant J. A. Burk, at Cheek's Ford, mouth of the Monocacy, crossed over and spent that night and next day in an attempt to destroy the locks and banks of the Chesapeake and

Ohio Canal; but the aqueduct, carrying the canal over the Monocacy, could not be destroyed for want of powder and tools.[1] While so engaged, on the 5th, Hill was directed by General Jackson, then crossing at White's Ford, to push forward that evening and unite with him where the Baltimore and Ohio Railroad crossed the Monocacy, near Frederick, to save or destroy the bridge, as circumstances should determine; but Hill could not see his way clear to carry out Jackson's instructions. Jackson, too, was delayed, and Hill remained near the mouth of the Monocacy until the morning of the 6th, when he followed Jackson's Division to near Frederick.

Jackson left Leesburg on the morning of the 5th, marched to White's Ford on the Potomac and began to cross before noon. The water was not deep and the passage was effected without much difficulty, though the progress was slow. An army correspondent writes: "When our army reached the middle of the river General Jackson pulled off his hat and the splendid band of music struck up the inspiring air 'Maryland, My Maryland,' which was responded to and sung by all who could sing; and the name of all who could then and there sing was legion."

What took place at the head of the column occurred its entire length. Each band as it came to the Potomac, or emerged from its waters, struck up the inspiring air, every regiment gave it vocal expression; the entire army was in the highest state of enthusiasm. Its historian says: "Its spirit, at this time was high. A series of brilliant successes had given it unbounded confidence in itself and its leaders, and the ragged and dirty soldiers hailed with joy the advance to the Potomac. The weather was fine, and on these splendid September days when the crossing was effected, the broad and placid river, with the long columns of wading infantry, and the lines of artillery and wagons making their way through it, and the men shouting and singing 'Maryland, My Maryland,' to give vent to their noisy delight, made a picturesque and animated scene."[2]

---

1    For D. H. Hill's crossing, see *OR* 19, pt.1; Hill's report, *ibid.*, p. 1,019; Lt. Binney's report, *ibid.*, pp. 532-3. It is clear that this crossing point is Cheek's Ford, although neither report mentions the name. Carman is incorrect in citing J. A. Burk. The correct person was Lt. Jerome B. Burke, Co. E, 1st Potomac Home Brigade. His name does not appear in the reports cited, so how Carman knew it is not known.

2    Quote from Allan, *The Army of Northern Virginia in 1862*, p. 325. Hill's report, OR 19, pt. 1, p. 1,019, is vague about this march, but see Jackson's report, *ibid.*, pp. 952-3. See also Henry Kyd Douglas, *B&L*, p. 620. The quotation about the brass band playing "Maryland, My Maryland" is from J. E. Cooke, *Life of Stonewall Jackson from Official Papers, Narratives and Personal Acquaintances* (New York: C.B. Richardson, 1863), p. 308, but is also included in Douglas, *B&L* account, although the wording is not exactly the same. Douglas also uses a similar description in *I Rode With Stonewall* (Chapel Hill: University of North Carolina Press, 1940), p. 147. Robertson, *Stonewall Jackson*, flatly denies that this incident took place, citing instead the incident where Major Harman cursed the mules to untangle a wagon tie-up, in *B&L*, 1, p. 238. The two stories

One of General Lee's biographers writes: "The fare of green apples and green corn, and the continuous bivouac and battle engaged in by the two corps of Jackson and Longstreet left thousands of stragglers behind. Clad in fluttering rags and with feet either bare or half shod, the depleted Confederate army moved forward in high spirit, with shout and song. They looked like a band of scarecrows. The groves and green fields of Maryland were made vocal with laughter as the gray-jackets marched toward Frederick."[3]

Jackson's spirits were as exuberant as those of a school boy. For months he had advocated a movement into Maryland and Pennsylvania, and as he saw before him fair fields laden with grain and orchards full of fruit, and his columns heading northward, he felt that the Confederate cause was brightening and looked forward to happy results. Not that he had any sentimental feeling regarding Maryland, but every step northward was taking him nearer the great industrial establishments, coal mines and railroads of Pennsylvania, that he would destroy, and the manufactures and commerce of Philadelphia and other cities and towns that he would annihilate. He was where he could subsist on the country and, once in Pennsylvania, would make unrelenting war upon her people, at their homes, and force them to understand the cost of holding the South in the Union at the point of the bayonet.[4]

On the afternoon of the 5th Stuart followed Jackson across the Potomac, Fitzhugh Lee's Brigade in the advance, and moved to Poolesville, near which place was encountered Captain Samuel E. Chamberlain, with a detachment of 100 men of the 1st Massachusetts Cavalry. This regiment had served in South Carolina; landed at Alexandria, Virginia, on the 2nd and, crossing the Potomac on the 4th, pushed out to Tennallytown, whence, on the morning of the 5th, Chamberlain was sent to watch the fords of the Potomac. As he marched through the principal street of Poolesville, some citizens, in sympathy with the Confederates, placed obstacles

do not necessarily contradict one another. It should be noted that many sources document the singing of "Maryland, My Maryland" on this march, making the Cooke story more believable. Prussian cavalryman Heros von Borke mentions it in *Memoirs of The Confederate War for Independence* (Philadelphia: J. B. Lippincott and Co., 1867), p. 127.

3   The quotation about green apples is from Henry Alexander White, *Robert E. Lee and the Southern Confederacy* (New York: G. P. Putnam and Sons, 1897), p. 199.

4   Jackson's intentions are not so clearly stated in any biographies, and his eagerness to invade the North is mentioned only in A. L. Long, *Memoirs of Robert E. Lee* (Philadelphia: J. M. Stoddart and Co., 1886), pp. 263-5. There is also the G. W. Smith anecdote of Jackson's intentions for the autumn of 1861 in Smith, *Confederate War Papers*, pp. 29-31. Nevertheless, this is not reason to doubt Carman's description as it may have come from his conversations with people who observed Jackson at the time. Note that Carman crossed out: "It was not the deliverance of Maryland, but the prospective desolation of Pennsylvania that aroused (gave) Jackson pleasure in crossing the Potomac."

of stones and other articles in the road behind him. He encountered Fitzhugh Lee just west of the town, was soon borne back by superior numbers, and, as he retreated rapidly through town, his men were thrown into confusion by the falling of the horses over the obstacles, resulting in the capture of Chamberlain and 30 of his men. None were killed; 8 or 9 were wounded. Lee's loss was 3 killed and 4 wounded. Lee went into camp about two miles east of Poolesville and Hampton followed to the same point. Fitzhugh Lee, impressed, no doubt, by the kindly assistance given by the citizens in overthrowing the Massachusetts Cavalry, reported that the reception of the Confederate troops in Maryland "was attended with the greatest demonstrations of joy, and the hope of enabling the inhabitants to throw off the tyrant's yoke, stirred every Southern heart with renewed vigor and enthusiasm."[5]

On the 6th, after paroling the Massachusetts prisoners, the two brigades of Lee and Hampton, the latter in advance, marched from Poolesville in direction of Frederick. Fitz Lee occupied New Market on the Baltimore and Ohio Railroad and felt out in the direction of Ridgeville, a gap in Parr's Ridge; Hampton took position at Hyattstown, with advanced posts at Damascus and Clarksburg in Parr's Ridge, while Robertson's Brigade, now under command of Colonel T. T. Munford, joining the command during the day, held the right at Sugar Loaf Mountain, and extended pickets as far as Poolesville. In this position from the mouth of the Monocacy on the right to the Baltimore and Ohio Railroad on the left, Stuart covered the front toward both Washington and Baltimore. This position was maintained until the 11th, Hampton being engaged in light skirmishing near Hyattstown, and Munford in more serious affairs at Poolesville and between that place and Sugar Loaf. Meanwhile the main body of Lee's army took position behind the Monocacy, and, covered by Stuart's enterprising cavalry, enjoyed a much needed rest.[6]

---

5    The Poolesville fight on September 5, 1862, is described in Stuart's report, *OR* 19, pt. 1, pp. 814-5; von Borke, *Memoirs of The Confederate War for Independence*, p. 128; and Pleasonton to Marcy, *OR* 19, pt. 2, p. 186. Pleasonton says "one killed and 1 wounded, Chamberlain and 21 missing." See Benjamin W. Crownishield, *A History of the First Massachusetts Cavalry Volunteers* (Boston: Houghton Mifflin & Co. 1891), pp. 71-2, for the obstacles placed in the streets and casualty numbers, which exactly match Carman's figures. The quotation about demonstrations of joy is not from Fitzhugh Lee, but is included in Stuart's report. In R. E. Lee's letter to Davis, September 7, 1862, he mentions capturing "31 of the enemy." *OR* 19, pt. 2, p. 597.

6    The disposition of Stuart's force on September 7 is roughly acknowledged in von Borke, *Memoirs of The Confederate War for Independence*, p. 131, although he has the date wrong. Stuart's report, *OR* 19, pt. 1, p. 815, gives the details, which are confirmed in Hampton's (*ibid.*, p. 822) and Munford's (*ibid.*, p. 825) reports, and Johnson, "Memoirs," *SHSP*. Although Brig. Gen. Beverly Robertson was transferred prior to the Maryland campaign, both Carman and Munford frequently refer to it as "Robertson's Brigade."

When Jackson crossed the Potomac on the 5th, it was his intention to make a rapid march and seize the Baltimore and Ohio Railroad bridge, over the Monocacy, near Frederick, that night, either to hold or to destroy it, and he called upon D. H. Hill, then engaged in the destruction of the canal, near the mouth of the Monocacy, to join him, but so much time was consumed in the crossing that Jackson could not accomplish the march. He halted at Three Springs near Buckeystown, six miles from the bridge and about nine miles from Frederick, a company of cavalry, under Captain Robert Randolph, moving in advance and scouting to the right, to observe any Union movement and keep connection with Stuart's cavalry. After going into bivouac Jackson sent orders to his division and higher commanders to let their men gather green corn for two days, which was all they now had to eat. He then sent for Captain E. V. White, of the cavalry, and directed him to accompany him in a ride. Starting after dark they went back, over the road marched that day, nearly to the Potomac, then back again to the bivouac, Jackson not speaking a word during the entire ride.[7]

Jackson resumed his march by the Frederick road on the morning of the 6th, arriving at the Frederick Junction of the Baltimore and Ohio Railroad, in the afternoon, where Ewell's Division was put in position covering the railroad and the approaches from the direction of Baltimore, and A. P. Hill's Division those from the direction of Washington. Jackson's old division went into camp on Best's farm, between the railroad junction and Frederick. Ewell seized the railroad bridge over the Monocacy, which had been held by the 14th New Jersey, until, under General Wool's orders, it retired in the direction of Baltimore.

D. H. Hill followed Jackson and camped near him. Colonel Bradley T. Johnson's Brigade, of Jackson's Division, occupied the town as a provost guard and Johnson, a former resident of the place, proclaimed to the citizens that he and his men came as their deliverers from a tyrannical oppression.

Frederick was held by a company of the 1st Maryland Regiment, Potomac Home Brigade, commanded by Captain W. T. Faithful. There were about 600 sick and wounded men in hospitals. When Faithful heard of the approach of Jackson he

---

7   The description of Jackson's intentions and actions are a composite from his report, *OR 19*, pt. 1, pp. 952-3, Early's report (*ibid.*, p. 966), and is corroborated by John Worsham, *One of Jackson's Foot Cavalry* (New York: Neale Publishing Co., 1912), p. 137. No source has been found for the green corn order, but it is too logical and commonplace on this campaign to question its authenticity. Carman may be referring to the documented case of Jackson purchasing a field of corn soon after crossing the river to subsist his men and animals. See Robertson, *Stonewall Jackson*, p. 587. Carman heard about Jackson's mysterious ride with "Lige" White directly from White. Carman's version is nearly word-for-word from a letter to Carman from White dated June 2, 1896, Carman Papers NYPL, Correspondence Files, Box 2, Folder 3.

removed the convalescents, set aside stores for those who could not be removed, sent all supplies possible to Pennsylvania and burned the remainder. Joined by Burk's detachment, which had fallen back from the mouth of the Monocacy, he led the party, about one hundred men, on the Harper's Ferry road, through Jefferson, Petersville and Knoxville, joining his regiment at Sandy Hook, a short distance [northeast] of Harper's Ferry, on the afternoon of the 6th.[8]

Longstreet crossed the Potomac at White's Ford, on the morning of the 6th, and, marching by way of Buckeystown and Frederick Junction, arrived at Frederick on the 7th. General Lee accompanied Longstreet. Hood's Division and Evans' Brigade followed Longstreet.[9]

General John G. Walker's Division had been left on the James River for the defense of Richmond. When it was ascertained that McClellan was leaving Harrison's Landing, Walker was ordered northward to reinforce Lee in his campaign against Pope, but when he reached the field of Second Manassas he found that the campaign in northeastern Virginia was closed and that Lee was pushing into Maryland. Walker followed and arrived at Leesburg on the evening of September 6th. The next morning he crossed the Potomac at Cheek's Ford, at the mouth of the Monocacy, about three miles above White's Ford. Here he overtook George B. Anderson's Brigade, which at been demonstrating on Point of Rocks and, marching with it, reached Buckeystown the same evening. On the 8th he marched his division to Frederick Junction and, riding ahead [Carman crossed out: "to Frederick"] reported to Lee, by whom he was informed of the plan to capture Harper's Ferry, in which he was to co-operate under orders not yet matured.[10]

---

8    The capture and occupation of Frederick is confirmed in reports filed by Jackson, *OR* 19, pt. 1, pp. 952-3, Early (*ibid.*, p. 966), and McGowan (*ibid.*, p. 987). Johnson's appointment as provost is also in Jackson's report. Johnson's proclamation can be found in the account of Dr. Lewis Steiner, who was in Frederick at the time. Lewis Steiner, *Report of Lewis Steiner M.D. Inspector of the Sanitary Commission, containing a Diary Kept During the Rebel Occupation of Frederick, MD* (New York: Anson D. F. Randolf, 1862), pp. 12-15. The proclamation was also printed in Evans, *CMH*, 2, pp. 90-91, which was printed in 1899. The record of the aptly-named Captain Faithful performing his duty is found in *OR* 19, pt. 1, pp. 533-4, and without naming Faithful, also in Steiner.

9    The march of Longstreet's and Walker's commands can be found in Longstreet's report, *OR* 19, pt. 1, p. 839, Walker, *B&L*, p. 604, and Longstreet, *Manassas to Appomattox*, p. 201.

10   Walker's route and his description of Lee's orders to destroy the aqueduct are taken from his account in *B&L*, pp. 201-2. Carman accepted Walker's later account even though some of the details differ markedly from Walker's contemporary report in *OR* 19, pt. 1, pp. 912-13. See Harsh, *Sounding the Shallows* (Kent,OH: Kent State University Press, 2000), Chapter 6. Harsh makes it clear that Walker is remembering things decades later that he did not mention (and probably could not have known about) in 1862.

On the morning of the 9th he was ordered by Lee to return to the mouth of the Monocacy and destroy the aqueduct of the Chesapeake and Ohio Canal, a duty which had been assigned to D. H. Hill and not performed. He arrived at the aqueduct a little before midnight and found it occupied by some cavalry pickets. These were driven away by the 24th and 25th North Carolina, which crossed the stream. Working parties were at once detailed and set to work drilling holes for blowing up the arches, but, after several hours labor, Walker met with no more success than had D. H. Hill; the aqueduct was so admirably constructed and cemented that it was found virtually a solid mass of granite. Not a seam or crevice could he discovered in which to insert the point of a crow-bar; and the drills were too dull and the granite too hard, so he was compelled to abandon the effort and before daylight of the 10th went into bivouac west of the Monocacy, having lost Captain Duffy of the 24th North Carolina, mortally wounded, and a few men taken prisoners.[11]

The high spirits with which Lee's army entered Maryland were intensified by cheering news from Bragg's army in Kentucky, essaying to carry the colors of the Confederacy to the Ohio River. Lee made the announcement in General Orders on the 6th:

> The general commanding takes pleasure in announcing to the brave soldiers of the Army of Northern Virginia the signal success of their comrades in arms in the West. The Confederate forces, under the command of Maj. Gen. E. Kirby Smith, defeated on August 30 the Federal forces commanded by General Nelson, capturing General Nelson and his staff, 3,000 prisoners, and all his artillery, small-arms, wagons, &c. This great victory is simultaneous with your own at Manassas. Soldiers, press onward! Let each man feel the responsibility now resting on him to pursue vigorously the success vouchsafed to us by Heaven. Let the armies of the East and the West vie with each other in discipline, bravery, and activity, and our brethren of our sister States will soon

11 For the movements of Walker's Division on September 9, Carman borrows language from Walker, *B&L*, p. 606. I have found no source that identifies the 25th North Carolina as the regiment assisting the 24th. Evidence may be in an unknown portion of Carman's papers. Carman was wrong about the mortal wounding of Capt. W. T. Duffy, who is mentioned as being severely wounded in Walker's report, *OR* 19, pt. 1, p. 912. See the accompanying biographical dictionary in Appendix 1 for the details. Duffy survived his wound, as noted in Louis H. Manarin and Weymouth T. Jordan, eds., *North Carolina Troops, 1861-1865: A Roster*, 17 Vols. (Raleigh, NC: State Division of Archives and History, 1973), 7, p. 266.

be released from tyranny, and our independence be established upon a sure and abiding basis.[12]

On the 7th Lee was holding the line of the Monocacy, and reported that he found plenty of provisions and forage in the country; that the community received his army with kindness, but hesitated to receive Confederate currency in payment for supplies; and "notwithstanding individual expressions of kindness that have been given, and the general sympathy in the success of the Confederate States, situated as Maryland is, I do not anticipate any general rising of the people in our behalf. Some additions to our ranks will no doubt he received, and I hope to procure subsistence for our troops."[13]

At the same time Lee could not conceal the fact that there was great and urgent necessity to correct some evils in his army, especially as it was in a state whose citizens it was his purpose to conciliate and bring to his cause; every outrage upon their feelings and property should be checked. The evils he complained of were "backwardness in duty, tardiness of movement and neglect of orders" on the part of officers, and straggling from the ranks among the men, and he begged Mr. Davis to find some tribunal under the law that could take cognizance of and punish such offenses. On September 7th he wrote Mr. Davis:

> I find that the discipline of the army, which, from the manner of its organization, the necessity of bringing it into immediate service, its constant occupation and hard duty, was naturally defective, has not been improved by the forced marches and hard service it has lately undergone. I need not say to you that the material of which it is composed is the best in the world, and, if properly disciplined and instructed, would be able successfully to resist any force that could be brought against it. Nothing can surpass the gallantry and intelligence of the main body, but there are individuals who, from their backwardness in duty, tardiness of movement, and neglect of orders, do it no credit. These, if possible, should be removed from its rolls if they cannot be improved by correction.
>
> Owing to the constitution of our courts-martial, great delay and difficulty occur in correcting daily evils. We require more promptness and certainty of punishment.

---

12 This was General Order #103, Army of Northern Virginia, and is found in *OR* 19, pt. 2, p. 596. There is some uncertainty about when Lee became aware of Bragg's campaign in Kentucky. It is tempting to assume the offensive operations of the Fall of 1862 were a coordinated effort, but evidence of Lee's knowledge of that plan is weak, at best. See Harsh, *Taken at the Flood*, pp. 28-31, 106-7.

13 This passage about the tepid support from Marylanders is from a letter to President Davis, September 7, 1862, *OR* 19, pt. 2, pp. 596-7.

One of the greatest evils, from which many minor ones proceed, is the habit of straggling from the ranks. The higher officers feel as I do, and I believe have done all in their power to stop it. It has become a habit difficult to correct. With some, the sick and feeble, it results from necessity, but with the greater number from design. These latter do not wish to be with their regiments, nor to share in their hardships and glories. They are the cowards of the army, desert their comrades in times of danger, and fill the houses of the charitable and hospitable in the march. I know of no better way of correcting this great evil than by the appointment of a military commission of men known to the country, and having its confidence and support, to accompany the army constantly, with a provost-marshal and guard to execute promptly its decisions.[14]

Six days later Lee wrote that his movement was much embarrassed by the reduction of his force by straggling which it seemed impossible to prevent with the present regimental officers. Although he had reason to hope that his casualties in battle in the recent campaign in Virginia did not exceed 5,000 men, his ranks were much reduced; he feared from a third to one-half of the original numbers. After the battle of Antietam he reported that the efficiency of his army "was paralyzed by the loss to its ranks of the numerous stragglers... A great many men belonging to the army never entered Maryland at all; many returned after getting there, while others who crossed the river kept aloof."[15]

Lieut. Col. Henderson in his elaborate *Life of Stonewall Jackson* says:

Many a soldier, who had hobbled along on his bare feet until Pope was encountered and defeated found himself utterly incapable of marching into Maryland. In rear of the army the roads were crowded with stragglers. Squads of infantry, banding together for protection, toiled painfully by easy stages, unable to keep pace with the colors, but hoping to be in time for the next fight, and amongst them were not a few officers. But this was not the worst. Lax discipline and the absence of soldierly habits asserted themselves. Not all the stragglers had their faces turned toward the enemy, not all were incapacitated by physical suffering. Many, without going through the formality of asking leave, were making for their homes, and had no idea that their conduct was in any way peculiar. They had done their duty in more than one battle, they had been long absent from homes and farms; their equipment was worn out, the enemy had been

14 Lee's concern for straggling and shirkers is expressed in a letter to Davis on the same day, September 7, 1862, *ibid.* pp. 597-8.

15 The concern about stragglers and casualties from Manassas was again expressed to Davis in a letter written September 13, 1862, from Hagerstown, Maryland, *OR* 19, pt. 2, pp. 605-6. Although Carman does not cite it, he used almost exactly the same wording Lee did.

driven from Virginia, and they considered that they were fully entitled to some short repose. And amongst these, whose only fault was an imperfect sense of their military obligations, was the residue of cowards and malingerers shed by every great army engaged in protracted operations.[16]

The sympathy of Jackson's biographer was with the Southern cause and the picture here presented of the straggling of Lee's army is in fortification of an argument for its comparatively small numbers engaged at Antietam, and yet, the picture is not much overdrawn, and it may be said, in addition, that many of the Confederate officers and men were opposed to an invasion of the North, or an incursion beyond the borders of the Southern Confederacy. They had been taught to believe that their duty lay entirely in defending their soil from invasion.[17]

As soon as it was known that Lee was across the Potomac the Confederate authorities at Richmond rose to a high state of exaltation, many believed that in ten days he would be dictating peace from the steps of the capitol at Washington. Mr. Davis went so far as to prepare a mission to propose terms of peace, and Henry S. Foote, in the House of Representatives, offered this resolution: "That the signal success with which Divine Providence has so continually blessed our arms for several months past would fully justify the Confederate government, in dispatching a commissioner or commissioners to the Government at Washington City, empowered to propose the terms of a just and honorable peace." By a vote of 59 to 26 the resolution was laid on the table.[18]

There was not entire unanimity in Confederate councils. When Mr. Davis communicated to the House of Representatives, Lee's dispatches, announcing his intention to cross the Potomac and that he had done so, the following resolution

16 The long quotation from Henderson is found Henderson, *Stonewall Jackson and the American Civil War*, p. 495. Carman misidentifies this as *Life of Stonewall Jackson*.

17 It is worth noting that Henderson, *ibid.*, does not add political reasons to the Confederate straggling, but Carman imposed his own. See Harsh, *Sounding the Shallows*, Chapter 6, A, for a discussion about reluctant Confederates in the Maryland Campaign. As a historian, Carman routinely alerted readers to the potential for bias in any source he quoted from. Although he seemed to accept Henderson's claim of reduced numbers from straggling, he added the concept of "conscientious objectors" to the mix. Harsh drew the distinction between being opposed to the movement and an outright refusal to obey orders. It is an important difference.

18 Foote's resolution was printed in the *Richmond Examiner* on September 20, 1862, as cited in Moore, *Rebellion Record*, 5, Diary, p. 83. The Moore entry does not include the vote tally, but it, and the resolution can be found in *Journal of the House of Representatives of the First Congress of the Confederate States of America, 1861-1865*, 5, September 16, 1862. These records are found in the 58th U.S. Congress, 2nd Session 1904, S. Doc. 234, Serial 4616, pp. 385-6, hereafter referred to as *Journal of the Confederate Congress*.

was offered: "that Congress has heard with profound satisfaction, of the triumphant crossing of the Potomac by our victorious army, and, assured of the wisdom of that masterly movement, could repose with entire confidence on the distinguished skill of the commanding general and the valor of his troops, under favor of the Great Ruler of nations, to achieve new triumphs, to relieve oppressed Maryland, and advance our standard into the territory of the enemy."[19]

The Confederate Congress had, in December 1861, declared, that no peace ought to be concluded with the United States, which did not insure to Maryland the opportunity of forming a part of the Confederacy. We have elsewhere noted the fact that, in February 1862, when the Confederate Government began to congratulate itself that it had convinced England and France that cotton was king, and that those two great powers were on the eve of armed intervention in American affairs, Mr. Mason, Confederate commissioner in London, was advised that no treaty of peace or settlement would be considered that did not secure the independence of the Confederate States, including Maryland, Kentucky, Virginia and Missouri. The liberation of Maryland and her alliance with the Confederacy had become the stated purpose of the South, and its Congress was willing to express and confirm it, in the resolution before the House, but a formidable minority would not go beyond that point and favor an invasion of Pennsylvania, and objection was made to the closing words of the resolution: "and advance our standards into the territory of the enemy" and a motion to strike out those words was warmly debated, by those who were not prepared to take the responsibility of going so far; they had not been invited even to enter Maryland, but had been invited to enter Kentucky and had been driven out by Kentucky steel. Others insisted that the North should taste some of the bitterness of war, the people demanded it, and Mr. Miles, of South Carolina, was sanguine that Jackson with half the Army of Northern Virginia, could scatter 600,000 of the enemy and gain peace. The motion to strike out the concluding words of the resolution was lost, by a vote of 29 to 62, and the entire resolution, as originally offered, committing the government to an invasion of the North, was adopted, September 12, 1862, by a vote of 56 to 13.[20]

19 *Ibid.*, pp. 371-2. This was also found in *SHSP*, 46, p. 120, which was published too late for Carman to have seen it.

20 For the Confederate States Congress on the inclusion of Maryland, see ORN Series 4, 1, pp. 805-6. The February 1862 instructions referred to are found in ibid., Series 2, 3, p. 333. Carman has the vote totals wrong. The motion to defeat the amendment was 29 to 61. The subsequent passage was voted 63 to 15. The debate over the resolution, amendment, and votes are found in *Journal of the Confederate Congress*, pp. 371-2. The resolution is found in *SHSP*, 46, pp. 120-5, with the correct vote total.

About the same time, to help Bragg's operations in Kentucky, it was proposed to make peace with the states of the Northwest and detach them from the Union, by offering them the free navigation of the Mississippi River, and a committee made a favorable report on the proposition that "such a proclamation . . . it is confidently believed, would have a tendency greatly to strengthen the advocates of peace in the northwestern states, be calculated to bring those states quickly into amicable relations with the states of the South, withdraw them ultimately from their injurious political connection with the states of the North and East, with which they have really so little in common, and thus enable us to dictate the terms of a just and honorable peace from the great commercial emporium of that region through whose influence mainly has this wicked and unnatural war been thus far kept in progress."[21]

A minority report was submitted, contending that the reported desire for peace in the northwest was delusive, and it advanced the opinion that: "the most effective mode of conquering a peace is not to be found in extending to the enemy propositions of reconciliation, but in the vigorous prosecution of the war." These reports were submitted September 19, 1862; Lee's army had then recrossed the Potomac and dreams of conquering a peace, at that time, vanished.[22]

The tone of the Southern press and what was expected to be accomplished by an invasion of the North is shown in the following editorial of the Richmond *Dispatch*, September 17, 1862:

> The road to Pennsylvania lies invitingly open. There are no regular soldiers on the route and it would be a task of little difficulty to disperse the rabble of militia that might be brought to oppose them.
>
> The country is enormously rich. It abounds in fat cattle, cereals, horse and mules. Our troops would live on the very fat of the land. They would find an opportunity, moreover, to teach the Dutch farmers and grazers, who have been clamorous for this war, what an invasion really is. If once compelled to take his own physic, which is a great deal more than he bargained for, Mynheer (Mein Herr) will cry aloud for peace in a very short time. For our own part we trust the first proclamation of Pope, and the manner in which his army carried it out, will not be forgotten. We hope the troops will turn the whole country into a desert as the Yankees did to the Piedmont country of Virginia.

21 *Ibid.*, p. 405.

22 *Ibid.*, pp. 406-7.

Let not a blade of grass, or stalk of corn, or barrel of flour, or bushel of meal, or a sack of salt, or a horse, or a cow, or hog or sheep be left wherever they were strong. Let vengeance be taken for all that has been done until retribution itself shall stand aghast. This is the country of the smooth spoken would-be gentleman, McClellan. He has caused to us in Virginia a loss of at least thirty thousand negroes, the most valuable property a Virginian can own. They have no negroes in Pennsylvania. Retaliation must therefore fall upon something else, and let it fall upon everything that constitutes property. A Dutch farmer has no negroes but he has horses that can be seized, grain that can be confiscated, cattle that can be killed and houses that can be burnt. He can be taken prisoner and sent to Libby's Warehouse as our people from Fauquier and Loudoun, Culpeper and the peninsula have been sent to Lincoln's dungeons in the North. Let retaliation be complete that the Yankees may learn that two can play at the game that they have themselves commenced.

By advancing into Pennsylvania with rapidity our army can easily get possession of the Pennsylvania Central Railroad and break it down so thoroughly that it couldn't be repaired in six months. They already have possession of the Baltimore and Ohio Railroad and the York River railroad. By breaking down these and the railroad leading from Philadelphia to Baltimore they will completely isolate Washington and Baltimore. No reinforcements can reach them from either North or West, except by the Potomac or the bay.[23]

Up to the 8th, Lee could not ascertain that any Union movement was being made to oppose him in Maryland, but that the entire Union army was concentrating about Washington. He was still purchasing ample supplies of provisions in the country, and still endeavoring to break up the line of communication as far back as Culpeper Court House, and turn everything into the Valley of Virginia, in accordance with the plan communicated to Mr. Davis.

Firmly established behind the Monocacy he held the Baltimore and Ohio Railroad and the principal roads to Baltimore, Washington, Harper's Ferry and the upper Potomac, and could operate on several of these. Those toward Harper's

23 This clipping, which Carman used to illustrate the feeling of the Southern press, is from an article titled "Our Army in Maryland," *Richmond Dispatch*, September 17, 1862, and was pasted in by Carman. It also appears in Moore, *Rebellion Record*, 5, Diary, p. 81. "Mein Herr" refers to the largely German and Republican farmers in Pennsylvania. "Pope's first proclamation" refers to the punitive orders issued by Gen. John Pope found in *OR* 12, pt. 2, pp. 50-51. The loss of blacks caused by Gen. McClellan was, at best, an unintentional outcome of the Peninsula campaign. McClellan deliberately stated that he had no intention of confiscating private property, including slaves. *Ibid.*, 11, pt. 3, pp. 345-6.

Ferry, Baltimore and Pennsylvania were unoccupied, while those in the direction of Washington were held by the Union army, now concentrating in his front.[24]

Lee now felt himself strong enough to develop one of the political objects of his Maryland campaign. Pollard, in his *Secret History of the Southern Confederacy*, says: "Mr. Davis had been persuaded that at the moment the Confederate armies were so visibly superior as to carry the war into the enemy's country, if he would then make any proposition showing the moderation of the designs of the South, it would furnish capital to the Democratic party in the North, widen the division of the party there, and excite a political division in favor of the South, beside making a moral exhibition to the world of great advantage to the cause."

It was for these reasons, to work on the feelings of the North and strengthen the hands of the Northern Democrats, that Mr. Davis gave the most stringent orders that Lee's army was to protect every right of private property in the North, to abstain from retaliation and to show the utmost regard for the humanities of war. "It was not," observed Pollard "so much to sentimentalism of Christian warfare, as the calculation of political effect . . . of operating on the division of parties in the North, and the weakening its resolution and temper in the contest."[25]

In his review of the Maryland campaign, Longstreet says: "It had been arranged that the Southern President should join the troops and from the head of his victorious army call for recognition," and indulges in roseate views of the effects: "Maryland would have put out some of her resources, and her gallant youth would have helped to swell the Southern ranks—the 20,000 soldiers who had dropped from the Confederate ranks during the severe marches of the summer would have been with us. Volunteers from all parts of the South would come, swimming the Potomac to find their President and his field marshal, while Union troops would have been called from Kentucky and Tennessee, and would have left easy march for Confederate armies of the West to the Ohio River. Even though the Confederates were not successful, the fall elections were against the administration. With the Southern armies victorious, the result of the contest at the polls would

---

24 Carman summarizes here from Lee's September 8, 1862, letter to Davis outlining this new route for supplies and communication for the army, found in *ibid.*, 19, pt. 2, pp. 600-1.

25 Pollard's book is Edward A. Pollard, *Life of Jefferson Davis, with a Secret History of the Southern Confederacy Gathered Behind the Scenes in Richmond* (Philadelphia: National Publishing Co., 1869), pp. 237-8, 239. Pollard made similar arguments in *Lost Cause and Southern History of the War* (New York: E. B. Treat and Co., 1867), but because of his bias, Pollard is not a reliable source. See also Allan, *The Army of Northern Virginia in 1862*, pp. 325-8, and Henderson, *Stonewall Jackson and the American Civil War*, pp. 497-8, about the potential results and reasons for Confederate operations in Maryland.

have been so pronounced as to have called for the recognition of the Confederacy."[26]

To what extent Lee shared these views is not definitely known, but we have Longstreet for authority, that it was Lee's deliberate and urgent advice to Mr. Davis to join him and be prepared to make a proposal for peace and independence from the head of a conquering army. But Mr. Davis had not joined the army and Lee, flushed with his victories in Virginia and quietly seated in the richest part of Maryland, wrote this letter:

HEADQUARTERS,
Near Fredericktown, Md., September 8, 1862.

His Excellency JEFFERSON DAVIS,
President of the Confederate States, Richmond, Va.:

Mr. PRESIDENT: The present position of affairs, in my opinion, places it in the power of the Government of the Confederate States to propose with propriety to that of the United States the recognition of our independence. For more than a year both sections of the country have been devastated by hostilities which have brought sorrow and suffering upon thousands of homes, without advancing the objects which our enemies proposed to themselves in beginning the contest. Such a proposition, coming from us at this time, could in no way be regarded as suing for peace; but, being made when it is in our power to inflict injury upon our adversary, would show conclusively to the world that our sole object is the establishment of our independence and the attainment of an honorable peace. The rejection of this offer would prove to the country that the responsibility of the continuance of the war does not rest upon us, but that the party in power in the United States elect to prosecute it for purposes of their own. The proposal of peace would enable the people of the United States to determine at their coming elections whether they will support those who favor a prolongation of the war, or those who wish to bring it to a termination, which can but be productive of good to both parties without affecting the honor of either.

I have the honor to be, with high respect, your obedient servant,

26 This quotation is excerpted from Longstreet, *From Manassas to Appomattox*, p. 285. According to Carman, Longstreet espoused the theory that Lee wanted Davis to join him in Maryland, which Carman accepted at face value. There is no corroboration of this view, no letters to Carman from Longstreet mention this theory, and Lee's actions and words seem to refute this claim. In fairness to Longstreet, the passages before this quotation suggest that he credited other factors necessary for success besides the presence of Davis.

R. E. LEE,
General.[27]

It was expected by Mr. Davis that when General Lee entered Maryland he would be joined by persons of influence, who would advise with him upon the political condition of the State and upon other matters of import, but Lee found no person of influence awaiting his arrival or coming forward to advise with him. It was a matter of grave concern to him how he should supply his army without money. The farmers of Western Maryland had no use for Confederate money and but little faith in the promises of the Confederate Quartermaster, and Lee reported that he anticipated some embarrassment in paying for necessities for the army, as it was probable that many individuals would hesitate to receive Confederate currency. He wrote to Mr. Davis: "I shall endeavor in all cases to purchase what is wanted, and, if unable to pay on the spot, will give certificates of indebtedness of the Confederate States for future adjustment. It is very desirable that the chief quartermaster and commissary should be provided with funds, and that some general arrangement should be made for liquidating the debts that may be incurred to the satisfaction of the people of Maryland, in order that they may willingly furnish us what is wanted. I shall endeavor to purchase horses, clothing, shoes, and medical stores for our present use, and you will see the facility that would arise from being provided the means of paying for them. I hope it may be convenient for ex-Governor Lowe, or some prominent citizen of Maryland, to join me, with a view of expediting these and other arrangements necessary to the success of our army in this State."[28]

Lee refrained from inducing men of prominence to come forward and openly, actively, espouse the Confederate cause and expressed himself averse to doing so. He was not confident of his ability to hold the State and was too considerate to compromise those who would suffer the moment his army failed to protect them. As none came forward and finding that the citizens were embarrassed as to the intentions of the army, he determined to delay no longer in making known the purpose of Confederate invasion and issued this proclamation:

---

27  Carman also included Lee's September 8, 1862, letter to Davis, OR 19, pt. 2, p. 600, which illustrated that Lee was looking for victory through defeat of the Union arms, at least in part, by defeat at the ballot box. Here, Lee's most optimistic opinion of the potential results of his campaign was expressed.

28  Lee to Davis, *ibid.*, p. 596.

HEADQUARTERS ARMY OF NORTHERN VIRGINIA,
Near Fredericktown, Md., September 8, 1862.
To the People of Maryland:

It is right that you should know the purpose that brought the army under my command within the limits of your State, so far as that purpose concerns yourselves. The people of the Confederate States have long watched with the deepest sympathy the wrongs and outrages that have been inflicted upon the citizens of a commonwealth allied to the States of the South by the strongest social, political, and commercial ties. They have seen with profound indignation their sister State deprived of every right and reduced to the condition of a conquered province. Under the pretense of supporting the Constitution, but in violation of its most valuable provisions, your citizens have been arrested and imprisoned upon no charge and contrary to all forms of law. The faithful and manly protest against this outrage made by the venerable and illustrious Marylander, to whom in better days no citizen appealed for right in vain, was treated with scorn and contempt; the government of your chief city has been usurped by armed strangers; your legislature has been dissolved by the unlawful arrest of its members; freedom of the press and of speech has been suppressed; words have been declared offenses by an arbitrary decree of the Federal Executive, and citizens ordered to be tried by a military commission for what they may dare to speak. Believing that the people of Maryland possessed a spirit too lofty to submit to such a government, the people of the South have long wished to aid you in throwing off this foreign yoke, to enable you again to enjoy the inalienable rights of freemen, and restore independence and sovereignty to your State. In obedience to this wish, our army has come among you, and is prepared to assist you with the power of its arms in regaining the rights of which you have been despoiled.

This, citizens of Maryland, is our mission, so far as you are concerned. No constraint upon your free will is intended; no intimidation will be allowed within the limits of this army, at least. Marylanders shall once more enjoy their ancient freedom of thought and speech. We know no enemies among you, and will protect all, of every opinion. It is for you to decide your destiny freely and without constraint. This army will respect your choice, whatever it may be; and while the Southern people will rejoice to welcome you to your natural position among them, they will only welcome you when you come of your own free will.

R. E. LEE,
General, Commanding.[29]

This address was received with cold indifference. The "ancient freedom of thought and speech" of the people of Maryland had not been so much curtailed as to anger them to the fighting point, and they doubted the power of Lee's ragged army to regain even the small moiety of the rights of which they were told they had been despoiled. Those of Frederick and adjoining counties were a thrifty people, entirely willing to dispose a reasonable share of their products at unreasonably high prices, but were not easily moved to rise to avenge the "wrongs and outrages" that had been inflicted upon them. They were not aware of the fact that they had been "deprived of every right and reduced to the condition of a conquered province." The temper of the people had been misjudged.

Bradley T. Johnson, a native of Maryland and resident of Frederick, an officer of Lee's army, who was designated as Provost Marshal of the town, was an ardent Confederate, and prone to judge others' thoughts by his own. He was sanguine of a Confederate rising and used his gift of oratory to that end upon his entrance into the town, with Jackson's advance on the 6th, he proclaimed himself and men as deliverers and called upon all to throw off the yoke of oppression and subjugation. In the evening he addressed a public meeting and assured his hearers that the Confederates had come into Western Maryland to stay; predicted that Washington and Baltimore would fall into their hands, and was sanguine that Lee would dictate terms of peace in Independence Square, Philadelphia. On the day that Lee issued his address to the people of Maryland, Johnson put forth this appeal:

To the People of Maryland:

After sixteen months of oppression more galling than the Austrian tyranny, the victorious army of the South brings freedom to your doors. Its standards now wave from the Potomac to Mason and Dixon's Line. The men of Maryland, who during the last long months have been crushed under the heel of this terrible despotism, have now an opportunity for working out their own redemption, for which they have so long waited, and suffered, and hoped.

---

29  Lee's proclamation is found in *ibid.*, pp. 601-2, and some of the language quoted is from Lee to Davis, *ibid.*, pp. 604-5, 605-6. Western Maryland's population was heavily German and there was little slavery in these counties. Thus, there was little local sympathy for the Confederates in the region. See Harsh, *Taken at the Flood*, pp. 113-114, 174.

The Government of the Confederate States is pledged by the unanimous vote of its Congress, by the distinct declaration of its President, the soldier and statesman, Davis, never to cease this war until Maryland has the opportunity to decide for herself her own fate, untrammeled and free from Federal bayonets.

The people of the South with unanimity unparalleled have given their hearts to our native State, and hundreds of thousands of her sons have sworn with arms in their hands that you shall be free.

You must now do your part. We have the arms for you. I am authorized immediately to muster in for the war, companies and regiments. The companies of one hundred men each. The regiments of ten companies. Come, all who wish to strike for their liberties and their homes. Let each man provide himself with a stout pair of shoes, a good blanket and a tin cup. Jackson's men have no baggage.

Officers are in Frederick to receive recruits, and all companies formed will be armed as mustered in. Rise at once.

Remember the cells of Fort McHenry! Remember the dungeons of Fort Lafayette and Fort Warren! The insults to your wives and daughters, the arrests, the midnight searches of your houses!

Remember these your wrongs, and rise at once in arms and strike for Liberty and right.

Bradley T. Johnson, Colonel C. S. A.
September 8, 1862[30]

The appeal was but feebly answered. A few enlisted; some, who came to enlist, upon seeing their liberators, officers as well as men, barefoot, ragged and filthy, changed their minds and went home. The result was disappointing to Johnson, who had impressed his sanguine views upon his superiors that, in that part of the state, the Southern cause would find recruits to march under its colors; that, freed from Federal bayonets and given the opportunity, they would decide for the South. Less than five hundred recruits were obtained, not enough to compensate for deserters.

It is said, "Lee expected volunteers to enroll themselves under his standard (25,000 or more says Longstreet), tempted to do so by the hope of throwing off the

---

30 Carman put the best face on the relations between Lee's army and the citizens of Frederick by suggesting that Lee acted to protect local Southern sympathizers. Lee's views can be found in his letters to Davis, cited above, including the letter of September 7, 1862, found in *ibid.*, 19, pt. 2, pp. 596-7, and especially in his desire to have Enoch Lowe present to rally supporters. Both Bradley Johnson's proclamation (Steiner, *Davis*, pp. 14-5, and Evans, *CMH*, 2, pp. 90-1), and Lee's less directly, refer to the February 1862 conditions laid out by the Confederate Congress for Maryland's independence as a condition of peace.

yoke of the Federal Government, and the army certainly shared this expectation. The identity of sentiment generally between the people of the State of Maryland and Virginia, and their strong social ties in the past, rendered this anticipation reasonable, and the feeling of the country at the result afterwards was extremely bitter."[31]

Had Lee entered Maryland by the Southern counties or had his army reached Baltimore, where the secession sentiment was strong, many would have flocked to his standards, but he was in a section of the State where there was an almost complete indifference if not open hostility to the Confederate cause, where, instead of being received with smiles, his ragged troops were regarded with aversion and ill-concealed dislike. The bad condition of the men had much to do with the character of their reception. General J. R. Jones, the commander of Jackson's Division, reports that "Never has the army been so dirty, ragged, and ill-provided-for as on this march."[32] In his Life of General Lee, John Esten Cooke thus writes:

> The condition of the army was indeed forlorn. It was worn down by marching and fighting. The men scarcely had shoes upon their feet, and above the tattered figures, flaunting their rags in the sunshine, were gaunt and begrimed faces, in which could be read little of 'the romance of war.' The army was in no condition to undertake an invasion, 'lacking much of the material of war, feeble in transportation, poorly provided with clothing and thousands of them destitute of shoes,' in Lee's description of his troops. Such was the condition of the better portion of the force, scattered along the hills, could be seen a weary, ragged, hungry and confused multitude, who had dragged along in rear of the rest, unable to keep up, and whose appearance said little of the prospects for the army to which they belonged. From these and other causes resulted the general apathy of the Marylanders and Lee soon discovered that he must look solely to his own men for success in his future movements. He faced that conviction courageously; and without uttering a word of comment, or indulging in any species of crimination against the people of Maryland, resolutely commenced his movement looking to the capture of Harper's Ferry and the invasion of Pennsylvania. The promises of his address had been kept. No one had been found to follow the

---

31  Cooke, *Life of Stonewall Jackson*, pp. 127-8.

32  The quotation from J. R. Jones is in his report, OR 19, pt. 1, p. 1,007. Jones included a clipping in his OR report from the *New York World* to substantiate the lack of Confederate looting. Other contemporary reports attest to the ragged condition of Lee's army. See Steiner, *Davis*, pp. 7-9. For the civilian sentiment, see Henderson, *Stonewall Jackson and the American Civil War*, p. 499.

Southern flag; and now when the people turned their backs upon it, closing the doors of the houses in the faces of the Southern troops, they remained unmolested.[33]

Lee was able to obtain forage for his animals and some provisions for his men, but there was some difficulty about the latter. Many of the farmers had not yet threshed their wheat, and there was reluctance on the part of millers and others to commit themselves in his favor or to receive pay in Confederate script. He obtained some cattle, but the inhabitants had driven most of their stock into Pennsylvania.

Reports reached him on the 9th that led him to believe that the Union forces were pushing a strong column up the Potomac, by Rockville and Darnestown, and by Poolesville toward Seneca Mills. Again he informed Mr. Davis that he was endeavoring to break up the line through Leesburg, which was no longer safe, and turn everything off from Culpeper Court House toward Winchester; and that he should move in the direction originally intended, toward Hagerstown and Chambersburg, for the purpose of opening the line of communication through Shenandoah Valley, in order to procure supplies of flour; and that his intention was to move on the 10th or 11th.

Lee now heard of Jefferson Davis's intention to visit his army, and was quick to inform him that while he "should feel the greatest satisfaction" in having an interview with him and consulting upon all matters of interest, he could not but feel great uneasiness for his safety. He would not only encounter the hardships and fatigue of a very disagreeable journey, but, also, run the risk of capture. He went so far as to send Major W. H. Taylor, of his staff, to explain how very hazardous would be the proposed visit. Taylor left Frederick at noon, on the 9th, with dispatches and verbal messages to Mr. Davis and suggestions to Ex-Governor Lowe, of Maryland, both of whom he expected to meet at Warrenton, but on his arrival on the 10th, Mr. Davis had returned to Richmond and Lowe did not put in an appearance.[34]

Ex-Governor Lowe of Maryland was an ardent sympathizer with the South and zealous in promoting and encouraging secession feeling in the State and in urging armed effort against the United States government. He was one of those who longed for the appearance of the "liberating army of the South" and was

---

33 See John Esten Cooke, *A Life of Robert E. Lee* (New York: D. Appleton and Co., 1871), pp. 131-2. Notice how Cooke mimics some of Lee's language from the letters found in *OR*.

34 These three paragraphs following Cooke's quotation, written by Carman, are reworded from Lee's letters to Davis, September 9, 1862, OR 19, pt. 1, pp. 602, 603. Lee did not identify what reports alerted him to the advance of the Union troops on September 9, but it may have come verbally from Stuart, or from northern newspapers, which he frequently scanned for information. The fact that Lowe did not appear in Warrenton is noted in Lee to Davis, September 12, 1862, found in *ibid*, pt. 2, pp. 605-6.

looked to give it moral and substantial assistance in its "holy mission" to redeem the soil from the foot of the "vandal invader." Before entering Maryland Lee asked Mr. Davis to have Lowe meet him, as he thought he would be of much service in many ways, and make arrangements necessary to the success of the army in its liberating march through the State. Lowe failed to reach Lee's messenger at Warrenton, on the 10th, but three days later made a speech at Winchester, in which he said Maryland long disappointed, had been perfectly taken by surprise on the entrance of the Confederate army, and that when it was seen to be no mere raid "25,000 men would flock to our standard and a provisional government would be formed."[35]

But the 25,000 men did not flock to the Southern standard; a storm of indignation swept over the South at the cold and indifferent treatment accorded the liberators; and Lowe rushed into print with an explanation of how it came about. He said that no notice had been given the Maryland people of Lee's intentions; his entrance into the State was a surprise to them, and it was impossible for them to know whether it was a mere raid or intended for permanent occupation. His army had entered the State where the Black Republican feeling was the strongest, but even in Western Maryland a free expression at the ballot box would show a decided majority for the secession cause; and the stay in Maryland was so short that the people had no chance to rally to the support of their liberators. Maryland wanted more time; how much time, measured in days he could not say: "All that she asks is to be set free and admitted into the Southern Confederacy. She wants such an occupation of her soil by the Southern army, and for such a reasonable length of time as will enable her people to dissolve the connection with the Federal Government, obtain admission into the Southern Confederacy, and arm and organize her quota of the Confederate army."[36]

We have said that Lee shared the sanguine views of Mr. Davis as to the result of an invasion of Maryland. The statement needs qualification. While it is quite true that he was convinced of military success in its initiative, he was fully aware of the immense resources of the North and the ability of the Union Government, should time be given it, to concentrate an overwhelming force against him. His enforced delay at Frederick and the failure to arouse the people of Maryland dashed even those hopes that he shared in a lesser degree with Mr. Davis, who, not looking at the obstacles in the way, was desirous of a speedy issue, with results much more important than those foreshadowed by Lee and which he has given us in his official report. Davis favored and hoped for a prompt march into Pennsylvania or on

35 *Richmond Dispatch*, September 20, 1862.

36 *Richmond Dispatch*, October 1, 1862.

Baltimore and Washington. Lee did not feel that he was free to make any advance with his army, north or east, until Harper's Ferry should have been reduced and in reply to Mr. Davis' suggestion as to the movement of his army, said: "I wish your views of its operations could be realized, but so much depends upon circumstances beyond its control and the aid we may receive, that it is difficult for me to conjecture the result. To look to the safety of our own frontier and to operate untrammeled in an enemy's territory, you need not be told is very difficult. Every effort, however, will be made to acquire every advantage which our position and means may warrant."[37]

The incursion of the Confederates into Maryland caused intense excitement in Baltimore and throughout the State and spread dismay beyond its border, extending into Pennsylvania as far northward as Harrisburg and Philadelphia. General Wool ruled Baltimore with a firm hand, volunteers were enrolled for the defense of the city and the forts surrounding it were strengthened. Governor Curtin, of Pennsylvania, called for 50,000 militia to defend the State and appealed to President Lincoln, Secretary Stanton and General Halleck, for competent generals and 80,000 disciplined men, to all of which reply was given that the men could not be furnished, that Harrisburg and Philadelphia were in no danger, and that the true defense of Pennsylvania lay in the strengthening of the Army of the Potomac, then marching after Lee in Maryland.[38]

Before crossing the Potomac Lee considered the advantages of entering Maryland east or west of the Blue Ridge. In either case it was his intention to march on Hagerstown and Chambersburg. By crossing east of the Blue Ridge, both Washington and Baltimore would be threatened, which he believed would insure the withdrawal of the mass of the Union army north of the Potomac, and the evacuation of Martinsburg and Harper's Ferry, thus opening his line of communication through the Shenandoah Valley. But, for reasons that will hereafter appear, Harper's Ferry was not abandoned. It was a great surprise to Lee, when he

---

37 Carman again used the exact language, as well as a direct quotation, from a letter written by Lee to Davis from Hagerstown, Maryland, on September 13, 1862, to describe the intentions and movements of Lee. It is found in OR 19, pt. 2, p. 606.

38 See Curtin to Lincoln, September 11, 1862, *ibid.*, pt. 2, p. 268. Lincoln's reply, including the idea of strengthening the Army of the Potomac, is in the same source, p. 276. Defensive measures were implemented in Pennsylvania as well as eastern Maryland. Maj. Gen. John Wool, the department commander in Baltimore, did take steps to defend the city, but also ordered the garrisons at Martinsburg and Harpers Ferry to defend to the last extremity, *ibid.*, pp.180-2. Curtin sent a flurry of telegrams to Lincoln, Halleck, Wool and anyone else he thought could help defend Pennsylvania. Halleck ordered Gens. John F. Reynolds and Andrew Porter to Pennsylvania to assist in organizing troops, *ibid.*, pp. 203, 253, but Lincoln's policy of not dispersing his trained troops obviously met with Carman's approval.

reached Frederick, to know that the place was still garrisoned, instead of being abandoned as he fully expected, and as it should have been had correct military principles been observed. It was more than a surprise to him, it was a keen disappointment, and it became necessary to dislodge the garrison from that post, on the direct line of communication of his army, before concentrating his army west of the Blue Ridge.[39] And yet, to reduce it was to retard his projected campaign and required a separation of his army, for, were he to use his whole force for the service and recross the Potomac, there was more than a strong probability that McClellan now in his immediate front, would prevent his return to Maryland. Lee came to the decision to divide his army and capture the Union forces at Martinsburg and Harper's Ferry should they not have retired. He says:

> To accomplish this with the least delay, General Jackson was directed to proceed with his command to Martinsburg, and, after driving the enemy from that place, to move down the south side of the Potomac upon Harper's Ferry. General McLaws, with his own and R. H. Anderson's division, was ordered to seize Maryland Heights, on the north side of the Potomac, opposite Harper's Ferry, and Brigadier-General Walker to take possession of Loudoun Heights, on the east side of the Shenandoah, where it unites with the Potomac. These several commands were directed, after reducing Harper's Ferry and clearing the Valley of the enemy, to join the rest of the army at Boonsborough or Hagerstown.[40]

The march of these troops began on the 10th, and at the same time the remainder of Longstreet's command and the division of D. H. Hill crossed the South Mountain and moved toward Boonsborough. General Stuart, with the cavalry, remained east of the mountains, to observe the enemy and retard his advance.

---

39  These insights into Lee's thinking come from Lee's letter to Davis, September 12, 1862, *OR* 19, pt. 2, pp. 604-5 and Lee's campaign report, *ibid.*, 19, pt. 1, pp. 144-5.

40  Carman borrowed words from Lee's letter to Davis, September 12, 1862, *ibid.*, Pt. 2, pp. 604-5, to open a discussion about the Harpers Ferry operation. Carman paraphrased Lee's expression of disappointment to Davis that the Shenandoah Valley garrisons of the Union forces were not withdrawn, then quoted directly from Lee report, *ibid.*, 19, pt. 1, p. 145. Because Lee's report was written after the battle, he made it sound like Jackson's operation against Harpers Ferry was intentional, when in fact it was not planned by Lee at all. See Special Order #191, *ibid.*, pt. 2, pp. 603-4, and Harsh, *Taken at the Flood*, pp. 152-67. It is worth noting that Carman's interpretation has guided historians of the campaign for nearly 100 years, and only recently has Harsh exposed the more extemporaneous nature of Lee's movements.

Two days before coming to a decision to send Jackson on this duty, Lee proposed to confide the capture of Harper's Ferry and its garrison to Longstreet. Upon this point Longstreet says:

> Riding together before we reached Frederick [Carman added "September 6th"], the sound of artillery fire came from the direction of Harper's Ferry, from which General Lee inferred that the enemy was concentrating his forces from the Valley, for the defense at Harper's Ferry, and proposed to me to organize forces to surround and capture the works and the garrison.
>
> I thought it a venture not worth the game, and suggested, as we were in the enemy's country and presence, that he would be advised of any move that we made in a few hours after it was set on foot, that the Union army, though beaten, was not disorganized; that we knew a number of their officers who could put it in order and march against us, if they found us exposed, and make serious trouble before the capture could be accomplished; that our men were worn out by very severe and protracted service, and in need of repose; that as long as we had them in hand we were masters of the situation, but dispersed into many fragments, our strength must be greatly reduced. As the subject was not continued, I supposed that it was a mere expression of passing thought, until, the day after we reached Frederick, upon going over to head-quarters, I found the front of the General's tent closed and tied. Upon inquiring of a member of his staff, I was told that he was inside with General Jackson. As I had not been called, I turned to go away, when General Lee, recognizing my voice, called me in. The plan had been arranged. . . . As their minds were settled firmly upon the enterprise, I offered no opposition.[41]

Two facts are here revealed: First, that the conception of surrounding Harper's Ferry and capturing the garrison was Lee's and not Jackson's, as has been claimed by some of his biographers. Second, that Jackson was selected to execute the movement because Longstreet was not in favor of it and had virtually refused it, and because Lee recognized the military impropriety of committing an important movement to a doubting commander.[42]

---

41 Carman emphasized the maturing of Lee's plans by relating the story about his suggesting the capture of Harpers Ferry to Longstreet. Carman most likely quoted from Longstreet's account in B&L, p. 663, or perhaps from his book *From Manassas to Appomattox*, pp. 201-2, to show how Lee then offered the command of the operation to Jackson. It is also noteworthy that Longstreet made no mention of McClellan in this account, reinforcing the suggestion that the Confederates were not yet aware who the Union commander was at that time.

42 Carman offered two "facts" here. First, that the idea that the Harpers Ferry operation was Lee's, is clear. Carman is referring to Robert Louis Dabney, *Life and Campaigns of Lieut. Gen.*

Referring to this period of the campaign Dr. Dabney, one of Jackson's biographers, says:

Lee now assembled his leading generals in council to devise a plan of operations. Harper's Ferry had not been evacuated, as he hoped. His first design, of withdrawing his army in a body toward Western Maryland for the purpose of threatening Pennsylvania and fighting McClellan upon the ground of his selection, was now beset with this difficulty, that its execution would leave the garrison at Harper's Ferry to re-open communications with their friends, to receive an accession of strength, and to set upon his flank, threatening his new line of supply up the valley of Virginia. Two other plans remained: the one was to leave Harper's Ferry to itself for the present, to concentrate the whole army in a good position and fight McClellan as he advanced. The other was to withdraw the army west of the mountains, as at first designed, but by different routes, embracing the reduction of Harper's Ferry by a rapid combination in this movement, and then to reassemble the whole at some favorable position in that region, for the decisive struggle with McClellan. The former was advocated by Jackson; he feared lest the other system of movement should prove too complex for realizing that punctual and complete concentration which sound policy required. The latter being preferred by the commander-in-chief was adopted.[43]

The final orders were as follows, and, as reports indicated that McClellan was advancing cautiously, but firmly, Lee impressed upon the officers in command of the columns the necessity for prompt action:

HEADQUARTERS ARMY OF NORTHERN VIRGINIA,
September 9, 1862.

*Thomas J. Jackson*, pp. 548-9. The second "fact" is not so obvious. Lee may have had several reasons for sending Jackson's men on this expedition, and in its final analysis, it was not entirely Jackson's men who undertook it. The most thorough analysis of this meeting between Lee, Jackson, and Longstreet is found in Harsh, *Taken at the Flood*, pp. 146-52. Longstreet had a tendency to elevate his own involvement with important decisions and events and seems to indulge that trait here. No other source suggests he was considered for leading the operation. According to Robertson, *Stonewall Jackson*, pp. 591-2, this meeting took place September 8, but Harsh makes it clear the meeting was on September 9.

43 Dabney, *Life and Campaigns of Jackson*, pp. 548-9. There are two points about Carman's use of the quotation about Lee's options taken from Dabney. First, Carman assumed Lee knew that McClellan was in command of the Union army pursuing him when he wrote Special Order 191. This is not at all certain. See Harsh, *Taken at the Flood*, pp. 141-2. Second, although Carman did not cite it specifically, he implied that Lee had received information about the advance of the Federal army. Harsh, *ibid.*, cited several other reasons for the accelerated pace of the operation.

The army will resume its march to-morrow, taking the Hagerstown road. General Jackson's command will form the advance, and, after passing Middletown, with such portion as he may select, take the route toward Sharpsburg, cross the Potomac at the most convenient point, and, by Friday night, take possession of the Baltimore and Ohio Railroad, capture such of the enemy as may be at Martinsburg, and intercept such as may attempt to escape from Harper's Ferry.

General Longstreet's command will pursue the same road as far as Boonsborough, where it will halt with the reserve, supply, and baggage trains of the army.

General McLaws, with his own division and that of General R. H. Anderson, will follow General Longstreet. On reaching Middletown he will take the route to Harper's Ferry, and by Friday morning possess himself of the Maryland Heights, and endeavor to capture the enemy at Harper's Ferry and vicinity.

General Walker, with his division, after accomplishing the object in which he is now engaged, will cross the Potomac at Cheek's Ford, ascend its right bank to Lovettsville, take possession of Loudoun Heights, if practicable, by Friday morning, Keys' Ford on his left, and the road between the end of the mountain and the Potomac on his right. He will, as far as practicable, co-operate with General McLaws and General Jackson in intercepting the retreat of the enemy.

General D. H. Hill's division will form the rear guard of the army, pursuing the road taken by the main body. The reserve artillery, ordnance, supply trains, &c., will precede General Hill.

General Stuart will detach a squadron of cavalry to accompany the commands of Generals Longstreet, Jackson, and McLaws, and with the main body of the cavalry will cover the route of the army and bring up all stragglers that may have been left behind.

The commands of Generals Jackson, McLaws, and Walker, after accomplishing the objects for which they have been detached, will join the main body of the army at Boonsborough or Hagerstown.

Each regiment on the march will habitually carry its axes in the regimental ordnance wagons, for use of the men at their encampments to procure wood, &c.

By command of General R. E. Lee

R. H. CHILTON,
Assistant Adjutant-General.[44]

---

44 This version of Special Order 191, found in *OR* 19, Vol. 1, pp. 42-3, and *ibid.*, pt. 2, pp. 603-4, is the final plan as amended by Lee and Longstreet on September 9. See Harsh, *Taken at the Flood*, pp. 45-52 for the evolution of this document.

Not satisfied with the organization of McLaws's column, Longstreet asked and obtained permission, on the morning of the 10th to strengthen it by three other brigades, Wilcox's, under Colonel Alfred Cumming; Featherston's and Pryor's, which were attached to R. H. Anderson's Division. The different columns marched as ordered. "It was a rollicking march," says Longstreet, "the Confederates playing and singing, as they marched through the streets of Frederick, 'The Girl I Left Behind Me.'"[45]

All movements were made as ordered, but, before following them, we must see what the Union Government was doing to meet the Confederate invasion of Maryland and why the garrison at Harper's Ferry was retained at that hazardous point.[46]

---

45 Carman said Longstreet added the three brigades mentioned (Cummings, Pryor, and Featherston) to McLaws' column to strengthen it. Longstreet, *From Manassas to Appomattox*, p. 205. The wording is almost an exact quotation.

46 The quotation about the "rollicking march" is a continuation of the citation above, now directly quoted. Carman said the marches were made as ordered, which of course ignored the fact that Special Order #191 sent Jackson to Martinsburg via Sharpsburg and Shepherdstown, and Jackson altered his route to use Williamsport and Hedgesville. *OR* 19, pt. 1, pp. 953.

# Chapter 4

# General McClellan and
# the Army of the Potomac

When General McClellan transported the Army of the Potomac to the York Peninsula, in April 1862, he left for the protection of Washington the commands of Generals Banks and McDowell, to which was subsequently added the army commanded by General Frémont. On the 26th of June, Stonewall Jackson, after defeating these three independent commands and driving them from the Shenandoah Valley, joined General Lee for that remarkable campaign, which, in seven days, forced McClellan from the front of Richmond to Westover on the banks of the James. On this same 26th of June, the defeated commands of Banks, McDowell and Frémont were consolidated into one army, known as the Army of Virginia, and General John Pope assigned to the command. With this army of about 45,000 men Pope was to cover Washington, assure the safety of the Shenandoah Valley, and so operate upon the enemy's lines of communications, in the direction of Gordonsville and Charlottesville, as to draw off, if possible, a considerable force of the enemy from Richmond, and thus relieve the operations of the Army of the Potomac against that city.[1]

There was much objection in Washington to the removal of McClellan's army to the Peninsula and, after its defeat, the Government was not entirely willing to reinforce it at the expense of troops thought necessary to insure the safety of the capital. Beyond this there was distrust of McClellan's capacity as a general and of his ability to take Richmond. These views were honestly entertained by some; by others they were put forward to shelve McClellan. There had grown up a hostility against him, soon after he was placed in command of the armies of the Union, with the result that, when he set out for the Peninsula, he left behind him, in Washington, hardly a friend among public men, with the exception of President Lincoln and two members of his cabinet. The Secretary of War, though profuse in expressions of friendship, was not friendly. Beyond all this it was manifest that the co-operation of the two armies acting in Virginia could not be relied upon and that they should have a common head. For this and other reasons, personal and political, General H. W. Halleck was assigned to the command of the land forces of the United States, July 11th, and ordered to Washington, where he arrived on the 22nd. [2]

In many respects the selection of Halleck was an unfortunate one for the country. He soon perceived what action would be most agreeable to Stanton and those who sided with him, and, on the 25th, visited the Army of the Potomac at Harrison's Landing. He came to the conclusion to withdraw McClellan from the Peninsula and unite his army with that of Pope in front of Washington and, August 3rd, orders were issued to that effect. McClellan made an earnest protest, setting forth the depressing effect which would follow the withdrawal of the army; representing that troops not necessary to the defense of Washington and Harper's Ferry were available to reinforce him, and contending that on the banks of the James the fate of the nation should be decided: "Here directly in front of this army, is the heart of the rebellion. It is here that our resources should be collected to strike the blow which will determine the fate of the nation. All points of secondary importance elsewhere should be abandoned and every available man should be brought here. A decided victory here, and the military strength of the rebellion is

---

1   The order creating the Army of Virginia is found in *OR* 12, pt. 1, p. 169, and the strategic mission is found *ibid.*, p. 21.

2   Since November 1, 1861, McClellan had been overall commander of all Union forces. His removal on March 11, 1862, is in *ibid.*, 10, pt. 2, p. 28. Halleck's appointment as commander of all Union field armies is in *ibid.*, Series 3, 2, p. 217. See also Gideon Welles (Howard Beale, ed.), *Diary of Gideon Welles, Secretary of the Navy Under Lincoln and Johnson*, 3 Vols. (New York: W. W. Norton and Co., 1960), 1, pp. 107, 119-22. After McClellan was removed as overall commander in March 1862, Lincoln and Stanton jointly exercised this power.

crushed. It matters not what partial reverses we may meet with elsewhere, here is the true defense of Washington."[3]

But McClellan's argument and protest made no impression upon Halleck, who replied on the 4th refusing to rescind the order. In a private letter to McClellan, August 7th, Halleck said,

> I fully agree with you in regard to the manner in which the war should be conducted. . . I deeply regret that you cannot agree with me as to the necessity of reuniting the old Army of the Potomac. I, however, have taken the responsibility of doing so, and am willing to risk my reputation on it. As I told you when I was in your camp, it is my intention that you shall command all the troops in Virginia as soon as we can get them together, and with the army thus concentrated I am certain that you can take Richmond. I must beg of you general to hurry along this movement; your reputation as well as mine may be involved in its rapid execution. I cannot regard Pope and Burnside as safe until you reinforce them. Moreover, I wish them to be under your immediate command, for reasons which it is not necessary to specify.[4]

McClellan very reluctantly withdrew from the Peninsula to unite his army with that of Pope, in front of Washington, but did not implicitly believe in the sincerity of Halleck's promise that the troops to be united would be placed under his command.

On August 23rd, while on his way up the Potomac, McClellan wrote these prophetic words: "I take it for granted that my orders will be as disagreeable as it is possible to make them, unless Pope is beaten, in which case, they will want me to save Washington again. Nothing but their fears will induce them to give me any command of importance or treat me otherwise than with discourtesy."[5]

McClellan arrived at Alexandria on the evening of August 26th and reported by telegraph to Halleck next morning. As fast as his troops arrived they were virtually

---

3  The order of August 3, 1862, to leave the James River, and McClellan's reply, quoted here, is found in *OR* 11, pt. 1, pp. 80-1. For an interesting discussion of Halleck's visit to the Army of the Potomac, see George B. McClellan, *McClellan's Own Story* (New York: Charles L. Webster and Co., 1887), pp. 490-7, and Ethan Rafuse, *McClellan's War: The Failure of Moderation in the Struggle for the Union* (Bloomington: Indiana University Press, 2005), pp. 44-7.

4  Halleck's reply is in *OR* 11, pt. 1, p. 82. The private letter mentioned by Carman is found in *ibid.*, pt. 3, pp. 359-60.

5  McClellan mentioned Halleck's promises in letters to his wife Ellen. See McClellan, Own Story, pp. 466, 467, 468, 470. The letter quoted here, McClellan to Ellen, August 23, 1862, is in *ibid.*, p. 471, and also in Sears, Stephen, ed., *The Civil War Papers of George McClellan* (New York: Ticknor and Fields), pp. 399-400.

taken from him and he was reduced to the command of a few orderlies, camp guards and construction parties, instead of being put in command of the combined forces of himself and Pope, as General Halleck had, on more than one occasion, indicated. He assured Halleck of his readiness to lend any assistance in his power, but complained of the extreme difficulty of doing anything while his power was curtailed and his position undefined. Meanwhile Secretary Stanton and his associates in the cabinet had formed a resolution that no more should McClellan command any army of the Union, and they were jubilant when Pope reported a great victory on the field of Second Manassas. They looked upon Pope as the coming man and could not conceal their intense pleasure in the apparent utter downfall of McClellan.[6]

There was a sudden transformation. Early on the morning of September 1st it began to dawn upon Halleck's mind that Pope's reported victories were defeats, and this impression was confirmed by a dispatch from Pope that the enemy was undeniably feeling for his right, upon which he telegraphed Pope: "If the enemy moves as your last telegram indicates, and you engage him to-day without a decisive victory, I suggest a gradual drawing of your army to Fairfax Court House, Annandale or, if necessary, farther south, toward Alexandria." He then sent for McClellan and gave him verbal directions to take charge of the defenses of Washington, expressly limiting his jurisdiction to the works and their garrisons, and prohibiting him from exercising any control over the troops actively engaged under Pope.[7]

During the day and night of September 1st alarming news from Pope's army reached Washington, and on the morning of the 2nd, between 7 and 8 o'clock, President Lincoln, asking Halleck to accompany him, called at McClellan's house, and Lincoln informed him that he had received alarming news; that affairs were in a very bad condition; much worse than had been reported to Halleck on the preceding day; that Pope's army was in confusion and in full retreat and the roads full of stragglers, and desired him to resume command and do the best he could to

---

6    Some of the telegraphic communications between McClellan and Halleck (August 26 and 27, 1862) are found in OR 12, pt. 3, pp. 672-3, 688-90, 773. See also McClellan, *Own Story*, Chapter 22, and especially Note A, pp. 538-48, and Rafuse, *McClellan's War*, pp. 259-63, for a full discussion of McClellan's activities at this time. The cabinet cabal against McClellan is described in Welles, *Diary*, 1, pp. 93-4, 120. See also Harold Hyman and Benjamin P. Thomas, *Stanton: The Life and Times of Lincoln's Secretary of War* (New York: Knopf, 1962), pp. 220-2. In the last sentence, after "upon Pope," Carman had written and crossed out "to succeed McClellan."

7    The telegram to Pope from Halleck dated September 1, 1862 is in OR 12, pt. 3, p. 785. For the panic in Washington and Halleck's verbal order, see *ibid.*, 11, pt. 1, p. 104, and McClellan, *Own Story*, pp. 532-4.

restore confidence and defend Washington. McClellan assured the President that he could save the capital and bring order out of chaos. This assurance was great relief to the President, who then verbally placed McClellan in entire command of the city and of the troops falling back upon it, with instructions to take immediate steps to stop and collect the stragglers; to place the works in a proper state of defense, and to go out to meet and take command of the army when it approached the vicinity of the works; then to place the troops in the best positions, in fact everything was committed to his hands. This action of the President was cordially approved, or at least accepted, by Halleck, who seemed glad to be rid of a great responsibility. Secretary Welles makes the statement that Lincoln said to him: "Halleck had no plan or views of his own, proposed to do nothing himself and fully approved his calling upon McClellan."[8]

The President's verbal orders to McClellan were supplemented, later in the day, by this written one:

General Orders
War Department, Adj. Gen's Office, No. 122
Washington, September 2, 1862.

Major-General McClellan will have command of the fortifications of Washington and of all the troops for the defense of the capital.

By command of Major-General Halleck,

E. D. Townsend
Assistant Adjutant-General

As originally drawn the order was worded as follows:

Headquarters of the Army
Adjutant-General's Office Washington
September 2, 1862

By direction of the President, Major-General McClellan will have command of the fortifications of Washington and all the troops for the defense of the capital.

---

8   For President Lincoln's visit to McClellan, see McClellan, *Own Story*, p. 535. The quotation from Lincoln about Halleck is in Gideon Welles, *Lincoln and Seward: Remarks Upon the Memorial Address of Charles F. Adams on the late Wm. H. Seward* (New York: Sheldon and Co., 1874), p. 196.

By command of the Secretary of War

E. D. Townsend,
Assistant Adjutant General[9]

There was no change in the substance of the order but a modification in form. Secretary Stanton would not permit it to be promulgated as "by order of the Secretary of War," nor would he have it appear that it was made "by direction of the President" and the order was issued with Halleck as its responsible author. He was made to assume the responsibility, though he had no knowledge that morning of President Lincoln's intentions. In a letter to General Pope, October 10, 1862, Halleck said: "The assignment of General McClellan to command, or rather his retention in it, was not my act, nor that of the War Department. It was the act of the President alone. I did not even know of his decision in the matter until he himself announced it to General McClellan."[10]

There has been much discussion upon the matter and the manner of McClellan's restoration to full command; we here note only the views expressed by the biographers of President Lincoln. Nicolay and Hay, in their *Life of Abraham Lincoln*, write:

> The majority of the cabinet were strongly opposed to it. The Secretary of War and the Secretary of the Treasury agreed, upon the 29th of August, in a remonstrance against McClellan's continuation in command of the Army of the Potomac. They reduced it to writing; it was signed by themselves and the Attorney General and afterwards by the Secretary of the Interior. The Secretary of the Navy concurred in the judgment, but declined to sign it, on the grounds that it might seem unfriendly to the President. In the cabinet meeting of the 2nd of September, the whole subject was freely discussed. The Secretary of War disclaimed any responsibility for the action taken, saying that the order to McClellan was given directly by the President, and that General Halleck considered himself relieved from responsibility by it, although he acquiesced and approved the order. He thought that McClellan was now in a position where he could shirk all responsibility, shielding himself under the President. Mr. Lincoln took a different view of the transaction, saying that he considered General Halleck as much in command of the army as ever, and that General McClellan had been charged with special functions, to command the troops for the defense of Washington, and that he

---

9  The final version of this order is in *OR* 12, pt. 3, p. 807. Both versions, and a discussion of them, are found in McClellan, *Own Story*, pp. 546-7.

10  Halleck's letter to Pope concerning Lincoln's decision is in *OR* 12, pt. 3, pp. 820.

placed him there because he could see no one who could do so well the work required.[11]

The writers quoted other reasons for President Lincoln's actions:

It was not alone for his undoubted talents as an organizer and drill-master that he was restored to his command. It was a time of gloom and doubt in the political as well as the military situation. The factious spirit was stronger among the politicians and the press of the Democratic party than at any other time during the war. Not only in the States of the border, but in many Northern States, there were signs of sullen discontent among a large body of the people that could not escape the notice of a statesman so vigilant as Lincoln. It was of the greatest importance, not only in the interest of recruiting, but also in the interest of that wider support which a popular Government requires from the general body of its citizens, that causes of offense against any large portion of the community should be sedulously avoided by those in power. General McClellan had made himself the leader of the Democratic party. Mr. Lincoln, for these reasons, was especially anxious to take no action against McClellan which might seem to be dictated by personal jealousy or pique; and besides, as General Pope himself had reported, there was a personal devotion to McClellan among those in high command in the Army of the Potomac which rendered it almost impossible for any other general to get the best work out of it. General Ethan Allen Hitchcock, one of the most accomplished officers of the old army, gave this as the reason for declining that command.[12]

The true reason for the restoration of McClellan was the unfitness of Halleck. One would naturally suppose that when the armies of McClellan, Pope and Burnside were concentrated in front of Washington, Halleck, as commander-in-chief, would have seized the opportunity of putting himself at their united head and

11 After the words "the biographers of President Lincoln," Carman wrote and crossed out "and Secretary Stanton." The quotation is in Nicolay and Hay, *Abraham Lincoln*, 6, pp. 21-2. A similar, although less precise version, is in Tyler Dennett, *Lincoln and the Civil War in the Letters and Diaries of John Hay* (New York: Dodd, Mead and Co., 1939), p. 47. Carman also wrote, but crossed out, the following: "Montgomery Blair, a member of the cabinet, made a statement April 3, 1889, that Stanton and Chase 'actually declared that they would prefer the loss of the capital to the restoration of McClellan to command.'" The correct date is in footnote 19.

12 The long quotation that continued describing the reasons for Lincoln's actions is from Nicolay and Hay, *Abraham Lincoln*, 6, pp. 22-5. This was not the first offer of command to Hitchcock. See W. A. Croffut, ed., *Fifty Years in Camp and Field: Diary of Ethan Allen Hitchcock* (New York: Putnam's Sons, 1909), p. 439, which stated that he was offered command March 15, 1862.

assume supreme control of affairs in the field. But he was either unequal to the responsibility or conscious of his lack of nerve and avoided the task, and it does not appear that the President urged the matter upon him, although when, at the instance of Pope, he appointed him to the command of the army, he expected that Halleck would exercise general command in the field, of operations in Virginia. This however, evidently, was not Halleck's idea, for when he visited the Peninsula, on July 25th, he promised McClellan that if the armies were speedily united he should command them.[13]

This promise to McClellan was studiously kept from the President and Secretary Stanton, also from Pope, who, as late as August 25th, while opposing Lee on the Rappahannock and vainly endeavoring to join hands with Burnside at Fredericksburg, dispatched Halleck: "I certainly understood that as soon as the whole of our forces were concentrated, you designed to command in person" and this was the understanding of the President and the Secretary of War. Somebody was being deceived, for Halleck had from the beginning, determined to manage the armies from his office at Washington. Lincoln soon saw this and the feebleness of his management, also the influences, other than military, that were surrounding him, and in his perplexity, turned to McClellan as one at least who was willing to accept responsibility and do what was required to bring order out of chaos, for whatever may have been the opinion of his military ability, or his failure to properly support Pope, it was well known that he alone had the power to restore confidence to the Army of the Potomac, and that as an organizer he had no superior in the army. Halleck assented to the arrangement with great good grace, if he did not actually court it, for he thought it relieved him of all responsibility, too obtuse in mind to comprehend that he had held at arms length an opportunity that most ambitious soldiers, would have given half a lifetime to have met and embraced.[14]

Halleck took upon himself the credit of saving Washington from capture, writing to his wife, September 5th: "I hope and believe I have saved the capital from

13 Here Carman clearly reveals his opinion of Halleck. His bias must be respected to some degree, however, since Carman was a Halleck contemporary and may have had contact with him. Whether Halleck was as duplicitous as Carman accuses him of being is arguable. See Sears, *McClellan*, pp. 248-51. Suffice it to say that Carman takes a rare positive view of McClellan here, and a negative one of Halleck.

14 For Pope's belief about unified command, see OR 12, pt. 2, p. 66. It is entirely possible that Halleck led Pope to believe that Halleck would assume command, and that he led McClellan to believe that he would exercise unified command over both armies.

the terrible crisis brought upon us by the stupidity of others. Few can conceive the terrible anxiety I have had."[15]

When the conference between the President and McClellan terminated Halleck hastened to inform Stanton of what had taken place. What occurred in Stanton's room we do not know, but we have the testimony of eye-witnesses as to what took place at the cabinet meeting that morning. In his private diary Mr. Chase, the Secretary of the Treasury, says:

> The Secretary of War came in. In answer to some inquiry the fact was stated by the President or the Secretary that McClellan had been placed in command of the forces to defend the capital, or rather, to use the President's own words, 'he had set him to putting these troops into the fortifications about Washington,' believing he could do this thing better than any one man. I remarked that this could be done equally well by the engineers who constructed the forts. The Secretary of War said that no one was now responsible for the safety of the capital; that the order to McClellan was given by the President direct to McClellan, and that General Halleck considered himself relieved from responsibility, although he acquiesced and approved the order; that McClellan could now shield himself, should anything go wrong, under Halleck, while Halleck, could and would disclaim all responsibility for the order given. The President thought General Halleck as much responsible as before, and reported that the whole scope of the order was simply to direct McClellan to put the troops into the fortifications and command them for the defense of Washington. I remarked that I could not but feel that giving command to him was equivalent to giving Washington to the rebels. This and more I said. The President said it distressed him exceedingly to find himself differing on such a point from the Secretary of War and the Secretary of the Treasury; that he would gladly resign his place; but that he could not see who could do the work wanted as well as McClellan. I named Hooker, or Sumner, or Burnside, either of whom would do the work better.[16]

In his account of the cabinet meeting Mr. Gideon Welles, Secretary of the Navy, says:

---

15 The quotation from Halleck's letters, September 5, 1862, can be found in James Grant Wilson, "General Halleck, a Memoir," *Journal of the Military Service Institution*, 36, p. 558. There is a pencil transcription of this letter in the Carman papers, Library of Congress, Box 4, Folder 3, which has this citation scrawled in the corner.

16 The quotation from Chase is from his diary. See Robert P. Warden, *An Account of the Private Life and Public Services of Chase* (Cincinnati: Wilstach, Baldwin and Co., 1874), p. 459. It is copied in McClellan, *Own Story*, pp. 544-5.

At the stated cabinet meeting on Tuesday, the 2nd of September, while the whole community was stirred and in confusion, and affairs were growing beyond anything that had previously occurred, Stanton entered the committee room a few moments in advance of Mr. Lincoln, and said, with great excitement, he had just heard from General Halleck that the President had placed McClellan in command of the forces in Washington. The information was surprising, and, in view of the prevailing excitement against that officer, alarming. The President soon came in, and, in answer to an inquiry from Mr. Chase, confirmed what Stanton had stated. General regret was expressed, and Stanton, with some feeling, remarked that no order to that effect had issued from the War Department. The President calmly, but with some emphasis, said that the order was his, and he would be responsible for it to the country. With a retreating and demoralized army tumbling in upon us, and alarm and panic in the community, it was necessary, the President said, that something should be done, but there seemed no one to do it. He therefore had directed McClellan, who knew this whole ground, who was the best organizer in the whole army, whose faculty was to organize and defend, and who would here act on the defensive, to take this defeated and shattered army and reorganize it. He knew full well the infirmities of McClellan, who was not an affirmative man; was worth little for an onward movement; but beyond any other officer he had the confidence of the army, and he could more efficiently and speedily reorganize it and put it into condition than any other general. If the Secretary of War, or any member of the cabinet, would name a general that could do this as promptly and as well, he would appoint him. For an active fighting general he was sorry to say McClellan was a failure; he had the 'slows'; was never ready for battle, and probably never would be; but for this exigency, when organization and defense were needed, he considered him the best man for the service, and the country must have the benefits of his talents though he had behaved badly. The President said he had seen and given his opinion to General Halleck, who was still general-in-chief; but Halleck had no plan or views of his own, proposed to do nothing himself, and fully approved his calling upon McClellan. . . . A long discussion followed, closing with acquiescence in the decision of the President, but before separating the Secretary of the Treasury expressed his apprehension that the reinstatement of McClellan would prove a national calamity.[17]

On the following Friday Secretary Welles had an interview with the President which he has put on record. He says:

---

17 This long quotation is from Welles, *Lincoln and Seward*, pp. 194-6. Welles's view of this important cabinet meeting, and the discussions of the key figures, is an often cited source. It also underscores Carman's antipathy toward Halleck.

The President said most of our troubles grew out of military jealousies. Whether changing the plan of operations (discarding McClellan and placing Pope in command in front) was wise or not, was not now the matter in hand. These things, right or wrong, had been done. If the administration had erred, the country should not have been made to suffer, nor our brave men been cut down and butchered. Pope should have been sustained but he was not. These personal and professional quarrels came in. Whatever may have been said to the contrary, it could not be denied that the army was with McClellan. He had so skillfully handled his troops in not getting to Richmond as to retain their confidence. The soldiers had certainly not transferred their confidence to Pope. He could, however, do more good in this quarter. It was humiliating, after what had transpired and all we know, to reward McClellan and those who failed to do their whole duty in the hour of trial, but so it was. Personal considerations must be sacrificed for the public good. He had kept aloof from the discussions that prevailed, and intended to, but 'said he' I must have McClellan to reorganize the army and bring it out of chaos. There has been a design, a purpose, in breaking down Pope, without regard to consequences to the country, that is atrocious. It is shocking to see and know this, but there is no remedy at present. McClellan has the army with him."[18]

Under date of April 22, 1870, Montgomery Blair, Postmaster General in President Lincoln's cabinet, wrote: "The bitterness of Stanton and (sic: "at") the reinstatement of McClellan you can scarcely conceive. He preferred to see the capital fall. McClellan was bound to go when the emergency was past and Halleck and Stanton furnished a pretense."

In a letter of April 3rd, 1879, Mr. Blair said: "The folly and disregard of public interests thus exhibited would be incredible but that the authors of the intrigue, Stanton and Chase, when the result of it came, and I proposed the restoration of McClellan to command, and to prevent the completion of ruin by the fall of this capital, actually declared that they would prefer the loss of the capital to the restoration of McClellan to command. Yet these are the men who have been accounted by a large portion of our countrymen as the civil heroes of the war, while McClellan, who saved the capital, was dismissed."[19]

After the President's departure from McClellan's house, McClellan stepped to the door of the room where his staff had assembled and said, with evident satisfaction, "Gentlemen, I am reinstated in command" and followed the

18 Once again Carman used a long excerpt from Welles, *Lincoln and Seward*, p. 197, to show the turmoil in the Lincoln government's inner circles.

19 The two quotations here from Blair are cited previously in note 11. McClellan, *Own Story*, p. 545. This time Carman had the dates correct.

announcement with orders to several staff members, who were sent in various directions.[20] McClellan's first step in complying with the President's instructions was a communication to Pope, wherein he advised him that he had been requested by Halleck to repeat the order given Pope early in the morning, to withdraw the army to Washington, without unnecessary delay, and he suggested the roads by which the withdrawal should be made and where the divisions should be posted: "Porter's Corps upon Upton's Hill, that it may occupy Hall's Hill; McDowell's to Upton's Hill; Franklin to the works in front of Alexandria; Heintzelman's to the same vicinity; Couch to Fort Corcoran, or, if practicable to the Chain Bridge; Sumner either to Fort Albany or to Alexandria, as may be most convenient." This order to Pope was carried by Lieutenant John M. Wilson, who found Pope at Fairfax Court House. Pope was greatly surprised cast down and betrayed in the expression of his countenance his pain and deep mortification.[21]

In a very short time McClellan had made all requisite preparations and, while the cabinet was still in angry session, was about to start to the front to assume command as far out as possible, when a message came from Halleck informing that it was the President's order that he should not assume command until the troops had reached the immediate vicinity of the fortifications. He, therefore, deferred the matter.

Meanwhile Halleck, as we have noted, had ordered Pope to fall back to the fortifications and advised him that McClellan had been put in charge of the defenses.

That afternoon McClellan crossed the Potomac and rode to the front and, at Upton's Hill met the advance of McDowell's Corps and with it Pope and McDowell. He gave Pope directions how best to place the respective divisions in the defensive works, made other dispositions and at a late hour of the night returned to Washington.[22]

20 The comment to his staff does not appear in any works discovered thus far. It is, however, in keeping with the events described in McClellan, *Own Story*.

21 McClellan's order to Pope is found, along with an explanation written by McClellan, in *OR* 11, pt. 1, pp. 104-5. There does not appear to be a source for the identity of the courier as Lt. Wilson. In his report, cited above, McClellan simply described him as "an aide." Perhaps Carman knew this from postwar discussions with Wilson, as letters from him have been found in the NYPL files. Because he was on McClellan's staff, it is very possible that Wilson was the source for both pieces of information.

22 Carman's description of McClellan's assumption of command was taken from McClellan's report, *OR* 11, pt. 1, p. 105. The order referenced by Carman is the one mentioned earlier, G. O. 122, found in *OR* 12, pt. 3, p. 807.

The assumption of command by McClellan was a grievous blow to Pope, who could not understand it. He thought it a great injustice to himself. He could not understand how the officer whom he held responsible for the reverse at Second Manassas, by his failure to forward help, when help was so much needed, should be entrusted with command and urged Halleck, if nothing else could be done, to command the army himself. Halleck could but reply that McClellan commanded all troops in the fortifications; that a reorganization for the field would immediately be made, till then, McClellan, as senior, would exercise general authority; and that as soon as his (Pope's) troops arrived within McClellan's command, he would report to his (Halleck's) headquarters.[23]

Halleck's functions were now reduced to mere routine work and the President assumed the entire responsibility, not only of McClellan's assignment, but, of all military affairs and, with his own hand, wrote this order for the organization of an army for the field:

Washington, D.C.
September 3, 1862

Ordered, that the General-in-Chief, Major-General Halleck, immediately commence, and proceed with all possible dispatch, to organize an army for active operations, from all the material within and coming within his control, independent of the forces he may deem necessary for the defense of Washington, when such active army shall take the field.

By order of the President:

Edwin M. Stanton
Secretary of War[24]

23 Carman evidently inferred from Pope's dispatch of September 3, 1862, written at 1:40 p.m., that Pope was calling on Halleck to take overall command. The wording is ambiguous: "Somebody ought to have supreme command here" could be taken to mean Pope himself, or perhaps Halleck. See OR 12, pt. 3, pp. 808-9. The next day, Pope wrote again proposing a reorganization of the armies with himself in overall command. The reply from Halleck is found in *ibid.*, p. 809. In this message Halleck made it clear that McClellan was in command. See also Pope to Halleck, *ibid.*, pp. 811-2, sent at 12:15 p.m. on September 5, 1862, in which he questioned who is to command and complained of McClellan giving him orders and scattering his troops. Halleck replied unequivocally the same day, *ibid.*, p. 813, that the armies were being combined and McClellan was in command.

24 Here, Carman pasted in Stanton to Halleck, September 3, 1862, from *ibid.*, 19, pt. 2, p. 169. This order was noted as being in Lincoln's handwriting and endorsed, "Copy delivered to

A copy of this order was delivered to Halleck at 10 o'clock that night, upon which he prepared this communication:

WASHINGTON, September 3, 1862.

Major-General MCCLELLAN, Commanding, &c.:

There is every probability that the enemy, baffled in his intended capture of Washington, will cross the Potomac, and make a raid into Maryland or Pennsylvania. A movable army must be immediately organized to meet him again in the field. You will, therefore, report the approximate force of each corps of the three armies now in the vicinity of Washington, which can be prepared in the next two days to take the field, and have them supplied and ready for that service.

H. W. HALLECK,
General-in-Chief.[25]

Meanwhile Pope's army had fallen behind the defenses of Washington and McClellan was concentrating everything for the defense of the capital and bringing order out of confusion. Burnside, with the remainder of his command, was ordered up from Aquia Creek and new regiments streamed in from the North.[26]

Pope's defeat startled Washington and the country and partially stunned the national authorities. Halleck was dazed: a member of President Lincoln's cabinet says both Stanton and Halleck were "filled with apprehension beyond others."[27] By direction of the President the clerks and employees of the Department were organized for the defense of the capital, the money in the Treasury and the contents of the arsenal were ordered to be shipped to New York, and a gun boat with steam

General Halleck September 3, 1862 at 10 p.m.," as Carman pointed out. This was an indication of Lincoln's desire to immediately launch a field army to pursue Lee, as Pope suggested, but not with Pope in command.

25 Carman pasted in a clipping here of Halleck's response that same night, preparing a field army, but not ordering anyone to command it. It is typical of Halleck's ambiguity.

26 A portion of Burnside's command was left at Aquia and did not fight at Second Bull Run, and the new regiments were responding to Lincoln's July 1862 call for more troops. See *OR* 12 pt. 3, pp. 799, 814-6, and *ibid.*, 19, pt. 2, pp. 196-7. The call for 300,000 new soldiers issued in July 1862 is discussed at length in Fred Albert Shannon, *Organization and Administration of the Union Army, 1861-1865* (Gloucester, MA: Peter Smith, 1965), pp. 269-76.

27 Although not an exact quotation, Welles, *Diary*, 1, p. 105, says Stanton and Halleck were apprehensive that Washington "was in danger."

up, lay in the river off the White House, giving the impression that the President was about to take flight. These things were seen by, and known to the public and a partial panic resulted. "Never before," says Swinton, "had the National Capital been in such peril—not even when the year before, the fugitive mob of McDowell rushed in panic beneath its walls."[28]

In view of this acute panic it may surprise the reader to know that, at the time, September 1st, there stood before the defenses of the capital full 40,000 veterans that had not fired a shot in Pope's campaign, and behind them in the defenses, 30,000 men of the garrison and reserves, of whom quite two-thirds were well-disciplined, though all were untried in battle. Add to them the 40,000 men Pope was leading back, gave McClellan 110,000 men for the defense of Washington, on September 2nd, and new regiments increased the number daily, so that, September 7th, when McClellan led an army of 74,000 men to meet Lee in Maryland, he left for the defense of Washington over 73,000 men with 120 field guns and about 500 heavy guns in position. Included in this number were the troops of the Third, Fifth and Eleventh Corps, commanded respectively by S. P. Heintzelman, Fitz-John Porter and Franz Sigel, covering the fortified line on the Virginia side of the Potomac, and numbering about 47,000 for duty; the garrisons of the works, 15,000; the city guard and Silas Casey's provisional brigade of newly arriving regiments, about 11,000—in all 73,000: "in brief nearly one-half of McClellan's entire army; a force a fourth or a third larger than Lee's; indeed, to all appearances, the identical command designed for McClellan himself, before the defense of the capital had made it necessary to resume operations in the field by the pursuit of Lee." And this force was daily increasing by the arrival of volunteers from the North.[29]

On June 28th, when it had become known that McClellan had suffered severe reverses on the Peninsula, Mr. Lincoln, in a communication to Secretary Seward, said "I expect to maintain this contest until successful, or until I die or am conquered, or my term expires, or Congress or the country forsakes me."[30] He was sanguine that there was strength enough in the country to put down rebellion and

---

28  The quotation is from William Swinton, *Twelve Decisive Battles of the War* (New York: Charles Scribner & Sons, 1882), pp. 149-50.

29  This passage citing strength figures for the troops around Washington, D.C., is from *B&L*. The first part is nearly word for word, from "Washington Under Banks," by Lt. Col. Richard B. Irwin (p. 541). The quoted portion is from the same article (p. 542).

30  The letter to Seward is in OR Series 3, 2, pp. 179-80, and also in Basler, Roy, *The Collected Works of Abraham Lincoln*, 5, p. 292. The proclamation and Lincoln's reply are in Moore, *Rebellion Record*, 5, Doc., pp. 547-8.

he would bring it out. He accepted a tender of 300,000 men from the Governors of the Loyal States. He was not mistaken in the reserve strength of the country and the call for volunteers brought it out. The governor of Connecticut replied: "Our losses before Richmond only stimulate this people to increased effort and firmer purpose to preserve the Union entire. Our armies may be checked and destroyed, but others will be organized and success is sure." Governor Andrew, of Massachusetts, reported that men swarmed the camps and that he would raise regiments until the Government cried "Hold." Charles S. Olden, the Quaker Governor of New Jersey, promptly responded: "I will bring forward every available man in the shortest possible time." In a month's time 25,000 men volunteered in Illinois and her Governor urged greater animus and energy in military movements and demanded that the President: "Summon to the standard of the Republic all willing to fight for the Union" including the colored man of the South. Ohio was ready with her men and her sturdy Governor, David Tod, recognizing the injury being done to the cause of the Union, by unseemly and disgraceful cabals at Washington, telegraphed Secretary Stanton, "For God's sake stop the wrangling between the friends of McClellan and yourself in Congress."[31] Other states were not behind in sending men to the front, by which it came about, in the first days of September 1862, that many thousands of new volunteers had reached Washington and many thousands more were on the way to guard the capital of the Republic and strengthen the advance against Lee in Maryland.

The fact that the Confederates had withdrawn from the front, on the 3rd, and information received during the day from Harper's Ferry and the signal officers on Sugar Loaf Mountain, in Maryland, led McClellan to believe that Lee intended to cross the upper Potomac into Maryland. "This," says McClellan: "materially changed the aspect of affairs and enlarged the sphere of operations; for, in case of a crossing in force, an entire campaign would be necessary to cover Baltimore, prevent the invasion of Pennsylvania, and clear Maryland."[32]

McClellan, therefore, on the 3rd, ordered the Second Corps, under Sumner, and Twelfth Corps, under A. S. Williams, to withdraw from the Virginia side of the Potomac and move to Tennallytown, on the Maryland side, and the Ninth Corps,

---

31 The letter to Seward is found in *OR* Series 3, vol. 2, pp. 179-80, and also in Basler, 5, p. 292. "In brief" quote is from *B&L*, p. 542. Connecticut Governor Buckingham's reply is *OR* Series 3, 2, p. 213; Andrew of Massachusetts is *ibid.*, p. 353; Olden of New Jersey, *ibid.*, p. 202; Yates of Illinois, *ibid.*, p. 218, and Ohio Governor Tod's, *ibid.*, p. 219.

32 McClellan's explanation of his movements relating to Lee's actions are found in *ibid.*, 19, pt. 1, p. 38, in his report of the campaign dated October 15, 1862. The troop dispositions described in the next paragraph are from the same report, except the specific details of the Ninth Corps, part of which was already in the Washington defenses.

then disembarking from the transports that had brought it from Aquia Creek, to a point on the Seventh Street road, near Washington. Pleasonton's cavalry was sent to the fords near Poolesville, Maryland, to watch and impede the enemy in any attempt to cross the river in that vicinity. The Second and Twelfth Corps cross the Potomac by the Aqueduct Bridge, on the 4th, and marched through Georgetown to Tennallytown, where they were joined by Couch's Division, Fourth Corps, and, on the next day, the Second and Twelfth Corps were advanced to Rockville. The Ninth Corps crossed the Potomac by the Long Bridge during the night and went into camp on Meridian Hill, early on the morning of the 5th.

When McClellan reported to Halleck that he had moved these troops into Maryland, he was asked what general had been placed in command of them, and, to McClellan's reply that he had made no such detail, as he should take command in person, if the enemy appeared in that direction, Halleck reminded him that his command included only the defenses of Washington and did not extend to any active column that might be moved out beyond the line of works; that no decision had yet been made as to the commander of the active army. McClellan says: "He repeated the same thing on more than one occasion before the final advance to South Mountain and Antietam took place."[33]

McClellan made no effort to force a decision as to who should command in the field. The present was in his own hands and he was hopeful that things would come his way, as the work of organization progressed and his prestige increased.

On the 5th Halleck sent to McClellan the following confidential note:

CONFIDENTIAL. WASHINGTON, September 5, 1862.
Major-General MCCLELLAN, Commanding, &c.:

GENERAL: The President has directed that General Pope be relieved and report to War Department; that Hooker be assigned to command of Porter's corps, and that Franklin's corps be temporarily attached to Heintzelman's. The orders will be issued this afternoon. Generals Porter and Franklin are to be relieved from duty till the charges against them are examined. I give you this memorandum in advance of the orders, so that you may act accordingly in putting forces in the field.

Very respectfully,

---

33 McClellan's assertion that he was never told that he was to command a field army is from McClellan, *Own Story*, p. 549, which Carman accepted uncritically. The point is open to debate since the general was never formally removed from command of the Army of the Potomac.

H. W. HALLECK,
General-in-Chief.[34]

Notwithstanding the fact that, as yet, no decision had been made as to the command of the active army and that McClellan's command was expressly limited to the defenses of Washington, the responsibility that should have rested with Halleck was thrust upon McClellan. Halleck would not order but proffered suggestions. On the 5th he wrote McClellan: "I think there can now be no doubt that the enemy are crossing the Potomac in force, and that you had better dispatch General Sumner and additional forces to follow. If you agree with me, let some troops move immediately."[35] McClellan had already placed Sumner north of the Potomac, with the Ninth and Twelfth Corps in support, preparatory to a movement northward.

At the same time McClellan ordered Pope to have his command ready to march with three days rations, to which Pope gave answer that he did not know what his command was nor where it was, as McClellan had ordered his troops to take post at various places, and he had not been notified in a single instance of their positions. He then asked Halleck if he was to take the field and under McClellan's orders, to which Halleck replied, the same day, September 5th: "The Armies of the Potomac and Virginia being consolidated, you will report for orders to the Secretary of War."[36]

Halleck lifted from his shoulders responsibility for the safety of Harper's Ferry, telegraphing General Wool, at Baltimore, September 5th: "I find it impossible to get this army into the field again in large force for a day or two. In the meantime

---

34 Other authors have been quick to point out that Halleck claimed in a meeting September 5, 1862, between himself, McClellan, and Lincoln, that the president positively gave McClellan instructions to take the field. On the other hand, Halleck was named by others as restoring McClellan to command. This controversy may be the result of neither Lincoln nor Halleck wanting responsibility for the action. See James Murfin, *Gleam of Bayonets* (New York: Thomas Yoseloff, 1965), pp. 78-80; Williams, T. Harry, *Lincoln and His Generals* (New York: Alfred A. Knopf, 1952), p. 165; Sears, *McClellan*, p. 263. Also, Welles said that Lincoln claimed Halleck gave the order. See Welles, *Diary*, 1, pp. 116, 122, 124, and Halleck to Pope, OR 12, pt. 3, pp. 819-20. Halleck's direction to McClellan about reassigning commanders, which Carman pasted in here from *ibid.*, 19, pt. 2, p. 182, only implies that McClellan is in command.

35 The letter from Halleck about troops crossing the Potomac, dated September 5, 1862, is also in *OR* 19, pt. 2, p. 182. It was this movement in response to Halleck's suggestion, and the ordering of Pope's troops, that sparked an angry outburst from Pope.

36 For Pope's angry dispatch and Halleck's reply to him, see *ibid.*, p. 183.

Harper's Ferry may be attacked and overwhelmed. I leave all dispositions there to your experience and local knowledge."[37]

The President's order of September 3rd directed General Halleck to proceed with all possible dispatch to organize an army for active operations and Halleck, in turn, advised McClellan that a movable army "must be immediately prepared to meet the enemy in the field." It was not the original intention that McClellan should command this army and, in the discussions of the matter, who should command it, there was developed in the cabinet and among the higher officers of the army an intense bitterness. Rivalries, petty jealousies and deep seated antipathies and animosities were active in all circles, especially among prominent general officers, concerning which Halleck wrote to Pope, September 5th 1862: "The differences and ill-feeling among the generals are very embarrassing to the administration and unless checked will ruin the country. We must all act together or we shall accomplish nothing, but be utterly disgraced." On the same day Halleck wrote to his wife: "The generals all around me are quarreling among themselves, while I am doing all in my power to conciliate and satisfy. It is sad to witness the selfishness of men at this time of sore trial.... I want to go back to private life as soon as possible and never again to put my foot in Washington."

It was at this time that the President Lincoln remarked to the Secretary of the Navy: "Most of our troubles grow out of military jealousies."[38]

The bitterness of feeling was not confined to the generals; it existed among the politicians and especially between what was known as the "radical" and "conservative" wings of the Republican party. The eastern press took sides and both factions seemed more intent upon political advantages than success in the field. On January 20, 1862, Halleck, who had been assigned to command in the west, wrote McClellan: "I take it for granted, general, that what has heretofore been done has been the result of political policy rather than military strategy, and that the want of success on our part is attributable to the politicians rather than to the

---

37 Carman's bias against Halleck is on display here in the discussion of the placement of the Harpers Ferry garrison. While Carman may indeed be correct, it is not as obvious from the full letter found in OR 19, pt. 2, p. 189. The full letter is more ambiguous—and more typical of Halleck—and less damning than Carman suggested.

38 Halleck's letter, which chided Pope's acrimonious behavior, is in *ibid.*, 12, pt. 3, pp. 812-3. That the strife between leaders in government and the army was obvious to many is borne out in Welles's diary references previously cited, and in McClellan's and Halleck's letters to their wives, as shown by Carman's citation for Halleck's letters. The actual wording is from Welles, *Lincoln and Seward*, p. 197. The passage attributed to Welles is a paraphrase of Welles, *Diary*, 1, p. 116. Halleck's letter to his wife is found in *Journal of the Military Service Institution of the United States*, 36 (NY: Governor's Island, New York Historical Society, 1906), p. 558.

generals' . . . pepper box strategy . . . movements having been governed by political expediency and in many cases directed by politicians in order to subserve particular interests." This feeling was observed by Halleck when he came to command the army; on July 30 he wrote to McClellan: "There seems to be a disposition in the public press here to cry down any one who attempts to save the country instead of party."[39]

Nor was this feeling confined to the politicians at large and the press. It was among the President's advisors and at the cabinet meetings, where personal ambition fought for partisan advantage and control of the administration. One of the first to recognize and criticize this political tendency of military direction was Edwin M. Stanton, who, July 26, 1861, after McDowell's defeat at Manassas and the arrival of McClellan from West Virginia, to assume command of the army in front of Washington, wrote to Ex-President James Buchanan of the condition of affairs and the arrival of McClellan saying: "Will not Scott's jealousy, cabinet intrigues and Republican interferences thwart him at every step."[40] A few weeks later we find Mr. Stanton urging McClellan to arrest Simon Cameron, Secretary of War, for inciting to insubordination because he had heartily endorsed an emancipation speech made by Colonel John Cochrane.

On November 13, 1861, Colonel John Cochrane, First United States Chasseurs, made a speech to his regiment, in which he took strong ground for arming the slaves in the war for the Union and for emancipation. Secretary Cameron was present and in a short speech endorsed the advanced views presented by Cochrane.

McClellan says, in his *Own Story*, pages 151-152, "he [Stanton] often advocated the propriety of my seizing the government and taking affairs in my own hands." Colonel A. K. McClure, in *Abraham Lincoln and Men of War Times*, says: "It is an open secret that Stanton advised the revolutionary overthrow of the Lincoln government, to be replaced by General McClellan as military dictator." Elsewhere McClure says: "Stanton was then the close friend and advisor of General McClellan, and it was well known in administrative circles, and to Lincoln himself, that Stanton earnestly urged McClellan to overthrow the constitutional

39 The quote from Halleck's January 20, 1862, letter to McClellan is in OR 8, pp. 508-11. With the phrase "pepper box strategy," Halleck was referring to a type of handgun that discharged several rounds simultaneously. The implication was that the policy lacked focus and was "scatter-shot" in its approach. Halleck's letter to McClellan of July 30, 1862, about the public mood is found in OR 11, pt. 3, p. 343.

40 Stanton's letter to Buchanan is found in George Ticknor Curtis, *Life of James Buchanan*, 2 Vols., (New York: Harper & Brothers, 1883), 2, p. 559, although Carman likely lifted it from McClellan, *Own Story*, in a note found on p. 67.

government because of weakness and incapacity and declare himself dictator."[41] He wrote freely of the "painful imbecility of Lincoln," and of the "venality and corruption of the government," expressing his belief that no better condition of things was possible "until Jeff Davis turns out the whole concern."[42] All this was before Mr. Stanton was called into the cabinet and up to that time he was in close and confidential relations with McClellan. When he entered the cabinet in January 1862, he believed that upon his shoulders rested the duty and responsibility of crushing the rebellion and it was with reluctance that he deferred to the authority of the President. He soon became a pronounced enemy of McClellan. He aspired to the military dictatorship that he had urged McClellan to assume.[43]

Under the President's order of March 11, 1862, McClellan was relieved from the command of the armies of the United States, his command being limited to the Department of the Potomac. No one was named as his successor or commander-in-chief, all department commanders being ordered to report "severally and directly to the Secretary of War," by which order the President virtually assumed command, the Secretary of War as his chief of staff.[44]

At the beginning of the war members of the cabinet believed themselves capable of managing military affairs and giving directions for the movement of armies in the field, but, recognizing the prestige of General Scott, refrained from an undue intrusion upon his prerogative, and contented themselves with recommending and urging the appointment of general officers and those of lower

41 Col. Cochrane's speech, and Cameron's comments endorsing it, are in Moore, *Rebellion Record*, 3, Doc., p. 373. The comment about Stanton urging Cameron's arrest is in McClellan, *Own Story*, p. 152, although Cochrane was not named. Carman may have put the two together to identify Cochrane, or had personal knowledge. Alexander K. McClure, a Philadelphia publisher and native of Franklin County, Pennsylvania, wrote *Abraham Lincoln and Men of War Times* (Philadelphia: Weekly Press, 1892). The quotation and information used by Carman are *ibid.*, pp. 155-8. Similar expressions about Stanton are found in McClellan, *Own Story*, p. 152. Here again is an example of Carman displaying his dislike of Stanton.

42 These specific quotes come from Alexander K. McClure, *Abraham Lincoln and Men of War Times* (Philadelphia: Weekly Press, 1892), p. 157.

43 Here, after the words "had urged McClellan to assume," Carman wrote and crossed out: "but was not strong enough to measure swords with Abraham Lincoln."

44 What Carman referred to here was Lincoln's Special War Order #3, which removed McClellan from overall command of the Union armies, *OR* 5, p. 54. Sears, *McClellan*, pp. 164-5, holds that McClellan interpreted the order as temporary until the end of the Peninsula campaign. Given Halleck's repeated assurances of joint command that can hardly be surprising. McClellan's relationship with Lincoln and his cabinet has occupied historians ever since the Civil War. Carman here seemed to take a slightly anti-McClellan stance, although not nearly as hostile as many other historians. See Sears, *McClellan*; Williams, *Lincoln and His Generals*; and McClellan, *Own Story*.

grade. When Scott was relieved and McClellan came to the command he was tendered any amount of advice that was coolly received and he went so far as to snub the President, when he inquired into proposed military movements, and this was one of the primary, underlying causes of his removal from chief command on March 11, 1862. Then the President's advisors came forward with their various plans and pushed their diverse views upon the President's attention, much to the annoyance and disgust of Stanton, who, as Secretary of War, was specially charged with the conduct of military affairs.

Prominent among those cabinet officers were William H. Seward and Salmon P. Chase. Seward assumed many duties outside of those connected with the foreign affairs of the government and was especially active in all pertaining to the military arm. He records in his diary: "I am consulting with the cabinet one hour, with the army officers next, the navy next, and I visit all the troops as fast as they come. I dare not, because I cannot safely, leave this post from which all supplies, all directions, all inquiries must radiate to armies and navies at home and legations abroad."[45]

He had entered upon the duties of his office with the idea that he was to be the ruling spirit of the administration and was to direct the affairs of the country in the name of the President. In carrying out this idea he trenched very largely and sometimes very offensively upon duties that pertained to other members of the cabinet, notably the Secretary of War and the Secretary of the Navy. Within a month after the inauguration of Mr. Lincoln we find that Mr. Seward "Exhibited his loose ideas of government, his want of system and defect of correct executive and administrative talent by preparing and sending out an irregular military expedition for the relief of Fort Pickens, without consulting the Secretary of War and without his knowledge or that of any of his associates."

Mr. Welles further says: "He took upon himself, as Secretary of State, to perform secretly and improperly the duties of Secretary of War without the knowledge of that officer. On one or two occasions when he attempted in total disregard of good government and correct administration, to intermeddle with naval affairs, the proceedings were, as with the War Department, disapproved as irregular, improper, and reprehensible."[46]

---

45 The direct quotation is from Welles, *Lincoln and Seward*, pp. 54-5. Carman relied principally on Welles's book for Seward, but in this case combined quotes from two letters into one. This juxtaposition is found in Frederic Bancroft, *Life of William H. Seward*, 2 Vols., (New York, Harper & Brothers, 1900), 2, p. 350.

46 Both quotes are from Welles, *Lincoln and Seward*, pp. 46, 54-6.

But Seward continued to take great interest in military affairs and pressed his views upon the President. He visited armies in the field and accompanied the President to the camps and grand reviews. He was particularly active in hastening the organization of New York volunteers and forwarding them to Washington and elsewhere in the field, and really did much good service; nor did he fail to see that New York had its fair and generous share of military appointments, from Major-Generals down to military store-keepers. But his interest grew less as the delicate condition of foreign affairs began to engross his attention and his intrusion upon the duties of the Secretary of War was not offensive. His influence was cast in favor of harmonizing the various elements of support to the administration by retaining McClellan in command.

His conservative course and friendship for McClellan brought upon him the condemnation of the radical wing of the administration and its supporters, one of whom wrote "McClellan in the field and Seward in the cabinet have been the evil spirits that have brought our grand cause to the very brink of death." McClellan's reverses on the Peninsula increased the severe criticisms on Seward and efforts were made by his former political supporters in New York, as Seward himself says: "to sow the seeds of dissension" in the relations between him and his colleagues in the cabinet, and the matter went so far that, early in September, after McClellan had taken the field against Lee in Maryland, a committee from New York journeyed to Washington to insist upon his enforced retirement from the cabinet, because of friendliness to McClellan and his conservatism upon the emancipation question, which was then agitating the cabinet and the country. The efforts of this self-constituted committee were met by Mr. Lincoln's very plain reply: "There is not one of you who would not see the country ruined, if you could turn Seward out."[47]

Chase was exceedingly active. He appeared to think that he had a peculiar and particular aptitude for military leadership. At the beginning of Mr. Lincoln's administration he was looked upon as the representation of the West, and as especially qualified to deal with the western Border States, and in Virginia and West Virginia he exercised a serious military responsibility; "in fact," says one of his biographers, "until Stanton became Secretary of War, Chase continued to consider himself administrator of operations in the west."[48]

---

47 The "member of the radical wing" quoted by Carman, was probably Chase. The quotations about seeds of dissension and turning Seward out can be found in Robert B. Warden, *Private Life and Public Services of Salmon Portland Chase* (Cincinnati: Wilstach, Baldwin & Co. 1874), p. 468.

48 Much of the information on Chase comes from A. B. Hart, *Salmon P. Chase* (Boston: Houghton Mifflin and Co., 1899), part of the American Statesmen series. The material begins on p. 212. The direct quotation about Chase's activities, and other material, are on pp. 212-4.

He looked to the appointment, assignment and promotion of western officers and these and western politicians were especially fond of seeking his military influence. For many months he felt quite as much responsibility for the military affairs of the country as he did for its finances, proof of which is found in his diaries and correspondence with officers in the field. As early as May 1861 he urged General Scott to occupy Manassas and compel the Virginians to evacuate Harper's Ferry. He urged McDowell to advance and give battle at Manassas in July 1861. When McClellan was called to the command of the army Chase requested him to confer with him regarding proposed military movements. On January 11, 1862, General McDowell inquired of Chase as to McClellan's plans and Chase gave him what he knew, in strict confidence and, on the following day, at a cabinet meeting to which McClellan was invited, insisted that the commander-in-chief should explain his military plans in detail, that they might be submitted to the approval or disapproval of the cabinet members. McClellan refused to discuss his plans and from that hour lost Chase's support.

In 1862 he began a correspondence with Colonel James A. Garfield, with whom he maintained intimate relations throughout the war. General Morgan asked him for regular troops; General Shields wanted him to confer in his behalf with the President; he was in direct and confidential correspondence with General Butler in New Orleans; General Banks sent him a message saying that he should like to join forces with him the two to be "Head and arm"; to McDowell, in March, he sent an article from the *Cincinnati Commercial* criticizing McClellan, who was then superior in rank to McDowell; to Colonel Key he expressed his reasons for approving Lincoln's orders to McDowell before McClellan's campaign of 1862.[49]

His biographer admits that, occasionally, Chase tried giving unasked counsel and cites that in June 1862, when McClellan was engaged on the Peninsula, he strongly urged the President to direct a column of troops, under McDowell, to Charlottesville and was much pained that his suggestion was not followed. A little later he was writing to General Pope and General Butler on the slavery question as affected by the military situation, and was trying to impress upon the President the necessity of a campaign against Vicksburg.

He favored the advancement of all Republican officers who had real merit, so as to counterpoise the too great weight already given to Democratic officers of little merit, who had been more pushed than Republicans, and to whom the administration had been more than generous, lavish even. He complained that generals had been placed and continued in command who never manifested the

49 *Ibid.*, pp. 295-296.

slightest sympathy with the Union cause as related to the controlling question of slavery. "These," he said, "naturally have never been more than half in earnest, and, instead of their being impelled to the most vigorous action, their influence has been suffered to paralyze in a great degree, the activity of the administration."[50]

Toward McClellan, Chase was, at the beginning, very friendly; indeed, he claimed a large share of credit for his appointment and suggested a plan of campaign for him; but, after McClellan's refusal to divulge his own plans to him and the failure of the Peninsula campaign, was very anxious to get rid of him. To Pope's suggestion that McClellan might be retained in command, and retrieve himself, by advancing on Richmond, Chase replied that if the movement were made and proved successful it "would only restore undeserved confidence and prepare future calamities."[51]

He did not regard him as loyal to the administration, although he did not question his general loyalty to the country."

Nor was Chase himself loyal to the administration. He was, writes McClure, in *Abraham Lincoln and Men of War Times*: "The merest plaything of the political charlatans who crossed his path, and he was thus made to do things unworthy of him, and which, with any other than Lincoln to judge him, would have brought him to absolute disgrace. He wrote many letters to his friends complaining of Lincoln's incompetency and of the hopeless condition of the war. From the day that Chase entered the cabinet he seems to have been consumed with the idea that he must be Lincoln's successor in 1864, and to that end he systematically directed his efforts and often sought, by flagrant abuse of the power of his department, to weaken his chief."[52]

On July 27th he spoke to the President "of the financial importance of getting rid of McClellan."[53]

When General Halleck was summoned to Washington and assigned to the command of the army, July 23rd, there was a partial repression of military suggestions from these members of the cabinet, not specially charged with the conduct of the war, and it was sought to confine the discussions and direction of

---

50 After the attributed quote from Hart, Carman began quoting from Warden, *Chase*, but the direct quote is from p. 454, not p. 545 as Carman cited it. Carman shortened the title to Warden's *Life of Chase*, or just *Chase*.

51 Chase's opinion that McClellan should be fired is from *ibid.*, pp. 439-40. McClellan did divulge his plans—somewhat—in December 1861 to Chase. See McClellan, *Own Story*, pp. 157-158.

52 The quotation is from McClure, *Abraham Lincoln and Men of War Times*, pp. 119-121.

53 Warden, *Chase*, p. 442.

military affairs to the President, Secretary Stanton and General Halleck. Chase tried hard to have it otherwise and complained that in the movements of the army: "We (the cabinet) have as little to do with it as if we were heads of factories supplying shoes or clothing" and when he called upon Halleck "judged it prudent not to say much of the war." He would have the war conducted upon intense anti-slavery lines and was much pained to hear Halleck say that he "did not think much of the negro."[54]

In the midst of these jealousies and contentions and the increasing pressure that the war should be conducted on anti-slavery lines, by anti-slavery generals, grew the alliance of Chase, Stanton and other members of the cabinet for McClellan's downfall, following the defeat of Pope, the order to McClellan of September 2nd, and the scene at the cabinet meeting, upon which occasion the President expressed his distress to find himself differing from the Secretary of War and Secretary of the Treasury, and that he would gladly resign his place.

Events did not move by the path desired by Chase, Stanton and the radical anti-slavery men of the country, but, strange as it may appear, the general whom they had most mistrusted, the only general of the Union army who had publicly declared against an emancipation policy, was the chosen instrument that made emancipation possible within twenty days, by the expulsion of the Confederate army from Maryland.[55]

McClellan having been assigned to the defenses of the capital and an order being given, September 3rd, for the organization of an army to take the field against Lee, there began a great pressure upon the President for the command of the movable army. Many names were presented and urged by members of the cabinet and others, and various arguments military, political and personal advanced for their selection. In the midst of the diverse views and insistence of his advisors the President kept his own counsel and seems, at first, to have considered General Pope for the command. According to Warden: "September 3rd. Pope came over and talked with the President, who assured him of his entire satisfaction with his conduct; assured him that McClellan's command was only temporary; and gave him reason to expect that another army of active operations would be organized at once which he (Pope) would lead."[56]

---

54  These three quotes are from A. B. Hart, *Salmon P. Chase*, p. 294, Warden, *Chase*, pp. 441, and 448, respectively.

55  The irony of Carman's paragraph about McClellan is striking. Carman may have used his own observation to foreshadow, but it was more or less true.

56  Warden, *Chase*, p. 460.

The idea was quickly abandoned if ever seriously entertained, and the command was again offered to General Burnside, by whom it had been refused in July, and who again refused and urged that McClellan be retained in command, and earnestly plead [sic] that good relations be restored between him and the War Department. He thought no one could do as well with the army as McClellan, if matters could be so arranged as to remove the objections held against him by the President and the Secretary of War. General Ethan Allen Hitchcock was then offered the command and declined it for reasons given elsewhere.[57]

This brings us to the evening of September 5th, when Halleck wrote Pope that the ill feelings and differences among the generals was very embarrassing to the administration, and when the President said to Mr. Welles "most of our troubles grow out of military jealousies." As the Confederate army was now crossing into Maryland and a decision was necessary, the President, accompanied by General Halleck, walked over to McClellan's residence, about 9 a.m., September 6th, and, after a short discussion upon the condition of affairs and the necessity for an immediate movement, the President said: "General, you will take command of the forces in the field." Until this moment Halleck did not know who was to command.

Early in the following October, Mr. Lincoln told W. D. Kelly that the command was given to McClellan, September 2nd, to reorganize a broken and demoralized army, and that his direction to take command of the forces in the field was due more to Lee than to himself.[58]

On the contrary, McClellan asserts that he was not placed in command of the forces in the field, but conducted the Maryland campaign with a halter around his neck. It is well to examine the record on this point. In his examination before the committee on the "Conduct of the War," McClellan said: "I asked the question two or three times of General Halleck, whether I was to command the troops in the field, and he said it had not been determined; and I do not think it ever was. I think that was one of these things that grew into shape itself. When the time came, I went

---

57 Warden claimed that Lincoln pondered restoring Pope to command of the field army gathering outside of Washington. Carman seemed to accept this claim by citing Warden's book. Welles was present when Lincoln and Pope met, which Welles said was on September 4, and he made no mention of Pope being offered or considered for command. See Welles, *Diary*, 1, p. 124. There does not seem to be any other substantiation of Warden's claim. Carman repeated the offering of command to Burnside and Hitchcock. See also Ambrose Burnside's testimony in the U.S. Congress' *Report of the Joint Committee on the Conduct of the War* (Washington, DC: GPO, 1863), pt. 1, p. 650, hereafter referred to as *CCW*.

58 Carman repeated the quotation from Welles about military jealousy, cited previously. The story about Lincoln and Halleck's visit to McClellan has been cited already as well. It is unclear why Carman repeated himself here. William D. Kelly, *Lincoln and Stanton: A Study of the War Administration of 1861 and 1862* . . . (New York: G. P. Putnam's Sons, 1885), pp. 73-74.

out." In his *Own Story*, McClellan says: "As the time had now arrived for the army to advance, and I had received no orders to take command of it, but had been expressly told that the assignment of a commander had not been decided; I determined to solve the question for myself, and when I moved out from Washington with my staff and personal escort I left my card with P. P. C. written upon it, at the White House, War Office, and Secretary Seward's house, and went on my way."[59]

The assertion by McClellan that he moved from Washington without orders, and with no assignment to command the army in the field is disputed by Halleck's testimony and contradicted by McClellan's *Own Story*. On October 9, 1862, General Halleck testified before the Miles Court of Inquiry that some days before McClellan went to the front, he had been directed to take the field against the enemy in Maryland. In his official report dated November 25, 1862, Halleck says:

> General McClellan was directed to pursue him (Lee) with all the troops which were not required for the defense of Washington." Before the Committee on the Conduct of the War, Halleck testified: "The order was given verbally to General McClellan by the President, at General McClellan's house about 9 o'clock in the morning, previous to General McClellan leaving the city for Rockville... The question was discussed by the President for two or three days as to who should take command of the troops that were to go into the field. The decision was made by himself, and announced to General McClellan in my presence. I did not know what the decision was until I heard it announced.... The day the President gave General McClellan directions to take command of the forces in the field we had a long conversation in regard to the campaign in Maryland. It was agreed between us that the troops should move up the Potomac, and, if possible, separate that portion of General Lee's army which had crossed the Potomac from the remainder on the Virginia side. There were no definite instructions, further than that understanding between us, as to the general plan of the campaign.[60]

---

59  The quotation about a halter around his neck is in McClellan, *Own Story*, as is the comment about taking command without written orders, on p. 551. The reference to leaving his card with P.P.C. on it was a common practice of 19th century military officers going on campaign. "P.P.C." stood for "pour prendre conge" ["to take leave"], and is explained in Sears, *McClellan*, p. 269. The testimony for *CCW* is from pt. 1, pp. 438-9.

60  The testimony in the Col. Dixon Miles Court of Inquiry is from *OR* 19, pt. 1, p. 786. Halleck's report is in *ibid.*, p. 4, and Halleck's testimony for the Committee on Conduct of the War is from *CCW*, pt. 1, pp. 453-454.

This testimony reveals the fact that not only was McClellan ordered to take command, but that the campaign was considered. That harmony prevailed is attested by a letter written by McClellan to his wife, on the afternoon of the 7th, in which he said: "I leave here this afternoon to take command of the troops in the field. The feeling of the Government toward me, I am sure, is kind and trusting. I hope with God's blessing, to justify the great confidence they now repose in me, and will bury the past in oblivion." In his preliminary report of the Maryland Campaign, submitted October 15, 1862, before relief from command had embittered his feelings, he said: "The disappearance of the enemy from the front of Washington and their passage into Maryland enlarged the sphere of operations, and made an active campaign necessary to cover Baltimore, prevent the invasion of Pennsylvania, and drive them out of Maryland. Being honored with the charge of this campaign, I entered at once upon the additional duties imposed upon me with cheerfulness and trust, yet not without feeling the weight of the responsibility thus assumed and deeply impressed with the magnitude of the issues involved."[61]

In the face of Halleck's testimony and McClellan's own letter and official report it is difficult to understand how he could make the statement that he fought the battles of South Mountain and Antietam "with a halter around his neck" unless we unhesitatingly accept the opinion advanced by McClellan and some of his friends some years later that, had the Maryland campaign ended in disaster to the Union armies, McClellan's enemies in the War Department would have taken advantage of the irregularity of his assignment to the command to bring charges against him.

Wrote McClellan: "I was afterwards accused of assuming command without authority, for nefarious purposes, and in fact I fought the battles of South Mountain and Antietam with a halter around my neck, for if the Army of the Potomac had been defeated and I had survived I would, no doubt, have been tried for assuming authority without orders, and, in the state of feeling which so unjustly condemned the innocent and meritorious F. J. Porter, I would probably have been condemned to death."

61 Underlining in the original text. McClellan's October report is found in *OR* 19, pt. 1, p. 25. Carman cited McClellan's letter to Ellen of September 7, 1862, in McClellan, *Own Story*, p. 567, as proof of his being ordered to field command, backed up by McClellan's report in *OR* 19, pt. 1, p. 25. In summary, several points seem clear: McClellan did receive at least verbal orders to take the field and also some ambiguous written orders, and other generals (Burnside, Hitchcock and possibly Pope) were also considered for field command.

This idea is adopted by the Compte [sic] de Paris who writes, that "the idle allegations which at a later date were made the pretext for deposing him give the impartial historian the right to entertain such a supposition."[62]

This view is also entertained by George T. Curtis, who, in an article in the North American Review for April, 1880, says:

General McClellan fought the battles of South Mountain and Antietam without any written order defining his command, excepting the ambiguous one of September 2nd, ambiguous, that is to say, after the date on which it was issued by the War Department. What, then, would have been his fate if he had lost those battles, and especially the last? We must carry the reader back to a period when mean rivalries, deep hatreds, and vengeful prejudices had their sway. It cannot be doubted that, if McClellan had been defeated in the battle of Antietam, he would have had to answer for it before a court-martial, and that his blood would have been demanded. We know what deeds were done in that period under the forms and mockeries of military justice. McClellan's bitterest enemies were among those, who, from their official stations, would have had the power, which they would not have scrupled to use, to arraign him for having assumed a command to which he had not been legally assigned. They could have pointed to the narrow scope of the order of September 2nd, and they would have pointed to the lives of brave men that had been lost and the public property that had been destroyed beyond what, they would have contended, was the scope of the only authority that he had received which could avail him as a legal order. In suffering McClellan to be thus exposed, President Lincoln would seem to have been unconscious of what a strain might be brought upon his own sense of executive justice if any disaster should befall the general who had taken the command at his earnest personal entreaty, and who had been left without a proper legal authority for the acts which he was expected to perform.[63]

---

62  Carman's Note: McClellan, *B&L*, p. 552. Some of the details of McClellan's appointment were confused when his literary executor compiled his memoirs. What is not clear is who ordered him to command. Halleck and Lincoln contradict one another, either by design or accident. It cannot be discounted that there was a sort of plausible deniability to the affair that would justify some of McClellan's hesitancy as expressed in the quotation from *B&L*, which is correct.

63  That Carman cited the Comte de Paris and the article by George T. Curtis in *North American Review* (April 1888) in support of McClellan's position may indicate Carman was leaning a little in favor of McClellan when forced to side with him or the cabinet members bent on removing him. The Comte de Paris quotation is found in Louis Phillippe d'Orleans, Comte de Paris, *History of the Civil War in America*, 2 vols. (Philadelphia: Porter and Coates, 1876), 2, pp. 305-06. The quoted portion from Curtis is found in the reprinted version of several of his articles,

It is admitted that President Lincoln, on the morning of September 6th, gave McClellan a verbal order to assume command of the army in the field. Why this verbal order was not supplemented by a written one, as was done September 2nd, can be explained only upon the supposition that in the dazed condition of Halleck and the confused state of affairs in the War Department it was forgotten. McClellan says he was fully aware of the risk he ran, if so, he was certainly very remiss in not asking for written orders. In after days when asked why he had not requested written orders, he replied: "It was no time for writing, and in fact I never thought of it."[64]

But why orders of any kind were necessary is not apparent. McClellan had never been relieved from command of the Army of the Potomac, and Halleck, when he ordered that army from the Peninsula, assured McClellan of his intention to have him assigned to the command of the consolidated armies of the Potomac and Virginia. McClellan brought the Army of the Potomac to Alexandria, and a part of it was sent to Pope. On September 5, Pope was relieved from command of the Army of Virginia, and that army was consolidated with the Army of the Potomac of which McClellan was in command. In addition thereto he had been, September 2nd, put in command of the defenses of Washington. Naturally and legally, therefore, McClellan was in full command and control of all troops inside of the defenses of Washington as well as those outside of them, belonging to the Army of the Potomac, including those formerly of the Army of Virginia.

It cannot be doubted that had McClellan been unsuccessful, his enemies would have pursued him unrelentingly and endeavored upon any pretext, to inflict upon him the severest punishment due to his taking the field without written orders, but we do not share the opinion that President Lincoln would have been unable to save him from any punishment due to his taking the field without written orders. He would not have permitted an act of such gross injustice. He would have assumed all the responsibility for any irregularity.

Be it as it may, whether McClellan had or had not reasons to anticipate severe punishment, should his campaign end in failure, he entered upon it with a full and patriotic determination to do his full duty and save the capital and the nation. Candor compels us to say that his efforts were not encouraged by those in authority

entitled *McClellan's Last Service to the Republic* (New York: D. Appleton and Co., 1886), pp. 57-59. Curtis claimed to have interviewed McClellan for his article.

64 Carman repeated the incorrect date of McClellan's restoration to command as September 6, 1862, but it was the 5th. For McClellan's claim that he did not think to ask for written confirmation, see his testimony in 1863 at the *CCW* hearing, pt. 1, p. 439.

who "actually declared that they would prefer the loss of the capital to the restoration of McClellan to command."[65]

The consolidation of the armies of the Potomac and Virginia, the relief of Pope and the assumption of command by McClellan, were followed by other changes. General McDowell, commanding a corps in the Army of Virginia, was relieved to await an investigation, self-sought, of cruel and unjust charges affecting his loyalty to the country, and Generals Fitz John Porter and William B. Franklin, commanding Fifth and Sixth Corps, Army of the Potomac, were ordered to be relieved, pending an investigation of their loyalty to Pope.

Major-General Joseph Hooker, commanding a division of the Third Corps, was, at first, assigned to command Porter's Corps, and Major General Jesse L. Reno, commanding a division of the Ninth Corps, was designated to command McDowell's Corps, while Franklin's Corps was ordered attached to Heintzelman's Third Corps. On September 6th McClellan represented to Halleck that it would save a great deal of trouble and invaluable time, if the investigation of the charges against Porter and Franklin was deferred until he could see his way out of the difficulties then confronting him. He desired to move Franklin's Corps to the front, at once, and, to avoid a change in the Ninth Corps, while on the march, by taking Reno from it, urged that Hooker be given command of McDowell's corps. To all of which Halleck promptly and properly assented, an act characterized by the enemies of McClellan as an abject surrender of the administration.[66]

Halleck's action in yielding to the request of McClellan had the sanction of the President, who reasoned logically that as, under the stress of circumstances, he had condoned the apparent remissness of McClellan in sustaining Pope, the condonation should extend to his subordinates. His self-abnegation, his personal feeling was nothing as weighed against the great interests of the country, and he undoubtedly felt at this time as when, upon a previous occasion, protest was made against his patient endurance of McClellan's exasperating conduct and sometimes

---

65 Carman summed up his conclusion about the legitimacy of McClellan's command, and acknowledged the political opposition, much of which was presented in McClellan, *Own Story*, pp. 538-47, and included the quotation from Montgomery Blair about the opposition preferring to see the loss of the capital, which was cited earlier.

66 The reshuffling of commanders is presented in OR 12, pt. 3, pp. 810-01, September 5, 1862, *ibid.*, pt. 2, pp. 188, 197-98, 279. Carman made no pretense of disguising his prejudices in this section. He characterized the charges against McDowell as cruel and unjust, and expressed approval of the judgment of McClellan on assigning other commanders.

absolute disrespect, he replied "I will hold his horse if he will only conquer the rebellion."The restoration of McClellan was hailed with joy by the army.[67]

McClellan had under his command, exclusive of the forces left for the defense of Washington, the First Corps, Major-General Joseph Hooker; the Second Corps, Major-General E. V. Sumner; a division of the Fourth Corps, under Major-General D. N. Couch; the Sixth Corps, Major-General W. B. Franklin; the Ninth Corps, Major-General A. E. Burnside, and the Twelfth Corps, Brig. Gen. A. S. Williams. Sykes's Division of the Fifth Corps, was an independent command at the beginning of the campaign; it was joined on the march near Frederick by Morell's Division and General Fitz John Porter assumed command. In addition to this infantry force there was a cavalry division led by Brigadier General Alfred Pleasonton, and an artillery reserve of seven batteries.

Including the two divisions (Sykes's and Morell's) of the Fifth Corps, and excluding Humphreys's Division, which did not leave Washington until the September 14th, the Army of the Potomac, in the field, numbered 75,800 infantry and artillery and 4,300 cavalry. The artillery had sixty batteries aggregating 326 guns. Nearly 30,000 men were new recruits, fresh from the stores, workshops and farms of the North. Over 48,000 were tried, seasoned veterans who had seen service on the Peninsula, in the Shenandoah Valley, in North Carolina, in West Virginia and in front of Washington.[68]

Before McClellan took the field there was an arrangement between Halleck and himself that the army should be divided into two wings and a reserve; that Sumner should command one wing of two corps and Burnside a wing of two corps,

67 The famous remark about holding McClellan's horse was used by Carman to illustrate what he saw as Lincoln's faith in McClellan and his determination to sustain him against the criticisms of certain cabinet members. It comes from Nicolay and Hay, *Life of Abraham Lincoln*, p. 469, note 1. After the words, "with joy by the army," Carman wrote and crossed out: "and when it was seen that the President had turned a deaf ear to those who were demanding his retirement from the service, stocks rose on Wall Street and the position on gold went down."

68 The listing of the elements of McClellan's command, and the formation of the wing commands, are partially reported in *OR* 19, pt. 2, p. 25, and McClellan's report, *ibid.*, pt. 1, pp. 39-40. Carman augmented these sources with his own research, listed in Chapter 14 of Carman's manuscript. See also, "The Opposing Forces at Antietam," *B&L*, pp. 598-603. The number of batteries and guns cited by Carman is slightly different from a modern study by Curt Johnson and Richard Anderson, *Artillery Hell: The Employment of Artillery at Antietam* (College Station TX: Texas A&M University Press, 1995), p. 36, which lists 64 batteries and 323 guns. The addition of the roughly 6,000 men of Humphreys's division would increase the total close to the 87,164 usually cited for McClellan's strength on September 17, 1862. See George McClellan, *Letter to the Secretary of War Transmitting Report on the Organization of the Army of the Potomac and of its Campaigns in Virginia and Maryland* (Washington, DC: GPO, 1864), p. 214. The figure of 30,000 new recruits is high. This editor's research arrives at a figure close to 18,000.

with Franklin's corps as a reserve, and that the two corps of the Army of Virginia should be separated, one to the right wing and one to the left. In the general advance McClellan observed this arrangement, but did not announce the formation of wing commands, in orders, until September 14th, and then suspended the orders within twenty-four hours; why, we shall tell elsewhere.[69]

The right wing commanded by Burnside, was composed of the First and Ninth Corps, in the latter was included the Kanawha Division from West Virginia; the center under Sumner was composed of the Second and Twelfth Corps; the left under Franklin was composed of the Sixth Corps and Couch's Division of the Fourth Corps. Of the Fifth Corps only Sykes' Division took the field as early as September 6th, to this was attached the Reserve Artillery. Morell's Division joined on the 13th, and the Fifth Corps constituted the reserve, under command of Fitz-John Porter. Humphrey's Division of the Fifth Corps did not join until September 18th.

Major-General Joseph Hooker, the commander of the First Corps, was one of the most positive and conspicuous characters of the War of the Rebellion and enjoyed the admiration of soldiers and of his countrymen. He was born at Hadley, Massachusetts, November 13, 1814, graduated at West Point in 1837 and was commissioned a Second Lieutenant in the First Artillery. He passed his first years of service in the Florida war. November 3, 1838, he was promoted to the rank of First Lieutenant. In 1841, he was adjutant at the Military Academy, and for the next five years was adjutant of his regiment. In 1846, at the beginning of the war with Mexico, he was assigned to staff duty and his brilliant services during the war won him the brevets of Captain, Major and Lieutenant-Colonel. After the war with Mexico he served on staff duty on the Pacific coast, and, in 1851, resigned his commission in the army and settled in California. When war broke out he hastened to Washington and offered his services to the Government, but met with but little encouragement. Finally, he decided to call upon President Lincoln, to whom he stated his case and that he was about to return to California, and added: "but before going I was anxious to pay my respects to you, sir, and to express my wish for your personal welfare, and for your success in putting down the rebellion. And, while I am about it, Mr. President, I want to say one thing more, and that is, that I was at the

---

69  It might seem these two structures of the Army of the Potomac are contradictory, however the order creating the wings, found in OR 19, pt. 2, p. 290, is imprecise about the structure and the two-wing-and-a-reserve that Carman described are not precisely detailed as such.

battle of Bull Run, the other day, and it is neither vanity nor boasting in me to disclose that I am a better general than you, sir, had on that field."[70]

This frank and characteristic declaration impressed Mr. Lincoln and Hooker was commissioned a Brigadier General of Volunteers to date from May 17, 1861. In the autumn and winter of 1861-1862, he was in command of the Second Division, Third Corps, stationed on the lower Potomac, in Maryland. In April 1862, his division went to the Peninsula and with the First Division, under Philip Kearny, formed Heintzelman's Corps.

These three commanders, all skillful and self-reliant, never awaited a second order to get into a fight. On May 5, 1862 occurred the battle of Williamsburg, conducted principally by Hooker, sustained by Kearny. This battle established the fame of Hooker as a fighting commander and he was justly rewarded by promotion to Major-General of Volunteers to date from May 5, 1862. In the battles before Richmond Hooker bore a prominent part. At Fair Oaks or Seven Pines, Glendale and Malvern Hill, his division was ably led and did heavy fighting. While the army lay at Harrison's Landing Hooker led a reconnaissance toward Richmond, the success of which was so marked, that he maintained that if properly supported, the Army of the Potomac could be placed at Richmond before the Confederates in Pope's front could return to prevent it. His suggestion was not acted upon, which caused him to express himself very freely and openly upon the incapacity of McClellan. Before the army withdrew from Harrison's Landing, Hooker urged McClellan to march again upon Richmond believing it could be taken and telling McClellan "that if we were unsuccessful, it would probably cost him his head, but that he might as well die for an old sheep as a lamb," that he knew of no better place to put an army than between the enemy in Pope's front and the defenses of Richmond.[71]

McClellan seems to have imbibed Hooker's spirit for, August 10th, he wrote his wife that he hoped to move on Richmond next day, crush or thrash Longstreet, and follow into Richmond, while they were hammering at Pope, but he was apprehensive that they would be too quick for him in Washington, and relieve him before he had the chance of making the dash.[72] At the last moment McClellan

70 Hooker's bold quotation to President Lincoln is discussed and cited in Walter H. Herbert, *Fighting Joe Hooker* (Indianapolis: Bobbs-Merrill Co., 1944), p. 312, note 7, but Carman took it from a unidentified "New York edition" newspaper clipping in the Library of Congress entitled "Gen. Hooker: His Intense Ego."

71 For his criticism of McClellan and desire to assault Richmond, see *CCW*, pt. 1, p. 579. Hooker repeated the story to Chase on September 3, 1862. See Chase, *Diaries*, 2, pp. 90-91.

72 McClellan's letter to Ellen is in McClellan, *Own Story*, p. 465.

shrank from the movement. When the army was transferred from the Peninsula to Alexandria, Hooker was among the first to report to Pope, and he needed no urging to find the enemy, and when the latter was encountered at Bristoe Station, August 27, a severe engagement resulted in a victory for Hooker. However much he may have criticized McClellan and however little the confidence he had in Pope, his loyalty to country made him loyal in action to his commanders: "he was by instinct and by education too much of a soldier to injure his cause or his commander by inefficient performance or disloyal deeds." He was handsome and knew it, had confidence in himself, was full of life, skillful on the field, of brilliant courage, was dead earnest in his fighting, and always on that part of the line where there was most of it; was courteous to those under him, and his genial kindness to the private soldier will not be forgotten by those who served under him. "Lofty patriotism, high conception of duty, and the loyal performance of it, consistently exerted and faithfully sustained by candid effort and fearless execution, this was Hooker." He was by far the best fighting corps commander of the army that McClellan was leading against Lee.[73]

Major-General Edwin V. Sumner, the commander of the Second Corps, was veteran officer of the regular army and the oldest of high rank in the Army of the Potomac, being over sixty-five years of age, though still vigorous and active. He was born at Boston, Massachusetts, January 30, 1797, entered the army from civil life as a Second Lieutenant in 1819, and served in the Black Hawk war. Upon the organization of the 2nd Dragoons, in 1833, he was appointed Captain in that regiment and was employed on the western frontier, where he took high rank as an Indian fighter. He was promoted major in 1846 and served in the Mexican War with great distinction. He led the famous cavalry charge at Cerro Gordo, April 1847, where he was wounded and obtained the brevet of Lieutenant-Colonel. He commanded the reserves at Contreras and Churubusco, where he won high honors, and at Molino del Rey commanded General Scott's entire cavalry force, and at its head checked the advance of a very superior force of Mexican Lancers, for which he was breveted colonel. In 1848, he was commissioned Lieut.-Col. of the 1st Dragoons. In 1851-3 he was (Territorial) Governor of New Mexico. In 1855 he was commissioned Colonel of the 1st Cavalry. He was in command of the Department

---

73 The quotations about Hooker's character have not been found. They sound like excerpts from a memorial volume or obituary, but are not in the clippings in the Library of Congress files. Similar, but not exact, language appears in William P. Shreve, *The Story of the Third Army Corps Union* (Boston: privately printed, 1910), p. 56, but this was printed after Carman was dead. Carman and Hooker corresponded frequently and warmly, underscoring Carman's clear admiration of "Fighting Joe."

of the West in 1858 and conducted affairs with great discretion during the Kansas border troubles. In March 1861, he was promoted Brigadier General in the regular army and ordered to San Francisco, California, to relieve General Albert Sidney Johnston in command of the Department of the Pacific, and his courage and loyalty did much to hold California true to the cause of the Union. He was recalled from California and was one of the five corps commanders designated by President Lincoln for the Army of the Potomac in March 1862, and commanded the left wing of the army at the siege of Yorktown. At Fair Oaks, May 31, 1862, where McClellan's army was attacked, when divided by the Chickahominy, on the first sound of battle, Sumner hurried the heads of his columns down to the bridges of the stream, in anticipation of orders to cross, and when orders came he was ready to cross and do great service. The Comte de Paris says that the army was saved "by the indomitable energy of old Sumner."[74] In the Seven Days he was twice wounded.

Sumner was of fine presence, consciousness of his high rank showed in all his movements; he was courageous as a lion; and self assertive (sic), whether for himself or his men, yet never arrogant, or unkind, and always accessible to his soldiers, who believed in and loved to follow him. Those who followed him testify to his honor, his courage, his chivalry, his patriotism, his magnanimity and his kindness. Meanness, falsehood, duplicity were more hateful than death to him. "If," said Walker,

the Second Corps had a touch above the common; if in the terrible ordeals of flame and death through which in those years of almost continuous fighting, they were called to pass those two divisions [Sedgwick and Richardson] showed a courage and tenacity that made them observed among the brave; if they learned to drop their thousands upon the field as often as they were summoned to the conflict, but on no account to leave a color in the hands of the enemy, it was very largely through the inspiration derived from the old chieftain who first organized them and led them into battle.

The same writer, while awarding praise and only praise to his transcendent soldierly virtues, says: "Much may be said on either side of the question whether, with his mental habits and at his advanced age, he should have been designated for

---

74 Comte de Paris, *History of the Civil War in America*, 2, p. 346. This is a paraphrase of the Comte's language, but the intimation is clear.

the command of 20,000 new troops in the field, against a resolute and tenacious enemy skillfully and audaciously led."[75]

General Palfrey says that he was a most excellent and every way respectable man, and had in the highest degree the courage of a soldier but was wanting in the courage of a general. He was apt to be demoralized by hard fighting, and to overestimate the losses of his own side and the strength of the enemy, and he seems to have possessed no judgment as a tactician. It is probable that his training as a cavalry officer had done him positive harm as a leader of infantry.

General McClellan pays him this tribute: "He was an old and tried officer; perfectly honest; as brave a man as could be; conscientious and laborious. In some respects he was a model soldier. He was a man for whom I had a very high regard, and for his memory I have the greatest respect. He was a very valuable man, and his soldierly example was of the highest value in a new army. A nation is fortunate that possesses many such soldiers as Edwin V. Sumner."[76]

Major General Fitz-John Porter, the commander of the Fifth Corps, was born at Portsmouth, New Hampshire, June 13, 1822, son of Captain John Porter, United States Navy. He graduated from the Military Academy at West Point in 1845 and was assigned to the 4th Artillery, in which he became Second Lieutenant a year later. He served in the Mexican War, particularly in the siege of Vera Cruz, the battles of Cerro Gordo, Contreras, and Molino del Rey, the storming of Chapultepec and the capture of the city of Mexico. For gallantry at Molino del Rey he was breveted Captain, September 8, 1849, and Major for Chapultepec. During the assault on the city of Mexico he was wounded at the Belen Gate. July 9, 1849, he was detailed an assistant instructor of artillery at West Point, and in 1853-4 served as adjutant at the academy. From May 1, 1854 to September 11, 1855, he was instructor of cavalry and artillery. In 1856 he was appointed assistant adjutant general with the rank of Captain, and served on the staff of General P. F. Smith, in the Kansas troubles of 1856, and, in 1857, reported to General Albert Sidney Johnston, under whom he served in the Utah expedition. In November 1860, he inspected the defenses of Charleston Harbor and advised against the occupation of Fort Sumter and Castle Pinkney by the United States troops. In April 1861, he was ordered by the Secretary of War to superintend the protection of the railroad between Baltimore and Harrisburg against the Baltimore rioters, and his services on

75 The citations from Francis Walker, *History of the Second Army Corps in the Army of the Potomac* (New York: Charles Scribner's Sons, 1887), are found on pp. 11-13. The direct quote is preceded by a paraphrased paragraph from the same source.

76 Francis Palfrey, *The Antietam and Fredericksburg* (New York: Charles Scribner, 1882), p. 54. The quotation about Sumner is from McClellan, *Own Story*, p. 138.

the occasion were marked by great energy and tact. He was then assigned as chief of staff to General Robert Patterson, near Harper's Ferry, and was, in fact, the most potent influence surrounding Patterson and remained with him until the close of that officer's term of service. He was appointed colonel of the 15th U. S. Infantry to date from May 14, 1861, and, at the request of General McClellan, was made Brigadier General of Volunteers, to date from May 17, 1861, and assigned to duty at Washington. McClellan says of him:

> Fitz-John Porter was on duty with Gen. Patterson, as Adjutant General, when I assumed command. As soon as possible I had him made a Brigadier General and gave him the command vacated by W. T. Sherman. Take him for all in all, he was probably the best general officer I had under me. He had excellent ability, sound judgment, and all the instincts of a soldier. He was perfectly familiar with all the details of his duty, an excellent organizer and administrative officer, and one of the most conscientious and laborious men I ever knew. I never found it necessary to do more than give him general instructions, for it was certain that all details would be cared for and nothing neglected. I always knew that an order given to him would be fully carried out, were it morally and physically possible. He was one of the coolest and most imperturbable men in danger whom I ever knew, like all his race.[77]

In the spring of 1862 Porter was in command of a division of the Third Corps and went to the Peninsula with it, where, April 27, McClellan appointed him director of the siege of Yorktown. On May 18th, with the consent of the President, McClellan formed two provisional corps, one for Porter and one for Franklin. Porter's was denominated the Fifth, and to it was attached the Artillery Reserve of the Army of the Potomac. McClellan's partiality for Porter had been observed by the older officers of the army and the fact was communicated to Mr. Lincoln, who, a few days before assenting to the formation of the new corps, wrote McClellan: "I am constantly told that you have no communication or consultation with them [the three corps commanders]; that you consult and communicate with no one but Gen. Fitz-John Porter and perhaps Franklin. I do not say that these complaints are true or just, but at all events it is proper you should know of their existence."[78]

He fought the battle of Mechanicsville, June 26th; made a splendid defense of his position at Gaines' Mill, June 27th; and commanded the left wing of the army at Malvern Hill, July 1st. In all these actions he displayed rare ability and unflinching

77  The quotation about Porter is also from McClellan, *Own Story*, p. 139.

78  The letter from Lincoln is in Basler, ed. *The Collected Works of Abraham Lincoln*, 5, pp. 208-9. A copy is also in the Stanton Papers.

courage. He was breveted Brigadier General in the regular army, June 27th, and on July 4th was made Major General of Volunteers. He was actively engaged and his corps fought nobly at Second Manassas, August 30th; but charges were brought against him for his inaction, on the 29th, and he was deprived of his command, but was restored to duty at the request of McClellan and took part in the Maryland campaign. The historian of the Fifth Army Corps says of him:

> Born a patriot; ambitious, but unselfish; self-respecting and self-denying; thoroughly equipped and void of ostentation; imperturbable and unflinching; self reliant but never egotistic; prudent without trace of fear; reserved, yet sympathetic; quiet, but quick to see, decide and act; cautious and careful to avoid offense, if possible, yet without strange oaths or other foreign aid, conveying with an order given the conviction that obedience must follow, his influence was ever present and controlling.[79]

And yet, conceding his eminent ability as a soldier, it is questionable, under the circumstances, if he should have been returned to command on the eve of an important campaign and if he gave strength to McClellan and the cause of the Union.[80]

Major General William B. Franklin, the commander of the Sixth Corps, was born at York, Pennsylvania, February 27, 1823. He graduated at the West Point Military Academy in 1843, at the head of his class and was assigned to the topographical engineers, in which he was commissioned Second Lieutenant, September 21, 1846. He accompanied the army to Mexico, served on the staff of General Zachary Taylor, as engineer, and for gallantry at Buena Vista received the brevet of First Lieutenant, February 23, 1847. After the close of the Mexican War he was engaged on surveys in the West, was for a time an assistant professor at the Military Academy, and when the war of the rebellion broke out was at Washington in charge of the construction of the capitol and other public buildings. Meantime he had been promoted First Lieutenant, March 3, 1853, and Captain, July 1, 1857. On May 14, 1861, he was appointed Colonel of the 12th U. S. Infantry and three days later was commissioned Brigadier General of Volunteers. He commanded a brigade in Heintzelman's Division at the First Manassas, July 21, 1861, and in April 1862, went to the Peninsula in command of a division. He was engaged at the siege

---

79 The "historian of the Fifth Corps" that Carman quoted is William H. Powell, *The Fifth Army Corps* (New York: G.P. Putnam's Sons, 1896), and the quotation about Porter is on p. 6.

80 Carman is almost certainly referring to Porter's controversial behavior at Second Manassas and the charges brought against him by Pope. Temporarily "rescuing" Porter from a court-martial fueled the criticism of McClellan's enemies.

of Yorktown and at the affair at West Point, on York River, and on May 18th, when two provisional corps were authorized, Franklin was given one, which was denominated the Sixth. It was a great corps in many respects. At the head of his corps he fought at White Oak Bridge, Savage Station and Malvern Hill. For distinguished service in these engagements he was breveted Brigadier General in the regular army, June 30th, 1862, and was made Major General of Volunteers, July 4, 1862. On the transfer of the Army of the Potomac from the Peninsula to Alexandria, Franklin fell under the displeasure of Pope, and, after Pope's defeat was, with Fitz-John Porter, relieved from command under serious charges. At the request of McClellan, Franklin was restored to his command and led it in the Maryland campaign. McClellan says of him:

> Franklin was one of the best officers I had; very powerful. He was a man not only of excellent judgment, but of a remarkably high order of intellectual ability. He was often badly treated, and seldom received the credit he deserved. His moral character was of the highest, and he was in all respects an admirable corps commander; more than that, he would have commanded an army well. The only reason that I did not send him to relieve Sherman, instead of Buell, was that I could not spare such a man from the Army of the Potomac.[81]

Major General Ambrose E. Burnside, the commander of the Ninth Corps, was born at Liberty, Indiana, May 23, 1824, and graduated at West Point in 1847. He was commissioned Second Lieutenant of Artillery, July 1 1847[82], and proceeded to Mexico. At the close of the war with Mexico he was ordered to Fort Adams, Newport, Rhode Island, and in 1849 transferred to New Mexico as First Lieutenant of the battery commanded by Braxton Bragg. After some service in repressing Indian troubles he returned to Newport and married. November 1, 1853, he resigned his commission in the army and entered into an arrangement with the National Government to manufacture and furnish an improved rifle, a breech loader. The enterprise failed, Burnside lost his all and was heavily in debt, and went west to retrieve his fortunes. Early in 1858 he obtained a position in the Land Department of the Illinois Central Railroad, of which his old friend and classmate, Geo. B. McClellan, was Vice President. [According to Augustus Woodbury:]

---

81 In this study of Franklin, Carman again quotes McClellan, *Own Story*, p. 138.

82 Carman omitted the word "Brevet" here, the common rank assigned USMA graduates. See Francis Heitman, *Biographical Register and Dictionary of the U.S. Army, 1789-1903*, 2 vols. (Urbana: Univesity of Illinois Press, 1965 reprint ed.), 1, p. 266.

He made his quarters with McClellan, and around a common fireside the two friends renewed the intimacy of former days. Burnside, limiting his expenses to a certain amount, devoted the remainder of his salary to the payments of his debts; and afterwards when he was able to free himself entirely from the claims of creditors, his unblemished integrity in business was as conspicuous as his fidelity in the field.

He had experienced poverty, disappointment, failure, then success, and was well and favorably known for his energy and skill in affairs, geniality in social intercourse, high sense of honor and honest simplicity.[83]

Though politically opposed to the administration of Mr. Lincoln he was intensely loyal to his country, and when war broke out entered the Union service. April 16, 1861, he was commissioned Colonel of the 1st Rhode Island Militia and on the 26th was in Washington with his regiment. At Bull Run, July 21, he commanded a brigade in Hunter's Division, which was severely engaged. On August 6, 1861, he was appointed Brigadier General of Volunteers and given a command composed of three years' regiments, then assembling in Washington. In January 1862, with John G. Foster, Jesse L. Reno and John G. Parke as brigade commanders, he landed a division and after some brilliant movements and severe fighting took possession of Roanoke Island. Newbern was taken on March 14th, the surrender of Fort Macon and Beaufort soon followed and Burnside was hailed as most successful of the Union leaders. This campaign was probably the most successful of any with which he was connected and much of this success was undoubtedly due to the skill of his subordinates. For his service in the campaign he was, March 18, 1862, promoted to Major General of Volunteers and assigned to command the Department of North Carolina, and administered its affairs in a business-like and conciliatory manner.

When McClellan was defeated before Richmond and the army was ordered withdrawn from the Peninsula, Burnside was ordered to Aquia Creek and Fredericksburg. He visited McClellan to consult in regard to future operations and found him surrounded by discord, petty jealousies and disagreement. He did not approve of Halleck's determination to evacuate the Peninsula, frankly told McClellan that he had enemies to contend with in the cabinet, and, after a full and free interchange of views, went to Washington convinced that McClellan had not been given a fair show, and hoping that the differences between Secretary Stanton

---

83 The quotation from Augustus Woodbury, *Major General Ambrose E. Burnside and the Ninth Corps: A Narrative of Campaigns in North Carolina, Maryland, Virginia, Ohio, Kentucky, Mississippi, and Tennessee During the War for the Preservation of the Republic* (Providence RI: Sidney S. Rider & Brother, 1867), pp. 10-12, continues with the next sentence.

and McClellan might be composed. Upon his arrival at Washington he was offered the command of the Army of the Potomac, but declined it.

After the defeat of Pope and the withdrawal of the army to Washington, Burnside was called into consultation with Mr. Lincoln and Halleck and again offered the command of the Army of the Potomac and again declined it, using his best endeavor to have McClellan retained. He was a tall and handsome man, of striking appearance, had fine eyes and a winning smile which showed a fine row of teeth. He was frank, sincere, captivating and true to his friends which won their confidence and esteem. He had a jovial, dashing way with him, as he rode through the camps or along the lines, a good humored cordiality toward everybody, which raised the enthusiasm of his soldiers to the highest degree. His personal character was without reproach, and his patriotism unquestioned. He was brave under fire and his courage was never doubted. He was modest and shrank from responsibility, because he had doubts of his ability to handle operations of magnitude. It is not going too far to say that the Union cause would have received no hurt and much blood saved had Burnside's own estimate of his ability been accepted by the administration.

When General Burnside was given command of the right wing, First and Ninth Corps of the army, Major General Jesse L. Reno was assigned to the command of the Ninth Corps. Reno was born at Wheeling, (West) Virginia, June 20, 1823, and when quite young removed to Pennsylvania. He entered West Point in 1842, graduated in 1846 and received his commission as Second Lieutenant[84] of Ordnance, July 1, 1846. He accompanied the army to Mexico and was at the battle of Cerro Gordo, April 18, 1847, where his gallantry won him the brevet of First Lieutenant. He was at Contreras and Churubusco. At the storming of Chapultepec, September 13, 1847, he was in command of a howitzer battery, was severely wounded and for gallantry was breveted Captain. January 9, 1849, he was detailed assistant professor of mathematics at West Point, and in July was detailed as secretary of a board to prepare a system of instruction for heavy artillery. He was on topographical duty in Minnesota in 1853-4 and Chief of Ordnance in the Utah expedition in 1857-9. He was in command of Mount Vernon Arsenal, Alabama, from 1859 until the seizure by state authorities January 1861. From February 2nd until December 6, 1861, he was in charge of the arsenal at [Fort] Leavenworth, Kansas. He was commissioned Brigadier General of Volunteers, November 12, 1861, and assigned to the command of one of the brigades composing the Burnside

---

84 Once again, Carman omitted the "brevet" in Reno's rank. See Hietman, *Biographical Register and Dictionary of the U.S. Army*, p. 823.

expedition. For distinguished gallantry at Roanoke Island and Newbern he was promoted Major General of Volunteers, April 26, 1862.

From April to August 1862, he was in command of a division in the Department of North Carolina. In Pope's August campaign he was at the head of the Ninth Corps in the field, and was engaged at Second Manassas and Chantilly. His services in this campaign were warmly eulogized by General Pope, who says: "I cannot express myself too highly of the zealous, gallant and cheerful manner in which General Reno deported himself from the beginning to the end of the operations. Ever prompt, correct, and soldierly, he was the model of an accomplished soldier and a gallant gentleman.[85]

"He was warm-hearted and cordial, yet quick-tempered, and always just and ready to recognize and reward merit. In person he was "of middle stature, stout, well knit and compact in frame. His forehead was high and broad, his face wore a genial expression, his eye beamed upon his friends with rare and quick intelligence, or, kindled in the excitement of conflict, flashed out in brave defiance of the foe. He had a magnetic kind of enthusiasm, and when leading on his men, he seemed to inspire his followers and make them irresistible in action. A dauntless soldier, whose like we rarely see."[86] His death at South Mountain, September 14, was a distinct loss to the army and a national misfortune.

Brigadier General Alpheus S. Williams, the commander of the Twelfth Corps, was born at Seabrook, Connecticut, September 20, 1810. He was of Puritan stock and his ancestors were men of note in the early colonies. In 1827 he entered Yale College and graduated in 1831. He then entered the Yale law school, where he spent three years, and then traveled two years in Europe, returning in 1836, and settling in Detroit, Michigan, where he began the practice of law. In 1839 he was elected judge of the court of probate of Wayne County, which position he held until 1844, when he was elected recorder of Detroit. Meantime he became connected with the press and conducted one of the leading journals of that city for about four years, when his editorial career was interrupted by the breaking out of the war with Mexico and his entering the volunteer service of his country as Lieutenant-Colonel of the 1st Michigan Infantry. At the end of the war he returned to Detroit and resumed his law practice and at the close of 1849 was appointed postmaster of that city, which position he held until 1853, when a change in the politics of the national administration was followed by his removal. In 1861, when the secession war broke out, Williams was one of the first to offer his services to the government, and as he

---

85 The praise for Reno by Pope is from the latter's report, *OR* 12 pt. 2, p. 48.

86 Woodbury, *Burnside and the Ninth Corps*, p. 131.

had always been an active member of the Democratic party, his example had great influence for good in a city where it was much needed. He first served as President of the State Military Board; then as commander of the camp of military instruction at Fort Wayne. On December 17, 1861, he was appointed Brigadier General of Volunteers and joined the Army of the Potomac.[87] He was assigned to the command of a brigade in General Banks's Division on the upper Potomac. In March 1862, he was given command of a division in Banks's Corps, and in the operations in the Shenandoah Valley displayed great skill and courage.

When Stonewall Jackson's aggressive movement on Banks's flank compelled him to fall back from Strasburg, Williams had full charge of covering the retreat and did so skillfully, retiring on May 24th, and, in a series of brilliant engagements, checking Jackson's advance at Newtown, Kernstown and Winchester, long enough to save part of the trains. The retreat was a disastrous and humiliating one, it would have been much more so had Williams not shown greater skill and judgment as a soldier than his immediate superior. At Cedar Mountain he handled his division admirably and in the subsequent campaign around Manassas was active and inspiring in effort. When General Banks assumed the command of the defenses of Washington, September 8th, Williams succeeded to the command of the corps, in which he had served as brigade and division commander.

Throughout his long and arduous service, which began with the beginning of the war and ended only when the final surrender was made, he never was taken by surprise, and when in action was cool and quick to see a faulty disposition or movement in his own army or in that of the enemy. He was not a brilliant soldier, but a safe one, he never sacrificed his men for the mere sake of winning to himself the attention of the newspaper correspondents and the plaudits of the public, but whenever hard work was to be done or hard knocks to be received he was ready. He was social in his habits; kind and considerate to officers and men; ever alive to their needs and comfort and always with them from the beginning to the end. He never received a furlough; his life was in camp with his men.

He never received the promotion to which his long and faithful service entitled him, but this did not lessen his honesty of purpose or diminish the energy with which he performed his duty. His ambition was more concerned with the welfare of his country and the triumph of her armies than his own promotion and advancement; and he was never above the work to which he was assigned, whether

---

87 Carman has the wrong date for Williams's commission as a brigadier general. See Ezra Warner, *Generals in Blue* (Baton Rouge: Louisiana State University Press, 1964), p. 560, and Heitman, *Biographical Register and Dictionary of the U.S. Army*, p. 1,039. The introduction to his published letters also cited his appointment to rank from May 17, 1861.

commanding a corps, a division, or a brigade. It has been truly said of him: "He was content that he did his duty, and in the satisfaction that he never committed an error, never misinterpreted an order, never relaxed his careful watchfulness and disinterested devotion to his country." Although this devotion to duty was not recognized by the Government, he never complained; "he never said aught in derogation of a fellow soldier; he was charitable even toward those who supplanted him or when advanced, when seemingly he was entitled to the promotion. He was a noble man as well as a gallant soldier."[88]

All these corps commanders had served in the Mexican War; five were graduates of West Point, two had resigned from the service and been reappointed; three had been in the service continuously. Sumner was not a graduate, but had been many years a soldier; Williams was appointed from civil life. Among the division and brigade commanders were many who subsequently rose to high command and fame; Meade to the command of a corps and the Army of the Potomac; Slocum to the command of a corps and the Army of Georgia; and Howard to the command of a corps and the Army of the Tennessee.

We have already stated that McClellan was the only general of the Union army who had publicly declared against the policy of emancipation; it is a noteworthy fact that every one of his corps commanders, six of whom were Democrats and one Republican, shared his views and were opposed to the attitude of the administration and to the action of Congress touching the question of slavery. More than two-thirds of the division and brigade leaders were of the same view.[89]

---

88 It is apparent that although Carman cited the usual laudatory character references, the warmth and personal tone here is stronger than with other biographical entries. This was probably because Carman commanded a regiment in Williams's division and knew him well. There may have been a bond between them for another reason: neither man was a West Point graduate. Carman commanded a brigade without getting promoted to brigadier general, while Williams commanded a division and a corps but was never promoted to major general. They corresponded regularly after the war until Williams's death in 1875. The source for the material Carman quoted has not yet been found.

89 Carman thought it important to note the political affiliation of the army commanders. He earlier mentioned the irony of McClellan's anti-emancipation stance, even though his victory made possible the announcement of the preliminary Emancipation Proclamation. Although McClellan discussed the proclamation with several people, he did not publicly oppose it. See Rafuse, *McClellan's War*, Chapter 15. On this page he commented on the leanings of the corps, division, and brigade commanders. While the corps commanders' political affiliations were documented, the division and brigade commanders would be more difficult to chart today. Carman must have thought this was important to the prosecution of the campaign, and perhaps used firsthand knowledge for this information. He may have used this political connection to underscore the strained relations between the Lincoln administration and McClellan's army.

# Chapter 5

# Advance of the Army of the Potomac from Washington to Frederick and South Mountain

The general theater of operations lay in Eastern Virginia and Western Maryland. The Potomac River crosses this area from the Northwest to Southeast, and, with the Chesapeake and Ohio Canal, which runs along it on the East, in the front of a vigilant enemy forms a military obstacle of some magnitude. The Monocacy and the Antietam enter the Potomac from the East, and the Shenandoah from the West, its waters mingling with those of the Potomac at Harper's Ferry. During the summer and early fall the Potomac is fordable, at several places above Conrad's Ferry, and presents no serious obstacle, when low, in the strategic conduct of a campaign.

The immediate theater of operations was Western Maryland, the physical features of which are determined by the great Appalachian system, which crosses that section nearly due North and South. The Blue Ridge, the eastern range of this system, is here broken into two well defined ranges, separated by a fertile valley of entrancing beauty, seven to nine miles in width, known as the Catoctin or Middletown Valley, the eastern range is known as the Catoctin, the western as

South Mountain. West of the South Mountain and crossing the Potomac at Harper's Ferry, is a lesser range known in Maryland as Elk Ridge. Where it borders the Potomac it presents a cluster or aggregation of lofty hills, known as Maryland Heights. It extends Northeast from the Potomac about ten miles and descends into and is lost in the general undulation of the country about one and a half miles southwest of Keedysville. The valley between it and South Mountain is happily known as Pleasant Valley and varies in width from one to three miles.

The three ranges are pierced by several gaps or passes, presenting opportunities for good defense, against superior numbers. The roads, both in the valleys and leading over the mountains, by the gaps, are generally good, most of them Macadamized turnpikes,[1] not excelled anywhere. The great number of roads gives easy access to all parts of the country. The entire field of operations is well wooded, springs and streams of pure, cool water abound, and there are no material obstacles, save in the mountain gaps, to hinder the movement of troops in any direction. The climate is healthy, the air invigorating, and supplies of all kinds, for men and animals, abundant.[2]

The movement of the Union army northward from Washington was initiated by the 1st Massachusetts Cavalry. This regiment had been in service in South Carolina and disembarked from steamers at Alexandria, September 2nd. Early that day Pope telegraphed Halleck from Fairfax Court House that it would be well for him to look out for his connections, as "the enemy from the beginning has been throwing his rear toward the North, and every movement shows that he means to make trouble in Maryland,"[3] whereupon orders were given that this Massachusetts regiment should move up the Potomac, watching all the fords between Great Falls and Harper's Ferry, and not a moment was to be lost in the execution of the order, as it was probable that the enemy might attempt to cross that night. Such was the confusion at Alexandria that the officers of the regiment could not be found on the 2nd and the orders were repeated on the 3rd, with the advice that it was not expected the regiment would engage the enemy, but simply watch carefully his operations and give timely notice should he appear on the Potomac above Great Falls. Three times was this order repeated on the 3rd, but not until the morning of

---

1  The "macadamized" turnpikes mentioned by Carman refer to a crushed rock road rather than the asphalt-based roads of modern times.

2  Carman's general description of the terrain and landscape of Western Maryland is very similar to Bradley T. Johnson's in *SHSP*, 12, pp. 512-14, but could also simply be taken from personal knowledge.

3  Pope's quotation is from *OR* 12, pt. 3, pp. 796-7.

the 4th did the regiment cross the Potomac by the Aqueduct Bridge and push out beyond Tennallytown, where it was halted for orders.[4]

On the evening of the 4th General Pleasonton, then in camp at Fort Albany, on the Virginia side of the Potomac, was ordered to Falls Church to ascertain, if possible, the intentions of the enemy. With the 6th United States Cavalry, Captain W. P. Sanders, and two companies of another regiment he reached the village, where he was joined by the 8th Illinois and 8th Pennsylvania Cavalry. The last two named skirmished with Munford's cavalry brigade about a mile north of the village. General J. D. Cox, commanding the Kanawha Division, at Upton's Hill, reported, early in the morning, an accumulation of evidence that the main body of the enemy had gone in the direction of Leesburg, and that the movements in his front were feints. Pleasonton came to the same conclusion and, at noon, dispatched his opinion that the Confederates were only making a show of force in his front to conceal their movement on the upper Potomac.[5]

Pleasonton was now ordered to withdraw from Falls Church and, with such forage and subsistence as could be carried on his horses, cross the Aqueduct Bridge, proceed to Tennallytown and await orders. He moved promptly with two regiments and on reaching Tennallytown received orders to move up the Potomac. Early on the 5th he was in motion, marching by way of Rockville to Darnestown, reconnoitering all the fords of the river as far north as Seneca Mills, and Chamberlain's detachment of the 1st Massachusetts, pushing ahead, encountered Fitz Hugh Lee's cavalry beyond Poolesville and came to grief, as we have seen. Exploration of the various fords south of the Seneca showed them to be unoccupied, and small parties were left to observe them, Pleasonton with his main force taking position on Muddy Branch, where it is crossed by the road from Rockville to Darnestown.[6]

---

4   Two of the orders to the regiment are found in OR 51, pt. 1, pp. 781, 783. There were only two battalions available and they and their horses were in poor condition. The commanding officers were not present initially, thus a senior captain eventually assumed command and led the unit into the field. Crownshield, *First Massachusetts Cavalry Volunteers*, pp. 68-71.

5   See Cox's report, OR 19, pt. 2, pp. 172, 176-77, 178. Again, Carman included more detail than the OR, indicating that he had knowledge from another source. For a general summary of this cavalry advance, see Pleasonton's report, *ibid.*, pp. 208-9. Pleasonton wrote only the barest of reports for September 4 to 6, 1862. The paucity of Union cavalry, compared to the Confederates, is striking at this point in the campaign. Pleasonton was relying on a few understrength regiments to not only discover the intentions of the Confederates, but also to guard the fords of the Potomac and screen the advance of the Union army. Carman does not directly mention this situation, but hints at it.

6   The placement of the cavalry is taken from Pleasonton's report, OR 19, pt. 1, pp. 208-9.

On the 5th, the 1st New York Cavalry, that had come up from Aquia Creek on the 3rd, marched through Washington and bivouacked near Rockville, reporting early next day to Pleasonton. It was immediately marched to Middlebrook and four companies were advanced to occupy Clarksburg and picket the line of the Seneca, scouting, at the same time, the country towards Hyattstown, near which place Wade Hampton's cavalry brigade was encountered. On the same day a squadron of the 1st United States Cavalry moved to Brookville and scouted to Unity, Goshen and Cracklintown, in the direction of the Baltimore and Ohio Railroad, and the 8th Illinois and 3rd Indiana pushed beyond Darnestown, picketing the roads in the direction of Poolesville and the fords of the Potomac.[7]

In every direction Stuart's cavalry pickets were encountered and from information obtained Pleasonton reported that Lee's entire army had crossed the Potomac with the evident intention of moving on Washington; Jackson by the Frederick road and another column by the road running through Poolesville and Darnestown.[8] Later in the day his information was that Jackson was to lead an advance on Baltimore, by way of Damascus, Clarksburg and Cooksville, whereupon he extended his right as far as Mechanicsville, and called for reinforcements. He had, September 6th, the 3rd Indiana and 8th Illinois in Darnestown; the 1st New York at Middlebrook; the 1st United States at Brookville and Mechanicsville, picketing and scouting the country thoroughly, from the Potomac at Seneca Mills to Cooksville, on [sic] Baltimore and Frederick turnpike. Sumner, with his own corps and that of A. S. Williams, was but a short distance in his rear.[9]

On the 7th a squadron of the 1st New York Cavalry moved from Middlebrook to reinforce the 1st United States and assist in scouting to Damascus and Cooksville. Two squadrons each of the 3rd Indiana and 8th Illinois, under command of Major George A. Chapman, of the Indiana regiment, made a dash on Poolesville and captured two cavalry videttes. On the next day Pleasonton sent Colonel John F. Farnsworth, with the 3rd Indiana and 8th Illinois regiments, and two guns of Battery M, 2nd U. S. Artillery, under Lieutenant Robert H. Chapin, to occupy Poolesville and picket the roads to Conrad's Ferry, Barnesville and the Monocacy. As Farnsworth approached Poolesville, Stuart's cavalry pickets were

---

7  *Ibid.,* pp. 208-9.

8  For Pleasonton's reports about the supposed plans of the Confederates, see *ibid.,* pt. 2, pp. 192-5.

9  The advance of the Federal infantry can be tracked in McClellan's report, *ibid.,* pt. 1, pp. 25, 38-40, and McClellan, *Own Story,* p. 550.

seen retreating on the road to Barnesville, and some of the 3rd Indiana pushed after them and soon came upon the 7th and 12th Virginia Cavalry and two guns of Munford's Brigade.[10]

Advised by the pickets of Pleasonton's advance, on the evening of the 7th, and divining his intention to occupy Poolesville, Stuart that morning, the 8th, had ordered Munford to advance from his camp, near Sugar Loaf, and drive the enemy from the place, and Munford's advance guard had barely entered the town when Farnsworth had appeared and drove it back to where Munford had drawn up to check further pursuit. Munford opened on Farnsworth with two guns of Chew's Battery; Chapin soon silenced them and a charge of the 3rd Indiana broke the 12th Virginia and sent it to the rear in some confusion, thus imperiling Chew's two guns, which were rescued by a gallant counter charge by the 7th Virginia, led by Captain S. B. Myers, that checked the Indiana men and enabled Chew to get off his guns.[11]

Munford retreated toward Barnesville, closely pursued by Farnsworth as far as Monocacy Church, where, about dark, Farnsworth was checked by the sharpshooters of the 2nd Virginia Cavalry, that had hastened from Barnesville to Munford's assistance. Munford's loss was 1 killed and 10 wounded, 8 of whom were of the 12th Virginia. Farnsworth had 1 killed and 10 wounded, the loss, with one exception, falling upon the 3rd Indiana.[12]

On the morning of the 9th Farnsworth resumed his advance, overtook, roughly handled and dislodged the 12th Virginia from position near Monocacy Church, captured its battle-flag and a few prisoners and, after a slight skirmish on the edge of Barnesville, entered that place and pursued the Virginians two miles beyond, the net result of the day's work being the capture of a battle-flag and 27 prisoners.[13] On the same day a battalion of the 1st New York Cavalry, under

10 Although Carman did not cite a source, a number of reports describe the fighting at Poolesville on September 7 & 8, 1862. For the Federal side, see Pleasonton's report, OR 19, pt. 1, pp. 208-9, and Pleasonton to Marcy, *ibid.*, 2, p. 201.

11 For the Confederates, see Stuart's report in *ibid.*, p. 815, Hampton's report, *ibid.*, p. 822, and Munford's report, *ibid.*, p. 825. Munford and Stuart cite different casualty numbers.

12 See the reports cited in the two footnotes above. Carman used each side's reports of their losses for the report of casualties, which seemed to be the most accurate.

13 The fighting at Barnesville on September 9 is related entirely from the Northern side. Confederate sources almost ignored the clash with the 12th Virginia Cavalry. Pleasonton, however, claimed the victory in his report, *ibid.*, pp. 208-9, and McClellan mentioned the fight on the 8th in his dispatches to Lincoln and Halleck, September 8 & 9, 1862, in *ibid.*, pt. 2, pp. 210, 219-20. Carman also did not include the Union advance, which was mentioned in Heros von Borke, *Memoirs of the Confederate War for Independence* (Philadelphia: J. B. Lippincott and Co., 1867), pp. 133-6, but Carman apparently did not use that source. Harsh, *Taken at the Flood*, p.

command of Major A. W. Adams, made a dash into Hyattstown and drove out some of Wade Hampton's cavalry. Hampton's men returned next day with artillery and a sharp encounter took place, the New York men being supported by a squadron of the 1st United States, under Captain M. A. Reno. Hampton's men were repulsed and the Union men fell back to Clarksburg.[14]

While Pleasonton was feeling the Confederate lines and seeking information of Lee's movements, McClellan was getting his army well in hand, supplying its needs, which were many, reorganizing the commands and providing for the defense of Washington. His corps on the Maryland side of the Potomac were moving cautiously in rear of Pleasonton and within supporting distance of him and of each other.

On the 6th the First Corps, under command of General Joseph Hooker, moved from Upton's Hill, Virginia, crossed the Potomac by the Long Bridge and marched through Washington to Leesborough. Cox's Kanawha Division moved from Upton's Hill, crossed the Potomac by the Aqueduct Bridge and, marching through Washington, went out on the Seventh Street road to the Soldiers' Home. The division was assigned to the Ninth Corps. The Sixth Corps, General William B. Franklin, moved from Alexandria Seminary, crossed the Potomac by the Long Bridge, and encamped near Georgetown. Sykes's Division, of the Fifth Corps, crossed the Potomac by the Long Bridge and took the road to Rockville. On the night of the 6th the army was thus distributed: the First Corps was at Leesborough; the Second Corps, under Sumner, and the Twelfth, under A. S. Williams, were at Rockville, and Sykes's Division of the Fifth Corps, on the march for that place. Three divisions of the Ninth Corps, under Reno, were on Meridian Hill and Cox's Division at the Soldiers' Home. Franklin, with the Sixth Corps, was between Georgetown and Tennallytown and Couch's Division of the Fourth Corps, was thrown forward to Offut's Cross Roads by the river road, thus covering that approach and watching the fords of the Potomac. Couch ultimately moved as a support to the Sixth Corps. The First and Ninth Corps constituted the right wing, under Burnside; the Second and Twelfth, under Sumner, the center; and the Sixth

---

166, is the first historian to speculate that perhaps Stuart's lapse in reporting these increasingly aggressive Union probes to his commander encouraged Lee to implement his Harpers Ferry operation in a mistaken sense of security.

14 The details of this Hyattstown skirmish may have come from James H. Stevenson, *"Boots and Saddles," A History of the First Volunteer Cavalry of the War, Known as the first New York (Lincoln) Cavalry* (Harrisburg PA: Patriot Publishing Co., 1879), p. 118. The wording is similar and confirms what Carman wrote. The skirmish is not described in any Union reports in the *OR*, or other sources searched. Hampton mentions it briefly in his report, found in *OR* 19, pt. 1, p. 822.

Corps and Couch's Division the left, under Franklin. Sykes's Division was designated as a reserve under the personal direction of McClellan.[15]

Cox's Division took the advance of the Ninth Corps, on the 7th, marching from the Soldiers' Home to Leesborough, Reno following from Meridian Hill with three divisions. The Sixth Corps moved from near Tennallytown to Rockville and was followed by Sykes's Division. The First Corps remained at Leesborough, the Second and Twelfth at Rockville, and Couch's Division at Offut's Cross Roads.

McClellan's avowed purpose of advancing from Washington was "simply to meet the necessities of the moment by frustrating Lee's invasion of the Northern States, and, when that was accomplished, to push with the utmost rapidity the work of reorganization and supply, so that a new campaign might be promptly inaugurated with the army in condition to prosecute it to a successful termination without intermission."[16]

With this purpose in view McClellan left Washington on the afternoon of September 7th, arriving at Rockville in the evening, where he established headquarters; and was joined by the Sixth Corps, which had advanced from Tennallytown. Before leaving Washington he received this dispatch from Halleck:

> I have just seen General Pleasonton's dispatch of 2.30. Until we can get better advices about the numbers of the enemy at Dranesville, I think we must be very cautious about stripping too much the forts on the Virginia side. It may be the enemy's object to draw off the mass of our forces and then attempt to attack from the Virginia side of the Potomac. Think of this. I will see you as soon as I can.[17]

Pleasonton's dispatch, referred to, was to the effect that paroled prisoners said Lee was moving on the road to Frederick, tearing up the rails on the road as he went, and that he had heard that, on the night of the 5th, the Confederates had 50,000 in the vicinity of Dranesville, that might be kept there, to cross the Potomac

---

15 The movement of the Union army from Northern Virginia to the western outskirts of Washington, and then to defensive positions guarding Washington, is in McClellan's reports, *ibid.*, pp. 25, 38. See also Jacob Cox, *Military Reminiscences of the Civil War* (New York: Charles Scribner & Sons, 1900), Chapter 13, for specific movements. Although Carman noted the "wing arrangements" for McClellan's army, formal orders creating them did not appear until September 14, and were disbanded shortly thereafter. See *OR* 19, pt. 2, pp. 290, 297. The assignments had been made earlier, as noted previously, and the written orders lagged behind.

16 The quotation from McClellan about his purpose in advancing is from McClellan, *Own Story*, p. 553.

17 Carman pasted in Halleck's dispatch to McClellan, September 7, 1862, from *OR* 19, pt. 2, p. 201.

in the direction of Rockville, after the Union advance had been engaged elsewhere; and that the enemy had already possessed themselves of Sugar Loaf Mountain, upon which they had established a signal station.[18]

In his elaborate report of August 4, 1863, McClellan says:

> At this time it was known that the mass of the rebel army had passed up the south side of the Potomac in the direction of Leesburg, and that a portion of that army had crossed into Maryland; but whether it was their intention to cross their whole force with a view to turn Washington by a flank movement down the north bank of the Potomac, to move on Baltimore, or to invade Pennsylvania, were questions which at that time we had no means of determining. This uncertainty as to the intentions of the enemy obliged me, up to the 13th of September, to march cautiously, and to advance the army in such order as continually to keep Washington and Baltimore covered, and at the same time to hold the troops well in hand, so as to be able to concentrate and follow rapidly if the enemy took the direction of Pennsylvania, or to return to the defense of Washington if, as was greatly feared by the authorities, the enemy should be merely making a feint with a small force to draw off our army, while with their main forces they stood ready to seize the first favorable opportunity to attack the capital.[19]

On the 8th the Ninth Corps advanced from Leesborough to Rockville; the Second and Twelfth Corps from Rockville to near Middlebrook, and the Sixth Corps from Rockville to near Darnestown. The First Corps remained at Leesborough; Couch's Division at Offut's Cross Roads and Sykes's at Rockville. McClellan says:

> Partly in order to move more freely and rapidly, partly in consequence of the lack of accurate information as to the exact position and intention of Lee's army, the troops advanced by three main roads; that near the Potomac by Offut's Cross Roads and the mouth of the Seneca, that by Rockville to Frederick, and that by Brooksville and Urbana to New Market. We were then in condition to act according to the development of the enemy's plans, and to concentrate rapidly in any position. If Lee threatened our left flank by moving down the river road or by crossing the Potomac at any of the fords from Coon's Ferry upward, there were enough troops on the river

---

18 The dispatch from Pleasonton, which Halleck mentions, is on *ibid.*, pp. 200-1.

19 The "elaborate report" of August 4, 1863, from which Carman pasted this paragraph into his manuscript, is found in *OR* 19, pt. 1, p. 39. McClellan wrote two reports for the *OR*, one dated October 15, 1862, and one on August 4, 1863. The second report is much more detailed and elaborate, as Carman suggested, but also contains more self-justification because it was written after McClellan had been removed from command.

road to hold him in check until the rest of the army could move over to support them; if Lee took up a position behind the Seneca, near Frederick, the whole army could be rapidly concentrated in that direction to attack him in force; if he moved upon Baltimore the entire army could rapidly be thrown in his rear and his retreat cut off; if he moved by Gettysburg or Chambersburg upon York or Carlisle we were equally in position to throw ourselves in his rear.[20]

On the 7th Halleck cautioned McClellan not to strip the defenses on the Virginia side of the Potomac; on the 8th he became satisfied that Lee was not to be feared in that quarter and suggested that McClellan should move rapidly forward to meet the enemy on the Maryland side, leaving a reserve in reach of him and Washington at the same time. To which McClellan replied that he was by no means satisfied that the enemy had crossed into Maryland in any large force; that his information was entirely too indefinite to justify definite action; that he was prepared to attack anything crossing south of the Monocacy, and to prevent any attack in force on Baltimore and at the same time cover Washington. He was ready to move in any direction, and, as soon as he found out where to strike, he would be after the enemy without an hour's delay. He did not feel sure that there was no force in front of Washington on the Virginia side of the river.[21]

During the evening he had become satisfied that Lee had crossed his entire army into Maryland, upon which he determined on a general advance for the morrow, the right wing under Burnside to Goshen and Cracklintown; the cavalry well out on the right and front; the center, under Sumner, near Middlebrook, and the left by Darnestown and Gaithersburg, the instructions being to occupy the line of the Seneca.[22]

The movement was made on the 9th as ordered. The cavalry pushed out in front, and on the right occupied Damascus and marched through Cooksville to Lisbon on the main road to Ridgeville and New Market; the Ninth Corps camped at Goshen and Cracklinton, with Hooker's First Corps in reserve at Brookville; the Second and Twelfth Corps remained at Middlebrook; the Sixth Corps at

20 Carman chose this quotation from McClellan, *Own Story*, p. 552, which provided insight into McClellan's actions. At this point in the campaign much uncertainty existed about what Lee was doing, and McClellan, in this passage, listed his options and motives. This rationale is interesting because many later authors miss this aspect of the advance of the Army of the Potomac. It also attests to Carman's thoroughness as a historian.

21 This exchange of telegrams between Halleck and McClellan, which Carman almost exactly copied, can be found in OR 19, pt. 2, pp. 201, 210-211.

22 These movements are described in *ibid.*, pp. 210-211.

Darnestown, and Couch's Division, leaving the 98th Pennsylvania at Offut's Cross Roads, marched to the mouth of Seneca Creek. The Confederate picket fell back without offering much resistance, some, who were taken prisoners reported that Stuart was at Urbana and Stonewall Jackson at New Market, indicating that a movement on Baltimore was intended, upon which McClellan dispatched Halleck that Jackson and Longstreet had almost 110,000 men of all arms near Frederick, covered by Stuart's cavalry; he was well prepared for anything except overwhelming numbers, but wanted more cavalry.[23]

The position taken by McClellan on the 9th, the ridge bordering Seneca Creek, was a defensive one. He had no intention of attacking Lee, his sole object being to interpose such a force in front of Washington as might best defend an advance from Lee at the head of overwhelming numbers.

These last dispatches to Halleck shows McClellan's serious defect as a commander in overestimating the numbers of the enemy. It was so in West Virginia in 1861, so on the Peninsula, in the spring and summer of 1862, and so on the Maryland campaign from the day he set out from Washington to the day that Lee's army, much inferior in numbers, recrossed the Potomac. At Rich Mountain he was convinced that he was greatly outnumbered, while in front of Washington in August 1861, he thought the enemy had three or four times his own force, and for many days was very apprehensive that Beauregard would attack Washington or cross into Maryland with very superior numbers; on the Peninsula he constantly contended that the Confederates outnumbered him two to one, his corps commanders accepted the estimate, and the Army of the Potomac was taught implicitly to believe the fiction. Nor was the fiction dispelled when Lee crossed into Maryland, McClellan reporting his belief that he had 120,000 men. It was a saying of Napoleon that the general who is ignorant of his enemy's strength and dispositions is ignorant of his trade. Judged by this standard, McClellan was not a great general.[24]

---

23 No source found confirms the detachment of the 98th Pennsylvania, which may have been temporary because the regiment was present on the march to Sharpsburg. Halleck's telegram and the reply from McClellan about needing more cavalry are in *ibid.*, p. 219. His troop dispositions are, for the most part, taken from *ibid.*, p. 220, but more information was added by Carman, perhaps taken from Palfrey, *The Antietam and Fredericksburg,* p. 13.

24 The rather severe judgment of McClellan made by Carman seems rooted more in 1890s historiography than fact, despite the many telegrams and messages and the quote from McClellan, *Own Story,* p. 9, which Carman used in the manuscript. McClellan's communication with Lincoln and Halleck, as well as his reports and postwar memoirs, make it clear that he was offensive-minded from the time he left Washington. He also received a communication from Halleck reprimanding him for moving too fast and leaving Washington uncovered. See *OR 19,*

We have noted General Lee's complaint of the prevalence of straggling from the ranks of the Army of Northern Virginia; the evil prevailed to a still greater extent in the Army of the Potomac. When it crossed from Virginia into Maryland many remained behind at Alexandria; when it moved from Washington many remained in the city or went to their homes and the country through which the march was made was overrun by stragglers. Halleck expressed the opinion that the straggling and demoralization was caused by the incapacity of officers, the want of proper discipline, and the action of Congress in the abolition and confiscation measures, which were very distasteful to the army of the West, and, as he understood, to the Army of the Potomac. There were many men belonging to the army that could not from absolute want of muscular tone follow its marches. Men never known to fall behind, upon previous marches, did so in Maryland, and what prevailed in the ranks of the old regiments to a great extent, prevailed to a like extent in the more than twenty new regiments that joined the army at Washington. The straggling was not confined to those who had lost muscular tone by hard service, nor to those who were dissatisfied with political ideas of the administration and Congress, but affected the entire organization. While some of the divisions and brigades lost a large fraction of their numbers, in their daily marches, falling so far

---

pt. 2, pp. 211, 216; *ibid.*, pt. 1, pp. 25-7, 39-41; and McClellan, *Own Story*, p. 553. This section of *Own Story* was compiled by McClellan's literary executor after his death. See Stephen Sears, *George B. McClellan, The Young Napoleon* (New York: Ticknor and Fields, 1988), pp. 403-06. The issue raised by Carman of McClellan's tendency to overestimate the numbers of the enemy was reported by the press and historians even while McClellan was in command. It is beyond the scope of these notes to investigate this issue in depth, but two comments may provide some understanding of the issue. First, the intelligence gathering system for army commanders in the Civil War was primitive, and for McClellan in this campaign, practically non-existent. McClellan received information from his cavalry, Confederate deserters, and from civilian observers of Lee's army. Estimates varied from 75,000 (General Wool, OR 19, pt. 2, pp. 214-5), to 200,000 (Governor Curtin, *ibid.*, p. 248). McClellan used the not unreasonable estimate of 120,000 as his best assessment, *ibid.*, p. 254. We know now that he was wrong, but not nearly as wrong as Carman suggested. For more on this, see Harsh, *Sounding the Shallows*, p. 138. Second, overestimation of the enemy was not a flaw limited to George McClellan. Virtually every commander in the Civil War over-reported enemy strength. For instance, Lee's September 3 letter to President Davis mentions "60,000 new levies posted in Washington," when in truth the number was closer to 30,000. Using the standard Carman adopted from Napoleon, there were very few great generals. The actual quote used by Carman has not been found after a search of many works on Napoleonic quotations. A reference in Elizabeth Longford, *Wellington: Pillar of the State*, 2 Vols. (New York: Harper and Row, 1969-1972), 2, states that the story is apocryphal, and may have originated with Julius Caesar in the Gallic Wars. Carmen ended this paragraph with these words: "When King Joseph wrote to Napoleon that he could not ascertain the position and strength of the enemy's army, the Emperor replied: 'Attack him and you will find out.'"

behind as to appear more numerous on the roadside than the marching column, there were other brigades and divisions in which the evil was almost unknown.

So great was the evil that on the 9th, before the army had moved far from Washington, McClellan issued stringent orders designed to abate it. He characterized the evil as habitually associated with cowardice, marauding and theft, and laid down stringent rules for numerous roll calls during a march, and that none should be allowed to leave the ranks save for necessary purposes or extenuating causes.

He observed that the evil was viewed without the least apparent concern by the officers of both high and low grades, and issued a circular calling attention to the fact of the frequent absence from their commands while in camp and from their columns on the march of superior officers; laxities that should be remedied. Inattention and carelessness on the part of those high in rank had been one futile source of the straggling and want of discipline then obtaining in the various camps. Attention was called to the fact that the safety of the country depended upon what the Army of the Potomac should achieve in the campaign; it could not be successful if its soldiers were one-half skulking to the rear, while the brunt of battle was borne by the other half, and its officer's inattention to observe and correct the grossest evils which were daily occurring under their eyes. He entreated all general officers to lend every energy to the eradication of the evil, and felt assured that their united determination could break up the practice in a single week.[25]

It was not broken up in a week, the orders were but partially and indifferently observed, and the army moved slowly to the front, leaving behind a swarm of stragglers, who did more damage to the property of friendly citizens than did the Confederates. So, while a host of Lee's stragglers were wandering around in Virginia, a larger number of McClellan's were wandering over Maryland.

Late in the evening of the 9th Burnside had his scouts at Ridgeville, within three miles of New Market, and obtained information that the main Confederate force was still at Frederick, but that Jackson with a considerable body was at New

---

25 The issue of Union stragglers is one seldom addressed in the Maryland campaign. Carman cited several factors contributing to the problem of stragglers, some of which seem to come from his personal experience. His diary in the New Jersey Historical Society collection recorded the dwindling numbers in his own regiment on the march from Washington, DC. to Frederick, Maryland. Another piece of evidence that would have come to his attention was an eloquent plea from his brigade commander Gen. S. W. Crawford, who decried the combat losses and recent marches as debilitating to his brigade. See OR 19, pt. 2, pp. 223-5. Also, notice that Carman borrowed the wording of McClellan's circular of September 9, 1862. Beginning with the phrase "safety of the country," through "in a single week," the words are copied directly from *ibid.*, p. 225. A strongly worded General Order #155 was published to correct the "evil" of straggling. See *ibid.*, pp. 226-7.

Market, threatening an advance on Baltimore; upon which McClellan ordered Burnside to push a reconnaissance beyond Ridgeville, using cavalry and artillery for that purpose, and should the enemy make any demonstration toward Baltimore, he was to allow him to get the columns well in motion, and then attack him vigorously on the flank; McClellan assuring him of his support with everything available.[26]

McClellan's intentions for the 10th were to occupy Ridgeville with a sufficient force to check an advance of the Confederates toward Baltimore; in view of this, early in the morning, the army was ordered to advance to the line of Parr's Ridge and along it from Ridgeville, through Damascus and Clarksburg, the extreme left to move to Poolesville and Barnesville, in the same high ridge. As these movements were "such as to uncover Washington slightly in the direction of Baltimore," McClellan ordered Banks, who had been left in command at Washington, to put his troops and works on the Maryland side of the Potomac in good position for defense.[27]

The movement began early in the morning; Cox's Division had gone but one mile on the road from Goshen to Ridgeville; Hooker's First Corps but a short distance on the road from Brookville to Poplar Springs and Cooksville; the Second Corps to within three miles of Clarksburg and the Twelfth to within two miles of Damascus, when the entire movement on the right and center was suspended, because McClellan received information that the mass of the enemy was still at Frederick, and he wished to verify this information by further reconnaissance.[28] He would not press his advance until satisfied whether the enemy intended to move toward Baltimore or Washington—in fact, the whole Confederate army was then on its "rollicking march" from Frederick to Harper's Ferry and Hagerstown.

No further advance was made by the right and center that day: the First Corps remained near Brookville; the Ninth Corps at Goshen, Seneca Ridge and Cracklinton, with an advance guard, the 30th Ohio and a section of McMullin's battery-at Damascus; the Second Corps was halted within three miles of Clarksburg and the Twelfth Corps about two miles of Damascus. Sykes's Division remained at Rockville. On the left the Sixth Corps, preceded by the 6th United States Cavalry,

---

26 Although not cited, Carman probably referred to Burnside to McClellan, September 9, 1862, 8:00 p.m., found in *OR* 19, pt. 2, pp. 222-3. The exact reply from McClellan is not found in the *OR*, but its intent can be discerned from McClellan's telegram to Lincoln, September 10, 1862, in *ibid.*, p. 233, and his order to Burnside the same day, *ibid.*, p. 239.

27 The concern for the defense of Washington is reflected in the order quoted by Carman. It was sent at 3:30 a.m. on September 10 to Banks, and is found in *OR* 19, pt. 2, p. 234.

28 The advance of the Ninth Corps and the subsequent suspension of the order to advance are found in *ibid.*, pp. 239-40.

pushed forward from Darnestown to Barnesville, covering the road from the mouth of the Monocacy to Rockville, and in position to connect with and support the center, should it become necessary, to force the line of the Monocacy. Couch's Division leaving the 7th Massachusetts at the mouth of the Seneca, marched to Poolesville, Cochrane's Brigade being advanced to Bell's Cross Roads, a short distance north of the town, while the 55th New York of Howe's Brigade, was sent to the mouth of the Monocacy, to support the 1st Massachusetts Cavalry in preventing the destruction of the aqueduct at that point.[29]

About three miles north of Barnesville, Sugar Loaf Mountain rises, in the shape indicated by its name, from the Monocacy Valley, to a height of 1281 feet above the level of the sea and about 750 feet above the general level of the surrounding country. It commands a view of the entire country east of Catoctin Mountains, watered by the Monocacy and looks far into Virginia, on the west. From its summit can be seen Frederick and the road over the Catoctin to Middletown, and no body of troops could move in any direction without being plainly seen and its numbers correctly determined. General Banks had early recognized its importance as a signal station and used it for that purpose. From one of his signal parties came the first authentic news that Lee had crossed the Potomac into Maryland, and one of the first acts of the Confederates in entering Maryland was to possess themselves of the mountain and establish a signal party on it.[30]

McClellan recognized the importance of its possession and, on the morning of September 9th, called Pleasonton's attention to the fact that, as a signal station, it was of great value, not only to him, but to the enemy, and should be taken, if not incurring too much risk. Late in the day McClellan received information that Pleasonton had carried Barnesville and the Sugar Loaf, but, early on the morning of the 10th, found that, as to Sugar Loaf, he had been wrongly informed, upon which he renewed his order to take it.[31]

---

29 The movements of the Union Corps are found in *ibid.*, pp. 238-9. The 55th New York was detached from Howe's brigade, and did not rejoin it. Second Corps movements are found in *ibid.*, p. 241. See also *ibid.*, pt. 1, pp. 39-41.

30 The importance of capturing Sugar Loaf Mountain is mentioned in *ibid.*, p. 238; Moore, *Rebellion Record*, 5, Diary, p. 77, mentions Sanders and the 6th U.S. Cavalry in their attempt to capture the signal tower. The message from the signal officer for Banks is found in *OR* 19, pt. 2, p. 184.

31 The fight for Sugar Loaf Mountain can be followed in Pleasonton's report, *ibid.*, pt. 1, p. 209, and in *ibid.*, pt. 2, pp. 258, and *ibid.*, 51, pt. 1, p. 801. McClellan's orders to Pleasonton and Franklin are in *ibid.*, pp. 802-3, 810-12. For a more colorful account that Carman may have used, see Abner Hard, *History of the Eight Illinois Cavalry Regiment* (Aurora: n.p., 1868), pp. 171-3.

Colonel Thomas T. Munford's cavalry brigade covered the right of the Confederate line and was specially charged with the defense of Sugar Loaf. The brigade was greatly reduced by detachments for service elsewhere; the 6th Virginia Regiment and the 17th Virginia Battalion had been left in Virginia, and, on the morning of the 10th, the 7th Virginia accompanied Jackson on his march to Harper's Ferry. This left the 2nd and 12th Virginia regiments, about 200 men each, and Chew's Virginia battery, in all about 500 men, with four guns. The 2nd Virginia, under Lieutenant Colonel J. S. Burks, was in position, covered by rail barricades, at the cross-roads, south-east of the base of the mountain, and the 12th Virginia, under Colonel A. W. Harman, on its right and rear.

In the early fore-noon of the 10th Captain William P. Sanders, 6th United States Cavalry, with a small cavalry force and two guns, attempted to dislodge the 2nd Virginia from its position, but found it too strongly posted to be driven by the force at his disposal and after the loss of a man killed and four wounded, withdrew as soon as the Sixth Corps came up and took position at Barnesville.[32] During the engagement the 9th Virginia Cavalry of Fitz Hugh Lee's Brigade came to Munford's assistance; it did not become engaged, and was held in reserve.

Pleasonton reported to McClellan that he had made three attempts to dislodge the enemy, that they had a very strong position and evidently intended to hold it, but that Franklin held an opposite opinion.[33]

McClellan was greatly disappointed and ordered Franklin to support Pleasonton with a brigade of infantry, and, at noon, Couch, who was at Poolesville, was directed to aid him with a brigade and, if necessary, with his entire division, and to assume charge of the movement. An hour later Couch was ordered to hasten the movement and advised that the mountain must be taken if it should require all of his available command and that of Franklin's also. Three urgent messages were sent to Pleasonton, impressing upon him the great importance of carrying the position

---

32 Pleasonton's report, OR 19, pt. 2, p. 258, lists one killed and three wounded, and in *ibid.*, 238, he claimed one man mortally wounded, which may account for the discrepancy in casualties. Confederate sources are nearly silent about the fight, and some of the details that Carman related are not in official sources. Jeb Stuart, in his report, says simply says the crossroads was held for three days. *Ibid.*, pt. 1, p. 815. The additional information came from several letters to Carman from Thomas Munford, found in NYPL, Correspondence Files, Munford Letters, December 16 and 19, 1894, Box 2, Folder 2, April 7, 1896, Box 2, Folder 3, and June 11 and 20, 1899, Box 2, Folder 5. Munford also referred Carman to Major Heros von Borcke's book that described the fight as a "sharp but unimportant affair." von Borke, *Memoirs of the Confederate War for Independence*, p. 137. Carman confused the name of Jesse Spinner Burks, who was out of the Confederate army by this campaign, and never served in the cavalry. Carman obviously meant his brother, R. H. Burks.

33 Pleasonton to Marcy, OR 19, pt. 2, p. 238.

and informing him that both Couch and Franklin had ordered to give him all the support required. At 3 p. m., Franklin was ordered to take control of the movement and accomplish the important object, if it could be done without the risk of losing his command.[34]

Not withstanding these urgent orders to Pleasonton, Couch and Franklin, no serious effort was made to carry Sugar Loaf on the 10th. Had Pleasonton put more force and persistence into his attack and carried the mountain, on the morning of the 10th, his lookout, from its summit, could have seen, on that clear, bright day, the long columns of Jackson, Longstreet, D. H. Hill and McLaws, as they marched out of Frederick and over the Catoctin, and Walker's division would have been seen marching from the mouth of the Monocacy northward to Point of Rocks and the mystery of Lee's whereabouts would have been solved. Or had one of the nine brigades of infantry supported Pleasonton on the afternoon of the 10th, the less than 800 cavalry at Munford's disposal could have been driven away before night and McClellan would have known the movements of his enemy and could have made dispositions for a rapid advance on the morrow.[35]

At 11.15 p. m. Franklin was ordered to put himself in communication with Sumner at Clarksburg and to carry Sugar Loaf if possible, but, if the enemy appeared too strong, he was authorized to await the result of Sumner's advance on Hyattstown and was told that "the earlier we gain the Sugar Loaf the better." After midnight the order was repeated and Franklin was advised that Sumner had been directed to co-operate with him.[36]

Partly, if not wholly, owing to the failure to carry Sugar Loaf Mountain, on the 10th McClellan's movements on the 11th were extremely cautious. Sumner, in the center, was directed to occupy Clarksburg and Damascus, as soon after daylight as possible; Burnside, on the right, was ordered to push a strong reconnaissance

---

34  These orders can be found in OR pt. 2, p. 238, and *ibid.*, 51, pt. 1, p. 807.

35  The weather on September 10, 1862, which Carman described as a "clear, bright day," was recorded at the Frederick Weather Station as 77 degrees at 2:00 p.m., as mostly cloudy in the morning, giving way to light clouds in the afternoon. These reports are from the Weather Bureau Records in the National Archives, as cited in Harsh, *Sounding The Shallows*, p. 12. Carman was perhaps exaggerating the clarity of the skies, or perhaps his memory was flawed. Thus, observing Confederate movements might have been a problem. Carman departed from being a historian here to speculate about what could have happened had Sugar Loaf been captured when McClellan had desired.

36  McClellan to Marcy, September 10, 1862, is in OR 19, pt. 2, p. 238, and Marcy to Franklin is in *ibid.*, 51, pt. 1, p. 815. McClellan's communication with Pleasonton and Franklin is found on *ibid.*, pp. 803-5, 807-8, 814-5, and shows his positive orders to them to carry Sugar Loaf Mountain. These movements are in keeping with his stated intent, found in *ibid.*, pp. 25-6. This contrasts with Carman's comments about McClellan's defensive posture (see note 24).

across the Frederick and Baltimore Turnpike and along the Baltimore and Ohio Railroad toward New Market, and, if he learned that the enemy had moved toward Hagerstown, to press on rapidly to Frederick, keeping his troops constantly ready to meet the enemy in force, but he was not to occupy New Market at the expense of an engagement. A corresponding movement was ordered on the left. These movements were made as ordered; in the center, the Second Corps moved three miles and occupied Clarksburg, and the Twelfth Corps marched two miles to Damascus; on the right, the Ninth Corps, under Reno, occupied Ridgeville and New Market, Reynolds' Division of the First Corps, marched from Brookville, by way of Cooksville and Lisbon to Poplar Springs; Hatch's Division to Lisbon, and Ricketts to Cooksville. Sykes's Division advanced from Rockville to Middlebrook. While these cautious and deliberate movements were made in the center and on the right, on the morning of the 11th, the left was held back, but, after the occupation of Damascus by the Twelfth Corps and Clarksburg by the Second, a movement was made on the left, and, in the afternoon, Farnsworth's Brigade of cavalry, supported by Hancock's infantry brigade of the Sixth Corps, dislodged Munford's rear guard from Sugar Loaf Mountain, which retired by the Buckeystown road in the direction of Frederick, bivouacking three miles from the last named place, the 9th Virginia Cavalry, pushing on through Urbana to New Market, where it rejoined its brigade. With the exception of Hancock's Brigade, the Sixth Corps remained at Barnesville and Couch at Poolesville; the 23rd Pennsylvania, the 1st New York Cavalry and a section of artillery relieved the 55th New York at the mouth of the Monocacy.[37]

At noon McClellan consulted Franklin as to the propriety of throwing a column over the Monocacy, at its mouth, to cut off Lee's retreat, but, information received shortly thereafter, by Cox at Ridgeville and Hooker at Cooksville, being to the effect that Lee had abandoned Frederick and was moving northward, which information was confirmed by dispatches received from Governor Curtin of Pennsylvania, that Jackson's command had already reached Hagerstown with the evident intention of moving into Pennsylvania, orders were given for a rapid movement on Frederick; the Ninth Corps, under Reno, by the direct road from New Market, the First Corps by way of Ridgeville and New Market, following

---

37 The movements described here for the various Union corps can be traced on the chart in McClellan's report, *ibid.*, 19, pt. 1, pp. 39-40. The information in *ibid.*, pt. 2, p. 255, and Pleasonton's 3:35 p.m. message of September 11, 1862, *ibid.*, p. 258, and *ibid.*, 51, pt. 1, p. 817, confirm the replacement of the troops at the mouth of the Monocacy, but not the specific regiments. However, in Special Order #252, McClellan, on September 10, 1862, ordered the 55th New York to proceed to Washington due to the regiment's "demoralized condition." *Ibid.*, 19, pt. 2, p. 242. Carman seemed to have overlooked this.

Reno, and a corresponding movement of all the troops in center and on the left in the direction of Urbana.[38]

McClellan reported up to this time his movements were for the purpose of feeling the enemy, "to compel him to develop his intentions, at the same time the troops were in position ready to cover Baltimore or Washington, to attack him should he hold the line of the Monocacy, or to follow him into Pennsylvania if necessary."[39]

Cautious and deliberate as was McClellan's advance there were reasons for it, beyond Halleck's warnings, in the condition of the transportation and artillery, the vigilance and superb handling of the Confederate cavalry and consequent ignorance of the Confederate movements.

The Quarter Masters [sic] Department was sadly disorganized. The trains of the Army of the Potomac, brought from the Peninsula, were not promptly disembarked, and when disembarked were not properly distributed to the divisions to which they belonged. The Army of Virginia had lost much of its transportation and there was not that systematic and perfect organization that, in general, characterized the conduct of the Quarter Masters service in the Army of the Potomac. In fact no information could be obtained as to the number of wagons belonging to that army, nor what Quarter Masters were on duty. In consequence, when the troops of both armies moved from Washington, there was some confusion and the trains were slow in coming up, and some brigades and divisions suffered accordingly; but, under the energetic and intelligent direction of Rufus Ingalls, aided by his corps and division chiefs, order was brought out of chaos, there was a uniform and efficient system and good service. This was done on the march and by the time the army reached Frederick it was well supplied, though its transportation was less than the usual allowance.[40]

The artillery was much disorganized. A number of batteries of the reserve were separated from their command, and attached to troops not only of the Army of the Potomac, but to those of the Army of Virginia. General Henry J. Hunt, who was

---

38 Curtin's dispatches about Jackson's march are in *ibid.*, 19, pt. 2, pp. 267-69. Curtin also reported the Confederate strength as "not less than 120,000 with a large amount of artillery."

39 The quotation about the intentions of McClellan was stated in his report, *ibid.*, pt. 1, pp. 25-26, and the wording about crossing the Monocacy is found in *ibid.*, 51, pt. 1, pp. 815-6.

40 Carman now reversed his course and offered several reasons, both tactical and logistical, for the "cautious and deliberate" advance of McClellan's army. He paraphrased a long report from Lt. Col. Rufus Ingalls, Chief Quartermaster of the Army of the Potomac, where the chaotic condition of supplying the newly amalgamated army is outlined. See *ibid.*, 19, pt. 2, p. 235. Also see Ingalls's report of the campaign, *ibid.*, 19, pt. 1, pp. 94-96.

designated chief of this arm of the service on September 5th, as the army was entering Maryland, was compelled to obtain on the roads the names and condition of the batteries and the troops to which they were attached. Not only were the batteries of the Army of the Potomac, brought from the Peninsula, dispersed and serving with other divisions than their own, but he had no knowledge of the artillery of the corps that had joined from the other armies, other than he could pick up on the road. Many had not been refitted since the August campaign under Pope; some had lost more or less guns; others were deficient in men and horses, and a number were wholly unservicable from all these causes combined.

Hunt was an energetic and efficient chief and threw his whole self into the work assigned him. The first measures were directed to procuring supplies of ammunition of which several hundred wagon-loads were ordered from the arsenal at Washington and reached the army at various points on the advance. Batteries were supplied from the Artillery Reserve to the corps and divisions deficient in guns. Horses were taken from baggage trains and men temporarily detached from the infantry, and by the time the artillery reached the Antietam it was, all things considered, in very good condition. Like the rest of the army, the artillery may be said to have been organized on the march and in the intervals of conflict.[41]

The Confederate cavalry completely masked Lee's movements. It occupied every avenue of approach and resisted every attempt to drive it. From the Potomac on its right to the Baltimore and Ohio Railroad on the left it covered Lee's entire front and no scout could penetrate it, consequently there was want of reliable information and McClellan knew neither the strength, position, nor purpose of his adversary.

Rumors of the most conflicting character came to him hourly, upon which he and his lieutenants built theories of the most plausible and irreconcilable kind. While a movement on Baltimore was considered entirely too hazardous, it was nevertheless borne in mind that Lee and his able lieutenants were prone to make hazardous movements with great success. Lee's masterly movements in front of Richmond by which McClellan had been driven to the James River were keenly remembered and Jackson's movement upon Manassas, in defiance of all ordinary rules of strategy, was not forgotten. There was nothing regarded as impossible to the Confederate leaders, who were men of military genius, quick to win campaigns by means not laid down in the art of war, rather than suffer defeat by following

---

41 Carman also reviewed the difficulties of Col. Henry J. Hunt, the chief of artillery, Army of the Potomac, in organizing, supplying and equipping his command while on the march. Like Ingalls, Hunt wrote about the tremendous task of providing an effective artillery force for the army. See his report, *ibid.*, p. 205. Again, Carman used some of Hunt's wording.

systems laid down in the books. It is true that the Union army had able generals, but they were not the equals of the Confederate chiefs in singleness of purpose, fertile resource, and swiftness of execution. It is not venturing too much to assert that McClellan felt this, therefore we say that there were reasons for his deliberate advance.[42]

Beyond the necessity for a reorganization of the artillery and the supply department, and the ignorance of Lee's movements, which were so effectually screened by Stuart's cavalry, it should be borne in mind that the question of relieving Harper's Ferry was an embarrassing one, giving some occasion for delay; and it should also be borne in mind that the orders and suggestions of Halleck were confusing, at times contradictory and unintelligible, and not easy to obey. McClellan's movements would have been much more rapid had he been not so tied to the telegraph wire that led from Halleck's office in Washington. Yet we see no good reason why he might not have advanced to the Monocacy as early as the 10th.

When McClellan took command in the field he was careful to leave in the defenses of Washington a force sufficient to insure its safety and quiet the fears of the administration. He had not forgotten his experience, earlier in the year, when he was called to account for leaving, what others thought to be, an insufficient force on the Virginia side of the Potomac. He had not forgotten how his army had been sliced off by divisions and corps to rectify the errors attributed to him, or to enlarge the commands of aspiring rivals, so, when he left Washington, September 7th, it was with the intention to leave intact those troops that he had assigned to the defense of the capital. Nor had he asked for the troops under General Wool—in whose department he was now operating—including the garrison in Harper's Ferry and detachments at Baltimore and at other points in Maryland. He had now come to the point where he thought he needed more men. His information led him to believe that Lee had not less than 120,000 men and was intent on giving battle, so, abandoning his purpose to ask no more men from the defenses of Washington, at noon of the 11th he telegraphed Halleck to order Peck's Division, upon it arrival from the Peninsula, to move at once to Rockville, and asked that one or two of the

---

42 Carman was quite complimentary about the effectiveness of the Confederate cavalry in masking Lee's movements, probably overly so. Most authors have repeated Carman's assessment, although Harsh, *Taken at the Flood*, pp. 230-1, 205, 208, 275-6, 278, calls into question this rosy view of Stuart's achievements. For example, Stuart evidently did not notify Lee of the proximity of Federal cavalry on the night of September 8, when an attack interrupted Stuart's "Sabers and Roses" dance at Urbana. See von Borke, *Memoirs of the Confederate War for Independence*, pp. 133-6. Lee issued Special Orders #191 the following day, splitting his army into five parts. If he in fact knew how close the Union army was to his own, it was a bold move even for Lee.

three corps on the Potomac, opposite Washington, be sent him.[43] In the following elaborate communication he sums up the situation and advises that Colonel Miles, at Harper's Ferry, be ordered to join him.

HEADQUARTERS,
Camp near Rockville, Md., September 11, 1862. (Received 6 p.m.)
Maj. Gen. H. W. HALLECK, General-in- Chief:

GENERAL: At the time this army moved from Washington, it was not known what the intentions of the rebels were in placing their forces on this side of the Potomac. It might have been a feint to draw away our troops from Washington, for the purpose of throwing their main army into the city as soon as we were out of the way, or it might have been supposed to be precisely what they are now doing. In view of this uncertain condition of things, I left what I conceived to be a sufficient force to defend the city against any army they could bring against it from the Virginia side of the Potomac. This uncertainty, in my judgment, exists no longer. All the evidence that has been accumulated from various sources since we left Washington goes to prove most conclusively that almost the entire rebel army in Virginia, amounting to not less than 120,000 men, is in the vicinity of Frederick City. These troops, for the most part, consist of their oldest regiments, and are commanded by their best generals. Several brigades joined them yesterday, direct from Richmond, two deserters from which say that they saw no other troops between Richmond and Leesburg. Everything seems to indicate that they intend to hazard all upon the issue of the coming battle. They are probably aware that their forces are numerically superior to ours by at least 25 per cent. This, with the prestige of their recent successes, will, without doubt, inspire them with a confidence which will cause them to fight well. The momentous consequences involved in the struggle of the next few days impels me, at the risk of being considered slow and overcautious, to most earnestly recommend that every available man be at once added to this army.

I believe this army fully appreciates the importance of a victory at this time, and will fight well; but the result of a general battle, with such odds as the enemy now appears to have against us, might, to say the least, be doubtful; and if we should be defeated the consequences to the country would be disastrous in the extreme. Under

---

43 Carman resumed his critique of McClellan's advance, citing the factors previously mentioned as sufficient to justify its pace, then suggested McClellan should have moved faster. In other words, he contradicted himself. McClellan indicated in his 1863 report how intrusive the telegraphic messages from Halleck and others were to his plans. A reading of the various messages in OR 19, pt. 2, sheds light on this point. The requests for Peck's and other troops are found in *ibid.*, p. 253.

these circumstances, I would recommend that one or two of the three army corps now on the Potomac, opposite Washington, be at once withdrawn and sent to re-enforce this army. I would also advise that the force of Colonel Miles, at Harper's Ferry, where it can be of but little use, and is continually exposed to be cut off by the enemy, be immediately ordered here. This would add about 25,000 old troops to our present force, and would greatly strengthen us.

If there are any rebel forces remaining on the other side of the Potomac, they must be so few that the troops left in the forts, after the two corps shall have been withdrawn, will be sufficient to check them; and, with the large cavalry force now on that side kept well out in front to give warning of the distant approach of any very large army, a part of this army might be sent back within the intrenchments to assist in repelling an attack. But even if Washington should be taken while these armies are confronting each other, this would not, in my judgment, bear comparison with the ruin and disaster which would follow a signal defeat of this army. If we should be successful in conquering the gigantic rebel army before us, we would have no difficulty in recovering it. On the other hand, should their force prove sufficiently powerful to defeat us, would all the forces now around Washington be sufficient to prevent such a victorious army from carrying the works on this side of the Potomac, after they are uncovered by our army? I think not.

From the moment the rebels commenced the policy of concentrating their forces, and with their large masses of troops operating against our scattered forces, they have been successful. They are undoubtedly pursuing the same now, and are prepared to take advantage of any division of our troops in future. I, therefore, most respectfully, but strenuously, urge upon you the absolute necessity, at this critical juncture, of uniting all our disposable forces. Every other consideration should yield to this, and if we defeat the army now arrayed before us, the rebellion is crushed, for I do not believe they can organize another army. But if we should be so unfortunate as to meet with defeat, our country is at their mercy.

Very respectfully, your obedient servant,

GEO. B. McCLELLAN,
Major-general.[44]

---

44 Carman pasted the clipping of the entire McClellan letter to Halleck dated September 11, 1862, from *ibid.*, pp. 254-5. In it, McClellan made some remarkable statements that caused concern in Washington. The fact that he considered losing Washington secondary to the defeat of his army may have made sense from a military point of view, but demonstrated his lack of political acumen. Likewise, the abandonment of Harpers Ferry and transfer of Miles's troops made sense militarily but, as events proved, was a disaster politically.

To McClellan's request of Peck's Division Halleck replied, within an hour, that it would not arrive from the Peninsula for some days, but that Weber's Brigade of the Seventh Corps, just arrived from Suffolk, Virginia, would be sent forward as soon as it could get transportation, and made this suggestion: "Why not order forward Porter's corps or Sigel's? If the main force of the enemy is in your front, more troops can be spared from here." McClellan was quick to act on this suggestion and sent this dispatch to Halleck at 3.45 p. m., September 11th:

> Please send forward all the troops you can spare from Washington, particularly Porter's, Heintzelman's, Sigel's, and all the other old troops. Please send them to Brookville, via Leesborough, as soon as possible. General Banks reports 72,000 troops in and about Washington. If the enemy has left for Pennsylvania, I will follow him rapidly.[45]

Halleck replied that Porter would be on the march next day to join him, and President Lincoln dispatched September 11, 6 p. m.: "This is explanatory. If Porter, Heintzelman, and Sigel were sent you, it would sweep everything from the other side of the river, because the new troops have been distributed among them, as I understand. Porter reports himself 21,000 strong, which can only be by the addition of new troops. He is ordered to-night to join you as quickly as possible. I am for sending you all that can be spared, and I hope others can follow Porter very soon."[46] Porter's two divisions, Morell's and Humphreys', were put in motion; Morell joined McClellan before the battle of Antietam, Humphreys the day after.

Early on the 11th, McClellan had sent this dispatch to Halleck:

> Camp near Rockville, September 11, 1862, 9.45 a. M.
>
> Colonel Miles is at or near Harper's Ferry, as I understand, with 9,000 troops. He can do nothing where he is, but could be of great service if ordered to join me. I suggest that he be ordered to join me by the most practicable route.

To this Halleck would not consent, he would not retire Miles from Harper's Ferry, nor would he permit his transfer to McClellan's command until the forward march of the army opened communications with him. He replied to McClellan,

---

45  The offer by Halleck of Weber's brigade is found in *ibid.*, pp. 253; for Halleck's reply, quoted here, see *ibid.*, pp. 253-4.

46  For Halleck's promise of Porter's corps, see *ibid.*, pt. 2, p. 255; Lincoln's dispatch is in *ibid.*, pp. 253-4.

September 11th: "There is no way for Colonel Miles to join you at present. His only chance is to defend his works till you can open communications with him. When you do so, he will be subject to your orders."[47]

Had Halleck, at this time, acceded to McClellan's request and placed Miles under his command, this history would not be called upon to narrate the fall of Harper's Ferry and the loss of an army. Miles would have had orders to abandon the place and join McClellan in the field; failing in that he would have been ordered to concentrate everything on Maryland Heights, fortify and hold out to the last, and he could have defied all efforts of the Confederates to dislodge him until relieved by the advance of McClellan. But it was not to be.[48]

The general advance ordered by McClellan, for the 12th, was not made with the spirit demanded. Early in the day the 6th New York Cavalry, Colonel Thomas C. Devin, attached temporarily to the Ninth Corps, was sent from New Market, off to the right to investigate the truth of reports that the enemy's cavalry were north of the column. Reno, with the advance of the Ninth Corps, moving directly from New Market, arrived at the Monocacy Bridge in the afternoon and Cox's Division was ordered to carry it. The bridge was defended by two squadrons of Wade Hampton's cavalry and a section of artillery. Cox brought up a battery and engaged the Confederate guns, while a regiment of infantry forced the cavalry back from the bridge, a regiment crossing the river by a ford a quarter of a mile to the right. As Cox had the advantage of position opposition was soon overcome and the bridge carried and crossed. Moor's Brigade, in the advance, was deployed on the right and left of the road, and Scammon deployed in second line, with the 11th Ohio in column in the road.[49]

We turn to the Confederates. When Lee marched from Frederick, on the 10th, Stuart's cavalry was directed to remain south of the Monocacy to cover his

---

47 McClellan's request to Halleck is in his report as Carman cited it. McClellan's report says this dispatch was on the morning of September 10, but the compiler of the *OR* says it was September 11, according to files of Headquarters of the Army. Halleck's response is on the same page, *OR* 19, pt. 1, p. 43. The reply from Halleck denying the request for Miles's troops is taken from the testimony in the Record of the Harpers Ferry Military Commission investigating the surrender of that place, *ibid.*, pt. 1, p. 758.

48 Carman took a position sympathetic to McClellan's view on the issue of evacuating Harpers Ferry. Carman was essentially pondering a hypothetical situation here, which is always dangerous.

49 Carman's statements about sending off the 6th New York Cavalry, and Reno leading the advance to the bridge, are mentioned in Cox, *Military Reminiscences*, Chapter 13. Cox does not mention the specific regiment, but Carman filled it in. The 6th New York Cavalry was attached to Cox's division. The account of the Union troops' attack into Frederick is from Cox, "At the Battle of Antietam," *B&L*, pp. 583-4.

movement and observe McClellan, but, upon the general advance of McClellan's army, its right on the Baltimore and Ohio Railroad [Carman added and crossed out, "its left on the Potomac"], Stuart was obliged to retire. On the morning of the 11th Fitz Hugh Lee's Brigade fell back from New Market to Liberty and crossed the Monocacy above Frederick, on the morning of the 12th; and Hampton's Brigade, falling back from Hyattstown and Urbana, occupied Frederick, with pickets thrown out on the various roads leading in the direction of the Union advance, and two squadrons with artillery at the Monocacy Bridge. About noon Hampton was notified of Cox's approach on the National road and placed a squadron of the 2nd South Carolina Cavalry to support the squadrons and battery at the bridge. This squadron was under command of Lieutenant John Meighan, who now began skirmishing with Cox's advance, Cox's men replying with a fire that killed two of Meighan's. Hampton withdrew his advance squadron slowly to the town, sending his guns to occupy a position commanding the road from Frederick to the foot of Catoctin Mountain.

As Hampton's men withdrew they were followed by Moor's Brigade, deployed on either side of the turnpike, Colonel Moor himself, with a troop of the Chicago Dragoons and a gun of Simmond's Kentucky Battery, being in the road abreast his line. Moor's movement was too deliberate to suit the views of a young staff-officer, attached to corps headquarters, who volunteered some criticism that angered Moor, who thought the criticism came from corps headquarters, whereupon he dashed ahead at a gallop, with escort, staff and the gun, and as he came to where the road turned, in the suburbs of the town, was brought to quick grief.

Hampton had seen Moor's movement, it was necessary to check it to insure the orderly withdrawal of his brigade and Colonel M. C. Butler was ordered to make a counter-charge. Lieutenant Meighan's squadron made the charge, supported by the brigade provost-guard of 40 men, under Captain J. F. Waring, rode down, unhorsed, and captured Moor and seven others, the gun was fired during the melee and capsized into a ditch, two men were killed and the survivors of staff and escort went back in disorder. This sharp encounter protected Hampton's rear, and his brigade was slowly withdrawn to Middletown, leaving the Jeff Davis Legion and two guns, under Lieutenant- Colonel W. T. Martin, to hold the gap in the Catoctin Mountains. As the rear of Hampton's cavalry went out at one end of the street, Cox's infantry came in at the other; passed through the town, amid joyous shouts, the waving of miniature Union flags and handkerchiefs, and encamped in the suburbs. The other divisions of the corps moved up and bivouacked about the town.[50]

Reynolds's Division of the First Corps, moved from Poplar Springs to the Monocacy bridge, Hatch's Division from Lisbon to New Market and Ricketts' Division from Cooksville to Ridgeville. The 3rd Pennsylvania Cavalry pushed north to Unionville, the Second Corps from Clarksburg to Urbana and the Twelfth Corps from Damascus to Ijamsville Cross Road.

On the left Farnsworth's Brigade of cavalry, with the horse batteries of Hains and Robertson, pushed past Sugar Loaf and through Urbana to Frederick, Munford's Virginia cavalry falling back to the gap in the Catoctins at Jefferson. The Sixth Corps marched from Barnesville to Licksville Cross Roads; Couch's Division from Poolesville to Barnesville, and Sykes's Division from Middlebrook to Urbana. Colonel A. T. McReynolds, 1st New York Cavalry, was put in charge of a brigade (1st New York and 8th Pennsylvania Cavalry and a section of Battery M, 5th U. S. Artillery) and ordered to Gettysburg, for which it was reported a body of Stuart's cavalry was moving.[51]

Morell's Division of the 5th Corps, moving from Upton's Hill and Arlington, crossed the Potomac and, marching through Georgetown, went out on the Seventh Street road as far as Silver Springs, where it bivouacked. The two brigades of Tyler and Allabach of Humphreys's Division, were ordered to start from their camps in Virginia and follow Morell, and Halleck directed Heintzelman, whom he had put in charge of the defenses on the Virginia side of the river, to ascertain by his cavalry the probable strength of the enemy south of the Potomac, as, "should there be no immediate danger on that side, I wish to send more forces to General McClellan."[52]

Heintzelman could find no trace of an enemy near Washington, nor could he hear of any considerable force south of the Potomac, but when McClellan ordered Banks, whom he had left in command of the defenses of Washington, to send from

---

50 Stuart's withdrawal from Frederick is chronicled in his report, *OR* 19, pt. 1, pp. 815-6. The fight on the eastern edge of Frederick is taken from Hampton's report, *ibid.*, pp. 822-3, and Johnson's memoir, in *SHSP*, 12, pp. 517-8. Carman seems not to have used a published response in *ibid.*, 13, pp. 417-8, which challenges the role of Lt. Meighan. For the Union accounts, see also an article in Moore, *Rebellion Record*, 5, Doc., pp. 606-8, and Cox, "At the Battle of Antietam," *B&L*, pp. 583-4, which Carman quotes from in places.

51 The Union advance to Frederick can be retraced through McClellan's report, *ibid.*, 19, pt. 1, pp. 40-42, and Pleasonton's report, *ibid.*, p. 209. Carman incorrectly cited Lt. Peter Hains commanding Battery M of the 5th U.S. Artillery. This battery was part of the 2nd U.S. Artillery. See Hain's report, *ibid.*, 51, pt. 1, p. 137.

52 The deployment of the Fifth Corps can be found on *ibid.*, 19, pt. 2, pp. 264, 271, and the quote from Halleck about reinforcing McClellan is found in *ibid.*, p. 274.

that place eight new regiments to relieve part of Couch's Division, left at Offut's Cross Roads, Seneca, Conrad's and Edwards' ferries, their presence at these points being deemed very necessary to guard his left and rear, Halleck interposed an objection and informed McClellan that Banks could not spare the regiments for that purpose, as nearly all new ones were being used to guard the railroad. In the same communication, he cautioned McClellan against moving from the river and thus uncovering the capital.[53]

Early in the day McClellan advised Halleck that his columns were pushing on rapidly to Frederick and that he was confident that the enemy were moving in two directions, viz., on the Hagerstown and Harper's Ferry roads, upon which Halleck dispatched in reply: "Is it not possible to open communications with Harper's Ferry, so that Colonel Miles forces can co-operate with you?" At 5.30 p. m., McClellan reported the movements of the day and said that cavalry had been sent toward Point of Rocks to ascertain whether there was any force of the enemy in that direction: "Should the enemy go toward Pennsylvania I shall follow him. Should he attempt to recross the Potomac I shall endeavor to cut off his retreat.... The troops have marched to-day as far as it was possible and proper for them to move." In a later dispatch he informed Halleck that in his orders of movement for the morrow he had arranged so that he could go to or send to Miles relief, if necessary, he had heard no firing in that direction and that if he made any resistance whatsoever, he could relieve him and place his assailants in great peril of capture.[54]

If McClellan had any doubts as to Lee's movements these were partially dispelled by the following by the following dispatch:

WASHINGTON CITY, D.C.
September 12, 1862—5.45 p.m.

Major-General McCLELLAN:

Governor Curtin telegraphs me:

I have advices that Jackson is crossing the Potomac at Williamsport, and probably the whole rebel army will be drawn from Maryland.

---

53 McClellan's request and Halleck's cautionary reply can be found in *ibid.*, pp. 271, 280-1.

54 Carman chose a few of the telegrams between Halleck and McClellan to develop McClellan's understanding of the Confederate army's movements as they left Frederick. They are found in *ibid.*, pp. 270-2.

Receiving nothing from Harper's Ferry or Martinsburg to-day, and positive information from Wheeling that the line is cut, corroborates the idea that the enemy is recrossing the Potomac. Please do not let him get off without being hurt.

A. LINCOLN.[55]

McClellan replied that the main body of his cavalry and horse artillery were ordered after the enemy's main column, with instructions to check its march as much as possible, that he might overtake it; if Harper's Ferry was still held he thought he could save the garrison; if the enemy were really marching into Pennsylvania, he should soon be up with them; but his apprehension was that they would make for Williamsport and get across the river before he could catch them.[56]

In explanation of the slowness and deliberation of his march to this point, McClellan says:

During these movements I had not imposed long marches on the columns. The absolute necessity of refitting and giving some little rest to troops worn down by previous long-continued marching and severe fighting, together with the uncertainty as to the actual position, strength, and intentions of the enemy, rendered it incumbent upon me to move slowly and cautiously until the headquarters reached Urbana, where I first obtained reliable information that the enemy's object was to move upon Harper's Ferry and the Cumberland Valley, and not upon Baltimore, Washington, or Gettysburg.[57]

Referring to the position of affairs at Harper's Ferry and the orders to McClellan of the 12th, Halleck reports:

As this campaign was to be carried on within the department commanded by Major-General Wool, I directed General McClellan to assume control of all troops within his reach, without regard to departmental lines. The garrisons of Winchester

55 *Ibid.*, 19, pt. 2, p. 270.

56 *Ibid.*, pp. 272.

57 The quotation about McClellan's deliberate marches and lack of firm intelligence is from McClellan's report, *ibid.*, pt. 1, pp. 27-8. McClellan seemed perplexed by Lee's objectives, although Carman suggested that Lincoln's dispatch cleared up all ambiguity. This dispatch, *ibid.*, p. 270, was answered by McClellan on the night of September 12, which is excerpted by Carman. Read in its entirety, it shows McClellan was still unsure of Lee's direction and intent. See *ibid.*, pp. 271-2.

and Martinsburg had been withdrawn to Harper's Ferry, and the commanding officer of that post had been advised by my chief of staff to mainly confine his defense, in case he was attacked by superior forces, to the position of Maryland Heights, which could have been held a long time against overwhelming numbers. To withdraw him entirely from that position, with the great body of Lee's forces between him and our army, would not only expose the garrison to capture, but all the artillery and stores collected at that place must either be destroyed or left to the enemy. The only feasible plan was for him to hold his position until General McClellan could relieve him or open a communication so that he could evacuate it in safety. These views were communicated both to General McClellan and to Colonel Miles.[58]

## In this same connection, McClellan reports:

It seems necessary for a distinct understanding of this matter to state that I was directed on the 12th to assume command of the garrison of Harper's Ferry as soon as I should open communications with that place, and that when I received this order all communication from the direction in which I was approaching was cut off. Up to that time, however, Colonel Miles could, in my opinion, have marched his command into Pennsylvania by crossing the Potomac at Williamsport or above, and this opinion was confirmed by the fact that Colonel Davis marched the cavalry part of Colonel Miles' command from Harper's Ferry on the 14th, taking the main road to Hagerstown, and he encountered no enemy except a small picket near the mouth of the Antietam.

Before I left Washington, and when there certainly could have been no enemy to prevent the withdrawal of the forces of Colonel Miles, I recommended to the proper authorities that the garrison of Harper's Ferry should be withdrawn, via Hagerstown, to aid in covering the Cumberland Valley, or that, taking up the pontoon bridge and obstructing the railroad bridge, it should fall back to the Maryland Heights and there hold out to the last. In this position it ought to have maintained itself for many days.

It was not deemed proper to adopt either of these suggestions, and when the matter was left to my discretion it was too late for me to do anything but endeavor to relieve the garrison. I accordingly directed artillery to be fired by our advance at frequent intervals, as a signal that relief was at hand. This was done, and, as I afterwards learned, the reports of the cannon were distinctly heard at Harper's Ferry. It was confidently expected that Colonel Miles would hold out until we had carried the mountain passes and were in condition to send a detachment to his relief. The left was

---

58 Carman pasted an excerpt from Halleck's report, *ibid.*, p. 4, in which Halleck seemed to be trying to pin blame for the loss of Harpers Ferry on McClellan, or at least deflect it from himself. Because this report was written after the fact, it is not unreasonable to suspect that Halleck may have been trying to avoid blame for his orders.

therefore ordered to move through Crampton's Pass in front of Burkittsville, while the center and right marched upon Turner's Pass in front of Middletown.[59]

On the night of the 12th McClellan knew that Harper's Ferry was in great danger and that Jackson had recrossed the Potomac, near Williamsport, but for what purpose was not clearly known. With this information in his possession what did McClellan do on the 13th? Captain W. P. Sanders, 6th U. S. Cavalry, who had reported his impression that Jackson was marching on Harper's Ferry, was directed to push his scouts in the direction of that place, and the 1st Rhode Island Cavalry, that had been sent him from Arlington on the 11th, and arrived at Frederick on the 12th, was, early on the 13th, sent to Seneca and Poolesville to watch all the fords from Seneca to the mouth of the Monocacy.

Before withdrawing from Frederick, Stuart ordered Fitzhugh Lee to feel the right and rear of McClellan's army, to ascertain the strength and meaning of its movements, and that enterprising officer was now heard from at Liberty; report came of his presence at Westminster on the march to Gettysburg, upon which Pleasonton, as we have seen, detached McReynolds's Brigade with a section of artillery to follow Lee in the direction of Gettysburg; and Rush's Lancers, supported by Fairchild's Brigade, Rodman's Division, Ninth Corps, were sent to Jefferson for Franklin's column, with which the 6th United States Cavalry and a battery of horse artillery were then acting.[60]

With the remainder of his command Pleasonton, at daylight of the 13th, pushed out of Frederick on the National road and had gone some three or four miles when Martin, who, with the Jeff Davis Legion and two guns of Hart's South Carolina Battery, had been left the night before on the road, where it passes over

59 Here, Carman pasted an excerpt from McClellan's report, *ibid.*, p. 44, to show that McClellan rightly contended that he had no authority over Miles and the Harpers Ferry garrison until it was too late to avoid their capture.

60 Carman's assurance of McClellan's state of mind on the night of September 12 is borne out by the general's actions. McClellan ordered an advance beyond Frederick to begin on the 13th, but also in obedience to Halleck's direction, held Franklin's force near the Potomac River, and with the cavalry units listed, guarded all the crossing points below Point of Rocks to prevent Confederates from swinging back into Maryland behind him. The reconnoitering toward Harpers Ferry was in fulfillment of Halleck's directive to relieve the garrison, if possible. For Sanders' report, see *ibid.*, 51, pt. 1, p. 824. The 1st Rhode Island Cavalry's orders are found in *ibid.*, p. 830. Stuart's order to Fitz Lee is mentioned in his report, *ibid.*, 19, pt. 1, p. 816, the report of him at Westminster is in *ibid.*, pt. 2, p. 271, and the deployments of the Ninth Corps cavalry and artillery are found in *ibid.*, pp. 47-48. In actuality, only Col. Tom Rosser's 5th Virginia Cavalry with John Pelham's two guns went to Westminster. See Gen. Thomas L. Rosser to Antietam National Battlefield Board, May 12, 1897, National Archives, RG 92:707, Antietam Studies, hereafter referred to as NA-AS.

the Catoctin, at Fairview, opened on his advance with his artillery, supported on either side of the road by his dismounted cavalry, favorably posted on the crest of the ridge.

Two sections from Robertson's and Hains' batteries were run forward and opened on Hart's two guns, and some squadrons of the 3rd Indiana and 8th Illinois cavalry were dismounted and sent up the ridge to the right as skirmishers, the 1st Massachusetts in support on the road.

McClellan's movements on the 12th were not understood by Stuart, who was watching him and guarding Lee's rear. All means were taken to ascertain their character, whether a reconnaissance, feeling for an opening, or an aggressive movement of the entire army. What information he did receive, the occupation of Frederick by Burnside's advance and his probable forward movement the next day, was promptly conveyed to D. H. Hill, then at Boonsboro, and he added to information the suggestion that the gap over the Catoctin, held by Martin, was a very strong position for infantry and artillery. The orders under which he was acting, in common with other subordinate commanders, contemplated the capture of Harper's Ferry on the 12th or 13th, and, as the garrison was not believed strong at that point, he supposed that it had already fallen, and then no importance would attach to the mountain gap. But, as he had received no intelligence from Harper's Ferry, he felt it important to check McClellan, as much as possible, and develop his force, so, on the morning of the 13th, he ordered Hampton to return from Middletown and support Martin in holding the gap in the Catoctin, while Fitzhugh Lee was feeling McClellan's right. Hampton moved as ordered, but it does not appear that he became actively engaged, leaving the fight to Martin, who conducted it with great skill, spirit and persistency, his skirmishers becoming actively engaged and Hart's guns annoying the Union batteries, causing them to make many changes of position.[61]

After some severe artillery firing and much brisk skirmishing Pleasonton's skirmishers, about 2 p. m. gained a position commanding Hart's guns as well as the road, upon which Hampton retired the two guns to near Middletown, barricaded the road in several places and drew up his entire brigade in the rear of the guns.

Pleasonton followed in pursuit, taking a number of prisoners, and came up to Hampton's second stand east of Middletown. Gibson's Battery was brought up and

---

61 Carman gave an account of the fighting on September 13 from the foot of Catoctin Mountain through Middletown. For the activities of the Confederate cavalry in this rearguard action, and for Stuart's reasoning as Carman conveys it, see Stuart's report, *OR* 19, pt. 1, pp. 816-7, and Hampton's report, *ibid.*, pp. 823-4. For the Union point of view, see Pleasonton's report, *ibid.*, p. 209. See also von Borke, *Memoirs of the Confederate War for Independence*, pp. 142-5.

a hot exchange of artillery fire was indulged in, the skirmishers, also, became engaged and the action continued a few minutes, when Stuart, having held his enemy in check sufficiently long to accomplish his purpose, which was to give D. H. Hill time to occupy Turner's Gap, again fell back, his rear covered by Colonel L. S. Baker's 1st North Carolina Cavalry.

Farnsworth's entire brigade (3rd Indiana, 8th Illinois and 1st Massachusetts) then advanced and drove Baker through Middletown and down the long slope which terminated at Catoctin Creek, a lovely stream winding through the valley to the Potomac. Here Baker made a stand. A section each of Gibson's and Hains' batteries engaged him and there was some skirmishing, but, in a few minutes, Baker blew up and destroyed the bridge over the creek and retreated rapidly to Turner's Gap of the South Mountain.

As the creek was easily fordable the destruction of the bridge did not long delay Pleasonton's advance to the foot of the mountain, which he found too strong a position to be carried by his cavalry, upon which, he sent back to Burnside for some infantry, awaiting which, he pushed some dismounted men ahead to reconnoiter.[62]

When Stuart arrived at the east foot of Turner's Gap he found, much to his relief, that D. H. Hill, in response to his suggestion, had occupied it with infantry— Colquitt's Brigade. Whereupon he ordered Hampton's Brigade, with the exception of the Jeff Davis Legion and two guns of Hart's Battery, to reinforce Munford at Crampton's Gap, which was considered by him the weakest part of his line and necessary to be held for the protection of McLaws's rear, who had gone through Brownsville Gap, one mile south, into Pleasant Valley, on the way to Maryland Heights. Stuart remained at Turner's Gap to put Colquitt's Brigade in position on the eastern slope of South Mountain. Colonel T. R. Rosser, who with the 5th Virginia Cavalry and two guns of John Pelham's Virginia battery, had left New Market on the morning of the 11th, moved through Liberty, Unionville, New Windsor, Westminster, Union, Middleburg, Utica and Hamburg, reaching Boonsboro after dark on the 13th, and was during the night thrown forward to

---

62 See Stuart's report, *OR* 19, pt. 1, pp. 816-7, and Hampton's report, *ibid.*, p. 823-4, for specific details of the units involved. For the Union point of view, see Pleasonton's report, *ibid.*, p. 209. Crownishield, *First Massachusetts Cavalry*, p. 74, uses wording very similar to Carman's for this action. The impact of this retreat of the Confederate cavalry across Middletown Valley is handled quite diffidently by Carman, who took Stuart's report at face value. It is worth noting that the loss of this valley exposed the Confederate army's rear while the operations at Harpers Ferry were far from complete, though McClellan did not know this. The danger of this situation for the Confederates, and also the fact that this aggressive Union action took place before McClellan issued any orders in response to coming into possession of the lost Confederate Special Order #191, can be followed in Harsh, *Taken at the Flood*, pp. 230-7.

Fox's Gap on Colquitt's right. Meanwhile, Fitz Lee, with three regiments of his brigade, was north and west of Frederick, endeavoring to ascertain the strength and intention of McClellan's movements.[63]

Munford, who, on the afternoon of the 12th, had been ordered to occupy the gap in the Catoctin near Jefferson, had two regiments only—the 2nd and 12th Virginia cavalry—the rest of his brigade being on detached service, two regiments had not crossed the Potomac with him and, two days before, the 7th Virginia went with Jackson in his movement against Harper's Ferry. Skirmishing began with him on the morning of the 13th and continued the entire day. Captain Sanders with the 6th United States Cavalry advanced by the main road from Licksville and, later in the day, Rush's Lancers, supported by Fairchild's Brigade of infantry and the battery of the 9th New York, moved from Frederick by the road, leading over a gap, which intersects the road leading to Middletown about one mile and a half north of Jefferson. Fairchild deployed the 89th and 103rd New York and advanced skirmishing, with the 9th New York in reserve; at the same time Sanders on the left made his presence known on the Licksville road. Munford was too feeble to resist this pressure and fell back to Burkittsville, encumbered with his brigade trains and pursued nearly the whole way by the Union cavalry. Colonel Harman, with the 12th Virginia, was hastened to Burkittsville to protect the main road leading from Jefferson to that point and to insure the passage of the wagon-train over Crampton's Gap, while Munford, with the sharpshooters of the 2nd Virginia, under Captain T. B. Holland, disputed the Union advance. Holland checked them until an advantageous position had been secured for the artillery on the mountainside beyond Burkittsville. Getting his trains safely over Crampton's Gap, Munford placed three guns in position and awaited the Union approach, momentarily expected.[64]

63 After the destruction of the bridge over Catoctin Creek, Stuart took steps to defend the road gaps in South Mountain, the last bulwark between Union advance and Lee's divided command. Stuart did not name Colquitt's Brigade in his report, but Carman may have obtained it from D. H. Hill's report, OR 19, pt. 1, pp. 1,025, or his account in B&L, p. 560. Carman continued the habit of filling in the opponent's identification for clarity of reading. Soldiers making reports seldom knew who they were fighting, but Carman frequently added it. The three regiments of Fitz Lee were the 1st, 2nd, and 9th Virginia Cavalry regiments, the 5th regiment on detached duty. See the reports of Colquitt, Stuart, Hampton, and Munford, OR 19, pt. 1, pp. 1,052, 817, 823-4, and 826-7, respectively. The details provided by Carman about Rosser's movements came from a printed map and letter from Gen. T. L. Rosser to Battlefield Board, May 12, 1897, NA-AS.

64 The description of the retrograde actions of Munford's Brigade toward Crampton's Gap is taken from his report, OR 19, pt. 1, pp. 826-7. For the Union report of this pursuit, see Fairchild's report, ibid., pp. 449-50. Company K of the 9th New York was equipped with naval

While Pleasonton, with the main body of his cavalry, was advancing to the foot of Turner's Gap a detachment of Farnsworth's Brigade, consisting of one squadron of the 8th Illinois and a part of the 3rd Indiana, both under command of Major Medill, 8th Illinois, left Middletown to reconnoiter in the direction of Harper's Ferry. The detachment took the road leading through Burkittsville. At the same time Hampton with his cavalry brigade was moving from Turner's Gap to Crampton's, by the road running near the foot of the mountain, all unaware of the pressure under which Munford was laboring and the presence of an enemy near his own line of march. When nearing Crampton's he saw the Union cavalry on a road parallel to the one on which he was moving. Hampton ordered Lieutenant-Colonel P. M. B. Young to charge it with the Cobb Legion; the order was carried out in gallant style, Young dispersing the body and capturing prisoners of the 3rd Indiana and 8th Illinois. Hampton's loss was 4 killed and 9 wounded, the Union loss was about the same. This attack gave needed relief to Munford. Fairchild's Brigade had, under orders of Reno, withdrawn and was on the return to Frederick and the Rush Lancers moved to the vicinity of Broad Run Village.[65]

The road was now clear for Hampton who, as he drew near from the direction in which Munford was looking for an attack, was not recognized by him. Waiting until the head of Hampton's column was in easy range, Munford's guns were shotted and the lanyards applied, when, fortunately, Hampton perceived the

howitzers. Again, the actions of Capt. Sanders (except for a brief mention in Franklin's report, *ibid.*, p. 378) appear only in Carman's manuscript. Somehow, Carman acquired a detailed account of the Union cavalry actions, especially those of Sanders. His name appears more often here than in the entire OR. Carman received letters from a soldier named Tullius Tupper who had served with Sanders. Tupper sent a map and letter about the 6th U.S. Cavalry at Antietam and mentioned his willingness to come to the battlefield if so ordered, as he was then a major in the U.S. Army. Carman may have arranged the orders and spoke with Tupper, but no notes of any conversation have been found. See Heitman, *Biographical Register*, pp. 858, 974, and Tupper letter, NA-AS.

65 The cavalry skirmish described here is known as the Quebec Schoolhouse fight. Union sources for it do not exist in the OR, and Carman used Hampton's and Munford's reports to narrate it. See OR 19, pt. 1, pp. 824, 825-6. Carman evidently did not use the account in Hard, *Eighth Illinois Cavalry*, p. 176, for this fight. According to Hard, the 8th Illinois lost eight men wounded and a "large number of the 3rd IN" were also wounded. A regimental history of the 3rd Indiana Cavalry decried Pleasonton's overlooking their efforts, and claimed the Hoosiers were in pursuit of Stuart's wagon train. However, Col. Marcy's order to Pleasonton of 11:30 p.m. on September 12, 1862, told him to ascertain the state of affairs in Harpers Ferry, which is the purpose Carman cited. See OR 51, pt. 1, p. 825. See also W. N. Pickerill, *History of the Third Indiana Cavalry* (Indianapolis: Aetna Printing Co., 1906), pp. 25-9. While this regimental history is helpful today, it was printed too late for Carman to have used it.

intention and, raising a white flag, made himself known as a friend. He bivouacked at the foot of the gap.[66]

The 3rd Pennsylvania Cavalry which had advanced to Unionville, on the 12th, in pursuit of Fitz Hugh Lee's cavalry, marched on the 13th to Woodsborough, Creagerstown, and Emmitsburg, returning to Frederick on the 14th.[67]

While the Union cavalry was pushing the Confederates from Catoctin Mountain and across the valley to South Mountain, the infantry columns slowly and cautiously advanced; the Ninth Corps, following Pleasonton, marched to and near Middletown; Hatch's and Ricketts's divisions, First Corps, closed up to Reynolds's, on the Monocacy, sixteen miles; the Second Corps moved from Urbana to Frederick; the Twelfth Corps from Ijamsville Cross Roads to Frederick, five miles; all these covering the direct road from Frederick to Washington. The Sixth Corps, under Franklin, continuing its movement by way of Barnesville, reached Buckeystown; Couch's Division replaced Franklin at Licksville and went into camp after a march of five miles. Sykes's Division and the Reserve Artillery, which habitually moved with it, pushed on from Urbana to Frederick. Morell's Division marched through Rockville to Middlebrook, thence its advance pushed on to Seneca Creek.[68]

The welcome extended by the citizens of Frederick to the Union army was not confined to the enthusiastic demonstration given the Ninth Corps. The Second Corps marched through the town on the morning of the 13th and its reception is told by its gifted historian:

> Probably no soldier who entered Frederick on the morning of the 13th will ever forget the cordial welcome with which the rescuing army was received by the loyal inhabitants. For five months the Second Corps had been upon the soil of Virginia, where every native white face was wrinkled with spite as the invaders passed; marching through or encamping in a region which, to a Northern eye, was inconceivably desolate and forlorn, barren fields affording the only relief to the dreary continuity of tangled thickets and swamp bottoms. Here, in the rich valley of the Monocacy, shut in by mountains of surpassing grace of outline, all nature was in bloom; the signs of

66 The withdrawal of Fairchild's brigade is verified by *OR* 19, pt. 1, p. 450, and the near-tragedy involving Hampton and Munford is narrated by Munford in his report found in *ibid.*, p. 826.

67 The movements of the 3rd Pennsylvania Cavalry are taken from a typed excerpt in the NA-AS labeled "From the Regimental Book and Journal of the 3d Penna. Cavalry."

68 The route taken by Union troops to Frederick can be followed through the chart in McClellan's report, *OR* 19, pt. 1, pp. 39-40, and *ibid.*, 51, pt. 1, pp. 824-26.

comfort and opulence met the eye on every side; while, as the full brigades of Sumner, in perfect order and with all the pomp of war, with glittering staffs and proud commanders, old Sumner at the head passed through the quaint and beautiful town, the streets resounded with applause, and from balconies and windows fair faces smiled, and handkerchiefs and scarfs waved to greet the army of the Union. Whether the ancient and apocryphal Barbara Fritchie had significantly recovered from the sentimental shocks of a poetical shower of imaginary musket-balls to appear again on this occasion may be doubted; but many an honest and many a fair countenance of patriot men and patriot women looked out upon the brave array of Sumner's Corps with smiles and tears of gratitude and joy. Amid all that was desolate and gloomy; amid all that was harsh and terrible, in the service those soldiers of the Union were called upon to render, that light day of September 13th, 1862 that gracious scene of natural beauty and waving crops, that quaint and charming Southern city, that friendly greeting, forms a picture which can never pass out of the memory of any one whose fortune it was to enter Fredericktown that day."[69]

McClellan's deliberate marches during the campaign have been severely and, in many cases, unjustly criticized, but, slow and deliberate as they were, they were too rapid to please Halleck, who trembled for the safety of Washington as McClellan's columns receded from it. So, while McClellan's cavalry was driving Stuart's from Fairview Gap, of Catoctin Mountain, Halleck, in his office at Washington, was preparing this dispatch which was received by McClellan during the day:

> Until you know more certainly the enemy's force south of the Potomac, you are wrong in thus uncovering the capital. I am of the opinion that the enemy will send a small column toward Pennsylvania, so as to draw your forces in that direction; then suddenly move on Washington with the forces south of the Potomac and those he may cross over. In your letter of the 10th (11th) you attach too little importance to the capital. I assure you that you are wrong. The capture of this place will throw us back six months, if it should not destroy us. Beware of the evils I point out to you.

Halleck repeated his caution on the 14th: "Scouts report a large force still on the Virginia side of the Potomac. I fear you are exposing your left and rear."[70]

---

69 The welcoming of the Union troops into Frederick is from Francis A. Walker, *History of Second Army Corps*, pp. 93-94. See also Steiner in Moore, *Rebellion Record*, 5, Doc., p. 608.

70 Carman used a number of telegrams between Halleck and McClellan to demonstrate what Carman believed were the reasons for McClellan's pace of advance and seemingly hesitant movements. As usual, Carman did not miss an opportunity to criticize Halleck, whose

Not as affecting the immediate movements of McClellan, but to show the apprehensions of Halleck, we anticipate our narrative by giving in this place a dispatch received by McClellan, on the afternoon of the 16th, when he was facing Lee on the Antietam: "As you give me no information in regard to the position of your forces, except that at Sharpsburg, of course I cannot advise. I think, however, you will find that the whole force of the enemy in your front has crossed the river. I fear now more than ever that they will recross at Harper's Ferry or below, and turn your left, thus cutting you off from Washington. This has appeared to me to be a part of their plan, and hence my anxiety on the subject."[71]

Halleck denies that he cautioned McClellan that he was moving too precipitately or too far from Washington. In his testimony before the Committee on the Conduct of the War, he says:

> In respect to General McClellan going too fast or too slow from Washington, there can be found no such telegram from me to him. He had mistaken the meaning of the telegram I sent him. I telegraphed him that he was going too far, not from Washington, but from the Potomac, leaving General Lee the opportunity to come down the Potomac and get between him and Washington. I thought General McClellan should keep more on the Potomac, and press forward his left rather than his right, so as the more readily to relieve Harper's Ferry.[72]

McClellan retorts that he can find no telegram from Halleck ordering him to keep his left flank nearer the Potomac, nor do the records show such instructions. Commenting upon Halleck's dispatches, McClellan says:

> The importance of moving with all due caution so as not to uncover the National Capital until the enemy's position and plans were developed was, I believe, fully appreciated by me, and as my troops extended from the Baltimore and Ohio Railroad to the Potomac, with the extreme left flank moving along that stream, and with strong pickets left in rear to watch and guard all the available fords, I did not regard my left or rear as in any degree exposed. But it appears from the foregoing telegrams that the General-in-Chief was of a different opinion, and that my movements were, in his

September 13 and 14 dispatches are found in *OR* 19, pt. 2, pp. 280-1, & 289, respectively. Carman selectively edited this telegram to make it sound more damning of Halleck than it really was, perhaps due to his personal antipathy toward the general.

71  This message from Halleck to McClellan, September 16, 1862, is not in the *OR* except in McClellan's report dated August 4, 1863, found in *ibid.*, pt. 1, p. 41.

72  *CCW*, pt. 1, pp. 451-2. This testimony is in McClellan's report, *OR* 19, pt. 1, pp. 41-2.

judgment, too precipitate, not only for the safety of Washington but also for the security of my left and rear…my left, from the time I left Washington, always rested on the Potomac, and my center was continually in position to re-enforce the left or right, as occasion might require. Had I advanced my left flank along the Potomac more rapidly than the other columns marched upon the roads to the right, I should have thrown that flank out of supporting distance of the other troops and greatly exposed it, and if I had marched the entire army in one column along the bank of the river, instead of upon five different parallel roads, the column, with its trains, would have extended about 50 miles, and the enemy might have defeated the advance before the rear could have reached the scene of action. Moreover, such a movement would have uncovered the communications with Baltimore and Washington on our right and exposed our right and rear. I presume it will be admitted by every military man that it was necessary to move the army in such order that it could at any time be concentrated for battle and I am of opinion that this object could not have been accomplished in any other way than the one employed. Any other disposition of our forces would have subjected them to defeat in detached fragments.[73]

Elsewhere McClellan writes:

Very few in the Army of the Potomac doubted the favorable result of the next collision with the Confederate army, but in other quarters not a little doubt prevailed, and the desire for very rapid movement, so loudly expressed after the result was gained, did not make itself heard during the movements preceding the battles; quite the contrary was the case, as I was more than once cautioned that I was moving too rashly and exposing the capital to an attack from the Virginia side.[74]

Considering the uncertainty of Lee's movements, the over estimate of his strength, and the apprehensions of Halleck and his warning dispatches, McClellan's excuses for deliberate movements are valid, but, on the 13th, by good fortune, he was put in possession of information that made everything clear—he emerged from the darkness in which he had been groping. Upon his arrival at Frederick he was handed a copy of Lee's "Special Orders No. 191," giving in detail the movements and position of every division of his army, and above all that Jackson,

---

73 Halleck's testimony to the Committee on the Conduct of the War was also in McClellan's report, as was the long quotation from McClellan defending his actions, *ibid.*, pp. 41-2. It is obvious that McClellan wrote this report to respond to Halleck's testimony before the Committee, and in defense of his reputation.

74 This quotation is from McClellan, *Own Story*, p. 551.

McLaws and Walker, were surrounding the garrison at Harper's Ferry. How that order came into his possession, and the means taken by McClellan to relieve Harper's Ferry shall be told elsewhere.[75]

The appearance of the Confederate army in Maryland caused intense excitement throughout the State and beyond its borders. Baltimore was in a fever when it became known that the Potomac had been crossed and excitement increased when it was reported that Lee had reached Frederick and the scouts of Stuart's cavalry were on the road leading to Baltimore. There were apprehensions on the part of Union men; and hopes indulged in by the Secessionists that Lee would march on the city, and rumors to that effect were freely circulated. Collisions on the street were frequent and more serious trouble was anticipated. Four hundred special policemen were sworn in, and the mayor requested the citizens to assemble and form themselves into military companies for the defense of the city. Prominent citizens published a request to all those who desired to join an independent military company, to be called the "Maryland Line," to register their names at the Post Office, and Governor Bradford, September 8th, issued a proclamation stating that the Confederates had crossed the border and calling upon the citizens of the state to organize and assist in defending "their homes and firesides against the assault of the invader."[76]

The Governor could arm and equip all the cavalry that would probably be offered, but was short of arms for infantry; he hoped that the loyal citizens would not wait for arms, but organize everywhere without delay, and "assist in driving from the State the invading host that now occupies its soil, armed with any weapon which opportunity may furnish."[77]

General John E. Wool, who was in command of the military department in which Baltimore was included, was instructed by General Halleck that he had full power for every emergency, and must exercise it for the maintenance of order in the city, and General John R. Kenly was ordered to report to him to organize and command a brigade of new troops. Under this order Kenly was assigned

---

75 Carman mentioned McClellan's coming into possession of Lee's Special Order #191, and that its appearance was a benefit to him. McClellan mentioned his acquisition of the order in his telegrams to Halleck and Lincoln of September 13, 1862. See OR 19, pt. 2, pp. 281-2.

76 Carman's description of Baltimore's unrest was evidently excerpted from the *Baltimore Sun*, September 9, 1862.

77 Following the theme set in his earlier chapters, Carman addressed the feelings and sympathies of the people in Maryland, and their reaction to the Confederate invasion. He did not cite any sources for his comments. See Moore, *Rebellion Record*, 5, Diary, p. 756, for Bradford's call for volunteers.

(September 8th) the duty of organizing the 1st, 4th, 6th, 7th and 8th regiments of Maryland Volunteers, then in process of formation near the city, and Captain F. W. Alexander's Battery of Baltimore Light Artillery. Wool was not apprehensive that Lee would move on Baltimore, but took all precautionary measures, planned some additional works and reported to Halleck that there were four roads by which the enemy could enter the city, but if they did enter, he would prevent their occupying it longer than to pass through it.[78] The explanation of the latter part of Wool's report is found in the fact that the forts were in readiness, as well as some war vessels, to lay the city in ashes, in case of a secession outbreak or its occupation by the Confederate army.

Notwithstanding the loyal resolutions and acts of the Legislature, and the action of the patriotic citizens of the State in swelling the ranks of the Army of the Union, and the patriotic response made by the citizens of Baltimore to the appeal by Governor Bradford and the mayor of the city, the military authorities had much mistrust of the strength of that loyalty in that city, and General Wool, whom it was proposed to transfer to Pennsylvania, to concert measures for the defense of that state, thought his absence from the city would lead to the most serious consequences and General Dix, who was more than two months in command, in the city, suggested that Federal Hill and other points should be more strongly fortified, as there was no city in the Union in which domestic disturbances had been more frequent, or carried to more fatal extremes. Although the great body of people were imminently distinguished for their moral virtues, there was in its midst a mass of inflammable material liable to ignite on the slightest provocation and a city prone to burst into flames should be controlled by the strong arm of the government.[79]

But there was no trouble in Baltimore. The increase in the police force, free enrollment of citizens in volunteer companies and the repressive measures of General Wool gave quiet to the city; Lee, meanwhile, was proposing to move in an opposite direction.

78 The order for Kenly's command is in *OR* 19, pt. 2, p. 280. Halleck's instructions to Wool about the safety of Baltimore are in *ibid.*, p. 198.

79 Wool's assignment to organize forces in Pennsylvania is in *ibid.*, p. 247. Wool argued against leaving the city and relieved himself from this assignment, and so was not sent. See *ibid.*, pp. 246, 276. Gen. Dix's recommendations for defense are found in *ibid.*, pp. 304-5. There were indeed desperate measures taken in Baltimore. See *ibid.*, pt. 2, pp. 286-7, for the mass arrests by the provost marshal and other stringent efforts to impede secessionist uprisings, although Wool characterized many of these arrests as "frivolous." Carman overstates Wool's repressive measures in the next sentence.

Lee's entrance into Maryland was the signal for intense excitement in Pennsylvania, particularly on her southern border and in the cities of Harrisburg and Philadelphia. The farmers, who had well filled barns and fine livestock, trembled for their safety and every effort was made to remove everything as far as possible from the grasp of the invader. Governor Curtin appealed to Washington for assistance and was assured that the military authorities would see to it that the Confederates would be checked long before they reached Harrisburg, and to the request that disciplined troops should be sent from the Army of the Potomac, Baltimore or Washington, the reply was made that it was not possible to send them and President Lincoln argued that the true defense of Harrisburg was to strengthen the column, which, under McClellan, was marching on the enemy in Maryland, and the suggestion was made that the men of the State should be called out and concentrated at or near Chambersburg. General Andrew Porter was ordered to report to Governor Curtin to organize volunteers and take measures for the defense of Harrisburg.[80]

The citizens of Philadelphia were thoroughly alarmed and appealed for help. Prominent men asked the President to send them a general of known energy and capacity "one who combines the sagacity of the statesman with the acuteness and skill of the soldier," to which Stanton gave answer: "If you know or have heard of any officer coming up anywhere near the description of the one you need, please make me happy by naming him, and I will make you happy by assigning him to your city." General O. M. Mitchel was then suggested as the very man for the emergency, but Stanton thought he "would not begin to fill the bill," besides he was required with his command in the South, and General Wool, whose command embraced Pennsylvania, was ordered to Philadelphia. Wool objected; he thought that Philadelphia was in no danger whatever, while Baltimore was threatened from within and without, and it would be extremely hazardous to relinquish his command of the city, under the intense excitement then prevailing. His objection availed and General J. F. Reynolds was then asked for and Halleck inquired of McClellan if he could be spared. McClellan objected to the detachment of one of

---

80 Carman described the excitement Lee's invasion caused in Pennsylvania. These notes about the situation in Pennsylvania are from Moore, 5, *Diary*, pp. 756-57, but they are not the source of Carman's language. Stanton's assurances to Curtin are in *OR* 19, pt. 2, p. 204, Curtin's request for veteran troops are in *ibid.*, p. 268, and Lincoln's reply is in *ibid.*, p. 276. It should be noted that Lincoln argued in favor of concentration of force and not dispersion, a point upon which he and McClellan had disagreed before. Here he appears to be in agreement with McClellan. Furthering this line of argument is McClellan's to Curtin, *ibid.*, p. 248, concerning gathering troops at Chambersburg. General Andrew Porter's assignment to command in Pennsylvania is found in *ibid.*, pp. 203, 214.

his best division commanders, then on important service, in the very face of the enemy, but his objection was overruled by Halleck's curt dispatch; "General Reynolds' division can be commanded by someone else. He has been designated for other duty, and must report here immediately." Reynolds was commanding a division in Hooker's Corps and that impetuous officer made a vigorous protest and advised McClellan not to heed Halleck's order, that "a scared Governor ought not to be permitted to destroy the usefulness of an entire division of the army, on the eve of important operations; it is only in the United States that atrocities like this are entertained," and he expressed an emphatic belief that the rebels "had no more intention of going to Harrisburg than they had of going to Heaven."[81]

On September 10th Governor Curtin called for 50,000 men to rally for the defense of the State; and, on the evening of that day Jackson left Frederick, moving northward. Swift footed rumor ran that the Confederates, 200,000 strong, ragged and filthy, but full of fight, were moving on Harrisburg and Philadelphia, consternation and dismay reigned on the border, and panic took possession of the Governor, who advised President Lincoln to put strong guards on the railway lines between Washington and Harrisburg and send over them to the last named place not less than 80,000 disciplined men, and order from New York and the Eastern States every available man to hasten to the same place, where he would concentrate in a few days as many of the Pennsylvania militia as he could muster; it was the "only hope to save the North and crush the rebel army." The Governor did not wish it supposed for one instant that he was unnecessarily alarmed, he believed Harrisburg in great danger, as his engineers, who had examined west of the Susquehanna, reported defensive works could not be created to stand against 50,000, and the enemy would bring against the city not less than 120,000, with much artillery. He concluded by advising the President that: "The time for decided action by the National Government has arrived." To which Lincoln promptly replied that he did not have to exceed 80,000 disciplined troops east of the mountains and most of them with many of the new regiments were then close in the rear of the enemy supposed to be invading Pennsylvania. "Start half of them to Harrisburg and the enemy will turn upon and beat the remaining half, and then reach Harrisburg before the half going there, and beat it, too, when it comes. The

81 The exchange of telegrams between Lincoln and the leaders of the city of Philadelphia are found in *ibid.*, p. 251, and *ibid.*, 51, pt. 1, p. 813. Stanton's denial of the request for Gen. Ormsby Mitchel is found on *ibid.*, 19, pt. 2, p. 251, as is Stanton's substitution with Wool. For Wool's protest, see *ibid.*, p. 266. Curtin's request for Reynolds is found on *ibid.*, p. 267, and McClellan's protest, along with Halleck's "curt" refusal, is on *ibid.*, p. 252. Hooker's impertinent (but correct) protest is on p. 273 of the same volume.

best possible security for Pennsylvania is putting the strongest force possible into the enemy's rear."[82] The Mayor of Philadelphia shared in the dire apprehensions of the Governor of the State, and wanted a general to command in the city; he was assured by President Lincoln that Halleck had made the best provision he could for generals in Pennsylvania, and hoped he would not take offense at his assurance that Philadelphia was in no danger. It was "more than 150 miles from Hagerstown, and could not be reached by the rebel army in ten days, if no hindrance was interposed."[83]

Nor was the partial panic confined to Pennsylvania and its chief cities. The Mayor of New York City was apprehensive of a visit by one or two Confederate iron-clads from Europe at any moment and requested heavy guns for the defense of the harbor and men to handle them.[84]

82 Curtin's and other Pennsylvania officials' panic can be sensed in his dispatches of the time. See OR 19, pt. 2, pp. 228-231, 248-253, 267-270, 276-77. The request for 80,000 troops, as well as the railway guards, is on p. 268; the reply from Lincoln is on p. 276. Some of Curtin's language, such as "ragged and filthy, but full of fight," found its way into Carman's narrative. The quotation beginning "only hope" is from the same dispatch.

83 See *ibid.*, p. 278, for Lincoln's reassurance of Mayor Alexander Henry of Philadelphia.

84 Carman lifted these phrases from Mayor George Opdyke of New York City to Edwin Stanton, Sept. 12, 1862, OR Series 3, 2, p. 540.

# Chapter 6

# Harper's Ferry

arper's Ferry is beautifully situated at the confluence of the Potomac and Shenandoah Rivers, where these streams, uniting, burst through the barriers of the Blue Ridge and roll their waters to the ocean. Thomas Jefferson said that the boldness and beauty of the view was worth a voyage across the Atlantic. At an early period the Government established an arsenal and armory at this point and much importance was attached to it as a military post; it was thought to be of great strategic value. The town itself is on the tongue of land at the junction of the Potomac and the Shenandoah which gradually rises to a table of land about 500 feet above the river levels. It is completely commanded by Maryland Heights, beyond the Potomac, and Loudoun Heights, across the Shenandoah, and by Bolivar Heights on the west; these three heights being separated from each other by a distance of nearly three miles. Although regarded, during the first two years of the war, as a place of great strategic importance, it was in fact, but a death trap. It was not defensible and could not be held by a garrison that did not absorb more men than could be spared for such a purpose. It was urged that its occupation was necessary for the protection of the railroad and canal running through it; both of these could have been cut elsewhere and whenever necessary; it was considered highly important to hold it, because it was the debouch from Virginia into

Maryland, but the Confederates had no occasion to pass through it, as good roads and fords led into Maryland above and below it. Its defects and dangers, as a military position, were early recognized by the Confederate officers; the Union authorities came to the same conclusion, at a later day, after much dear and mortifying experience.[1]

Simultaneously with the secession of Virginia, Harper's Ferry, with the United States arsenal, armory, arms and munitions of war, were seized by Virginia troops and Thomas J. Jackson, who came to the command, determined to hold possession "with the spirit which actuated the defenders of Thermopylae," but he saw that Maryland Heights was the key to the position, and these he preceded to occupy and fortify in face of the caution of General Robert E. Lee, then commanding the Virginia troops, who wrote him that it was "not considered advisable to intrude upon the soil of Maryland," lest it might interrupt the friendly relations with that State and arouse a spirit of hostility to the Confederate cause. But Lee was of Jackson's opinion that Harper's Ferry should be strongly held; he opposed the suggestion of abandoning it, as a measure depressing to the Southern cause. He was aware that the position could be easily turned by crossing the Potomac, at Williamsport and at Shepherdstown, thus threatening the communications of the garrison with Winchester, but he would be prepared to take a strong offensive against any such movement.[2]

Joseph E. Johnston succeeded Jackson in command, in the latter part of May 1861, and promptly reported the place as untenable against a large force moving on it. He proposed to abandon it and take position at Winchester, but Mr. Davis objected. A few days later, when General Patterson advanced from Chambersburg, Pennsylvania, toward the Potomac, Johnston, not intending to be caught in a trap, promptly abandoned the position and retired to Winchester. At the same time, he destroyed all the bridges over the Potomac as far up as Williamsport.[3]

---

1   Carman's description of the geography of the terrain around Harpers Ferry probably came from his own observation and local knowledge. He spent a lot of time around the area during and after the war and came to know it intimately. Because of his military background, and his service as regimental and brigade commander, he was also well qualified to judge advantages and disadvantages of the terrain as it pertained to the armies.

2   The quotation from Jackson's letter to Lee, May 5, 1861, is in *OR 19*, pt. 2, p. 814; Lee's reply is in *ibid.*, p. 822. It is worth noting that Jackson requested Lee to come to Harpers Ferry and view the site himself. Clearly Lee was thinking strategically and politically, while Jackson was thinking operationally and tactically. In a later letter Lee wrote, "The true policy is to act on the defensive . . ." *Ibid.*, p. 825.

3   For Johnston's abandonment of Harpers Ferry, see *OR 19*, pt. 2, pp. 970-2.

After the Confederates abandoned the place it was re-occupied by the Union forces, the military authorities attaching much importance to its retention as a protection to the railroad and canal passing through it, and as the eastern debouch of the Shenandoah Valley. On March 29, 1862, Colonel Dixon S. Miles, 2nd United States Infantry, was assigned to the protection of the Baltimore and Ohio Railroad, from Baltimore to the western limits of the Department of the Potomac, with headquarters at Harper's Ferry, and this assignment by General McClellan was continued by General John E. Wool, when he came to command of the Eighth Army Corps, with headquarters at Baltimore. Wool soon relieved him of the care of the railroad from Baltimore to Point of Rocks, but put him in special charge of Harper's Ferry, the railroad immediately west of it and the railroad east to Point of Rocks.[4] Miles had disgraced himself at the first battle of Bull Run, July 20 (sic), 1861, where he was in command of one of the reserve divisions, and had shown an utter lack of military capacity. Wool says: "I did not think he had the capacity to embrace so large a command as he had there; but he appeared to be very zealous.... Indeed, he was the only one I could place there, the only regular officer." Why a confessedly incompetent regular officer should be preferred to a good volunteer does not appear.[5]

While McClellan was operating on the Peninsula and Pope in front of Washington outposts were kept at Winchester and Martinsburg to hold the lower valley and protect the Baltimore and Ohio Railroad. There was but a small force at Martinsburg, but at Winchester a brigade, under command of General Julius White. White was assigned to this command by General Pope, July 26th; on the 31st his brigade numbered 3600 and he had fifteen pieces of artillery. His brigade consisted of the 39th New York Infantry, Colonel F. G. D'Utassy; the 32nd Ohio Infantry, Colonel Thomas H. Ford; the 60th Ohio Infantry, Colonel William H. Trimble; the 9th Vermont Infantry, Colonel George J. Stannard; the Seventh Squadron, Rhode Island Cavalry, Major A. W. Corliss; the First Independent Indiana Battery, Captain Silas F. Rigby, and Captain Benjamin F. Potts' Ohio Battery. There was added to

---

4   The order to Miles is found in *ibid.*, 12, pt. 3, pp. 30-1.

5   Carman recorded the wrong date for the battle of First Manassas (Bull Run). It was July 21, 1861. Miles had command of the reserve division of McDowell's army, but was accused of drunkenness by a subordinate. A hearing found insufficient evidence to convict Miles, but his relegation to guarding railroads was construed as sufficient punishment and a form of professional exile. See *ibid.*, 19, pt. 2, pp. 438-9.

this command, August 20th, a battalion of Maryland cavalry, commanded by Captain Charles H. Russell.[6]

The troops at both Winchester and Martinsburg were kept constantly on the alert by three or four small detachments of Virginia cavalry which, when Jackson marched from the Shenandoah Valley, to join Lee before Richmond, had been left to observe the movements of the Union army. These small detachments, numbering less than one hundred men each, ran in White's outposts, captured and burned railroad cars and caused some uneasiness. On August 11th twenty-five men of the 12th Virginia Cavalry dashed into Front Royal and captured two officers. On the 23rd a detachment of the same regiment captured a train of cars on the Winchester and Potomac Railroad, about two miles south of Summit Point, with ten prisoners and $8000. The train was burned and the telegraph line cut. On the same day the command of Lieutenant R. H. Milling, Cole's Maryland Cavalry, at Smithfield, west of Winchester, was captured by Captain George Baylor's company, 12th Virginia Cavalry. These and other spirited attacks gave credence to reports that a column of Confederates was marching up the valley, leaving Winchester to the left.[7]

Miles had no adequate force on the railroad between Harper's Ferry and Point of Rocks, to resist an attack of any considerable body of men. There was one company of infantry at Sandy Hook, one at Berlin, one at Point of Rocks, and another, ten miles south, at Edwards Ferry; these four companies belonging to Colonel Maulsby's regiment, Maryland Potomac Home Brigade. On the 27th of August Wool ordered Miles to increase the force at Point of Rocks with infantry and two guns, which Miles did by sending 200 men of the 87th Ohio and two guns of Graham's New York Battery.[8]

There was but one small regiment, the 11th New York Militia, to keep open communication between Harper's Ferry and Winchester, and the term of service of this regiment was about to expire. On the 28th of August Wool ordered the 8th

---

6  For White's order to command, see *ibid.*, 51, pt. 1, p. 728. The information about his strength is in *ibid.*, 12, pt. 3, p. 523.

7  Few of these actions mentioned by Carman were reported in the *OR*. The Smithfield Raid is covered in *OR* 12, pt. 2, pp. 764-5, *ibid.*, 19, pt. 1, 532, and *ibid.*, 51, pt. 1, p. 784. The capture of a train near Summit Point is mentioned in *ibid.*, 12, pt. 3, p. 650, and *ibid.*, 19, pt. 1, pp. 737, 797. The 12th Virginia Cavalry left the 1st Squadron, Companies B & I, in the Shenandoah Valley when Jackson departed in June. This force under Capt. George Baylor conducted the raid on Front Royal and the capture of the train. See NA-AS letters from W. L. Wilson, May 21, 1897, and George Baylor, May 21, 1897, for the details provided by Carman.

8  Cautionary orders as early as July 21, 1862, to Miles are in his report of the dispositions of his command, and found in *OR* 51, pt. 1, pp. 723-5, 747, 764-8.

New York Cavalry, then at Relay House, to report to Miles, who, on the 31st, ordered it to Summit Point, on the Winchester Railroad, to watch the Confederate cavalry, especially the 12th Virginia, operating in that vicinity, and to give timely notice should White be attacked at Winchester; but the primary duty of the regiment was to protect the Winchester Railroad. If cut off from Harper's Ferry the regiment was to retreat to Martinsburg, cross the Potomac at Shepherdstown, and join Miles by the left bank of the river. Four companies of the 12th Illinois Cavalry were ordered from Martinsburg to Smithfield, six miles north of Summit Point, and Captain Cole's Maryland Cavalry and Means' company of partisans were to operate in Loudoun County from Hillsboro and Leesburg to Snicker's Ferry. If too heavily pressed by the enemy Cole was to fall back on Berlin or Point of Rocks. The 3rd regiment (infantry) Potomac Home Brigade, held Kearneysville and Shepherdstown, with orders, if attacked, to cross the Potomac at Shepherdstown Ford and occupy Maryland Heights.[9]

Halleck was looking for a movement of the Confederates into the Shenandoah Valley and instructed White to keep him advised of any information coming in from that quarter, upon which White replied on the 25th (before the arrival of the New York Cavalry), that want of cavalry prevented him from obtaining information of importance, but that Union men in and around Winchester constantly informed him that the movement of the Confederates on Pope's right were to keep the valley clear for their real attack on Maryland.[10]

Subsequent movements of Lee's army brought it nearer the valley and, on the morning of September 2nd, Halleck telegraphed White: "You will immediately abandon the fortifications at Winchester, sending the heavy guns under escort by rail to Harper's Ferry. If this cannot be done, they should be rendered unservicable. Having sent off your artillery, you will withdraw your whole force to Harper's Ferry."[11] Simultaneously with this order came news of Pope's defeat and

---

9  The order to Miles from Wool is in *OR* 51, pt. 1, p. 764. The expiration of the 11th New York Militia's term of service is mentioned, *ibid.,* pp. 767-8. The order from Wool concerning the 8th New York Cavalry is also on p. 768. The orders from Miles to screen the Valley approaches to Harpers Ferry are found in *ibid.,* pp. 772-3. Shepherdstown Ford is one of three names Carman used interchangeably for the crossing of the Potomac below Shepherdstown. It is also called Blackford's Ford and Boteler's Ford, after the two farms on the north and south bank of the river next to the ford.

10  For the exchange of telegrams between White and Halleck, see *ibid.*, 12, pt. 3, p. 665. With the spring campaign of Jackson in the Shenandoah Valley still fresh in their minds, Stanton and Halleck expected Lee to move west into the Valley and then north, as Jackson had done earlier.

11  The evacuation of Winchester was examined by a Special Military Commission in September of 1862. The communications mentioned here were included in the testimony,

information that a column of 20,000 Confederates was coming down the Valley. This column of 20,000 was, in fact, the 17th Virginia Cavalry Battalion, moving for Snicker's Gap, in the Blue Ridge. White was not deceived by this report and sent out some cavalry to assure himself if there was anything in it to hasten his movements; meanwhile, he telegraphed Halleck that if rapid movement was necessary much ammunition would be abandoned, and suggested that the time be given him to remove it. He waited for an answer until 10 o'clock that night, none coming, he evacuated Winchester, abandoning four siege guns, blowing up his magazine, burning some buildings, containing military stores, and fell back to Harper's Ferry; the retreat being covered by the Seventh Squadron, Rhode Island Cavalry. The four siege guns, a few prisoners, and some supplies, fell into possession of the Confederates next day, when Lieutenant Colonel Funk, commanding a detachment of Virginia cavalry, entered the town.[12]

Miles immediately notified Wool that White had abandoned Winchester and assured him that he (Miles) had everything in readiness for any demonstration on Harper's Ferry, to which Wool replied: "I must leave the course you ought to pursue to your own sound discretion. Take care of your position and not expose it to surprise. Watchfulness, vigilance, and a sound discretion must be your guide at the present moment."[13]

On the 3rd General Wool was directed by Secretary Stanton to send to Cumberland all paroled prisoners, then at Point of Rocks, and was advised that there were strong indications that the Confederates intended to cross the Potomac below and cut off Harper's Ferry. On the evening of the same day Wool was notified by the officer commanding a detachment of the 87th Ohio, at Point of Rocks, of the dispersion of Cole's and Means' cavalry at Leesburg, and of Munford's dash into Waterford on the afternoon of the 2nd.[14]

That same evening White, with his brigade, arrived at Harper's Ferry from Winchester and reports came to Miles that Confederate cavalry were at Lovettsville,

---

which runs from *ibid.*, pt. 2, pp. 766-804. White was cleared of culpability in losses incurred by the evacuations. The original message is found in *ibid.*, pt. 3, p. 800.

12 White's telegram to Halleck is found in *ibid.*, p. 801. Carman implies there was no answer when, in fact, the answer was not received. See the testimony in the Special Military Commission. See also *OR* 12, pt. 2, p. 768, for the message, and *ibid.*, pp. 789-90, for the testimony that the lines was inoperable to Winchester.

13 Miles's message to Wool and Wool's reply about using his discretion are quoted almost in entirety from *ibid.*, 51, pt. 1, 784.

14 Stanton's instructions were funneled through Halleck. See *ibid.*, 19, pt. 2, p. 173. The officer at Point of Rocks was Lt. Col. John Faskin, 87th Ohio, whose telegram is in *ibid.*, p. 173.

Hillsboro, and on the Potomac below him, and that infantry and artillery were approaching Leesburg. Similar reports came in, on the 4th. Colonel H. B. Banning, who had been sent to Point of Rocks, with the greater part of the 87th Ohio, abandoned that place, upon hearing that D. H. Hill had crossed the Potomac below, and Miles promptly ordered him back from Berlin, with instructions to retreat, only when compelled to, and to obstruct the advance of the enemy as much as possible.[15]

Wool was informed by Miles on the 5th, and again, on the 6th, that Lee's army was crossing the Potomac and Wool promptly responded that Miles must "be energetic and active, and defend all places to the last extremity. There must be no abandonment of a post, and shoot the first man that thinks of it, whether officer or soldier.... The position on the heights ought to enable you to punish the enemy passing up the road in the direction of Harper's Ferry. Have your wits about you, and do all you can to annoy the rebels should they advance on you. Activity, energy, and decision must be used. You will not abandon Harper's Ferry without defending to the last extremity." To all of which Miles replied, on the 7th: "The enemy is steadily pressing on my pickets and establishing batteries on the plateau opposite Point of Rocks, but I am ready for them." And this was the last communication Wool had from Miles, for the telegraph was now cut and the Baltimore and Ohio obstructed near Frederick.[16]

When Stanton and Halleck realized the fact that their administration of military affairs had endangered the safety of the capital they sought to unload the responsibility upon the shoulders of others. President Lincoln took charge of affairs and assumed the responsibility of placing McClellan in command of the army to save Washington, notwithstanding the protest of Stanton and Chase that "they would prefer the loss of the capital to the restoration of McClellan to command," and Halleck, in the following paper, abdicated direction of affairs in Maryland and the Shenandoah Valley to General Wool:

15 Miles to Halleck, *ibid.*, p. 174. Messages from Banning and others about Confederate activities are found in *ibid.*, pp. 179-81. Miles's message to Wool is in *ibid.*, p. 188.

16 Miles's message of September 5 is in *ibid.*, p. 188. No message on the 6th has been found, but Wool's firm message about shooting anyone thinking of surrender is in *ibid.*, 19, pt. 1, p. 523, and is repeated in the testimony of the Military Commission, *ibid.*, p. 790. The second part of the quotation from Wool is in a subsequent telegram from Wool, and is in the Military Commission testimony immediately following the other telegram, p. 790. Miles's reply of the 7th about being ready is quoted in Wool's report, *ibid.*, 19, pt. 1, p. 520. A slightly different version is in the Record of the Harper's Ferry Commission, *ibid.*, p. 791.

HEADQUARTERS OF THE ARMY,
Washington, D.C., September 5, 1862.


Major-General WOOL, Baltimore, Md.:

    I find it impossible to get this army into the field again in large force for a day or two. In the mean time Harper's Ferry may be attacked and overwhelmed. I leave the dispositions there to your experience and local knowledge.

    I beg leave, however, to suggest the propriety of withdrawing all our forces in that vicinity to Maryland Heights. I have no personal knowledge of the ground, and merely make the suggestion to you.


H. W. HALLECK,
General-in-Chief[17]


We have quoted McClellan as saying that, before he left Washington, when there was no enemy to prevent the withdrawal of Miles, he recommended that the garrison at Harper's Ferry should be withdrawn via Hagerstown, to aid in covering the Cumberland Valley; or that, taking up the pontoon bridge, and obstructing the railroad bridge, it should fall back to Maryland Heights and then hold out to the last. Halleck did not deem it proper to adopt either suggestion, unless the dispatch of September 5, was the result. The matter was again brought to Halleck's attention in the manner and with the result as here given in McClellan's words:

Before I went to the front Secretary Seward came to my quarters one evening and asked my opinion on the condition of affairs at Harper's Ferry, remarking that he was not at ease on the subject. Harper's Ferry was not at this time at any sense under my control, but I told Mr. Seward that I regarded the arrangement there as exceedingly dangerous; that in my opinion the proper course was to abandon the position and unite the garrison (10,000 men, about) to the main army of operations, for the reason that its presence at Harper's Ferry would not hinder the enemy from crossing the Potomac; that if we were unsuccessful in the approaching battle Harper's Ferry would

---

17 Carman's obvious bias against Stanton and Halleck is evident here. He blamed them for the miscues that led to the capture of the garrison at Harpers Ferry, and seldom overlooked an opportunity to criticize Halleck. The quote about Stanton and Chase appeared in Chapter Three and came from McClellan, *My Own Story*, p. 545, but originated with Montgomery Blair. In his testimony before the Miles court of inquiry, Gen. Wool said he had no recollection of the dispatch of September 5. Even if he had received it, he would not have approved it, because he thought Miles's troops could have defended themselves where they were, in Harper's Ferry, particularly after he had ordered a block-house to be constructed on Maryland Heights.

be of no use to us, and its garrison necessarily lost; that if we were successful we would immediately recover the post without any difficulty, while the addition of 10,000 men to the active army would be an important factor in insuring success. I added that if it were determined to hold the position the existing arrangements were all wrong, as it would be easy for the enemy to surround and capture the garrison, and that the garrison ought, at least, to be withdrawn to Maryland Heights, where they could resist attack until relieved. The Secretary was much impressed by what I said, and asked me to accompany him to General Halleck's quarters and repeat my statement to him. I acquiesced, and we went together to Gen. Halleck's quarters, where we found that he had retired for the night. But he received us in his bed-room, where, after a preliminary explanation by the Secretary as to the interview being at his request, I said to Halleck precisely what I had stated to Mr. Seward. Halleck received my statement with ill-concealed contempt; said that everything was all right as it was; that my views were entirely erroneous, etc., and soon bowed us out, leaving matters at Harper's Ferry as they were.[18]

On the day that McClellan left Washington to take command in the field Halleck, notwithstanding his telegram to Wool, on the 5th, that he had no knowledge of the topography around Harper's Ferry and that he, Wool, must look to the safety of that place, telegraphed directly to Miles, Sept. 7th: "Our army is in motion. It is important that Harper's Ferry be held to the latest moment. The government has the utmost confidence in you, and is ready to give you full credit for the defense it expects you to make." And to this order and the strict construction put upon it by Miles is due the loss of Maryland Heights and Harper's Ferry, or, as Halleck officially stated it: "the disgraceful surrender of the post and the army."[19]

---

18 The wording that Carman used to describe McClellan's recommendations for Harpers Ferry was taken from both of McClellan's reports, *OR* 19, pt. 1, pp. 26, 44.

19 The telegram Carman referred to, *ibid.*, p. 757, was from Halleck to Miles dated September 7, 1862, and is given in its entirety. The "disgraceful surrender" comment is from Halleck's report, *ibid.*, p. 5. Notice that Carman criticized Halleck for shirking responsibility, then damned him for giving rigid orders that Carman believed dictated Miles's inflexible conduct of the operation. The way in which Carman reported Halleck's position reflects the author's bias. The quote from the report, put in context, reads: "As this whole matter has been investigated and reported upon by a military commission, it is unnecessary for me to discuss the very disgraceful surrender of the post and army under Colonel Miles's command." Thus, Halleck condemned Miles's actions but puts the blame, testifying to the commission, on Miles rather than his own order.

On the 4th General White, who had come in from Winchester the preceding day, was ordered to the command of Martinsburg, his brigade remaining at Harper's Ferry. On the 5th the troops at Harper's Ferry were thus brigaded:

First Brigade (right wing, line of battle Bolivar Heights, Va.)
Col. F. G. D'Utassy (39th N. Y.), commanding:
39th N. Y.
111th N. Y. (Garibaldi Guard), Col. Segoine
115th N. Y., Col. Sammon
15th Independent Indiana Battery, Capt. Von Sehlen

Second Brigade (left wing, line of battle Bolivar Heights, Va.)
Col. Trimble (60th Ohio), commanding
60th Ohio
126th New York, Col. Sherrill
9th Vt., Col. Stannard
Potts' Battery (substituted Rigby's subsequently)

Third Brigade (Maryland Heights, Md., including siege guns thereon)
Col. Thomas H. Ford (32nd Ohio), commanding
32nd Ohio
Battalion, 1st Potomac Home Brigade, Maj. John A. Steiner
Co. F, N. Y. Heavy Artillery, Capt. McGrath
Battalion, Rhode Island Cavalry, Maj. Corliss
Detachment Maryland Cavalry, Capt. Russell

Fourth Brigade (entrenchments on Camp Hill, Va.)
Col. W. G. Ward (12th N. Y. Militia)
12th N. Y. Militia (three months)
Co. A, 5th N. Y. Heavy Artillery, Capt. Graham
Rigby's Battery (Potts substituted afterwards)
87th Ohio (three months), Col. Banning

Independent commands:
1st Maryland Potomac Home Brigade, Col. Maulsby, Sandy Hook, Md.
8th N. Y. Cavalry, Col. B. F. Davis, Harper's Ferry, Va.

Detachment Maryland Potomac Home Brigade Cavalry, Capt. Cole, Sandy Hook, Md.[20]

On September 6th Colonel Maulsby, at Sandy Hook, was ordered to the utmost vigilance in guarding the fords below Harper's Ferry and to concentrate five companies of his regiment as near the ford at Sandy Hook as he could get to command it and the roads leading to Maryland Heights. He was advised that Captain Faithful, who had abandoned Frederick, was on the march to join him and that "the position of Sandy Hook was to be held if it took half the force at Harper's Ferry, and under no circumstance was it to be abandoned."[21] Colonel Banning of the 87th Ohio, then at Berlin, was ordered to defend that point as long as possible, but, if obliged to fall back, he was to stop at Sandy Hook, which was to be defended at all hazards. The commanding officer of three companies of the 29th Pennsylvania Infantry at Hagerstown was ordered by General Wool to send all stores and two Parrott guns to Chambersburg, Pennsylvania, and, on the same day the orders were repeated to Lieutenant F. B. Crosby, who was permitted to use his discretion in the matter, governed by the movements of the enemy.[22]

Banning, who had been ordered to return to Point of Rocks on the 4th, and who took with him two howitzers of Graham's 5th New York Artillery, was shelled from the opposite side of the Potomac, on the 6th, by George B. Anderson's command, and pressed on the Monocacy road by Longstreet's skirmishers, whereupon, he again fell back to Berlin and thence to Sandy Hook, where he formed a junction with Colonel W. P. Maulsby's 1st Maryland Potomac Home Brigade. On the 7th Miles visited Sandy Hook and Weverton and directed cavalry reconnaissances on the different roads. Some of the detachments started out, heard rumors and returned, but Lieutenant H. T. C. Green with a small party of Cole's Maryland Cavalry, pushing through Petersville and Middletown to within 2 1/2

---

20 The organization of the Union troops in Harpers Ferry is found in Lt. Binney's report, *OR* 19, pt. 1, p. 533. Binney was an aide-de-camp of Gen. White and wrote a very detailed after-action report.

21 The quotation from the orders received by Col. Maulsby related to defending Sandy Hook is found in *ibid.*, 51, pt. 1, pp. 794-5. Carman slightly altered the wording.

22 The orders to Maj. Scott Banning of the 29th Pennsylvania, and Lt. Crosby, 4th Artillery, the latter two at Hagerstown, are in *ibid.*, pp. 795-6.

miles of Frederick, ran into Confederate pickets, took some prisoners and returned without loss, to report that Lee's army was at Frederick.[23]

This definite information inspired Miles with much energy and he was now constantly in the saddle. On the 8th he visited Colonel Ford, who, three days before, had been sent to Maryland Heights, instructed him and his officers as to the importance of the position, giving them to understand that they must retain it at all hazards, with them held he could defy an army of 25,000 men on his front. Finding himself short of forage and subsistence, he seized all the flour in the stores and mills in the vicinity, and sent out foraging parties on various roads. Major A. W. Corliss, of the Rhode Island Cavalry, made a reconnaissance into Solomon's Gap on Elk Ridge, thence down through Jefferson, driving in the enemy's pickets, capturing 25 prisoners, and pushing on to within two miles of Lee's army at Frederick. Again, on the 9th, Miles was at Sandy Hook, Weverton, Maryland Heights and Bolivar Heights, and rumors of the enemy were heard in every direction.[24]

On the 10th authentic reports came in, thick and fast, that the Confederates had crossed the South Mountain and were in motion northward. Lieutenant-Colonel Downey of the 3rd Maryland Potomac Home Brigade, with Captain Francis Shamburg's company (20 men) of the 1st Maryland Cavalry, scouting in Pleasant Valley, encountered Jackson's advance, near Boonsboro, with a loss of 1 man killed and three men wounded. He ascertained that the whole Confederate army was on the move but whether on Hagerstown or to recross the Potomac below he could not tell. White, who received the same information at Martinsburg, reported it to Halleck at Washington and Wool at Baltimore and telegraphed to Miles: "The enemy will be whipped in Maryland, and we will be gobbled up in their retreat." But from his lookout or observatory on Maryland Heights, Miles could see no indication of the enemy in any direction.[25]

On the 11th Miles again went onto Maryland Heights and soon ascertained that the Confederates had come into Pleasant Valley, by Brownsville Gap and made

---

23 The chronology of Banning's movements can be found in Binney's report, *ibid.*, 19, pt. 1, pp. 533-5, and also in Maj. McIllvaine's (5th New York Artillery) report, although McIllvaine mistook the date of the shelling as September 7, *ibid.*, p. 546, and D. H. Hill's report, *ibid.*, 1,019.

24 For Miles's visit to Sandy Hook on September 7, the reaction to the information of the Confederate advance, and the scouting of Corliss, Downey, and Shamburg, see Lt. Binney's report, which Carman's wording closely paraphrased, in *ibid.*, pp. 534-6.

25 The cavalry actions are continued in *ibid.*, pp. 534-6. The telegraph message from White to Miles about being gobbled up is also quoted in Binney's report; the messages to Halleck and Wool are in *ibid.*, pt. 2, p. 249.

a lodgment at Solomon's Gap; and later came the startling news from White at Martinsburg that he was surrounded.[26]

When Halleck, September 2nd, ordered General White to evacuate Winchester and retire to Harper's Ferry, he consulted neither Wool nor Miles about the matter, he was simply stampeded, nor did he advise either of the step. Wool received his first information from Miles and, naturally, was greatly surprised that such an important outpost, generally regarded as the key to the valley, had been abandoned "without the approach or presence of an enemy."[27]

As White ranked Miles his presence at Harper's Ferry was not agreeable to Wool, who wanted a regular officer at that place, so he promptly detached White from his brigade and ordered him to the command of the small garrison at Martinsburg, with instructions to guard the Baltimore and Ohio Railroad, to exercise "sleepless energy" and take "active measures" to defend the place to the last extremity. White could not see that Martinsburg was of more importance than Winchester, from which he had been ordered to beat a somewhat precipitous retreat, nor could he see how the position could be any better held against a superior force. The assignment was much to his astonishment and extremely distasteful, and he asked to be returned to his rightful command of the brigade that he had organized at Winchester, but this was denied him and he was ordered to remain at Martinsburg and Wool repeated the admonition to defend himself to the last extremity and that there must be "no running before the enemy is coming." When Halleck was appealed to he informed White that no orders had been sent by him (Halleck) to go to Martinsburg but, as in falling back from Winchester to Harper's Ferry, he had come under Wool's orders, he must be governed by them.[28]

On September 6th Miles advised White that communication with Baltimore and Washington was cut off; that Frederick was occupied by Confederates in force; that rumor said a column was moving on Williamsport and to "look out for squalls." On the same day (Sept. 7) White informed both Wool and Halleck that his outposts had been attacked that morning; to Wool he made an additional remark that he should obey the order to fight, "though with no hope of support." Again, on

26 *Ibid.*, pt. 1, pp. 535-6.

27 *Ibid.*, pt. 2, p. 182.

28 The process of how Gen. White and Col. Miles determined the command structure at Harpers Ferry was related by Carman, perhaps to show the confused state of affairs in the Union high command. Carman again highlighted the roles of Wool and Halleck to build his case against the latter as the villain of the Maryland campaign. Halleck's order for White to retreat to Harpers Ferry is in *ibid.*, 12, pt. 3, p. 800. Wool's surprised telegram, including the phrase "without approach or presence of an enemy," is in *ibid.*, 19, pt. 2, p. 182.

the morning of the 7th, he reported the repulse of an attack on his outposts, which gave Secretary Stanton the opportunity to commend him and to say: "It is expected that no post will be surrendered, but that every officer and every man shall fight as if the fate of the Government depended upon him."[29]

The orders of Wool and Stanton to hold on to Martinsburg to the last extremity; that there must be "no running before the enemy is coming," and that "no post will be surrendered," may be taken as criticism of Halleck's order for the abandonment of Winchester.

White's outposts were daily attacked and the 12th Illinois and a detachment of the 8th New York Cavalry were active in repelling them, all of which was reported to Wool, with a request for reinforcement of four regiments of infantry and two batteries, as he had but a small force of cavalry and infantry and three 6-pounder guns. Wool could not spare the reinforcement nor would he permit Miles to give it, but he telegraphed White: "If 20,000 men should attack you, you will of course fall back. Harper's Ferry would be the best position I could recommend, but be sure that you have such a force against you or any other that would overwhelm you."[30]

On the 8th two companies of the 8th New York Cavalry scouted to Bunker Hill, Smithfield, and Summit Point, capturing a few pickets, but ascertaining no general movement of the enemy in that direction. Colonel Downey, who scouted from Kearneysville and returned without incident, was ordered to remain there and to protect the road and the bridge over the Opequon, unless severely pressed by the enemy, in which case he would retreat to Shepherdstown, cross the Potomac to Maryland Heights and report for duty to Colonel Ford. Two days later the 8th New York Cavalry made a reconnaissance toward Winchester and saw nothing, and Downey, crossing the Potomac, ran into Jackson's advance near Boonsboro, as we have seen, and gave White information of the danger menacing him.[31] What action White now took is told in his official report:

29 The communication between Miles and White on September 6 and 7, along with the message from Wool about "look out for squalls," can be found in *ibid.*, 51, pt. 1, pp. 794, 798, and *ibid.*, 19, pt. 2, p. 205, which included the admonition about the fate of the government, respectively. Notice that Carman again sided with those critical of Halleck, and portrayed Halleck as avoiding responsibility at all costs.

30 The message to White from Wool about "no running" is in *ibid.*, 19, pt. 1, p. 520, and the "no post surrendered" message is from Stanton to White, *ibid.*, 51, pt. 1, p. 798. White's request for infantry and artillery is in *ibid.*, 19, pt. 2, p. 205, and also in *ibid.*, 51, pt. 1, p. 798. Wool's directive about falling back if attacked by 20,000 men is in *ibid.*, 19, pt. 1, pp. 520 and 791 as part of Wool's report and his testimony at the Military Commission.

31 Although there are other reports in the *OR*, Carman leans heavily on Binney's report, and his wording nearly matches Binney's. See *ibid.*, 19, pt. 1, pp. 534-5.

On the 11th instant reports reached me, through scouts and others, that the enemy were crossing the Potomac into Virginia at or about Williamsport and Cherry Run in force; also, that they were passing to the west of Martinsburg, between it and North Mountain, thus cutting off our retreat in that direction.

It being ordered by Major-General Wool that the place should be held to the last extremity, at noon on the 11th instant I sent out one section of Captain Phillips' battery and four companies of the Sixty-fifth Illinois, together with half a company of cavalry and two teams, with axes, &c., the whole under command of Colonel Cameron, of the Sixty-fifth Illinois, with orders to proceed out upon the Williamsburg [Williamsport] road, as far as practicable, and to obstruct the roads, tear up the bridges, and, in every way possible, retard the advance of the enemy.

At night-fall, it having been well ascertained that the enemy were between us and North Mountain, and were in very large force near Falling Waters, on the Williamsport road, some 7 miles from Martinsburg, and were still crossing, it became evident that with the small force at my disposal the position could not longer be held.

Colonel Cameron's party was accordingly recalled, and every exertion made to convey the public property to Harper's Ferry, that being the only line of retreat left open.

The railroad agent had, the previous day, sent off some 11 empty cars, in defiance of my orders for them to be retained, but I had detained the train up from Harper's Ferry that day, consisting of but 6 cars, and I caused all the surplus arms, clothing, ammunition, and camp equipage to be conveyed to the railroad depot, to be sent thence by rail to Harper's Ferry, as but one of the regiments under my command was provided with transportation. This was done mostly by the men themselves, the transportation (being divided as equally as possible between the several regiments) being wholly insufficient for the purpose.

The railroad train was loaded to the extent of its capacity and sent to Harper's Ferry, where it arrived in safety. The transportation was then employed to haul the most valuable property remaining, and the troops and wagons took up their line of march at 2 o'clock on the morning of the 12th.

But little public property was abandoned, consisting mostly of tents and camp equipage, which could not be conveyed with the means at disposal.

Upon the march, the pickets of the enemy were encountered at Hall-town, but they were driven back to Charlestown, the command arriving safely at Harper's Ferry on the afternoon of the 12th.[32]

---

32 The long quotation explaining White's retreat from Martinsburg is from his report, *ibid.*, 19, pt. 1, p. 524. Carman pasted eight paragraphs from it into the manuscript.

On the 12th a detachment of the 8th New York Cavalry was observing Knott's Ford, near the mouth of the Antietam, but, upon the approach of Jackson's column from Martinsburg withdrew to Harper's Ferry. On the same day the Seventh Squadron Rhode Island Cavalry set out from Maryland Heights on a reconnaissance to Sharpsburg. It passed the mouth of the Antietam, saw the New York Cavalry at Knott's Ford, and advanced nearly to Sharpsburg when, finding that its retreat by the road was cut off by the occupation of Solomon's Gap, by Kershaw and Barksdale, returned to camp by way of the canal tow path.[33]

As ranking officer White was entitled to the command of all the forces now assembled and should have assumed it, but, believing it the intention and desire of both Halleck and Wool that Miles should retain it, he waived his right, at least for the present, and put himself and staff at Miles's disposal and gave him loyal help. This action was more to the credit of his heart than his head, but he justified himself in the fact that fighting had already commenced, that Miles knew the topography of the vicinity and that there was no probability that the interests of the service would suffer.[34]

When White arrived skirmishing had begun on Maryland Heights and distrust was growing as to Miles' capacity. Brigade and regimental commanders generally approved White's course, under the circumstances, yet wished that he had done otherwise. Immediately upon his arrival White asked Miles what his plans were, but received no definite reply. He had no specific plan beyond the defense of Bolivar Heights and the bridges; that these positions being defended, Harper's Ferry was secure, and that his orders were to hold Harper's Ferry. White then suggested that Maryland Heights appeared to be the key to the position and offered the only feasible line of retreat, should that become necessary, as well as the most defensible position should it become necessary to concentrate the entire force at any one

---

33 The order for the 7th Rhode Island Squadron reconnaissance is found in *ibid.*, 51, pt. 1, p. 804. No report of these two expeditions appears in the OR. An account by William Luff, "March of the Cavalry From Harpers Ferry September 14th, 1862," in *Military Order of the Loyal Legion of the United States* (MOLLUS Papers), Volume 2, Illinois Commandery, pp. 33-5. Carman's source was Isaac Heysinger, a corporal in the same command who stated in an August 17, 1905 letter (NYPL, Correspondence Files, Box 3, Folder 5) the almost identical story Carman related here, but said it was on Saturday, September 13. Why Carman accepted Heysinger's account, but kept the date as the 12th, is unclear. McLaws's report, OR 19, pt. 1, p. 852, confirms the presence of Joseph Kershaw's and William Barksdale's brigades in Solomon's Gap.

34 Binney's report included the arrival of White and his deferring of command to Miles, *ibid.*, p. 536, and White's reasoning is in his report, *ibid.*, p. 525, and his appendix to the Military Commission, *ibid.*, pp. 774-5. White also defended his view in this appendix that Maryland Heights was the key to the Union defense.

point, and that it should be defended at all hazards and with the entire force if necessary. In the main Miles agreed with White, but thought Camp Hill best commanded the bridges and the approaches from that side and stated that there was no water on Maryland Heights; that the objection to taking the entire force over there was that and the difficulty of getting up subsistence and artillery, and when they got there the difficulty of remaining there for want of water. But Miles' great objection was the orders he had received to hold Harper's Ferry to the last extremity and that to leave Harper's Ferry, even to go to Maryland Heights, would be disobeying the instructions he had received from both Halleck and Wool. Other officers made like suggestions but to one and all he made the same reply-he had been ordered to hold Harper's Ferry.[35]

The defenses of Harper's Ferry comprised an unfinished line of rifle-pits on Bolivar Heights. These heights, two miles and more beyond the town, a low ridge extending from near the Potomac southward to the Charlestown road, where a small work for the protection of a battery was thrown up, thence the line dropped to a lower plateau near the Winchester road, then rising again onto a slight eminence finally sloped steeply to the Shenandoah. This line was over one and a half miles long and was held by 7000 men. In the rear of this line, eastward, in the upper part of the town, was an earthwork, on elevated ground known as Camp Hill, and in this work were about 800 men. About 1000 men guarded the bridges and other points on the river.

Maryland Heights beyond the Potomac, rising over 1000 feet above it, completely commanded Harper's Ferry; looking up from the town they seem ready to drop upon it. On the crest of these, one and a half miles north of the railroad bridge, there was a small work, called the stone fort; well down their western slope was a battery of heavy guns that could throw shot down upon Bolivar Heights [ink blot: probably "and"] beyond it; a line of entrenchments ran across this slope terminating at a work near the Potomac, called Fort Duncan—but this line was not occupied for the upper end. For the defense of these heights Miles assigned 2000 men.[36]

35 Carman accepted White's testimony at the Harpers Ferry Military Commission to explain why Miles did not follow White's ideas, *ibid.*, p. 716. Carman allowed White to put his interpretation on the events after the fact. Obviously this puts White in a better position, and should thus be accepted with caution.

36 Carman's general description of the defenses of Harpers Ferry and positioning of troops is accurate. The 2,000 men on Maryland Heights was the brigade of Thomas Ford, augmented by the 3rd Maryland Potomac Home Brigade and the 39th New York from D'Utassy's brigade. The 1,000 men on Camp Hill comprised Ward's brigade, and the 7,000 arrayed along Bolivar Heights were the commands of Trimble and D'Utassy. The description is lifted from White's

The eastern approaches to Maryland Heights were guarded by Colonel William P. Maulsby, 1st Maryland Potomac Home Brigade, who was at Sandy Hook, where the railroad and canal, hugging the Potomac, and the country roads, leading down Pleasant Valley, united. A zig-zag and difficult road leading from Harper's Ferry over the southern end of the heights, came into Pleasant Valley at the hamlet of Sandy Hook. Maulsby had under his command five companies of his own regiment; eight companies of the 87th Ohio, Colonel H. B. Banning; Cole's Maryland Cavalry, and three pieces of artillery, under Captain B. F. Potts.[37] These forces were placed to prevent surprise and repel attack upon the eastern side of Maryland Heights from the direction of Pleasant Valley, as well as to guard the approach to the ferry around the bend of the Potomac. On the 11th, the greater part of this command was withdrawn to the slope of Maryland Heights and one gun added to the three already under Potts' charge.

We now return to the Confederates who, in high feather, left Frederick on the evening of the 10th, on their "rollicking march" to surround and capture the prey that Halleck had already corralled for them. To repeat the orders under which they were acting: Jackson, with fourteen brigades, was to march on the morning of the 10th, by way of Middletown and Boonsboro in the direction of Sharpsburg, crossing the Potomac at the most convenient point, and, by Friday morning, the 12th, take possession of the Baltimore and Ohio Railroad, capture such of the enemy as were at Martinsburg and intercept those attempting escape from Harper's Ferry. Walker, with his two brigades, after destroying the Monocacy viaduct, was to cross the Potomac at Cheeks' Ford, near the mouth of the Monocacy, ascend the west bank of the river to Lovettsville, and take possession of Loudoun Heights, overlooking Harper's Ferry from the Virginia side of the Potomac, but separated from the town by the Shenandoah River. Walker was to be in place by Friday morning, the 12th, Key's Ford on his left, and the road between the end of the mountain and the Potomac, on his right. As far as possible he was to co-operate with Jackson and McLaws and intercept the retreat of the enemy. McLaws, with his own division and that of R. H. Anderson—ten brigades in all—was to turn to the

---

article in *B&L*, p. 612. In borrowing White's account Carman allowed the erroneous statement into his manuscript that the Stone Fort existed during this time. The structure was not built until 1863. Likewise, Fort Duncan was not in existence yet. In fact, it was the disaster at Harpers Ferry that prompted more defensive construction there. Writing to Halleck on September 26, 1862, McClellan stated, "I have just returned from Maryland Heights, and have determined to fortify them, as well as the heights on the opposite side of the river, in order to avoid a similar catastrophe to the one which happened to Colonel Miles." *OR* 19, pt. 2, pp. 360-1.

37 The dispositions and withdrawal of Maulsby's command to the foot of Maryland Heights is found in his testimony to the Military Commission, *ibid.*, 19, pt. 1, pp. 556-8.

left on reaching Middletown, cross the South Mountain, traverse Pleasant Valley and seize Maryland Heights, overlooking Harper's Ferry from the Maryland side of the river. He, also, was to be in position by Friday morning, the 12th.

Although separated from both Maryland Heights and Loudoun Heights, by the Potomac and the Shenandoah respectively, Harper's Ferry was commanded by both Heights and at the mercy of a plunging fire from them. Jackson was to prevent the escape of the garrison in the direction of Martinsburg and close in from the west; McLaws and Walker were to prevent escape across the Potomac and Shenandoah. After the capture of Harper's Ferry, Jackson, Walker, and McLaws were to join Lee at or near Hagerstown.[38]

The divisions of D. H. Hill, D. R. Jones and John B. Hood, and the brigade of N. G. Evans, in all fourteen brigades, and the greater part of Stuart's cavalry, were retained by General Lee to watch and delay the march of McClellan until Harper's Ferry should be taken, a matter considered as requiring not more than three days, when the army, reunited at Hagerstown, would continue its advance into Pennsylvania, or if possible and advisable, give McClellan battle west of the South Mountain. There was such absolute confidence in the continued slow and cautious movement of McClellan that Lee apprehended no serious interference with his plans. He had not entertained the intention of offering or receiving battle at Frederick or of delaying McClellan at the passes of South Mountain; quite the contrary; his plan was to draw him beyond South Mountain and give battle in the valley west of it, where the Army of the Potomac would be farther removed from its resources of men and supplies at Washington, and where a disaster to it would be well nigh irretrievable.[39]

When the order for this movement was issued Walker's Division was on detached service in vain effort to destroy the aqueduct of the Chesapeake and Ohio Canal at the mouth of the Monocacy. D. H. Hill had been instructed to do this when he crossed into Maryland, on the 4th, but finding it impracticable abandoned

38 Carman repeated from Chapter Five the movements of the various Confederate divisions pursuant to Lee's S.O. #191. His language mimics the actual order, but he made two errors. First, he presumed Jackson was to move eastward from Martinsburg, which S.O. #191 did not mention, and second, Carman presumed the object of the operation was the capture of Harpers Ferry, when the stated objective was the Union forces blocking the Shenandoah Valley. It appears Lee believed these Union troops would retreat, but as Carman presented it, Miles's literal interpretation of Halleck's orders forced him into defending the town.

39 Carman seemed to accept that Lee was calculating on McClellan's advance, when recent studies demonstrate that he was unaware of who was commanding the Union army, and how close Union forces really were. See Harsh, *Taken at the Flood*, pp. 129-31. Carman states that Lee did not intend to defend the passes in South Mountain because he wanted the Union army to follow him into the Cumberland Valley, as per Lee's report, OR 19, pt. 1, p. 145.

it, whereupon Walker was ordered back to do it effectively. He worked from 11 p. m. of the 9th to early morning of the 10th, but with no better success than Hill, the work was one of days instead of hours, and, as he had been informed by Lee that the army would march from Frederick toward Hagerstown on the 10th, thus leaving his small division in the immediate presence of a strong force of the enemy, he determined to rejoin his chief by way of Jefferson and Middletown as he had been instructed. Before marching, however, he received Lee's orders to cross the Potomac at Cheek's Ford and proceed towards Harper's Ferry to co-operate with Jackson and McLaws.*

> * September 9, 1862. Marched four miles to within two miles of Frederick. After sunset marched to the aqueduct across the Monocacy River. This regiment, with the 25th N. C., was thrown across the river. In a slight skirmish with the enemy's pickets, Capt. Duffy (Co. B) was mortally wounded, and two privates of Co. K missing supposed to have been taken prisoners. During the night withdrew to the position occupied the evening before. (Muster Roll of 24th North Carolina, October 31, 1862.)[40]

When ready to move on the morning of the 10th he found that the aqueduct and its approaches, as well as Cheek's Ford, were commanded by artillery, supported by the 1st Massachusetts Cavalry, upon which he marched up the east bank of the Potomac and crossed at Point of Rocks, during the night of the 10th, but with much difficulty, owing to the destruction of the bridge over the canal and the steepness of the river banks. A heavy rain now set in and as his men were exhausted by their night march, Walker allowed them rest during the 11th and resumed march on the morning of the 12th, camping at Hillsboro that night.

At 10 o'clock on the morning of the 13th Walker arrived at the foot of Loudoun Heights and reconnaissance disclosed that they were unoccupied, upon which Colonel John R. Cooke, with the 27th North Carolina and 30th Virginia, took possession of them and held them during the night. Upon his arrival in the morning, Walker was joined by a detachment of signal men and Captain White's

40 This description of Walker's march and his attempt to destroy the aqueduct are lifted from Walker's report, *ibid.*, pp. 912-3. It should be noted that Carman ignored Walker's *B&L* account, in which Walker claimed he already knew he was to march to Loudoun Heights based on a conversation with Lee. See Harsh, *Taken at the Flood*, pp. 133-45. Carman cited the Muster Roll of the 24th North Carolina Infantry, which evidently he had access to in Washington, D.C. Several muster rolls and notes from records of Confederate units appear in the Battlefield Board Papers. Carman erred in writing that Captain Duffy was mortally wounded. Duffy lived several more years.

company of Maryland cavalry, the former went with Cooke to open communications with Jackson, the latter scouted the approaches from Harper's Ferry and the Maryland side. Cooke, on reaching the summit of Loudoun, put his men in hiding from the view of the Harper's Ferry garrison.

Meanwhile McLaws had gained the summit of Maryland Heights, which commanded Harper's Ferry as well as Loudoun Heights, and Walker's entire Division, except that portion occupying Loudoun Heights, was placed in a strong position to prevent the escape of the Union forces down the west bank of the Potomac.[41]

Jackson left his bivouac, near Frederick early on the morning of the 10th, passed through Frederick and Middletown and, with the divisions of A. P. Hill and Jackson, went over Turner's Gap and bivouacked one mile from Boonsboro; Ewell's Division bivouacking between Middletown and the Gap.[42]

A staff officer riding with Jackson that day writes:

At Frederick he asked for a map of Chambersburg and its vicinity, and made many irrelevant inquiries about roads and locations in the direction of Pennsylvania. Having finished this public inquiry, he took me aside, and after asking about the different fords of the Potomac between Williamsport and Harper's Ferry, told me that he was ordered to capture the garrison at Harper's Ferry, and would cross either at Williamsport or Shepherdstown, as the enemy might or might not withdraw from Martinsburg.... On the march that day the captain of the cavalry advance, just ahead, had instructions to let no civilians go to the front, and we entered each village we passed before the inhabitants knew of our coming."[43]

---

41 Carman relied, practically word for word, on Walker's report for the actions of his command, *OR* 19, pt. 1, p. 913. The only additions to Walker's report are the specific naming of the enemy unit, 1st Massachusetts Cavalry, which was detailed to guard the Potomac fords. See *ibid.*, 51, pt. 1, p. 783. For the specific time they arrived at the foot of Loudoun Heights and the presence of White's men, see Walker's account in *B&L*, p. 608.

42 Jackson's march from Frederick was traced by Carman using Jackson's report and a few other sources. Harsh, in *Taken at the Flood*, pp. 175-6, offered convincing evidence that A. P. Hill's Division followed Ewell's, and thus both divisions camped east of South Mountain on September 10.

43 Carman's Note: Henry Kyd Douglas, in *B&L*, p. 620. Carman's footnote for Douglas's account of Jackson's deceptive ruse and subsequent questioning of Douglas is actually on p. 622. Douglas implied the entire command camped near Boonsboro on the 10th. He also claimed Jackson was ordered to capture Harpers Ferry, which was not stated in S.O. #191, but Douglas seems to be reading what happened backward to make it all appear intentional.

Jackson had now to determine whether to go on to Williamsport or turn toward Shepherdstown, and Captain Douglas, of his staff, was directed to ride into Boonsboro and make inquiries as to the whereabouts of the Union troops, more especially whether White was still at Martinsburg. As Douglas, with but a single cavalryman, rode into the village, he encountered Captain Shamburg's detachment of 1st Maryland Cavalry and was quickly driven back without obtaining the desired information.[44]

The next morning, the 11th, having learned that the Union troops still held Martinsburg. Jackson marched through Boonsboro, and, taking the direct road to Williamsport, recrossed to the Potomac into Virginia, at Light's Ford, during the afternoon, the troops singing and the bands playing "carry me back to Ole Virginny." A. P. Hill's Division took the direct road to Martinsburg, while Jackson, to prevent the escape of White from Martinsburg northward and northwestward, led the divisions of Jackson and Ewell by a side road, to North Mountain Depot, on the Baltimore and Ohio Railroad, about seven miles northwest of Martinsburg, where they bivouacked that night; and Major S. B. Myers, commanding the cavalry, sent a detachment of his command as far south as the Berkeley and Hampshire Turnpike. White, advised of Jackson's approach, abandoned Martinsburg during the night, as we have seen, and joined Miles at Harper's Ferry. [45]

On the morning of the 12th Jackson's cavalry entered the town, followed during the day by the entire command, took a large quantity of abandoned quartermaster and commissary stores and, moving on, camped that night on the

---

44 Carman evidently accepted the story from Douglas, *B&L*, p. 620, concerning his encounter with Federal cavalry in Boonsboro. It may be significant that Carman did not include the portion that detailed Jackson's close brush with capture. The story has been called into serious question by modern authors, who cite sources by soldiers whom Carman knew personally, including Jed Hotchkiss. See Dennis Frye, "Henry Kyd Douglas Challenged by His Peers," in *Civil War: The Magazine of the Civil War Society*, Vol. IX, No. 5 (Sept. Oct. 1991). Thus, Carman may have known the story's inaccuracy, but left it to later historians to rediscover. Douglas did not mention that it was Shamburg's company of the 1st Maryland Cavalry, but its reconnaissance was mentioned in *OR* 19, pt. 2, p. 249. Lt. Col. Downey, the regimental commander, accompanied Shamburg on this reconnaissance. Curiously, and perhaps revealingly, instead of being congratulated for his boldness, he was reprimanded by Col. Miles. See *ibid.*, 51, pt. 1, p. 820.

45 Jackson's choice of using Williamsport and Light's Ford deviated from the instructions of S.O. #191, something Carman did not mention. See Harsh, *Taken at the Flood*, Chapter Four, for a discussion of the reasons and implications of this action. Carman relied on Douglas's account for the march of Jackson's command, which is slightly more detailed than Jackson's report. However, Carman's wording on this page almost duplicates Jackson's report. See *OR* 19, pt. 1, p. 953, which refers to Myers as a major, but later correctly cites his as a captain. Myers was promoted to major on October 30, 1862. Compiled Military Service Record, National Archives.

banks of the Opequon. On the morning of the 13th the march was resumed on Harper's Ferry and, at 11 o'clock A. P. Hill's Division, in the advance, came in view of Miles' forces drawn up on Bolivar Heights. Hill went into camp near Halltown, about two miles from Miles' position, Jackson's and Ewell's divisions encamping near by. The reasons why Jackson delayed attack are thus stated in his official report:

> The commanding general having directed Major-General McLaws to move, with his own and General R. H. Anderson's divisions, to take possession of the Maryland Heights, overlooking Harper's Ferry, and Brig. Gen. J. G. Walker, pursuing a different route, to cross the Potomac and move up that river on the Virginia side and occupy the Loudoun Heights, both for the purpose of co-operating with me, it became necessary, before making the attack, to ascertain whether they were in position. Failing to learn the fact by signals, a courier was dispatched to each of those points for the required information. During the night the courier to the Loudoun Heights returned with a message from General Walker that he was in position. In the mean time General McLaws had attacked the Federal force posted to defend the Maryland Heights; had routed it and taken possession of that commanding position. The Potomac River flowed between the positions respectively occupied by General McLaws and myself, and the Shenandoah separated me from General Walker, and it became advisable, as the speediest mode of communication, to resort to signals. Before the necessary orders were thus transmitted the day was far advanced. The enemy had, by fortifications, strengthened the naturally strong position which he occupied along Bolivar Heights, extending from near the Shenandoah to the Potomac. McLaws and Walker, being thus separated from the enemy by intervening rivers, could afford no assistance beyond the fire of their artillery and guarding certain avenues of escape to the enemy, and, from the reports received from them by signals, in consequence of the distance and range of their guns, not much could be expected from their artillery so long as the enemy retained his advanced position on Bolivar Heights.[46]

Longstreet followed Jackson from Frederick, bivouacking on the night of the 10th between Middletown and Turner's Gap. Next morning he marched over South Mountain and, with D. R. Jones' and Hood's divisions and Evans' Brigade moved on the road to Hagerstown to procure some needed supplies and to meet a force of Pennsylvanians reported to be advancing from Chambersburg.

---

46 Carman pasted in here a long paragraph from Jackson's report, OR 19, pt. 1, p. 953, to explain Jackson's dispositions for capturing Harpers Ferry. Note that the report gives no details of why Jackson chose to pursue the fleeing Federals under White.

General D. H. Hill, who had followed Longstreet from Frederick, was left at Boonsboro, with five brigades, to guard the immense wagon train of the entire army, support Stuart's cavalry in holding the passes in rear, and to prevent the escape of any part of the garrison from Harper's Ferry, by the road of Pleasant Valley.[47]

Hagerstown is pleasantly situated in the center of a rich farming country, abounding in supplies, and is a place of considerable local importance. Good roads radiate from it in every direction and the fords of the Upper Potomac were accessible over roads not likely to fall into possession of the enemy. It was sufficiently far from Harper's Ferry and South Mountain to enable Lee to concentrate his army, in the event of disaster at either of these places, and a good point from which to conduct offensive operations in Maryland or into Pennsylvania, therefore a place of considerable strategic value.[48]

Longstreet indulges in the criticism that the change of his position from Boonsboro to Hagerstown, further misled Stuart and the commanders of the divisions at Boonsboro and Harper's Ferry into a feeling of security that there could be no threatening by the Union army moving from Washington.[49]

On the morning of the 9th McLaws received verbal instructions from Lee as to the part he was to play in this complicated, yet simple, movement. He was to follow with his own division and that of R. H. Anderson in the rear of the army as it marched from Frederick until, reaching Middletown, he would take up the left hand road leading to Harper's Ferry and by Friday morning, the 12th, possess himself of Maryland Heights and endeavor to capture the garrison at Harper's Ferry. When informed by McLaws that he had never been to Harper's Ferry and knew nothing of the surrounding country Lee replied to the effect that it did not matter, but that 7000 or 8000 of the enemy were there and their capture a matter of some importance and troops enough would march with him to accomplish this purpose.

---

47 Longstreet's and D. H. Hill's marches are summarized from their *B&L* accounts, pp. 560 and 663-4, respectively.

48 The discussion of the resources and road network around Hagerstown are cited by Carman as the basis for Lee's determination to use Hagerstown for the center of his operations. While Lee implied that possibility in his letter to President Davis dated September 12, 1862, *OR* 19, pt. 2, pp. 604-5, it was not a stated goal of the campaign. Nevertheless, Carman's assessment of its strategic value makes sense in light of Lee's plans, as stated in this letter.

49 Some of Longstreet's criticism is in his *B&L* account, pp. 663-4, and *Manassas to Appomattox*, pp. 219-20 and Chapter 20. Carman copied Longstreet's language from this source.

Following these verbal instructions there came to McLaws, that evening, his written orders—Special Orders No. 191.[50]

Late on the morning of the 10th McLaws marched out of Frederick in rear of D. H. Hill. If he had had a clear road he could have reached Pleasant Valley early on the 11th and Maryland Heights next day, as it was, he moved in the rear of a slow marcher, he turned to the left on reaching Middletown and, passing through Burkittsville, bivouacked between that place and Brownsville Gap. On the next day he marched through Brownsville Gap to Pleasant Valley and bivouacked near the foot of the pass.[51]

Pleasant Valley is appropriately named. It is rolling and highly cultivated, the home of a highly prosperous and contented farming community, whose good stock and well filled barns give evidence of intelligent thrift. The valley runs north and south, and is bounded on the east by the South Mountain, on the west by Elk Ridge; the distance across, in an airline between the summits of the ridges, being about 2 or 3 miles, narrowing as it approaches the Potomac River and increasing as it extends north to Keedysville. A main road runs along or near the foot of South Mountain, and another along the base of Elk Ridge, at the time very much out of repair and not much used.

The South Mountain is a continuous ridge from 800 to 1000 feet high and abuts on the Potomac in a lofty, almost perpendicular mass of rocks, overhanging the small hamlet of Weverton, the canal to Washington, the Baltimore and Ohio Railroad and the turnpike from Harper's Ferry to Frederick, there being just enough space for them between the mountain and the river. Four miles north of Weverton Pass is Brownsville Gap, by which the road through Burkittsville debouches into Pleasant Valley, and one mile north of this is another pass, known as Crampton's Gap. Six miles north of Crampton's is Turner's Gap through which the National Road pursues its way from Frederick to Hagerstown; the turnpike

---

50 McLaws's movements conform to instructions per S.O. #191. The personal aspects of Carman's narrative came from McLaws, "The Capture of Harper's Ferry," *Philadelphia Weekly Press*, September 5, 1888. The article continued on September 12 and 19. Much of the language is identical to Carman's wording.

51 Carman made a rare error here. McLaws's and Anderson's divisions left Frederick behind Longstreet, not D. H. Hill. The latter general was commanding the rearguard and did not march through Frederick until September 11. Whether Carman intended to indict Hill as the "slow marcher," or someone else, is unclear. In his 1888 article, McLaws indicated that he was forced to wait for "the advance troops to get off," and that he "could not push on at ordinary marching gait." On this particular day it was Jackson's march, which while relatively quick, ended prematurely just short of Boonsboro at 10:00 a.m., and thus backed up everyone else. See Harsh, *Taken at the Flood*, pp. 172-9. Note also that Carman wrote, "Pass" after each mention of Brownsville, then crossed it out. "Pass" is the term used today on maps and in common usage.

from Frederick to Harper's Ferry passing through Weverton as already stated. About half way between Weverton and Harper's Ferry is Sandy Hook. A road from Sandy Hook runs about the middle of Pleasant Valley and joins the main road along the foot of South Mountain about two miles from the Potomac. Passing from the valley, going west, were two roads—one along the south end of Maryland Heights, and another through Solomon's Gap, a slight depression in Elk Ridge, about four miles north of the first.

Elk Ridge bounds Pleasant Valley on the west; its southern extremity is more specially designated and generally known as Maryland Heights, dominating both Harper's Ferry and Loudoun Heights; its northern extremity dips down into, and is lost in, the rolling country about a mile southwest of Keedysville. Where the railroad, canal and turnpike, after passing Weverton, go under the south end of Maryland Heights, the crowded space for them was made by blasting the almost perpendicular rocks for a considerable distance. The railroad bridge crosses the Potomac, here about 400 yards wide, just under the frowning precipice of Maryland Heights; and about fifty yards above the bridge was a pontoon bridge, for wagons and infantry, by which communication was kept up between Harper's Ferry and the Maryland shore. The railroad bridge was defended by cannon placed on the farther end; the narrow causeway along the river, under Maryland Heights, by guns placed under the precipice and on the road.

The Potomac River then runs along the south ends of both South Mountain and Elk Ridge and between it and those high ridges run the Baltimore and Ohio Railroad, the Chesapeake and Ohio Canal and Frederick Turnpike, all centering at Harper's Ferry, on the Virginia side of the river. [52]

Harper's Ferry is at the confluence of the Potomac and Shenandoah, but commanded by Maryland Heights. So long as Maryland Heights was occupied by Union troops Harper's Ferry could not be occupied by the Confederates. If McLaws gained possession of these heights, Harper's Ferry was not tenable to Miles. With this view in mind McLaws made his dispositions.

Ascertaining that there was a rugged road running from the top of Solomon's Gap along Elk Ridge to the heights commanding Harper's Ferry, he directed Kershaw with his brigade and Barksdale's to ascend the ridge, march along its summit and carry the heights, using infantry alone, as the character of the ground forbade the use of either cavalry or artillery.

---

52 McLaws's official report contained a detailed geographical description of Pleasant Valley and the area around Harpers Ferry. While not identical to Carman's description, there is some similarity in the wording. See *OR* 19, pt. 1, pp. 852-3.

Wright's Brigade was directed to ascend South Mountain, with two pieces of artillery, and move down it to the point overlooking Weverton, to command the approaches to the pass there, the route by which McClellan's left column might be expected to attempt the relief of the garrison at Harper's Ferry.

Cobb's Brigade was directed to cross the valley and, marching along the base of Elk Ridge, keep in communication with Kershaw above, and as to his advance to support it if necessary and to serve as a rallying force in case of disaster.

Semmes's and Mahone's brigades were left at the west foot of Brownsville Gap, to protect the rear of Kershaw and guard the approaches over South Mountain by Crampton's and Brownsville gaps.

These dispositions made and columns in motion early on the morning of the 12th, McLaws, with the four brigades of Cummings, Armistead, Pryor, and Featherston, moved down the valley toward the Potomac, by the road along the base of South Mountain, keeping in advance of Kershaw and communicating with him by signal parties moving with Kershaw on Elk Ridge. As McLaws marched down the valley the citizens impressed him with the idea that the crest of Maryland Heights was lined with cannon for a mile or more overlooking Harper's Ferry.[53]

Kershaw marching early reached Solomon's Gap without opposition, where he discovered Union cavalry pickets, under Captain Charles H. Russell, 1st Maryland Cavalry, and it behooved him to advance cautiously, with skirmishers thrown well out to the right and left, for the ground was favorable to an ambuscade and a stout resistance. This being done and an advance made Russell withdrew after a few scattering shots, his object being not so much to resist a Confederate movement as to observe it. Upon reaching the summit of the ridge Kershaw's skirmishers were thrown well down its side on the right, the main column filing to the left along the ridge, which, in places was not more than 25 yards in width. The skirmishers on the right soon received a volley from a party under command of Major Hildebrandt, 39th New York, and upon the return fire Hildebrandt fell back with slight loss. About a mile farther on Major Bradley, 13th Mississippi, commanding the skirmishers in advance of the main column, reported an abatis across the ridge, from which he had been fired upon. He was ordered forward and passed the obstruction without resistance, the Union pickets, some men of the

---

53 Carman paraphrased McLaws's report as he outlined the placement of his and Anderson's divisions. Much of McLaws's language was directly copied by Carman and can be found in *ibid.*, pp. 852-3. Carman neglected to include McLaws's directive to send the brigades of Semmes and Mahone to guard Solomon's Gap in the rear, and did not mention several brigades in Anderson's Division, yet it is clear that McLaws's report is the source for this part of the chapter. Perhaps because Mahone soon marched to Crampton's Gap and Semmes to Brownsville, Carman omitted this minor activity.

32nd Ohio and Potomac Home Brigade, falling back upon the main body. Leaving the path, which at this point passed down the ridge to the right, the Confederates filed along the crags along the ridge, the natural obstacles being so great, that they only reached a point, a little more than a mile from the point of the mountain, about 6 p. m. Here another abatis was encountered, extending across the narrow ridge, flanked on either side by ledges of precipitous rocks. A sharp skirmish ensued, Kershaw became satisfied that the enemy occupied the position in force, and ordered Bradley to withdraw his skirmishers, not, however, before they had been quite roughly handled, and deployed his own brigade in two lines, extending across the entire practicable ground on the summit of the mountain, Barksdale's Brigade immediately in rear. It was now dark and further operations were suspended.[54]

Wright moving down South Mountain, his two mountain howitzers drawn by one horse each, gained his position, on the bold heights overlooking Weverton, without opposition. At sunset Pryor's Brigade was pushed forward from McLaws' main column, took possession of Weverton and deployed to close and defend the pass between the mountain and the river. The brigades of Armistead and Cobb were moved up and formed a line across the valley, commanding the road from Sandy Hook, upon which Colonel Maulsby, who, with 1100 men and four guns, was holding that place as an outpost, fell back to Harper's Ferry and disposed his command to guard both the railroad bridge and the pontoon crossing. [55] McLaws had now closed well in on all sides and Kershaw was about to grasp the key to Harper's Ferry, and it is time to consider what dispositions had been made to defend these heights and what had been left undone.

Early in August, General Wool, while on an inspection visit to Harper's Ferry, gave verbal orders to Colonel Miles to build a block-house on the heights, but Miles did not do so, as he thought it unnecessary, and appears not to have visited the heights until September 7th, when he inspected the position but gave no orders to throw up works, contenting himself by directing the officers in command to hold the heights at all hazards, as he considered them the key to his entire position.[56]

54 The details about Russell and Maj. Hildebrandt skirmishing with Kershaw's men at Solomon's Gap is from *ibid.*, pp. 545, 536, 601-2. Maj. Bradley's actions can be traced in Kershaw's report, *ibid.*, pp. 862-4. Carman often copied Kershaw's wording.

55 Wright's occupation of the "bold heights" of Weverton, and the sealing off of escape routes through Weverton and Sandy Hook, are found in McLaws's report, *ibid.*, p. 853.

56 Carman relied on several accounts of this event, mostly heavily on Col. Thomas Ford's report, *ibid.*, pp. 541-4, and White's article in *B&L*, pp. 611-5. For Wool's recommendation of a block house and entrenchments, see Wool's report, *OR* 19, pt. 1, p. 519, Miles's order to hold the heights at all costs was mentioned by Lt. Binney, who wrote Miles's report, *ibid.*, pp. 532-40.

Colonel Thomas H. Ford, of the 32nd Ohio, who had withdrawn from Winchester, two days before, was, on the 5th, put in command on Maryland Heights and the troops there stationed—the 32nd Ohio, Major S. W. Hewitt, commanding; a squadron of Rhode Island Cavalry, Major A. W. Corliss; three companies of the 1st Maryland Potomac Home Brigade, under command of Major John A. Steiner; two companies of the 1st Maryland Cavalry, under command of Captain Charles H. Russell; about 12 men of Means' Loudoun Rangers, and Captain Eugene McGrath's Battery, 5th New York Heavy Artillery. McGrath's Battery was nearly half way up the west slope of the heights and had two 10-inch Columbiads, which could throw shot into Halltown, about two miles beyond Bolivar Heights, and one 50-pounder rifled gun. To these three guns were subsequently added four 12-pound howitzers. In all Ford had 1150 men and seven guns.

Ford found that no preparation had been made for defense, and the eastern and northern slope of the mountain open and easy access by way of Solomon's Gap, where a battery might be so placed as to repel a large force, but repeated applications for guns to be placed at that point were refused by Miles. Examination of the top of the mountain, at a point known as the "Lookout," satisfied him that, if he could procure two guns, he could make a stand at that point and possibly prevent any enemy from ascending the mountain, either on the eastern or northern slopes through the gap, but a second earnest appeal for two guns was met with the remark that if Ford and McGrath, his artillery officer, had their way, all the artillery would be withdrawn from Harper's Ferry to Maryland Heights, whereupon Ford abandoned this project and utterly neglected to throw up any defensive works, seemingly content with a small picket a short distance north of the "Lookout" and a few cavalry in observation at Solomon's Gap. On the 11th Ford was informed that the Confederates were in Pleasant Valley, directly opposite Solomon's Gap. He reinforced the picket at the "Lookout" by one company of the 32nd Ohio and two companies of the 1st Regiment Potomac Home Brigade. Captain Russell, who was observing Solomon's Gap, reported Kershaw's advance, and Ford called upon Miles for reinforcements, and a battalion of the 39th New York, under Major Hugo Hildebrandt; the 126th New York, Colonel Eliakim Sherrill, and one company of the 111th New York was sent to him; Hildebrandt coming up early enough to skirmish with Kershaw near Solomon's Gap. Sherrill arrived just before night and became partially engaged in front of the barricade beyond the "Lookout."

A short mile above where the railroad crosses the Potomac, there leads up around the western slope of the mountain a rather difficult road. It was about halfway up this road that McGrath's guns were placed. Along the ridge of the mountain ran a rough path for nearly a mile to the highest point, where the "Lookout" was constructed, and north of this was a log-work part way across the crest of the mountain, thrown up by Captain Whittier, when he heard of Kershaw's appearance in Pleasant Valley. A company of the 32nd Ohio and two companies of the 126th New York were disposed to guard the approach from Pleasant Valley, by the Sandy Hook Road, and Hildebrandt, with a part of the 39th New York and two companies of the 32nd Ohio, to support McGrath's guns. Colonel Sherrill, with eight companies of his regiment, one company of the 111th New York, and Major Hewitt, with five companies of the 32nd Ohio, were sent to the top of the mountain to reinforce Captain Whittier at the barricade of chestnut-logs before which Kershaw had been brought to halt and lay down within 500 yards of its defenders, whose advance pickets could hear the talk of his men and the rattling of their canteens.[57]

It was apparent that the contest would be renewed in the morning and Ford was apprehensive of the result. He made a pressing call on Miles for reinforcements, at least three regiments during the night, or all would be lost in the morning. He enforced repeated messages to this effect by sending Major Hewitt, who had been over the ground and knew the situation, to press upon Miles the importance of immediate help, and Miles promised to have reinforcements on the ground at daybreak, two regiments and two guns to report to Ford and one regiment to go up the west side of the mountain and come in on the enemy's right flank.[58]

The heights are very rugged, unsuitable for the movement of troops, and, in great part covered with dense woods and undergrowth, impeding movement and obscuring the vision.

We left Kershaw at dark on the 12th, in check, some distance north of the barricade. At sunrise of the 13th he advanced his first line, the 7th South Carolina, Col. D. W. Aiken, on the right, the 8th South Carolina, Colonel John W. Henagan,

---

57  The organization of the garrison into brigades and their placement is covered in *OR* 19, pt. 1, p. 533. The request for more artillery and the comment from Miles refusing to put more guns on Maryland Heights is in Ford's report, *ibid.*, p. 542. Much of the wording is borrowed from Ford's report, including the reference to Whittier's barricade. The composition of the barricade (chestnut logs) is from the report of Col. Nance, 3rd South Carolina Infantry, *ibid.*, p. 868. Carman used the contemporary reports of the participants and did not repeat his earlier miscue about the existence of the Stone Fort and Ft. Duncan. The comment about the Confederates talking and canteens rattling comes from Maj. Hewitt's 32nd Ohio testimony, *ibid.*, p. 567.

58  Ford's call for reinforcements and their arrival are also in Ford's report, *ibid.*, p. 542. Carman used Ford's report despite his dismissal from the service for the poor defense of Maryland Heights. Ford blamed Miles for not supporting him properly, while the Harpers Ferry Military Commission focused on the lack of stout fighting by the troops on Maryland Heights and Ford's order to retreat. It is possible Carman chose this source because it was the most complete, but it is possible he was offering subtle support of Ford.

on the left. Henagan soon came to a ledge of rock which cut him off from further participation in the attack at that point, but Aiken, moving briskly forward through the dense woods, under a heavy and telling fire of musketry, forced some slashings and, at the end of little more than half an hour, drove the skirmish line and its supports, consisting of nearly the whole force on the summit, back 300 to 400 yards to the barricade, behind which they confusedly rallied under the immediate command of Colonel Sherrill, an inexperienced but gallant officer, and some of the subordinate officers.

At the beginning of the attack Kershaw had directed Barksdale to form his brigade down the eastern face of the mountain to his left, in prolongation of the two lines of the South Carolina brigade on the summit, to oppose that part of the Union line extending down the slope of the mountain. When Aiken had forced the slashings Barksdale was ordered to advance and attack the Union line on that flank, and in rear, and the two Carolina regiments again pressed forward in front. The Carolinians met with a most obstinate resistance and a fierce and destructive fire was kept up for some time, entailing a heavy loss, which fell principally upon the 7th South Carolina, and it became necessary to send in the 3rd South Carolina, Colonel J. D. Nance, to its support. This gallant regiment marched over their not less gallant comrades of the 7th, to carry the barricade and met the same stout resistance and severe loss, from those who had held the barricade and its approaches since early morning and a valiant reinforcement just arrived.[59]

About 10 o'clock Lieutenant-Colonel S. W. Downey, at the head of eight companies of the 3rd Maryland Potomac Home Brigade came over from Harper's Ferry and reported to Ford, who retained four companies to go around on the eastern slope of the mountain, and ordered Downey, with the other four companies and three companies of the 32nd Ohio, under Captain William A. Palmer, up the western slope to the assistance of the troops engaged. Downey marched up by a difficult by path and just as he reached the "Lookout" came under a rattling fire which wounded several of his men. Pressing on he came up to the barricade and ranged his men behind it and with others there began his work. The firing was very brisk and heavy and brought the South Carolinians to check. Colonel Nance, seeing the difficulty of forcing the position by a direct attack, suggested a flank movement by the 8th South Carolina on the Union left, but,

---

59 This narrative continues to rely on Kershaw's report, *ibid.*, p. 863. Kershaw was the senior officer and commanded this attack.

before his suggestion could be acted on resistance ceased and the Union men were in retreat.[60]

Meanwhile word had come from Barksdale that, after much difficulty and hard labor, he had reached the desired position on the Union right flank, but could not bring his men to the crest of the mountain without coming under the fire of the South Carolinians, as he was partially in rear of the Union line, upon which Kershaw, hoping to capture the enemy before him, if Barksdale could get up, ordered a cessation of firing, but before the order had been carried to all parts of the line, the right company of the 17th Mississippi, of Barksdale's Brigade, fired into a body of the 126th New York, posted on a rocky and inaccessible position, a severe fusillade began along the whole line, Colonel Sherrill was badly wounded and carried from the field, a partial panic followed and many of the troops left the field in wild disorder, despite all efforts to stay them.[61]

"After Colonel Sherrill was wounded there appears to have been no field officer in responsible command on the heights, and contradictory and confusing orders followed one another. The larger portion of the men were just from home and had not had their arms long enough to have learned to load and fire. It was a bad place in which to match green troops against veterans, and though some of the green troops went to the rear rather precipitously, there were many instances of conspicuous bravery among them."[62]

The defense of the heights was badly managed. Ford did not go to the top of the mountain, where the contest was carried on, and entrusted the direction of affairs to Major Hewitt of his regiment, who, far in the rear, saw the stricken

60 For the arrival time of Downey on the mountain, see his testimony to the Commission, *ibid.*, pp. 614-5.

61 For Nance's suggested flank attack, see *ibid.*, pp. 867-8, and the position of Barksdale's Brigade, see Kershaw's report, *ibid.*, p. 863. Carman pieced together the opposing forces reports to put specific unit names to the action. For example, Kershaw only wrote "Colonel Fisher's regiment," but Carman filled in "17th Mississippi." Likewise, he was able to discern the Union regiment receiving this fire to be the 126th New York. See Ford's report, *ibid.*, p. 542.

62 William H. Nichols, "Siege and Capture of Harper's Ferry," Rhode Island Soldiers and Sailors Historical Society (1889), p. 26. Carman's quote is from Nichols (7th Squadron, Rhode Island Cavalry). The panic and confusion Carman describes is apparent from reading the Harper's Ferry Military Commission transcripts, *OR* 12, pt. 2, pp. 549-800. Throughout this testimony, claims, accusations, and counterclaims abound. Some soldiers claimed there was an order from Miles to withdraw, but it was never found nor proven. Carman referred to the inexperience of the majority of regiments in Miles command. Most were either 90-day troops or recently raised regiments. Miles's judgment can be called into question for allowing a new commander like Ford to control such a vital spot as Maryland Heights, but Miles had very few seasoned officers to call upon.

fugitives and judged it time to abandon the heights. Without making a personal examination he sent orders for those at the barricade to retreat. This order conveyed to the troops nearest him was promptly obeyed. The remaining troops, either hearing that an order had been given to retreat or, judging from the general retrograde movement that such had been given, began to fall back down the mountain, crowding to and past McGrath's Battery.[63] This was about 11 0'clock and the Confederates, seeing the first indications of retreat, gave a joyous shout, poured in a parting volley and advanced to the possession of the barricade that had cost them dear, for they lost 35 killed and nearly 200 wounded before it.[64]

In the meantime a stand had been made south of the "Lookout" by some companies of the 126th New York, 32nd Ohio, and parts of other regiments, and a line was formed across the ridge and down the west side.

It was at this critical state of affairs that Miles came on the field with reinforcements and endeavored to turn the tide of retreat and rally the fleeing troops, but, says, Ford: "As fast as we forced them up one mountain path they returned by another until all seemed to be lost."[65] There were, however, some who had not lost head and heart and by the exertion of many officers partial order was restored and a part of the retreating troops, men of all regiments, returned to the front and formed on the line near the "Lookout," and orders were given to retake the barricade, but an advance in that direction was met by the fire of the enemy, who had taken possession of the abandoned work and were in the act of moving forward. Miles now returned to Harper's Ferry. Ford understood him to say that if it became necessary to abandon the heights, the guns were to be spiked, dismounted, and rolled over the crags, so they could not be used against Harper's Ferry.

About 12 o'clock Colonel Simeon Sammon arrived on the heights with seven companies of the 115th New York; five companies under the Colonel were placed

---

63 Hewitt insisted in his testimony that Miles gave him discretionary orders to withdraw; others denied this was so. See Hewitt's testimony, *OR* 19, pt. 1, pp. 568-9, which is countered by that of Clemans, 115th New York, *ibid.*, pp. 576-8, Lt. Binney. *ibid.*, pp. 577-9, and Ford, *ibid.*, pp. 777-8. White claimed that Miles did not authorize a retreat, but simply mentioned that if there was a retreat, the heavy guns should be spiked. *Ibid.*, pp. 526, 718.

64 McLaws's casualty figures, *ibid.*, 19, pt. 1, pp. 860-1, do not agree completely with Carman's figures. McLaws states the losses in the brigades of Kershaw and Barksdale as 37 killed and 182 wounded.

65 The comment about Miles's arrival and Ford's attempt to rally fleeing soldiers comes from Ford's report, *ibid.*, p. 543. Ford reiterates that Miles gave him permission to withdraw, if necessary.

on the side of the hill, near an old house and spring, beyond McGrath's Battery, and two companies were sent to the mountain top.

Severe skirmishing continued at all points on the mountain as McLaws's two brigades cautiously advanced, but, without pressing the fighting. When, about 3.30 p. m., it was discovered that the Confederates were advancing on both flanks, as well as in front, Ford, it is said, "in obedience to the positive orders of Colonel Miles, ordered the guns spiked and dismounted and the forces withdrawn to the opposite side of the river, all of which was done in good order." Ford rode down the mountain at the head of the 126th New York.[66]

"It is said that McGrath, who commanded the battery, after receiving orders to spike his guns refused to obey and would not do so until he saw the infantry deserting him. . . . It was supposed that Ford had orders to hold the heights to the last extremity, which had not then arrived. Colonel Miles told General White immediately after the evacuation that he gave no orders to withdraw from the heights."[67]

Barksdale was now directed to occupy the point of the heights, which he did without encountering more than a retiring skirmisher and by 4.30 p. m., McLaws's two brigades had possession of the entire heights, the Union troops retreating down a road, invisible to the Confederates in the valley, and fired on by their skirmishers from the high ground, as they crossed the bridge to the Harper's Ferry side of the Potomac.[68] The western slope of the heights was so fully swept by artillery fire from Camp Hill, in Harper's Ferry, that the Confederates did not occupy it, from which it resulted that, on the next day, a detachment of the 39th New York and 65th Illinois, under command of Major John Wood, of the last named regiment, crossed the bridge and recovered the four field guns abandoned, with a load of ammunition and other stores.[69]

Most of the Union troops engaged in the defense of Maryland Heights behaved well, some of them most gallantly; heavy and undeserved censure fell upon a greater part of the 126th New York, a new regiment, raw and undrilled, suddenly

---

66 Sammon's reinforcement and Ford's retreat, including the quote about Miles's positive order, are taken from Ford's report. *Ibid.*, p. 544.

67 Nichols, "Siege and Capture of Harper's Ferry," pp. 27-8.

68 The story of Barksdale's advance and the occupation of the heights and Union retreat come from McLaws's report, *OR* 19, pt. 1, p. 854.

69 The removal of the field guns and ammunition is from testimony by Col. Cameron during the Commission's inquiry of the surrender, ibid., pp. 636-7, and by Lt. Bacon, *ibid.*, p. 665.

placed in a trying position, where it suffered severe loss—its subsequent record was a good and honorable one.[70]

Colonel Miles was justly censured for the loss of Maryland Heights and Colonel Ford was dismissed from the service. Ford did not personally direct the movements of his men, many of whom were new recruits, nor did he ascend the mountain while they were engaged, in fact he never went to the crest where the barricade was thrown up, either before, during or after the engagement, but, remaining near McGrath's Battery, on the west slope of the mountain, entrusted the conduct of affairs to Major Hewitt of his regiment, a venerable gentleman with a long white beard; who had exchanged the practice of medicine for the profession of arms, and it was this nervous officer, who, from the vicinity of the "Lookout," heard the rattle of musketry, saw wounded officers and men borne past him, was unduly impressed by the usual confusion in rear of a fighting line and, believing that the time had come for retreat, ordered the abandonment of the barricade. This order was fatal to the possession of Maryland Heights and sealed the fate of Harper's Ferry.[71]

Maryland Heights secured, the Confederate troops in Pleasant Valley were advanced. Cobb's Brigade occupied Sandy Hook; Maulsby's infantry and four guns having abandoned the place and fallen back to Harper's Ferry. At the same time the main Confederate column, near South Mountain, moved down to close all avenues of escape from Harper's Ferry and tighten the grasp on that place.[72]

Up to this time McLaws had received no notice of the advance of either Jackson or Walker, except that a courier from Jackson brought a dispatch to the effect that his leading division would be near Harper's Ferry about 2 p. m., and some firing in that direction led to the belief that he was advancing. During the day

70 The regiment that most sources identify as leading the panic, the 126th New York—subsequently known as the "Harpers Ferry Cowards"—redeemed its honor at Gettysburg in July 1863, when it made a stubborn stand against a determined Confederate attack. See William Fox, *New York at Gettysburg* (Albany: Lyon & Co. 1900), pp. 895-903. Carman's wording indicates that he knew of their later service.

71 Carman's analysis criticizing the performance of Ford and Hewitt is not surprising and echoes the finding of the Commission. See *OR* 12, pt. 2, pp. 794-800. More important, there is a clear sense in Carman's tone that his judgment was that of a veteran infantry officer who knew firsthand what Ford and Hewitt had witnessed. Also, most modern studies agree that Maryland Heights was the key to the position. See also Dennis Frye, "Drama Between the Rivers; Harpers Ferry in the Maryland Campaign," in Gary Gallagher, ed., *Antietam: Essays on the Maryland Campaign* (Kent, OH: Kent State University Press, 1989), pp. 14-34.

72 The Confederate occupation of Sandy Hook, the closing of the escape routes, and McLaws's isolated situation, are taken from McLaws's report, *OR* 19, pt. 1, p. 854.

heavy cannonading was heard to the east and northeast, and cavalry scouts were constantly reporting the advance of Union troops from various directions.

At night of the 13th McLaws had the two brigades of Semmes and Mahone guarding the passes at Brownsville and Crampton; Wright's and Pryor's at Weverton; Cobb's and Armistead's at Sandy Hook; Kershaw and Barksdale on Maryland Heights, and Cummings and Featherston's in Pleasant Valley, as reserve.

During the night McLaws received a dispatch from Lee with information of his belief that McClellan was moving toward Harper's Ferry to relieve Miles, and urging him to expedite matters and, when completed, to move to Sharpsburg; that Longstreet would the next day, the 14th, move down from Hagerstown and take position on Beaver Creek, and that Stuart had been directed to keep him informed as to the enemy's movements. On the same night came another dispatch from Lee that he had not heard from him since he had left the main body of the army; that the enemy had abandoned Martinsburg and retreated to Harper's Ferry, 2500 to 3000 strong; that Stuart occupied Middletown Valley; D. H. Hill was a mile or two west of Boonsboro, at the junction of the Boonsboro and Hagerstown roads; Longstreet at Hagerstown. This dispatch directed him to watch well the main road from Frederick to Harper's Ferry through Weverton, and to communicate freely; above all that Harper's Ferry would be speedily disposed of and the various detachments returned to the main body of the army.[73] When it became known that Ford had abandoned Maryland Heights there was much astonishment among officers and men in Harper's Ferry and on Bolivar Heights, and Miles was appealed to by White and others, to reoccupy them at any cost, but he pleaded the orders under which he was acting, besides which, he argued, that, as the guns had been spiked and dismounted, the heights were of no further consequence. After the withdrawal of the troops they took position on Bolivar Heights.[74]

It was evident to Miles and his officers that they could not hold out much longer in the position where the troops were now crowded, and, hearing nothing from McClellan, yet believing him near, Miles sent for C. H. Russell of the 1st Maryland Cavalry, and asked if he could not go with two or three men, pass the enemy's lines and "try to reach somebody that had ever heard of the United States

---

73 The position of the troops on September 13 came from McLaws's *Weekly Press* article, September 5, 1888 (the wording is almost exactly the same). McLaws's memory was faulty for he anticipated some events. In his report, McLaws wrote that he did not order Semmes to withdraw his brigade from Solomon's Gap until the morning of September 14. McLaws narrated the positions on the 14th in his report. OR 19, pt. 1, p. 855.

74 For the surprise and disappointment about the retreat from Maryland Heights, see White, *ibid.*, p. 537 and 775, D'Utassy, *ibid.*, p. 597-8, and findings of the Commission, *ibid.*, p. 796.

Army, or any general of the United States Army, or anybody that knew anything about the United States Army, and report the condition of Harper's Ferry." Russell was willing to make the trial, upon which Miles told him that if he could get to any general of the United States Army, or to a telegraph station, or, if possible, get to General McClellan, whom he supposed was at Frederick, to report that Maryland Heights had been lost; that he thought he could hold out forty-eight hours; that he had subsistence for forty-eight hours, but if not relieved in that time, he would have to surrender. Russell selected nine men, went through the Confederates on the Virginia side, moved across fields near the river, and crossed the Potomac near the mouth of the Antietam, where he dashed past a Confederate picket, and by by-roads and trails reached South Mountain, where another picket was met and avoided. Russell crossed South Mountain by a wood road, reached Middletown and informed General Reno of his mission; passing on, by 9 o'clock on the morning of the 14th, he had delivered his message to McClellan, by whom he was informed that Franklin was on the way to relieve Miles. Nearly three hours later at 11.45 a. m., McClellan wrote Franklin, from Middletown, that he had heard from Miles, who had abandoned Maryland Heights; and said, in concluding his dispatch: "Continue to bear in mind the necessity of relieving Colonel Miles if possible." This dispatch was delivered to Franklin while he was making leisurely arrangements to force Crampton's Gap. What other measure McClellan took to relieve Miles shall appear elsewhere.[75]

On the morning of the 14th Miles held the bridges across the Potomac, Camp Hill, and the line of Bolivar Heights, with the ridge on the prolongation of the heights between the Charlestown Turnpike and the Shenandoah River. The bridges were guarded by eight companies of the 1st Maryland Potomac Home Brigade, the 87th Ohio Infantry, and one section of Captain Potts' Battery, all under command of Colonel Maulsby.

Bolivar Heights form the base of a triangle, of which the Potomac and the Shenandoah are the other two sides. They rise quite abruptly from the town on the west, spread out in a plain and, again rising, form a sort of parapet, sloping down to the surrounding country, the level of which is of much lower grade.

The right of Bolivar Heights was held by the 39th New York Infantry, Major Hugo Hildebrandt; the 111th New York, Colonel Jesse Segoine; the 115th New

75 The account of the daring ride of Capts. Russell and Cole was taken from Russell's testimony to the Commission, *ibid.*, pp. 720-1. Russell was repeating what Miles said to him, which Carman quoted. Without mentioning Cole or Russell, McClellan reported this incident, and his reply to Miles and his instructions to Franklin are found *ibid.*, pp. 45-6. Carman's comment about "leisurely arrangements" foreshadows his view on Franklin's efforts to drive the Confederates from Crampton's Gap.

York, Colonel Simeon Sammon; the 65th Illinois, Colonel Daniel Cameron; Captain John C. Phillips' battery (6 rifled guns) Illinois Light Artillery, and Captain J. C. von Sehlen's battery (6 rifled guns) Indiana Artillery. These troops were brigaded under command of Colonel F. G. D'Utassy, 39th New York Infantry. The 65th Illinois was on the extreme right of the brigade, where the bluff descended abruptly to the Potomac, Von Sehlen's battery about the center of the brigade and Phillips' on its left, slight earthworks having been thrown up for their protection. On the forenoon of the 14th three heavy guns of Captain John A. Graham's New York battery moved from Camp Hill and took position on the extreme right, supported by the Illinois regiment.

The left of Bolivar Heights was held by the brigade commanded by Colonel William H. Trimble, 60th Ohio Infantry, consisting of the 60th Ohio; the 9th Vermont, Colonel George J. Stannard; the 126th New York, Captain P. D. Phillips; and Captain Silas F. Rigby's Battery, Indiana Artillery. Rigby's Battery was on the left of the line about 50 yards from the Charlestown Turnpike and a slight earthwork was constructed to shelter the men. The 60th Ohio Infantry was on the immediate right of the battery.[76]

Miles had utterly neglected to entrench the heights and failed to cut down the woods in front which gave good shelter and cover to an enemy's advance. Ax-men were now set to work felling trees and, without orders from superior officers, regimental and company commanders began to throw up intrenchments. They were thrown up on the evening of the 14th, of logs and earth, filled in with tents, cast off clothing, army blankets and any thing else that would break the force of a ball.[77]

The ground to the southwest of the Charlestown Turnpike, and between it and the Shenandoah, full of ravines and quite heavily wooded, was held by the 3rd Maryland Regiment, Potomac Home Brigade, under command of Lieutenant Colonel S. W. Downey. Other troops were placed on the plateau adjacent to Bolivar Heights and, as much as possible, under cover of ravines. Camp Hill, rising immediately from the town of Harper's Ferry, was surrounded by an inner line of intrenchments to fall back upon in the event of being driven from the more advanced position of Bolivar Heights. This position was occupied by Captain John A. Graham's Battery A, 5th New York Artillery, and four guns—two 24-pounder howitzers, and two 20-pounder Parrott guns—of Captain Potts' Ohio Battery,

---

76 Carman used White's report, *ibid.*, pp. 526-7, to describe the defenses of Bolivar Heights, Camp Hill, and the town of Harpers Ferry.

77 Wool's testimony to the Commission confirmed that he had ordered entrenchments and none were erected. *Ibid.*, pp. 788-9.

supported by the 12th New York State Militia, under command of Colonel William G. Ward. As we have seen, three of Graham's guns, on the morning of the 14th, were sent to the extreme right of the line on Bolivar Heights, the remainder, upon the precipice overhanging the Shenandoah, commanding the approaches by the Shenandoah road and also up the Potomac from Sandy Hook. They commanded also the position on Bolivar Heights and raked the whole plain, across which troops must approach to the inner intrenchments, and they had range of Maryland Heights and Loudoun Heights. Potts' guns were north of the main road running from Harper's Ferry to Bolivar. In addition to the batteries of Graham and Potts a number of howitzers were mounted along the intrenchments.[78] Jackson, as we have seen, encamped on the evening of the 13th, two miles in front of Miles' position on Bolivar Heights. This was after McLaws had possession of Maryland Heights and had driven the Union forces from them and into the blind alley, of which Jackson held the key, and had to but advance and gather the fruit of McLaws' enterprise.

Before moving, however, he wished to satisfy himself that all avenues of escape were closed to Miles, and deferred attack until he could communicate with McLaws and Walker. Early in the morning he acknowledged receipt of McLaws' dispatch of the 13th, informed him that Loudoun Heights was in the possession of Walker, and directed McLaws to take complete possession of Maryland Heights, hoped that he could establish batteries to fire upon Miles, and to let him know when they were ready so that he could make a demand for the surrender of the place before opening fire on it. There was much difficulty in communicating with McLaws and Walker. McLaws did not receive the dispatch until late in the day, and forenoon of the 14th passed with but little movement on Jackson's part, partly attributable to the fact that he could not be made to believe that McClellan's whole army was in movement and partly because Bolivar Heights was so strong that he desired to remain quiet until McLaws and Walker drew attention from him. The following were the orders for the day:

HEADQUARTERS VALLEY DISTRICT,
September 14, 1862.

I. To-day Major-General McLaws will attack so as to sweep with his artillery the ground occupied by the enemy, take his batteries in reverse, and otherwise operate against him, as circumstances may justify.

---

78 The position of the batteries is found in White's report, *ibid.*, pp. 526-7.

II. Brigadier-General Walker will take in reverse the battery on the turnpike, and also sweep with his artillery the ground occupied by the enemy, and silence the battery on the island in the Shenandoah should he find a battery there.

III. Maj. Gen. A. P. Hill will move along the left bank of the Shenandoah, and thus turn the enemy's left flank and enter Harper's Ferry.

IV. Brigadier-General Lawton will move along the turnpike for the purpose of supporting General Hill and otherwise operating against the enemy on the left of General Hill.

V. Brigadier-General Jones will, with one of his brigades and a battery of artillery, make a demonstration against the enemy's right; the remaining part of his division will constitute the reserve and move along the turnpike.

By order of Major-General Jackson:

WM. L. JACKSON,
Acting Assistant Adjutant-General

These orders were prepared in the morning and sent to the signal officer near midday; they were not received by McLaws and Walker until action had been opened.[79]

We left Walker, on the evening of the 13th, in possession of Loudoun Heights and closing all avenues of escape down the west bank of the Potomac. At daylight of the 14th he ordered Captain Thomas B. French, with three Parrott guns of his battery and two rifled pieces of Captain J. R. Branch's Battery, under Lieutenant M. A. Martin, to ascend Loudoun Heights, and Walker accompanied him to place the guns in a good, yet masked, position. This was done by 8 o'clock and Walker sought to open communication by signal with Jackson, but it was after 10 o'clock before he could advise him of his readiness to attack and ask whether, before opening fire, he should wait for McLaws, to which Jackson replied: "Wait"; and then prepared the following, which was signaled to both McLaws and Walker:

If you can, establish batteries to drive the enemy from the hill west of Bolivar and on which Barbour's house is, and any other position where he may be damaged by your artillery, and let me know when you are ready to open your batteries, and give me any suggestions by which you can operate against the enemy. Cut the telegraph line down the Potomac if it is not already done. Keep a good lookout against a Federal advance

---

79 Jackson's arrival at Halltown and his reconnoitering on September 14 are mentioned in his report. The position of the batteries is found in White's report, *ibid.*, pp. 526-7, 953. See also Walker's report, *ibid.*, p. 913. Carman pasted in the special order of September 14, signed by William L. Jackson. The position of the batteries is found in White's report, *ibid.*, pp. 526-7.

from below. Similar instructions will be sent to General Walker. I do not desire any of the batteries to open until all are ready on both sides of the river, except you should find it necessary, of which you must judge for yourself. I will let you know when to open all the batteries.[80]

The sound of heavy guns was heard by Walker in the direction of Turner's Gap and McLaws signaled him that the enemy was in his rear, upon which he again communicated with Jackson, giving him the information he had received from McLaws and again reporting that his guns were ready to open, to which Jackson replied: "Do not open until General McLaws notifies me what he can probably effect. Let me know what you can effect with your command upon the enemy."

As the sound of artillery in the direction of South Mountain grew louder and apparently nearer, at noon, indicating McClellan's advance, Walker again asked permission to open fire and about the same time signaled that he had information the enemy were advancing in his own rear, by way of Purcellville and had possession of the passes from the valley.

About this time Jackson signaled both McLaws and Walker to "fire at such positions of the enemy as will be most effective." But, before the receipt of this, indeed Walker says that he never received it, Walker had opened fire. The signal station and two North Carolina regiments, under Colonel M. W. Ransom, who had relieved Cooke, had attracted the attention of the batteries on Camp Hill and Bolivar Heights, which opened their guns upon them. Walker construed Jackson's order not to fire until it became necessary, as now operative.

Two days after this Jackson and Walker were riding from the Potomac to join Lee at Sharpsburg. Walker says: "As we rode along I mentioned my ruse in opening fire on Harper's Ferry. Knowing the strictness of Jackson's idea in regard to military obedience, I felt a little doubtful as to what he would say. When I had finished my confession, he was silent for some minutes, and then remarked, 'It was just as well as it was; but I could not believe that the fire you reported indicated the advance of McClellan in force. It seemed more likely to be a mere cavalry affair.' Then, after an interval of silence as if to himself, he continued, 'I thought I knew McClellan but this movement of his puzzles me.'"[81]

---

80 The somewhat muddy picture of Walker's circumventing Jackson's instructions was addressed by Carman, who began his explanation by pasting in the manuscript the text from the message in *ibid.*, p. 958.

81 Carman's Note: *B&L*, 2, p. 611. These messages and the others quoted here are found in *ibid.*, pp. 958-9. Walker's account of his conversation with Jackson concerning his preempting the order to open fire is highly doubtful. Postwar controversy erupted about Walker's claim of

Fully impressed with the idea that McClellan was advancing with much more speed than either Lee or Jackson had anticipated and anxious to expedite matters with Miles, he opened his five guns on the batteries on Bolivar Heights and Camp Hill, disabling some of them and stampeding their infantry support. Colonel Willard of the 125th New York, reports that: "The fire was rapid and all the troops on the plateau made a speedy and somewhat disorderly retreat. My regiment, in spite of my efforts, and subjected for the first time to a hot fire, retreated in a good deal of disorder toward the ravine running south from the battery on Bolivar Heights." The long range guns near the Barbour House on Camp Hill and Van Sehlens' Battery on Bolivar Heights answered the fire, but ineffectively, and were soon silenced.[82]

An hour after Walker opened his batteries those of Jackson joined in from the right and left of his line and, still an hour later, McLaws added to the attack, the combined fire disabling four of Miles guns, blowing up two caissons, and discouraging the cavalry and infantry, helpless to defend themselves a heavy fire of artillery in front and a plunging fire from the rear. Leaving Hill, for a moment, now in motion closing in from the Charlestown road, we return to McLaws.[83]

The engineers that had been examining the ground during the evening of the 13th, had reported that it was impracticable to carry cannon to the top of the heights, owing to the steepness of the ascent and the numerous walls of rock that could not be passed, but Major A. H. McLaws, Quarter-Master of the division, in coming from Kershaw's command that evening had accidentally struck an old wood road, which wound up a part of the way, and by using that as far as it went the men could by lifting the guns over the ledges and hauling them by hand in other places get the guns up. So McLaws employed the morning of the 14th in cutting and improving the wood road to the top of the heights, and, overcoming the difficulties

Jackson's intent to offer a 24-hour delay for any surrender. Bradley Johnson and Henry Kyd Douglas both wrote articles in *B&L*, pp. 615-8, refuting Walker's contention that Jackson wanted a 24-hour delay before firing. Their accounts and records make it clear that Walker is wrong. The report of Jackson's signal officer is in OR 19, pt. 1, pp. 958-59. He acknowledged the difficulty in establishing communication with Walker and McLaws, but he also listed all the messages sent by Jackson. The other two authorities cited above refute it, and Walker's credibility is severely damaged by examination of other claims that have been deemed unreliable.

82  The quotation from Willard about the damage of Walker's fire came from his report in *ibid.*, pp. 540-1. For Confederate activities, see McLaws's report, *ibid.*, p. 854, Crutchfield's, *ibid.*, p. 962, and Walker's, *ibid.*, p. 913.

83  Carman's phrase "Leaving Hill" was a mistake. This paragraph was pasted onto the page, suggesting that material about A. P. Hill originally preceded this paragraph before Carman physically rearranged it.

of the ascent, and between 2 and 3 o'clock in the afternoon, Captains John P. W. Read and H. H. Carlton, commanding batteries of Kershaw's and Barksdale's brigades, under the direction of Major S. P. Hamilton, chief of artillery, had two Parrott guns from each battery in position, overlooking Bolivar Heights, Camp Hill, and the town. Fire was opened at once, driving the Union troops from Camp Hill and their works on the right of Bolivar Heights. This in connection with Walker's fire from Loudoun Heights, and from Jackson's' advancing line, was kept up all the afternoon.[84]

A. P. Hill, on the right was ordered to move along the left bank of the Shenandoah, around the base of the hill, turn Miles' left and enter Harper's Ferry. Lawton, commanding Ewell's Division, was directed to move along the turnpike in support to Hill and, also, to operate against Miles' line to the left. J. R. Jones, commanding Jackson's Division, was directed to take one brigade and a battery of artillery, and make a demonstration against Miles' right, while the remaining brigades of his division, as a reserve, moved along the turnpike.

Major T. B. Massie, who, with two companies of the 12th Virginia Cavalry, joined Jackson while on the road from Martinsburg, was instructed to keep upon the left flank for the purpose of preventing the escape of the Union forces in that direction.[85]

The movement began late in the afternoon by the advance of Winder's (Stonewall) Brigade, under Colonel A. J. Grigby, on the Union right, by which a cavalry detachment was quickly dispersed and a commanding hill secured near the Potomac, from which, subsequently, the batteries of Poague and Carpenter did admirable execution. Toward night Jones moved nearer the Potomac and, when darkness concealed the movement, Starke's Brigade was moved in still closer proximity, resting on the river road, overlooking the river, to prevent the Union troops from making escape.

Having first shelled the woods through which his route lay and flushed the Union skirmishers, Hill, in execution of his orders, moved obliquely to the right

---

84 The reference to Maj. A. H. McLaws by Carman is found in McLaws's report, *ibid.*, p. 854. The major was the general's younger brother Abraham Huguenin McLaws, who served as major & quartermaster on Gen. McLaws's staff. See Robert E. L. Krick, *Staff Officers in Gray: A Biographical Register of the Staff Officers in the Army of Northern Virginia* (Chapel Hill: University of North Carolina Press, 2003), p. 210. The references to the artillery commanders are on the same page of McLaws' report.

85 A letter dated May 21, 1897, from W. L. Wilson, Company B, 12 Virginia Cavalry and another from Col. T. B. Massie, 12th Virginia Cavalry, dated May 14, 1897, NA, Antietam Studies, confirm this point. Massie states he was in command of all of Jackson's cavalry at Harpers Ferry. He had Companies B & I of the 12th and two companies of Maryland cavalry.

until he struck the Shenandoah River. Observing an eminence crossing the extreme left of the Union line, occupied by infantry, but without artillery, bare of all earthworks and protected only by an abatis of slashed timber, Pender, Archer, and Brockenbrough, brigade commanders, were directed to gain the crest of this hill, while Branch and Gregg were directed to march along the river road, during the night, taking advantage of the ravines cutting the precipitous banks of the river, and establish themselves on the plain to the left and rear of the Union line. Thomas' Brigade was to follow in reserve.

The execution of the movement on the hill by the three brigades of Pender, Archer, and Brockenbough, was entrusted to Pender, his own brigade being commanded by Colonel R. H. Brewer. Pender moved briskly forward, his own brigade in advance, and soon encountered the skirmishers of Downey's 3rd Maryland Potomac Home Brigade and drove them. General White was on this part of the field and perceiving the danger of Pender's movement, ordered the 9th Vermont to support Downey and, subsequently, reinforced the two regiments with the 32nd Ohio and one section of Rigby's Battery. One of Rigby's guns opened fire with good effect, the other was unable to limber. Later the 125th New York was put on a cross road extending from Bolivar Heights to the Shenandoah, as a reserve and to extend the left of the line as far as the railroad and connect with the 87th Ohio, and two guns of Potts' Battery were hastened from Camp Hill and placed on the turnpike. Pender continued the engagement until after dark but did not gain the coveted ground, although within one hundred yards of it. No troops being within supporting distance he ordered his brigade back a few yards; White claims it that was repulsed by the Union troops behaving very handsomely.

Lieutenant-Colonel R. L. Walker, chief of artillery of Hill's Division, brought up the batteries of Pegram, McIntosh, Davidson, Braxton and Crenshaw and, during the night, established them on the ground gained by Pender's advance. Branch and Gregg, moving down the Winchester and Harper's Ferry Railroad, the 7th North Carolina in advance, drove down sharpshooters from a high point overlooking the railroad and gained the position indicated for them. This was not accomplished until after midnight, and daylight found them in rear of the Union line, between Bolivar Heights and the Shenandoah.

As directed, Lawton led Ewell's Division, in the center, along the turnpike in three columns, one on the road and another on either side of it, until he reached Halltown, where he formed line of battle; Lawton's and Trimble's brigades on the right of the turnpike, and Hays' on the left.

Early's Brigade was in rear of Lawton. In this order he advanced to School House Hill, fronting Bolivar Heights, in easy range for artillery. The troops laid on their arms during the night.[86] While engaged in getting his guns in position on Maryland Heights, on the 14th, McLaws was startled by news that McClellan was forcing Crampton's Gap in his rear. This he communicated to Jackson, but Jackson could not credit the information, he thought only of cavalry affairs in this quarter, and directed McLaws to notify D. H. Hill of the enemy's position and request him to protect his rear, and to send the same message to Lee, near Hagerstown. At the same time he requested McLaws to let him know what he could probably effect with his artillery, and also with his entire command. Early in the day he received a message from Lee that Longstreet would move back from Hagerstown to occupy the Boonsboro or Pleasant Valley so as to protect his flank, until the operations at Harper's Ferry were finished, and desired him to push those operations as rapidly as possible and join the main army by way of Pleasant Valley. Still later McLaws knew that Crampton's Gap had been forced, so, when night came he withdrew Kershaw and Barksdale from Maryland Heights and hastened to form a line across Pleasant Valley, leaving only the 13th Mississippi Regiment and two guns of Read's Battery on the heights, overlooking Harper's Ferry.[87]

While in the execution of this movement McLaws received this dispatch from Lee dated September 14th, 8 p.m.:

---

86 The deployment of Jackson's three divisions and the attack on the Union left by troops under A. P. Hill was taken from Jackson's and Hill's reports, OR 19, pt. 1, pp. 854 and 980, respectively. White reported the shift in troops to repel Pender's attack (which he claimed he did) in his report, *ibid.*, p. 527. Pender simply said his men advanced within 60 yards of the enemy and stopped. Pender wrote that he ordered a slight withdrawal to a better position at dark, knowing support was near at hand. *Ibid.*, p. 1,004. "Col. R. H. Brewer" is actually Lt. Richard Henry Brewer. The reference to the 7th North Carolina is in OR 19, pt. 1, p. 985. The march of Ewell's Division, under Alexander Lawton, is taken from Jackson's report. Carman copied it literally before crossing out a portion that was redundant. *Ibid.*, p. 954.

87 There is no question that McLaws was startled to find the Federal army pressing the gaps in his rear. His report, *ibid.*, p. 854, bears that out. There is also no question that he notified Jackson. The message is included in the report of Capt. J. L. Bartlett, Jackson's signal officer, in *ibid.*, p. 958. What is a mystery is why Carman accepted Walker's story that Jackson assured McLaws it was only cavalry. McLaws was in a much better position than Jackson to know the situation at the gaps, and how Jackson could advise McLaws was not explained. More telling is the comment in McLaws's report, *ibid.*, p. 854, that Jeb Stuart was with McLaws and told him he had just come from that area and that there was a Union infantry brigade there. The evidence is against Carman on this issue. The message from Lee about Longstreet's return is in *ibid.*, pt. 2, p. 607.

GENERAL: The day has gone against us and this army will go by Sharpsburg and cross the river. It is necessary for you to abandon your position to-night. Send your trains not required on the road to cross the river. Your troops you must have well in hand to unite with this command, which will retire by Sharpsburg. Send forward officers to explore the way, ascertain the best crossing of the Potomac, and if you can find any between you and Shepherdstown leave Shepherdstown Ford for this command. Send an officer to report to me on the Sharpsburg road, where you are and what crossing you will take. You will of course bring Anderson's division with you.

McLaws received another dispatch from Lee dated at 11.15 p. m.:

In addition to what has already been stated in reference to your abandonment of Weverton, and routes you can take, I will mention you might cross the Potomac, below Weverton, into Virginia, I believe there is a ford at the Point of Rocks, and at Berlin below, but do not know whether either is accessible to you. The enemy from Jefferson seem to have forced a passage at Crampton's Gap, which may leave all on the river clear. This portion of the army will take position at Centreville, commonly called Keedysville, 2½ miles from Boonsborough, on the Sharpsburg road, with a view of preventing the enemy that may enter the gap at Boonsborough turnpike from cutting you off, and enabling you to make a junction with it. If you can pass to-night on the river road, by Harper's Ferry, or cross the mountain below Crampton's Gap toward Sharpsburg, let me know. I will be found at or near Centreville, or Keedysville, as it is called.

McLaws reasoned that to obey these orders would leave open a way for Miles to escape; that Lee did not know the real condition of affairs in Pleasant Valley, so, he sent a courier to inform him that his position was a strong one, and he would take the risk of remaining where he was and relied upon him to get him out of the difficulty he was in by maneuvering McClellan away from the support of Franklin, who had come through Crampton's Gap, McLaws considering himself able to take care of Franklin.[88]

McLaws says in his report:

The enemy having forced Crampton's Gap, thereby completely cutting off my route up the valley to join the forces with General Lee, as Solomon's Gap, the only road over

---

88  The dispatches from Lee, the first of which Carman copied, and the second he pasted into the manuscript, were dated September 14 and are found in *ibid.*, 51, pt. 1, pp. 618-9, and *ibid.*, 19, pt. 2, p. 608, respectively. McLaws's reasoning and his efforts to send a message back to Lee are found in his report, *ibid.*, pt. 1, p. 856.

Elk Ridge, was just in front of the one over the Blue Ridge occupied by the enemy, I had nothing to do but to defend my position. I could not retire under the bluffs along the river, with the enemy pressing my rear and the forces at Harper's Ferry operating in conjunction, unless under a combination of circumstances I could not rely on to happen at the exact time needed; could not pass over the mountain except in a scattered and disorganized condition, nor could have gone through the Weverton Pass into the open country beyond to cross a doubtful ford when the enemy was in force on the other side of the Blue Ridge and coming down in my rear. There was no outlet in any direction for anything but the troops, and that very doubtful. In no contingency could I have saved the trains and artillery. I therefore determined to defend myself in the valley, holding the two heights and the two lower passes in order to force a direct advance down the valley, to prevent co-operation from Harper's Ferry, and at the same time to carry out my orders in relation to the capture of that place.[89]

Lee's instructions to Jackson were similar to those given McLaws; he informed him of McClellan's advance and impressed upon him the necessity of completing the work at Harper's Ferry and hastening to join him. To which Jackson replied at 8.15 p.m.:

Through God's blessing, the advance, which commenced this evening, has been successful thus far, and I look to Him for complete success to-morrow. The advance has been directed to be resumed at dawn to-morrow morning. I am thankful that our loss has been small. Your dispatch respecting the movements of the enemy and the importance of concentration has been received.[90]

The tone of this characteristic dispatch indicates that Jackson did not fully realize the fact that McClellan's entire army was abreast both passes of South Mountain and that Lee and all his detachments were in great jeopardy.

Had he so thought, it is inconceivable how he could have run the risk of remaining another hour in front of Harper's Ferry, but he would have abandoned

---

89 Carman copied this paragraph from McLaws's report, *ibid.*, to show McLaws's further thinking on what must have been a difficult decision. See also the *Weekly Press*, September 5, 12, and 19, 1888.

90 No copy of the dispatch survives that shows Jackson received the same message that McLaws did, yet Jackson's famous reply, which Carman copied from OR 19, pt. 1, p. 951, shows he must have been aware of Lee's anxiety. As Carman pointed out, the dispatch illustrated Jackson's ignorance of the situation north of the Potomac. It is illogical for Carman to acknowledge Jackson's lack of information, but repeat the Walker story suggesting Jackson had some knowledge of Gen. McClellan and his movements.

operations and immediately marched to rejoin his chief. But he correctly reasoned that to relinquish the opportunity of gaining the prize before him and march to join Lee would make his brilliant move a vain one; and knowing it was with McClellan that Lee had to deal, concluded that instead of marching to join Lee that night, he would hold on a few hours longer and reap the fruits of his enterprise.[91]

Jackson worked with great energy to get his guns in position by daylight to crush out all resistance. During the night, Colonel Crutchfield, his chief of artillery, crossed ten guns from the batteries of Brown, Dement, Garbor and Latimer over the Shenandoah at Key's Ford, and, moving on the west side, established them on a plateau at the foot of Loudoun Heights, so as to enfilade the entire position on Bolivar Heights and take the nearest and most formidable work, an embrasure battery for four guns, but open in the rear, in reverse. These ten guns were of Ewell's Division; the other guns of this division were placed in position on the crest of School House hill, on either side of the road.[92]

When night came, on the 14th, Miles's officers felt that they were in desperate straits and many of them favored an attempt to cut a way out or retake Maryland Heights. Of what use was it, they argued, to remain there and be butchered, and they made their views known to Miles, who drew from his pocket and read to them Halleck's order to defend Harper's Ferry to the last extremity, and this order, he emphatically declared, he intended to obey to the letter. When the suggestion was made to make the defense on Maryland Heights, assuming that they could be retaken, Miles insisted that it was not Maryland Heights that he had been ordered to defend, but Harper's Ferry.

White then secured approval of his suggestion to mass all the artillery on Bolivar Heights and fight it out there, but, when the batteries were about to be moved to that point, two obstacles presented themselves. There were no horses to haul the guns and Miles had changed his mind and countermanded the order. He yielded to a suggestion that the cavalry might attempt escape.

---

91 Unlike McLaws, Jackson did not explain in his report his thoughts on remaining at Harpers Ferry, so this assertion by Carman is speculative. Carman thinks Jackson reasoned correctly, an assertion proven more by circumstances than fact. By "both passes," Carman likely meant Crampton's *and* Turners/Fox's, since he conflated the latter two into one chapter in his original manuscript.

92 The paragraph describing Crutchfield's deployment of artillery is taken nearly verbatim from Jackson's report, *ibid.*, p. 954. Carman referred to the Staunton Artillery as both "Balthis'" and "Garber's" battery. Capt. Balthis left the battery in September because of wounds received at Malvern Hill on July 1, 1862. Garber was the actual commander, but Carman refers to the battery by both names. See also Robert J. Driver Jr., *The Staunton Artillery—McClanahan's Battery* (Lynchburg, VA: H.E. Howard, 1988), pp. 21-27.

During the afternoon of the 13th Colonel B. F. Davis, 8th New York Cavalry, and Lieutenant-Colonel Hasbrouck Davis, 12th Illinois Cavalry, waited upon General White, then in temporary command of all the cavalry, and suggested that, as the cavalry was of no use there and forage short, it cut its way out, as, if obliged to surrender, the horses and equipment would be a great prize to the enemy, and that an effort to reach McClellan ought to be made. That evening a conference of all the cavalry commanders was held at Miles' headquarters, and Miles agreed that if they would consult together and propose means of getting out, and a road to go by, he would consider the matter and, if he deemed proper, issue orders. The question whether the whole force, cavalry, infantry and artillery, might not escape was considered, but came to a negative conclusion on the ground that the infantry and artillery could not march fast enough, and by the objection of Miles that, under his orders, he had no right to abandon the post.[93]

There was considerable disputation as to the road to be taken; Colonel B. F. Davis desired to go up on western or Virginia side of the Potomac, as far as Kearneysville, and then cross the river at Shepherdstown; others favored a crossing of the Shenandoah and a march down the Potomac in the direction of Washington, or to recross at or below Point of Rocks and join McClellan by way of Frederick. Miles represented that there was extreme danger in both these routes. He and Davis had much talk about it, and there were some sharp words between them, which was finally cut short by a decision of Miles to issue an order directing the column to go across the pontoon bridge and then up the Maryland side of the river by what was known as the Sharpsburg route. All were cautioned by Miles to preserve secrecy, from the infantry officers, because, if they became aware of the intention, it would cause a stampede among them and their men. White proposed to go with the cavalry, as most of it had been under his command but, under the circumstances,

---

93 Carman let his bias against Halleck skew his objectivity. Miles's citing of the order to defend Harpers Ferry to the "last extremity" came from Wool, not Halleck. OR 19, pt. 1, pp. 522-3. On pages 294 and 302, Carman wrote that Halleck abdicated responsibility for the post. Since no dispatch of Halleck's used the "last extremity" language, it is unfair to blame him for the order. The conference in Harpers Ferry concerning the first discussion of the breakout and its difficulties comes from testimony of several officers to the Military Commission. See *ibid.*: White, pp. 530-1, Willard, pp. 559-66, Cameron, p. 635, Curtis, p. 687, Trimble, p. 745 and the finding of the Commission, p. 796. White reiterated much of his testimony in his *B&L* account, p. 613. All sources agreed that Miles steadfastly interpreted the letter of his instructions. White's suggestion to mass guns on Bolivar Heights is in McIlvaine's report, OR 19, pt. 1, p. 584. The request from the cavalry officers to attempt an escape and Miles's reluctant acquiescence, as well as his insistence that the rest of the garrison remain at the post, come from White's account in *B&L*, p. 613. This long paragraph loosely paraphrases White's article. White repeated here the impracticality of taking the infantry and artillery along.

thought it his duty to remain at Harper's Ferry, so, the command devolved upon the senior officer, Colonel Arno Voss, 12th Illinois Cavalry.[94]

The following orders were issued and sent, late in the afternoon, to each cavalry commander:

Headquarters, Harper's Ferry, September 14, 1862
Special Order No. 120.

The cavalry force at this post, except detached orderlies, will make immediate preparations to leave here at 8 o'clock to-night, without baggage-wagons, ambulances, or led horses, crossing the Potomac over the pontoon bridge, and taking the Sharpsburg road. The senior officer, Colonel Voss, will assume command of the whole, which will form the right at the quartermaster's office, the left up Shenandoah Street, without noise or loud command, in the following order: Cole's cavalry, Twelfth Illinois Cavalry, Eighth New York Cavalry, Seventh Squadron Rhode Island Cavalry, and First Maryland Cavalry. No other instructions can be given to the commander than to force his way through the enemy's lines and join our own army.

By order of Colonel Miles
H. C. Reynolds, Lieutenant and A. A. G.[95]

There was not much preparation required, so, as soon as it was dark, and the Confederate fire had ceased, supper was eaten, forage divided among the horses and the several commands moved silently down to the rendezvous in the main street, running close to the Shenandoah, and took their places in the column, which was ready to march at the designated time. The command numbered about 1500, officers and men, in good condition, well mounted and armed.

---

94 The dispute over which route the cavalry was to take came from an account cited by Carman: Luff, "March of the Cavalry From Harper's Ferry," pp. 33-49. White's *B&L* account is the source for the "sharp words" with Miles. Luff said White was "invited" to go but declined. See also Hasbrouck Davis' testimony to the Commission, *OR* 19, pt. 1, pp. 629-631.

95 Although Carman did not mention it, there was also a dispute after the fact about who had been in command of the column. Credit is usually given to Col. Benjamin Davis. See Sears, *Landscape Turned Red*, p. 151. Murfin, however, in his *Gleam of Bayonets*, p. 147, was correct. Davis was superseded in seniority by Col. Voss of the 12th Illinois Cavalry, who was designated by Miles as the commander, per S.O. #120. For a more detailed study of this issue and the cavalry escape, see Allan Tischler, *The History of the Harpers Ferry Cavalry Expedition, September 14 & 15, 1862* (Winchester VA: Five Cedars Press, 1993). S.O. #120 does not appear in the *Official Records*, but is reproduced in Luff, "March of the Cavalry From Harper's Ferry," pp. 33-49.

"Although the enemy was believed to be in strong force on the road chosen, and there were unknown dangers to be met in the darkness of night, it was an immense relief to be once more in motion with a chance for liberty.

Hemmed in on all sides as they had been, harried by shot and shell without being able to strike back, and with the gloomiest forebodings for the future, the spirits of officers and men had been depressed to the point of despondency; but all now recovered cheerfulness, and pressed forward, full of hope and courage, and equal to any emergency."

The command was formed in columns of two's and led by Lieutenant H. T. C. Green, 1st Maryland Cavalry, who knew the country, and another experienced guide, the two Davis' riding at the head of the column and giving it immediate direction, took up the line of march in intense darkness, crossed the pontoon bridge, turned to the left and passed up between the canal and Maryland Heights nearly a mile, and then turned to the right into the woods and by a narrow road moved in the direction of Sharpsburg, closing up as rapidly as possible into columns of four. Near the road leading up Maryland Heights from the river the head of the column encountered a picket guard, which was scattered by a charge, the Confederate shots doing no damage. The pace was now increased and the movement was rapid, sometimes at a trot, sometimes at a gallop, at times in the road, at times across fields, with an occasional picket shot to accelerate speed and increase confusion. The last of the Confederate pickets was cleared near the Antietam Iron Works, just beyond which, the stone bridge, near the mouth of the Antietam, was crossed and the direct road to Sharpsburg followed, which place was reached near midnight and a halt made in the quiet streets of that sleepy place for the rear to close up and the horses to gain breath.[96]

Here the officers heard of new dangers that increased their caution and shortened their stay. Lee's army had fallen back from South Mountain, some of it was at Keedysville, but three miles distant, and advance parties still nearer, with some scouts in the town. Commanders were quietly informed of this and a reconnoitering party was sent out on the Keedysville road, which was fired upon from the hill just beyond the town. The column was now massed as closely as possible and the march resumed on the Mercerville road, west of the Hagerstown

---

96 The quotation Carman included is also from Luff, "March of the Cavalry From Harper's Ferry," p. 40, and the following paragraph is condensed or extrapolated from pp. 40-41. Carman evidently used Luff's account as his main source for this ride. Luff does not include the specifics about the events in Sharpsburg on the night of September 14 that Carman provided here; Carman's are similar in wording to Heysinger's letter, August 17, 1905, Correspondence Files, Box 3, Folder 5. Luff described a greater collision of Union and Confederate troops in Sharpsburg than Carman. Luff's memoirs might be overly dramatic on this point.

pike; once on the road they broke into a brisk trot, went through New Industry and Mercerville on the Potomac, traversing hills and ravines, through cornfields and meadows, over fences and water courses, with an occasional halt to breathe the horses and determine the route. [Carman wrote and then crossed out: Many dropped out of the column and did not join their command for some days.]

Before it was yet day the column came out near St James College and a halt was made to blow the horses and close up, when the march was resumed and the advance entered the woods, skirting the turnpike from Hagerstown to Williamsport.[97] It was now in the gray of the morning, the bivouac fires of the Confederate camps, near Williamsport, were plainly visible, and the column was on the point of crossing the turnpike, about two and a half miles from Williamsport, when the low, rumbling sound of heavy carriage wheels was heard.[98] The column was halted, and the leader of the advance reported a large wagon train in sight, coming from Hagerstown. It was promptly decided to surprise and capture the train. The 8th New York and 12th Illinois were formed in line near the turnpike, the Maryland and Rhode Island cavalry in reserve, while Colonel B. F. Davis, with a squadron of the 8th New York, quietly advanced and took possession of the turnpike to intercept the passing of the train to Williamsport. When the head of the train came up, it was discovered that four or five infantrymen guarded each wagon. The first wagon was halted and the guard ordered to surrender, which it did without much parley or the firing of a shot on either side. With but a short halt the foremost wagon was turned to the right, driven a short distance over a dirt road to the Greencastle turnpike, and then driven northward on that road at a rapid pace.

Major William M. Luff, "March of the Cavalry from Harper's Ferry Sept. 14, 1862":

> As each wagon successively reached the point where Colonel Davis was posted, it
> shared the fate of its predecessors. Its escort was noiselessly captured, and, with

---

97 Carman's wording in the paragraph beginning with "Here the officers heard," sounds as if he was quoting someone else, but my research has not identified any source thus far. In Heysinger's letter of August 17, 1905, he emphatically denied passing through Mercerville and said the column did not turn off the Hagerstown Pike until two miles north of town, and then it was into a field, not a road. Heysinger also stated that he grew up near Sharpsburg and knew the area well. Why Carman chose not to use his account here, after using it in the previous paragraph, is unclear.

98 An account by Francis W. Dawson, a Confederate officer leading the wagon train, confirmed the visible campfires beyond Williamsport, but it is doubtful Carman was aware of these memoirs. Francis W. Dawson, *Reminiscences of Confederate Service 1861-1865* (Baton Rouge: Louisiana State University Press, 1993), p. 64.

scarcely another halt or check of the column, the whole train was transferred to the Greencastle road and traveling northward faster than a wagon train ever moved before. The capture was effected so quietly that after the foremost wagon had been taken and turned toward Greencastle the escort of the remainder were in complete ignorance of what had taken place until they reached the point where the change of direction was made. Many of the drivers rebelled against driving into captivity; but with a trooper on each side with drawn revolver, they had little opportunity to hesitate. Several wagons were purposely ditched by their drivers, but these were promptly set on fire and destroyed. After the whole train had passed, and was on the road to Greencastle, the cavalry formed in its rear to prevent recapture. The rebel cavalry escort had not before ventured to attack; but being reinforced, they now several times charge the rear of our column, without effect, however, as they were in each instance met and driven back.[99]

The Confederate cavalry followed as far as the Pennsylvania line and two light guns which they brought up annoyed the Union rear. It was now broad day and as the sun rose bright and warm the scene upon the road is described as very enlivening; "The long train of heavily loaded wagons rumbling over the hard smooth road as rapidly as they could be urged forward, enveloped by throngs of cavalry-men with a solid column in their rear, the clouds of dust, the cracking of whips, the cries of the drivers, and the shouts of officers and men, formed a striking contrast to the long march in silence and darkness of the previous night." The column reached Greencastle, Pennsylvania between 9 and 10 o'clock in the morning of the 15th, with the captured train of 97 wagons, about 600 prisoners, and a good supply of beef cattle. The wagons proved to be those of Longstreet's ordnance train, which, under charge of Captain Francis W. Dawson, had left Hagerstown during the night to cross into Virginia.[100]

99 See Luff, "March of the Cavalry from Harper's Ferry," p. 43. Carman again relies almost completely on Luff's account. Beginning with the words, "It was now in the gray...," Carman virtually quoted Luff. The section Carman set off in quotation marks begins on p. 44 and continues onto p. 45 in Luff's article.

100 After a brief excerpt from an account that closely matches the wording in Samuel P. Pettingill, *The College Cavaliers* (Chicago: Ft. McAllister & Co. Printers, 1883), pp. 79-87 (which includes Col. Voss' unofficial report), Carman returned to Luff's account, "March of the Cavalry from Harper's Ferry," p. 45, for the rest of his quotation. Carman's figures for the success of the capture of Confederate resources differ from Luff, *supra*, in terms of prisoners, but agree in the number of wagons captured (97). Carman reported 600 prisoners; Luff says 200. Both mention a herd of beef cattle and agree on the time of arrival in Greencastle. There is considerable dispute about the details of this cavalry expedition. Everything from the route taken to the number of wagons captured has been argued in various accounts. No commander

The escaping cavalry narrowly missed a novel encounter with the Reserve artillery of Lee's army, under command of General W. N. Pendleton, which crossed its track between eight and nine miles north of Sharpsburg, about sunrise on the 15th. On the 14th Pendleton accompanied Longstreet on the march back from Hagerstown to Boonsboro, but was halted on reaching Beaver Creek four miles northwest of Boonsboro, and ordered to put his guns in position on the heights covering the National Road and the crossings of the stream. After the day had gone against Lee at South mountain, Pendleton was ordered to take two battalions of the artillery by the shortest route to Williamsport and cross the Potomac, to guard the fords of that river. He started during the night and thus reports:

> By sunrise, Monday, 15th, we had reached the intersection of the Hagerstown, Sharpsburg, Boonsborough, and Williamsport roads, and there received reliable intelligence of a large cavalry force of the enemy not far ahead of us. I immediately posted guns to the front and on the flank, sent messengers to General Toombs, understood to be at Sharpsburg, for a regiment or two of infantry, set to work collecting a band of armed stragglers, and sent scouts to the front. These latter soon returned and reported the road clear for some 2 miles. I therefore determined to advance cautiously, without waiting for infantry, in order to protect the large wagon train proceeding by the Hagerstown road through Williamsport. The cavalry, which consisted of three regiments, escaped from Harper's Ferry, crossed our road perhaps less than an hour ahead of us. We thus narrowly missed a rather strange encounter. My

---

involved left an official report, and several published versions differ. See, generally, Tischler, *Harpers Ferry Cavalry Expedition*. Carman relied upon Luff's account, and perhaps William H. Nichols, "The Siege and Capture of Harper's Ferry by the Confederates," *Soldiers and Sailor's Historical Society of Rhode Island*, 4th Series (Providence: The Providence Press, 1889), and Heysinger letter, August 17, 1905. Why Carman did not use Nichols' "A Cavalry Escape," *The National Tribune* (Washington DC: The National Tribune), April 12, 1894, is unknown, although the latter work by Nichols appears to be a revision of his earlier work. There are other sources, some published later, that dispute Luff's version. See also Pettingill, *The College Cavaliers*, which Carman did not cite, but evidently did use here. Carman also provided the name of the Confederate officer in command of the train, while Luff only described the capture of an unnamed officer in command of the escort. Carman referred to Dawson as a captain in charge of General Longstreet's wagon train. Dawson was a lieutenant and ordnance officer at the time, appointed September 10, 1862. (He did not make captain until April 2, 1864.) Joseph Crute, *Confederate Staff Officers* (Powhatan, VA: Derwent Books, 1982), p. 123. Tischler, *supra.*, p. 251, cited Dawson's service record and his book *Reminiscences of Confederate Service*, which confirmed his rank as lieutenant, but claimed he was appointed brigade ordnance officer on August 13, 1862, while, Robert E. L. Krick, *Staff Officers in Gray: A Biographical Register of Staff Officers of the Army of Northern Virginia* (Chapel Hill, NC: University of North Carolina Press, 2003), p. 112, puts his rank as lieutenant.

purpose was, of course, if we met, to attempt the destruction of those retiring invaders.[101]

The escaping Union cavalry narrowly missed another encounter, and this with a regiment of Confederate cavalry and a light battery of six guns. When Wade Hampton's brigade of cavalry marched from Burkittsville, on the morning of September 14, part of it went along the east base of South Mountain to Knoxville on the Potomac, and picketed the roads leading to Berlin and Frederick. Two regiments crossed Brownsville Gap into Pleasant Valley one of these, the Jeff Davis Legion, with Hart's South Carolina Battery of six guns, was placed at Solomon's Gap, in Elk Ridge. Lieutenant Colonel W. T. Martin, commanding the regiment, threw out pickets in the direction of the Potomac; some of these were encountered and brushed away by the Union cavalry, about 10 p.m., as it neared the bridge spanning the Antietam near its mouth. This information was quickly carried to Martin, who was surprised at the news of an enemy in that direction, and after a hasty conference with some of his officers the conclusion was reached that McClellan's left wing had interposed between Jackson's forces besieging Harper's Ferry and the Confederates at Turner's Gap, Boonsboro and Hagerstown.

Martin did not know the result of the day's fighting at South Mountain and his scout reported a large Union force south and west, he decided to fall back towards Hagerstown and quickly set out in that direction, throwing scouts to the crossroads to the left, that reported the Union column, the cavalry from Harper's Ferry, moving parallel to him up the Potomac. Hart placed some of his guns in advance to cover all cross-roads and kept one or more at the rear of the column. Skirting the east base of Elk Ridge, the column, leaving Keedysville to the right, went over the Antietam by the bridge above Pry's Mill and, going through Smoketown and Bakersville, came to Downsville, where, just before sunrise, it was learned that the Union cavalry had passed that point. From Downsville Martin followed rapidly after the retiring force, and soon after sunrise saw the explosions from the burning of a part of Longstreet's ordnance train, which had been intercepted. After a short pursuit, past the burning wagons, Martin withdrew to Williamsport, crossed the Potomac, went down the Virginia side, recrossed the river at Shepherdstown Ford, on the afternoon of the 16th and rejoined his brigade at Sharpsburg on the 17th.[102]

---

101 Information about the near-miss with Confederate artillery on the night of September 14, along with the quotation, are from General Pendleton's report, OR 19, pt. 1, pp. 829-30.

102 The second brush with Confederates on the Federal cavalry odyssey is taken from letters from to Carman from Capt. James Hart dated March 27, 1900, (NA-AS) and April 7, 1900 (NYPL). A modern regimental history, Donald Hopkins, *The Little Jeff: The Jeff Davis Legion*

[In the margin, without indication where it was to be inserted, Carman wrote: When Jackson heard that the cavalry had escaped from Harper's Ferry, he was much disappointed, saying: "I would rather have had them than anything else in the place."][103]

We return to the beleaguered garrison at Harper's Ferry. When it became known that the cavalry had passed out, some of the leading officers of the infantry waited upon Miles and suggested that the entire force be withdrawn to Maryland Heights. As we now know these would have been found held by but one regiment of Confederate infantry and two guns. Colonel Willard thought that by falling back during the night to the town there would be found many old walls, stone fences, and rocks which could be made available for a stout resistance, others thought that a retreat by the road through Sandy Hook possible, but Miles negated all such suggestions. Still later in the night, when it was reported that Jackson was placing batteries in position, beyond the Shenandoah and also opposite the right of the line, these suggestions were earnestly renewed, and Miles's emphatic reply was: "No, I cannot listen to any such proposition; I am ordered to hold Harper's Ferry at all hazards." If Miles had not been tied down by his orders to hold Harper's Ferry at all hazards, his nearly 12,000 infantry could have followed the cavalry and escaped. McLaws could not have barred their passage, and their junction with Franklin, in Pleasant Valley, could have been readily accomplished.[104]

"After dark on Sunday (14th), the various batteries that were then in position, especially those from Loudoun and Maryland Heights, continued their fire on Harper's Ferry, and this, together with the Federal guns replying from Bolivar, constituted a magnificent display of fireworks, which was visible for many miles. All night were Jackson's troops making movements...and his artillery officers placing guns

*Cavalry Army of Northern Virginia* (Shippensburg PA: White Mane Pub. Co., 1999), placed the legion elsewhere and made no mention of Hart's battery. His citations from letter collections are confusing and refer to towns not in existence. Tischler's *Harpers Ferry Cavalry Expedition* suggests Hart's battery was separated and two guns and a portion of the legion were sent to Solomon's Gap. Since these accounts do not cite Hart's letters, Carman is likely the most accurate source.

103 The source of this quote is Heysinger's August 17, 1905 letter, in which he wrote that he heard this from General John G. Walker. Jackson's capture of large amounts of artillery, infantry weapons, and other stores makes it unlikely that he would favor instead the capture of 1,500 cavalry. Walker has been proven to be an unreliable source, and this might be another tall tale.

104 Carman based his statements about options for the Federal troops at Harpers Ferry on the testimony of Cols. Willard and Trimble to the Commission, OR 19, pt. 1, pp. 559-66, and 741-9. Trimble repeated Miles strict adherence to his orders, as Carman quoted it.

in position. The devoted garrison awaited with apprehension and without hope the fearful hail of fire which the day would surely bring. The Confederates were spurred to prompt action by the important events of the 14th elsewhere. The advance on that day of McClellan, the battle of South Mountain, and the seizure of Crampton's Gap and Pleasant Valley in rear of McLaws...all showed the vigorous efforts making to relieve Harper's Ferry, and earnest dispatches from Lee represented to his lieutenant the necessity of speedy success and of a speedy reunion of his scattered forces, to make head against the overwhelming advance of McClellan's army."[105]

Before daylight Starke's Brigade fell back from its close proximity to the Potomac to its position of the evening before, in support of Brockenbrough's Battery, which re-opened with telling effect; in the near vicinity the batteries of Poague and Carpenter poured an incessant fire upon the right of Bolivar Heights and the batteries of Von Sehlen and Phillips; Lawton advanced his division to the front of the woods to support the advance. A. P. Hill, and Lieutenant-Colonel R. Lindsay Walker, Hill's chief of artillery, opened a rapid enfilade fire from all his batteries at about 1000 yards range, the batteries on School House hill firing upon Miles's line in front.

As Crutchfield was obliged to cut a road for his guns beyond the Shenandoah, he did not get them into position by daybreak, as intended, but in a short time after Lindsay Walker's guns had opened, the ten guns of Brown, A. W. Garbor, Dement and Latimer poured an accurate fire upon the left and rear of Miles' defenses. This concentrated fire from many guns, bearing most heavily upon Rigby's Battery, on the left of the line, near the Charlestown Turnpike, and upon Potts' Battery, nearby, which White had ordered up and placed into position to reply to Hill's and Lawton's guns in front, soon silenced the Union guns; the men running from them, but returning as the fire slackened, again to abandon them as the fire strengthened.

The artillery upon Loudoun Heights, under French, which had silenced the guns on Camp Hill and near the Barbour House, on the afternoon of the 14th, again opened fire, but, as it was foggy, their shots were at random. The two guns on Maryland Heights joined in the attack, by a plunging fire, which added to the Union discomfort and demoralization.[106]

For more than a full hour this heavy direct, enfilading and plunging fire, from front, flank and rear, was responded to by all the Union guns which could be brought to bear, but Phillips and Von Sehlen soon were out of ammunition,

---

105 Carman's Note: Allan, *The Army of Northern Virginia*, p. 339.

106 Most of the information about Jackson's forces on the morning of September 15 comes from Jackson's report, *ibid.*, pp. 954-5, and Crutchfield's report, *ibid.*, p. 962.

Graham, on Camp Hill, exhausted the ammunition for the 20-pounder Parrott, but Rigby and Potts, moving nearer the Shenandoah, still kept up a sharp and effective fire which availed but little, however, against the superior weight of the Confederate fire. At this point White says: "The long-range ammunition had now almost entirely failed, and it became evident that from the great preponderance of the enemy's artillery and his ability to keep up a fire at long range to which we were no longer able to reply, our ability to hold the position became a mere question of time, and that our defense could only be continued at great sacrifice of life without any corresponding advantage."[107]

The fire now slackened, for ammunition was momentarily running low, and believing resistance nearly at an end, Hill's batteries were ordered to cease their fire which was the signal for the infantry to storm the works. Pender had moved his three assaulting brigades, his own, Archer's and Brockenbrough's, to within 150 yards of Miles' works, sheltered as much as possible from fire by the inequalities of the ground, and had commenced to advance to the assault when the Union fire again opened with full force and Pegram and Crenshaw pushed their batteries to within 400 yards of Miles' works and poured a rapid fire into them, over the heads of their own infantry, in which they were joined by the guns beyond the Shenandoah, which, since the return of the battery men to their guns, had been paying particular attention to Rigby's Battery on the Charlestown road and Potts' guns between it and the Shenandoah. Under this fire Hill was gathering for a determined assault; when the white flag was seen on Miles' works his guns ceased their fire and his infantry came to a halt.[108]

When Miles saw the circle of fire by which he had been surrounded and felt its effect, when the Confederate guns had opened upon him, he realized that it was only a question of time as to the final result, unless aid came from McClellan, but when one battery after another reported ammunition running low and then exhausted, he knew that the time had come earlier in the day than he had anticipated. White says; "During the afternoon of the 14th our guns at Harper's Ferry, engaged with Jackson's forces, were cheeringly responded to by those of General Franklin at Crampton's Gap, but after 4 p.m. and on the morning of the 15th, there was no sound of conflict in that direction, and the hope of relief from McClellan which the proximity of the firing had inspired, was abandoned." Without ammunition for his guns, much of his infantry disorganized and demoralized, all

---

107  White's direct quotation is from his report, *ibid.*, p. 528.

108  Most of the Confederate description of the bombardment and surrender flags being seen are from A. P. Hill's report in *ibid.*, p. 980.

hope lost of help from McClellan, Miles at 8.30 a. m., called a council of his brigade commanders and conferred with them upon the propriety of an immediate surrender. There was some opposition to this course but an interchange of opinion resulted in the unanimous conclusion that it was useless to continue the contest and that, if reasonable terms could be obtained, it was best to stop further waste of life by surrender. Accordingly the white flag was raised on Bolivar Heights and General White was directed to arrange terms of capitulation.[109]

The Confederate batteries across the Shenandoah and those in front on the Charlestown road, ceased firing upon the display of white flags on Bolivar Heights, but the men of Brockenbrough's Battery did not see them and continued their fire until a courier stopped them; the gunners on Loudoun Heights did not immediately see the signals, through a heavy fog and powder smoke, and continued their work for some minutes; and from Maryland Heights the white flag was seen on Bolivar and the United States flag on Camp Hill, upon which the two guns were trained upon the latter, until it was replaced by the white flag; and from one of these points a shell was thrown which struck Miles in the leg, inflicting a mortal wound.[110]

When the white flag was displayed and the firing ceased Jackson was at the church in the wood on the Bolivar and Halltown turnpike. He sent Captain Henry Kyd Douglas, of his staff, up the turnpike and into the Union lines to ascertain the purpose of the white flag. On his way, and when near the top of the hill, Douglas met General White and staff and told his mission. White replied that Miles had been mortally wounded, that he was in command and desired an interview with Jackson. At that moment A. P. Hill came up from the direction of his line and the whole party went back to the church where Jackson was found sitting on his horse. "He was not, as the Comte de Paris says, leaning against a tree asleep, but exceedingly wide awake. The contrast in appearance there presented was striking. General White, riding a handsome black horse, was carefully dressed and had on untarnished gloves, boots and sword. His staff were equally comely in costume. On the other hand, General Jackson was the dingiest, worst-dressed, and worse-mounted general that a warrior who cared for good looks and style would

---

109 White's quotation is from his *B&L* account, pp. 614-5. According to White, the sound of cannon from Franklin ended at 4:00 p.m., the time most accounts note that the fighting at Crampton's Gap began. See Chapter Seven for the details of this action. Once again, Carman failed to correct an inaccurate source.

110 The language for the discussion of the Union surrender comes from White, *ibid.* The specific references to Confederate batteries and the shell that fatally struck Miles are not clear. Most Confederate accounts mention the fog, and Walker mentioned being unsure of a surrender. See his report, *OR* 19, pt. 1, pp. 912-3. Brockenbrough's firing after the flag was seen comes from Pendleton's report, *ibid.*, p. 1,016.

wish to surrender to. The surrender was unconditional, and then General Jackson turned the matter over to General A. P. Hill." Hill granted liberal terms. The officers were allowed to go on parole with side arms and private property, and the privates with everything except equipment and guns.[111]

Jackson sent a brief dispatch to Lee announcing the surrender and then rode up to Bolivar and down into Harper's Ferry. The Union prisoners lined the sides of the road and their curiosity to see him was keen and kindly. Many of them uncovered as he passed and he immediately returned the salute. Some cheered him, and one man had an echo of response all about him, when he said aloud: "Boys, he's not much for looks, but if we'd had him we wouldn't have been caught in this trap."[112]

There were surrendered including the wounded, over 12,000 officers and men, 73 pieces of artillery, 3,000 small arms, about 200 wagons and a large amount of quartermaster and commissary stores.[113]

\* \* \*

Return of casualties in the Union forces at Maryland Heights and Harper's Ferry[compiled from the nominal list of casualties, returns &c.:

| | Killed | | Wounded | | Captured | | |
|---|---|---|---|---|---|---|---|
| Command | Officers | Men | Officers | Men | officers | Men | Total |
| General Staff | | | 1 | | 6 | | 7 |
| 12 IL Cav. | | | | 2 | 4 | 153 | 159 |
| M, 2 IL Lt. Art. | | | | | 3 | 97 | 100 |

111 The general information and the long quotation are from Douglas' *B&L* article, which extends to p. 626.

112 This dispatch is found in *OR* 19, pt. 1, p. 951. The description and quote about Jackson's appearance is from Douglas, *B&L*, p. 627.

113 The number of men, arms, cannon, and other supplies captured varies by report. Gens. Lee, Hill, Jackson, and Henry Douglas, all mention similar but slightly different numbers. Carman's figures of "over 12,000 officers and men" correlated well to the official number of 12,737 given in the table in the "Return of Casualties in the Union Forces at Maryland Heights and Harper's Ferry," *OR* 19, pt. 1, p. 549, which Carman pasted into his manuscript.

| | | | | | | |
|---|---|---|---|---|---|---|
| 65 IL Inf. | | | 1 | 6 | 32 | 778 | 817 |
| 15 IN Bat. | | | | 3 | 4 | 114 | 121 |
| Rigby's IN Bat | | | | | 4 | 109 | 113 |
| 1 MD Cav (detach) | | | 1 | 2 | 1 | 19 | 23 |
| Cole's Bttn MD Cav. | | | | | | | |
| 1st MD PHB Inf. | | | 6 | 6 | 32 | 747 | 791 |
| 3 MD PHD Inf | 1 | 2 | 1 | 8 | 24 | 510 | 546 |
| 8 NY Cav. | | | | | 5 | 87 | 92 |
| 5 NY Bats. A & F | | | | | 9 | 256 | 267 |
| 12 NY Inf (militia) | | | | | 30 | 530 | 560 |
| 39 NY Inf. | | | | 15 | 10 | 520 | 545 |
| 111 NY Inf. | | 5 | | 6 | 36 | 934 | 981 |
| 115 NY Inf. | | | 1 | 10 | 28 | 950 | 989 |
| 125 NY Inf. | | 2 | | 1 | 38 | 881 | 922 |
| 126 NY Inf. | 1 | 12 | 4 | 38 | 30 | 946 | 1,031 |
| Potts OH Bat. | | | | | 2 | 82 | 84 |
| 32 OH Inf. | 1 | 9 | 3 | 55 | 31 | 643 | 742 |
| 60 OH Inf. | | 2 | 1 | 5 | 38 | 867 | 913 |
| 87 OH Inf. | | 1 | | | 38 | 976 | 1,015 |
| 7 Squad'n RI Cav. | | | | | | | |
| 9 VT Inf. | | | | 3 | 30 | 714 | 747 |
| Unatt'd, in hospital | | | | | | 1,172 | 1,172 |
| TOTAL | 3 | 41 | 13 | 160 | 435 | 12,085 | 12,737 |

Officers Killed—Capt. Jacob Sarbaugh, Third Maryland Potomac Home Brigade Infantry, Samuel R. Breese, Thirty-Second Ohio Infantry, and Lieut. Alfred R. Clapp, One Hundred and Twenty-Sixth New York Infantry.

Died of Wounds—Col. Dixon S. Miles, Second U.S. Infantry, and Lieut. Daniel C. Hiteschew, First Maryland Cavalry.

A number of wounded fell into the enemy's hands, and are also counted with the captured.[114]

Of the 217 killed and wounded four-fifths are chargeable to the defense of Maryland Heights on the 12th and 13th. The Confederate loss was 41 killed and 247 wounded, of which McLaws had 35 dead and 178 wounded on Maryland Heights; Walker 1 killed and 3 wounded on Loudoun Heights; Jackson 5 killed and 66 wounded in front of Bolivar Heights.[115]

Miles would not permit the destruction of the Government property, which fell into enemy hands. He would not destroy the pontoon bridge across the Potomac, after the abandonment of Maryland Heights, but left it intact and, by its use, McLaws was enabled to cross and reach the field of Antietam, some hours earlier than he could, otherwise, have done, and in time to deliver that telling blow upon Sedgwick's flank in the Dunkard Church woods.[116]

Lee's necessities did not present much rest to Jackson's troops. Leaving Hill to receive the surrender of the Union troops and take the requisite steps for securing

---

114 Carman pasted in this recapitulation of the Union casualty return from *ibid.*

115 Carman's Confederate casualty figures are not correct. Carman said McLaws lost 35 dead and 178 wounded, but this does not include the two killed and 17 wounded from Barksdale's Brigade. See McLaws's report, *ibid.*, pp. 860-1; Walker's figures are the same as his report, *ibid.*, p. 913; the figures for Jackson's Division differ only by listing two more killed than A. P. Hill's report; neither J. R. Jones nor Jubal Early reported casualties. It is possible that the two additional deaths are from one of those divisions. The numbers of captured guns vary also; official sources say 47 guns, but most Confederate sources say 73. Most puzzling is the figure of 3,000 small arms cited by Carman. This must be a mistake, for almost all other sources put the figure between 11,000 and 12,500. Since most of the soldiers who surrendered were armed, and there was a small reserve supply there as well, 3,000 is much too low. Carman probably omitted a "1" in front of the 3,000 (i.e., 13,000).

116 Carman's judgment against Miles about the government property may be correct, but the pontoon bridge comment was speculative and probably a bit unfair. Miles might have left the bridge expecting it to be used by Franklin, who was supposedly coming to rescue the garrison. It was already established that Miles strictly interpreted his orders, and the destruction of the bridge might be construed in that light. McLaws's actions after crossing allowed him plenty of time to reach Sharpsburg, so the bridge might not have made much difference.

the captured stores, Jackson moved to rejoin Lee with the remaining divisions of his command. By a severe night march he reached the vicinity of Sharpsburg on the morning of the 16th. Walker followed Jackson. He crossed Loudoun Heights, the Shenandoah, and the Potomac, reached the neighborhood of Sharpsburg on the 16th and reported to Lee.[117]

So far Lee's plans had been carried out with complete success, but with a delay that he did not anticipate and that was nearly fatal to that part of his army north of the Potomac. McLaws was but little behind time, Walker was a day late, and Jackson more than a day late in closing in on Harper's Ferry; and nearly two days more were consumed in reducing the place; what it was thought could be accomplished by the evening of the 13th, was not consummated until the morning of the 15th. Meanwhile events were taking place at the South Mountain passes, threatening not only the operations at Harper's Ferry, but imperiling the entire Confederate army.[118]

## Note to Chapter VI

On the 23rd of September 1862, a Military Commission was organized to investigate and report upon the conduct of certain officers connected with and the circumstances attending the abandonment of Maryland Heights and the surrender of Harper's Ferry. The Commission, after a session of forty days and the examination of many witnesses, reported, November 3rd, that the conduct of General Julius White merited approbation. (Here Carman wrote a sentence that appears to be critical of D'Utassy and Sherill, but he crossed it out.) It called attention "to the disgraceful conduct of the 126th New York Infantry" and therein did a gross injustice. As to Colonel Thomas H. Ford, commanding Maryland Heights, it was perfectly clear that he should not have been placed in that command, and that he had "a discretionary power to abandon the heights or not, as his better judgment might dictate, with the men and means then under his

---

117 The efforts to rejoin Lee are taken from the reports of Jackson, *ibid.*, p. 954, from whom Carman borrowed the sentence about the "severe night march"; and from Walker, *ibid.*, p. 914, for his route and time.

118 Lee's report did not criticize anyone for tardiness in the Harpers Ferry operation, and Lee did not personally chastise his subordinates. Carman's description of the timing was flawed. The original intent of S.O. #191 called for the time that each objective was to be reached, i.e. "Friday morning" (September 13), but there was no set time for the rejoining of the commands. If Lee expressed a time verbally to these officers, they did not record it. It appears that Carman was conjecturing about regrouping by the evening of the 13th.

command, and it is believed from the evidence, circumstantial and direct, that the result did not, to any great extent, surprise, nor in any way displease the officer [Colonel Miles] in command at Harper's Ferry." It found that under these discretionary powers Ford had mismanaged affairs; that he had conducted the defense of the heights without ability, and abandoned them prematurely and without sufficient cause, and that throughout he displayed such a total lack of military capacity as to disqualify him for a command in the service. Colonel Ford was dismissed November 8, 1862, as also, was Major Baird of the 126th New York. In the case of Major Baird, it was subsequently proven that his conduct, far from being disgraceful, was most meritorious; he was restored to command and fell in front of Petersburg, June 16, 1864.[119]

In the case of Colonel Miles the following report was made:

The Commission has approached a consideration of this officer's conduct, in connection with the surrender of Harper's Ferry, with extreme reluctance. An officer who cannot appear before any earthly tribunal to answer or explain charges gravely affecting his character, who has met his death at the hands of the enemy, even upon the spot he disgracefully surrendered, is entitled to the tenderest care and most careful investigation. These this Commission has accorded Colonel Miles, and, in giving an opinion, only repeats what runs through our nine hundred pages of evidence, strangely unanimous upon the fact that Colonel Miles' incapacity, amounting to almost imbecility, led to the shameful surrender of this important post.

Early as the 15th of August he disobeys orders of Major-General Wool to fortify Maryland Heights. When it is attacked by the enemy, its naturally strong positions are unimproved, and, from his criminal neglect, to use the mildest term, the large force of the enemy is almost upon an equality with the few men he throws out for their protection.

He seemed to have understood and admitted to his officers that Maryland Heights was the key to the position, and yet he placed Colonel Ford in command with a feeble force; made no effort to strengthen him by fortifications, although, between the 5th and the 13th of September, there was ample time to do so; and to Colonel

---

119  What Carman entitled as "Note to Chapter VI" amounted to several pages. It is mainly an examination of the aftermath of the Harpers Ferry operation, as far as the Union investigation was concerned. The group was called The Harper's Ferry Military Commission, and was authorized by Special Order #256, Adjutant General's Office, September 23, 1862, OR 19, pt. 1, pp. 549-50. The members of the commission were Maj. Gen. David Hunter; Maj. Gen. George Cadwalader; Brig. Gen. C. C. Augur; Capt. Donn Paitt, assistant adjutant general; Capt. F. Ball, Jr., aide-de-camp; and Col. J. Holt, judge advocate general. The testimony of the witnesses fills pages 553 to 794 in OR 19, pt. 1. Their final report is in *ibid.*, pp. 794-800. Much of Carman's language comes from this report, including his direct quotations.

Ford's repeated demands for means to intrench and re-enforcements to strengthen the position, he made either inadequate return or no response at all. He gave Colonel Ford discretionary power as to when he should abandon the heights, the fact of the abandonment having, it seems, been determined on in his own mind, for, when the unhappy event really occurred, his only exclamations were to the effect that he feared Colonel Ford had given them up too soon. This, too, when he must have known that the abandonment of Maryland Heights was the surrender of Harper's Ferry. This leaving the key of the position to the keeping of Colonel Ford, with discretionary power, after the arrival of the capable and courageous officer who had waived his rank to serve wherever ordered, is one of the more striking facts illustrating the utter incapacity of Colonel Miles.

Immediately previous to and pending the siege of Harper's Ferry he paroled rebel prisoners, and permits, indeed, sends them to the enemy's headquarters. This, too, when he should have known that the lack of ammunition, the bad conduct of some of our troops, the entire absence of fortifications, and the abandonment of Maryland Heights were important facts they could, and undoubtedly did, communicate to the enemy. Sixteen of these prisoners were paroled on the 12th, and a pass given them in the handwriting of Colonel Miles, and some of them left as late as the 14th ; while a rebel officer, by the name of Rouse, after an escape, is retaken, and subsequently has a private interview with Colonel Miles, is paroled, and after the surrender appears at the head of his men, among the first to enter Harper's Ferry.

It is not necessary to accumulate instances from the mass of evidence that throughout scarcely affords one fact in contradiction to what each one establishes, that Colonel Miles was unfit to conduct so important a defense as that of Harper's Ferry.

This Commission would not have dwelt upon this painful subject were it not for the fact that the officer who placed this incapable in command should share in the responsibility, and in the opinion of the Commission Major-General Wool is guilty to this extent of a grave disaster, and should be censured for his conduct.[120]

It is safe to say that, at the time, ninety-nine out of every hundred Union men in the North believed that Colonel Ford was an arrant coward and Colonel Miles a

---

120 Carman pasted these six paragraphs from the final report, *ibid.*, pp. 799-800, to show how the Commission placed an ample portion of the blame on Miles, Ford, and Baird. Yet Carman acknowledged in his commentary that, in the heat of the moment, the Commission may have gone too far. Beyond incapacity, there were rumors of treason and collusion afloat at the time, charges Miles could not answer. Carman seemed to realize that the loss sprang more from mistakes and an indefensible position than conspiracy. While some blame attached itself to Gen. Wool for putting an "incompetent" in command at such an important post, Carman thought Miles and Ford were slandered by the report and recognized the political need to chastise McClellan, too.

designing traitor, and the conclusions of the Commission were approved and would have been commended had it suggested that Ford be shot and the body of the unfortunate Miles exposed as food for vultures. Time has softened the asperities of those hot hours; and a clearer light leads to a calmer judgment, and there are many who doubt that whether the finding of the Commission was a just one. They have come to the conclusion that it was unduly severe; that while Miles committed a blunder in abandoning Maryland Heights, the blunder was exceeded by that of General Halleck, in retaining the garrison at Harper's Ferry, after it was known that General Lee had crossed into Maryland.

Having covered Ford and Miles with disgrace and justly censured General Wool, it proceeded to give its opinion of General McClellan and his share of the blame:

> The Commission has remarked freely on the conduct of Colonel Miles, an old officer, killed in one of the battles of our country, and it cannot, from any motives of delicacy, refrain from censuring those in high command when it thinks such censure deserved. The General in-Chief has testified that General McClellan, after having received orders to repel the enemy invading the State of Maryland, marched only 6 miles per day on an average when pursuing the invading enemy. The General-in-Chief also testifies that, in his opinion, General McClellan could, and should, have relieved and protected Harper's Ferry, and in this opinion the Commission fully concur.
>
> The evidence thus introduced confirms the Commission in the opinion that Harper's Ferry, as well as Maryland Heights, was prematurely surrendered. The garrison should have been satisfied that relief, however long delayed, would come at last, and that 1,000 men killed in Harper's Ferry would have made a small loss had the post been secured, and probably save 2,000 at Antietam. How important was this defense we can now appreciate. Of the 97,000, composing at that time the whole of Lee's army, more than one-third were attacking Harper's Ferry, and of this the main body was in Virginia. By reference to the evidence, it will be seen that at the moment Colonel Ford abandoned Maryland Heights his little army was in reality relieved by Generals Franklin's and Sumner's corps at Crampton's Gap, within 7 miles of his position, and that after the surrender of Harper's Ferry no time was given to parole prisoners even, before 20,000 troops were hurried from Virginia, and the entire force went off on the double-quick to relieve Lee, who was being attacked at Antietam. Had the garrison been slower to surrender or the Army of the Potomac swifter to march,

the enemy would have been forced to raise the siege or have been taken in detail, with the Potomac dividing his forces.[121]

The findings of the Commission were cordially approved by Halleck. He cared but little for the censure of Wool and the condemnation of Miles and Ford, but was more than pleased at the censure of McClellan. The Commission had done what is was organized to do, to condemn McClellan; it had failed to declare, that which the evidence proved, that the guilty party was General H. W. Halleck.

A curious and caustic commentary upon the animus of the Commission and its findings is made by one of its members, Captain Donn Piatt, who says:

We had not been in session twenty-four hours before it was understood at the Executive Mansion, and in the War Department it was well known, that the fault was in McClellan. How this came to be the opinion of the board no one could explain. It seemed to pervade the atmosphere. Now we all know, as well as facts could control convictions, that Harper's Ferry was lost, not through any fault of McClellan, but from the treachery, cowardice and stupidity of the officers left there for the defense. Had not Maryland Heights been abandoned the place could have easily been held until McClellan came to the rescue.

McClellan was not only a Democrat, but he had forced his political opinions into the army, and instead of fighting the country's battles with some sense and a little success, he had imprudently elevated his shallow mind to the post of advisor on political subjects. This was enough to brush aside Miles' treachery and Ford's cowardice. The writer of this, the younger member, was called on to write the opinion of the Court. It was not his opinion, and so he embodied in the judgment Halleck's testimony, which said, true enough, that had McClellan marched an hour more or a mile farther a day, he would have reached Harper's Ferry in time to rescue the garrison. The fact was that McClellan, after advising the evacuation of the place, was feeling his way along in utter ignorance of the enemy's whereabouts or intentions. The finding of the board, as far as McClellan is concerned, is an historical infamy, and so impressed with such a conclusion was he that he inserted a sentence in the finding that rendered the entire judgment a ludicrous absurdity. It read: 'By reference to the evidence it will be seen, that at the very moment Colonel Ford abandoned Maryland Heights his army

---

121 Carman pasted these two paragraphs from *ibid.*, p. 800, to finish the Commission's censure of those it blamed for the loss of Harpers Ferry. The Commission was made up of several officers loyal to the Lincoln government, and their animus toward McClellan is evident. Hunter was a staunch Republican. See Warner, *Generals in Blue*, p. 244. Although a Democrat prior to the war, Gen. Joseph Holt, *ibid.*, pp. 232-233, faithfully supported the more radical actions of Lincoln and vigorously enforced the suspension of habeas corpus and other actions.

was in reality relieved by General Franklin's Corps at Crampton's Gap, within seven miles of his position."'[122]

It will be observed in the report of the Commission that it made no effort to ascertain through McClellan or any of his experienced officers the condition of the army on its march, or why it made short marches or slow ones, but accepted, without question, Halleck's testimony that "General McClellan after having received orders to repel the enemy invading the State of Maryland, marched only six miles per day, on average, when pursuing the invading army."[123]

This testimony given by a man jealous of McClellan and desiring to placate and please his enemies, invites comparison.

On the 2nd of September McClellan was assigned to the command of the forces for the defense of Washington, on the 3rd he was ordered to prepare an army for active operations in the field. By the evening of the 5th, in less than four days, the defeated, disorganized and partially demoralized army lying around Washington was ready for the field. On the morning of the 6th McClellan was verbally assigned to the command of the army in the field; on the morning of the 19th, after marching seventy miles and fighting the battles of Crampton's Gap, Turner's Gap and Antietam, he telegraphed to Halleck: "I have the honor to report that Maryland is entirely free from the presence of the enemy who have been driven across the Potomac."[124]

The battle of Shiloh was fought by Grant and Buell, April 6-7, 1862, and resulted in a Confederate defeat. On the 10th General Halleck arrived and assumed command. It took him until the 30th, twenty days, to get his victorious army in readiness to pursue the defeated Confederates. On the 30th, at the head of a grand army of 100,000 men he began an advance on Corinth, distant about twenty miles, digging intrenchments and creeping along behind them. He threw up works every few hundred yards and occupied seven strongly entrenched camps. For thirty days he so marched and entrenched, making not to exceed two-thirds of a mile a day.

---

122  Donn Piatt, *Life of George H. Thomas*, p. 349. It is interesting that Carman included the account from Capt. Piatt. His suggestion that the outcome was predetermined is unsupported, but plausible given the outcome. In other writings, Piatt is critical of McClellan and cannot be labeled as a McClellan sycophant. See, generally, his scathing treatment of McClellan in *Memories of Men Who Saved the Union* (New York & Chicago: Belford, Clark and Company, 1887). Because Halleck appointed it, the Commission's finding may be included in the manuscript as further evidence of Carman's animus toward Halleck, more than his support for McClellan.

123  Halleck's testimony to the Commission is in *OR* 19, pt. 1, pp. 786-7.

124  This is from McClellan's August 1863 report, *ibid.*, p. 68.

During the last week of the campaign, when everybody in the army, except Halleck, knew that Beauregard was getting out of Corinth as rapidly as possible, with his immense supplies, the most arduous work was done in entrenching. On the 29th Beauregard evacuated Corinth, and Halleck ignorant of the fact, on the morning of the 30th, announced in orders that an attack by the enemy all along the line was expected. When the place was occupied it was found that Beauregard had carried away everything, except a few Quaker guns, made of wood. This was the extent of Halleck's service in the field.

In view of the snail like pace of Halleck at the head of a powerful, victorious army, at the rate of two-thirds of a mile a day, it ill became him, who never commanded an army in battle, and was never under fire during the war, to criticize McClellan or any other officer for not marching more than six miles a day against a victorious army commanded by General Robert E. Lee.

The commission reported also: "The General-in-Chief [Halleck] also testified that, in his opinion, General McClellan could, and should, have relieved and protected Harper's Ferry, and in this opinion the Commission fully concur."[125]

There is no question that up to September 12th General McClellan was in no way responsible for the situation of affairs at Harper's Ferry; on the contrary, he had made honest effort to impress General Halleck the danger at that point. He had, on more than one occasion, protested against the bad judgment that kept a garrison there after Lee had crossed the Potomac, had suggested that it be withdrawn in the direction of Hagerstown to cover the Cumberland Valley or concentrated on Maryland Heights, as it was in imminent danger of capture, but to these suggestions Halleck gave a flat and contemptuous refusal; finally September 11th, McClellan requested that Miles be ordered to leave Harper's Ferry and join the army in the field by the most practicable route, to which Halleck replied, that there was no way for Miles to join him. "His only chance is to defend his works till you can open communication with him. When you do so he will be subject to your orders."[126]

---

125 The excerpt from the Commission is from their report, *ibid.*, p. 800. Carman cannot be considered a McClellan supporter, yet it seems for reasons of fairness or history, or perhaps simply to use McClellan as a lever to tilt at Halleck, he included this comparison. Whatever his reasons, Carman presents a counterbalance to the Commission's bias, a different view of McClellan's campaign, and a lambasting review of Halleck's record as field commander. For a brief confirmation of Halleck's Corinth campaign, see McPherson, *Ordeal By Fire*, pp. 232-4.

126 The communication between McClellan and Halleck regarding the Harpers Ferry garrison was referenced earlier in this chapter. The direct quote is from OR 19, pt. 1, p. 758. A shortened version is found in McClellan's report, *ibid.*, p. 44.

Had Halleck given a candid reply to McClellan's request it would read: "In defiance of all sound military principles we have kept Colonel Miles so long at Harper's Ferry to hold an indefensible position, that he is now surrounded and cannot escape, and is peremptorily ordered not to escape if he could, but if you can relieve him from the trap in which we have placed him you are welcome to his services." Halleck could not have been of more service to the Confederates had he been Lee's chief of staff, with authority to issue orders from the head of the Union army.[127]

127 Carman's scathing final paragraph made it clear who he blamed for what was, until 1942, the largest surrender of United States forces in the nation's history. The analysis and judgments offered by Carman in the last few pages of this long "note" raise questions about him as a historian. Seldom do modern historians engage in the extremely critical censure of a subject, as Carman did with Halleck. Nineteenth century historians often passed judgments in this fashion, but more importantly, Carman had been a participant in the operation and had some firsthand knowledge of the people about whom he wrote. This "note" is an example of what makes his manuscript so compelling and valuable: he commented on situations and people he experienced firsthand.

# Chapter 7

# South Mountain (Crampton's Gap)
## September 14, 1862

ongstreet followed Jackson from Frederick, on the morning of September 10, and bivouacked that night near the east foot of Turner's Gap. On the morning of the 11th he resumed his march by the National Road to Hagerstown, D. H. Hill's Division, of five brigades, being left behind near Boonsboro. Longstreet's advance, the 1st Virginia Cavalry, Lieutenant-Colonel L. Tiernan Brien, dashed into Hagerstown about midday, followed in the afternoon by Toombs's Brigade, which passed through the town and encamped near the railroad. The main body of Longstreet's command camped a short distance southeast of town, between it and Funkstown.[1]

---

1  The source for the 1st Virginia Cavalry's dash into Hagerstown, as described by Carman, comes from the "Confederate Occupation of Washington County," *Hagerstown Herald of Freedom and Torchlight*, September 10, 1862, p. 2, Section A. Although the date of the newspaper is one day before the event happened, the newspaper of September 10 was not finished and published until long after the battle of Antietam. No official sources place Brien and the

Lee accompanied Longstreet and awaited the result of operations upon Martinsburg and Harper's Ferry, when, if successful, he proposed to concentrate his army at Hagerstown for a further advance, into Pennsylvania, or to give battle to McClellan should he follow west of South Mountain. On the 13th he sent Jefferson Davis, copies of his proclamation of the 8th, and orders "191." He reported that his advance pickets were at Middleburg, on the Pennsylvania line; that his army had been received with sympathy and kindness, and he had found in the town about 1500 barrels of flour and had hopes of a further supply from the mills in the surrounding country, though he feared he should have to haul from the Valley of Virginia. His supply of beef was small and he had not been able to procure bacon. One thousand pairs of shoes had been obtained at Frederick, 250 pairs in Williamsport, and about 400 pairs in Hagerstown, but they "were not sufficient to cover the barefeet of the army."[2]

The 13th found him still waiting for news from McLaws and Walker; to the first named he expressed his anxiety for the speedy accomplishment of the duty assigned him and the quick return of the various detachments to the main body of the army. He informed him that Stuart, with his cavalry, occupied Middletown Valley, D. H. Hill was near Boonsboro and, that by noon, Jackson would be at Harper's Ferry. He wrote Mr. Davis that every effort would be made to acquire all advantages which his position and means might warrant, and called attention to the great embarrassment in the reduction of the army by straggling. His ranks were very much diminished: "I fear," he wrote, "from a third to one-half of the original numbers."[3]

Meanwhile, events were transpiring beyond the South Mountain that culminated in the entire failure of Lee's campaign and its expected results—the

---

regiment there, but the newspaper's wording is almost identical to Carman's description. Union reports place the Confederate cavalry in Hagerstown by 9:00 a.m. *OR* 19, pt. 2, pp. 267-68. These marches and arrivals are found in Toombs's report, *ibid.*, pt. 1, p. 888.

2  Lee's intention to engage McClellan, and to lure him away from the Federal supply base, is taken from Lee's report, *ibid.*, p. 145. The description of Lee's position and the precarious logistical situation was taken from Lee to Davis, September 12, 1862, *ibid.*, pt. 2, pp. 604-5.

3  Carman also used Lee's communication to Davis and McLaws, *ibid.*, pp. 605-6, to confirm that events were rapidly spinning out of control for Lee as his army was widely spread out to answer a number of real or perceived threats. The portions in quotation marks are from these sources, but as usual, Carman used much of the language of the letters verbatim.

liberation of Maryland and its alliance with the South; English and French intervention, and the recognition of the Southern Confederacy.[4]

On the night of September 12th, the Twelfth Army Corps, Brig. Gen. A. S. Williams, commanding, bivouacked at Ijamsville Cross Roads, five miles from Frederick. On the morning of the 13th it marched in the direction of Frederick and, at early noon, reached the outskirts of the city, where the converging columns of other commands caused it to halt in a meadow. The weather was warm, the march had been tiresome, arms were stacked and the men threw themselves on the grass for rest. Sergeant John M. Bloss and Private B. W. Mitchell of the 27th Indiana Infantry were separated by a few feet and Bloss noticed near Mitchell a long envelope, one end showing above the tall grass and, at his request, Mitchell handed it to him. The envelope was not sealed and as it passed into Bloss's hands two cigars and a paper fell out. The cigars were properly divided and the two men were about to indulge in a quiet smoke, when Bloss picked up, opened, and proceeded to read, the paper that had fallen from the envelope, and as the reading progressed he recognized its great value; barely completing the reading he hastened with it to his captain, Peter Kop. The Captain, accompanied by Bloss and Mitchell went to Colonel Silas Colgrove, commanding the regiment, and Bloss explained how the paper came into his possession. Colgrove, who had not yet dismounted from his horse, rode over to General Williams's headquarters, not far distant, and handed the paper to Samuel E. Pittman, Acting Adjutant General of the corps. It was addressed to Maj.-Gen. D. H. Hill and signed by R. H. Chilton, Assistant Adjutant General. Pittman recognized the signature of Chilton as genuine; as a teller in the Michigan State Bank, at Detroit, where, a few years before, Chilton had kept his account, as a Paymaster in the United States Army, he had paid many of his checks and thus become well acquainted with his signature. Pittman wrote a brief note to McClellan's Adjutant General, to accompany the transmission of the paper, and was about to copy the paper itself, recognizing that the finding of such an important document was likely to become an interesting fact of history, but General Williams would not permit a moment's delay and the paper was immediately taken by Pittman to McClellan's headquarters and delivered to General McClellan.[5]

---

4   Carman offered his judgment that the events that caused Lee's campaign to fail were in motion before the battle of Antietam. The intentions he listed for Lee's entrance into Maryland should be compared with Harsh, *Taken at the Flood*, Chapter One.

5   The story of the discovery of the famous S.O. #191, the "Lost Order," has been a source of controversy since the day it was found. The description of the march of the Twelfth Corps came from Sgt. John H. Bloss, who read a paper before the Kansas Commandery of MOLLUS, January 6, 1892, copy in Battlefield Board Papers, dated May 26, 1897. Carman used Bloss's

Sergeant Bloss states that he found the paper not later than 10 o'clock, he thinks it was really an hour earlier, in this he is evidently mistaken, accounts generally agree that Williams's Corps arrived near Frederick and halted about noon, very early noon, and this agrees with the recollection and papers of the writer.[6]

The effect that the paper had on McClellan is shown in the telegram that was immediately sent to President Lincoln:

HEADQUARTERS, Frederick, September 13, 1862—12 m.

To the PRESIDENT:

I have the whole rebel force in front of me, but am confident, and no time shall be lost. I have a difficult task to perform, but with God's blessing will accomplish it. I think Lee has made a gross mistake, and that he will be severely punished for it. The army is in motion as rapidly as possible. I hope for a great success if the plans of the rebels remain unchallenged. We have possession of Catoctin. I have all the plans of the rebels, and will catch them in their own trap if my men are equal to the emergency. I now feel that I can count on them as of old. All forces of Pennsylvania should be placed to co-operate at Chambersburg. My respects to Mrs. Lincoln. . . . All well, and with God's blessing will accomplish it.

GEO. B. McCLELLAN.[7]

---

words almost verbatim. There are several discrepancies between Carman's account and the account given by Col. Colgrove in *Century Magazine*, as reprinted in *B&L*, p. 603. Colgrove credits Mitchell with finding the order, and claimed that Chilton and Pittman served together before the war. Carman did not repeat these statements, and in fact contradicted them. Carman is correct. First, Bloss, in the early 20th Century attended a reunion of the 27th Indiana and discussed the finding with other veterans. Several gave sworn affidavits that Bloss pointed out the envelope to Mitchell and asked him to retrieve it. See Richard Carroll Datzman, "Who Found Lee's Lost Dispatch," Lost Order File, Antietam National Battlefield, Sharpsburg, MD. Second, Pittman never served with Chilton, who was a U.S. Army Paymaster before the war. Pittman did not join the U.S. military until Chilton had resigned. See the letters to Carman from Samuel Pittman, May 7, 24, and 28, 1897, Chapin Library, Williams College, Williamstown MA.

6  The only portion not addressed by Datzman—the time of the finding—Carman put at around noon. This is one of the rare occasions when Carman cited himself as a source. Capt. Kop was killed at Antietam, and Bloss (a sergeant) and Mitchell (a corporal who was later reduced to the rank of private, as Carman described him) were both wounded. Edmund Randolf Brown, *The Twenty Seventh Indiana Volunteer Infantry in the War of the Rebellion* (Monticello: n.p., 1899), pp. 252, 597-598.

7  McClellan's telegram to Lincoln is found in *OR* 19, pt. 2, p. 281. This telegram is noted as being sent at September 13 at "12 m." received at 2:35 a.m. September 14. In the terminology of the 19th Century, "m" stood for meridian or midday, i.e., noon, but the original telegram found

At 3 p. m. a copy of the order found was sent to General Pleasonton, who was directed to ascertain whether the order of march, as given in it, had been followed, and he was cautioned to approach the pass through the Blue Ridge [South Mountain] with circumspection, as his advance might be disputed by two columns.

At 3.35 p. m. General Cox was ordered to march his division to Middletown and support Pleasonton; an hour later Captain W. P. Sanders, commanding 6th U. S. Cavalry, was ordered to send one company to Noland's Ferry, on the Potomac, to assist General Couch in guarding it, and with his main body push out from Licksville to Jefferson, using his discretion whether to go by way of Point of Rocks or Adamsville [sic]. From Jefferson he would throw out scouts as far as possible towards Harper's Ferry, and he was to open communication with Pleasonton, who could be found on the National Road, between Middletown and South Mountain.[8]

When Lee's order was taken to McClellan there still remained seven hours of good daylight. His troops had done but little marching during the day; quite half of them were in bivouac by noon. They were in good condition, well fed and well clothed, the weather clear and pleasant and the broad roads excellent. Yet, beyond the orders given Pleasonton, Cox and Sanders, not a move was made, nor was an order of movement prepared until 6.20 p.m., and this was very far short of the occasion.

The order of 3 p.m. to Pleasonton is suggestive that McClellan had suspicions that the lost order was not a genuine one, that it was not lost in reality, but that it was left where he would find it, that it was intended to deceive. Upon no other theory can his inaction be accounted for; yet the order confirmed the reports he was receiving from Governor Curtin and others of the movement and position of the Confederate army, and these reports should have been promptly accepted as guaranties of the genuine character of the order.

If for a moment, a few minutes, an hour, or nearly a full afternoon he doubted, the truth was finally accepted and there was revealed to him Lee's designs and knowledge of his intended movement for days to come. It told him that Lee's army was divided, and where its divisions were and what doing, that Walker was on

---

in the Lincoln Papers, Library of Congress, has "midnight" written out as the time it was sent. This timing is more logical as McClellan was still evaluating the validity of the document at noon, and notifying Lincoln before Halleck would break the military chain of command. For a more detailed explanation, see Timothy Reese, *High Water Mark: The Maryland 1862 Campaign in Strategic Perspective* (Baltimore: Butternut & Blue, 2004), pp. 24-25.

8   The directions to Pleasonton are found in OR 51, pt. 1, p. 829. Cox's instructions are *ibid.*, p. 827, and to Sanders, *ibid.*, p. 830, which should read "Adamstown" for "Adamsville." Apparently Carman miscopied it.

Loudoun Heights, beyond the Potomac, that Jackson, also, was on the Virginia side of the Potomac, facing Bolivar Heights, and that McLaws was on Maryland Heights, on the Maryland side of the Potomac, and that Walker, Jackson and McLaws were surrounding, indeed had surrounded Harper's Ferry. It also told him that Lee, Longstreet and D. H. Hill were just beyond the South Mountain and that with them were the Reserve Artillery and the trains, and that in his immediate front was Stuart's cavalry to delay his advance, and that all were awaiting the issue at Harper's Ferry, preparatory to a concentration of the army at Boonsboro or Hagerstown. It was revelation that permitted him to smile at Halleck's fears of a sudden dash on Washington and to exult that Lee had put himself in great peril, and this, unquestionably, Lee had done.[9]

There has been much criticism on Lee's conduct of the campaign against Harper's Ferry and the danger in which he put the various divisions of his army, all of which has been ably answered by Colonel William Allan. In a paper read before the "Military Historical Society of Massachusetts, December 10, 1888, he said:

Lee has been severely criticized for dividing his army at this time, and in one sense he is fairly exposed to it. But at the bottom the criticism in this case is the common one to which a bold leader is always exposed who attempts by superior energy and skill to make up for inferiority of men and resources. General Lee's whole course during the summer of 1862, and indeed during the war is open to this kind of criticism. There were no aggressive movements possible to an army so inferior in strength as was the

---

9   Carman indulged in some criticism of McClellan at this point. He accused him of tardiness in moving troops in response to the information conveyed in the "Lost Order." He then concluded that the only reason McClellan delayed was doubt about the authenticity of S.O. #191. Carman also mentioned that the order confirmed Governor Curtin's fear of Confederate movements toward Pennsylvania. Carman's conclusions ignore several other very real possibilities. First, the order did not indicate numbers for the separate arms of the Lee's forces. If, as Curtin also advised, Lee's army numbered 150,000 to 200,000 men, then McClellan's caution was logical. Beyond the numbers, two other factors may have influenced McClellan. The order was four days old and described movements supposed to be completed by the 12th or 13th. McClellan knew that Harpers Ferry had not fallen, but he did not know the situation there other than the message brought by Capt. Russell. Also, the position of Lee's troops could have been drastically altered since the order was drafted, and the order itself was vague about the composition and location of "the main body of the army." Thus, Pleasonton's scouting expedition could be justified as a reconnaissance to confirm intelligence, a standard military procedure. Carman is too critical in his assessment, and allowed what he knew after the fact to color his judgment of what should have been done beforehand. For more on these points, see Rafuse, *McClellan's War*, pp. 291-3, although he mistimes McClellan's message to Lincoln on September 13. It is interesting to note that Carman, a former Union officer, criticized McClellan while defending Lee's actions in the campaign. His evaluation may be open to question, but this example is evidence of his balance as a historian.

Confederate that may not be condemned as rash, while on the other hand a strictly defensive war against the resources and facilities of the attacked possessed by the North, pointed to certain and not distant collapse. Lee's expectation in regard to the reduction of Harper's Ferry was a reasonable one and the risk he assumed in dividing his army to effect it, was less than the risk he incurred in the operations against Pope three weeks before. A single day's time would probably have rendered unnecessary the struggle at the South Mountain passes: two days would certainly have done so. And the Confederate army, loaded with the spoils of Harper's Ferry, would have reunited at Hagerstown with difficulty. No one can read the history of this campaign, no one can study McClellan's career, no one can see the doubt, the anxiety, of the Federal administration as shown by Halleck's dispatches, without feeling that those two days and more, would have been Lee's had the course of events not been affected by the accident of the lost dispatch.[10]

Longstreet says that the copy of order "191" sent him was carefully read then used as some persons use a little cut of tobacco, to be assured that others could not have the benefit of its contents. When Walker received his copy he was so impressed with the disastrous consequence which might result from its loss that he pinned it securely in an inside pocket.

There has been discussion as to how and by whom Lee's order was lost. It was addressed to D. H. Hill and the statement of that officer is conclusive, so far as he is concerned. He says, February 24 1888:

I went into Maryland under Jackson's command. I was under his command when Lee's order was issued. It was proper that I should receive that order through Jackson and not through Lee. I have now before me the order received from Jackson. . . . My Adjutant-General made affidavit twenty years ago, that no order was received at our office from General Lee. But an order from Lee's office, directed to me, was lost and

---

10 Allan's remarks, "Strategy of the Campaign of Sharpsburg or Antietam, September 1862," can be found in *Papers of the Military Historical Society of Massachusetts* (Boston: Griffith-Stillings Press, 1903), 3, pp. 85-6. The assessment that the finding of S.O. #191 changed the whole campaign, and that another day or two would have allowed Lee to occupy Hagerstown unmolested may indeed be true, but that line of thinking can be applied to many other battles and situations. In other words, it is a moot point. The operation was behind schedule, and wishing for yet more time is no justification for what Lee undertook. He had no right to expect more time. There is much debate about how dramatic the impact of the Lost Order was on the campaign. Many authors, notably Sears, *Landscape Turned Red*, and Murfin, *Gleam of Bayonets*, claimed this discovery was a watershed of the campaign. A careful analysis of the movements of the two armies shows that the initiative was slipping from Lee before September 13 (when the order was found), and that McClellan moved more rapidly before it was found than afterward. See Harsh, *Taken at the Flood*, pp. 237-52.

fell into McClellan's hands. Did the courier lose it? Did Lee's own staff officers lose it? I don't know."[11]

Jackson was so careful that no one should learn the contents of the order that the copy he furnished Hill was written by his own hand and entrusted to a careful member of his staff for delivery. Colonel Venable of General Lee's staff says, "One copy was sent directly to Hill from headquarters, General Jackson sent him a copy, in his own handwriting, which General Hill has. The other was undoubtedly left carelessly by some one at Hill's headquarters."[12]

But, however lost, the find was a valuable one. The possibilities it opened to McClellan were great; possibilities that come to a commander seldom, and not to one man more than once in a life time. How did he approach them; did he even meet them half-way? He had three courses presented to him; he could move to the relief of Harper's Ferry by the road leading through Jefferson and Knoxville and thence up the east bank of the Potomac; he could force his left under Franklin, by way of Burkittsville, through Crampton's Gap, and then come directly upon the rear of McLaws on Maryland Heights, and interpose between him and Lee; or he could press his right under Burnside and his center under Sumner, by way of

---

11  Carman's Note: *B&L*, p. 570.

12  The question of how the Lost Order became lost was a mystery in Carman's era, and remains so today. Several modern writers have addressed the issue: see Stephen Sears, "The Last Word on the Lost Order," *Military History Quarterly*, Special Issue: The Civil War (1995), and Wilbur D. Jones Jr., "Who Lost the Lost Order? Stonewall Jackson, His Courier, and Special Order 191," *Civil War Regiments: A Journal of the American Civil War*, Vol. 5, no. 3, pp. 1-26. Jones added a convenient table that lists the various explanations of the participants and authors. No author has reached an unimpeachable conclusion. Carman added the actions of a few other officers impressed with the importance of the order. Longstreet's recollection that he chewed up his copy is from *From Manassas to Appomattox*, pp. 213-4, and almost a direct quote. Walker's story is in *B&L*, p. 607, not only related what he did with it, but confirmed Longstreet's version. The D. H. Hill quote is accurate. The quote from Col.Charles Venable is from Armistead L. Long, *Memoirs of Robert E. Lee: His Military and Personal History*, p. 213. Despite the many articles elevating the importance and unique aspects of S.O. #191, it was but one of several such exchanges of intelligence in the summer of 1862. On August 18, Union cavalry intercepted orders from Lee at Verdiersville, Virginia. Less than a week later Jeb Stuart captured orders and plans from John Pope. In both cases, these had a significant effect on the course of events. S.O. #191 was simply one of several intercepted orders and probably not much more important than any of the others, at least in influencing events. Postwar writers interested in burnishing Lee's image used the Lost Orders to explain Lee's lack of success in Maryland. See Pope, *OR* 12 pt. 2, p. 29; Edwin C. Bearss's introduction in John Michael Priest, *Before Antietam: the Battle for South Mountain*, p. vii; Lee, *OR* 12 pt. 3, p. 942; William B. Talliaferro, "Jackson's Raid Around Pope," *B&L*, p. 507; Johnson, Bradley T., *OR* 12 pt. 2, p. 664; and Ambrose Powell Hill, *ibid.*, p. 670.

Middletown, through Turner's Gap, then interposing between Lee, Longstreet and D. H. Hill and all the reserve artillery and trains on the one side, and the troops beyond the Potomac on the other; and the chances were that those 55,000 Union soldiers would utterly crush the 15,000 that the Confederates had to oppose them. All depended, however, on celerity of movement and vigor of attack.

McClellan determined not to move by the direct road through Jefferson and Knoxville and he gives his reasons; in his official report:

> It may be asked by those who are not acquainted with the topography of the country in the vicinity of Harper's Ferry why Franklin, instead of marching his column over the circuitous road from Jefferson via Burkittsville and Brownsville, was not ordered to move along the direct turnpike to Knoxville and thence up the river to Harper's Ferry. It was for the reason that I had received information that the enemy were anticipating our approach in that direction, and had established batteries on the south side of the Potomac which commanded all the approaches to Knoxville. Moreover the road from that point winds directly along the river bank at the foot of a precipitous mountain, where there was no opportunity of forming in line of battle, and where the enemy could have placed batteries on both sides of the river to enfilade our narrow approaching columns. The approach through Crampton's Pass, which debouches into Pleasant Valley in rear of Maryland Heights, was the only one which afforded any reasonable prospect of carrying that formidable position. At the same time the troops upon that road were in better relation to the main body of our forces.

McClellan was wrongly informed that the enemy had batteries on the south side of the Potomac, commanding the approaches to Knoxville, and he magnified the difficulties of reaching Harper's Ferry by that route; in the main his reasons for not choosing it are sound; it is enough to say that they were convincing to him, and that he chose a route promising better results.[13]

The plan that he adopted had two purposes, the controlling one to relieve Harper's Ferry, as speedily as possible, by moving through Crampton's Gap and breaking the line of investment that McLaws had thrown across Maryland Heights and the foot of Pleasant Valley; the other to force Turner's Gap, fall upon and

---

13 The summary Carman presented of McClellan's options regarding S.O. #191 is a fair assessment, although predicated on the assumption that McClellan knew the number of Confederate troops he faced and where they were and could be expected to be. This was not the case. As Carman noted earlier, McClellan's best estimate of Confederates in Maryland exceeded 100,000. McClellan had even less knowledge of the fluid and vague organizational structure of Lee's army. Carman copied the paragraph from McClellan's second report, OR 19, pt. 1, pp. 44-5, to show the general's reasoning, which was also sound.

destroy that part of the Confederate army Lee had retained at Boonsboro. The plan was a good one and in the hands of an able general and enterprising subordinates should have produced greater results.

McLaws had ten brigades, and those were not concentrated, nor were they in close supporting distance, and there remained to Lee, beyond the South Mountain, but fourteen brigades, aggregating, according to D. H. Hill, about 15,000. Five brigades, under D. H. Hill, were at Boonsboro, nine brigades under Longstreet were twelve miles in the rear near Hagerstown, and this division of commands was an advantage to McClellan, had he known it, but he did not, as the lost order indicated that Lee, Longstreet, D. H. Hill and all the reserve artillery and trains were at Boonsboro.[14]

Having concluded to move by Crampton's Gap McClellan sent this letter of instructions to Franklin, then at Buckeystown:

HEADQUARTERS ARMY— OF THE POTOMAC
Camp near Frederick, September 13, 1862——6.20 p.m.

Maj. Gen. W. B. FRANKLIN, Commanding Sixth Corps:

GENERAL: I have now full information as to movements and intentions of the enemy. Jackson has crossed the Upper Potomac to capture the garrison at Martinsburg and cut off Miles' retreat toward the west. A division on the south side of the Potomac was to carry Loudoun Heights and cut off his retreat in that direction. McLaws, with his own command and the division of R. H. Anderson, was to move by Boonsborough and Rohrersville to carry the Maryland Heights. The signal officers inform me that he is now in Pleasant Valley. The firing shows that Miles still holds out. Longstreet was to move to Boonsborough and there halt with the reserve corps, D. H. Hill to form the rear guard, Stuart's cavalry to bring up stragglers, &c. We have cleared out all the cavalry this side of the mountains and north of us.

The last I heard from Pleasonton he occupied Middletown, after several sharp skirmishes. A division of Burnside's command started several hours ago to support him. The whole of Burnside's command, including Hooker's corps, march this evening and early to-morrow morning, followed by the corps of Sumner and Banks and Sykes's division, upon Boonsborough, to carry that position. Couch has been ordered to concentrate his division and join you as rapidly as possible. Without waiting

---

14 The figures for the fourteen brigades cited by Carman and the position of those Confederate troops were indeed unknown to McClellan. Put in this light, McClellan's actions look much more logical.

for the whole of that division to join you, you will move at daybreak in the morning, by Jefferson and Burkittsville, upon the road to Rohrersville. I have reliable information that the mountain pass by this road is practicable for artillery and wagons. If this pass is not occupied by the enemy in force, seize it as soon as practicable, and debouch upon Rohrersville, in order to cut off the retreat of or destroy McLaws's command. If you find this pass held by the enemy in large force, make all your dispositions for the attack and commence it about half an hour after you hear severe firing at the pass on the Hagerstown pike, where the main body will attack. Having gained the pass, your duty will be first to cut off, destroy, or capture McLaws's command and relieve Colonel Miles. If you effect this, you will order him to join you at once with all his disposable troops, first, destroying the bridge over the Potomac, if not already done, and, leaving a sufficient garrison to prevent the enemy from passing the ford, you will then return by Rohrersville on the direct road to Boonsborough if the main column has not succeeded in its attack. If it has succeeded, take the road by Rohrersville to Sharpsburg and Williamsport, in order either to cut off the retreat of Hill and Longstreet toward the Potomac, or prevent the repassage of Jackson. My general idea is to cut the enemy in two and beat him in detail. I believe I have sufficiently explained my intentions. I ask of you, at this important moment, all your intellect and the utmost activity that a general can exercise.

General McClellan appears to have intended the completion of the letter at this point, but, before signing, he received a dispatch from Franklin, that the enemy was in some force at Petersville, whereupon he continued to write:

Knowing my views and intentions, you are fully authorized to change any of the details of this order as circumstances may change, provided the purpose is carried out; that purpose being to attack the enemy in detail and beat him. General Smith's dispatch of 4 p.m. with your comments is received. If, with a full knowledge of all the circumstances, you consider it preferable to crush the enemy at Petersville before undertaking the movement I have directed, you are at liberty to do so, but you will readily perceive that no slight advantage should for a moment interfere with the decisive results I propose to gain. I cannot too strongly impress upon you the absolute necessity of informing me every hour during the day of your movements, and frequently during the night. Force your colonels to prevent straggling, and bring every available man into action. I think the force you have is, with good management, sufficient for the end in view. If you differ widely from me, and being on the spot you know better than I do the circumstances of the case, inform me at once, and I will do my best to re-enforce you. Inform me at the same time how many more troops you think you should have. Until 5 a.m. to-morrow general headquarters will be at this place. At that hour they will move upon the main road to Hagerstown."[15]

This letter is here given in full because of its importance as showing the information McClellan had in his possession and how he proposed to profit by it, and invites attention. As far as it went it was good, but it did not go far enough. It did not set Franklin and the entire army in instant motion, and there were no valid reasons why this should not have been done. It had not been wearied by long marches, nor exhausted by lack of sleep. It was well clothed, well fed, and ready to respond to any call upon it. It had confidence in most of its officers and idolized McClellan.[16]

On the day in question, September 13th, Hooker's First Corps moved from Lisbon and Cooksville, by the National Road, to the Monocacy, the average march of the divisions being about sixteen miles; no other division covered half this distance. Sumner's Second Corps marched from Urbana to Frederick, about six miles; Williams's Twelfth Corps from Ijamsville Cross Roads to Frederick, five miles; Sykes's Division from Urbana to Frederick, about six miles; Franklin's Sixth Corps from Licksville to Buckeystown, about six miles, and Couch's Division from Barnesville to Licksville, about five miles.

---

15 Carman thought the long and detailed instructions to Franklin were important enough to include in total. Evidently, McClellan thought Franklin's mission was critical because the order is detailed and complete. The first part is from OR 19, pt. 1, pp. 45-6 in McClellan's report, but is incomplete. They appear as two separate dispatches in the *OR*; Carman pasted the long final paragraph from *ibid.*, 51, pt. 1, pp. 826-7. It appears as one long message in Sears, *McClellan Papers*, p. 455. Whether this was sent as one long message or two separate ones is unknown. Franklin replied at 10:00 p.m. that he had received it, which implies one message. *McClellan Papers*, A-79:31. Sears provides a transcript of a signed letter that indicates the document was a single piece of correspondence. It is possible that McClellan deliberately held back the second portion of the message as it seemed to give Franklin free rein to ignore the Harpers Ferry mission imposed on him by Halleck. Given the Committee on Conduct of the War's investigations, McClellan might well have passed on only the first portion of the message to the compilers of the *OR*. Until volume 51 appeared, the second part had not been published.

16 The main criticism Carman made of McClellan's dispositions for the advance against Lee is the timing. In Chapter Five, Carman described the disorganized and poorly supplied Union soldiers and their straggling march from Washington. Now, in Chapter Seven, these same soldiers are characterized as ready, rested, and awaiting command. It could be argued that more vigorous marching on September 13 would make these troops even less combat-ready, as they were already in motion before S.O. #191 was found. A march that night might also have alerted D. H. Hill to reinforce the gaps sooner than he did, making a tougher fight in the morning. This is not to say Carman's analysis is wrong, but that the situation was more obvious to him when he wrote his manuscript then it was to McClellan at the time he wrote the orders.

Farnsworth's cavalry brigade marched out of Frederick, by the National road, on the morning of the 13th, drove Wade Hampton's cavalry from Fairview Gap of the Catoctins, followed through Middletown, overtook Hampton's rearguard on Catoctin Creek, brushed it away and pursued nearly to the foot of Turner's Gap, of South Mountain. A detachment of Farnsworth's Brigade scouted in the direction of Burkittsville and was roughly handled by Hampton's cavalry.

The 1st and 6th United States Cavalry advanced from Licksville to Jefferson and threw out scouts in the direction of Crampton's Gap and Petersville, and the Rush Lancers, supported by Fairchild's Brigade, Rodman's Division, Ninth Corps, moved from Frederick to near Burkittsville, skirmished with Munford's cavalry; which was driven to Burkittsville, at the foot of Crampton's Gap, and then drew off to near Broad Run Village; Fairchild's Brigade, by some singular misapprehension of orders, returning to Frederick. The 1st Rhode Island Cavalry examined the fords of the Potomac, below Point of Rocks. Cox's Kanawha Division, Ninth Corps, moved from Frederick to Middletown and thence a mile beyond, seven miles, and Sturgis's and Willcox's divisions, of the same corps, marched to within one mile of Middletown.

With the exception of some of the cavalry and Fairchild's Brigade of infantry, none of the army came in touch with the enemy; more than two-thirds had marched less than seven miles, and all, save the cavalry, the First and part of the Ninth Corps, was in bivouac by noon, consequently by sunset well rested.

The cavalry was close up to Turner's Gap, and the Ninth Corps but a few miles in its rear; the Second and Twelfth Corps and Sykes's Division, of the Fifth Corps, were at Frederick, twelve miles from Turner's Gap and the same distance from Crampton's, and the First Corps was on the Monocacy, a short distance east of Frederick. Franklin's Sixth Corps was at Buckeystown, twelve miles from Crampton's Gap and ten from Burkittsville, and Couch's Division, at Licksville was the same distance from the two places, by roads running nearer the Potomac, either through Jefferson or Petersville.

From Frederick the broad National road had been cleared to the foot of Turner's Gap by the cavalry, and they had cleared the road to Burkittsville to within two miles of that place. On the left Sanders's regular cavalry had marched to Jefferson, and beyond, and there was nothing to prevent a rapid advance of the entire army. Nothing was wanting but the order to march. The afternoon had been practically lost, the loss should have been retrieved by an order to march at sunset. The roads were good, the nights were cool, and the evening dews, which fell early, partially laid the dust; a night march would have been welcomed by the soldier, and the twelve miles, between Frederick and the foot of Turner's Gap, over a broad road as smooth as the floor; the ten miles from Frederick to Burkittsville, and the ten miles from Buckeystown and Licksville to Burkittsville could have been completely made before midnight, and all would have had a good rest and been in good condition to begin work at daylight of the 14th. And as far as McClellan and Franklin supposed then, and, as we know now, there was nothing to oppose or in any way interfere with this night march, save a few Confederate cavalry scouts, thrown out in front of Burkittsville, that could have been brushed away without halting the column, and this night march would not have been as severe a one as Jackson made on the night of the 15th from Harper's Ferry to Shepherdstown.[17]

Had the Ninth, Second and Twelfth Corps marched that night and reached the foot of Turner's Gap by midnight and rested until morning, they would have found to oppose them one of Stuart's cavalry regiments, Colquitt's and Garland's small infantry brigades, and eight pieces of artillery, and the gap could have been forced

17 Carman supported his vigorous argument for rapid movement on the September 13 with a detailed examination of the location of the various Union forces and their marching up to that time. Part of this assessment bears a close resemblance to Palfrey's account in *The Antietam and Fredericksburg*, pp. 29-30. Carman seemed to be influenced more by Palfrey's critique than the facts. The claim that McClellan failed to capitalize on the discovery by rapidly moving his army out of Frederick that same day ignores not only that the army was already in motion, but the obstacle presented by Frederick itself. The movements of the Federal Army on September 13 were a direct result of orders issued on September 12—orders already underway to move a portion of the army into the Middletown Valley. Most the army was in motion already when Special Order #191 was found, the First Corps arriving east of Frederick throughout the day, and a portion arriving late in the day. OR 19, pt. 1, p. 249. The Second Corps and Ninth Corps were in a traffic jam in the streets of Frederick throughout September 13. Because of that situation, the Twelfth Corps was forced to halt east of town. And, of course, nobody could march westward until early afternoon, when Hagan's or Fairview Gap was cleared of Confederate rearguard forces. Carman also ignored two divisions of the Ninth Corps marching into Middletown Valley on the night of September 13, which McClellan mentioned in the 6:20 p.m. order to Franklin, *ibid.*, 51, pt. 1, pp. 826-7. In short, Carman criticizes McClellan for not getting his army through Frederick in a day, something Lee had been unable to do with a much smaller army. In addition, as in the previous note, Carman ignored a basic factor that makes his speculative assessment just that. At this time we cannot know what course Lee or McLaws might have taken had they learned of a rapid advance by a large Union force on September 13. It is possible that the siege of Harpers Ferry might have been abandoned, or at least its garrison rescued. It is also possible, however, that Lee might have rushed Longstreet's men back from Hagerstown that night and used them to substantially increase the defenders of the gaps. If so, McClellan probably would not have carried any of them the next day. It is also worth noting that on September 14, Halleck was still notifying McClellan about large numbers of troops in Virginia, and warning him about exposing his flank and rear. See *ibid.*, 19, pt. 2, p. 289. What Carman wanted McClellan to do was not only boldly attack what he believed was a superior force, but also ignore the advice of his superior officer. In hindsight, both of these movements make sense, but if they had been undertaken at the time, they might have been considered bold to the point of rashness. The specific information about the location and marching of troops is found in McClellan's report, *ibid.*, 19, pt. 1, p. 40; Pleasonton's report, *ibid.*, pp. 209-10, and dispatch *ibid.*, 19, pt. 2, p. 290; orders to Sanders and 1st Rhode Island Cavalry, *ibid.*, 51, pt. 1, p. 830; and Fairchild's report, *ibid.*, 19, pt. 1, pp. 449-51. The snippets taken from McClellan's telegram to Lincoln are found in the previously cited whole message, *ibid.*, 19, pt. 2, p. 281.

before D. H. Hill could have brought up his support from beyond Boonsboro, five miles away; or had Franklin marched at the same time he would or could have taken Crampton's Gap next morning, with but little opposition, and descended into Pleasant Valley, early in the forenoon, with the consequent result of relieving Miles at Harper's Ferry, interposing between Lee and McLaws, and moving on the flank and rear of the Confederate forces, engaging the main body at Turner's Gap, providing, always, that he took advantage of opportunity.[18]

McLaws might have rejoined Lee by descending the west side of Maryland Heights and marching north by Antietam Furnace and Sharpsburg, which would have permitted Miles to re-occupy the heights and join Franklin; he might have re-crossed the Potomac by Knott's Ford, at the mouth of the Antietam, and joined Jackson, or he might have descended the southeastern extremity of the height, and, uniting his command at Weverton, marched by Knoxville and re-crossed the Potomac at some of the fords below, which would have been hazardous; in fact, all of these movements would have been attended with great risk and entailed the loss of many stragglers and much material; in any event the abandonment of Maryland Heights would have been imperative.

But McClellan did not rise to the occasion; he did not take advantage of the long afternoon; he did not order the night march and thereby missed the opportunity of his life. At noon he dispatched President Lincoln that his "army was in motion as rapidly as possible" and that knowing the plans of the rebels he would "catch them in their own trap," if his men were "equal to the emergency." As matter of fact nearly the entire army, at that hour, was at a dead halt, and McClellan did not rise to the occasion to lead it forward. The failure to be "equal to the emergency" was on the part of the commander of the army and not on the part of the men.[19]

We turn from the contemplation of what might or should have been done to the narration of what actually was done. Before this, however, we shall note what occurred after the order was prepared for Franklin at 6.20 p. m., and how Lee came to the knowledge that McClellan had a copy of some important paper that had been

18 Boonsboro is about two miles from Turner's Gap, not five miles as Carman states it.

19 Once again, Carman ignores Sturgis's and Willcox's march on the night of September 13, something that was rare during the Civil War. If McClellan's dispatch was not sent until midnight, as mentioned previously, then Carman's criticism is even less valid. Carman's jaundiced assessment of McClellan's hesitation leading to his ultimate failure has become the theme for many future studies. See Sears, *Young Napoleon*, and *Landscape Turned Red*, and Murfin, *Gleam of Bayonets*. For a more balanced view, see Thomas J. Rowland, *In the Shadow of Grant and Sherman: George B. McClellan and Civil War History* (Kent, OH: Kent State Univ. Press, 1998) or Rafuse, *McClellan's War*.

found, and the preparations that had been made to meet and delay the Union advance.

Pleasonton was ordered to fire occasionally a few artillery shots, even though no enemy appeared in his front, so that Miles, at Harper's Ferry, would know that the Union army was near, and, after orders were issued for the advance of the several corps at daylight next day, McClellan's time was occupied receiving reports from the front, writing a letter to the Adjutant General of the army about the artillery service in the regular army and preparing a long and by no means clear dispatch to Halleck. He told Halleck that he had found Lee's order addressed to D. H. Hill; that its authority was unquestionable, and that the order disclosed that the main Confederate army was before him and that the genuineness of the order was attested by the fact that "heavy firing has been heard in the direction of Harper's Ferry this afternoon, and the columns took the roads specified in the order." He had good reasons for believing that Lee had 120,000 men or more, and that it was his intention to penetrate Pennsylvania. He informed Halleck that the army would make forced marches on the morrow to relieve Miles, but he feared it was too late. He then proceeded to allay Halleck's fears for the safety of Washington.[20]

He assured him that there was very small probability of the enemy being in much force south of the Potomac. He agreed with Halleck that the holding of Washington was of great consequence, but insisted that the fate of the nation depended upon the success of his army, and it was for this reason he had said that everything else should be made subordinate to placing his army in proper condition to meet Lee's army in his front. In conclusion he said: "Unless General Lee has changed his plans, I expect a severe general engagement to-morrow. I feel confident that there is now no rebel force immediately threatening Washington or Baltimore, but that I have the mass of their troops to contend with, and they outnumber me when united." This dispatch was dated September 13th, 11 p. m.[21]

---

20 Carman added: Halleck had telegraphed McClellan that day, Sept. 13–10.45 a. m.: "Until you know more certainly the enemy's force south of the Potomac, you are wrong in thus uncovering the capital. I am of the opinion that the enemy will send a small column toward Pennsylvania, so as to draw your forces in that direction; then suddenly move on Washington with the forces south of the Potomac and those he may cross over." *OR* 19, pt. 1, p. 41.

21 These messages from McClellan's headquarters to various people are found as follows: Pleasonton's artillery firing to alert Miles, *ibid.*, 51 pt. 1, pp. 829-30; orders to advance, see Franklin's letter cited above; Burnside, Cox, Sumner, Sykes, and Humphreys, see *ibid.* pp. 826-9; letter to Thomas concerning artillery, *ibid.*, 19, pt. 2, pp. 282-3; McClellan's dispatch to Halleck, *ibid.*, 19, pt. 1, pp. 785-6. This dispatch includes the closing lines quoted by Carman, "Unless General Lee changes his mind . . ."

When McClellan came into possession of the lost order a citizen, friendly to the Southern cause, was present and observed the great satisfaction it gave him and the exuberant spirits of the staff. He listened to some talk of what was to be done by the Union army and noted the activity of aids and orderlies. He did not know the character of the paper, whether it was an order to McClellan or some report from one of his corps commanders, but he knew that it was of some importance and that a rapid forward movement of the army was to be ordered. It was but a few minutes till he was speeding out of Frederick in the direction of Stuart's cavalry outposts, and before sunset had found Stuart, near Turner's Gap, and told him what he had seen and heard.

Stuart hastened a swift courier with the news to Lee, at Hagerstown, fifteen miles away, and was able to confirm them by reporting increased activity on the part of Pleasonton's cavalry during the afternoon; that cavalry affairs had taken place near Burkittsville and Jefferson and that Pleasonton had driven him back and then was in the immediate front of the gap. All this unlooked for and unpleasant information Lee received early in the evening and he acted promptly. He concluded that McClellan was acting with energy for the relief of Harper's Ferry and determined to press matters there to a conclusion and to protect and support the troops he had detached to reduce it, and to thwart McClellan in his efforts to divide his army and beat it in detail, as he divined that McClellan was endeavoring to do.[22]

22  The story of the unnamed civilian is from Allan, *Army of Northern Virginia in 1862*, p. 345, but no other source confirms it. Although Lee stated in his report that he knew the order had been lost, it is likely that he did not know that until after the Maryland campaign was concluded. His postwar conversation with Gordon also indicated that the order to Hill was found by Union troops, and included the quote by an unnamed source that McClellan, when presented with it, remarked, "Now I know what to do!" Gary Gallagher, ed., *Lee the Soldier* (Lincoln: U. of Nebraska Press, 1996), pp. 25-7. Lee wrote to D. H. Hill on February 21, 1868: "Early on the morning of the 14th I rec'd at Hagerstown a dispatch . . . that he [McClellan] was in possession of the order directing the movement of our troops." See Harsh, *Sounding the Shallows*, pp. 171-172. In his September 16, 1862, letter to Davis, however, Lee made no mention of the Lost Order, nor that it had been found by McClellan, stating only that the enemy was advancing more "rapidly than convenient." OR 19, pt. 1, p. 140. Longstreet's memoir mentions only that Lee knew of the Union advance; see the quote beginning on the next page, which comes from *From Manassas to Appomattox*, pp. 219-20. Carman's assertion that Lee only knew of Union activities, and not their motivation, came from Charles Marshall's November 22, 1900 letter to Carman. Marshall, Lee's aide-de-camp, flatly stated that Lee did not know about the loss of the orders until he read it in McClellan's report. NYPL Correspondence Files, Box 5, Folder 1. A tantalizing possibility is an article by Scott Sherlock, "The Lost Order and the Press," *Civil War Regiments* (January, 2000), Vol. 6, No. 2, which documented that news of the Lost Order's discovery was published in a Washington newspaper on September 15. Lee often read Union newspapers for intelligence and may have seen this item. It is interesting that Carman castigated McClellan for not acting promptly on the 13th, then cited accelerated Union actions of the 13th as reason for Lee to believe the Union forces possessed special intelligence information.

Longstreet argued against this course and advised an immediate withdrawal behind the Antietam, of all forces north of the Potomac. Lee was not prepared to yield his grasp on Harper's Ferry, the surrender of which was hourly looked for, nor was he willing to risk the march of McLaws to join him by the Boonsboro or Pleasant Valley, and his position at Turner's Gap would not only give support to McLaws, but it would check the advance of McClellan long enough to insure the surrender of Harper's Ferry, so, he concluded not to yield his hold on that place and concentrate behind the Antietam, as Longstreet advised. Longstreet says:

It seems that up to the night of the 13th most of the Confederates were looking with confidence to the surrender at Harper's Ferry on the 13th, to be promptly followed by a move farther west, not thinking it possible that a great struggle at and along the South Mountain was impending; that even on the 14th our cavalry leader thought to continue his retrograde that day. General Hill's attention was given more to his instructions to prevent the escape of the fugitives from Harper's Ferry than to trouble along his front, as the instructions covered more especially that duty, while information from the cavalry gave no indication of serious trouble from the front.

A little after dark of the 13th General Lee received, through a scout, information of the advance of the Union forces to the foot of South Mountain in solid ranks. Later information confirmed this report, giving the estimated strength at ninety thousand.

General Lee still held to the thought that he had ample time. He sent for me and I found him over his maps. He told me of the reports, and asked for my views. I thought it too late to march on the 14th and properly man the pass at Turner's, and expressed preference for concentrating D. H. Hill's and my own force behind the Antietam at Sharpsburg, where we could get together in season to make a strong defensive fight, and at the same time check McClellan's march towards Harper's Ferry, in case he thought to relieve the beleaguered garrison by that route, forcing him to first remove the obstacle on his flank. He preferred to make the stand at Turner's Pass, and ordered the troops to march the next morning, ordering a brigade left at Hagerstown to guard the trains. . . . The hallucination that McClellan was not capable of serious work seemed to pervade the army, even to this moment of dreadful threatening.[23]

Lee sent a note of warning to Jackson and ordered him to press his attack at Harper's Ferry. D. H. Hill, who had been left near Boonsboro, was informed of the condition of affairs and directed to see that Turner's Gap was defended, and

---

23 Longstreet's account in *B&L*, pp. 664-6, closely paralleled his memoir, *From Manassas to Appomattox*, pp. 219-20. In both accounts Longstreet claimed he argued against the return to Boonsboro, but was overruled by Lee. Both of these sources were memoirs written after the war and must therefore be used with caution. Neither source mentions the civilian account.

Longstreet, who had taken position near Hagerstown to gather supplies and keep an eye on Governor Curtin's militia, was ordered to march at an early hour in the morning to Hill's support, while Stuart, holding the gaps over South Mountain, was ordered to delay McClellan's advance as much as possible and to keep McLaws informed of his movements. At 10 p. m. this communication signed by Major Talcott was sent to McLaws:

> General Lee directs me to say that, from reports reaching him, he believes the enemy is moving toward Harper's Ferry to relieve the force they have there. You will see, therefore, the necessity of expediting your operations as much as possible. As soon as they are completed, he desires you, unless you receive orders from General Jackson, to move your force as rapidly as possible to Sharpsburg. General Longstreet will move down to-morrow and take a position on Beaver Creek, this side of Boonsborough. General Stuart has been requested to keep you informed of the movements of the enemy.[24]

Early the next morning Lee transferred his headquarters from Hagerstown to Boonsboro; before doing so he sent another dispatch to McLaws:

> General Longstreet moves down this morning to occupy the Boonsborough Valley, so as to protect your flank from attacks from forces coming from Frederick, until the operations at Harper's Ferry are finished. I desire your operations there to be pushed on as rapidly as possible, and, if the point is not ultimately taken, so arrange it that your forces may be brought up the Boonsborough Valley. General Stuart, with a portion of General D. H. Hill's forces, holds the gap between Boonsborough and Middletown, and Hampton's and Munford's brigades of cavalry occupy Burkittsville and the pass through the mountains there. If Harper's Ferry should be taken, the road will be open to you to Sharpsburg. Around the mountains from Sharpsburg the road communicates with Boonsborough and Hagerstown.

---

24 Of the messages sent by Lee to the commanders at Harpers Ferry on the night of September 13, only the one to McLaws survives. Allan, *The Army of Northern Virginia*, p. 345, implied there was a message to Jackson, and D. H. Hill said he received one. *B&L*, p. 560. Carman copied the entire dispatch from OR 19, pt. 2, p. 607. The messages Hill and Jackson received must have been similar.

It would appear from this dispatch that Lee was not aware of the fact that McLaws had any infantry at Crampton's Gap, and the dispatch was received by McLaws when his troops were in touch with Franklin's advance.[25]

Franklin's orders were to move at daybreak, on the morning of the 14th, by Jefferson and Burkittsville, as soon as practicable, and debouch upon Rohrersville, in Pleasant Valley, in order to cut off the retreat of or destroy McLaws's command. He started from Buckeystown at 6 o'clock and marched to Jefferson, where he halted to await the arrival of Couch from Licksville. At the end of an hour he learned that Couch was still some distance in the rear, and resumed the march to within two miles of Burkittsville, where he arrived at noon and, thinking that Crampton's Gap was occupied by the enemy in strong force, made elaborate preparations for an attack. He says: "The enemy was strongly posted on both sides of the road, which made a steep ascent through a narrow defile, wooded on both sides, and offering great advantages of cover and position. Their advance was posted near the base of the mountain, in rear of a stone wall, stretching to the right of the road at a point where the ascent was gradual, and, for the most part, over open fields. Eight guns had been stationed on the road, and at points on the sides and summit of the mountain to the left (south) of the pass."[26]

It was evident to Franklin that the position could be carried only by an infantry attack and General H. W. Slocum, a splendid soldier, commanding the First Division, was assigned that duty. He was directed to move his division through and to the right of Burkittsville, and begin his attack on the right. Wolcott's 1st Maryland Battery, of eight guns, was put in position on the left of the road and to the rear of the village, where it maintained a steady fire until the close of the

---

25 Carman pasted the entire Lee to McLaws dispatch from *ibid.*, 19, pt. 2, p. 608, into his manuscript here. This dispatch demonstrates Lee's thoughts about protecting the most vulnerable elements of his command (McLaws's and Anderson's divisions), and also his faulty information about the South Mountain passes. He believed Crampton's Gap was held by Munford and Hampton, but Hampton had been moved to Knoxville and Weverton by Stuart. Lee's instruction for the route to Sharpsburg likewise provides a clue that he was already anticipating moving on that town, although there is no indication he had decided to make a stand there. As Carman pointed out, Lee did not know that McLaws had placed infantry in the gap, nor how few men comprised that infantry force.

26 Carman repeated some of McClellan's instructions, previously cited, about the march and included Franklin's dispatch, *OR* 19, pt. 1, p. 375. Although McClellan's orders specified he should not wait for Couch's division, or at least "the whole of that division," Franklin did wait. Carman said he delayed an hour, while Franklin described it in his report as "a short delay." Mark Snell, *From First to Last: The Life of Major General William B. Franklin* (New York: Fordham University Press, 2002), p. 176, states that Franklin wrote to his wife from Jefferson that morning, so Carman's estimate of an hour seems reasonable.

engagement. Ayres's regular battery, of Smith's Division, was posted on commanding ground on the right of the road, some distance in Wolcott's rear, and near Franklin's headquarters, where it kept up an uninterrupted fire upon the Confederate artillery, on the side of the mountain, nearly two miles distant.

Smith's Division was held in reserve, on the east side of the village, ready to co-operate with Slocum, or support his attack as occasion might require.

Slocum's skirmishers met the pickets of the enemy at 12 o'clock, noon, near Burkittsville, upon which he deployed the 96th Pennsylvania, Colonel H. L. Cake, of Bartlett's Brigade, and ordered it forward. Cake drove in Munford's cavalry pickets and advanced to the village, drawing the fire of Grimes' and Chew's batteries on the roads to Crampton's Gap and that of Manly's Battery, in Brownsville Gap, one mile south, which was kept up during the greater part of the afternoon, the shots being divided between the skirmishers and the main body of the regiment, drawn up in line on the road leading out of Burkittsville, southwest to Knoxville.[27]

The other regiments of Slocum's Division were advanced to a position about a half mile east of the village, where they were completely concealed from the view of the enemy and covered from the fire of his artillery. Here the command halted quite two hours, while the men ate their rations and the officers considered preparations for attack. In an article in the *National Tribune*, December 19, 1889, General Bartlett writes:

> Here everything was halted, and while the men were having their midday meal, the General commanding came up and established his headquarters in the edge of the little woods, at a point from which he could overlook the intervening valley, which stretched up to the base of the mountain, and had the road leading up to the Pass and the Pass itself plainly in vision. After resting perhaps an hour in this position, the Adjutant General of the Division, Major H. C. Rodgers, came to me with a message from General Slocum, saying he would like to see me at General Franklin's headquarters, where I immediately reported.
>
> I found grouped there, resting upon the ground, in as comfortable positions as each one could assume, after lunch, smoking their cigars, Gen. Franklin, commanding

27  The timing is confirmed from Slocum's report, *OR* 19, pt. 1, p. 380, while Franklin's report, *ibid.*, pp. 374-5 is the source for the general information and the quote about "the enemy was strongly posted…" The deployment of the artillery and the skirmishers' advance against the Confederates is taken from the same two reports mentioned above. As before, Carman supplied the names and position of the Confederate forces to render a more complete description of the action. Franklin's report was written to make it sound like the assault on the Confederate line was immediate; Slocum gives the proper timing.

the corps; General Slocum and W. F. Smith (Baldy), commanding respectively the First and Second Divisions; Gen. Hancock, commanding First Brigade, Smith's Division; Gen. W. T. H. Brooks, commanding Vermont Brigade, Smith's Division, and Gen. John Newton, commanding Third Brigade, Slocum's Division. After a preliminary conversation, not touching upon the battle before us, Gen. Slocum suddenly asked me on which side of the road leading through and over the Pass I would attack.

Without a moment's hesitation I replied, "On the right."

"Well, gentlemen, that settles it," said Gen. Franklin.

"Settles what, General," I exclaimed.

"The point of attack."

I was naturally indignant that I should be called upon to give even an opinion upon such an important matter without previously hearing the views of such old and experienced officers upon such an important question. Gen. Slocum then explained the situation. In discussing the question, it seems that they were equally divided in their opinions between the right and left of the road for the main attack. Gen. Franklin then asked Gen. Slocum who was going to lead the attack. Gen. Slocum replied, "Bartlett." "Then," said Gen. Franklin, "send for Bartlett and let him decide." This settled the question as to where the principal attack was to be made; and later, when we were alone, I asked Gen. Slocum what formation to make with the division. He said: "As Gen. Franklin has allowed you to decide the point of attack, on the ground that you were to lead it, it is no more than fair that I should leave to you the formation."

I suggested the formation of the three brigades in column of regiments deployed, two regiments front, at 100 paces interval between lines (that would give us six lines); that the head of the column should be directed toward a point I indicated to him, at nearly right angles to the road which crossed the mountain, and in a direction to strike the highest point the road reached at the crest, it being the shortest line; that I would deploy the 27th New York (his old regiment and mine also) as skirmishers at the head of the column and skirmish into the teeth of their line of battle, following with the head of the column at 100 paces; that I would not halt after giving the order forward until we reached the crest of the mountain, if possible. These suggestions met with the general's approval, and he based his written orders upon them. I was to attack at the point and in the manner indicated, take the crest of the mountain, and throw out a picket line for the night. The enemy's artillery had now opened upon everything in sight."[28]

---

28  It was during this lull while troops arrived from Jefferson and preparations were undertaken that Bartlett's story from the *National Tribune* takes place. While Bartlett's tone in this article has been construed as critical of Franklin, the policy of allowing subordinates who have knowledge of the ground and who will lead the attack to determine the method and point of assault was

The road from Burkittsville to Rohrersville and Pleasant Valley runs northwest from Burkittsville a good half mile, when it begins to ascend the mountain in a northerly direction by a laborious grade. It runs in this northerly direction another good half mile when it turns gradually to the west and reaches the summit of the gap at an elevation of 400 feet above the level of Burkittsville. Though of heavy grade, the road is good. All the time the mountain, on either side of the road, was heavily wooded from base to summit.

About one third of a mile west of Burkittsville and 250 yards short of where the road turns northerly in ascending the mountain, a narrow country road leads from the right, northerly along the base of the mountain. On both sides of this narrow road were stone-walls or fences, not continuous on both sides, nor continuous on either side, but, on one side or the other, they furnished good cover for infantry and were skillfully utilized for defense of the gap. On the west side of this road were several houses, behind which the mountain slope was well wooded.[29]

McLaws did not share in the belief, entertained by Lee, Jackson, Stuart and others, that McClellan would give them no serious trouble while in the execution of their plans, although he did not anticipate the prompt movement that was made. He had been informed by Lee, at Frederick, that Stuart would take care of the mountain gaps after he had passed them, but was rightly minded to look to this matter himself, so, when he marched through Brownsville Gap, on the 11th, and marched on Elk Ridge and Maryland Heights, he left General Semmes with his brigade and Mahone's in Pleasant Valley, opposite the Gap, to guard both Crampton's and Brownsville Gap, with instructions to send a regiment to protect the rear of Kershaw, who had ascended Solomon's Gap in Maryland Heights. As we have seen, Wright's Brigade, of Anderson's Division, proceeded down the South Mountain and took position on the heights above Weverton Pass, as ordered the night before. Cobb was directed to cross Pleasant Valley and, marching along the eastern base of Elk Ridge, keep in communication with Kershaw, above and up to his advance, ready to give him support, if needed, and serve as a rallying force, should Kershaw be worsted, which McLaws asserts Cobb failed to do because of some misconception of orders. Anderson pushed forward Pryor's Brigade and

---

not unusual nor bad practice for Civil War armies. J. J. Bartlett, "Crampton's Pass: The Start of the Great Maryland Campaign," *National Tribune* (Washington D.C.), December 19, 1889.

29 The physical description of the terrain near Crampton's Gap is probably from Carman's personal knowledge. It does not appear in the reports of the commanders, McLaws's address, or in any articles found in *B&L*. Because he spent so much time studying the campaign firsthand, Carman undoubtedly traveled to Crampton's Gap and Burkittsville to examine the field.

took possession of Weverton and disposed the troops of Wright and Pryor to defend that Pass.[30]

McLaws ordered a picket of one infantry company posted at Brownsville Gap, which, on the 12th, Semmes increased to three regiments and five pieces of artillery, thus employing his entire brigade, except for the 10th Georgia, which was picketing the Rohrersville road and other avenues leading down Pleasant Valley, in the direction of Harper's Ferry. On the 13th, Colonel William A. Parham, commanding Mahone's Brigade, reported to Semmes, and the 41st Virginia Regiment was sent as a picket to Solomon's Gap to cover Kershaw's rear.

Having familiarized himself with the roads and passes, Semmes, on the morning of the 14th, ordered Parham, with his skeleton brigade and Grimes' Portsmouth Battery to support Colonel Munford's cavalry at Crampton's Gap, and instructed him, if he needed support, to call upon Major Willis C. Holt, commanding 10th Georgia, for his regiment, then posted on the Rohrersville road. Munford had been gradually forced back to the gap on the 13th, by Pleasonton's cavalry and, late the same day, had been joined by Hampton's Brigade of cavalry.

Stuart, believing that Crampton's Gap was the weakest point in his line, left Rosser, with the 5th Virginia Cavalry, at Fox's Gap; saw that two brigades of D. H. Hill's Division were put in Turner's Gap and, early on the morning of the 14th, rode down to Crampton's. Here he saw no signs of a Union advance in force and fearing a movement along the Potomac, towards Harper's Ferry, sent Hampton in that direction, thus leaving Munford with but two small cavalry regiments (2nd and 12th Virginia) and a part of Mahone's infantry brigade at Crampton's. Hampton went down the east side of South Mountain, halted at the south end at Knoxville, and threw out pickets on the roads to Point of Rocks and Frederick. Stuart proceeded to McLaws's headquarters, to acquaint him with the situation of affairs, and rode with him to Maryland Heights, to assist in the reduction of Harper's Ferry, as he was familiar with the topography of the country, from his connection with the John Brown raid. He says: "I explained to him the location of roads in the vicinity and repeatedly urged the importance of his holding with an infantry picket the road leading from the Ferry by the Kennedy farm toward Sharpsburg; failing to do which, the entire cavalry force of the enemy, at the Ferry, escaped during the night

---

30 The review of the Confederate situation in Pleasant Valley and the gaps was covered in detail in Chapter Six. Most of it is found in McLaws's report, OR 19, pt. 1, pp. 852-4. The criticism of Cobb misinterpreting his orders is not in his report, but appears in McLaws's postwar address, "The Capture of Harpers Ferry."

by that very road, and inflicted serious damage on General Longstreet's train in the course of their flight."[31]

While Stuart was thus prompting McLaws on Maryland Heights trouble was brewing for Munford, who, as senior officer, had been ordered to take command at Crampton's Gap and hold it at all hazards. The morning was rife with rumors of the Union advance and his scouts confirmed them. Munford prepared to receive it; he posted the 6th, 12th and 16th Virginia regiments, of Mahone's Brigade, commanded by Colonel William A. Parham, 41st Virginia, behind the stone walls and rail fences of the road, at the eastern base of the mountain, and running parallel with it, and the 2nd and 12th Virginia Cavalry were dismounted and disposed on the flanks of the infantry as sharpshooters, the 2nd on the right, the 12th on the left. Captain R. P. Chew's Virginia Battery and a section of navy howitzers, of Grimes' Portsmouth Battery, were placed in rear, about half way up the slope of the mountain, in the most eligible position that could be found. Major Willis Holt, commanding 10th Georgia Infantry, was ordered by Semmes to Munford's support and took position at the base of the mountain, but was almost immediately ordered by Semmes to fall back and take position at the Colored Church on the road to Rohrersville. Holt had reached the summit of the mountain when Parham halted him, allowed him to send two companies to the church, at the junction of the roads, and gave him peremptory orders to return and go into position on the left of the line as he had formed.

Colonel E. B. Montague, 32nd Virginia, Semmes' Brigade, holding Brownsville Gap, one mile south of Crampton's, stationed a picket of 200 men at the base of the mountain and a line of skirmishers along his whole front, connecting with Munford's right. These were more spectators than participants in the action about to ensue, as they were not engaged.

Including the 300 men of Semmes' Brigade, on the right of his command, Munford had about 1200 men to meet the advance of five brigades of Franklin's

---

31 Stuart's deployment of the cavalry and his admonition to McLaws about the Harpers Ferry Road are taken from Stuart's report in OR 19, pt. 1, pp. 817-9. Written after the fact, Stuart's report may be self-serving in places. There is no evidence of his warnings in contemporary reports or orders. The placement of the troops is a compilation from the reports of Stuart, *ibid.*, p. 818, Munford, *ibid.*, pp. 826-7, McLaws, *ibid.*, p. 854, Hampton, *ibid.*, pp. 823-4, Cobb, *ibid.*, pp. 870-1, and Holt, *ibid.*, pp. 876-7. There were not two brigades in Turner's Gap on the night of September 13. Garland's Brigade did not join Colquitt until the morning of September 14. Hill's report, *ibid.*, p. 1,019. As will be shown in the next chapter, Stuart did not tell D. H. Hill about posting Rosser in Fox's Gap.

Corps, numbering nearly 12,000 men, but he had the advantage of position and 13 pieces of artillery.[32]

As elsewhere stated reconnaissance had decided that the Union attack should be made on the right and flank of the road leading over the mountain and Bartlett was to direct and lead the advance. Bartlett conducted his brigade, as secretly as possible, to a large field near the base of the mountain, where the formation was to be made in a ravine, screened from view by a hedge and large cornfield.

About this time Captain Russell arrived upon the field with a dispatch from McClellan to Franklin, and Russell informed Franklin of the condition of affairs at Harper's Ferry.[33]

It was three o'clock before the column of attack was formed in this order: the 27th New York, Lieutenant-Colonel A. D. Adams, was deployed in skirmishing order, to be followed at a distance of 200 yards by two regiments in line of battle, the 16th New York, Lieutenant-Colonel Joel J. Seaver, on the right; the 5th Maine, Colonel N. J. Jackson, on the left. These three regiments were of Bartlett's Brigade.

General John Newton's Brigade was to follow Bartlett's and was formed in two lines. In the first line the 32nd New York, Col. R. Matheson, was on the right, and the 18th New York, Lieutenant-Colonel George Myers, on the left; in second line the 31st New York, Lieutenant-Colonel Francis E. Pinto (32nd New York), was on the right, and the 95th Pennsylvania, Colonel George W. Town,[34] on the left.

The New Jersey Brigade, Colonel A. T. A. Torbert, was also formed in two lines; in first line, the 1st New Jersey, Lieutenant-Colonel M. W. Collett[35] (3rd New Jersey), on the right, the 2nd New Jersey, Colonel Samuel L. Buck, on the left; in second line, the 3rd New Jersey, Colonel Henry W. Brown, on the right, and 4th New Jersey, Colonel William B. Hatch, on the left.

Including the skirmish line the column was six lines deep, the four leading lines being separated by intervals of 200 yards; the New Jersey Brigade took intervals of 150 yards. The 96th Pennsylvania of Bartlett's Brigade, that had advanced into the

---

32 The figures Carman cited for the Confederates are confusing. He can only achieve a total of 13 guns by adding the Troup Artillery, which arrived with Cobb, but he did not count the men of Cobb's Brigade. The troop positions come from the reports of Kershaw, *ibid.*, p. 855, Semmes, *ibid.*, pp. 872-3, Holt, *ibid.*, p. 977, and Munford, *ibid.*, pp. 826-7.

33 The presence of Capt. Russell with Franklin during the battle is confirmed by Russell's testimony in the Harpers Ferry Commission, *ibid.*, pp. 720-730.

34 Carman elsewhere listed his name properly as Gustavus W. Town.

35 Elsewhere he is correctly listed as "Collet." (Carman added an extra "t" to his name.)

village, joined the column as it went forward, following the Jersey men; the 121st New York was held as reserve.[36]

McClellan's order to Franklin was to seize the pass immediately upon his arrival before it, if not occupied by the enemy in force; if held in force he was to make his dispositions and begin the attack half an hour after hearing severe fighting at Turner's Gap. The sound of heavy fighting came down the valley before Franklin had reached Burkittsville and continued during his leisurely preparations; it was not necessary to wait, and the day was well spent when the orders were given to advance. As soon as it began the Confederate opened a heavy and well directed fire from their artillery, half way up the mountain and in Brownsville Gap, but the troops advanced steadily, preceded by the skirmishers, that soon drew the fire of the Confederate infantry and dismounted cavalry, posted behind the stone fences and houses, which afforded them admirable cover. Having thus developed the Confederate position, Slocum withdrew the skirmishers, and the first line, the 5th Maine and the 16th New York, moved to a rail fence, on a rise of ground, within 300 yards of the Confederates, an open field intervening, and a severe engagement ensued, in which the two regiments lost heavily, while the Confederates having greatly the advantage of position, had few casualties.[37]

Bartlett advanced his line promptly and in good order, but, for some unexplained and unaccountable reason, Newton did not promptly follow, and there was more than 600 yards interval between the two lines. When Newton did come up, Bartlett's men, that had been engaged nearly an hour, had suffered severely and were out of ammunition. Newton advanced the 32nd and 18th New York to relieve Bartlett's two regiments, that fell slightly to the rear, and his second line, the 31st New York and 95th Pennsylvania, soon came up and formed on the left.

When first examined the position at the pass made it evident to Slocum that the attempt to carry it must be made by infantry alone, therefore, the artillery had been

36 The formation on Slocum's division is detailed in Slocum's report, *ibid.*, p. 380, and the reports of his brigade commanders: Torbert, *ibid.*, pp. 382-3, Bartlett, *ibid.*, p. 388-9, and Newton, *ibid.*, pp. 396-7. The 96th Pennsylvania formed on the right of Bartlett's brigade, *ibid.*, p. 39.

37 For the account of the fighting, Carman used Slocum's and Bartlett's reports (see previous note). Carman suggested Franklin's attack was behind schedule, according to the orders to coordinate his attack with the one at Turner's Gap. See McClellan to Franklin, September 13, 1862, in *ibid.*, 19, pt. 1, pp. 45-6. Subsequent authors have noted Franklin's deliberate pace and held him responsible for the failure to relieve Miles. See Palfrey, *The Antietam and Fredericksburg*, p. 44; Murfin, *The Gleam of Bayonets*, Chapter 6, and Sears, *Landscape Turned Red*, pp. 146-9, and Timothy Reese, *Sealed With Their Lives: The Battle of Crampton's Gap* (Baltimore: Butternut and Blue, 1998), pp. 248-56.

left behind, but the stone walls, covering the enemy, presented such an obstacle to the advance of his lines, that further effort was suspended until the artillery could be brought up and used against them. A battery was sent for, it came at a gallop, but before fairly in position, there was no use for it, the Confederate position at the base of the mountain had been carried.[38]

While awaiting the arrival of artillery, Torbert's New Jersey Brigade came up on the left in two lines, the 1st and 2nd, in advance, opening a rapid and accurate fire; and the 96th Pennsylvania took position on the extreme right, but no impression seemed to be made on the enemy, while the Union line, much exposed, was severely suffering. It was apparent to everyone, officers and private, that nothing but a quick rush, a united charge of the entire line, would dislodge the enemy and win the day. Bartlett and Torbert, young and gallant soldiers, had a moment's consultation, and, as the artillery was not yet in sight, decided to charge immediately without waiting for it or further orders from Slocum. Everything was in readiness; the 96th Pennsylvania, of Bartlett's Brigade, was on the right of the whole line; on its left were the 32nd and 18th New York, of Newton's Brigade, and on the left of these two New York regiments the 16th and 27th New York, and 5th Maine of Bartlett. On the left of Bartlett's three regiments were the 31st New York and 95th Pennsylvania, of Newton, and on the left of the 95th Pennsylvania was Torbert's Jersey Brigade, the left of the division. The left of Torbert's line was about 200 yards north of the Burkittsville road. From right to left the length of the line was about a mile.

Thus formed, the order was passed along the line to "cease firing" and the command given to charge double-quick. Instantly the troops were in motion and the sight was a grand and thrilling one. The mile of brightened muskets glistened in the evening sun, and the regimental colors, stirred by a gentle breeze, waved proudly over the well aligned ranks as they went forward over mostly open fields, swept by musketry and shot and shell.

The fields through which the 96th Pennsylvania charged, on the extreme right, presented many obstacles and, in order not to meet the enemy with disordered lines, Colonel Cake twice halted for a moment, under cover of stone fences, to reform. The last of the many fields over which it had to charge was a marshy meadow and tall standing corn, and, as it emerged from the corn and came into open field, officers all in place and cheering the men onward, the men well aligned

---

38 Slocum made no mention of the delay in Newton's advance, and Newton said Bartlett advanced before he did. Even though Bartlett formulated the plan for the attack, it appears not to have been well communicated to brigade commanders. The comment about bringing up artillery is from Slocum's report, *OR* 19, pt. 1, p. 380.

on the colors, which were proudly carried by stalwart bearers, it received a murderous fire from the stone-walled road, but 20 paces distant, that laid low a large number of men and for a moment staggered it. The men threw themselves flat on the ground to avoid as much as possible the destructive rain of minie balls pouring in their ranks, but it was for a moment only, they raised as one man, the colors pointed forward, the road was gained, and the enemy sent in confused retreat up the mountain. The left of the Confederate line was routed and, without stopping, the Pennsylvanians pressed on in eager pursuit.

To the left of the 96th Pennsylvania the men of Bartlett's and Newton's brigades had less natural obstacles to contend with, but the rain of musketry was severe and thinned the charging lines, though it did not stop them; they swept over the open field, drove the Virginians from cover and followed them up the mountain side.

When the order to advance was given, the 3rd and 4th New Jersey were in second line to the 1st and 2nd New Jersey, and about 100 yards distant, protected by a slight rise in the ground. The 1st and 2nd regiments ceased firing, and the 3rd and 4th, with wild cheers, went forward on a run, jumped the rail fence, behind which the 1st and 2nd had been fighting, and faced the leaden storm, which swept over the grass field between them and the stone-wall, bordering the road. When they had covered about 150 yards, the 1st and 2nd regiments charged in the same handsome manner as did their comrades, both lines reaching the stone wall about the same time, the Virginians breaking and retreating up the side of the mountain closely pursued by the Jersey men.

While Slocum's men were making their successful charge on the right of the road, Brooks's Vermont Brigade, of Smith's Division, moved on the left. After passing through Burkittsville, under the fire of the artillery in Brownsville Gap, the Confederate skirmish line was encountered. Brooks deployed the 4th Vermont as skirmishers, with the 2nd in support, the other three regiments remaining as a reserve on the edge of the village, and advanced, the Confederates quickly retreating, leaving some of their number as prisoners. [39]

While the Virginians are retreating up the mountain, closely pursued by the Union lines, we must see what dispositions were made to relieve them at the top

[39] In his report, Torbert said it was Newton who ordered the charge, but Bartlett claimed he gave the command. Newton was on Bartlett's left, a good distance away from Torbert, who was probably mistaken. The advance of the Federals can be traced in the brigade commander's reports: Torbert, *ibid.*, pp. 382-3; Bartlett, *ibid.*, pp. 388-9; and Newton, *ibid.*, pp. 396-7. Carman also borrowed from the report of Col. Cake of the 96th Pennsylvania Volunteers, *ibid.*, pp. 94-5, but mentioned a few details not in the report.

and meet the Union pursuit. When McLaws descended into Pleasant Valley, three days before, he ordered General Semmes to take care of his rear by occupying both Crampton's and Brownsville gaps, and two brigades were placed at his disposal—his own and Mahone's. Brownsville Gap seemed to Semmes of the first importance and he placed there three regiments of his own brigade and a battery of artillery, leaving Mahone's Brigade in the valley, west of the mountain. Becoming familiar with the roads and passes he recognized the great importance of Crampton's Gap, and, on the morning of the 14th, ordered Parham, commanding Mahone's Brigade, with three regiments and a battery, to move into it, and authorized him, in case of need, to call upon the 10th Georgia, then on the Rohrersville road. By this time he had become so thoroughly impressed by what he had heard of the Union advance in heavy force, that he rode in hot haste to acquaint McLaws of the danger threatening his rear. He found him on Maryland Heights, about noon, told him that scouts were constantly reporting the Union advance from Frederick and suggested an increase of force at Crampton's Gap, whereupon McLaws sent an order to Cobb, near Sandy Hook, to march back to the camp near the foot of Brownsville Gap, and directed Semmes to withdraw the regiment of Mahone's Brigade from Solomon's Gap, leaving a small rear-guard to give notice should a force of the enemy approach that position. Semmes was instructed, also, to tell Cobb, on his arrival in the vicinity, to take command at Crampton's Gap. Semmes rode back to his command, disposed his brigade for action and Cobb, receiving McLaws's order at one o'clock, set out on the return march from Sandy Hook, reaching his old camp, about two miles from Crampton's Gap, at four o'clock, where he was immediately waited upon by Semmes, who gave him the instructions he had received from McLaws; but Cobb was sluggish and remained a full hour, without making the least effort to acquaint himself of what was going on, nor did he give sign of interest, until he spurred to action by a message from Munford, recommending him to move up to the gap, as the enemy was pressing his small force. McLaws says:

> Cobb was inexperienced enough not to realize that, as ranking officer, he was responsible for everything that might happen in the rear, where his inferiors in rank were stationed, unless they were under immediate orders of others superior to himself. He was sent to the camp ground upon which I camped on the evening of the 11th, when my command came into the valley, so as to be able to throw his troops either to Brownsville Gap or Crampton's, or to any other forces in this area where they were most needed; and of this he was to be the judge, as he was superior in rank to General Semmes and to all others in that neighborhood. If he had had more experience as to the responsibility which rank confers he would not have waited an hour in camp upon

contingencies, but would have gone in person in advance to inform himself as to the best way to provide against misfortune."[40]

Cobb was finally moved by the advice of Semmes and the appeals of Munford and sent two of his strongest regiments to Munford's support. These had hardly taken up the line of march when a message was received from Parham to the effect that the enemy was pressing him hard with overwhelming numbers, and appealing for all the support he could bring him, upon which he ordered the two remaining regiments of his brigade to march and accompanied them in person. As he started he received McLaws's orders to hold the gap if it cost the life of every man in his command.

In his official report McLaws says: "I was on Maryland Heights, directing and observing the fire of our guns, when I heard cannonading the direction of Crampton's Gap, but I felt no particular concern about it, as there were then three brigades of infantry in the vicinity, beside the cavalry of Colonel Munford, and General Stuart, who was with me on the height and had just come in from above, told me that he did not believe there was more than a brigade of the enemy. I, however, sent my Adjutant General to General Cobb, as also Major Goggin, of my staff, with directions to hold the gap, if he lost his last man in doing it, and shortly afterward went down the mountain and started toward the gap."[41]

Thus impressed with the importance of the position, Cobb went forward as rapidly as possible. When he went by the road to the top of the mountain Munford and Parham were still engaged. Below, and through an opening in the woods, where he stood, and over the top of the trees below him, could be seen the long Union lines charging and overlapping the Confederate flanks. Munford explained the position of his troops and yielded the command; as he did so the Virginians broke and began to come up the mountain. The Cobb Legion and 24th Georgia were now up and Cobb requested Munford to put them in position, which he promptly did, on the road just east of the summit, and where it turns to the right in descending the

---

40 Carman's wording is somewhat ambiguous, but it appears that he drew most of this information from Semmes's report, *ibid.*, 19, pt. 1, pp. 872-3. There was no mention of Semmes riding to talk to McLaws on Maryland Heights in his or in McLaws's report. Instead, McLaws simply wrote, "Hearing of an advance of the enemy . . . about noon I ordered Cobb," so Semmes's timing would appear correct. *Ibid.*, p. 854. Confirmation of Semmes's ride to McLaws is found in McLaws, "The Capture of Harper's Ferry." Carman used excerpts of the September 12 issue of the Philadelphia *Weekly Times* verbatim in his manuscript to describe Semmes's and McLaws's meeting. The 10th Georgia was recalled from Rohrersville and in position before Bartlett's attack. See Holt's report, *ibid.*, pp. 876-7.

41 McLaws's report, *ibid.*, pt. 1, p. 854.

mountain to Burkittsville. The 15th North Carolina and 16th Georgia soon came up and, at Cobb's request, Munford placed them on the road running to the left, after crossing the gap, but, says Munford, "They behaved badly and did not get into position before the wildest confusion commenced, the wounded coming to the rear in numbers and more well now coming with them."[42]

The unsteadiness in the ranks of these two regiments was caused by the retreat of the Virginians through them, and the on-coming of Slocum's line. The 96th Pennsylvania and other regiments on the right and center, did not halt, for breath even, at the foot of the mountain, but, scaling the stone walls and fences, went on close upon the heels of the Virginians and, as the most long-winded and fleet-footed neared the summit, they saw the new line of battle on the road, and, taking cover of rocks and trees, immediately engaged it. As the Union firing line increased by others coming up, the two regiments broke and retreated, leaving many prisoners in the hands of their enemy, and were pursued as rapidly as Slocum's men could climb the hill to the summit, and then down it.

Like disaster overtook the Cobb Legion and 24th Georgia at the hands of Torbert's Brigade and the left of Newton's. As the Jersey men climbed up the shingly side of the mountain they took many prisoners from the Virginians; when they reached near the crest, on the left of the road, it was seen that the Georgians were forming a new line on their right, upon which the right regiment wheeled to the right and poured a murderous volley into them, which dispersed them and sent them in disorder through the gap and down the west side of the mountain, closely followed by the Jersey men, the 31st New York and the 95th Pennsylvania.

Cobb, aided by Semmes, Munford, Parham and others, made great effort to rally the men; the 10th Georgia and the Virginia cavalry and infantry, a few being collected, endeavored to stay them, but without the least effect. Munford says: "It would have been as useless to attempt to rally a flock of frightened sheep," and, as it

---

42 The delay in Cobb's move to Crampton's Gap and McLaws's criticism derived by Carman, in part, from McLaws's newspaper article. The direct quote of McLaws was taken from the September 12 issue. Cobb said he was in camp one hour when he received the message to reinforce the gap and started two regiments immediately. *Ibid.*, p. 870. Munford said he sent four couriers and there was "much delay." *Ibid.*, p. 826. Reese, *Sealed With Their Lives*, argued that Cobb was unfairly blamed by Stuart, Munford, and McLaws, and that the poor deployment of the Confederate defenders was more to blame. Longstreet was more supportive of Cobb and obliquely criticized Munford, remarking in his memoirs, "cavalry commanders do not always post artillery and infantry to greatest advantage." Longstreet, *From Manassas to Appomattox*, p. 230. It appears that Carman favored McLaws's account. The Confederate defense of the gap was taken from the reports of McLaws, whose report, *OR* 19, pt. 1, p. 854, Carman quoted concerning Cobb's inexperience, and Munford's report, which Carman used heavily and quoted as saying Cobb's men "behaved badly." *Ibid.*, pp. 826-7.

was evident that the gap could no longer be held, he formed his own command and moved down the Rohrersville road, to where his horses had been left, "the infantry still running in great disorder on the Harper's Ferry road," with no apparent idea of stopping until met by McLaws and Stuart coming from Maryland Heights.

Stuart says: "Hearing the attack at Crampton's Gap, I rode at full speed to reach that point, and met General Cobb's command just after dark, retreating in disorder down Pleasant Valley. He reported the enemy as only 200 yards behind, and in overwhelming force. I immediately halted his command, and disposed men upon each side of the road to meet the enemy, and a battery, which I had accidentally met with, was placed in position commanding the road. The enemy not advancing I sent out parties to reconnoiter, who found no enemy within a mile. Pickets were thrown out, and the command was left in partial repose for the night."[43]

The Union pursuit was halted by darkness, the weariness of the men, and the dislocation of the commands, consequent upon the broken character of the field. Slocum's Division gathered along the road to Rohrersville, at the western foot of the gap. Brooks' Vermont Brigade which had participated in the charge up the mountain, moved on Slocum's left. When the summit was reached the 4th Vermont followed the crest of the mountain to the left, where Manly's Battery had been, and the 2nd Vermont continued on down the western slope and reached the base of the mountain just as Slocum's men had scattered the enemy. The 4th Vermont proceeded along the crest about a half mile and captured the battle-flag, Major Holladay and many men of the 16th Virginia, and then descended the west side of the mountain, where it was joined by the other regiments of the brigade, and all bivouacked in the valley at the point where Slocum's Division ceased pursuit, on the Harper's Ferry road, about one half mile south of the gap. Irwin's brigade went over the mountain by the gap and bivouacked on Brooks' right. Hancock's brigade was in reserve, did not participate in the engagement and remained east of the mountain.[44]

43 See Cobb's report, *ibid.*, p. 870-1; Semmes's report, *ibid.*, pp. 872-3; and Major Holt, 10th Georgia, *ibid.*, pp. 876-7. Carman also quoted from Stuart's report, *ibid.*, pp. 818-9, on his rapid ride to meet Cobb. As usual, Carman wove in the names of the Union regiments and commanders making the assault to enhance the readability of the text. By using primarily the Virginia reports, Carman may be accused of slanting his text toward their point of view. Either he ignored Cobb's report, *ibid.*, pp. 870-1, or was exercising his historiographer's authority. Either way, Carman chose to believe the Virginians and doubt Cobb.

44 Carman's wrap-up of the battle and the Union pursuit came from Slocum's report, *ibid.*, pp. 380-1, and Brooks' report, ibid., pp. 407-8, which Carman paraphrased to describe the pursuit by the Vermonters. Carman supplied the name of Major Holladay to fill out the report.

The operations of the day resulted in a Union victory, and the capture of 600 prisoners, 700 stand of arms, a piece of artillery from the Troup battery and four colors. The piece of artillery had been abandoned at the foot of the mountain because of the hot pursuit of the 95th Pennsylvania, and was captured by the skirmishers of the Vermont Brigade. The victory was purchased at the expense of 113 killed, 418 wounded, and 2 missing, an aggregate of 533.[45]

\*    \*    \*

## Return of Casualties in the Union Forces at the Battle of Crampton's Gap:

| | Killed | | Wounded | | Captured | | |
|---|---|---|---|---|---|---|---|
| Command | Officers | Men | Officers | Men | officers | Men | Total |
| General Staff | | | 1 | | | | 1 |
| 5th Maine | | 4 | 1 | 27 | | | 32 |
| 1st NJ Inf. | | 7 | 3 | 31 | | | 41 |
| 2d NJ Inf. | | 10 | 1 | 44 | | | 55 |
| 3d NJ Inf.. | | 11 | 2 | 27 | | | 40 |
| 4th NJ Inf. | 1 | 9 | 3 | 23 | | | 36 |
| 16th NY Inf. | | 20 | 1 | 40 | | | 61 |
| 18th NY Inf. | 1 | 10 | 1 | 40 | | 2 | 54 |

45 The Union casualty returns are taken from *ibid.*, p. 183. Reese points out mathematical errors in the Union table that reached total casualties of 538, and then used his own methodology to arrive at 152 killed and 289 wounded for a total of 441 casualties. Reese also included those who died of wounds shortly after the battle with those killed outright. Reese, *Sealed With Their Lives*, Appendix B. The number of Confederates captured is unclear. Franklin's report said 400 men were captured from seventeen different organizations, as were 700 stands of arms, three colors, and one gun. OR 19, pt. 1, p. 375. Slocum reported only 300 captured, but this would not include any men captured by Brooks because he was in Smith's division. Neither Smith nor Brooks gave a firm number of prisoners captured. *Ibid.*, pp. 402-3, 408-9. Reese's research, which challenges Carman's numbers, puts the Confederate losses much higher at 179 killed, 317 wounded, and 377 captured for a total of 873 casualties. Reese makes no mention of differentiating between wounded and unwounded prisoners, so it is possible Carman's figure is accurate. Reese, *Sealed With Their Lives*, Appendix B.

| | | | | | | |
|---|---|---|---|---|---|---|
| 27th NY Inf. | | 6 | 2 | 25 | | | 33 |
| 31st NY Inf. | | 1 | | 3 | | | 4 |
| 32d NY Inf. | 1 | 10 | 3 | 37 | | | 51 |
| 95th PA Inf. | | 1 | | 14 | | | 15 |
| 96th PA Inf. | 2 | 18 | | 71 | | | 91 |
| 2d VT Inf. | | | | 5 | | | 5 |
| 4th VT Inf. | | 1 | | 10 | | | 11 |
| 6th VT Inf. | | | 1 | 2 | | | 3 |
| Total | 5 | 108 | 19 | 399 | | 2 | 533 |

The defense of the Confederates at the east foot of the mountain, against the heavy odds they faced was a brilliant one. Outnumbered eight to one they held position until fairly overwhelmed. Nor must the actions of the men of Cobb's Brigade be too harshly criticized. They came upon the field when it was practically lost, pursued and pursuers nearly commingled, were thrown into some disorder by the unexpected, murderous fire poured into them from front and flank, and yielded only when one-fourth of their number were killed or wounded, and the survivors nearly surrounded. Their severe losses attest their gallantry.[46]

46 Carman paid due homage to the Confederate defenders at Crampton's Gap. His ratio of Union troops to Confederate, 8:1, is based on the figure of 1,200 Confederate defenders, (Reese, *Sealed With Their Lives*, Appendix B, arrived at a figure of 1,514) against the Sixth Corps total of 12,800, minus the brigades of Irwin and Hancock, leaving roughly 9,500 men, or odds of 8:1. Carman's figure of 550 in Mahone's Brigade, not counting the 41st Virginia, compares favorably with Reese's research in Appendix B. Reese discovered that the Compiled Service Record for Peter Bird in the National Archives, the soldier listed as killed in the 2nd Virginia Cavalry, in fact died of typhoid fever at a much later date. Reese, *Sealed With Their Lives*, p. 370n. The figures cited by Carman for Cobb's Brigade and the 10th Georgia come from a chart on the page cited by Carman. McLaws kept unusually accurate figures for Confederates in the Maryland campaign. Reese, who gave no indication of using Carman's manuscript, listed figures only slightly different.

## Casualties in the Confederate Forces at Crampton's Gap, South Mountain, September 14, 1862

| Command | Killed | Wounded | Missing | Total | Notes |
|---|---|---|---|---|---|
| 2d VA Cav. | | 1 | 2 | 3 | OR 19, pt. 1, p. 827 |
| 12th VA Cav. | | 2 | 3 | 5 | Note 1 |
| Mahone's Brigade | 5 | 74 | 124 | 203 | Note 2 |
| 10th GA Inf. (Semmes) | 3 | 21 | 37 | 61 | OR 19, pt. 1, p. 877 |
| Troup Arty. | 1 | 3 | | 4 | OR 19, pt. 1, p. 861 |
| Cobb's Brigade | 58 | 186 | 442 | 696 | OR 19, pt. 1, p. 861 |
| Total | 70 | 289 | 602 | 962 | |

Note 1: From information given by survivors of the regiment.[47]

Note 2: From the best obtainable information Mahone's Brigade had about 550 officers and men at Crampton's Gap. The report in W. R., XIX, pt. 1, p. 843, gives its losses September 14-17 1862, as 8 killed, 92 wounded, 127 missing, an aggregate of 227. At Antietam, September 17th the brigade had 3 killed, 18 wounded, 3 missing, thus leaving the loss at Crampton's Gap as stated. The muster roll of the 12th Virginia (October 31 1862) shows its loss as 86.

Night was fast falling as McLaws, hastening from Maryland Heights, drew near Cobb's retreating forces. On the way he met his Adjutant General, who informed him that Franklin had carried the Gap and that Cobb needed help, upon which he at once ordered up Wilcox's Brigade from down the valley, and rode on to Cobb's camp, where there was much apprehension, notwithstanding that Stuart had averted a panic and measurably allayed fear. McLaws remarked to Stuart that it looked very much as if he had been caught in a trap, and asked what he thought of the situation. Stuart advised that an effort be made to retake Crampton's Gap, but McLaws would not consider the proposition, and came to the conclusion to make

---

47 The 12th Virginia Cavalry did not report any casualties, nor do any turn up in Dennis Frye, *Twelfth Virginia Cavalry* (Lynchburg: H. E. Howard, 1988). Either Carman spoke with a veteran who knew those who were injured, or he was mistaken.

preparations to resist an advance down Pleasant Valley, to keep guard over the passes below, and to push the attack on Harper's Ferry. General R. H. Anderson concurred in McLaws views and they were carried out. McLaws says:

> Fortunately night came on and allowed a new arrangement of the troops to be made to meet the changed aspect of affairs. The brigades of Generals Kershaw and Barksdale, except one regiment of the latter and two pieces of artillery, were withdrawn from the [Maryland] Heights overlooking the town [Harper's Ferry] and formed line of battle across the valley, about one and a half miles below Crampton's Gap, with the remnants of the brigades of Generals Cobb, Semmes, and Mahone, and those of Wilcox, Kershaw and Barksdale, which were placed specially under the command of General Anderson. Generals Wright and Pryor were kept in position guarding the Weverton Pass, and Generals Armistead and Featherston that from Harper's Ferry. That place was not yet taken, and I had but to wait and watch the movements of the enemy. It was necessary to guard three positions: First, to present a front against the enemy advancing down the valley; second, to prevent those forces from escaping from Harper's Ferry and acting in conjunction with their troops in front; third, to prevent an entrance at Weverton Pass. . . . The loss in those brigades engaged was, in killed, wounded, and missing, very large, and the remnant collected to make front across the valley was very small. I had dispatched Lieutenant Tucker, my aide-de-camp, with a courier and guide, to report to General Lee the condition of affairs, but, on getting beyond our forces, he rode suddenly on a strong picket of the enemy, was halted, and fired on them as he turned and dashed back. The courier was killed, but Lieutenant Tucker and the guide escaped. General Stuart had, however, started couriers before that, and sent others from time to time during the night, and I, therefore, was satisfied that General Lee would be informed before morning."[48]

None of these couriers ever reached General Lee, and McLaws was left to work out his own salvation. Meanwhile we turn to affairs at Turner's Gap.

---

48 For the details of McLaws meeting his adjutant and ordering Wilcox to support Cobb, see OR 19, pt. 1, pp. 854-5. This was also the source of the long quote from McLaws concerning his desperate circumstances.

# Chapter 8

# South Mountain (Fox's Gap)

## September 14, 1862

While Franklin, with the Sixth Corps, was forcing Crampton's Gap, Burnside, at the head of the First and Ninth Corps, was severely engaged at Turner's Gap, six miles northeast of Crampton's. The engagement was most severe at and south of Fox's Gap, a mile and more south of Turner's, and there was a sharp and fierce contest north, but as both these were for the possession of the main road, which ran through Turner's Gap, this place has given the Union name to the battle. The Confederates call it the battle of Boonsboro.

At this point the South Mountain runs, in a general direction northeast and southwest, and its crests are about 1300 feet above sea-level and 1000 feet above the general level of the Catoctin or Middletown Valley. The National road or turnpike between Frederick and Hagerstown crosses the mountain at Turner's Gap, a depression some 300 feet below the crests on either side.

The mountain on the north side of the turnpike is divided into two crests or ridges, by a narrow valley, which, though deep at the gap, becomes a slight depression about a mile to the north. There are country roads, both to the right of the Gap and to the left, which give access to the crests overlooking the National road. The principal one on the left, or south, called the Old Sharpsburg road, is nearly parallel to, and about three-fourths of a mile distant from the road through the Gap, until it reaches the crest of the mountain at Fox's Gap, where it bends to the left and, leaving Boonsboro far to the right, goes to Sharpsburg. A road on the right, known as the Old Hagerstown Road, passes up a ravine in the mountain about a mile from the National road and, bending to the left over and along the first crest, enters the National road just east of the Mountain House. By the National road the summit of the Gap is reached by easy grades. On the east side of the mountain, on either side of the road, almost to the very summit, the land was cleared and under cultivation. At the summit, on the south side of the road, is the Mountain House or old Inn, a famous hostelry of the olden days, when stage-coach and wagon formed the chief means of communication between Baltimore and Wheeling.

Some years after the war Mrs. Dahlgren, widow of Adm. John A. Dahlgren, purchased the Mountain House and much of the surrounding field and forest. The house was renovated, the field and forest improved, and a charming summer home established. North of the road and nearly opposite the house a modest memorial chapel was erected, in which were placed the remains of Adm. Dahlgren and Col. Ulric Dahlgren. In May 1898, the remains of Mrs. Dahlgren were laid to rest by the side of those of her husband and son.[1]

From the opposition displayed by the Confederates to his advance from Frederick, on the 13th, Pleasonton was convinced that they would make a determined stand at Turner's Gap, with an accession of force, and called upon Burnside for infantry support; awaiting its arrival he utilized the declining hours of the day (the 13th), by sending some dismounted cavalry up the mountain, on the right of the National road, to examine the position. This brought on some skirmish and caused the Confederates to concentrate on that flank. Pleasonton learned of the two roads, one on the right, another to the left of the Gap, both entering the National road beyond it, and favoring the movement of turning both flanks of the Confederate position. As the infantry support requested of Burnside did not come up on the 13th, Pleasonton made no effort to force the Gap and bivouacked in the valley, near its foot.[2]

---

1   Carman's description of the terrain follows the pattern established earlier in the manuscript. The "Mountain House" as Carman called it, is today a restaurant and the postwar chapel is restored. Carman is mistaken, however: Ulric was never buried there. For more information, see generally, Eric J. Wittenberg, *Like a Meteor Blazing Brightly: The Short but Controversial Life of Colonel Ulric Dahlgren* (Roseville MN: Edinborough Press, 2009).

2   See Pleasonton's report, *OR* 19, pt. 1, pp. 209-10.

Early on the morning of the 14th Pleasonton renewed his reconnaissance of the Gap and soon ascertained that the Confederates were in some force, upon which he awaited the arrival of infantry. Meanwhile Benjamin's and Gibson's batteries had come up to within a short distance of Bolivar and took position to the left of the National road, on a high knoll, about a half mile beyond the forks of the Old Sharpsburg road with the turnpike, commanding a portion of the Gap, and began an engagement with the Confederate artillery well up in the Gap.[3] Later in the day McMullin's Ohio battery came up and engaged the Confederates, about a mile distant.

General J. D. Cox, commanding the Kanawha Division, of the Ninth Corps, bivouacked on the night of the 13th, a little west of Middletown. He did not receive an order from Burnside to support Pleasonton on the evening of the 13th, as Pleasonton was led to believe, but was ordered that evening to support him with a brigade next morning. Cox detailed the brigade, commanded by Colonel E. P. Scammon, to report to Pleasonton and, at 6 a. m., Sunday, September 14th, it left camp and marched out on the National road. The brigade consisted of the 12th, 23d and 30th Ohio regiments and numbered nearly 1500 men. Cox was on the road when Scammon marched out and, impelled by a laudable curiosity, to know how Pleasonton intended to use the brigade, rode forward with Scammon, when, just after crossing Catoctin Creek, he was greatly surprised to see, standing at the road is Colonel Moor, who, two days before, had been taken prisoner in the streets of Frederick. Cox asked for an explanation and Moor replied that he had been paroled and was on the way back to the Union camps. Upon learning that the object of Scammon's movement was a reconnaissance into the Gap, Moor made an involuntary start and uttered an unintended note of warning, then, remembering that he was under parole, checked himself and turned away.[4]

The incident was not lost on Cox, who now realized that there was more serious work to be done by his brigade than merely supporting a cavalry reconnaissance. He says:

> I galloped to Scammon and told him that I should follow him in close support with Crook's Brigade, and as I went back along the column I spoke to each regimental commander, warning them to be prepared for anything, big or little,—it might be a skirmish, it might be a battle. Hurrying back to the camp, I ordered Crook to turn out his brigade prepared to march at once. I then wrote a dispatch to General Reno, saying

3   Cox, B&L, p. 585, and Burnside's report, *ibid.*, p. 417.

4   Cox, *ibid.*, pp. 585-6, and Cox, Reminiscences, p. 280.

I suspected we should find the enemy in force on the mountain-top, and should go forward with both brigades instead of sending one. Starting a courier with this, I rode forward to find Pleasonton, who was about a mile in front of my camp, where the old Sharpsburg road leaves the turnpike. I found that he was convinced that the enemy's position in the gap was too strong to be carried by a direct attack, and that he had determined to let his horsemen demonstrate on the main road, supporting the batteries (Benjamin's and Gibson's) while Scammon should march by the Sharpsburg road and try to reach the flank of the force on the summit. Telling him of my suspicion as to the enemy, I also informed him that I had determined to support Scammon with Crook, and if it became necessary to fight with the whole division I should do so, in which case I should assume the responsibility myself as his superior officer. To this he cordially assented.

One of my batteries (Simmonds') contained a section of 20-pounder Parrotts, and as these were too heavy to take up the rough mountain road, I ordered them to go into action beside Benjamin's battery, near the turnpike, and to remain with it till further orders. Our artillery at this time was occupying a knoll about a half mile in front of the forks of the road, and was exchanging shots with a battery of the enemy well up toward the gap. It was about half past 7 o'clock when Crook's column filed off on the old Sharpsburg road, Scammon's having perhaps half an hour's start. We had fully two miles to go before we should reach the place where our attack was made and, as it was a pretty steep road, the men marched slowly with frequent rests. On our way up we were overtaken by my courier who had returned from Reno with approval of my action, and the assurance that the rest of the Ninth Corps would come forward to my support."[5]

The engagement about to be opened by Cox was confined entirely to the south of the National road. It began early in the day and continued until after dark and shall be first considered.

When General Cox left the column, to order out Crook's Brigade, Scammon continued the march and reported to Pleasonton, on the National road, about a mile beyond the Catoctin. By this time Pleasonton had come to the conclusion to send him to the left, by the old Sharpsburg road, to feel the enemy and ascertain whether they held the crest of South Mountain, on that side, in any considerable force. About 7 a. m. Scammon turned off the National road at Ripp's and taking a cross road, passing a school house, entered the old Sharpsburg road, which was followed a quarter of a mile beyond Mentzer's Mill, when an artillery shot from the summit of the mountain, revealed the presence of an enemy and compelled more caution in movement. A detachment of the 30th Ohio continued the direct

5   *Ibid.*, p. 586.

movement up the mountain by the main road, and the main column turned off, at what is now the Reno school house, into a country road, leading still farther to the left and running nearly parallel to the crest of the mountain. It had the advantage of cover of the forest. When the head of the column reached the extreme southern limit of the open fields south of the gap on the east slope of the mountain, the 23d Ohio, Lieutenant-Colonel Rutherford B. Hayes, was deployed to the left to move through the woods on the left of the road and up to the crest of the mountain, gaining, if possible, the enemy's right to attack and turn it. The remainder of the brigade advanced on Hayes' right and rear, the 12th Ohio, Colonel C. B. White, in the center, and the 30th Ohio, Colonel Hugh Ewing, on the right. The entire line soon became engaged with an enemy, whose preparation we now note.[6]

We have seen that General D. H. Hill, with five brigades, was halted near Boonsboro, on the night of the 10th, to guard the wagon trains and park of artillery of the Confederate army and to watch all the roads leading from Harper's Ferry up Pleasant Valley. This required a considerable separation of his command on the various roads; his headquarters were about the center of his five brigades, and not less than three miles from Turner's Gap. As Stuart, with his cavalry, had been charged with the duty of observing the movements and checking the advance of the Union army, Hill did not consider it necessary to leave any infantry to defend the Gap but, when, on the forenoon of the 13th, he received a message from Stuart that he was being pushed back by two brigades of Union infantry, and requesting that a brigade of infantry be sent back to check the Union pursuit at Turner's Gap, Hill sent him the two brigades of Garland and Colquitt and the batteries of Bondurant and Lane, of four guns each, and it was the presence of this force that caused Pleasonton to pause in his advance on the evening of that day and call upon Burnside for a brigade of infantry.[7]

---

6  Carman did not state how he knew the details of Scammon's route, but he was a friend of Rutherford B. Hayes and visited him many times. Hayes was there, so he may have told Carman the details. The places mentioned are in the OR *Atlas*, Plate XXVII, 3, which shows the battle of South Mountain and the roads near it. The troops and movements are found in Scammon's report, OR 19, pt. 1, pp. 461-2, and the cannon shot alerting the Union soldiers is found in a letter from R. B. Wilson, 12th Ohio Infantry, Library of Congress, Manuscript Division, Ezra Carman Papers. The 23rd Ohio leading the column is also confirmed in a letter to Carman from President Rutherford B. Hayes, on Executive Mansion stationery, NYPL, Box 10, Folder 23.

7  D. H. Hill, *B&L*, p. 560. Hill's *OR* report is vague, but other sources show the second brigade, Garland's, was not sent until later in the evening and did not arrive at the Mountain House until the morning of the 14th. Garland did, however, go up to the Mountain House and spoke with D. H. Hill that night. See McRae's report, *ibid.*, 19, pt. 1, p. 1,039; and George Grattan, "Battle of Boonsboro Gap or South Mountain," *SHSP*, 39 (April 1914), pp. 37-8. Although not printed until after Carman was dead, it is obvious that Carman knew of Grattan's

At the same time Hill ordered the three other brigades to be drawn in nearer to Boonsboro and directed Ripley to send, at daybreak next morning, a regiment to hold the Hamburg Pass road, between two and three miles north of Turner's Gap. About midnight Hill received a note from General Lee saying that he was not satisfied with the condition of things on the National road and directing him to go in person to Turner's Gap, next morning, and assist Stuart in its defense. Hill made an early start and, upon reaching the Mountain House, at the summit of the Gap, between daylight and sunrise of the 14th, received a message from Stuart that he had gone to Crampton's Gap. The cavalry pickets had all been withdrawn and, as far as Hill then knew, Stuart had taken all his command with him. Garland's Brigade was found at the Mountain House and Colquitt's at the foot of the mountain, on the east side, without cavalry videttes in front, and with no information of the Union forces but under the impression that they had retired, when, in fact, says Hill: "General Cox's Federal division was at that very time marching up the old Sharpsburg or Braddock road, a mile to the south, seizing the heights on our right and establishing those heavy batteries which afterwards commanded the pike and all the approaches to it."[8]

Nor did Hill know of or suspect this movement and he was ignorant of the topography of the country. He has been criticized as being slow to learn the character of his surroundings and for not accompanying his two brigades to the mountain on the afternoon of the 13th, and examining the ground upon which, it was probable, he would be called upon to fight. He had, however, depended entirely upon Stuart to defend his rear, and Stuart parries criticism by reporting that the Gap was no place for cavalry operations; that he had put Hill's two brigades in position, directed Rosser with a detachment of cavalry and the Stuart Horse Artillery, to occupy Braddock's Gap and then started to join the main position of his command at Crampton's Gap. He says:

---

account. Grattan also mentioned in the article that he corresponding with Carman. Several Grattan letters appear in the various repositories, and it is obvious that the position description came from these letters. E. M. Dugand, 5th North Carolina Infantry, to John A. Gould, April 1892, "We arrived at the gap at sunrise. . ." NYPL Carman Papers, Box 9, Folder 2.

8   Ripley sent the 4th Georgia Infantry to guard what he called "Hamburg Pass." This slight gap in South Mountain is shown on local maps as Orr's Gap, after a nearby property owner. Apparently Ripley confused this gap with a gap ten miles to the east in Catoctin Mountain, where a village named Hamburg was located. See Ripley's report, *OR* 19, pt. 1, p. 1,031, Dennis Griffith map of Maryland 1794, and Varle Map 1808 (Washington County Free Library). Historians seem to have perpetuated this mistake. In addition to the direct quote, much of this paragraph comes from Hill, *B&L*, pp. 560-1.

I had not, up to this time, seen General D. H. Hill, but about midnight he sent General Ripley to me to get information concerning roads and gaps in the locality where General Hill had been lying for two days with his command. All the information I had was cheerfully given, and the situation of the gaps explained by maps. I confidently hoped by this time to have received the information which was expected from Brig. Gen. Fitz Lee. All the information I possessed, or had the means of possessing, had been laid before General D. H. Hill and the commanding general. His troops were duly notified of the advance of the enemy, and I saw them in line of battle awaiting his approach, and, myself, gave some general directions concerning the location of his lines during the afternoon, in his absence."[9]

Once on the ground, it took Hill but a hasty examination to decide that the Gap could only be held by a force larger than he had at his disposal and was wholly indefensible by a small one. General Lee was so informed and Hill ordered up General George B. Anderson's Brigade back near the summit and ordered it in line of battle, on either side of the National Road, three regiments on the right and two on the left.[10] Having posted Colquitt across the road, he then rode to the right, on a ridge road, to reconnoiter and, much to his surprise, found Colonel Thomas L. Rosser with the 5th Virginia Cavalry and two guns of Pelham's Battery, guarding Fox's Gap on the old Sharpsburg or Braddock road. Rosser had been ordered to that point by Stuart, who had not informed Hill of the fact, nor had Rosser been told that he would have infantry support. While here Hill became convinced that there were movements of troops on the mountain side below, screened from view by the forest, and, at the foot of the mountain, Cox's men could be seen advancing.

This was a menacing condition of affairs and Hill took measures to meet it. He rode back to the Mountain House and found Garland prepared for action. That gallant and enterprising officer had heard the report of a gun on the right front and the hurtling of a shell, and put his brigade under arms. Hill explained the situation to him and ordered him to sweep through the woods, on the right, to the old Sharpsburg road and hold it all hazards, as the safety of Lee's large trains depended upon its retention. He had already ordered up George B. Anderson to assist Colquitt and Garland, but was reluctant to order up Ripley and Rodes from the

---

9   Stuart's report, OR 19, pt. 1, p. 817. Carman made no comment, but it appears that Hill and Stuart were not acting in complete concert on the night of September 13. Hill's tone in his B&L account, pp. 560-1, is mildly critical.

10  Carman confused George B. Anderson's Brigade, perhaps with Garland's Brigade. Anderson only had four regiments, and he could not have posted five regiments as Carman described. See Chapter Eleven, which contains the Order of Battle for the two armies.

important points held by them near Boonsboro, until something definite was known of the strength and designs of the Union advance.[11]

From the National road or turnpike, at the Mountain House, where Garland was drawn up, a rough road runs southerly, first on the east slope and then along the crest of the mountain, nearly a mile, where it is intersected, at right angles, by a road diverging from the National road, about a mile west of Middletown. This road was followed by General Braddock in his march on Fort Duquesne, in 1755, and for many years was known as the Braddock road, later it became known as the old Sharpsburg road. The point where this road intersects the road on the crest of the mountain is generally known as Fox's Gap—sometimes as Braddock's Gap.[12]

About three-quarters of a mile beyond Fox's Gap, another road reaches the mountain top and connects with the crest road. This road branches from the old Sharpsburg road at the foot of the mountain, runs southerly some distance along its base and reaches the crest by a northwest course. It was by this road that Scammon marched. From Fox's Gap the crest road runs southerly a half mile, then follows the terrain of the mountain westerly, a quarter of a mile, and intersects the road reaching the crest by the northwest course, and at the point of this intersection on the crest, several wagon roads and trails lead down the west side of the mountain, into the valley south of Boonsboro. West of the crest road there is a slight depression beyond which are spurs and ridges covered by a dense forest. In front of Fox's Gap, and between it and the roads farther south, is a plateau of open ground; at the time some was wheat stubble, some in corn and some in grass. The ground sloping eastward from this plateau was open and under cultivation and heavy stone fences separated many of the fields.[13]

Garland's orders were to move quickly to the right and defend Fox's Gap and the road south of it, where it crossed the mountain. He was immediately in motion and, passing through the first belt of woods, south of the National road, found Rosser and, after a short conference with him, formed line. He had five regiments of North Carolina infantry, aggregating about 1000 men, and Bondurant's Alabama battery of four guns. The 5th North Carolina was placed on the left [right], north of

---

11  Hill, *B&L*, pp. 561-2. Hill's postwar memoirs make it clear that Hill did not know Rosser was at Fox's Gap. Hill's report, *OR* 19, pt. 1, p. 1,020, states that "Rosser, who had reported to me," is ambiguous. Likely, only later in the day did Hill learn of Rosser's presence there.

12  This description is from Jacob Cox, *Military Reminiscences of the Civil War* (New York: Charles Scribner & Sons, 1900), pp. 281-2.

13  This byroad, viable in its day for horses and artillery, was noted by Cox in his book, *ibid.*, p. 282 and in his *B&L* article, p. 587. The rest of the description is similar to Col. Duncan McRae's in *OR* 19, pt. 1, pp. 1,039-40. Part of the crest road is now the path of the Appalacian Trail.

the farther road and quite near it. The 12th and 23d North Carolina were on the left of the 5th on the mountain or crest road, the 12th on the open ground, the 23d behind a low stone wall. These three regiments filled the line between the two roads crossing the mountain south of Turner's Gap. Then came the 20th and 13th North Carolina on the left, north of Fox's Gap. From the nature of the ground and the duty to be performed by an inadequate force, the regiments were not in contact with each other, the 13th being 250 yards to the left of the 20th. There were intervals between the regiments south of Fox's Gap also, but this part of the line was strengthened by Bondurant's Alabama battery of four guns, which took position near the right, in a small clearing with a stone fence on either flank. Later, as we shall see, the 20th and 13th North Carolina were moved to the right, south of the Gap, but the interval between them was not closed.[14]

Garland and Colonel D. K. McRae, commanding 5th North Carolina, went forward to reconnoiter. McRae reports:

> Immediately in front of the ridge road were stubble fields and cornfields, and, for about forty paces to the front, a plateau, which suddenly broke on the left into a succession of ravines, and, farther beyond and in front a ravine, of greater length and depth, extended from the road which ran along the base of the mountain far out into the fields, and, connected with the ravine on our left, formed natural parallel approaches to our position. Between and beyond these ravines to our right was a dense growth of small forest trees and mountain laurel, through which the intersecting road ran for some distance, and on the mountain side to the top this growth was continued. General Garland and I had been but a few moments in the field when our attention was directed to persons moving at some distance on this road, and, apprehending that the enemy might be preparing to make a lodgment upon the mountain side, he ordered me to advance a body of fifty skirmishers into the woods to our right oblique front to go as far as possible to explore. This was done, and they had not passed fifty steps ... when they encountered the enemy's skirmishers and the fight commenced."[15]

The skirmishers then encountered were those of the 23d Ohio and the time was 9 a. m. Hayes was moving through the woods on the left of the road, by the

14 The placement of the 5th North Carolina is an error by Carman, who obviously meant the "right." Hill, *B&L*, p. 563. See also McRae, *OR* 19, pt. 1, p. 1,040. Bondurant's position description is from a letter by John Purifoy dated July 15, 1899, LOC, Carman Papers.

15 McRae's report, *OR* 19, pt. 1, p. 1,040.

right flank, one company deployed in front as skirmishers, one on the right and another on the left as flankers.[16]

As soon as the skirmish lines became engaged Garland ordered McRae to support those of the 5th North Carolina and McRae led his entire regiment forward. The forest growth of small trees was so dense that it was almost impossible to advance in line of battle, and, as he cleared some of it, coming into partly open ground and approaching the near edge of another woods, he was met by the advance of the 23d Ohio. Hayes had seen McRae coming down hill on his right, and, while yet in the woods, faced his regiment by the rear rank and pushed through the thicket and over the rocky, broken ground to meet the advancing 5th North Carolina. The skirmishing at close quarters was very severe, many falling on both sides. As the skirmishing soon involved his whole regiment, Hayes ordered an advance, which was quickly responded to, and some conscripts on the right of the 5th North Carolina, never before under fire, fled from the field, upon which McRae fell back a short distance. Hayes halted, reformed line, and the engagement was soon resumed and became so hot that he ordered a charge, which was made in gallant style, driving the Confederates clear out of the woods, the 5th North Carolina falling back to its original position. While this was transpiring, the 12th North Carolina, numbering about 70 men, came to the support of the 5th North Carolina, gave one wild volley and retreated in disorder. About half the regiment halted on the line of the 13th North Carolina and continued with it the remainder of the day. The 23d North Carolina now advanced from the crest road about 40 yards into the field in front of the 23d Ohio, and, under cover of a hedge row and an old stone fence, partly fallen down, opened with some effect upon it and upon the 12th Ohio on the right of the 23d. This advance of the 23d North Carolina was followed by Garland's order to the 20th and 13th North Carolina to move from the left to the right to support the 5th North Carolina.[17]

The 23d Ohio halted at a stone fence, just out of the woods, and kept up a brisk fire upon the 23d North Carolina behind the old stone fence, on an opposite hill, not more than 100 yards distant. Its loss was heavy, among the wounded was its gallant commander. Soon after giving the command to charge, and when but a few

16 The information about skirmisher and flank companies is inferred in R. B. Wilson's letters and maps, July 11 and 22, 1899, NA-AS, but not directly stated. It is confirmed by Hayes's memoirs of South Mountain sent to Carman. See Hayes, undated letter, NYPL Collection, Box 10, Folder 23.

17 The description of the fighting comes from the reports of Scammon's brigade, *OR* 19, pt. 1, pp. 461-2; Hugh Ewing, *ibid.*, p. 469; James M. Comley, *ibid.*, pp. 466-7; Carr White, *ibid.*, pp. 464-5; and McRae, *ibid.*, p. 1,040.

yards out of the woods, Hayes was severely wounded, a musket ball shattering the bone of his left arm, above the elbow, but he remained in command. Weak from loss of blood, he was compelled to lie down. Fearing an attack on the left he ordered his regiment to leave the stone fence and fall back to the edge of the woods. In falling back he was left in the field; requesting to be carried back a few men stepped out of the woods for that purpose, but drew upon themselves such a heavy fire from the 23d North Carolina that Hayes ordered them back. A few moments later Lieutenant Benjamin W. Jackson ran forward, brought his wounded commander back into the woods and laid him down behind a log. Here he relinquished the command to Major J. M. Comly; had his wound dressed and walked to the Widow Coogle house, near a mile distant, and taken to Middletown.[18]

On the right of the 23d, and in the center of the brigade line, was the 12th Ohio, which, after moving nearly a fourth of a mile through a pine wood, was obliged to advance over open pasture ground, under a most galling fire from the 23d North Carolina. It was halted and ordered to lie down for shelter and await the coming up of the 30th Ohio on its right, when a general advance of the entire brigade was to be made.

The movement convinced McRae that a strong Union force had been massed in the woods, with the intention to turn his right, and he suggested that the woods be shelled, but there were no guns available, as Bondurant's Battery had been so heavily pressed by the Ohio skirmishers, who advanced to the stone fence on its right and opened fire on its flank, that Garland ordered it away. Garland now rode to the left to bring up the 20th and 13th North Carolina, that he had ordered to the support of the 5th. He met these two regiments after they had crossed the Sharpsburg road, when, perceiving that some of the skirmishers of the 30th Ohio were apparently endeavoring to turn the left of his line, he halted the 13th North Carolina at the Wise house, and the 20th North Carolina 250 yards farther to the right. The 13th was in an open field, upon the brow of a hill and, immediately in front of it, in a dense wood, were the Ohio skirmishers, some of whom, farther to the left, were threatening the flank of the 13th. Not being able to see those in the

---

18 Carman may have been deceived here by "old soldier's stories." It is unlikely from reading the reports mentioned in the previous footnote that the like-numbered regiments ever directly opposed one another. Carman described Rutherford B. Hayes's wounding in words strikingly similar to his diary, which was not published until 1922, but was taken from Hayes's undated memoir. See NYPL Carman Papers, Box 10, Folder 23. The "Widow Koolge house" (Carman's spelling is incorrect, but is more correct than Hayes's diary, which has "Kugler"), where Hayes was taken, is shown on OR *Atlas* Plate XXVII-3. See Charles R. Williams, ed., *Diary and Letters of Rutherford B. Hayes, Nineteenth President of the United States* (Columbus: Ohio State Archeological & Historical Society, 1922), vol. 2, p. 357.

immediate front the whole fire of the 13th was directed upon those on the left, who were driven from that part of the field, but while thus engaged the Ohio skirmishers in front poured in a hot fire by which General Garland was mortally wounded. Garland was a fine soldier of whom D. H. Hill says: "I never knew a truer, better, braver man. Had he lived, his talent, pluck, energy, and purity of character must have put him in the front rank of his profession, whether in civil or military life."[19]

Not deeming it prudent to advance down the hill, into the woods, in face of an enemy supposed to be very strong, and it being very much exposed, the 13th North Carolina was withdrawn about 50 yards from the brow of the hill, which brought it in advance of and to the right of the Wise house.[20]

Upon the fall of Garland the command passed to Colonel McRae. As soon as he saw the condition of affairs, and had been convinced of the enemy's determination to turn both his flanks, he notified D. H. Hill that the force at his disposal was wholly inadequate to hold the position. Very soon thereafter Colonel C. C. Tew, with the 2d and 4th North Carolina, of General George B. Anderson's Brigade, reported to McRae, and was about taking position on the immediate left of the 13th, when he received an order from Anderson to move off to the left. Hill was advised of this movement and of the wide gap thus made in the line, and McRae, believing that he would immediately respond by sending troops to fill it, in anticipation of their arrival, ordered the 13th North Carolina to follow Tew to the left and keep connection with him. McRae then rode to the right, intending if time allowed, to move the 5th North Carolina to the left and with it fill the vacant space in the line, but found, that, under a previous order given by him, this regiment had already been advanced into the field, on the right of the 23d, and it was then dangerous to withdraw it.[21]

While dispositions were being [made] on both sides, during which there was a comparative lull, a section of McMullin's Battery, under Lieutenant George L. Crome, was advanced by hand to the top of the slope, in front of the 12th Ohio, and opened fire on the 20th North Carolina, in position behind a stone fence about 400 yards distant. The position of the section was an exposed one, the men were soon struck down, and the skirmishers of the Carolina regiment, under Captain James B. Atwell, killed the gallant Crome as he was sighting a gun. After firing but

---

19  See McRae's report, *OR* 19, pt. 1, pp. 1,040-41, and Col. Thomas Ruffin Jr.'s report, *ibid.*, pp. 1045-6. Hill's quote, and much of this wording, is from his *B&L* article, p. 562.

20  This is almost a direct quote from Ruffin's report, *OR* 19, pt. 1, p. 1,046.

21  This paragraph is directly quoted from McRae's report, *ibid.*, p. 1,041.

four rounds of canister the guns were abandoned, but the Confederates were unable to capture them.[22]

Of the Confederates at this time Colonel McRae reports:

> The 5th North Carolina, on the extreme right, was nearest the intersecting road, which was threatened. It was advanced into the field, sheltered in some degree by a fence, which ran perpendicularly to its line next in the field, under cover of the piles of stones, was the 23d North Carolina. Back on the ridge road to the left and rear of the 23d, was the 20th North Carolina. This regiment could not be advanced with the others because of the exposed position and because this would discover to the enemy at once the vacuum in our line. Between this and the 13th North Carolina was the open space which I had been anxious to fill."[23]

The skirmishers of the 30th Ohio, after persistent efforts against those of the 13th North Carolina, had now come up on the right of the 12th Ohio. Crook's Brigade, led by Cox, came up in close support to Scammon, the division was united, and Cox gave the order for a general advance of the whole line. Scammon moved promptly with the 1400 men of his brigade, the entire line giving a loud and prolonged yell. On the left the 23d Ohio, led by Maj. J. M. Comly, sprang out of the woods, passed through a cornfield and, under a deadly volley of musketry, struck the 23d North Carolina. Many of both regiments were killed and wounded in a hand to hand contest over the stone fence, through an opening of which the Ohio men pressed. Many met death or wounds at the very muzzle of the musket. Bayonets were freely used and men on both sides fell under the cutting thrusts, among these were three North Carolinians and Sergeant Major Eugene L. Reynolds of the Ohio regiment. The contest was most obstinate and sanguinary but the North Carolina men were finally driven from the field, followed by the 23d Ohio, which established itself firmly on the crest.[24]

---

22  Hill, B&L, p. 563; Lt. Crome's death is mentioned in Capt. James R. McMullin's report, OR 19, pt. 1, p. 464, the details are from R. B. Wilson's July 22, 1899, letter in NA-AS. Carman has filled in the actions of Captain Atwell and the guns abandonment from OR 19, pt. 1, p. 1,041.

23  McRae's report, ibid., pp. 1,041-2.

24  Exact sources have not been found. The NA Battlefield Board Papers include a copy of The News and Observer (Raleigh, NC) for April 11, 1897. The article "Thirteenth Regiment (later the Twenty-Third) of Infantry," by H. C. Wall, mentions Union troops surging through a wall and bayonets and clubbed muskets used freely. The same language was in Hill, B&L, p. 566. The wording is very similar to part of Hayes's letter, and may be taken from that source. Hayes's statement mentions "3 men bayoneted by Pvt. Stevens, Co. K, and Sgt. Major Reynolds was killed by a bayonet thrust." Hayes, NYPL, Box 10, Folder 23.

On the right of the 23d, the 12th Ohio charged up the slope with the bayonet, the 20th North Carolina in its front stood firm and kept up a steady fire until the Ohio men were within a few yards, then it broke and fled over the crest into the shelter of a dense laurel thicket skirting the other side, leaving 15 to 20 dead and wounded on the field. The 12th Ohio dashed over the crest and into the thicket in pursuit, halted 300 yards beyond the crest and lay for some time under a severe fire of shell and canister.[25]

The quick overthrow of the center of Garland's Brigade, and the Union pursuit, cut off the 5th North Carolina and part of the 23d, who escaped by moving to the right and rear, thence by a circuitous route to the turnpike, where they reported to D. H. Hill. The 20th North Carolina and the greater part of the 23d rallied on the west side of the mountain and, at Rosser's request, occupied an adjacent height to support a battery which he proposed to put in position to command the old Sharpsburg road. Four regiments of Garland's brigade were now out of the fight; Hill says they had been "too roughly handled to be of any further use that day."[26]

The commander of the brigade reports that:

> The enemy...with a long extended yell, burst upon our line, surrounding the 20th on both flanks, and passing to the rear of the 23d. The distance was so short that no opportunity was given for more than a single fire, which was delivered full in the enemy's face, and with great effect, for his first line staggered and some of his forces retreated. A portion of the 23d received his advance upon their bayonets, and men on both sides fell from bayonet wounds; but the enemy's strength was overpowering, and could not be resisted. The 20th and a portion of the 23d, finding themselves surrounded, were compelled to retreat, and this they did, under a severe fire, down the mountain side."[27]

It remains to note the movements of the 30th Ohio, on the right of the brigade. This regiment was ordered to attack and turn the left of Garland's Brigade, held by the 13th North Carolina, and to seize Bondurant's Battery on that part of the line. It succeeded in driving back the heavy skirmish line and reaching the top of

---

25  Much of this paragraph is from the report of Col. White, 12th Ohio, OR 19, pt. 1, p. 464.

26  Hill, *B&L*, p. 566. Hill and Carman treated this morning fight as one continuous action. A detailed study of the reports and memoirs suggest it more complicated than that, but given that Carman was not directly charged with explaining this battle, it is not surprising that he summarized some of it.

27  McRae's report, OR 19, pt. 1, p. 1,042.

the slope in the face of showers of canister and spherical case from Bondurant's guns. Line was formed to charge the battery and its supports; the 36th Ohio of Crook's Brigade, was rushed forward as a support and formed on the right of the 30th, and an advance made, but the 13th North Carolina was so advantageously posted, so skillfully handled, and made such a determined resistance, that the Ohio men could not reach the battery, which was, however, soon driven away by the 12th Ohio, nor could they pass the plateau that lay between them and the mountain road in front.[28]

When the 12th Ohio stopped its pursuit of the Confederates in the woods, about 300 yards west of the ridge road, it came under a heavy fire from Bondurant's guns and as these could not be reached by the 30th and 36th, the 12th was ordered to charge them. The guns were near a stone fence about 600 yards to the front and right. The regiment pushed through the dense thicket, under a heavy fire, and gained the flank of the battery at a garden, enveloped by a stone fence, where a severe fight occurred, with the result that the Confederate infantry supporting the battery were driven away, leaving many prisoners with the Ohio men, but the battery escaped by the road leading to the Mountain House.[29]

While engaged in checking the advance of the 30th and 36th Ohio, Lieutenant Colonel Ruffin, commanding the 13th North Carolina, sent his adjutant to the right to see what was transpiring in that quarter. The adjutant returned with information that the center and right of the brigade had disappeared and that the Union troops had gained the ridge and were coming down from that direction; he now discovered that his left was in the air, Colonel Tew, with the two regiments of Geo. B. Anderson's brigade, having been ordered away, upon which Ruffin marched his regiment to the old Sharpsburg road and joined Anderson's right and acting under his orders the rest of the day.[30]

Hill, believing that Cox was about to advance to the Mountain House by the road, running south from it on the summit of the mountain, and having nothing to oppose him, ran two guns down from the Mountain House and opened a brisk fire on the advanced Ohio skirmishers, and a line of dismounted staff-officers, couriers, teamsters and cooks, was formed behind the guns to give the appearance of battery

28  This paragraph, although not directly quoted, is a compilation of the reports of Col. Ewing, 30th Ohio, *ibid.*, p. 469; Col. White 12th Ohio, *ibid.*, pp. 464-5; Col. Crook 36th Ohio, *ibid.*, p. 471; and Col. Ruffin, 13th North Carolina, *ibid.*, pp. 1045-6.

29  White's report, *ibid.*, p. 465, and R. B. Wilson letter, NA-AS, July 22, 1899. Wilson adds many vivid details Carman did not include.

30  Ruffin's report, *OR* 19, pt. 1, p. 1,046.

supports. He states that some of the advancing Union skirmishers encountered Colquitt's skirmishers under Capt. W. M. Arnold, and were driven back.[31]

Had Cox pressed his advantage there is little room to doubt that he could have seized and held Fox's Gap and the old Sharpsburg road; but he knew nothing of the enemy's strength; did not know what he might encounter in the woods and dense thickets lying beyond the ridge road; naturally supposed that his enemy was in force to hold the position against his small division; was ignorant of the fact that he had thoroughly disposed of four regiments of Garland's Brigade and that there was scarcely anything to oppose him; furthermore, he was moved to caution by threatening movements on both flanks. Therefore, the advance parties were recalled from the woods, the line made more compact and the expected reenforcements(sic) awaited.[32]

To meet the movement on his left, where the enemy, principally Rosser's cavalry and artillery and a few of Garland's rallied men, extended beyond the flank of the 23d Ohio and poured canister into the line, the 11th Ohio of Crook's Brigade had been moved to the left of the 23d, skirmished towards the woods, beyond the open field, and, on nearing them, received a heavy fire on its right and rear from the enemy in the woods and behind a stone fence, upon which it charged into the woods, suffering severely until relieved by the advance of the 23d Ohio. This was near the northwest corner of the open field and the opposing force was Rosser's, concerning which Hill says: " Rosser retired in better order, not, however, without having some of his men captured, and took up a position from which he could still fire upon the old road, and which he held until 10 o'clock that night."[33] This position was across the ravine by which the old Sharpsburg Road went down the west side of the mountain, and on a hill in rear of the heights at the Mountain House, where there was some open ground. On the right two 10-pounder Parrott guns of Simmond's battery, Lieutenant D. W. Glassie, were pushed forward to an

31 This is taken from Hill, *B&L*, p. 566. Hill was probably overstating the desperation of his situation, as the reports of some of Garland's regiments state meeting troops of Gen. George B. Anderson's Brigade in their retreat toward the Mountain House. McRae, *OR* 19, pt. 1, p. 1,041, and Ruffin, *ibid.*, p. 1,046. Significantly, no commander, including Hill, reported anything about the line of cooks and teamsters or confirmed the additional artillery.

32 Carman's assessment, although colored by the postwar accounts of Cox & Hill, *B&L*, pp. 587 and 567, respectively, offers good reasons for the mid-day lull on the mountain as both sides brought up fresh troops.

33 See 11th Ohio Major Lyman Jackson's report, OR 19, pt. 1, p. 472, and Cox, *Reminiscences*, p. 283. The quote is from Hill, *B&L*, p. 566. Evidently artillery fire was kept up for some time between Bondurant's (AL) Battery and Simmonds' (KY) battery. Joseph E. Walton, "At South Mountain," *National Tribune*, October 6, 1898.

open spot in the woods in front of the 30th Ohio, where they remained until the close of the battle, supported, later in the day, by Lieutenant Belcher and 100 men of the 8th Michigan, who, during the confusion of battle became separated from their brigade and reported to Cox for duty, with the request for an assignment where they could render service.[34]

Cox reports:

> The enemy made several attempts to retake the crest, advancing with great obstinacy and boldness. In the center they were at one time partially successful, but the 36th Ohio, Lieut. Col. Clark, was brought forward, and with the 12th, drove them back by a most dashing and spirited charge. The whole crest was now held by our troops as follows: the left by the 11th and 23d Ohio, the center by the 12th Ohio, supported by the 36th, formed in reserve, and the right by the 30th Ohio, supported by the 28th, Lieut. Col. G. Becker commanding."[35]

The line then formed ran diagonally across the mountain top, conforming somewhat to the shape of the ground, making the formation a hollow curve: the 11th and 23d on the left, clinging to the hill that the 23d had first carried, their line nearly parallel to the old Sharpsburg road; the right was in the air exposed to an annoying artillery fire from Pelham's guns on a hill to the northwest and from some guns near the Mountain House, also from a battery on a hill north of the turnpike. Referring to this stage of the action, Cox says:

> We had several hundred prisoners in our hands, and learned from them that D. H. Hill's Division, consisting of five brigades, was opposed to us, and that Longstreet was said to be in near support. Our own losses had not been trifling, and it seemed wise to contract our lines a little, so that we might have some reserve and hold the crest we had won till the rest of the Ninth Corps should arrive. Our left and center were strongly posted, but the right was partly across Fox's Gap, at the edge of the woods beyond Wise's house, around which there had been a fierce struggle. The 30th and 36th were therefore brought back to the crest on the hither side of the gap, where we still commanded the old Sharpsburg road, and making the 30th our right flank, the 36th and 28th were put in second line. My right then occupied the woods looking northward into Wise's fields. About noon the combat was reduced to one of artillery, and the enemy's guns had so completely the range of the sloping fields behind us that

---

34 Lt. Glassie's position is taken from Cox's report, *OR* 19, pt. 1, p. 459. The details about the men from the 8th Michigan are found *ibid.*, p. 461.

35 Cox, *ibid.*, p. 459.

their canister shot cut long furrows in the sod, with a noise like the cutting of a melon rind."[36]

In this position Cox awaited reenforcements. Meanwhile the Confederates were gathering in his front. First to arrive was G. B. Anderson's Brigade. A part of this had engaged the right of Cox's line and given some assistance to the 13th North Carolina which, as we have seen, fell in on Anderson's right, in the old Sharpsburg road. Anderson's men did not become seriously engaged; they did some skirmishing late in the forenoon during which a few men of the 30th North Carolina were wounded.[37]

Ripley followed G. B. Anderson. At 9 a. m., while occupying a position northeast of Boonsboro, he received an order from Hill to send forward his artillery. A few minutes later came an urgent order to march his brigade to Turner's Gap. Upon arriving at the Mountain House, with the 1st and 3d North Carolina and 44th Georgia, Hill directed him to move on the ridge road and form on Anderson's left. He found Anderson in the Old Sharpsburg road, his left at the Wise house, and it was arranged that Anderson should extend farther to the right and make room for Ripley on his left, then the two were to advance and attack the Union line, then occupying the crest of the ridge to the south.[38]

While making these dispositions Hill came up with G. T. Anderson's and Drayton's brigades, the advance of Longstreet's command, which had arrived at the Mountain House about 3.30 p. m. and reported to Hill. The two brigades aggregated about 1900 men. As Hill was very anxious to dispose of the Union force on his right, before the main attack, which he apprehended would be made on his left, north of the National road, these brigades were ordered to move to the right until they came to Rosser's first position, or reached Ripley's left, when they were to come to a front and, marching in line of battle, Ripley on their right, sweep

---

36 This information, and the disposition of troops preceding the quotation, is Cox, *B&L*, p. 587.

37 Maj. William Sillers's report, *OR* 19, pt. 1, p. 1,051, lists one officer and three privates wounded. Evidence from sources other than Sillers, including Col. Bryan Grimes of the 4th North Carolina, suggest that the two regiments, the 2nd and 4th North Carolina, were hotly engaged in the late morning near the Wise Cabin. Walter Clark, *Histories of the Several Regiments and Battalions from North Carolina in the Great War*, 5 Vols. (Raleigh: Uzzell, Printer and Binder, 1901), 1, p. 266, and Grimes' report, *OR* 19, pt. 1, p. 1,049. Why Carman chose only Sillers's report to document this statement in unknown.

38 Gen. Roswell Ripley's report, *ibid.*, pp. 1,031-2. The other regiment in the brigade, the 4th Georgia, was detached earlier to guard "Hamburg Pass," actually Orr's Gap, north of Turner's Gap.

everything before them, and, to facilitate the movement, a battery was brought forward and shelled the woods in various directions. After these directions had been given and the advance was moving off by the flank, Hill concluded to accompany it and upon reaching Ripley's position, in the old Sharpsburg road, called Ripley, G. T. Anderson, and Drayton together and again gave the nature of the movement that he wished executed. He ordered G. B. Anderson and Ripley to extend still farther to the right, to make room in the Sharpsburg road for G. T. Anderson and Drayton, and then returned to the Mountain House to await the coming of Lee and Longstreet, leaving Ripley in command of the four brigades—G. B. Anderson's, Ripley's, G. T. Anderson's and Drayton's, and in the order named from right to left—with instructions to make the advance and a vigorous attack as soon as the brigades were properly formed. G. B. Anderson and Ripley had moved some distance to the right, G. T. Anderson was moving to overtake Ripley's left and had opened an interval of nearly 300 yards between his left and Drayton's right, when Drayton, not yet in position, was attacked.[39]

We return to the Union preparations for this attack. When Cox notified Reno, early in the morning, that he was going forward with his entire division, instead of one brigade as had been ordered, and that there was a probability that the enemy would be encountered at the mountain top, he was promptly assured by Reno that the rest of the Ninth Corps would move forward to his support. The first to move was Willcox's Division, which, on the night of the 13th, bivouacked a mile and a half east of Middletown. At 8 a. m. it was on the march by the National road and, near Bolivar, Cox advised Willcox to consult Pleasonton as to taking position. Pleasonton indicated an attack along the slope of the mountain, on the north of the National road and Willcox marched on and formed for an attack upon the wooded spur southeast of the Mountain House, when Burnside rode up and ordered him to withdraw, cross over to the Sharpsburg road, march up it and take position near Cox.[40]

Much valuable time was lost and it was 2 o'clock when Willcox came up and found Cox a few hundred yards to the left of the road, skirmishing with the enemy on the wooded slope. He halted on the road where it turns to the left, and where the mountain slopes down toward the National road, on the right, which he looked

---

39 The details of these dispositions are taken from Hill's report, OR 19, pt. 1, p. 1,020.

40 Gen. Orlando B. Willcox's report, cited by Carman, is found *ibid.*, pp. 427-8. Cox's "correction" to Willcox's report is from Cox, *B&L*, pp. 587-8. Carman added: "In stating this movement, we have followed Willcox's report. Cox says Willcox movement to the north of the National road was because of "a mistake in the delivery of a message to him," and that he was "recalled and given the right direction by Reno, who had arrived at Pleasonton's headquarters."

down upon. His left was covered by the eastern slope of the mountain. Under Cox's direction he sent the 8th Michigan, Lieutenant-Colonel Frank Graves, and the 50th Pennsylvania, Major Edward Overton, to follow up Cox's line on the left, and, with the rest of his division, was about taking position on the immediate right of Cox, facing the summit, when he received an order from Reno to take position overlooking the Sharpsburg road, his left near Cox's right but his line drawn back at nearly right angles to it.[41]

Meanwhile a section of Cook's Massachusetts Battery had been advanced near to the turn of the road, and at the angle of the line made by Cox and Willcox, about 400 yards from the summit, and opened fire upon Lane's Georgia Battery, about a mile distant, across the National road. After a few good shots one of Cook's guns became disabled, and another was going up the road to replace it, when the Confederates opened a rapid and heavy fire of canister and shell from Bondurant's battery, in a small field partially surrounded by woods, near the Wise house. This sudden and unexpected fire at less than 600 yards drove some of Cook's men from their guns, the drivers with the limbers went wildly to the rear, down the narrow, gullied road, and through the ranks of the 17th Michigan and other troops in it, creating great confusion, which was increased by the exploding shells that followed the sudden stampede. Cook and some of his men stood some time by the guns, but, unable to serve them, after a loss of 1 killed and 4 wounded, they were abandoned, Cook ordering his men to the shelter of the woods on the slope of the hill.[42]

This sudden attack came when the entire division was in motion, changing position, and a temporary panic was the result, which was stayed by the exertion of the officers and the prompt transfer of the 79th New York and 17th Michigan, from the left to right, to face the enemy, who were so close that it was thought a charge on Cook's guns was contemplated. Cox, who was senior officer on the line ordered Wilcox to close in on his (Cox's) right and make the line continuous at the same time holding strongly the Sharpsburg road, upon which Willcox made a new disposition of his division. The 79th New York, Colonel David Morrison, was advanced to a stone fence on the left of the road and of Cook's guns, the 17th

---

41 Willcox's report, OR 19, pt. 1, pp. 427-8. The "valuable time lost" remark is understood more fully by reading Willcox's explanation of the travels of his division. Coincidently, Willcox was preparing a charge up the National Road against Colquitt's small brigade when he was recalled to march to Fox's Gap. Had the attack been made as intended, it might have dramatically changed the course and outcome of the battle.

42 Most of this information came from Capt. Asa Cook's report, *ibid.*, pp. 433-4, with Carman supplying the information on their opponents. The "stampede" is mentioned in John Robertson's *Michigan in the War* (Lansing: W.S. George & Co. State Printers and Binders, 1882), p. 375. Carman may have used this source to augment the drama of the situation.

Michigan, Colonel W. H. Withington, being in great part to the right of the road and a little to the rear of the guns. Welsh's Brigade formed on the left of the road, the right of the 45th Pennsylvania, Lieutenant Colonel John I. Curtin, resting on the road, the 46th New York, Lieutenant Colonel Joseph Gerhardt, on its left, extending to the right of Cox's Division. Christ's Brigade formed on Welsh's right, across the Sharpsburg road. The 100th Pennsylvania, coming up later, was held in reserve. The entire division was now under cover of the hill-side, at the eastern edge of the wood looking into the open ground at Fox's Gap, and two companies of the 45th Pennsylvania went forward to reconnoiter, preparatory to swinging forward the right of the line up to the wooded hills running south from the Mountain House. Upon reaching the top of the hill, the Pennsylvanians saw the Confederates in force; a battery commanding the approach, and infantry, covered by trees and stone-fences, supporting the battery.[43]

The Confederate force was Drayton's Brigade, which we left coming on the field, and had taken position at and around the Wise house, availing itself of the stone fences at and on both sides of the house. The road from the Mountain House comes into the Sharpsburg road at the Wise house. From the house northward about 550 yards this road was bounded on the east by a stone fence three feet high, overlooking cleared fields on the east, the summit of the mountain being in these fields, beyond which was another stone fence, running northeast from the Sharpsburg road, but not visible from the fence on the Mountain House road, the slight ridge forming the summit intervening. On the south side of the Sharpsburg road, 40 yards east from where the Mountain House road comes into it, commences a lane or ridge road running southerly. For about 300 yards this narrow lane was flanked on both sides by stone fences, then a single stone fence ran nearly its entire length, separating the woods from the cleared fields. East of the double stone-walled lane was a cleared field of about four acres, bounded on the north by the Sharpsburg road, and on the east and south by forest. West of the lane was a garden of about one acre, bounded on the east, south and west by a stone fence, and on the north by an ordinary rail fence, running along the Sharpsburg road, and in this garden was the Wise house—a small log cabin—a few feet from the road. Directly north of the Wise house, across the Sharpsburg road, was a partially cleared spot of about an acre, in which was Bondurant's Battery. It was behind these stone fences, running north and south from the Sharpsburg road, at the Wise house, and behind the garden fences that Drayton formed, and sent a heavy body of

43 Carman compiled the reports of Willcox, OR 19, pt. 1, p. 428; Col. Benjamin Christ, a brigade commander, ibid., p. 437; and Col. Thomas Welsh, 45th Pennsylvania, also commanding a brigade, ibid., pp. 439-40, to create this summary.

skirmishers well to the front—to the stone fence beyond the field north of the Sharpsburg road, and into the woods east of the small field south of the Sharpsburg road, the Wise field.[44]

Meanwhile the Confederate guns had kept up a furious fire of canister and shell, to escape which their opponents lay close to the ground. The shot rattled against the stone wall, behind which lay the 79th New York, knocking the stones about, and those which went over made gaps, here and there, in the lines of the reinforcing troops as they came up. Willcox soon received an order to silence the guns in his front, and proposed to do so by a charge of the 79th New York directly upon them, but, on seeing the thin line of the regiment, and recognizing the fact that a strong infantry force was supporting the guns, concluded to relieve the 79th New York by the 45th Pennsylvania, a larger regiment, and deploy the 17th Michigan, a new, large, regiment, on the right of the road, and move it on the flank of the guns, and to support the movement with his entire division. His dispositions were quickly made; the 45th Pennsylvania took its place behind the stone fence, the 79th New York falling to its rear as a support, the 17th Michigan formed on the right of the road and the advance was ordered. The 45th Pennsylvania leaped over the stone fence and double-quicked up the hill, the 46th New York advancing in échelon on its left. As the Pennsylvanians came to the crest of the hill they met the advancing Confederate skirmishers and the action began.[45]

After a sharp contest the Confederates were driven back to their main line, behind the stone fences, in front of the Wise house, where a determined stand was made and many Pennsylvanians laid low, for the latter were on open ground and at close quarters. The fighting was fast and furious, extending on the left to the center of Cox's Division; on the right the 17th Michigan went forward in gallant style. The Michigan men had lain a long time exposed to fire without being able to reply, and were impatient at the delay, and the order to advance was received with shouts of enthusiasm. The tangle of dense undergrowth in which they lay, and through which

---

44 This description evidently is from Carman's own observations and investigation. Modern research shows that the "heavy body of skirmishers" was the 50th, 51st, and Phillips' Georgia Legion of Thomas Drayton's Brigade. Kurt Graham, "Death of a Brigade," *The Society of the Descendents of Frederick Fox of Fox's Gap Maryland* (June 1, 2000), Issue 9, Vol. 1. Carman omitted Phillips Legion from his order of battle, but this article proves the unit was there.

45 Christ's report, OR 19, pt. 1, p. 437, and Welsh's report, *ibid.*, p. 440. Carman included more detail from William Todd, *Seventy-Ninth Highlanders, New York Volunteers in the War of the Rebellion, 1861-1865* (Albany: Press of Brandow, Barton & Co., 1886), p. 232, some of it directly quoted. The same information, and wording appears in notes in "79th Highlanders at South Mountain," from the NYPL, Carman Papers, 10, Folder 23. The advancing skirmishers were from Phillips Georgia Legion. See Graham, *Death of a Brigade.*

they had to pass, somewhat destroyed formation, but they went rapidly forward a short distance and as they came to the edge of the woods saw a stone fence in the open ground in front, behind which were Drayton's skirmishers, who at once opened a heavy and accurate fire, inflicting much loss. At the same time artillery on the right opened upon them, but, under the fire of musketry and artillery they pressed on, drove Drayton's men from the fence and across the open ground, back to the stone fence, bordering the forest and the ridge road, north of the Wise house. The batteries in the direction of the Mountain House, now fairly swept the open field, into which the regiment had advanced, and this caused the line to crowd to the left, across the Sharpsburg road and into the woods, on the right of the 45th Pennsylvania, where the contest was maintained with the enemy, square in front, behind the double stone fence in front of the Wise house.[46]

The Confederate guns now played upon the woods bringing down broken limbs, and the discharge of musketry from the stone fence was a continuous blaze. The artillery fire soon relaxed and the greater part of the Michigan regiment moved back into the open field, across the road, and advanced upon the stone fence north of the Wise house, which was quickly abandoned by Drayton's men, upon which the right wing of the Michigan regiment swung to the left and opened an enfilading fire upon Drayton's men behind the stone fence south of the Sharpsburg road. This was more than Drayton's men could stand. They had maintained a most heroic fight against great odds, but, with the fire of the left wing of the 17th Michigan, and the 45th Pennsylvania, supported by the 79th New York, in front; the 46th New York and the right of Cox's line on their right, and the terrible enfilade fire of the Michigan men on their left, they broke in disorder and went streaming to the rear, down the west side of the mountain, leaving many dead, wounded, and prisoners, in the hands of the Union men, who closely pursued, down the slope far into the woods. The battery, for the capture of which the charge had been made, escaped by the road to the Mountain House.[47]

Before the order for the advance had been given, the 46th New York, on the left of the 45th Pennsylvania, was under cover of a stone fence. When the order was given, it sprang forward, under a heavy fire, to the woods, where the right of Cox's Division was engaged, and joined in the fight, which it kept up, until the 9th New

46 Welsh's report, OR 19, pt. 1, p. 440, Gabriel Campbell, 17th Michigan, letter dated August 23, 1899, NA-AS.

47 Carman used Welsh's report, *ibid.*, p. 440, for the Pennsylvanians' attack, and the Campbell letter for the 17th Michigan's charge. Hill's report, *ibid.*, p. 1,020, mentions the destruction of Drayton's command. Modern studies of the fight suggest Drayton ordered his men to abandon the stone wall and file into Old Sharpsburg Road. Carman had no way of knowing this.

Hampshire charged past it, upon which it again advanced over an open field, on the extreme left of the division and joined the 9th New Hampshire in pursuit of the enemy beyond the stone-walled lane and into the woods. The right of Cox's Division participated in this charge, but its center and left were not seriously engaged, coming under the skirmishing fire only.[48] It was early in this engagement that the head of Sturgis's Division came up.

Sturgis moved from near Middletown about 1 p. m.; it was 3.30 p.m. when he reached the field. The 2d Maryland and 6th New Hampshire had been sent along the National road, in the direction of Turner's Gap, and, at the foot of the mountain, Clark's Battery (E, 4th United States) was detached and sent to the support of Cox's left. Arriving near the crest of the mountain, while the contest was raging, Ferrero's Brigade was deployed on either side of the Sharpsburg road, and, coming under fire, suffered some loss. Nagle's 48th Pennsylvania and 9th New Hampshire were, for a time, held in reserve, but soon went forward and participated in the final charge. Durrell's Battery was put in position on the right of the road and quickly silenced Lane's Battery, which, from a point near the Mountain House, was enfilading the Union line. About the same time Cook's guns, abandoned earlier in the day, re-opened fire upon the Confederates at Turner's Gap. The right of the Union line was reformed to avoid the enfilading fire from the Confederate artillery near the Mountain House, and presented to General D. H. Hill's view the appearance of an inverted V. Hill says: "The V afforded a fine target from the pike, and I directed Captain Lane to open on it with his battery. His firing was wild, not a shot hitting the mark. The heavy batteries (Durell's and Cook's) promptly replied, showing such excellent practice that Lane's guns were soon silenced."[49]

Referring to the action just described, General Cox, in his official report, says:

About 4 p. m. most of the reinforcements being in position, the order was received to advance the whole line and take or silence the enemy's batteries immediately in front. The order was immediately obeyed, and the advance was made with the strongest enthusiasm. The enemy made a desperate resistance, charging our advance line with firmness, but they were everywhere routed and fled with precipitation. In this advance the chief loss fell upon the division of General Willcox, which was the most exposed,

48 Lt. Col. Joseph Gerhardt's report, *OR* 19, pt. 1, p. 442. Carman gave the 9th New Hampshire the benefit of a doubt. Gerhardt claimed that in their eagerness to attack they fired into his regiment from behind.

49 Gen. Samuel Sturgis's report, *ibid.*, p. 443. Carman, as usual, supplied the name of the enemy unit referred to in the report. The quote from Hill, *B&L*, p. 571.

being on the right, but it gallantly overcame all obstacles, and the success was complete along the whole line of the corps."[50]

Elsewhere Cox says:

"Their strongest attack fell upon the angle of Wilcox's command, and for a little while there was some confusion, during the raking artillery fire which came from the right, but Willcox soon reformed his lines, and after a very bloody contest, pushed across the Sharpsburg road, through Wise's field, and into the wooded slope beyond. Along the front of the Kanawha Division the line was maintained and the enemy was repulsed with severe loss. At nearly 4 o'clock Sturgis's Division arrived and relieved the left wing of Willcox's Division, the latter taking ground a little more to the right and rear."

When Sturgis relieved the left of Willcox he formed line just at the top of the mountain, facing Fox's Gap and on the left of the Sharpsburg road: Ferrero's Brigade on the right and two regiments of Nagle's on the left, and as Cox reports: "occupying the new ground gained on the farther side of the slope."[51]

Rodman's Division came on the field after Sturgis. It marched from Frederick at 3 a. m., and arrived at Middletown at 10 a. m., where it remained four hours, until 2 p. m., when the march resumed and the field reached between 4 and 5 p. m. The division was now divided: Harland's Brigade, under the supervision of Rodman, being posted on the extreme right, in support to Willcox, while Fairchild's Brigade was sent by Cox to the extreme left to strengthen the flank of the Kanawha Division and support Clark's battery of four guns, that had been ordered in that direction. Fairchild arrived at the designated place and took a position in rear of the guns; the 9th New York on the right, the 103d in the center, and 89th on the left.[52]

It is now time to return to the Confederate movements. When the Union line struck Drayton, the brigade of George T. Anderson, over 400 yards to the right, was moving by the right flank, following Ripley, down the Sharpsburg road. Upon the first sound of the firing Ripley ordered Anderson to move by the left flank into the wood, south of the road; the skirmishers having no orders to the contrary, continued moving to the right, thus uncovering the front of the brigade, which, having moved some distance up the wooded mountain side, came to a halt and Anderson, finding his front uncovered and that the firing was more to the left than

50 This quote is from Cox's report, *OR* 19, pt. 1, p. 460.

51 Cox, *B&L*, p. 588; Cox's report, *ibid.*

52 *Ibid.*, Cox's report, p. 459, and Col. Harrison Fairchild's report, *ibid.*, p. 450.

to the front, changed front forward on the left and ordered Colonel W. J. Magill to deploy half of the 1st Georgia Regulars as skirmishers, feel forward and locate the enemy, but before Magill could get in motion, it was ascertained that Drayton's right had been completely turned and that the Union troops pursuing Drayton were on his own left and rear. At the same time Anderson learned that Ripley was more than 400 yards to the right and rear; finding that he was unsupported and almost isolated, he recrossed the Sharpsburg road to the left, reformed his line, and was advancing to find the right of Drayton, when his skirmishers reported that the Union troops were crossing the road and were already on his left, upon which he again moved by the left, diagonally to the rear, to intercept them, and met Hood's two brigades coming up through the tangled forest to recover the ground lost by Drayton. Anderson reported to Hood for orders and formed on his left; he had not been engaged, his skirmishers only firing a few shots.[53]

Ripley, who had been left by D. H. Hill in command of four brigades, appears to have been unequal or disinclined to the task. Upon the rout of Drayton, he concluded he was entirely cut off from Hill and, upon a report from the skirmishers of his own brigade, that a heavy body of troops was moving across his front, supposed to be those of the enemy, in reality those of George B. Anderson of his own command, he ordered an immediate retreat down the mountain, without coming in contact with an enemy or firing a shot, leaving the commanders of the other brigades, placed by D. H. Hill under his orders, to wonder what had become of him. Hill says that Ripley uselessly employed his brigade in marching and countermarching, for some cause was not engaged, and "did not draw a trigger."[54] After stating that Drayton and George T. Anderson had been placed on Ripley's left and a forward movement ordered, Hill continues: "In half an hour or more I received a note from Ripley saying that he was progressing finely; so he was, to the rear of the mountain on the west side. Before he returned the fighting was over, and his brigade did not fire a shot that day."[55]

---

53  This information was taken almost word-for-word from Col. George T. Anderson's report, *OR* 19, pt. 1, pp. 908-9, except that Anderson said the separation from Ripley was 300 yards. Whether Carman used another source for this change or simply miscopied it is unclear.

54  This phrase is lifted from Hill's report, *ibid.*, p. 1,021.

55  D. H. Hill's writings are filled with sarcasm and criticism of others. Carman hints at Hill's opinion of Gen. Ripley. The Battlefield Board Papers have letters from Col. Stephen Thruston and Lt. Col. William De Rossett, 3rd North Carolina (many addressed to Hill) offering negative comments about Ripley and his unfitness for command. See their letters in NA-AS. A portion of this feud is printed as a footnote in Hill, *B&L*, p. 569, directly below Hill's quote cited here. To be fair, the terrain was not practicable for the large-scale movement Hill conceived of when he ordered Ripley to attack.

George B. Anderson, whose movement across Ripley's front caused the latter's withdrawal, was not so remiss in duty. After he had moved by the right flank some distance down the Sharpsburg road, he recognized the fact that he was moving far away from his enemy, and, without prompting, faced to the left and moved up the mountain. He had the 2d, 4th and 30th North Carolina of his own brigade, and the 13th North Carolina of Garland's. The 14th North Carolina had become detached earlier in the day and had fallen in with Ripley. It was an arduous march up the mountain side, covered with huge boulders, laurel thickets and tangled vines. When the top was reached, it was at the crest road and some distance beyond Cox's left. Finding nothing in his immediate front he sent the 2d and 4th North Carolina to reconnoiter. Captain E. A. Osborne, commanding the skirmishers of the 4th, on coming to the open ground on the left, saw Clark's Battery and infantry support; all facing nearly north. He hastened back to his regimental commander and told him that they could deliver a flank fire upon the infantry support before it could change position to meet them, upon which the 2d, 4th and 13th North Carolina were marched along the ridge road to the left, until they came to a dense cornfield on the right of the road, where they saw the guns and the infantry in support. An instant charge was ordered, the North Carolinians sprang out of the laurel thicket and over the fence into the open and this at the moment that the 89th New York, its left in the corn, was just coming into position on the left of its brigade. The 89th and the battery opened fire and the North Carolinians were quickly repulsed with great loss, and fell back into the woods, leaving their dead, wounded, 30 prisoners and 150 stand of arms in the hands of the 89th New York, which had but one wing engaged, and lost 2 killed and 18 wounded. The 9th and 103d New York report no casualties. It was near sunset and the fighting on the left was over.[56]

The historian of the 9th New York gives an account of this action:

The brigade was formed like the letter L, the 9th New York being the base line, while the 103d and 89th New York were formed at right angles to it, extending toward the rear. The battery faced down the line toward the left. The 9th and 103d, with about two companies of the 89th had arrived on the line when the enemy, who were concealed in a close thicket of laurel on the west slope of the mountain, suddenly dashed from cover, and made an impetuous charge on the battery, yelling and discharging their

---

56 Some elements of this paragraph can be gleaned from Hill, *B&L*, p. 567, and the reports of Hill, *OR* 19, pt. 1, p. 1,020, Ripley, *ibid.*, pp. 1031-2, and McRae, *ibid.*, p. 1041, but Carman includes more details from Clark, *North Carolina Regiments*, 2, p. 245. The latter portion comes from Col. Harrison Fairchild's report, *OR* 19, pt. 1, p. 450.

muskets as soon as the forces were sighted. Without hesitation Colonel Kimball gave the order: 'Right wing, attention! Fix bayonets! By the right flank by file left, double quick. March!' and led the way through and between guns and limbers into the thick brush on the right of the battery beyond the rear of the remainder of the regiment, to a position where he could strike the flank of the charging rebels. Meanwhile the battery was firing double charges of canister at point blank range, the enemy being so close that it was unnecessary to aim but simply point the guns after each discharge. The 103d after a momentary unsteadiness stood up to the work like good fellows, firing volley after volley, while the two companies of the 89th opened a steady, well directed fire, the other companies joining in as each arrived on the line, the entire movement being as coolly and methodically performed as though on drill in camp."[57]

This encounter on the left was quickly followed by an affair on the right, near the Wise house. Hood, with his two brigades, arrived at the Mountain House about 4 p. m., and took position on the left of the National road, but was soon ordered to the right to support the troops there reported as giving way. On his way he met Drayton's men coming out and reporting that the enemy had succeeded in passing to their rear. He then inclined more to the right, over very rugged ground, came up to George T. Anderson's Brigade and took position to engage and check the Union advance, Anderson forming on his left. No enemy appearing, he fixed bayonets and swept through the woods, drove back a few Union stragglers, and, regaining part of the ground lost by Drayton, came to the stone fence running north from the Wise house. Fire was opened by him and upon him but he held his ground, with small loss; among his mortally wounded was Lieutenant Colonel O. K. McLemore, 4th Alabama.[58] In this encounter, as the shades of night were falling, the gallant and loved Reno, commanding the Ninth Corps, lost his life. It will be remembered that when Sturgis relieved the left of Willcox, he formed on the left of the Sharpsburg road. Nagle's two regiments on the right and Ferrero's Brigade on the left, in column of regiments: the 51st Pennsylvania in front, 51st New York second, 35th Massachusetts, third and 21st Massachusetts in rear. The head of the column was on the west edge of the woods overlooking the field of four acres separating the woods from the Wise house. At near sunset the 35th Massachusetts was sent into the woods, north and west of the Wise house, to reconnoiter. It went some

57  Matthew J. Graham, *History of the Ninth New York Volunteers, Hawkins' Zouaves, Being a History of the Regiment and Veteran Association from 1860 to 1900* (New York: E. P. Cohy & Co., 1900), pp. 271-2.

58  Report of Brig. Gen. John B Hood, *OR* 19, pt. 1, p. 922.

distance, came back, reported that no enemy was in the immediate front, and resumed its place in the third line of the brigade.

Up to this time Reno had not been up the mountain, but had remained with McClellan and Burnside, at Pleasonton's position, near the heavy batteries in the valley. He now rode up to see why it was that the right of the line could not get forward to the summit at the Mountain House. After a brief conference with General Cox, during which he was informed of the condition of affairs and the obstacles in the way to an advance to the Mountain House, he rode on to where Sturgis had formed his division, went forward to examine the ground in the immediate vicinity of the Wise house, saw a few men around the house and in the small opening across the road from it, succoring the wounded, and was told by some of these men, that there seemed to be a movement of some kind in the woods, out of which the 35th Massachusetts had just come. He rode back to Ferrero's Brigade, ordered the 51st Pennsylvania to the right of the Sharpsburg road and its skirmishers to the stone fence, north of the Wise house, and into the woods beyond. His order was being promptly executed, the 51st was crossing the road and its skirmishers pushing obliquely to the front, when Hood's men opened fire from behind the stone fence; the fire being promptly returned. The sudden rain of bullets from the woods, where no enemy was expected came as a surprise and one of Sturgis's regiments became panic-stricken, broke, and opened indiscriminate fire. Reno and others hastened to rally the men and, while so doing, Reno received a mortal wound. [59]

59 The position and order of the regiments is not listed in any of the reports of the commanders involved. A hand-copied account by Carman from the Carman Papers in the Library of Congress identified as "Report of Maj. Gen. Robert B. Potter to the Adjutant General of the Army," includes the same order of regiments and much of the same details about the movements of the units in Ferraro's brigade. This document does not mention the advance of the 35th Massachusetts as skirmishers, and instead states that the 51st Pennsylvania went forward as skirmishers, obliquing to the right and uncovering the front of Potter's regiment. Carman also had a hand-copied excerpt written by a committee of the regimental association entitled *History of the Thirty-Fifth Regiment, Massachusetts Volunteers* (Boston: Mills, Knight & Co. 1884), pp. 27-30, in his files that provided some of the details about the 35th he used here; NYPL, Box 10, Folder 23. Cox, *B&L*, pp. 588-9, confirms Reno's arrival and the desire to push forward on the Union right. Carman filled in the identification of Hood's men firing the shots that killed Reno, and the rest of the account follows Potter's report. Other accounts of Reno's fatal wounding exist, including the Gabriel Campbell NA-AS letter, but Carman chose this one to present in his version. Subsequent authors have cited Campbell's letter, which states that Reno believed he was shot by his own men. See, for example, John Priest, *Before Antietam: The Battle for South Mountain* (Shippensburg, PA: White Mane Publishing Co, Inc., 1992), pp. 216-8. Note, however, that the Campbell letter also states that Reno was mistaken. The NYPL Ezra Carman Papers, Box 11, contains at least four accounts by veterans refuting the premise that Reno was killed by friendly fire.

The 51st Pennsylvania had now crossed to the right of the road, the men from the 51st New York sprang to their feet and advanced to the crest of the plateau, on a line with the 51st Pennsylvania, and the entire front opened on the enemy, the contest ceasing only when darkness came on, but a desultory fire was kept up all along the line until 10 p. m.[60]

On the Confederate side George T. Anderson had come up on Hood's left; George B. Anderson still held ground on the right, and Ripley, returning to the front after the fighting was over, filled the interval between George B. Anderson and Hood, and this line was held until the retreat was ordered.

The casualties in the Ninth Corps numbered 157 killed, 691 wounded, 41 missing, a total of 889. The Confederate loss in killed and wounded, in front of the Ninth Corps, was about 600, and many were captured, the Kanawha Division alone, claiming the capture of 600, in which, however, must be included some of the wounded.[61]

---

60 The source for this advance by the 51st Pennsylvania, and the uneasy night of skirmishing, is mentioned in Thomas H. Parker, *History of the 51st P.V. and V.V.* . . . (Philadelphia: King & Baird, Printers, 1869), pp. 225-6. The advance of the 51st New York is implied there also. Carman's note concerning the random fire of the 35th Massachusetts likely came from this source as well.

61 A detailed account of casualties is appended to the chapter, but the Union totals here are taken from OR 19, pt. 1, p. 187. The Confederates did not report separate casualties for each battle in the Maryland campaign, and are thus necessarily imprecise.

# Chapter 9

# South Mountain (Turner's Gap)
## September 14, 1862

Cox started from camp in the morning to support a cavalry reconnaissance, became engaged at 9 a. m., with an enemy whose presence was suspected only, carried the crest of a mountain early in the forenoon and was left unaided till 2 p. m., when Willcox came up, followed an hour and more later by Sturgis and Rodman. It was not until 3 p. m., that any movement was made on the right of the national road, at which hour Hooker, at the head of the First Corps, reached the eastern base of the mountain, at Mt. Tabor church, and began his deployment.

Let us return, briefly, to the Confederates at Hagerstown, whom we left, on the night of the 13th, under orders to march back to Turner's Gap next morning. At daybreak, the column—the brigades of Drayton, Kemper, Garnett, George T. Anderson, Evans, Jenkins, Hood and Law, with artillery—marched as ordered, leaving Toombs' Brigade and the 11th Georgia of Georgia T. Anderson, that had all night been on picket, and the 1st Virginia cavalry, at Hagerstown. The day was very hot and the roads dusty; the march, consequently, a severe one, and nearly one-half of the command became stragglers and did not reach the field of action. The artillery battalions of S. D. Lee, J. Thompson Brown and William Nelson were left on the heights of Beaver Creek, four miles north of Boonsboro. The brigades of George T. Anderson, Drayton, Hood and Law engaged the Ninth Corps, as we have seen; the remaining four brigades of Kemper, Garnett, Evans and Jenkins, went to the north to make head against Hooker's advance.[1]

At daybreak of the 14th, Hooker marched from his camp, on the Monocacy, by the National road, passed through Frederick and Middletown and, about 1 p. m., halted on Catoctin Creek, one mile west of Middletown, where the men were directed to rest and make coffee. Hooker rode forward to examine the country in the neighborhood of where it was proposed to make an attack on the north side of Turner's Gap. He says:

> In front of us was South Mountain, the crest of the spinal ridge of which was held by the enemy in considerable force. Its slopes are precipitous, rugged and wooded, and difficult of ascent to an infantry force, even in the absence of a foe in front. The National road (running northwest and southeast) crosses the summit of this range of mountain through a gentle depression, and near this point a spur projects from the body of the ridge, and running nearly parallel with it about a mile, where it is abruptly cut by a rivulet from the main ridge and rises again and extends far to the northward. At and to the north of the pike this spur is separated from the main ridge by a narrow valley, with cultivated fields, extending well up the gentle slope of the hill on each side. Here the enemy posted his infantry and a few pieces of artillery. Through the break in the spur at the base of the principal ridge, were other cleared fields occupied by the enemy."[2]

For convenience sake we shall call the main ridge, the "north ridge" and the spur projecting from it the "south spur." At the summit of Turner's Gap and 80 yards east of the Mountain House, a road branches from the National road and runs in a northeasterly direction along the southeast slope of the "north ridge"; at the distance of nearly a mile it inclines to the right, passes down a gorge, dividing the

---

1  Maj. Gen. David R. Jones's report, *ibid.*, p. 885, confirms that Toombs's Brigade and the 11th Georgia were left behind, but does not mention the 1st Virginia Cavalry. Fitzhugh Lee's report (mentioned by Stuart in his own report) has never been published, but several veterans of the 1st Virginia Cavalry confirm they were in Hagerstown. See NA-AS. The artillery on Beaver Creek is mentioned (although not named specifically) in Brig. Gen. William N. Pendleton's report, OR 19, pt. 1, p. 830. Carman probably filled in the battalions and their commanders. He refers to Hood's Brigade, although he made it clear elsewhere that Hood was commanding two brigades of a small division. Hood's Brigade will subsequently become known as Wofford's Brigade, after the senior colonel who assumed command.

2  Hooker's account is from his report, *ibid.*, pp. 213-4. Carman paraphrased the report for the first portion before he began quoting directly.

"south spur" from the eastern part of the 'north ridge" and curving around to the right, at the hamlet of Frosttown, goes south by the Mt. Tabor church, and enters the National road at Bolivar, at the eastern foot of the mountain, two miles east of where it leaves the summit, near the Mountain House. This is the old Hagerstown road. There are other roads branching from this and leading over the mountain; these shall be noted as occasion requires.[3]

Before Hooker had completed his reconnaissance, Meade's Division, at 2.30 p.m., was ordered to make a movement north of the National road, to divert attention from Reno, who was operating south of it. Hatch and Ricketts were ordered to follow Meade and support him. The three divisions moved from the Catoctin, turned to the right at Bolivar and marched by the old Hagerstown road to the vicinity of Mt. Tabor church, where they turned into the fields west of the road and took position to support Cooper's Battery, which it was proposed to establish on an adjoining eminence near the base of the mountain. As soon as the divisions arrived they were successively deployed for action, Meade on the right, Hatch to the left, and Ricketts in reserve.[4]

The 3d Pennsylvania Reserves, Lieutenant Colonel John Clark, was detached to watch a road running to the right, from the old Hagerstown road, about three-fourths of a mile north of Mt. Tabor church, where it remained until, late in the day, it was relieved by the movement of the 1st Massachusetts Cavalry, higher up the valley.[5]

The Confederates, perceiving these movements, opened fire from a battery on the mountain side, but without inflicting any injury, upon which Cooper's Battery was quickly put in position on elevated ground and opened on such bodies of the enemy as were visible. At the same time, the 13th Pennsylvania Reserve, the

---

3   Carman's description of the road network is flawed. The Old Hagerstown Road left the National Road farther to the east near Catoctin Creek. Mt. Tabor Church Road intersected the National Road at Bolivar. The road dividing the "south spur" and the "north ridge," now known as Dahlgren Road, was not the "official" Old Hagerstown Road. That road, according to the 1858 Isaac Bond map of Frederick County, continued north and west passing through South Mountain north of Turner's Gap at Orr's Gap. The road Carman describes here is now called Dahlgren Road, but it is possible someone told Burnside or McClellan, both of whom use the term in their reports, that this road bore that name. See OR 19, pt. 1, pp. 48, 51 for McClellan, and *ibid.*, p. 417 for Burnside.

4   Maj. Gen. Joseph Hooker's report, *ibid.*, p. 214, and Brig. Gen. George Meade's report, *ibid.*, p. 267.

5   Lt. Col. John Roberts's report, *ibid.*, 51, pt. 1, p. 143. Roberts did not identify the cavalry regiment. Carman fills it in from Hooker's report, *ibid.*, p. 214, but the regimental history says it was on the main road during the 14th. See Crowninshield, *First Massachusetts Cavalry Volunteers*, pp. 74-5.

"Bucktails" deployed as skirmishers and advanced to feel for the enemy. Becoming satisfied that the mountain was held in force, Hooker ordered Meade to extend his division to the right, outflank the Confederates and then move to the attack. Hatch and Ricketts followed Meade's movement to the right. The right of Meade's division now rested a mile and a half from the National road, at a point, where, a mile beyond Mt. Tabor church, a road branching to the right from the old Hagerstown road, runs over the mountain, coming out at the National road at Zittlestown, about a half mile west of the Mountain House. Seymour's Brigade was on the right of this road, the brigades of Gallagher and Magilton between it and the old Hagerstown road.[6]

In front of Meade was a succession of parallel ridges, alternating with deep, irregular valleys and broken ravines. Those nearest him were wooded, beyond these it was quite clear all the way to the summit. The hills increased in height and their eastern slopes became more abrupt and rugged, as they neared the crest of the mountain, which was of irregular crescent front, in many places jutting out in rugged prominences of difficult access. Gorges or small ravines bisected the ridges, running parallel to the crest. Favorable positions were occupied by small Confederate outposts, well protected by rocks and trees, and the numerous stone fences separating the fields.

Early in the morning R. E. Rodes' Brigade (3d, 5th, 6th, 12th and 26th Alabama) relieved George B. Anderson's North Carolina brigade a half mile west of Boonsboro. As it neared noon Rodes was ordered to follow Ripley up the mountain. Upon arriving at the Mountain House he was ordered by Hill to occupy the "south spur" immediately to the left of the National road. He held this position about three-quarters of an hour, under artillery fire from the batteries of Benjamin, Gibson and McMullin, near Bolivar, when he was ordered to occupy a bare hill on the "north ridge" about three-quarters of a mile to the left. The entire brigade was moved to the hill, crossing, in doing so, a deep gorge, which separated the "north ridge" from the "south spur." This left a large interval between the right of the brigade, which rested in the gorge, and the rest of the division, which was filled by sending back the 12th Alabama, Colonel B. B. Gayle, to cover the ground to the National road and support Lane's Georgia battery.[7]

---

6    Hooker's report, *OR* 19, pt. 1, p. 214, has some of this information. The details about the 13th Pennsylvania Reserves, which Carman frequently called by their nickname "the Bucktails," came from Meade's report, *ibid.*, p. 267, and Brig. Gen. Truman Seymour's report *ibid.*, p. 272.

7    Brig. Gen Robert Rodes's report, *ibid.*, pt. 1, pp. 1,033-4. Carman supplied the commander's names.

By this time Hooker's lines were well developed and in full view, and it was evident to D. H. Hill and Rodes that it was Hooker's intention to attack the main ridge, the south spur and the gorge between them, and that from the length of his line it would extend a half mile beyond Rodes' left. Immediately upon his arrival on the extreme left Rodes had discovered that the hill there was accessible to artillery, and that a good road, passing by his left from Hooker's line, continued immediately in his rear and entered the National road about a half mile west of the Mountain House. Therefore, he sent for artillery and determined upon the only promising plan by which Hooker could be prevented from taking immediate possession of this road, and thus marching in his rear, and that was to extend his own line as far as possible to the left, keeping his right in the gorge, and to send for reinforcements to fill out from his right to the National road, an interval of three-fourths of a mile. Skirmishers were sent to the left, and Lieutenant Robert E. Park, 12th Alabama, led 40 men to the foot of the mountain to delay Hooker' advance.[8] Hooker was very deliberate in making his dispositions and it was nearly 5 p. m. before the assault on the mountain was ordered.[9]

It began by throwing forward heavy skirmish lines, which Meade and Hatch were to support with their entire divisions. The battle that ensued resolved itself into two attacks, one, led by Meade, for the possession of the "north ridge," the other, led by Hatch, for the possession of the "south spur." Ricketts assisted each with a brigade.

We follow the assault led by Meade upon Rodes. Seymour's Brigade, on the right, under cover of the forest, at the base of the mountain, was ordered to move on and near the road over the mountain to Zittlestown, the road watched by Rodes. The "Bucktails" 275 men, Colonel Hugh W. McNeil commanding, advanced as skirmishers, supported by the 2d Pennsylvania Reserves and two companies of the 1st, moving 50 yards in the rear, the remainder of Seymour's Brigade closely following. Soon after advancing through open woods and over cultivated ground on the right of the road, Seymour could see the two detached heights on which Rodes was posted, the 12th Alabama on the one, and the 3d, 5th, 6th and 26th Alabama on the other, and reported to Meade that he could take the "north ridge,"

---

8  The information about Lt. Park is found in *SHSP*, 1, No. 6, "Diary of Captain Robert E. Park, Twelfth Alabama Infantry," pp. 435-6, but more likely came from Hill *B&L*, pp. 572-3.

9  "I had to order him [Hooker] four separate times to move his command into action and I had to myself order his leading division (Meade's) to start before he would go." Burnside to Gen. S. Williams, *OR* 19, pt. 1, pp. 422-423. Burnside was answering criticisms made in Hooker's report of Cox's and Reno's behavior in the battle. Hooker had a deserved reputation for contentiousness, but it is surprising that Carman (who usually spoke highly of Hooker) chose to include this in his manuscript.

along which ran the road, and then advance across the ravine to the "south spur" taking it in flank, and Meade directed him to do so.[10]

The two brigades of Gallagher and Magilton advanced on the left of Seymour, and simultaneously with him and, as Meade's entire division swept into the open, Rodes was convinced that his own 1,200 men were opposed to a force that would flank them completely on either on side. Particularly did he fear the danger menacing the peak on the Zittlestown road, a danger so imminent that he ordered his left regiment, the 6th Alabama, Colonel John B. Gordon, to move along the brow of the hill, under fire, still farther to the left, which was done in good order. Once during the movement Gordon essayed a charge that checked Seymour's onward movement, and a severe skirmish fire followed, which, on the Confederate side, was assisted by the fire of artillery up the mountain to the left, and some of Seymour's men, on open ground, greatly exposed, fell under this fire.[11]

While Seymour was moving on the right to take Rodes in reverse, Gallagher and Magilton went straight to the front. At first Gallagher moved obliquely to the right and front to keep in touch with Seymour, by which he came under a harmless artillery fire. The 9th Reserve, on the right of the brigade, gained a stone wall, near the foot of the mountain, behind which it remained some twenty minutes, engaged with Confederate skirmishers, sheltered by a log home in the ravine. Finally, a charge was made, the house carried, and a few prisoners captured, when the 9th Reserve was relieved by the 10th. In advancing on the left of the 9th Reserve, the 11th, when approaching the ravine, received a volley that laid low more than half of its commissioned officers and many men. The 12th Reserve, on the left of the brigade, crossed the ravine and came under the fire of an unseen enemy, but did not suffer as severely as the 11th. In this spirited affair, Colonel Thomas T. Gallagher, commanding the brigade, was wounded, and Lieutenant Colonel Robert Anderson, 9th Reserve, succeeded to the command.[12]

Of this affair in the ravine, Rodes says: "In the first attack of the enemy up the bottom of the gorge, they pushed on so vigorously as to catch Captain Ready and a portion of his party of skirmishers, and to separate the 3d from the 5th Alabama

---

10 These paragraphs are a compilation from Meade's report, *ibid.*, pt. 1, pp. 214-5, and Seymour's report, *ibid.*, p. 272. The order of Rodes's Brigade is from his report, *ibid.*, p. 1034.

11 Rodes's report, continued, *ibid.*

12 Carman used parts of the reports of Capt. Samuel Dick, 9th Pennsylvania Reserves, Lt. Col. Samuel Jackson, 11th Pennsylvania Reserves, and Capt Andrew Bolar, 12th Pennsylvania Reserves, to write this paragraph. These reports are found in *ibid.*, 51, pt. 1, pp. 149-50, 153, and 154, respectively.

Regiment. The 3d made a most gallant resistance at this point, and had my line been a continuous one it could never have been forced."[13]

In the movement to the ravine Magilton advanced on the left of Gallagher, his three regiments deployed in one line, and with Gallagher engaged the Confederates at the foot of the mountain and was opposed, also, by Lieutenant Park and his 40 skirmishers.[14]

Meade's men were very persistent. When they drove the Alabamians from the bottom of the ravine, they followed them closely up the mountain side, pushed them from every point of vantage, behind trees, rocks and stone walls, penetrated their thin and broken line, worked in on their flanks, and continued swinging around their left. Rodes' efforts to meet and repel Meade's steady advance are well told in his admirable report:

> By this time the enemy, though met gallantly by all four of the regiments with me, had penetrated between them, and had begun to swing their extreme right around toward my rear, making for the head of the gorge, up the bottom and sides of which the whole of my force, except the Sixth Alabama, had to retreat, if at all. I renewed again, and yet again, my application for reenforcements, but none came. Some artillery, under Captain Carter, who was moving up without orders, and some of Colonel Cutts', under a gallant lieutenant, whose name I do not now recollect, was reported by the last-named officer to be on its way to my relief; but at this time the enemy had obtained possession of the summit of the left hill before spoken of, and had command of the road in rear of the main mountain. The artillery could only have been used by being hauled up on the high peak, which arose upon the summit of the ridge just at the head of the gorge before mentioned. This they had not time to do, and hence I ordered it back.
>
> Just before this, I heard that some Confederate troops had joined my right very nearly. Finding that the enemy were forcing my right back, and that the only chance to continue the fight was to change my front so as to face to the left, I ordered all the regiments to fall back up the gorge and sides of the mountain, fighting, the whole concentrating around the high peak before mentioned. This enabled me to face the enemy's right again, and to make another stout stand with Gordon's excellent regiment (which he had kept constantly in hand, and had handled in a manner I have never heard or seen equaled during this war), and with the remainder of the Fifth, Third, and Twelfth Alabama Regiments. I found the Twelfth had been relieved by other troops and closed in toward my right, but had passed in rear of the original line

13 See Rodes's report, *ibid.*, 19, pt. 1, p. 1,035.

14 *SHSP*, 1, No. 6, Park's Diary, p. 436.

so far that, upon re-establishing the line on the main peak, I found that the Third Alabama came upon its right. The Twenty-sixth Alabama, which had been placed on my right, was by this time completely demoralized; its colonel ([E. A.] O'Neal) was wounded, and the men mingled in utter confusion with some South Carolina stragglers on the summit of the hill, who stated that their brigade had been compelled to give way, and had retired. Notwithstanding this, if true, left my rear entirely exposed again (I had no time or means to examine the worth of their statements), I determined, in accordance with the orders I received about this time, in reply to my last request for re-enforcements, to fight on the new front.

My loss up to this time had been heavy in all the regiments except the Twelfth Alabama. The Fifth Alabama, which had occupied the left center, got separated into two parts in endeavoring to follow up the flank movement of Gordon's regiment. Both parts became engaged again before they could rejoin, and the right battalion was finally cut off entirely. The left and smaller battalion, under Major Hobson's gallant management, though flanked, wheeled against the flanking party, and, by desperate fighting, silenced the enemy so far as to enable his little command to make its way to the peak before mentioned. In the first attack of the enemy up the bottom of the gorge, they pushed on so vigorously as to catch Captain Ready and a portion of his party of skirmishers, and to separate the Third from the Fifth Alabama Regiment. The Third made a most gallant resistance at this point, and had my line been a continuous one it could never have been forced. Having re-established my line, though still with wide intervals, necessarily, on the high peak (this was done under constant fire and in full view of the enemy, now in full possession of the extreme left hill and of the gorge), the fight at close quarters was resumed, and again accompanied by the enemy throwing their, by this time apparently interminable right around toward my rear.[15]

Seymour, while advancing and still working on Rodes' flank, saw, as he looked to the left, an extended field of corn, leading directly to the position Rodes had taken, and determined to carry it. The "Bucktails" continued on in the direction they were then moving, straight for the 6th Alabama to turn its left, while the 1st, 2d and 5th Reserves, changed direction to the left, and, supported by the 6th Reserve, ascended the slope. After a stubborn resistance the whole division line—Seymour, Anderson and Magilton—gained the crest of the "north ridge," the loss being severe on both sides; among the Confederates, Colonel B. B. Gayle, 12th Alabama,

---

15  Rodes's report, *OR* 19, pt. 1, pp. 1,034-5.

was killed. Seymour was first to gain the crest and follow the Confederates to the left, where the latter came under the fire of Anderson and Magilton.[16]

Soon after the action began, Meade, having reason to believe that the Confederate line was being extended to the left, to flank Seymour's right, sent to Hooker for help. Duryea's [sic] Brigade of Ricketts' Division was sent him, but, owing to the distance to be marched, Duryea did not arrive until just at the close of the engagement, and was then thrown in on Seymour's left and in front of Anderson's Brigade.[17]

It was now dark and the Confederates retreated. Magilton, moving up the mountain on the left of Anderson faced somewhat the National road and met an obstinate resistance, the 8th Reserve, on the extreme left, fighting its way at every step and sustaining a heavier loss than that of all the other regiments of the brigade combined. Because of this stout resistance made by Evans' South Carolina Brigade, it did not gain the crest quite as early as the brigades on the right; when it did get up it was quite dark, the Confederates had fallen back, and, with the other two brigades of the division, but separated from them by Duryea's Brigade, it bivouacked on the commanding eminence won.[18]

The efforts made by the Confederates to defend their last position in the report of General Rodes:

The Sixth Alabama and the Twelfth suffered pretty severely. The latter, together with the remainder of the Third Alabama, which had been well handled by Colonel (C. A.) Battle, was forced to retire, and in so doing lost heavily. Its Colonel (B. B. Gayle) was seen to fall, and its Lieutenant-Colonel (Samuel B. Pickens) was shot through the lungs; the former was left on the field, supposed to be dead; Pickens was brought off. Gordon's regiment retired slowly, now being under an enfilading as well as direct fire and in danger of being surrounded, but was still, fortunately for the whole command, held together by its able commander. After this, I could meet the enemy with no organized force except Gordon's regiment. One more desperate stand was made by it from an advantageous position. The enemy by this time were nearly on top of the

16 Seymour's report, *ibid.*, p. 272, the source of this paragraph, only mentions driving the Confederates from the hill top. Carman supplied the death of Col. Gayle from Rodes's report, *ibid.*, p. 1,035.

17 Meade's report, *ibid.*, p. 267. Carman routinely misspells Duryee's name as "Duryea." Gen. Abram Duryee's original regiment, the 5th New York, contained two Duryees and two Duryeas among the officer ranks. This fact has confused many historians. See, generally, Alfred Davenport, *Camp and Field Life of the Fifth New York Volunteer Infantry, Duryee's Zouaves* (New York: Dick and Fitzgerald, 1879), and Warner, *Generals in Blue*, p. 133.

18 Maj. Silas Baily's report, 8th Pennsylvania Reserves, *OR* 51, pt. 1, p. 149.

highest peak, and were pushing on, when Gordon's regiment, unexpectedly to them, opened fire on their front and checked them. This last stand was so disastrous to the enemy that it attracted the attention of the stragglers, even, many of whom Colonel Battle and I had been endeavoring to organize, and who were just then on the flank of that portion of the enemy engaged with Gordon, and for a few minutes they kept up a brisk enfilading fire upon the enemy; but, finding his fire turning from Gordon upon them, and that another body of Federal troops were advancing upon them, they speedily fell back. It was now so dark that it was difficult to distinguish objects at short musket range, and both parties ceased firing. Directing Colonel Gordon to move his regiment to his right and to the rear, so as to cover the gap, I endeavored to gather up stragglers from the other regiments. Colonel Battle still held together a handful of his men. These, together with the remnants of the Twelfth, Fifth, and Twenty-sixth Alabama Regiments, were assembled at the gap, and were speedily placed alongside of Gordon's regiment, which by this time had arrived in the road ascending the mountain from the gap, forming a line on the edge of the woods parallel to and about 200 yards from the main road. The enemy did not advance beyond the top of the mountain, but, to be prepared for them, skirmishers were thrown out in front of the line."[19]

Rodes' loss was 61 killed, 157 wounded, and 204 missing. He sums up the result of his fight: "We did not drive the enemy back or whip him, but with 1200 men we held his whole division at bay without assistance during four and a half hour's steady fighting, losing in that time not over half a mile of ground."[20]

Although Rodes reports that he had no assistance, he refers to the fact that he heard that some Confederate troops had joined his right, nearby, and that some South Carolina stragglers were on the peak with him, and D. H. Hill says: "Evans, who was supporting Rodes, fought gallantly and saved him from being entirely surrounded, but he got on the ground too late to effect anything. He had but about 550 men."[21]

Evans marched that day from Hagerstown in command of a "provisional" division, composing the two brigades of Hood's Division and his own South Carolina brigade. When nearing the Mountain House he was informed that Hood's two brigades were to be detached to support the right, at Fox's Gap, and that he,

---

19 Rodes's report, *ibid.*, 19, pt. 1, pp. 1,035-6.

20 *Ibid.*, p. 1,036.

21 Hill, *B&L*, p. 574.

with his own brigade, was to support Rodes and hold the position assigned him on the left of the National road, and that reinforcements would be sent him.[22]

His brigade was under the command of Colonel P. F. Stevens, of the Holcombe Legion. When Stevens arrived at the summit of Turner's Gap, about 4 p. m., he was ordered by Longstreet, who had just come up, to report to D. H. Hill, and was conducted to him by Colonel J. W. Fairfax, of Longstreet's staff. Hill ordered him to the position held by Rodes and when he had gone about half way and was on the slope of the mountain, he was overtaken by an order from Evans to halt; at about the same time came a message from Rodes to press on to his assistance. While awaiting new instructions from Evans he discovered that the Union forces were in the valley below, on his right. Throwing the Holcombe Legion to the right as skirmishers, he disposed the brigade along the brow of the hill, the left regiment, 23d South Carolina, Captain S. A. Durham, very nearly joining Rodes' right. Before Stevens received further instructions from Evans his skirmishers were driven in and his brigade engaged with Magilton's Brigade of Pennsylvania Reserves. The 23d South Carolina, the left of the brigade, was on the left of the old Hagerstown road, its left extending along the summit of the ridge. It advanced a short distance, met the skirmishers coming in, was quickly driven back and rallied on the left of the 22d South Carolina, Lieutenant Colonel T. C. Watkins. The two regiments made an effort to stop the Union advance, but were soon driven in some disorder. Watkins endeavored to rally his regiment, was killed, the men became confused, were partially rallied three times by Major Hilton, but the Union pressure upon them was so persistent that they fell back to the National road. The 23d, after being twice rallied, finally fell in with the 6th Alabama and marched off the field with it. The 18th South Carolina, Colonel W. H. Wallace, in the right center, shared much the same fate as the 22d.[23] Wallace reports that when it arrived near Rodes's Brigade that brigade was retiring:

22 Report of Gen. Nathan G. Evans, OR 19, pt. 1, p. 939. Evans and Gen. Hood had been feuding since late August. Harsh, *Taken at the Flood*, pp. 68-9, 306, 256. Evans had Hood arrested and on the way to Turner's Gap, Lee, acquiesing to shouts from the Texas troops, released Hood from arrest. Lee's solution was to split Evans's Brigade from the other two, giving Hood command of a small division and Evans an independent brigade. This was a direct affront to Evans, who ranked Hood. Carman consistently avoids controversial topics and here glossed over this famous rift in the Army of Northern Virginia. As an "official historian" Carman needed cooperation from survivors of the war, and stirring up controversy might antagonize some veterans. Lee's order of restoration is found in OR 19, pt. 2, p. 609.

23 See the report of Col. P. F. Stevens, *ibid.*, pt. 1, p. 941, for the first portion of this paragraph. The details come from the reports of Col. F. W. McMaster, 17th South Carolina, *ibid.*, p. 945; Col. W. H. Wallace, 18th South Carolina, *ibid.*, pp. 946-7; Maj. M. Hilton, 22nd South Carolina, *ibid.*, pp. 948-9; and Capt. S. A. Durham, 23rd South Carolina, *ibid.*, pp. 949-50. Col. Thomas C.

Under orders from Colonel Stevens, commanding the brigade, the 18th was then ordered to change front forward on first company and advance, with the view of taking a column of the enemy in flank which was advancing upon the point first occupied by the 18th, and which it had left to go to Rodes's support. A sharp engagement ensued, when, a heavy column of the enemy appearing upon our left flank, and the enemy, continuing to press upon Rodes's Brigade, were gaining ground toward our rear, the 18th was ordered to face back toward the top of the mountain and form on the right of the 22d South Carolina. The enemy advancing, we engaged them in this position until, the troops upon the left giving way, the enemy gained a point from which they enfiladed us again. Whereupon the regiment fell back to the turnpike, where it remained until the march to Sharpsburg began."[24]

The 17th South Carolina, Colonel F. W. McMaster, on the extreme right, beyond the gorge road leading down the mountain, was tenaciously holding ground against the 7th and 8th Pennsylvania Reserves, but seeing its brigade go in disorder; pressed in front by the 8th Reserve and flanked by the 7th, it retired to form a new line some 300 yards to the rear, but, again flanked by the steady Union advance, continued its retreat, with but 36 men in its ranks, leaving wounded on the field Lieutenant Colonel R. S. Means. McMaster was now ordered to form on the left of Jenkins' Brigade, before being able to do so, night came and, under Evans' order he fell back to the National road. The brigade having been rallied on the National road, near the Mountain House, the Holcombe Legion was thrown to the front as a picket, deployed about a skirt of woods, on the south foot of the hill from which the brigade had been driven. Of the 550 men taken into action it lost 171 killed and wounded, and 45 missing.[25]

When Evans was sent to help Rodes he was given to understand that the interval between his right and the National road would be filled. The only troops available for the purpose were the brigades of Kemper, Garnett and Jenkins of D. R. Jones' Division. When the two brigades of Drayton and George T. Anderson were detached and sent directly up the mountain, to report to D. H. Hill, these three small brigades were ordered by Longstreet to march from Boonsboro, in a southerly direction and then ascend the mountain to assist in the defense of Fox's Gap, which, it was reported, Reno was about to carry. After marching and

---

Watkins was not killed immediately, but died of his wounds on the 20th. Krick, *Lee's Colonels*, p. 388; *Confederate Veteran*, July, 1910, p. 329, lists the date of Watkins's death as September 26.

24  *OR* 19, pt. 1, p. 947.

25  McMaster's report, *ibid.*, p. 945, and Stevens's report, *ibid.*, p. 942.

countermarching it was ascertained that the Confederates on that part of the line were fairly holding their own, but that north of the National road affairs were more threatening and needed more attention. Jones was ordered to move his three brigades, as speedily as possible, back to the main road, and thence to the mountain top. When, after more blind marching, he reached the main road, not more than a third of a mile from where he had left it, his men were well nigh exhausted by miles of useless marching, added to the hot, dusty and fatiguing march from Hagerstown; he lost many men by straggling, beyond this, he lost much valuable time. Under Longstreet's orders he placed Kemper and Garnett, supported by Jenkins, in position, on the ridge to the right of Rodes and Evans.[26] Hill says:

> Major-General Longstreet came up about 4 o'clock with the commands of Evans and D. R. Jones. I had now become familiar with the ground, and knew all the vital points, and, had those troops reported to me, the result might have been different. As it was, they took wrong positions, and, in their exhausted condition, after a long march, they were broken and scattered."[27]

Kemper's Brigade formed chiefly across the old Hagerstown road: Garnett followed Kemper and took position about 200 yards to his right, the 8th Virginia, only 34 men, under Colonel Eppa Hunton, on the right, resting in a thick wood, the ground descending quite abruptly in front. The left, which, at first, was held by the 56th Virginia, Colonel W. D. Stuart, then by the 28th Virginia, Captain W. L. Wingfield, was in a field of standing corn. In front of the 19th Virginia, Colonel J. B. Strange, the left center was an open space, beyond which, about 18 yards, was a stone fence.

As soon as the line had been formed, Garnett sent out skirmishers to ascertain the position of the enemy. It was near sunset, when Garnett received an order to send the 56th Virginia from his left to strengthen the right of Kemper, about 200 yards distant, and to withdraw the rest of the brigade to a wooded ridge a little to the left and the rear. The 56th Virginia had scarcely been detached, leaving the 28th Virginia on the left, and Garnett was about to move to the position designated for him, when the Union skirmishers of Hatch's Division made their appearance, immediately followed by their main body and, at once, the action became general.

---

26  Carman borrowed much of the language used here from Gen. David R. Jones's report, *ibid.*, p. 886, and Gen. Richard Garnett's report, *ibid.*, p. 894.

27  Carman's Note: D. H. Hill's report, *ibid.*, p. 1,021.

Before considering this, we briefly note the position and formation of Kemper's Brigade on Garnett's left.[28]

When leaving the National road at the Mountain House Kemper moved to the left by the old Hagerstown road, Kemper and staff riding ahead some distance to see the lay of the ground. He had gone about 100 yards, beyond a backbone to a ridge running nearly north and south, when he was fired upon by the advancing enemy upon which he galloped back and formed his brigade across the old Hagerstown road. The brigade had come up under a severe shelling from Durell's Pennsylvania battery, on Reno's line, south of the National road, this enfilading fire causing some loss. It was formed from right to left in the following order: the 17th Virginia, Colonel M. D. Corse; 11th Virginia, Major Adam Clement, 1st Virginia, Captain Geo. F. Norton, 7th Virginia, Major Arthur Herbert, of the 17th Virginia, and the 24th Virginia, Colonel W. R. Terry. The 24th and 7th Virginia and part of the 1st were in rocky woods on the left of the road, the remainder of the brigade on the right of the road. On the extreme right the 17th Virginia, advanced about 100 yards to the far edge of a cornfield, a wood in front, and sent out skirmishers. Then it moved to the left, in the corn, to connect with the 11th Virginia, when the 56th Virginia of Garnett's Brigade, closed in on its right, the three regiments being in the same cornfield.[29]

The combined strength of the two brigades of Garnett and Kemper did not exceed 850 men[30], and they were about to be struck by Hatch's fine division.

When Hatch left the National road at Bolivar, to follow Meade to the right, he had the three brigades of Patrick, Phelps and Doubleday, with an effective force of about 3500 men. He arrived in the vicinity of Mt. Tabor church about 3.30 p. m. and formed on Meade's left.

The general order of battle was for two regiments of Patrick's Brigade to precede the main body, as skirmishers, supported by the two remaining regiments

---

28 These paragraphs are taken from Jones's report, *ibid.*, p. 886, Col. Eppa Hunton's report, *ibid.*, p. 898, Maj. Cabell's report, *ibid.*, p. 899, and Gen. Richard Garnett's report, *ibid.*, p. 894.

29 The latter portion of this description is from Col. Montgomery Corse's report, *ibid.*, p. 904. The specific details of Kemper's actions and the deployment of the brigade came from a letter by William H Palmer, 1st Virginia Infantry, August 26, 1899, NYPL, Box 2, Folder 5.

30 Carman's strength figures, tabulated in Chapter 23 for Sharpsburg, are 704 men for these two brigades. Adding to that sum the casualties lost at South Mountain (271, as stated at the end of the chapter and cited from the *OR,*) the total is 975—well above the 850 cited here. Col. Henry T. Owen, 18th Virginia Infantry, "Incidents of the Battle of South Mountain," *Philadelphia Weekly Times* (July 23, 1880), states that Garnett's Brigade at the Mountain House had 407 men present, so perhaps he is discounting stragglers. NYPL Box 11.15.

of the brigade, these to be followed at 200 paces by Phelps' Brigade, and Phelps in turn by Doubleday's, at the same interval.

Following this arrangement Patrick deployed the 21st New York, under Colonel William F. Rogers, as skirmishers, with orders to move up a ravine on the right, leading to a depression on the mountain top, and the 35th New York, Colonel Newton B. Lord, to move on the left of the 21st directly to the summit of the "south spur." The 21st New York was supported by the 80th Lieutenant Colonel Theodore B. Gates, and the 35th New York, by the 23d, Colonel Henry C. Hoffman, the objective point was the "south spur" and all the movements of the division were on the left, south, of the old Hagerstown road; Meade's Division operating, at the same time, on the right of that road.[31]

Rogers, with the 21st New York, supported by the 80th, ascended the ravine which partially divided the eastern slope of the mountain, throwing skirmishers to the right and left; the 35th New York, supported by the 23d, being on the left and, eventually, diverging so much farther to the left as to overlook the National road at the foot of the "south spur." These movements were made with some deliberation, under a fire of artillery described by D. H. Hill "as harmless as blank cartridge salutes in honor of a militia general" and which "the enemy did not honor by so much as a dodge."[32] Hill states that at this time the advance of Hatch's Division in three lines, a brigade in each, was grand and imposing. Hatch's general and field officers were on horseback, his colors were all flying, and the alignment of the men seemed to be perfectly preserved. Hooker looking at it from the foot of the mountain describes it as a beautiful sight. From the top it was grand and sublime. Hill states also that "there was not a single Confederate soldier to oppose the advance of General Hatch," and that he obtained some guns from the reserve artillery of Colonel Cutts to fire at the three imposing lines, but the cannonade, owing to the large angles of depression and the limited practice of the gunners was "the worst he ever witnessed." It was while this harmless cannonade was going on that Longstreet appeared with three small brigades and assumed direction of affairs,

31 Both Gen. John Hatch, the division commander, and Gen. Abner Doubleday, who replaced Hatch when he was wounded, wrote reports for South Mountain. See OR 19, pt. 1, pp. 220-223. Carman used elements of both reports to narrate this portion of the fighting. Phelps's brigade was known as the Iron Brigade, a term subsequently applied to John Gibbon's brigade. See Thomas Clemens, "The Other Iron Brigade," Civil War Times (April 2009), pp. 54-59.

32 Doubleday's report, ibid., pp. 221-2, and Gen. Marsena Patrick's report, ibid., pp. 241-2. The quote from Hill is from his B&L account, pp. 573-4.

Evans being sent to aid Rodes, and Garnett and Kemper to meet and check Hatch, advancing, so far, without opposition.[33]

Before these brigades had fairly taken position Hatch was well on his way up the "south spur." When nearing a road, part way up the spur, parallel to its crest, and just at the edge of a wood, it was discovered that there was a considerable interval between the right of the 35th New York and the left of the 21st, upon which the 80th New York was brought up to the left of the 21st and the left wing of the brigade, 35th and 23d New York, reaching this road at about the same time that the 21st struck it, was ordered to change direction to the right, to close the opening, which had not been accomplished, when Phelps' Brigade came up, in column of divisions, and passed through it. Phelps saw that no skirmish line was in front, halted, and advised Hatch of the situation. Hatch, who was close at hand, came up, rode to the front, saw that the gap was closed, and the skirmishers and entire line again pushed ahead, Phelps following 30 yards in rear of the skirmishers. Soon the ascending column came under fire of Garnett's and Kemper's skirmishers. Phelps deployed his brigade in line of battle, the skirmishers of the 35th New York and their support, the 23d New York, which had again drifted far to the left, were again drawn in to the right and merged into the general line of battle, now moving steadily toward the summit of the "south spur" under a galling fire from the Confederates above, posted behind trees, among rocks and under the shelter of stone walls. The steepness of the ascent and the heat of the day, added to the long march of the morning, caused a slow advance up the rough side of the spur.[34]

The skirmishers soon developed the position of Garnett's Brigade, behind a stone fence on the summit of the spur, running north and south, fronted by a wood and backed by a cornfield, full of rock ledges. Phelps now ordered his men to attack and Hatch rode through the lines to urge them forward. But they needed no urging, they leaped forward with a hearty cheer, poured in a hot fire, were given a hot volley in return, followed by a heavy and continuous fire, which was as heavily responded to and, after a contest of about fifteen minutes, in which Garnett's men displayed much courage and obstinacy, the line began to yield, the 28th Virginia on the left gave way and fell back on Kemper's right and the 8th Virginia, on the right, despite all efforts of Hunton, was obliged to yield ground and form on Jenkin's Brigade, just coming into position as Garnett's support. Phelps now ordered a charge, the

---

33 Carman once again used Hill's B&L account, verbatim, although Carman added in a quote from Hill's official report about the poor artillery practice (*OR* 19, pt. 1, p. 1,020). Hill's reference of Hooker's opinion may be a supposition taken from Hooker's report, *ibid.*, p. 215.

34 This paragraph is taken almost verbatim from the reports of Col. Walter Phelps, Jr., *ibid.*, pp. 231-2, and Patrick, *ibid.*, pp. 241-2. Carman supplied the identity of the opposing force.

stone fence was carried, and the entire line of Garnett driven back some 200 yards, leaving many prisoners in Phelps' hands. In this contest at the fence, Colonel J. B. Strange, 19th Virginia, was killed and General Hatch wounded. Doubleday succeeded to the command of the division.[35]

Captain H. T. Owen of Garnett's Brigade, after a graphic description of the march to the field and the appearance of the steadily advancing Union line, says:

> A heavy fire was soon opened upon the enemy, but they neither paused nor faltered, and a brief, fierce contest took place along the ridge until the enemy brought up a second line of reinforcements when the Confederates, being greatly outnumbered, gave way and rushed back down the hill and out in the open field. There was great confusion, and the broken ranks were hard to rally and reform, so that had the enemy followed up closely behind they could have taken the gap but the enemy halted . . . and this gave the Confederates time to rally and reform in separate squads and detachments behind the rocks and fences and reopen a brisk fire.
>
> . . . Still falling back and fighting as we retreated, we reached the fence across the field, and although half of the brigade had disappeared the survivors made a stand along the fence and endeavored to hold the enemy back until reinforcements could be brought up. There was now probably, not 200 men left in the brigade, and they were fighting in squads of a dozen or more, with great gaps between them, and were scattered along behind the fence and bushes for half a mile, while the enemy had a strong line in front and outflanked our position on both the right and left. On the right Colonel Eppa Hunton, with some 30 or 40 men, was trying to keep the enemy back, then a gap in the line, perhaps of 50 yards, and a dozen men were found together, and then another gap and another squad, then a gap of two or three hundred yards, and on the other side, but in line came Major Cabell (18th Virginia) and General Garnett with perhaps, a hundred men more. The sun was now behind the mountains and the somber shadows of night were settling down over the smoky, blood-stained field."[36]

While the main fight was in progress at the stone fence, between Phelps and Garnett, Patrick's divided brigade came up on either side of Phelps, the 21st and 80th New York on his right, the 35th and 23d New York on his left. Colonel Rogers, with his two regiments, 21st and 80th New York, co-operated with Phelps

---

35 Carman compiled information from Phelps's report, *ibid.*, pp. 231-2, and the reports of Hunton, *ibid.*, p. 898, Cabell, *ibid.*, p. 899, Brown, *ibid.*, p. 901, and Garnett, *ibid.*, p. 895. Owen, "Incidents of the Battle of South Mountain," p. 4, also confirms the actions of Garnett's Brigade.

36 Owen, "Incidents of the Battle of South Mountain," p. 4.

by cautiously advancing his right, forcing back part of Kemper's brigade skirmishers, and seizing and holding the fence bounding the northeast side of the cornfield. Phelps' fierce attack upon Garnett did not extend to Kemper's Brigade on Garnett's left, between whose right and Garnett's left was an interval of quite 200 yards. Kemper's skirmishers were driven in but the brigade front was not seriously engaged. Fearing, however, for the right flank, threatened by the fierce attack upon Garnett, the 56th Virginia, which had joined his right, changed front with its right wing prepared to meet the Union advance in that direction. It was now quite dark and almost impossible to see anything of Phelps' men, or of Garnett on his right front, but when, at the end of a few minutes, Garnett's 28th Virginia fell back onto Kemper's right, and it was ascertained that Union troops (21st and 80th New York) were advancing and forcing back the left, Colonel Corse, who was commanding the right wing (56th, 17th and 11th Virginia) fell back about 20 yards to the shelter of a fence, separating the cleared field and cornfield, which position was held until long after dark, under a severe fire of musketry, obliquely on his right and upon his front.[37]

On the left the 23d and 35th New York came up to the fence that Phelps had carried and opened fire through the cornfield. After a few rounds the Confederate fire slackened, the two regiments were ordered to cease firing and the alignment corrected about five yards back of the fence. It was then quite dark and there was much confusion, which was increased by the renewal of the Confederate fire and, Doubleday coming up ordered the regiments back to the fence.[38]

At this time Phelps' Brigade, much reduced in number by casualties and meeting a determined resistance from the Confederates, was relieved by Doubleday's Brigade, now under command of Colonel William P. Wainwright, 76th New York. This brigade had ascended the spur in close support to Phelps and numbered about 1000 men. It took position behind the stone fence from which Garnett had been driven, but who had rallied in knots and squads, in the cornfield,

---

37 Carman has combined the reports of Patrick, OR 19, pt. 1, pp. 241-2, and William Stuart, *ibid.*, pp. 902-3. That Patrick's brigade was split by Phelps's command is inferred from Lt. Col. Theodore Gates's report, *ibid.*, pp. 245-6. The 200-yard gap between Gens. Kemper and Garnett is not reported in the OR.

38 Carman may have found this account in Pound Sterling (William P. Maxson), *Campfires of the Twenty-third* (NY: Davis Kent Printers, 1863), p. 99, but that source quotes Henry C. Hoffman's unpublished report of the battle of South Mountain. A handwritten (by Carman) copy of Hoffman's Antietam report is in the NA-AS collection. Although the South Mountain report is not there, he may have obtained both accounts from this source.

still showing a determined, although broken, front. Wainwright's left extended beyond Garnett's right and was threatened by Jenkins.[39]

Jenkins' Brigade, commanded by Colonel Joseph Walker, Palmetto Sharpshooters, followed Garnett, reached the field shortly after 4 p.m. and formed on Garnett's right, but some distance in rear, and but a short distance beyond the Mountain House. When the attack developed upon Garnett it moved, under Jones' order, farther up the mountain, obliquely to the right, and formed line, still on Garnett's right and to his rear. The 1st, 6th and 5th South Carolina were quickly advanced 200 yards to the front, behind a stone fence, where the 8th Virginia, of Garnett's Brigade, driven from its position at the front, fell in on their left, small parties of Kemper and Garnett's men rallied upon the line and kept up an irregular fire upon the 23d and 35th New York and Doubleday's Brigade, which had relieved Phelps.

It was the movement of Jenkins in the fading light that led Wainwright to believe that an effort was being made to turn his left, though no such movement was intended, upon which he changed front with the 76th New York and 7th Indiana. A severe fire was kept up for some time, by both sides, Garnett's and Jenkins' position being known only by the flashes of fire from their muskets, when, almost out of ammunition, Wainwright was relieved by Christian's Brigade of Ricketts' Division and fell back a few paces.[40]

Christian's Brigade fired a few volleys and, in about a half hour, the Confederates withdrew and the Union troops lay on their arms for the night. Hartsuff's Brigade of Ricketts' Division was brought up after dark and formed line across the gorge, connecting Hatch's right with Meade's left and the entire corps was ordered to sleep on its arms.[41]

While the contest was its height on the crest of the "south spur," Gibbon's and Colquitt's brigades were severely engaging each other on the National road, which ran past the south foot of the spur. Colquitt, as has been noted, had been withdrawn from the east foot of the mountain nearer to the summit and placed in line on either side of the road. About 700 yards in a direct line from the Mountain House, or about 850 yards by the winding road, the 23d Georgia, Colonel W. P. Barclay, and the 28th Georgia, Major Tully Graybill, each with about 300 men, were

39 Wainwright was wounded at South Mountain, so the report was prepared by Lt. Col. J. William Hoffmann, 56th Pennsylvania, who commanded the brigade. OR 19, pt. 1, pp. 234-5.

40 The first paragraph is taken from the report of Col. Joseph Walker, commanding Jenkins's brigade, ibid., pp. 905-6, except the mention of the 8th Virginia falling in on its left. The change of front to repulse an attack is mentioned in Hoffmann's report, ibid., p. 235.

41 Carman borrowed this summary from Hooker's report, ibid., p. 215.

on the left, north of the road. The 23d, its right resting on the road, was under cover of a stone fence and a channel or shallow ravine worn by water down the slope of the "south spur." The 28th, on the left of the 23d, was about one-fourth behind the same stone fence, the other three-fourths in the woods higher up the spur. The position held by the two regiments was a very strong one. The 23d was under cover and out of sight until the enemy mounted a gentle rise of ground about 40 yards in front, of which and the ground to its right front, the 23d had complete command, while the 28th, on its left, on the wooded slope of the spur, had command of the approaches to the front of the 23d and, by advancing its left could enfilade any line attacking it. Two companies of each regiment were detached as skirmishers. The 6th and 27th Georgia and 13th Alabama were on the right of the road, on lower ground than the 23d Georgia, nearly the entire line in woods, extending across a deep ravine, and under instructions to connect with Garland on the right, but the force in the three regiments was not sufficient to reach that distance, and there was a gap of quite 400 yards between the two brigades, and this gap Colquitt was to cover should it become necessary to do so. Upon the right of the road, about 400 yards in advance of Colquitt's right, was a thick growth of woods, with fields opening in front and around them. In these woods were concealed four companies of Colquitt's skirmishers, under command of Captain W. M. Arnold. The strength of Colquitt's Brigade was about 1350 officers and enlisted men.[42]

When Hatch's Division turned to the right at Bolivar, Gibbon's Brigade was detached from it, and, moving on the National road a short distance, was halted. After two hours, or about 5 p. m., when the general advance was made by Hooker, on the right, and Reno, on the left, Gibbon was ordered by Burnside to move directly up the road and attack the Confederates in position at Turner's Gap. One section of Campbell's Battery, under command of Lieutenant James Stewart accompanied the brigade. The 7th Wisconsin, Captain John B. Callis, formed on the right of the road, and the 19th Indiana, Colonel Solomon Meredith, on the left, Captain W. W. Dudley's company of the 19th being thrown to the left as flankers. One company each from the 2d and 6th Wisconsin, under command of Captain Wilson Colwell, of the 2d, were thrown 100 yards to the front, and the two advance regiments followed, formed in double columns at half distance, the section of artillery in the road a short distance in rear of the infantry. The 7th Wisconsin was

---

42 Grattan, "Battle of Boonsboro Gap or South Mountain," pp. 36-8, and Gen. Alfred Colquitt's report, OR 19, pt. 1, pp. 1,052-3. In Chapter 23, "Strengths of the Union and Confederate Armies," Carman credits Colquitt with 1,250 men at South Mountain, but also states that details for camp guards, etc. were left in Boonsboro. Perhaps he added an estimated number for them to the total.

supported by the 6th, Lieutenant Colonel Edward S. Bragg, and the 19th Indiana by the 2d Wisconsin, Colonel Lucius Fairchild, each following about 200 yards in rear.[43]

When Colquitt saw those well regulated movements he sent an urgent request for support, but D. H. Hill had none to give and he was left to his own resources.[44]

The Wisconsin skirmishers soon encountered those of Colquitt and were closely supported by the 7th Wisconsin and 19th Indiana, while Stewart's two guns moved on the road until within range of the Confederate guns, firing from the summit of the gap, when they opened with good effect. The 19th Indiana, in advancing on the left of the road, was much annoyed by a skirmish fire from a house and outbuildings, surrounded on the southwest and north by woods. This fire was soon silenced by a few shots from Stewart's guns, but the Georgians, seeking the cover of the woods, re-opened fire, upon which Colonel Meredith ordered his regiment forward and engaged them at close quarters. The Georgians soon yielded and were closely followed, when coming to a stone fence they rallied on Arnold's skirmish battalion, and the Indianians were checked by a severe fire. Captain Clark's company was wheeled to the left and gaining a position enfilading the line behind the fence, speedily dislodged Arnold's skirmishers, Clark taking 11 prisoners, including three officers. The 2d Wisconsin supported the 19th Indiana by moving upon its right, its right resting on the National road.[45]

On the right of the road the 7th Wisconsin moved about 100 yards in rear of the skirmishers, went, by the right of companies to the front, through a cornfield nearly a half a mile, and emerged into an open field, where the skirmishers met such a sharp fire from those of the 23d and 28th Georgia that farther progress was checked, the open field affording no shelter from the fire of the Georgians, behind one of the stone walls bounding the winding road. The regiment soon formed line of battle and advanced, its left touching the road, the right extending north to the edge of the woods on the slope of the "south spur." It immediately came under the fire of the enemy from the stone fence on the left of the road, from which, as yet, they had not been driven by the 19th Indiana and 2d Wisconsin, which fire was returned by a left oblique volley, followed by a scattering fire, when the 19th Indiana and 2d Wisconsin coming up on that side of the road and dislodging the Confederates, as we have seen, the 7th Wisconsin kept on until an enfilading fire

---

43 This information is from Gen. John Gibbon's report, *ibid.*, p. 247. Carman filled in the names of the commanders.

44 Colquitt's report, *ibid.*, p. 1,053.

45 Col. Solomon Meredith's report, 19th Indiana, *ibid.*, pp. 249-50.

from the 28th Georgia, in the woods on the right, and a direct fire, at 40 yards, from the 23d Georgia, behind the stone fence in the ravine, again checked it; it did not give back and the fire on both sides was rapid and deadly.[46] Colquitt says:

> Confident in their superior numbers, the enemy's forces advanced to a short distance of our lines, when, raising a shout, they came to a charge. As they came full into view upon the rising ground, 40 paces distant, they were met by a terrific volley of musketry from the stone fence and hill side. This gave a sudden check to their advance. They rallied under cover of the uneven ground and the fight opened in earnest. They made still another effort to advance, but were kept back by the steady fire of our men."[47]

Meanwhile the 19th Indiana and 2d Wisconsin had come up on the left and, having driven the Confederates from their own front, opened a right oblique fire upon the 23d Georgia, engaging the 7th Wisconsin. The 2d Wisconsin, with its right wing changed front to the right, parallel to the road, and opened fire, but its ammunition was soon exhausted, when it was relieved by the left wing, the left wing being relieved, in turn, by the 19th Indiana. From the fact that the 23d Georgia was well protected by the stone fence and that the 19th Indiana and 2d Wisconsin were on much lower ground their firing was not effective and the 7th Wisconsin could make no progress. Callis, commanding the regiment, made an effort to drive the Georgians from behind the fence, by advancing by his right wing and getting an enfilade fire upon them, but there burst from the woods on the right a flame of musketry from the 28th Georgia followed by such a shower of bullets into the rear of the right wing that it was driven back and enforced the impression that the Confederates were making effort to flank the line, upon which Bragg, who was but a few yards in rear, was ordered to form the 6th Wisconsin on the right of the 7th and check the movement. Bragg moved double quick and became engaged with the 28th Georgia. He used some effective tactics, the details of which he gives in his official report:

> The skirmishers soon found the enemy in front, and an irregular fire commenced. This was past twilight. The Seventh moved to the support of the skirmishers, and was soon engaged with the enemy, who was concealed in a wood on their left and in a ravine in front. So soon as the Seventh received the fire of the enemy and commenced replying, I deployed the Sixth, and with the right wing opened fire upon the enemy concealed in

---

46 This is from the report of Capt. John Callis, 7th Wisconsin, *ibid.*, p. 256.

47 Colquitt's report, *ibid.*, p. 1,053.

the wood upon the right. I also moved the left wing by the right flank into the rear of the right wing, and commenced a fire by the wings alternately, and advancing the line after each volley.

At this time I received an order from the general, directing me to flank the enemy in the wood. The condition of the surface of the ground, and the steepness of the ascent up the mountain side, rendered this movement a difficult one; but without hesitation the left wing moved by the flank into the wood, firing as they went, and advancing the line. I directed Major Dawes to advance the right wing on the skirt of the wood as rapidly as the line in the wood advanced, which he did. This movement forward and by the flank I continued until the left wing rested its right on the crest of the hill, extending around the enemy in a semicircular line, and then moved the right wing into the wood so as to connect the line from the open field to the top of the hill. While this was being done, the fire of the enemy, who fought us from behind rocks and trees, and entirely under cover, was terrific, but steadily the regiment dislodged him and kept advancing. Ammunition commenced to give out, no man having left more than four rounds, and many without any. It was dark, and a desperate enemy in front.

At this moment I received an order from General Gibbon to cease fire and maintain the position, and the battle was won. I directed my men to reserve their fire, unless compelled to use it, and then only at short range, and trust to the bayonet. No sooner did the time of fire erase than the enemy, supposing we were checked, crept close up in the wood and commenced a rapid fire. I directed a volley in reply, and then, with three lusty cheers for Wisconsin, the men sat cheerfully down to await another attack; but the enemy was no more seen.[48]

Gibbon held his ground until late in the night, when all his command, except the 6th Wisconsin, which occupied the field all night, was relieved by Gorman's Brigade of Sumner's Corps. He had lost 37 killed, 251 wounded, and 30 missing. Among the killed was Captain Wilson Colwell, 2d Wisconsin, an officer of rare merit, who commanded the skirmishers with signal ability and bravery.[49]

Colquitt's loss was about 110 killed, wounded and missing, falling principally upon the 23d and 28th Georgia. He closes his official report with the statement that "The fight was continued with fury until after dark. Not an inch of ground was

48 Before he included the long quote from Lt. Col. Edward Bragg's report, 6th Wisconsin, *ibid.*, pp. 253-4, which Carman pasted into the manuscript, he included information from Col. Lucius Fairchild's report, 2nd Wisconsin, *ibid.*, pp. 252-3, and Callis's report, *ibid.*, pp. 256-7.

49 The summary and casualty figures are from Gibbon's report, *ibid.*, p. 248, and the mention of Capt. Colwell's death is taken from Fairchild's report, *ibid.*, p. 253. Although Carman corresponded with Dawes and Gibbon, neither mentioned details of South Mountain.

yielded. The ammunition of many of the men was exhausted, but they stood with bayonets fixed." He quietly withdrew about 10 p.m. and marched for Sharpsburg.[50]

When night put an end to the day's conflict the Confederates still held the National road, leading over Turner's Gap, but both flanks had been forced back. On the right Fox's Gap was held, but Cox held the crest in front and south of it, and the roads leading into Pleasant Valley, south of Boonsboro. North of the National road Hooker had completely turned the position, seized the commanding heights from which he had driven Rodes and Evans, and their supports, and was waiting for daylight, to advance to the rear of the Mountain House, to which Lee's entire left wing had been driven.

It was an anxious and disheartened group that gathered at General Lee's headquarters that night. D. H. Hill, who was more conversant with the situation than either Lee or Longstreet, expressed his decided opinion that the position was no longer tenable and advised an immediate retreat. Longstreet concurred with Hill. Lee had not entirely abandoned hope and, before giving orders for a retreat, ordered a small detachment back to the ground on the left, to ascertain whether it was still held by Hooker, or whether he had retired, as reported. A picket officer, Lieutenant W. P. Dubose, of the Holcombe Legion, was charged with the duty, went forward and was captured. Hooker's pickets were found alert and strongly posted on the heights overlooking the Mountain House, and a prisoner gave information that Sumner had arrived at Bolivar and that the Twelfth Corps was on the march for that place. Lee then ordered a retreat.[51]

Longstreet reports: "It became manifest that our forces were not sufficient to resist the renewed attacks of the entire army of Gen. McClellan. He would require but little time to turn either flank, and our command must then be at his mercy. In view of this, the commanding general ordered the withdrawal of our troops to the village of Sharpsburg."[52]

In a letter to Jefferson Davis, written at Sharpsburg, September 16, 1862, Lee reports:

---

50 The quote is from Colquitt's report, *ibid.*, p. 1,053, but the casualty figure comes from an extensive note later in this chapter, which actually totals 109 casualties.

51 Longstreet's memoirs seems to be the source for this story of the meeting of Hill, Lee, and himself, which Harsh explores more fully in *Sounding the Shallows*, p. 181. See Col. P. F. Stevens's report, *OR* 19, pt. 1, p. 942, for the disappearance of his adjutant, Lt. William Porcher DuBose. His capture was confirmed in a letter by Henry J. Sheafer, 107th New York, who referred to him as commanding the Holcolme Legion. Letter to Gould, Gould Papers, Dartmouth, NH.

52 Longstreet's report, *OR* 19, pt. 1, p. 840.

My letter to you of the 13th instant informed you of the positions of the different divisions of this army. Learning that night that Harper's Ferry had not surrendered, and that the enemy was advancing more rapidly than was convenient from Fredericktown, I determined to return with Longstreet's command to the Blue Ridge, to strengthen D. H. Hill's and Stuart's divisions, engaged in holding the passes of the mountains, lest the enemy should fall upon McLaws' rear, drive him from the Maryland Heights, and thus relieve the garrison at Harper's Ferry. On approaching Boonsborough, I received information from General D. H. Hill that the enemy in strong force was at the main pass on the Frederick and Hagerstown road, pressing him so heavily as to require immediate re-enforcements. Longstreet advanced rapidly to his support, and immediately placed his troops in position. By this time Hill's right had been forced back, the gallant Garland having fallen in rallying his brigade. Under General Longstreet's directions, our right was soon restored, and firmly resisted the attacks of the enemy to the last. His superior numbers enabled him to extend beyond both of our flanks, and his right was able to reach the summit of the mountain to our left, and press us heavily in that direction. The battle raged until after night; the enemy's efforts to force a passage resisted, but we had been unable to repulse him.

Learning later in the evening that Crampton's Gap (on the direct road from Fredericktown to Sharpsburg) had been forced, and McLaws' rear thus threatened, and believing from a report from General Jackson that Harper's Ferry would fall next morning, I determined to withdraw Longstreet and D. H. Hill from their positions and retire to the vicinity of Sharpsburg, where the army could be more easily united. Before abandoning the position, indications led me to believe that the enemy was withdrawing, but learning from a prisoner that Sumner's corps (which had not been engaged) was being put in position to relieve their wearied troops, while the most of ours were exhausted by a fatiguing march and a hard conflict, and I feared would be unable to renew the fight successfully in the morning, confirmed me in my determination. Accordingly, the troops were withdrawn, preceded by the trains, without molestation by the enemy, and about daybreak took position in front of this place.[53]

## In his official report, August 19, 1863, Gen. Lee says:

The effort to force the passage of the mountain had failed, but it was manifest that without reinforcements we could not hazard a renewal of the engagement, as the enemy could easily turn either flank. Information was also received that another large body of Federal troops had during the afternoon forced their way through Crampton's

53 *Ibid.*, p. 140. Lee's knowledge of Jackson's situation was much more complete on September 16, when he wrote this letter, than it was on the night of September 14.

Gap, only 5 miles in rear of McLaws. Under these circumstances, it was determined to retire to Sharpsburg, where we would be on the flank and rear of the enemy should he move against Mclaws, and where we could more readily unite with the rest of the army."[54]

The retreat began about 10 o'clock, the troops near the Mountain House retiring by the National road and Boonsboro, those confronting Cox generally by the old Sharpsburg road to the foot of the mountain, and thence to Boonsboro. Jenkins' South Carolina Brigade covered the withdrawal from Turner's Gap. When Colquitt was withdrawn from the foot of the mountain, about 10 o'clock, the 2d South Carolina went down the National road from the Mountain House, and threw out a strong line of skirmishers on either side of it, Walker, commanding the brigade, remaining at the Mountain House with the other regiments, until 4 a. m. of the 15th, when the 2d South Carolina was withdrawn, the brigade relieved by Fitzhugh Lee's cavalry and marched to Sharpsburg, where it rejoined its division. Rosser, with the 5th Virginia cavalry, covered the withdrawal of the troops from Fox's Gap.[55]

During the day the Union troops in the rear closed up on the First and Ninth corps. The Second Corps moved from Frederick by the Shookstown road, north of the National road, to Middletown, thence by the National road to Bolivar. Richardson's Division was pushed ahead to Mt. Tabor Church to the support of the First Corps, one brigade of Sedgwick's Division was ordered to relieve Gibbon, the other two brigades and French's Division remained at Bolivar.[56]

The Twelfth Corps, near Frederick, was ordered to move at 7 a.m., it was somewhat later when it drew out on the road. It marched through Frederick as the church bells were calling to worship the followers of the Prince of Peace. The Stars and Stripes floated over the most prominent buildings, hung from windows and were waved by fair hands, demonstrating that the brief Confederate occupation of the ancient borough had not impaired its love for the old Flag, nor diminished its sympathies for its defenders. Through the streets of Frederick-town, "green-walled by the hills of Maryland," rendered immortal by Whittier's undying verse, on that beautiful Sabbath morning amid the ringing of church bells and the waving of flags, thousands of men pressed on to conquer a peace and to illustrate to all coming

---

54 *Ibid.,* p. 147.

55 Walker's report, *ibid.,* p. 906. Rossser's rearguard position is confirmed in a letter by him to Carman dated May 12, 1897, and found in NA-AS.

56 McClellan's report, *OR* 19, pt. 1, p. 52.

time, to all Christian nations, that the truth of Julia Ward Howe's most beautiful sentiment that as Christ died to make men holy, the highest duty of a citizen-soldier is to die to make men free. Presently a voice strikes up the song of "John Brown's body," the bands join in, it is taken up regiment after regiment, is carried from the leading brigade through the whole division, from one division to another, until the grand chorus, swelling from thousands of voices, fills the whole air and produces an effect beyond the comprehension of those who know not, from experience, the capability, power and richness of a man's voice when a man's heart is in it.[57]

It was thus that the Twelfth Corps marched through and out of Frederick, then it climbed the Catoctin Mountain and saw from its summit the beautiful Middletown or Catoctin Valley, bathed in a flood of sunlight. Beyond this peaceful and charming valley, a garden in the highest state of cultivation, could be seen the powder smoke as the shells exploded in air at and near Turner's Gap. Descending into the valley the corps went into bivouac but, after a brief rest, was again ordered forward. The road was crowded with artillery, ordnance and baggage wagons, and the troops were compelled to take to the fields, and through corn higher than the heads of the men. It was now dark and the march was through fields and woods and over ditches and fences—north, south, east and west—in fact if there is a point of the compass, toward which the heads of the column did not march that evening and in the darkness it is unknown to us. Finally the advance struck a road that led to Middletown, thence it took the road leading back to Frederick, went some distance, found somebody had blundered and marched back to Middletown, where, worn out by the unnecessary marching, the men lay down in the streets awaiting orders, and while waiting they slept, not the sleep of the righteous for they swore worse than the army in Flanders. Again they were urged forward and about midnight halted near Bolivar; the organizations were there but more than one half the men were sleeping in cornfields along fences and in the tortuous trail of the march.[58]

Sykes' Division and the reserve artillery marched from Frederick and halted for the night at Middletown. Thus, reports McClellan: "On the night of the 14th the

---

57  It appears that this paragraph (and probably the next one) is one of the few times Carman injected his own memoirs and opinions into his manuscript. He commanded a regiment in the Twelfth Corps and experienced the march toward South Mountain from Frederick. No other source has been found for it.

58  It is interesting that Carman ignored this march when he castigated McClellan for not making a night march after discovering S.O. #191. In fact, there were two nights where at least part of (or an entire) corps was night marching: Rodman's division on the September 13, and this instance. Both were made with difficulty and unsatisfactory results. Swearing in Flanders was a common phrase in 19th Century writing. It refers to the Spanish Army in the 16th Century, which was notorious for mutinying.

whole army was massed in the vicinity of the field of battle, in readiness to renew the action next day or to move in pursuit of the enemy."[59]

The Confederates indulged in many regrets that affairs at South Mountain were not differently managed. Longstreet, speaking only of his own troops, says: "Had the command reached the mountain pass in time to have gotten into position before the attack was made, I believe that the direct assault of the enemy could have been repulsed with comparative ease. Hurried into action, however, we arrived at our position more exhausted than the enemy."[60] D. H. Hill contends that had Longstreet's men been directed to report to him the result might have been different, and further says:

> Had Longstreet's division been with mine at daylight in the morning, the Yankees would have been disastrously repulsed; but they had gained important positions before the arrival of reinforcements. These additional troops came up, after a long, hurried, and exhausting march, to defend locations of which they were ignorant, and to fight a foe flushed with partial success, and already holding key points to farther advance. Had our forces never been separated, the battle of Sharpsburg would never have been fought, and the Yankees would not have even the shadow of consolation for the loss of Harper's Ferry."[61]

These are vain regrets and apologies for defeat, but Hill derives some consolation from the satisfactory work of his own division and makes it the subject of official report:

> Should the truth be known, the battle of South Mountain, as far as my division was concerned, will be regarded as one of the most remarkable and creditable of the war. The division had marched all the way from Richmond, and the straggling had been enormous in consequence of heavy marches, deficient commissariat, want of shoes, and inefficient officers. Owing to these combined causes, the division numbered less than 5,000 men the morning of September 14, and had five roads to guard, extending over a space of as many miles. This small force successfully resisted, without support, for eight hours, the whole Yankee army, and, when its supports were beaten, still held the roads, so that our retreat was effected without the loss of a gun, a wagon, or an ambulance. Rodes's brigade had immortalized itself; Colquitt's had fought well, and

---

59  McClellan's report, *OR* 19, pt. 1, pp. 52-3.

60  Longstreet's report, *ibid.*, p. 839.

61  D. H. Hill's report, *ibid.*, p. 1,022.

the two regiments most closely pressed (Twenty-third and Twenty-eighth Georgia) had repulsed the foe. Garland's brigade had behaved nobly, until demoralized by the fall of its gallant leader, and being outflanked by the Yankees. Anderson's brigade had shown its wonted gallantry. Ripley's brigade, for some cause, had not been engaged, and was used with Hood's two brigades to cover retreat.[62]

A Confederate historian makes this criticism:

Hill's troops were badly handled. The field was not understood, and the troops not promptly enough put into position. Though with such odds against the Confederates as demanded the services of every man, Ripley's Brigade was not engaged at all, and the half of G. B. Anderson's very slightly. The condition of affairs was not improved after Longstreet's arrival, though of course it should be remembered that he came hurriedly upon an unknown battlefield in the midst of a fight. Three of his brigades lost valuable time and valuable strength in marching first two or three miles towards the south side of the battlefield, and then retracing their steps. Others seem to have been badly placed. G. T. Anderson's Brigade was not engaged, and Jenkins' but slightly. It seems probable that had Hill's troops been in position in the early morning, and had Longstreet arrived some hours sooner, the Federal army would not have succeeded in taking and holding any of the Confederate positions.[63]

On the other hand McClellan cannot escape criticism. His movements were so slow that he failed in the object of his movement—the relief of Harper's Ferry. We have referred to his failure to take advantage of his knowledge of Lee's plans and press forward on the afternoon and night of the 13th. Affairs were not better conducted on the morning of the 14th. Cox went promptly forward and engaged the enemy, on the summit of the mountain, at 9 o'clock and, notwithstanding the assurance given him that the entire corps would promptly follow, it was five hours later, at 2 p. m., when Willcox came to his support. He had camped one mile east of

62 *Ibid.*, pp. 1,021-2. Rather than "vain regrets and apologies," both Longstreet's and D. H. Hill's comments can be read as criticisms of Lee's handling of the army during these crucial days of the campaign. Apparently Carman did not want to interpret them in that vein.

63 Allan, *Army of Northern Virginia*, p. 360. While D. H. Hill's troops may have been badly handled, much blame also belongs to Stuart, for he was designated by Lee to oversee the rearguard. Hill never had any orders to fight at South Mountain, and was only directed there to assist Stuart in defending Turner's Gap. Allan was part of the Southern Historical Society, which sought to exonerate Lee from all blame, and thus he pinned the loss at South Mountain on D. H. Hill, much the way this organization blamed Longstreet for the loss at Gettysburg. These writers, including Jubal Early, vigorously defended Lee's performance from any blemish, and Carman seemed to accept their accounts at face value.

Middletown, and had but six miles to march, yet, in doing so, consumed six hours of most valuable time. Sturgis' Division, which had camped near Middletown was not ordered forward until 1 p. m. and arrived on the field at 3.30 p. m. We now know that had Willcox and Sturgis joined Cox before noon, as they could and should have done, Cox could have carried Fox's Gap and flanked the position at Turner's Gap before the arrival of Lee's foot-sore men from Hagerstown. And Hooker's movements on the right were entirely too deliberate for the occasion. Burnside never went beyond his headquarters at Bolivar, from what McClellan says, and, was listless and indifferent. McClellan was late on the field and fairly responsible for the delay of his subordinates in not energetically pushing matters and for Burnside's neglect to reinforce Cox and carry the passes before night.[64]

The result of the day's work was that the Confederate invasion of the North was thwarted: Lee ordered McLaws to recross the Potomac by the most practicable ford; the Reserve artillery, which had been halted on Beaver Creek, was, except S. D. Lee's Battalion, ordered back to Virginia, by way of Williamsport; Lee led that part of the army with him to cross the Potomac by the Shepherdstown Ford, and Jackson was ordered up from Harper's Ferry to cover his crossing.[65]

64 This analysis of the activities of the two armies appears to be Carman's own, or perhaps the consensus of the members of the Antietam Battlefield Board. While Carman blames Willcox, and ultimately McClellan, for a lack of speed and forcefulness at South Mountain, he was using hindsight to reach that conclusion. Cox's initial orders did not anticipate battle at all on September 14. Cox was sent to take and hold Turner's Gap. When the battle erupted, it required time for orders to reach Willcox, for him to get his men prepared to move, and to march to the fight. Carman's retrospective view assumes that Willcox should have been prepared to march immediately to Cox's aid. Burnside's position is arguable as well. Moving closer to either gap (Fox's or Turner's) would cause him to lose sight of the other, and make it more difficult to control his two corps. Carman included this quote from McClellan's memoir: "Burnside never came as near the battle as my position. Yet it was his command that was in action. He spent the night in the same house that I did." McClellan, *Own Story*, p. 583.

65 While criticizing McClellan's alleged inactivity, and that of his subordinates, Carman does credit him (almost in passing) with achieving a decisive result that changed the momentum of the campaign. Whatever else Lee lost at South Mountain, he certainly lost the initiative, although arguable this happened when McClellan arrived at Frederick. In addition, McClellan forced Lee into a retreat, the first the Union had seen of Lee's Confederates, and made an invasion of Pennsylvania much less likely. Lee's dispatch to McLaws, OR 51, pt. 2, pp. 618-619, continued the information that Lee was returning to Virginia and ordered McLaws to break off the siege of Harpers Ferry. Harsh, in *Sounding the Shallows*, pp. 181-182, and *Taken at the Flood*, pp. 287-95, offers a detailed study of the decision to retreat. Pendleton's report, *ibid.*, 19, pt. 1, pp. 829-30, contains the orders for the Reserve Artillery. No order to Jackson about covering Lee's crossing has been found, although Henry Kyd Douglas claims there was one. Douglas, *I Rode with Stonewall* (Chapel Hill: University of North Carolina Press, 1940), p. 164. Carman, in the next chapter, positively states there was such an order, perhaps influenced by Douglas. Although Douglas' memoir was printed long after Carman was dead, Douglas and Carman

The Union troops engaged at Turner's Gap numbered about 26,000 men and their loss was 1,813 killed, wounded and missing.

The Confederates engaged consisted of one cavalry regiment under Rosser, of the five brigades under D. H. Hill and of the eight brigades which came up with Longstreet. Hill's Division numbered 5,000. It is doubtful if Longstreet's brigades were as strong as Hill's, but averaging them at the same, the Confederates had in all some 13,000 or 14,000 men on the field."[66]

Their loss was about 1950 killed, wounded and missing. Though tactically defeated in the engagements at Crampton's Gap and Turner's Gap, the Confederates were strategically successful and D. H. Hill was correct in his statement that they had "accomplished all that was required, the delay of the Yankee army until Harper's Ferry could not be relieved."[67]

## Casualties in the Union Forces at the Battle of South Mountain (Turner's and Fox's Gaps), September 14, 1862

| Command | Killed | Wounded | Missing | Total |
|---|---|---|---|---|
| First Army Corps | | | | |
| Hatch's Division | 63 | 390 | 43 | 496 |
| Rickett's Division | 9 | 26 | | 35 |
| Meade's Division | 95 | 296 | 1 | 392 |
| Ninth Army Corps (staff) | 1 | | | 1 (Gen. Reno) |
| Willcox's Division | 63 | 287 | | 350 |
| Sturgis' Division | 10 | 117 | 30 | 157 |
| Rodman's Division | 2 | 18 | | 20 |
| Cox's Division | 81 | 269 | 11 | 361 |

communicated often and Douglas shared many stores with him and other writers. That Jackson would receive an order similar to that sent to McLaws seems logical.

66 Allan, *Army of Northern Virginia*, p. 360.

67 Hill's report, *ibid.*, p. 1,021. Carman accepted Hill's view, but it can also be argued that this was the first time a portion of Lee's army had been beaten and driven from the battlefield. That alone might have been the cause for cheering by the successful Union soldiers.

| Cavalry Division | 1 | | | 1 |
| Total | 325 | 1,403 | 85 | 1,813[68] |

## Casualties in the Confederate Forces at South Mountain (Turner's and Fox's Gaps), September 14, 1862

| Command | Killed | Wounded | Missing | Total |
|---|---|---|---|---|
| D. H. Hill's Division—Staff | 1 | | | 1 (Gen. Garland) |
| Rodes's Brigade | 61 | 157 | 204 | 422[69] |
| Ripley's Brigade | | | | 0 |
| G. B. Anderson's Brigade | 7 | 54 | 29 | 90[70] |
| Garland's Brigade | 37 | 168 | 154 | 359[71] |
| Colquitt's Brigade | 18 | 74 | 17 | 109[72] |

68 This chart is a summary of the more detailed returns posted after the Union losses. It is unclear why Carman arranged them in this manner.

69 *OR* 19, pt. 1, p. 1,036.

70 Carman's Note: In *ibid.*, p. 1,026 the loss in Geo. B. Anderson's Brigade during the Maryland campaign, is given as 64 killed, 299 wounded, 202 missing. On page 1,048, Col. R. T. Bennett gives the loss of his brigade at Antietam as 57 killed and 245 wounded, but does not give the number missing, which was very large. D. H. Hill, in *B&L*, p. 579, says Anderson had 29 missing at Turner's Gap, and this estimate we accept, making the loss at Turner's Gap, as tabulated.

71 Carman's Note: In *ibid.*, p. 1,026, the loss of Garland's Brigade, in the entire campaign is given as 46 killed, 210 wounded, 187 missing, an aggregate of 443. It is known that at Antietam this brigade was not long or severely engaged, while at Turner's Gap, it was both long and severely engaged. We estimate that four-fifths of its loss, as recorded for the entire campaign, was sustained at Turner's Gap, which gives the result as tabulated.

72 Carman's Note: In *ibid.*, p. 1,026, the loss of Colquitt's Brigade for the entire campaign is given as 129 killed, 518 wounded, 184 missing. D. H. Hill, after an extended correspondence with the officers of the brigade, estimates its loss at Turner's Gap as 92 killed and wounded and seven missing, in which estimate is not included 10 missing of the 6th and 27th Georgia and 13th Alabama. This estimate we believe to be approximately correct and adopt. Allowing one killed to four wounded and adding the 10 missing in the 6th and 27th Georgia and 13th Alabama, we have 18 killed, 74 wounded, 17 missing.

| | | | | |
|---|---|---|---|---|
| Bondurant's Battery | | 3 | | 3[73] |
| D. H. Hill's Division Total | 124 | 456 | 404 | 984 |

| Command | Killed | Wounded | Missing | Total |
|---|---|---|---|---|
| D. R. Jones' Division | | | | |
| G. T. Anderson's Brigade | | 3 | 4 | 7[74] |
| Garnett's Brigade | 35 | 142 | 19 | 196[75] |
| Drayton's Brigade | 49 | 164 | 176 | 389[76] |

73 Carman's Note: The loss of the artillery of D. H. Hill's Division is given as four killed, 30 wounded, three missing, for the entire campaign. Of this number, Bondurant's Battery had three wounded. We cannot learn that the other batteries had any casualties.

74 Carman's Note: General Geo. T. Anderson informs us that his loss at Turner's Gap was six or seven men wounded and missing. [Although several letters from G. T. Anderson to Carman exist, none found yet mention South Mountain casualties.]

75 Carman's Note: Garnett's Brigade, OR 19, pt. 1, p. 898, gives the loss of the 8th Virginia as 11 killed and wounded; 18th Virginia (p. 900) 7 killed, 27 wounded, seven missing; 19th Virginia (p. 901) 63 killed, wounded and missing; 56th Virginia (p. 903) 40 killed and wounded and five missing. There are no reports from the 28th Virginia, but its strength was about 95 men. Assuming that its loss was in the same proportion as the other regiments of the brigade, would give 41 killed, wounded and missing. Estimating the ratio of one killed to four wounded, the 8th Virginia had two killed and nine wounded. Assuming that the 19th Virginia had the same proportion of missing as had the 18th and 56th Virginia, and that the ratio of killed to wounded was one to four, the loss in the 19th Virginia was 11 killed, 46 wounded and six missing. The 56th Virginia reports 40 killed and wounded, of which, in the usual ratio, eight were killed and 32 wounded. Of the 41 killed, wounded, and missing of the 28th Virginia, we estimate that seven were killed, 28 wounded and seven missing.

76 Carman's Note: The official reports in OR 19, pt 1, pp. 843, 888, show a loss in Drayton's Brigade during the Maryland Campaign of 82 killed, 280 wounded, 179 missing, for an aggregate of 541. An extensive correspondence with survivors of the brigade indicates that its loss at Antietam was 33 killed, 106 wounded, and three missing, or 142. Deduct these figures from those given as the loss in the entire campaign, we have the loss at Turner's Gap as 49 killed, 164 wounded, and 176 missing, an aggregate of 389 out of the 650 men taken into action. Little correspondence has been found, none mentioning casualty figures. As pointed out earlier, Carman also missed the Phillips (Georgia) Legion in this brigade.

| | | | | |
|---|---|---|---|---|
| Kemper's Brigade | 11 | 57 | 7 | 75[77] |
| Jenkins' Brigade | 3 | 29 | | 32 |
| Total D. R. Jones' Division | 98 | 395 | 206 | 699 |

| Command | Killed | Wounded | Missing | Total |
|---|---|---|---|---|
| Hood's Division | | | | |
| Wofford's Brigade | | 3 | 2 | 5[78] |
| Law's Brigade | 3 | 11 | 5 | 19[79] |
| Total Hood's Division | 3 | 14 | 7 | 24 |

| Command | Killed | Wounded | Missing | Total |
|---|---|---|---|---|
| Evans's Brigade (unattached) | 23 | 148 | 45 | 216[80] |

77  Carman's Note: Kemper's Brigade carried about 400 men into action; there are no official reports of its losses. The muster rolls of the 1st Virginia note a loss of one lieutenant and four men wounded and one man captured. From D. E. Johnston's history of the 7th Virginia and correspondence with survivors of the regiment, we put its loss at 32 killed, wounded and missing—five killed, 24 wounded, three missing. [David E. Johnston, *Four Years a Soldier* (Princeton WV: n.p., 1887). Several letters from members of the 7th Virginia are in the NA-AS collection, but none mention South mountain casualties.] The 11th Virginia was very small, and its loss, as gleaned by correspondence with survivors, was one killed, 7 wounded and two missing. George Wise, *The History of the 17th Virginia* (Baltimore: Kelly, Piet, & Company, 1870), gives the names in eight companies, of three killed and 10 wounded. The 24th Virginia was a small regiment and sustained a severe loss, which, from information derived from its members, was two killed, 11 wounded and one missing. The total loss of the five regiments was 11 killed, 57 wounded and seven missing.

78  Carman's Note: The muster rolls of the 18th Georgia give one man wounded; muster rolls of the 1st Texas give one man wounded and one missing, and those of the 4th Texas give one man wounded and one missing.

79  Carman's Note: The official reports give three killed and 11 wounded. The muster rolls of the 4th Alabama note five men captured.

80  Carman's Note: There are official reports from three regiments of Evans' Brigade: the 17th South Carolina (*OR* 19, pt 1, p. 945) had seven killed, 27 wounded, 17 missing; the 22nd South Carolina (p. 949) had 10 killed, 57 wounded, four missing; the 23rd South Carolina (p. 950) had four killed, 16 wounded, four missing. According to *OR* 19, pt 1, p. 811, the Holcombe Legion

## Return of Casualties in the Union Forces at the Battle of South Mountain (Turner's Gap), September 14, 1862

| Command | Killed | | Wounded | | Capt./Missing | | Total |
|---|---|---|---|---|---|---|---|
| | O | M | O | M | O | M | |
| **First Corps** | | | | | | | |
| First Division-Staff | | | 1 | | | | 1-Gen. Hatch |
| First Brigade | | 20 | 44 | 63 | | 8 | 9595 |
| Second Brigade | | 3 | 4 | 48 | | 4 | 59 |
| Third Brigade | | 3 | | 19 | | 1 | 23 |
| Fourth Brigade | 1 | 36 | 6 | 245 | | 30 | 318 |
| Second Division | | | | | | | |
| First Brigade | | 5 | 1 | 15 | | | 21 |
| Second Brigade | | 2 | 1 | 5 | | | 8 |
| Third Brigade | | 2 | | 4 | | | |
| Third Division | | | | | | | |
| First Brigade | 4 | 34 | 7 | 126 | | | 171 |
| Second Brigade | 1 | 24 | 1 | 62 | | 1 | 89 |
| Third Brigade | 2 | 30 | 8 | 92 | | | 132 |
| **Total First Corps** | 8 | 159 | 33 | 679 | | 44 | 923 |
| **Ninth Corps** | 1 | | | | | | 1-Gen. Reno |
| First Division | | | | | | | |

had 18 men wounded in the entire campaign, assuming that two-thirds of this number is chargeable to Turner's Gap, would give 12 as the number there wounded. The 18th South Carolina (p. 811) is reported to have had three killed and 39 wounded during the entire campaign, two-thirds of this loss is fairly chargeable to Turner's Gap, which gives two killed and 26 wounded. The missing in the 18th South Carolina is estimated by us, from incomplete data, as 13; and in the Holcombe Legion as seven, thus making an aggregate in the brigade of 216—23 killed, 148 wounded and 45 missing.

| | | | | | | | |
|---|---|---|---|---|---|---|---|
| First Brigade | | 26 | 5 | 131 | | 7 | 162 |
| Second Brigade | | 35 | 8 | 143 | | 23 | 188 |
| Second Division | | | | | | | |
| First Brigade | | | | 34 | | | 41 |
| Second Brigade | | 9 | 5 | 78 | | | 116 |
| Third Division | | | | | | | |
| First Brigade | | 2 | 1 | 17 | | | 20 |
| Second Brigade | | | | | | | |
| Kanawha Division | | | | | | | |
| First Brigade | 1 | 62 | 11 | 190 | | 8 | 272 |
| Second Brigade | | 17 | 3 | 61 | | 3 | 84 |
| **Total Ninth Corps** | 5 | 152 | 33 | 658 | | 41 | 889 |
| **Cavalry Division** | | 1 | | | | | 1 |
| **Grand Total** | 13 | 312 | 66 | 1,337 | | 85 | 1,813[81] |

| Recapitulation | Killed | Wounded | Missing | Total |
|---|---|---|---|---|
| D. H. Hill's Division | 124 | 456 | 404 | 984 |
| D. R. Jones' Division | 98 | 395 | 206 | 699 |
| Hood's Division | 3 | 14 | 7 | 24 |
| N. G. Evans's Brigade | 23 | 148 | 45 | 216 |
| Total | 248 | 1,013 | 662 | 1,923[82] |

81 Carman laboriously copied the casualty returns for the First and Ninth Corps from Union Consolidated Return in *ibid.*, pp. 184-87.

82 Again Carman provided a summarized return and then a more detailed chart. Carman's Note: This does not include the loss sustained by the 5th Virginia Cavalry, the artillery acting with it, and Cutts's artillery, which would probably increase the aggregate to 1,950.

# Chapter 10

# From South Mountain to Antietam

When General Lee, after September 14th, realized that the action at Turner's Gap had gone against him he abandoned, temporarily at least, his idea of further invasion of the North, into Pennsylvania, or even of remaining in Maryland, and took immediate measures to reunite with McLaws and recross the Potomac into Virginia. Those who were with Lee say that he gave no sign of disappointment and depression that his campaign had ended in failure, but we can imagine it was with a swelling heart that, at 8 p.m., he sent this dispatch to McLaws:

GENERAL: The day has gone against us and this army will go by Sharpsburg and cross the river. It is necessary for you to abandon your position to-night. Send your trains not required on the road to cross the river. Your troops you must have well in hand to unite with this command, which will retire by Sharpsburg. Send forward officers to explore the way, ascertain the best crossing of the Potomac, and if you can find any between you and Shepherdstown leave Shepherdstown Ford for this command. Send an officer to report to me on the Sharpsburg road, where you are and what crossing you will take. You will of course bring Anderson's division with you.[1]

At about the same hour he sent a dispatch to Jackson to march up from Harper's Ferry and cover his passage of the Potomac at Shepherdstown Ford. These orders to McLaws and Jackson contemplated the abandonment of operations against Harper's Ferry, but these had so far progressed that the place was then virtually, in the grasp of Jackson and McLaws.[2]

Longstreet and D. H. Hill was directed to push such of their commands and trains as were at or near Hagerstown across the Potomac at Williamsport; and the three reserve artillery battalions at Beaver Creek, four miles north of Boonsboro, were ordered to move; two battalions by Williamsport into Virginia, one battalion to Keedysville.

Two hours later, about 10 p. m., Lee had information that Franklin had forced Crampton's Gap and interposed between himself and McLaws, upon which he sent McLaws a message to make a way, if possible, over Elk Ridge to Sharpsburg, if not practicable, then to cross the Potomac near Weverton. At about the same time, 10.15 p.m., he sent this order to Colonel Munford at Rohrersville: "Hold your position at Rohrersville, if possible, and if you can discover or hear of a practicable road below Crampton's Gap by which McLaws, at Weverton at present, can pass over the mountains to Sharpsburg, send him a messenger to guide him over immediately."[3]

Munford knew no road by which McLaws could escape over the mountain and so informed Lee, he gave the same information to McLaws when he forwarded to him Lee's dispatch.

---

1   After paraphrasing it, Carman pasted in the manuscript Lee's dispatch to McLaws, *OR* 51 pt. 2, pp. 618-9, which contained the order for McLaws to break off the siege of Harpers Ferry. Carman's description of Lee's demeanor is not found in postwar accounts of his staff or senior commanders. Carman met with Marshall and Venable and may have learned this from them. Marshall's letter, November 22, 1900, NYPL Correspondence Files, Box 5, Folder 1, implies this calm behavior, but does not directly state it.

2   This order to Jackson is not in the *Official Records* and its existence is known only by H. K. Douglas and Carman referring to it. Yet, it seems logical that it was given, and is discussed in Harsh, *Sounding the Shallows*, pp. 181-2, and Harsh, *Taken at the Flood*, pp. 289-90.

3   Pendleton's report, *OR* 19, pt. 1, pp. 829-30, contains the orders for the Reserve Artillery, and D. H. Hill's report, *ibid.*, p. 1,025, mentions wagons sent across the river on Sunday. The 10:15 p.m. message to Munford, *ibid.*, pt. 2, p. 609, is pasted in the manuscript. It was forwarded by Munford to McLaws, although it is unclear why this order said McLaws was at Weverton.

Up to 10.30 p. m. Lee had no idea of departing from his intention to cross the Potomac as speedily as possible, but the unwelcome news that Franklin had interposed between him and McLaws necessitated a change in his plans. McLaws could not now join him by the road up Pleasant Valley, and it would not do to leave him to his fate; his extrication was of grave necessity. To accomplish this he concluded to halt, on the road to the Potomac, at Keedysville, 5 1/2 miles from Turner's Gap and 3 miles southwest of Boonsboro, for the purpose of covering McLaws' movement from Pleasant Valley by way of Weverton, or across Elk Ridge to Sharpsburg, thence by some ford across the Potomac. Then he proposed an immediate crossing of the army he had with him—Longstreet and D. H. Hill—by the Shepherdstown Ford. To that end, before he received Munford's reply to his dispatch of 10.15 p. m., he again wrote McLaws at 11.15 p.m.:

> In addition to what has already been stated in reference to your abandonment of Weverton, and routes you can take, I will mention you might cross the Potomac, below Weverton, into Virginia, I believe there is a ford at the Point of Rocks, and at Berlin below, but do not know whether either is accessible to you. The enemy from Jefferson seem to have forced a passage at Crampton's Gap, which may leave all on the river clear. This portion of the army will take position at Centreville, commonly called Keedysville, 2½ miles from Boonsborough, on the Sharpsburg road, with a view of preventing the enemy that may enter the gap at Boonsborough turnpike from cutting you off, and enabling you to make a junction with it. If you can pass to-night on the river road, by Harper's Ferry, or cross the mountain below Crampton's Gap toward Sharpsburg, let me know. I will be found at or near Centreville, or Keedysville, as it is called.[4]

How McLaws received these instructions and his action in regard to them have already been noted and shall again be referred to, meanwhile we follow the withdrawal of Lee's immediate command.

At 10 p. m., General Toombs, at Hagerstown, received an order from General D. R. Jones, his division commander, to march immediately to Sharpsburg, leaving the 11th Georgia, of George T. Anderson's Brigade, to conduct the large wagon train across the Potomac at Williamsport. Toombs started from beyond Hagerstown about midnight and, marching by the Hagerstown turnpike, reached Sharpsburg before daybreak of the 15th and took position on the high ground

---

4   This order, also pasted into the manuscript, is found in *ibid.*, 19, pt. 2, p. 608. The reasoning Carman states is consistent with modern scholars' view of the event. See Harsh, *Taken at the Flood*, pp. 293-4.

southeast of the town. Upon the arrival of his division commander, a few hours later, he was ordered to detail two regiments from his brigade and direct them to march immediately and in haste to Williamsport for the protection of the wagon train crossing over into Virginia. Toombs selected the 15th and 17th Georgia regiments and placed them under command of Colonel W. T. Millican, a brave and energetic officer, who reached Williamsport, after a severe march of 13 miles, to find that the train had already crossed into Virginia; he followed it across the river, overtook and remained with it, until the 17th, when, with the two regiments and five companies of the 11th Georgia, he recrossed the river at Shepherdstown Ford and rejoined his brigade, while it was in action, on the field south of Sharpsburg.[5]

Longstreet's reserve ammunition train was near Hagerstown and started for the Potomac at midnight, without apprehension of danger and very lightly guarded. Near Funkstown was a train of supplies, collected in Maryland, and other commissariat and quartermaster stores. There were also many wagons belonging to D. H. Hill's Division that had been pushed forward from near Boonsboro to Funkstown, late in the evening, and with these were cooking details from the several brigades. Longstreet's ordnance train moved directly from Hagerstown toward the Potomac; the general supply train, about 50 wagons, guarded by the 11th Georgia, Major F. H. Little, marched west from Funkstown by the Williamsport road, and, intercepting Longstreet's train, at the intersection of the Hagerstown and Williamsport road, fell in behind it. The men were scattered along behind, of what they supposed to be, the regimental or brigade wagons, and in the confusion of haltings and startings, became weary, sleepy, and listless, and, apprehending no danger, paid no attention to the wagons and overlapped Longstreet's train, as they neared Williamsport, when Colonel B. F. Davis, with his cavalry, was upon them and turning a part of Longstreet's train off the Williamsport road onto the road leading to Greencastle, Pennsylvania.

The historian of the 11th Georgia writes that the regiment, with one of cavalry, the 1st Virginia, was detailed to guard the transportation train and

> accordingly moved back [from Hagerstown] to Funkstown, in order to meet a portion of the returning wagons, and take the Williamsport road from that place. The train extended for several miles and our small force was of necessity wholly inadequate to cover the line of its movements. But Major Little made the best possible disposition of his men. He divided the regiment, placing Captain Mitchell in command of the right wing towards the front, and moving himself with the left, in rear of the wagons. Before

---

5  Toombs's report, *OR* 19, pt. 1, pp. 888-91, Benning's report, 17th Georgia, *ibid.*, 51 pt. 1, pp. 161-4.

day, next morning, the right wing was in motion. About the time of their starting, two brigades (so reported) of fugitive Yankee cavalry from Harper's Ferry, crossed the track of the train at the junction of the Funkstown [Greencastle] and Hagerstown roads, and began to conduct the wagons in the direction of the former place. At first the wagoners thought they were Confederate soldiers and obeyed instructions with their usual cheerfulness. But as daylight was dawning, the secret soon leaked out, and a messenger was hastened to communicate the intelligence to Captain Mitchell. Knowing it was impossible, with his handful of men, to contend against such a force, the Captain (after consultation with his officers) wisely resolved to fall back and connect with the left wing. But the Federals meditated nothing more than a passing notice, they were too thoroughly panic-stricken to tarry, and he had not, consequently, retreated a great way before information came that the road was again clear, and he resumed his march and reached Williamsport without further interruption. We had lost a number of wagons and some valuable stores by this raid.[6]

The train, save the wagons captured by Colonel Davis, crossed the Potomac at Williamsport. Later, Colonel Millican, with the 15th and 17th Georgia, came up and took charge of the train and added the 11th Georgia to his command. The rations cooked for D. H. Hill's Division, near Boonsboro, on the night of the 14th, were given them on the field of Sharpsburg, September 17th.[7]

General Lee made the report of the loss of a part of Longstreet's train:

I regret also to report that on the night of the 14th instant, when I determined to withdraw from the gap in front of Boonsborough to Sharpsburg, a portion of General Longstreet's wagon-train was lost. When his division was ordered back from Hagerstown to the support of D. H. Hill, his train was directed to proceed toward Williamsport, with a view to its safety, and, if necessary, to its crossing the river. Unfortunately, that night the enemy's cavalry at Harper's Ferry evaded our forces, crossed the Potomac into Maryland, passed up through Sharpsburg, where they encountered our pickets, and intercepted on their line of retreat to Pennsylvania General Longstreet's train on the Hagerstown road. The guard was in the extreme rear of the train, that' being the only direction from which an attack was apprehended. The

6 Kittrell J. Warren, *History of the Eleventh Georgia Volunteers, Embracing the Muster Rolls, together with a Special and Succinct Account of the Marches, Engagements, Casualties, etc.* (Richmond: Smith, Bailey & Co. 1863), p. 50. As usual, Carman uses the source for the preceding paragraph before he introduced it.

7 Part of this paragraph comes from Benning's report, OR 51, pt. 1, pp. 161-4.

enemy captured and destroyed 45 wagons, loaded chiefly with ammunition and subsistence.[8]

The 1st Virginia Cavalry that had been detached from its brigade at New Market, on the 10th, to accompany Jackson (Carman obviously meant Longstreet) and protect his flank and rear from a possible movement from Pennsylvania, remained in the vicinity of Hagerstown, scouting and picketing up to the Pennsylvania line, until the 14th, when its scouts and pickets were withdrawn, the regiment concentrated at Hagerstown and followed the trains across the river after daybreak of the 15th, camping that night at Hainesville. On the 16th, it marched through Martinsburg to Shepherdstown Ford, where it recrossed the river and rejoined Fitzhugh Lee's Brigade on the left of the Confederate line.[9]

Late at night, General W. N. Pendleton, commanding the Reserve Artillery, who, with three battalions, had, late in the afternoon, taken position on the heights of Beaver Creek, four miles north of Boonsboro, was summoned to Lee's headquarters and directed to send Colonel Stephen D. Lee's Battalion to Keedysville and to move with the battalions of Colonel J. Thompson Brown and Major William Nelson by the shortest route to Williamsport and across the Potomac to guard the fords of the river. Pendleton hastened back to his camp and moved promptly to the Boonsboro and Williamsport road, and, by sunrise, reached Jones's Cross Roads, where the Williamsport road intersects the Hagerstown and Sharpsburg turnpike. Here he was informed that a large force of Union cavalry was not far ahead of him, upon which he placed some guns in position commanding the road leading to Williamsport, and the Hagerstown pike on either flank, sent to Toombs, who had passed down to Sharpsburg, for a regiment or two of infantry, and set to work collecting a band of armed stragglers to support his guns. Meanwhile he had sent out scouting parties; these soon returned with information that the road was clear for some two miles, upon which, without waiting for infantry from Toombs, he resumed the road to destroy the "retiring invaders" with his artillery and protect the large wagon train proceeding by the Hagerstown road through Williamsport. Colonel Davis' cavalry had passed on the road and attacked

8   *Ibid.* p. 142, Lee to Davis.

9   Letter to Carman, May 7, 1897, from William N. Lemon provided the itinerary of the 1st Virginia Cavalry.

Longstreet's train, and Pendleton, without meeting an enemy or further delay, reached Williamsport and crossed the Potomac by Light's Ford, into Virginia.[10]

Colonel Brown, with his battalion of five batteries, was ordered to guard Light's Ford and a ford two miles below. Major Nelson's battalion of five batteries, went down the river to Shepherdstown, which he reached on the 16th, and took position commanding Boteler's or Blackford's Ford, a mile below town.[11]

General D. H. Hill's Division was the first to retire from South Mountain. At 10 p. m., Colquitt's Brigade, relieved by the 2nd South Carolina Rifles of Jenkins' Brigade, withdrew from the east foot of the mountain and, uniting with Rodes' Brigade at the Mountain House, the two brigades, General Rodes in command, began the descent of the mountain at 11 p. m., passed through Boonsboro and, marching on the Boonsboro and Sharpsburg turnpike, reached Keedysville about 1 a. m. of the 15th, where, under Lee's orders, Rodes halted. After resting about an hour he was ordered to proceed to Sharpsburg with the two brigades under his command to drive out a Union cavalry force reported there. He was soon on the road and quickly overtaken by Colonel Chilton of Lee's staff with contrary orders, which required him to send only a part of his force; he selected the 5th and 6th Alabama, under Colonel John B. Gordon. In a few minutes, however, he received an order from Longstreet to go ahead, and did so with the two brigades, but found no cavalry at Sharpsburg; it had passed through the town.[12]

Colquitt's Brigade passed through the town to Blackford's or Shepherdstown Ford on the Potomac; Rodes halted his brigade on the high ground southwest of the town and cooked breakfast at a very early hour, for both brigades arrived at Sharpsburg some time before daylight.

The three brigades of Garland, Ripley and G. B. Anderson, in the order named, moved on by-roads from the old Sharpsburg road to the vicinity of Boonsboro, then followed Rodes over the Boonsboro and Sharpsburg pike to Keedysville, where they were halted an hour, then, continuing the march, crossed the Antietam between daybreak and sunrise, and formed line on the high ground a short mile beyond the stream and north of the Boonsboro pike.

---

10 Carman summarized Pendleton's report, OR 19, pt. 1, pp. 829-30, for this description of events.

11 Pendleton's report, *ibid.*

12 See Walker's report to confirm the 2nd South Carolina relieving Hill's men, *ibid.*, 19, pt. 1, p. 906. The latter portion of this paragraph is taken from Rodes's report, *ibid.*, p. 1,036. Chilton's actions are narrated in an excerpt from Charles Venable, *Personal Reminiscences of the Confederate War* (University of Virginia accession # 2969-a, September 28, 1889), p. 65.

D. H. Hill, who accompanied the three brigades of Garland, Ripley and G. B. Anderson, placed the right of his line, G. B. Anderson, on the Boonsboro pike; Ripley's Brigade a short distance in rear, and Garland's, now commanded by Colonel D. K. McRae, 5th North Carolina, on the high ground, and in the Sunken Road, now known as Bloody Lane, with its left resting on the lane running north from the Sunken Road to Roulette's house. Rodes and Colquitt were brought back from beyond the town and placed on the line, Rodes on a plateau on the right of Garland's Brigade and at right angles to it, and in his immediate rear was a cornfield (Piper's?). "Here," says Rodes, "subsisting of green corn mainly and under an occasional artillery fire, we lay until the morning of the 17th."[13] Colquitt took position on Garland's left, in the Sunken Road, between the mouth of Roulette's lane and the Hagerstown pike. G. B. Anderson, Ripley and Rodes faced the Antietam and the east. Garland and Colquitt faced north, looking upon groves and fields in grass, luxuriant corn or freshly plowed for seeding. Captain Thomas H. Carter's Virginia battery was placed in the interval between Rodes and Garland and in Garland's front, two guns on Rodes' left, facing the Antietam, two guns in front of Garland's right and one in front of his center, the three guns facing north. Captain W. B. Jones' Virginia battery and Hardaway's Alabama battery were in reserve, and Bondurant's Alabama battery, still east of the Antietam, was, when it arrived, kept with the reserve artillery beyond the town and not brought to the front until the 17th.

Following D. H. Hill's Division came the trains of the army, quartermaster and commissary wagons, ordnance wagons, and ambulances, and some of the reserve artillery. These passed through Sharpsburg and beyond more than half way to the Potomac, where they halted for rest, near Blackford's Ford, still under instruction to cross the Potomac, for, as yet, Lee had not come to the determination to give battle at Sharpsburg.

With the trains came Colonel S. D. Lee with his battalion of six batteries. Lee had been unable to reach Keedysville from Beaver Creek by the road through Boonsboro and was obliged to go across fields and on by-roads to reach the main road, about midway between Boonsboro and Keedysville, which was found crowded with infantry, artillery and wagons, making their confused way to the rear. It was with difficulty he gained a place in the road; this done he preceded on his way to Keedysville. Here he was ordered to push on to Sharpsburg. He crossed the Antietam at 8 a. m. and, under Longstreet's orders, went into position with five

---

13 The direct quote is from Rodes's report, *OR* 19, pt. 1, p. 1,036. Carman may have deduced the order of retreat and troop placement from the official reports, but it reads more like he used a source not yet identified.

batteries on the ridge north of the Boonsboro pike, on D. H. Hill's line, facing the Antietam. The left of his line was near Rodes' Brigade and the right extended to the Boonsboro pike, occupying positions most favorable for artillery. Eubank's battery was detached from the battalion and reported to General Toombs, who, about this time, was moving to his position to cover the Rohrbach Bridge, now known as the Burnside Bridge.[14]

Longstreet did not closely follow D. H. Hill. It was necessary to give time for the wagon train and other impedimenta to get on the road, and this delayed Longstreet's withdrawal until midnight and later. Drayton's Brigade, on the old Sharpsburg road, near the foot of Fox's Gap, marched in lanes and on by-roads and across fields to Boonsboro; Kemper and Garnett, leaving Jenkins to retire last, took the National road, down the mountain, and George T. Anderson, being ordered to report to Hood for rearguard, was left near Fox's Gap, the brigades of Drayton, Kemper and Garnett marched by the Boonsboro turnpike to Keedysville.[15]

The retreat was not affected without much disorder and some demoralization, and the number of stragglers was very large, particularly in Longstreet's command, which had made a severe march from Hagerstown, been needlessly marched about the field, some of it very roughly handled by the enemy, and all of it much jaded.

General John B. Hood had under his command for rear guard the two brigades of his own division and the brigades of N. G. Evans and George T. Anderson. Evans descended the mountain by the National road to Boonsboro; then followed the main army to Keedysville. Hood's two brigades and G. T. Anderson withdrew from Fox's Gap about 1 a. m. of the 15th, and by roads and farm lanes reached the Keedysville road, a mile south of Boonsboro, and halted until after daylight, when the march was resumed. The roads were filled with stragglers, and broken down and belated wagons, which made the march slow and tedious. Colonel Joseph Walker, commanding Jenkins' Brigade, who had been ordered by General D. R. Jones to cover the withdrawal of the troops from the vicinity of the Mountain

---

14 This information is from a letter from Capt. Tom Carter, November 14, 1896, NYPL Carman Papers, Correspondence Files, Box 2, Folder 3. See also Stephen D. Lee's report, *OR* 19, pt. 1, p. 844, and Toombs's report, *ibid.*, p. 888. Carman mentions both names for the lower of the three bridges across the Antietam near Sharpsburg. Because Henry Rohrbach owned a farm on the east bank of the creek just past the bridge, locals used his name for it. The earliest documented use of the name "Burnside" for this bridge is a broadside advertising the sale of the farm owned by Noah, Henry's son. The broadside describes the farm as "one and one quarter mile past Burnside's Bridge." Both Rohrbachs appear on the 1859 Thomas Taggert Map of Washington County, author's collection. The broadside is in the Earl Roulette Collection, Sharpsburg, Maryland.

15 G. T. Anderson's report, *OR* 19, pt. 1, p. 908, confirms his rearguard activity.

House, remained until 4 a. m. of the 15th, when he descended the mountain, passed through Fitzhugh Lee's cavalry brigade, and followed the route taken by the army.[16]

When General Lee withdrew from Turner's Gap it was with the intention of halting his entire army at Keedysville for the purpose of assisting McLaws out of Pleasant Valley and forming a junction with him at Keedysville or at Sharpsburg, and this he had in view when he dispatched him at 11.15 p. m., just as he was leaving his headquarters to fall back, that the army would take position at Keedysville "with a view of preventing the enemy that may enter the gap at Boonsboro turnpike from cutting you off, and enabling you from making a junction with it."[17]

Soon after this dispatch was written General Lee started from his headquarters at the foot of South Mountain. He had been disabled by a fall on the field of Second Manassas, and was unable to use his bridle arm, so rode in an ambulance, officers of his staff riding in front, guiding him through the troops, artillery and trains, which were moving toward the Potomac. He arrived at Keedysville about an hour before daybreak, and not hearing from McLaws and doubtful if the dispatches already sent had reached him, immediately sent him another dispatch: "We have fallen back to this place to enable you more readily to join us. You are desired to withdraw immediately from your position on Maryland Heights, and join us here. If you can't get off any other way, you must cross the mountain. The utmost dispatch is required. Should you be able to cross over to Harper's Ferry, do so and report immediately."[18]

After this dispatch had been sent, Lee heard from Munford that McLaws could not come up the valley and that the difficulties in getting over Elk Ridge and Maryland Heights were very great. Upon the receipt of this communication Lee determined not to make a stand at Keedysville, and there were sound reasons for his conclusion. First, that as McLaws could not come up the valley, thus exposing his flank to Franklin, the position at Sharpsburg was a good one to help McLaws

---

16 Much of this is not in official reports, memoirs, or letters examined thus far. Carman may have gotten this from one of Lee's staff members, or from a letter not yet discovered.

17 Chilton's dispatch to McLaws, *OR* 19, pt. 2, p. 608. Lt. Col. William Allan, in his address "Strategy of the Campaign of Sharpsburg or Antietam," Military Historical Society of Massachusetts, December 10, 1888, p. 19, supports this view as Lee's.

18 Lee's fall and injuries are discussed at length in Harsh, *Taken at the Flood*, pp. 66, 72, 85. Confirmation of Lee riding in an ambulance and his staff guiding him is found in a letter to Carman from Marshall, NYPL Correspondence Files, Box 3, Folder 1. The second dispatch is found in *OR* 19, pt. 2, pp. 609-10.

over the mountain or by the Weverton Pass, as was that at Keedysville; second, that it was a better defensive one against McClellan's larger army.[19]

Later, Lee was confirmed in his conclusion by additional information from Munford, upon which he ordered Munford to hold his position near Rohrersville until morning and then follow the army beyond the Antietam.[20] Lee had heard nothing from McLaws and still hoping to hear from him, and that by some means he would be able to elude Franklin and join him at Keedysville; he remained there, while Longstreet's command was closing up, until 8 o'clock in the morning.

There can be no question that when the sun rose that morning it was an anxious hour for Lee. He had not heard from either McLaws or Jackson and was in profound ignorance of how they were progressing and when and by what route they could join him. It was understood that both, Harper's Ferry being reduced, were to come up Pleasant Valley and join him at Hagerstown. Circumstances had changed all this and it was reasonably sure that some time during the day he would have heard from Jackson, who would come to his relief from the Virginia side of the Potomac, in response to his urgent dispatch of the night before, but of McLaws nothing was assured.

While resting here in a meadow by the roadside, on the high ground nearly a mile west of the village, near where McClellan afterwards had his headquarters, a farmer's kindly wife sent him a pot of hot coffee and, but a few minutes later, a courier rode up with the belated dispatch from Jackson, dated 8.15 p. m. of the 14th: "Through God's blessing, the advance, which commenced this evening, has been successful thus far, and I look to Him for complete success to-morrow. The advance has been directed to be resumed at dawn to-morrow morning....Your dispatch respecting the movement of the enemy and the importance of concentration has been received."[21] Both the coffee and the dispatch had an

---

19 Lee's report, *OR* 19, pt. 1, p. 147, states that should the Union troops from Turner's Gap move toward McLaws, Lee at Sharpsburg would be on their flank and rear. This alone is not a reason to fall back to Sharpsburg. Lee would have been a more potent threat at Keedysville. Harsh speculates that Lee was concerned about protecting McLaws no matter which way he left Pleasant Valley, and that Keedysville was not as defensible as Sharpsburg Ridge. Harsh, *Taken at the Flood*, pp. 299-301. Carman evidently supplied his own reasoning here.

20 A letter from Thomas T. Munford, December 10, 1894, NA-AS, states he reported to Lee at Keedysville by orderly and was directed at 2:00 a.m. by orders from Chilton to "hold that place. I stayed there at the forks of the road near H. Weir's place until day." The actual order has not been found.

21 Jackson's famous dispatch announcing his success at Harpers Ferry is found in *OR* 19, pt. 1, p. 951. Carman knew about the coffee and Lee's elation at Jackson's message from a November 22, 1900 letter from Marshall, NYPL, Correspondence Files, Box 3, Folder 1. This may have been on the Phillip Pry farm, later used as McClellan's headquarters.

invigorating effect upon Lee. He looked southward, where, fourteen miles away, he could see Maryland Heights and Loudoun Heights, sloping east and west down to the Potomac, but he could not heard the sounds of Jackson's guns; then turning to the east he saw, by aid of his glass, the head of the Union advance coming down the slope of South Mountain. To the west, beyond the Antietam, he saw D. H. Hill's Division going into position and the wagon train moving over Cemetery Hill and down into Sharpsburg.[22]

Then, when the long trains had nearly passed, Lee, leaving Longstreet to bring up his command, was assisted into his ambulance and driven across the Antietam where D. H. Hill was forming his command. He stopped on Cemetery Hill, examined the ground and gave general direction for the formation of the line and the placing of the artillery. Longstreet followed Lee, crossed the Antietam at 9.30 a.m., and joined his chief on Cemetery Hill.[23]

General D. R. Jones' Division, the advance of Longstreet's command, crossed the Antietam at 10.00 a. m., and as the brigades arrived on the field were put in position under Longstreet's direction, on the south side of the Boonsboro and Sharpsburg Turnpike, on the high ground just east and southeast of Sharpsburg. This high ground or ridge, rising 185 feet above the Antietam, and running nearly north and south, is very commanding. South of the turnpike, and very near the highest point of the ridge, is an old burying ground or cemetery, in which stood, but a few feet from the turnpike, a modest, log-built home of worship—the Lutheran Church. We shall call the ridge south of the turnpike Cemetery Hill, the ridge running north from the turnpike, and on which is now a citizens' cemetery-the Cemetery Ridge. (At the close of the war a National Cemetery was laid out, a short distance east of the old Lutheran Church and Cemetery, in which rest the remains

22 Carman's citing of Lee using a "glass" or a telescope to survey the terrain is not specifically mentioned in Marshall's November 22, 1900, letter, NYPL, Correspondence Files, Box 3, Folder 1. Lee's hands were injured on August 31 and he could not write or hold utensils. The most thorough treatment of Lee's injury is found in Harsh, *Confederate Tide Rising*, pp. 205-7. It is possible the additional details arise from several conversations between Marshall and Carman. Carman may also have meant an aide held the glass for Lee, although Marshall says he fell asleep while Lee drank his coffee. Lee had his servant wait with coffee for Marshall when he awoke, while he continued west to Cemetery Hill.

23 Once again, Carman cites specific times and order that has not been verified through other sources. Longstreet's report and memoirs, for instance, offer no specific time for his crossing Antietam Creek. Marshall was responding to Carman's request for a specific time when Lee crossed the Antietam. These times mentioned here may also have been from their discussions.

of 4,742 Union dead. Just opposite the National Cemetery, on the north side of the road has been laid out a citizens' cemetery.)[24]

At first D. R. Jones' Division, except Toombs Brigade, was formed in double line on Cemetery Hill, facing east and southeast, Kemper's, Jenkins', and Drayton's brigades in first line, Garnett's in second line; G. T. Anderson, being with Hood as rearguard, had not yet arrived. Toombs Brigade—2nd and 20th Georgia—were ordered to occupy the most eligible position that could be found on the Antietam, near Rohrbach's Bridge—now known as Burnside Bridge—to prevent the enemy from crossing it and to hold it for the passage of McLaws, should he cross Elk Ridge, near Solomon's Gap, and approach Sharpsburg by the road coming from the East and South. From this position Toombs was ordered to fall back when it should become necessary, by his right flank, and hold a hill about 400 yards below the bridge and immediately on the Antietam, as long as practicable, and then to fall back and take position on the right of Jones' Division, in the line of battle of the other brigades. With these orders Toombs took place on the ground indicated, with the 20th Georgia, Colonel John B. Cumming, and the 2nd Georgia, Lieutenant-Colonel William R. Holmes, (400 muskets) both under the immediate command of Colonel Henry L. Benning. Eubank's Virginia battery took position on the high ground in Toombs' rear and commanded the approaches to the bridge. The Wise Artillery, Captain J. S. Brown, was put on the high ground south of the town and west of the road running from Sharpsburg to Burnside Bridge.[25]

Colonel John (James)[26] B. Walton's Washington (Louisiana) Artillery Battalion of four batteries crossed the Antietam about 11 a. m. and took position on the line held by Longstreet on Cemetery Hill, on the south side of the Boonsboro pike. The first company, Captain C. W. Squires was on the left and close to the pike; the third company, Captain M. B. Miller to the right of Squires. The position occupied by these two batteries is now in the enclosure of the National Cemetery and between the entrance gate and the statue of the American soldier. To the right of Miller,

---

24 Carman's description of the ground and features is accurate to the time. The Lutheran Church was pulled down after the battle and its replacement now occupies the corner of Hagerstown and Boonsboro-Shepherdstown pikes. The civilian cemetery is still there, and the National Cemetery now contains 4,776 graves of Union veterans.

25 The details here come from the reports of D. R. Jones, *OR* 19 pt. 1, p. 886; Toombs, *ibid.*, p. 888, James Walker, *ibid.*, p. 906, and G. T. Anderson, *ibid.*, p. 909. Eubanks' position is confirmed by a letter dated January 20, 1900, from H. H. Perry, a member of the battery, NA-AS. Wise's Battery position is confirmed by James W. B. Frazier, a member of the battery, in a letter to Carman dated October 22, 1895, NA-AS. William H. Palmer, 1st Virginia Infantry, confirmed that battery was on his left facing the lower bridge. Letter in NA-AS, April 22, 1895.

26 Carman incorrectly gave his name as John. See Krick, *Confederate Staff Officers*, p. 386.

across a ravine, down which runs the road to Burnside Bridge, in an apple orchard, were placed the Second Company, Captain J. B. Richardson and the Fourth Company, Captain B. F. Eshleman. Squires and Miller commanded the middle bridge over the Antietam; Richardson and Eshleman the Burnside Bridge and its approaches.[27]

As the batteries came up and took position Longstreet said: "Put them all in, every gun you have, long range and short range;" the object being to make a formidable a showing as possible and impress the enemy that they were going no farther backward and were at bay.[28]

Hood with the rearguard of four brigades of infantry and a few batteries of artillery, halting near Boonsboro until after daybreak, crossed the Antietam a little after 11 a. m. and, at noon, took position on Cemetery Hill. George T. Anderson's Brigade formed in rear of Squires and Miller's batteries, its left resting on the Boonsboro road. N. G. Evans' Brigade formed on the north side of the Boonsboro road, opposite Anderson's left. Boyce's South Carolina Battery of Evans' Brigade was held in reserve, in a ravine, on the right rear of Anderson. Law's and Wofford's Brigades of Hood's Division, formed on D. R. Jones' right; two of Hood's batteries also, were on Cemetery Hill, Bachman's South Carolina on the right of Miller's with its guns pointing to the bridge by which the army had crossed the Antietam, Reilly's North Carolina Battery facing Burnside Bridge. Garden's South Carolina Battery was held in reserve at the west foot of the hill, close to the road running from Sharpsburg to Burnside Bridge, prepared to resist the advance of the enemy by the road crossing the bridge.[29]

Colonel Thomas L. Rosser, with the 5th Virginia Cavalry and Captain John Pelham with two guns of his battery, was ordered to cover the withdrawal from Fox's Gap of South Mountain. At daybreak he moved down the old Sharpsburg road to the foot of the mountain, thence to Boonsboro, passing through the eastern outskirts of the town to the Sharpsburg pike, just as Fitzhugh Lee entered the place by the National road. He pushed before him many stragglers and, as no cavalry

---

27 Carman's inclusion of the cemetery shows his efforts to orient readers to modern landmarks. The positions are found in Col. James Walton's report, *OR* 19, pt. 1, p. 848.

28 The quote is from William M. Owen, *In Camp and Battle with the Washington Artillery: A Narrative of Events During the Late Civil War...*(Boston: Ticknor & Co. 1885), p. 138.

29 Basic information about the infantry brigades is found in the reports of G. T. Anderson, *OR* 19, pt. 1, p. 909; Hood, *ibid.*, p. 922; Wofford, *ibid.*, p. 927; Law, *ibid.*, p. 937; and Evans, *ibid.*, p. 939. Artillery placements came from Maj. B. W. Frobel's report, *ibid.*, p. 925. Several sources confirm the locations and the arrival time of noon, as do Hood & Frobel in their reports. See the letters of James Simons dated August 25, 1897, and May 25, 1896, NA-AS.

pursued him, moved back leisurely , detaining the Union advance— Richardson's Division—by causing it to deploy from time to time, and thus spent a good part of the morning covering only a few miles. On reaching Keedysville all the Confederate infantry had gone and the road was clear. He sent frequent written reports to General Lee, as he fell back, of the character of McClellan's advance, informed him of Fitzhugh Lee's misadventure and that he had been cut-off, and, without incident of note, crossed the Antietam about 12 o'clock noon, leaving a few skirmishers east of the stream. As his was the only cavalry command on the field he threw out detachments on both flanks of the army, south beyond Burnside Bridge and north on the Hagerstown pike, beyond the Dunkard Church and down the Smoketown road in the direction of the upper crossings of the Antietam.[30]

Colonel T. T. Munford (2nd and 12th Virginia Cavalry), who was at Rohrersville and near the intersection of the Rohrersville and Old Sharpsburg road, had been ordered by General Lee to hold his position until daylight. It was after sunrise, when, menaced by Franklin, he started to withdraw. He marched by the Old Sharpsburg road over the nose of Elk Ridge and through Porterstown to Burnside Bridge, crossing which, he formed on Toombs right and covered all the approaches to Sharpsburg from the east and south, his right being at the Antietam Furnace, beyond the stone bridge at the mouth of the Antietam.[31]

Cutts' Battalion of reserve artillery and Bondurant's Battery, of D. H. Hill's Division, were actively engaged at Turner's Gap. They were relieved just before nightfall and sent to the train near Boonsboro to replenish ammunition and bivouac for the night. When morning came the train had gone and they were without orders. Soon it was learned that the army had retreated and that Fitzhugh Lee was covering the retreat. Lee was found just at the time that some of Richardson's skirmishers were reported on the Boonsboro road, west of the town, and he ordered the batteries to make their way to Sharpsburg by the best practicable route, and as speedily as possible. They took a settlement road, running nearly parallel with the Boonsboro and Sharpsburg pike and, after an exciting and rapid march, crossed the Antietam at a ford near Pry's Mill, thence by the Williamsport road to the Hagerstown pike, thence down the pike. Cutts' Battalion came to a halt

---

30 Rosser's actions are described in a letter to Carman dated July 10, 1897, NA-AS, though not to the extent of detail Carman includes. It is possible they conversed or had further correspondence not yet discovered.

31 Munford's actions are taken from a letter to Carman dated June 29, 1897, and is in the NA-AS files. Munford mentions that his position was ordered personally by Lee, and that Col. Matthew C. Butler's 1st South Carolina Cavalry was added to his command. The Old Sharpsburg Road mentioned here is a different road than the one passing through Fox's Gap. Munford's route was most likely what is now called the Burnside Bridge Road.

near the Dunkard Church; Bondurant's Battery went through Sharpsburg to the Grove farm, more than a mile beyond town, where it remained until the 17th.[32]

By middle noon all the Confederate infantry and artillery—except Cutts' Battalion and Bondurant's Battery—Rosser's 5th Virginia Cavalry and Munford's cavalry were across the Antietam, and their retreat had been conducted without loss, except in stragglers. But Fitzhugh Lee, who covered the retreat from Turner's Gap was not so fortunate.

After a week spent among the rich pastures and generous cornfields of Frederick County and the adjoining county Fitzhugh Lee, then at New Market, received orders on September 11th to operate with his cavalry on the right and rear of McClellan's army and ascertain what his advance indicated. He moved at 11 a. m. and marched that day to Liberty where he bivouacked for the night. On the 12th he moved toward Frederick, hovered in the vicinity all day, and, marching all night, reached the foot of Catoctin Mountain, at Shookstown, early in the morning of the 13th. Here he remained until 2 p. m., when he moved north along the base of the mountain to the entrance to Hamburg Pass, which was reached at sunset. He bivouacked at dark part way up the Pass. At dawn the march was resumed over the Catoctin, and down its western slope to the beautiful valley below, the peaceful Catoctin Creek, bordered on either side with well tilled farms, winding gracefully through it. After a march of several hours the brigade halted near a large grist-mill, and rested under the shade of an apple orchard, until 4 p. m., when the march was resumed over the South Mountain to Boonsboro, which was reached after nightfall, and a halt ordered to rest and feed horses. Here Fitz Lee soon received an order to report to General Lee, who told him that he was about to withdraw his army from South Mountain and Boonsboro, and directed him to move his brigade up as close as possible to the front and relieve by dismounted cavalry the infantry pickets; to cover the retreat of the infantry from Turner's Gap and to resist and retard as much as possible the advance, which it was anticipated that McClellan would make in the morning.[33]

It was near midnight when Fitzhugh Lee marched out of Boonsboro on the National road in the direction of Turner's Gap. The disaster to Confederate arms

---

32 Lt. Col. Allen S. Cutts did not write a report for either South Mountain or Sharpsburg. This information came from his article, "Cutts's Battalion at Sharpsburg," *SHSP*, 10 (1882), pp. 430-1. The reference to a "settlement road" and the movement of Bondurant's Battery are taken from a letter to Carman from John Purifoy of Alabama dated April 28, 1896, NA-AS.

33 This section is paraphrased from "The Cavalry Fight at Boonsboro Graphically Described," *SHSP*, 25 (January-December 1897), pp. 276-7, and taken from the *Richmond Dispatch*, July 16, 1897, by G. W. Beale. For details of this march, see the letter to Carman from R. B. Lewis, 9th Virginia Cavalry, dated May 8, 1897, NA-AS.

was apparent as infantry, in detached parties from 10 to 200, apparently without organization, artillery wagons and ambulances were met in a confused retreat down the mountain. The brigade was halted about a mile and a half out of Boonsboro and remained in readiness for a charge until daylight of the 15th.

The nature of the ground was not favorable to the operations of cavalry, but formation was made to command the road down the mountain. A good position, on a swell of ground, was selected for the artillery—two guns of Pelham's Battery—and dismounted skirmishers were pushed well to the front. The 3rd Virginia Cavalry, Lieutenant-Colonel John T. Thornton, held the front and flanks, the 9th Virginia, Colonel W. H. F. Lee, was in column on the road, a little in rear of the guns, and the 4th Virginia, Colonel William C. Wickham, in the same formation, was in the rear of the 9th, near Boonsboro. A little before daybreak Jenkins' South Carolina Brigade filed down the road from the Mountain House, the last of the Confederate infantry, and there was nothing between Fitzhugh Lee and the advance of the Union army.[34]

When the contest was closed by darkness, on the 14th, McClellan had good reason for believing that when morning came the Confederate army would not been seen in his front. Evidently the reasons, so apparent to others, did not so impress him, or orders would have been given for an immediate pursuit, but, beyond orders to his corps commanders to press forward their pickets at early dawn, he gave no orders for an energetic aggressive movement.[35]

At dawn of the 15th the skirmishers of Hartsuff's Brigade, of the First Corps, overlooking the Mountain House, went forward and discovered that the Confederates had fallen back towards Boonsboro, leaving their dead and badly wounded. Soon after Hartsuff's advance, Richardson's Division, of the Second Corps, came up and was ordered to take the place of Hartsuff and give pursuit,

---

34 Carman continued copying from G. W. Beale's narrative here, but added details from Richard R. L. T. Beale, *History of the Ninth Virginia Cavalry, War Between the States* (Richmond: B. F. Johnson Publishing Company, 1899), pp. 38-39.

35 Carman demonstrates again his impatience with McClellan's progress, an attitude much more indicative of the scholarship of the time Carman wrote than was suggested at the time of the battle. Cox's and Hooker's reports do not mention a lost opportunity to go forward on the night of September 14 or rapid pursuit the next day. Hooker said the fighting was hard, and that "the resistance of the enemy continued until after dark." He believed his corps had achieved a great victory. OR 19, pt. 1, p. 215. Cox also described fighting until well after dark, and did not suggest any night or early dawn pursuit. *Ibid.*, p. 460. Carman was likely influenced by Palfrey, *Antietam and Fredericksburg*, pp. 34-35, who takes McClellan to task for a slow pursuit. It should be mentioned also that on September 14, the First Corps had marched from east of Frederick and fought its way up South Mountain through the afternoon. Continuing a pursuit that night, or even at dawn, would have been a daunting physical challenge.

leaving Hooker's First Corps to make coffee and draw subsistence, of which they had had none since leaving the Monocacy twenty-four hours before, save a cup of coffee at Catoctin Creek.[36]

At night of the 14th Richardson's Division was ordered to report to Hooker and did so, halting at Mt. Tabor Church. At 9 p. m. Hooker was ordered to hold his position on Lee's flank, and commanding the Mountain House, at all hazards, and advised that Richardson was placed under his orders, and, at the same hour, Sumner was advised of these orders and directed to notify Richardson to obey them.

Hooker, knowing that there would be "a fight or a foot race" early in the morning, ordered Richardson to move at daybreak up the old Hagerstown road to support him in either case. And this, as we know, was the only order given, on the night of the 14th, to prepare for the work to be done early on the 15th.[37]

Richardson moved promptly, as ordered, up the sometimes very steep and always rough and very rocky road from Mt. Tabor Church to the Mountain House, seeing nothing of the Confederates, except their dead and wounded, and, Meagher's Brigade in advance, passed Hartsuff's advance and descended the mountain towards Boonsboro. Fitzhugh Lee's officers say it was about sunrise when Richardson's head of column descended from the gap and engaged the cavalry skirmishers, who were slowly driven back until the position held by Pelham's guns was uncovered; the fire of the guns being withheld until the head of the Union column was within easy range, when shells were exploded in it so rapidly as to cause it to halt. Richardson now formed line of battle, on either side of the road, extending beyond both of Lee's flanks, and again advanced and again halted.[38]

36 Carman practically contradicted his criticism of the previous paragraph with information from Hooker's report, *ibid.*, p. 215, to explain why the First Corps needed to rest.

37 Hooker's report, *ibid.*, mentions Richardson's arrival and position. Although Carman used quotation marks for the words "fight or foot-race," it is likely a common expression rather than a direct quote. The phrase appears once in the OR 38, pt. 4, p. 459, in relation to Sherman's march of 1864. Carman is incorrect about pursuit orders, as McClellan's report of August 1863 states: "on the night of the battle of South Mountain orders were given to the corps commanders to press forward the pickets at early dawn." *Ibid.*, 19, pt. 1, p. 53. McClellan also wrote to Halleck on the night of the 14th that he was unsure what the enemy would do in the morning, but was hurrying troops forward to be prepared to fight or pursue in the morning. *Ibid.*, pt. 2, p. 289. In short, Carman engaged in hindsight more than valid criticism.

38 Fitzhugh Lee letter, February 11, 1896, NA-AS, confirms his dismounted troopers replaced the infantry pickets and the advance of the Union troops on the morning of September 15. Much of the description of Confederate disposition is strikingly similar to H. B. McClellan's account in *The Life and Campaigns of Major-General J.E.B. Stuart, Commander of the Cavalry of the Army of Northern Virginia* (Secaucus NJ: Blue & Gray Press, 1993), pp. 124-5. McClellan first

In the march that morning the 5th New Hampshire, Colonel Edward E. Cross, was rearguard. This excellent regiment was now brought to the front and Richardson ordered Cross to deploy it as skirmishers and cover the advance. Four companies were deployed on either side of the road and two in the road. Before the steady advance and rattling fire of this line the Confederate guns were retired, followed by their supports, the 4th Virginia leading, the 9th Virginia following, and the 3rd Virginia in the rear, nearest Richardson. The 4th and 9th Virginia continued on to Boonsboro and, passing beyond the center of the town, halted in the narrow street. As the 3rd Virginia was retiring through the town the ranks of Richardson's infantry suddenly opened and six companies of the 8th Illinois Cavalry, led by Colonel John F. Farnsworth, dashed past at a gallop, charging down the road and into the street. The 3rd Virginia, led by Fitzhugh Lee in person, met the charge and checked it handsomely, forcing the Illinois men back upon the infantry.[39]

Pleasonton had bivouacked near Bolivar on the night of the 14th, and at daylight of the 15th galloped to the front with the 8th Illinois, 1st Massachusetts, and 3rd Indiana, the 8th Illinois in front. Four companies of the Illinois regiment were ordered to take a road to the left. Farnsworth leading the six companies on the National road, as here stated, beyond Richardson's infantry.[40]

Farnsworth's check was but momentary. His men quickly faced about, made another charge and the 3rd Virginia was driven pell-mell down the street closely followed by the Illinois horsemen.

The men of the 4th and 9th Virginia had been so long in the saddle during the four days past, that when they halted in the street they were permitted to dismount, and for some time remained in this way, standing by their horses or sitting on the curb-stones and holding the bridle reins. Suddenly the cry Mount! Mount! resounded down the street and simultaneously a rapid fire of pistols and carbines were heard near at hand. Colonel W. H. F. Lee ordered the rear squadrons of the 9th Virginia to face about, but before the order could be executed, even before the men could mount, the rearguard, the 3rd Virginia, retreating at full speed, dashed

---

published this book in 1885 and corresponded with Carman at least twice, but only addressed Sharpsburg and not Boonsboro. At the time, McClellan was still a private in Company G, but was acting as adjutant of the regiment. Letter from McClellan dated June 30, 1898, NA-AS.

39  This advance is mentioned in Edward E. Cross's report, *OR* 19, pt. 1, p. 287. The details of the Confederate cavalry movements are taken from Beale, *Ninth Virginia Cavalry*, p. 39.

40  See Pleasonton's report, *OR* 19, pt. 1, p. 210, states that the 1st Massachusetts and 3rd Indiana were detached to serve with the First Corps. Crowninshield, *A History of the First Regiment of Massachusetts Cavalry Volunteers*, p. 75, suggests they were part of the pursuit; Carman's notes on the 3rd Indiana say they were "not seriously engaged" on September 15, NA-AS.

into the already confused column and, in an incredibly short time the street became packed with a mass of horses and horsemen, so jammed together as to make motion impossible. Had the 4th Virginia promptly fallen back there would have been some relief, but it did not do so. Very soon a pistol fire was opened upon the Virginians from the upper windows of some of the houses, and clouds of dust covered everything. The Illinois cavalry, quickly taking in the situation, dashed up boldly and discharged their carbines into the struggling and helpless mass of humanity and horse.

Meanwhile the 4th Virginia had gotten underway and thus opened the way for the 9th and 3rd, upon which a general stampede ensued, the whole force, closely followed by the Illinois men, who were using their carbines, rushing from the town along the Hagerstown road at the highest speed, many escaping through the fields. This disorderly movement was increased by the report that some of Richardson's infantry skirmishers were moving upon their flank and threatening to cut off their retreat.

The fleeing men had scarcely cleared the town when Colonel W. H. F. Lee tried to rally them, but his horse was killed and, in falling, severely injured his rider, who, dirt-covered and bruised, laid some time on the ground, unable to move, ridden over by friend and foe, finally to escape through the fields and find shelter in a cornfield. Captain Hughlett's horse fell in like manner at the edge of town and he, leaping the rail fence on the roadside found concealment in a cornfield, from which he emerged after dark and rejoined his regiment next day.

In the middle of the turnpike were piles of broken stone placed there for repairing the roadway. On these, amidst the impenetrable dust, many horses blindly rushed and falling piled with their riders on one another, crushing, mangling and killing many. Here and there in the pell-mell race, blinded by the dust, horses and horsemen dashed against telegraph poles and fell to the ground to be trampled by those behind.

When the open fields were reached and beyond the range of the infantry, a considerable part of the 9th Virginia was rallied by Lieutenant-Colonel R. L. T. Beale, who led a charge with the saber, when his horse was killed within a few paces of the Union cavalry line, deployed across the pike and the field on the Confederate left. Captain Thomas Haynes assumed command and, continuing the charge, forced back the Illinois men a short distance and brought out 3 or 4 prisoners. The charge was participated in by a squadron of the 4th Virginia Cavalry and cost it several killed and wounded, among the latter was the sergeant-major of the regiment.[41]

The gallant charge checked the ardor of the Illinois men and gave Fitzhugh Lee an opportunity to rally his men around the colors of the three regiments. This was about a mile and a half beyond the town and near the intersection of a road running to Keedysville. He then withdrew followed by a few shells from a section of Captain John C. Tidball's Battery, which Pleasonton had brought up. Finding that he was not pursued he turned to the left and following by-roads crossed the Antietam north of Keedysville and reached the left of General Lee's line, near the Dunkard Church, that evening.[42] Some of his men fell in with Cutts' Battalion and Bondurant's Battery on their march.

Pleasonton, in obedience to instructions, moved across country and came up with Richardson's Division in line of battle beyond Keedysville. He reported a loss of 1 killed and 15 wounded, "among the latter the brave Captain Kelley of the 8th Illinois Cavalry who was shot while gallantly charging at the head of his squadron." He also reported that he captured 2 guns and a very large number of prisoners, among whom were several hundred stragglers; and that Fitzhugh left 30 dead on the field and some 50 wounded. He claimed that the Confederates outnumbered him two to one and that the number of personal encounters demonstrated the superiority of the Union cavalry. He commended Colonel Farnsworth, Captains Kelley, Medill and Adjutant Hynes of the 8th Illinois Cavalry, and Captain George A. Custer of McClellan's staff for conspicuous gallantry.[43]

The Confederate loss is not definitely known. That of the 9th Virginia was 2 lieutenants and 16 privates killed and mortally wounded, and 10 privates captured. Many of the killed and mortally wounded were trodden to death, several slightly wounded and bruised are not numbered. The 4th Virginia had several killed and wounded and there was severe loss in the 3rd Virginia.[44]

---

41 G. W. Beale, *SHSP*, pp. 277-78. The history of the 9th Virginia Cavalry, by Col. R. L. T. Beale, and an article in *SHSP*, 25, p. 276, has been freely used in the preparation of the preceding pages.

42 This information is a letter to Carman from Fitz Lee, February 11, 1896, NA-AS. Carman supplied the name of the battery, which Lee only mentioned as a Union battery.

43 Pleasonton's report, *OR* 19, pt. 1, p. 210. "Capt." Medill was actually major. He was promoted on September 10, 1862. There is no record in Abner Hard, *History of the Eighth Illinois Cavalry Regiment* (Aurora: n.p., 1868), pp. 331-2, or Hyne's "Official Register" when he was serving as adjutant.

44 Both of Beales's accounts repeat the losses in the 9th Virginia. Letters in the NA-AS from men in the 3rd and 4th Virginia cavalry regiments only vaguely mention losses. Beale's *SHSP*

Richardson's Division did not become engaged at Boonsboro, when Pleasonton's cavalry uncovered the road turning west to Keedysville—the Boonsboro and Sharpsburg pike, on which it was learned the Confederate infantry had retreated—Richardson without a cavalryman or gun in advance followed the trail of the enemy. Fairly out of town two companies of the 5th New Hampshire were deployed as skirmishers on either side of the road, Captain C. H. Long commanding on the right, Captain J. W. Bean on the left. Rosser's cavalry skirmishers were encountered and gradually forced back from one position after another, and at 2 p. m., had all fallen back beyond the Antietam, closely followed by the New Hampshire men, who ascended the bluff bordering the east bank of the Antietam and skirmished with the enemy beyond. They were soon joined by the skirmishers of Meagher's Brigade and a lively fusillade kept up, during which Richardson's entire division went into position on the north side of the Boonsboro pike and at the east foot of the bluff bordering the Antietam.[45]

Pleasonton soon came up and as none of Richardson's artillery had arrived, he ordered Tidball's Battery to reply to the enemy's batteries, those of S. D. Lee, which had opened from four different points of their line. Tidball quickly ascended the bluff on the right of the road and opened fire. He was soon followed by Pettit's New York Battery of six guns, and both engaged the Confederate artillery until nearly dark. Lee's guns engaged were two rifles of Parker's Battery, two of Rhett's Battery, and one of Jordan's Battery. Lee reports that "they were exposed to a hot fire, several men slightly wounded and several horses disabled."[46]

On the night of the 14th McClellan's headquarters were at Bolivar, two miles east of Turner's Gap. Next morning he gave Pleasonton an early start, but gave no other order until 8 a. m., when he ordered Burnside to advance upon Boonsboro by the old Sharpsburg road, as far as the intersection of the Boonsboro and Rohrersville road, and then place himself in communication with the troops

---

account mentions losing two flags, which Pleasonton does not mention, but no Confederate source mentions losing the two guns claimed by Pleasonton.

45 Some of this detail came from Col. Cross' report of the 5th New Hampshire, *OR* 19, pt. 1, p. 287, although Carman supplies details here not yet located. Meagher's report of the Irish Brigade, *ibid.*, p. 293, said they led the pursuit, but more sources confirm Cross's account.

46 Pleasonton mentions Tidball's support of Richardson, *ibid.*, pt. 1, pp. 210-11. Pettit's actions appear in his report, *ibid.*, p. 283. Carman, citing members of the battery, said they remained there until relieved at 5:00 a.m. by Kusserow's battery. Carman cited Lt. Robert Sheldon of Pettit's battery as saying that Richardson spent the night with the first section, sleeping under a canvas. Carman Papers, NYPL. The Confederate guns and the quote come from S. D. Lee's report, *OR* 19, pt. 1, p. 844. Typescript in Antietam Battlefield Library, with notes in Carman's handwriting.

advancing by the Boonsboro pike, and also with Franklin, if he had reached Rohrersville, and lend assistance to either, if required, or to advance straight upon Keedysville and Sharpsburg to cut off the retreat of the enemy. After writing this, but before delivery, he heard that Richardson had taken the advance from the Mountain House, and added a postscript, directing Burnside to keep the head of his column as near parallel as possible to Richardson, and to move promptly, keeping his skirmishers well to the front and flanks until he came to open ground. An hour later McClellan advised Burnside that Fitz-John Porter would follow on the same road to support him, and that he desired to impress upon him "the necessity for the utmost vigor" in the pursuit. How Burnside obeyed these orders shall be shown later.[47]

At 8.45 a. m. McClellan ordered Sumner to move with the Second Corps (Sedgwick's and French's divisions) and the Twelfth Corps, from Bolivar on the National road to Boonsboro, following Pleasonton and Richardson. He informed him that Burnside had been ordered to advance on his left. He directed Sumner, should Boonsboro be abandoned, to take a strong position in the vicinity. Before sending this order he heard from citizens beyond the mountain and from Hooker that Lee was making a demoralized retreat for the Potomac, whereupon he gave additional orders that, should such be the case, he was to pursue the enemy as rapidly as possible. Hooker was ordered to get rations from his train and if Sumner was closed up, when he reached Turner's Gap, to allow him to pass, but to follow Sumner.[48]

Sumner and Hooker moved as ordered, the advance of the columns reaching Keedysville about 3 p. m. Instead of massing the brigades and divisions on either side of the road as they came up, the entire column was halted in the road and remained there. Consequently the road was congested for miles back, some of the troops did not get up until midnight, some not until next morning, and the Twelfth Corps, starting from Bolivar late in the forenoon, after marching through Boonsboro, and a short distance beyond, turned into the fields and bivouacked at

---

47 McClellan's two reports vary somewhat about this pursuit. His first report claims that "as soon as it was definitively known that the enemy had abandoned the mountain the cavalry, and the corps of Sumner, Hooker, and Mansfield, were ordered to pursue them." His later report, as cited previously, states that the orders went out on the night of September 14. *OR* 19, pt. 1, pp. 29, 53. The specific orders to Burnside, Hooker, Franklin, and Sumner are found in *ibid.*, 51, pt. 1, pp. 834-7, dated between 8:00 a.m. and 8:45 a.m., but make it clear that Richardson and the cavalry were already moving. Once again it appears that Carman let hindsight slip into his critique of the campaign.

48 This order to Sumner is included in the group cited above, *ibid.*, p. 834.

Nicodemus' Mill, nearly two miles southeast of Keedysville, on the old Sharpsburg road.[49]

Hearing that the Confederates had made a stand beyond Keedysville, Hooker rode forward and found Richardson and Pleasonton at the front, with Tidball's and Pettit's guns replying to those of the Confederates beyond the Antietam. He saw the Confederate infantry ostentatiously deployed, with many batteries posted to resist the passage over the bridge crossing the Antietam, and estimated that 30,000 men were thus deployed and that his own command was too weak in numbers and morale to attack them.

Meanwhile, Major D. C. Houston, of the engineers, had gone up the stream in search of bridges and fords by which a crossing could be made. He found a practicable bridge and two fords, which, with a little labor, were made practicable for infantry, but it was now 5 o'clock, the infantry column had not closed up and Hooker decided that he could not cross, and in this opinion Sumner concurred.[50]

Leaving the column strung along the road at 5.30 p.m., at a halt, awaiting orders, we turn to the movements of Burnside and Fitz-John Porter. McClellan's early orders to Burnside, to pursue with the "utmost vigor" have been noted. Porter was at Middletown, with Sykes' Division and the Reserve Artillery; Morell's Division was at Frederick. Sykes was ordered to march at daybreak and Morell at 3 a. m. of the 15th.[51] Porter, with Sykes' Division and the Reserve Artillery, moved from Middletown about 9 a.m., passed through Bolivar and up the old Sharpsburg road to Fox's Gap, where he arrived about 12 noon, and to his great surprise found that Burnside, whom he had been ordered to follow, had not yet moved, nor displayed any intention of doing so. McClellan now rode up and Porter reported the condition of affairs and asked for orders to pass Burnside and take the advance. McClellan gave the orders at 12.30:

---

49  McClellan's reports, *ibid.*, 19, pt. 1, pp. 29, 53 confirm the delay in getting the corps into position. The Twelfth Corps march and bivouac may be evidence of Carman's local knowledge. The words "Nicodemus Mill" do not appear in the *Official Records*, however "Nicodemus" appears on maps in the *Official Records Atlas*, 38-1 (1862) and 39-2 (1867). The latter map was prepared by Bvt. Brig. Gen. N. Michler, whose maps were used by the Antietam Battlefield Board. Because Carman was in the Twelfth Corps, he could easily remember, or discover, where his corps was bivouacked on September 15-6, 1862.

50  This language is taken almost verbatim from Hooker's report, *ibid.*, 19, pt. 1, p. 217. Sumner's concurrence was implied as his orders had urged attack, if possible. *Ibid.*, 51 pt. 1, p. 835.

51  The orders to Porter and Morrell are found in *ibid.*, p. 832.

HEADQUARTERS ARMY OF THE POTOMAC,
September 15, 186212.30 p.m.

Major-General PORTER:

GENERAL: General McClellan desires me to say that Burnside's corps has not yet marched. Should the march of Sykes' division be obstructed by Burnside's troops, direct General Sykes to push by them and to put his division in front.

I am, general, very respectfully, your obedient servant,

R. B. MARCY,
Chief of Staff.

Indorsements [sic]

Burnside's corps was not moving three hours after the hour designated for him, the day after South Mountain, and obstructed my movements. I, therefore, asked for this order, and moved by Burnside's corps.

F. J.P.[52]

Burnside was ordered to follow Porter as closely as possible, and give the reason for delay in not marching under the orders of the morning. McClellan, in his *Own Story*, page 587, says:

Early in the morning I had directed Burnside to put his corps in motion on the old Sharpsburg road, but to wait with me for a time until more detailed news came from Franklin. About 8 o'clock he begged me to let him go, saying that his corps had been sometime in motion, and that if he delayed longer he would have difficulty overtaking it, so I let him go. At about midday, I rode to the point where Reno was killed the day before and found that Burnside's troops—the 9th Corps—had not stirred from bivouac, and still blocked the road for the regular division. I sent to Burnside for an explanation, but he could not be found. He subsequently gave as an excuse the fatigue and hungry condition of his men.[53]

52  This order is found in *ibid.*, 19, pt. 2, p. 296.

53  The quote is from McClellan, *Own Story*, p. 586. It is unclear where and when Burnside made this excuse. Perhaps Carman grasped its implication from their meeting later that day.

It appears that part of the corps had marched without rations the day before, and during the night had sent back for them. Burnside took the responsibility for allowing the corps to wait until these supplies came up and the men could be fed before marching again. Meanwhile orders were given to bury the dead and send the wounded and prisoners to Middletown, and it was nearly noon when Cox, who was commanding the corps, got his orders to march, and then Porter had come up.[54]

Porter filed past Burnside and taking the old Sharpsburg road, at 5.30 p. m., reached Porterstown and the intersection of the turnpike from Boonsboro to Sharpsburg. He found Richardson in position and formed Sykes' Division on his left, at the base of the bluff bordering the Antietam. Skirmishers were sent to the left, also to the top of the bluff, and the 3rd U. S. Infantry, Captain John D. Wilkins, was advanced and deployed on either side of the Sharpsburg pike, near the Antietam, to guard the stone bridge, which, it was apprehended the enemy might attempt to destroy. The Reserve Artillery, having been cut off by Burnside's Corps, arrived later, and was massed in rear of the right of Sykes' Division.[55]

Burnside's Ninth Corps, following Porter's infantry, marched down the mountain and was soon overtaken by orders to move on Rohrersville, connect with Franklin, and attack and defeat McLaws, then to move on and join in the attack on Sharpsburg. Under these orders Burnside halted near the junction of the Rohrersville and old Sharpsburg roads. Here he heard that McLaws was leaving Franklin's front; at 4.30 p. m. he was ordered to resume his march to Sharpsburg. He passed through Springvale and over the nose of Elk Ridge, his head of column halting at sunset close to the hills on the southeast side of Antietam Valley, and on the left of the old Sharpsburg road, in rear of the left of Sykes' Division.[56]

Richardson, delayed in his advance by Rosser's cavalry, arrived at the front in reasonably good time; Pleasonton, after a severe affair, promptly followed Richardson; and Porter, marching from Middletown and delayed by Burnside, made a good day's work, and these officers escape criticism. Sumner and Hooker

54 Cox, *Reminiscences*, 1, p. 297, confirmed the delay in receiving the marching orders and the orders to bury the dead. It is difficult to understand why the order sent at 8:45 a.m. from two miles away at McClellan's Headquarters did not reach Cox until nearly noon. Carman did not explain why Cox was now commanding the corps. Reno's death left a vacancy, and Cox was the senior among the four division commanders. Burnside was still commanding the Right Wing of the army.

55 See Porter's report, *OR* 19, pt. 1, p. 338.

56 It appears Carman combined his knowledge of the local area with the itinerary of the First Division, Ninth Corps, in creating this paragraph. The itinerary, *ibid.*, p. 432, notes the pause. The mention of Mt. Carmel is in H. S. Fairchild's report, *ibid.*, p. 450, and on Michler's map, *Official Records Atlas*, 39-2, which shows Springvale and the roads mentioned by Carman.

were very remiss in halting their commands on the road, instead of massing them as they came up, and thus delaying the arrival of the center of the column until long after dark and the rear until next morning, and the trains until late in the day.

McClellan says: "It had been hoped to engage the enemy during the 15th. Accordingly, instructions were given that if the enemy were overtaken on the march, they should be attacked at once, if found in heavy force and in position, the corps in advance should be placed in position for attack and await my arrival."[57]

Where was McClellan during the advance of his divisions to the Antietam and where when his columns arrived there and awaited his orders? In the morning he was at Bolivar, where in addition to the orders issued to his corps commanders he dispatched Halleck at 8 a. m. that he had just learned from Hooker that Lee was "making for Shepherdstown in a perfect panic" and that he (McClellan) was hurrying everything forward to press Lee's retreat to the utmost.[58] In another dispatch, of the same hour, he reported Franklin's success at Crampton's Gap as complete as that at Turner's Gap and that "the morale of our men is now restored."[59] At 9 a. m. he sent a dispatch to General Banks, whom he had left in command of the defenses of Washington, that, under the present circumstances, it would be well to move the greater part of his command to the south side of the Potomac, as he did not consider that any danger to Washington was to be found from the north side of the river.[60]

At 9.30 a. m. he sent a second telegram to his wife that he had won a glorious victory, and a half hour later he sent a second dispatch to Halleck confirming the report of the rout and demoralization of Lee's army and giving some further details.[61] At Bolivar he heard that Miles had probably surrendered and awaited news from Franklin. He left Bolivar about noon and rode to Fox's Gap, saw where Reno had been killed, ordered Porter to pass Burnside, rode over to Turner's Gap, passed over Hooker's battlefield of the previous day and talked to the wounded:

More than one will remember the morning after the battle of South Mountain, when headquarters of the army moved westward over the mountain by the turnpike road

---

57 McClellan's August 1863 report, *OR* 19, pt. 1, p. 53. It is worth noting that many authors overlook this logjam of troops when they suggest McClellan should have attacked Lee on September 15.

58 McClellan to Halleck, 8:00 a.m., September 15, *ibid.*, pt. 2, p. 294.

59 McClellan to Halleck, 8:00 a.m., September 15, *ibid.*, second message.

60 McClellan to Banks, September 15, *ibid.*

61 McClellan, *Own Story*, p. 612.

through Turner's Gap to Boonsboro and Keedysville. As the cavalcade was riding rapidly up the eastern approach to Turner's Gap they came to a two-story farm house on the right of the road, which had been occupied as a hospital, and some wounded men were lying outside on the grass because the house was entirely taken up by the surgeons with the more serious cases. In front of this house McClellan suddenly halted, dismounted, and, accompanied by General Marcy, walked among the men lying on the grass outside, taking the hands of many and telling them how valuable and timely a victory their bravery had won, and that he thanked them in the name of their country. He then went into the house and remained some minutes, and when he reappeared and passed rapidly to the road, though his face was unmoved, tears were trickling down his cheeks, and as he came to his horse he dashed them away with his hand, mounted hastily and rode on.[62]

From Turner's Gap he rode on to Boonsboro and telegraphed General Scott, at West Point, of the battles of the 14th and that he was pursuing Lee closely taking many prisoners.[63] Here he received reports from the signal station near the Washington Monument, on South Mountain, that the forces of the enemy were visible near Sharpsburg, forming line of battle beyond the Antietam. At 4.30 p. m. he was yet at Boonsboro, sending messages and orders to Franklin in Pleasant Valley to hold his own without attacking McLaws, and to Burnside, on the old Sharpsburg road, to move on Sharpsburg at once and that he would be at the front to meet him.[64] It was quite 5 o'clock when he mounted his horse and rode out of Boonsboro on the Sharpsburg road, where he overtook the rear of the column,

62 This article cited by Carman was "Recollections of McClellan," by William F. Biddle, a captain and aide-de-camp to McClellan, printed in *United Service Magazine*, vol. 9, #5 (May 1894). Biddle's rank is listed in Heitman, 2, p. 217.

63 McClellan to Scott, September 15, *OR* 19, pt. 1, p. 295.

64 The messages to Franklin and Burnside, both timed at 4:30 p.m., are found in *ibid.*, 51 pt. 1, pp. 836, 838. In his *Own Story*, McClellan makes it sound much earlier than Carman's time of arrival at the front. Carman did not give the source of his timing, but it should be noted that although the message was marked from Boonsboro, that does not necessarily mean that was where McClellan was located. Jacob Cox claims he met McClellan on the east bank of Antietam Creek at 3:00 p.m. Cox, *Reminiscences*, 1 p. 298. Rafuse, *McClellan's War*, accepts that McClellan did not reach the front until 5:00 p.m., thus rejecting Cox's timing. Carman's tone and language are quite critical of McClellan. His attitude is reflective of the historiography of the time he was writing, but as has been shown, his narration is open to challenge and shows no real analysis of where McClellan should have been. In short, he follows the crowd rather than logic. McClellan had issued pursuit orders, had made his intent clear to his subordinates, and had every expectation of a coordinated pursuit and attack, if practicable. That a traffic jam resulted from failure to obey of orders cannot be laid entirely at his feet, and Carman's criticism is perhaps undeserved.

either at a halt or laboriously creeping to the front, and his presence became known, the wearied men parted a way for him, threw up their caps, cheered and yelled until their throats were sore. An eye-witness, a gallant officer of the 20th Massachusetts, thus writes of what took place near the head of the column:

> On the afternoon of the hot 15th September, while the long columns of the Federal army were resting along the Boonsboro road, General McClellan passed through them to the front, and had from them such a magnificent reception as was worth living for. Far from the rear the cheers were heard, faintly at first, and gradually the sound increased and grew to a roar as he approached. The weary men sprang to their feet and cheered and cheered, and as he went the cheers went before him and with him and after him, until the sound receding with the distance at last died away.[65]

When McClellan emerged from this tumult of enthusiasm it was at the foot of a hill nearly a mile beyond Keedysville and on which, subsequently, he had his headquarters. Here he was met by Sumner and others and they ascended the hill. This he reports as the condition of affairs:

> I found but two divisions, Richardson's and Sykes' in position. The other troops were halted in the road, the head of the column some distance in the rear of Richardson. The enemy occupied a strong position on the heights on the west side of Antietam Creek, displaying a large force of infantry and cavalry, with numerous batteries of artillery, which opened on our columns as they appeared in sight on the Keedysville and Sharpsburg turnpike.... After a rapid examination of the position I found that it was too late to attack that day, and at once directed the placing of the batteries in position in the center and indicated the bivouacs for the different corps, massing them near and on both sides of the Sharpsburg turnpike. The corps were not all in their positions until the next morning after sunrise.[66]

In his *Own Story* McClellan says:

> Near Keedysville I met Sumner, who told me that the enemy were in position in strong force, and took me to a height in front of Keedysville whence a view of the position could be obtained. We were accompanied by a numerous staff and escort; but no sooner had we shown ourselves on the hill than the enemy opened upon us with rifled

---

65 Carman's Note: Palfrey, *The Antietam and Fredericksburg*, p. 56.

66 McClellan's August 1863 report, *OR* 19, pt. 1, pp. 53-4.

guns, and, as his firing was very good, the hill was soon cleared of all save Fitz John Porter and myself.[67]

The natural inference from this plain statement that "the hill was soon cleared of all save Fitz John Porter" and McClellan himself is that they only braved the fire and that the rest, Hooker, Sumner, Burnside and Cox, for all were there, sought safety elsewhere. The fact is that McClellan directed that all but Porter and himself should retire behind the ridge, while he and Porter continued the examination of Lee's position.[68] The discarded officers did not hear what passed between McClellan and Porter, but one, at least, came to the quick conclusion, that there would be no aggressive action that night or next day should McClellan listen to the advice of Fitz John Porter.[69]

Others looked upon the notorious partiality of McClellan for Porter as disrespectful to them, and as bad for McClellan and the Union cause, for, however brilliant as had been Porter's services on the Peninsula, there was a strong feeling that he had acted badly towards Pope. He was known to be intensely hostile to the administration; and by many his loyalty was distrusted.[70]

Late in the evening McClellan was considering the advisability of sending a large force of Pleasonton's cavalry with artillery to Jones' Cross Roads—the intersection of the Keedysville and Williamsport road with the Hagerstown and Sharpsburg turnpike—four miles north of Sharpsburg, but finally concluded not to send them so far off, but ordered Colonel B. F. Davis, who had escaped from Harper's Ferry, to return from Greencastle to that point and unite with about 300 Pennsylvania cavalry, under Colonel W. J. Palmer, which had marched through Hagerstown during the day and awaited orders at the cross roads; and Governor

---

67 Carman's Note: McClellan, *Own Story*, p. 586.

68 Carman seemed to go out of his way to read insult into an ambivalent statement. Cox, *Reminiscences*, 1, p. 298, make it clear McClellan ordered everyone except Porter from the hill. The passage in McClellan, *Own Story*, implies no disrespect to the other generals.

69 Gen. Hooker made this statement to Carman. No written evidence in the Carman Papers supports this statement. However, Hooker made other, somewhat outrageous, statements contained in newspaper clippings and letters found in the Carman Papers, NYPL. In short, Hooker is not always a reliable source.

70 No other general mentioned this disrespect until many years later. Carman ignores that Porter was eventually cleared of the charges brought by Gen. Pope, and his loyalty was never seriously suspected or challenged. William Marvel, *Burnside* (Chapel Hill: University of North Carolina Press, 1991), p. 128, suggests that this was a slight to Sumner and Burnside who ranked Porter and were wing commanders. Only circumstantial evidence supports this interpretation. For a complete record of Porter's courts-martial, see *OR* 12, pt. 2.

Curtin was requested to send all the troops he could spare from the Cumberland Valley to the same place.[71]

Under McClellan's direction, placing the troops in bivouac, the First Corps marched to the right, crossed the Little Antietam by a stone bridge and bivouacked in the forks of the Big and Little Antietam. The divisions of French and Richardson [Carman obviously meant Sedgwick] of the Second Corps went into position, after dark, in rear of Richardson and on either side of the Sharpsburg turnpike, Sedgwick on the right and French on the left. The Twelfth Corps remained at Nicodemus Mills until next day. Burnside was directed to move still farther to the left and McClellan sought his headquarters at Keedysville with the satisfactory belief that he "delivered Pennsylvania and Maryland."[72]

We sum up the operations of the day. Harper's Ferry was surrendered early in the morning. Franklin lay inactive in Pleasant Valley, while McLaws quietly withdrew from his front; and McClellan moved the main body of his army from the east side of Turner's Gap to the banks of the Antietam.

In his *Antietam and Fredericksburg*, General Palfrey says:

The fact of the surrender [of Harper's Ferry], and the hour it took place, were speedily made known to McClellan. It was remarkably certain that the troops assigned by Lee's Special Order 191 to capturing the garrison at Harper's Ferry, were then around that place, and most of them far from Lee, and all of them separated from him either by distance and the Potomac, or by Union troops, or both. Whatever his estimate may have been of the amount of force so employed, he knew that it comprised all or part of Jackson's command, and the divisions of McLaws, R. H. Anderson, and Walker. If he looked for no aggressive action on the part of Franklin and Couch, he could at least look to them to hold in check and neutralize the forces of McLaws and R. H. Anderson, and thus left him free to use the First, Second, Ninth, and Twelfth Corps, with all of the Fifth Corps that was with him, and Pleasonton's cavalry command, against Longstreet and D. H. Hill. In other words, in fine country and in fine weather,

71 Telegram to "The President," from Gov. Andrew G. Curtin citing a telegram from Palmer, *ibid*, pt. 2, p. 311. Neither McClellan nor Pleasonton make any mention of this pondered movement. Curtin refers to him as Capt. Palmer, his rank in the Anderson troop, but Carman used his rank as colonel, appointed September 8, 1862, as commander of the 15th Pennsylvania Cavalry. See Roger Hunt, *Brevet Brigadier Generals in Blue* (Gaitehrsburg, MD: Olde Soldier Books, 1990), p. 462.

72 Carman may be "filling in gaps" from his personal knowledge as McClellan and the corps commanders were not specific about their locations on September 15. McClellan, OR 19, pt. 1, p. 54, simply said they were not in position until after dawn on September 16. The quote about "delivered Maryland and Pennsylvania" is from a letter to Ellen in McClellan, *Own Story*, p. 612. Carman implies it was on the evening of the 15th, but the letter is dated September 16.

he had 35 brigades of infantry to use against Longstreet's 9 brigades and D. H. Hill's 5 brigades. Pleasonton's cavalry and the reserve artillery were probably as numerous as Stuart's and Rosser's cavalry and their artillery. We assume this in the absence of figures.... Here again was a great opportunity. With a long day before him, a force that outnumbered his foe as five to two, and probably as six to two, and the knowledge that the large detachments his opponent had made could not join him for twenty-four hours, and might not join him for forty-eight or more, it was a time for rapid action. It would seem that he ought to have pressed his troops forward untiringly till they reached cannon shot distance from the enemy, and made his reconnaissance as his columns were advancing. He would speedily have learned the length of the enemy's line, and as the distance from the summit of Turner's Gap to Sharpsburg is only seven or eight miles, it is not easy to see why he might not have attacked in force early in the afternoon. He had every reason for believing that delay would strengthen the enemy much more proportionately than it would strengthen him, and he might be sure that delay would be at least as serviceable to the enemy as to him in acquiring knowledge of the ground, and much more so in putting that knowledge to account. But it was not to be. With all his amiable and estimable and admirable qualities, there was something wanting in McClellan. If he had used the priceless hours of the 15th September, and the still precious, though less precious hours of the 16th as he might have, his name would have stood high in the roll of great commanders; but he let those hours go by.[73]

In his admirable *History of the Second Army Corps*, General Francis A. Walker commends Palfrey's views; shows that not one of Lee's detached divisions could, by the most strenuous exertion be brought up, through the long, round-about way which was alone open to them to support Lee on the Antietam, before the morning of the 16th, while a portion could not be expected before the 17th. In this situation the most strenuous exertions should have been made to carry the four corps (1st, 2nd, 9th and 12th) and Sykes' Division, constituting the right and center, clean and fast across the space, not more than seven miles as the line of march was, which intervened between the base of South Mountain and the banks of the Antietam. The staff should have been out upon the road all day, full of life and all alert to

73 Palfrey, pp. 46-7. Palfrey's analysis, which Carman seems to accept unreservedly, was made in 1882, when he had much more information about Lee's army, its order of battle, and the general situation than McClellan had in 1862. Carman did not include a footnote, where Palfrey acknowledged McClellan's dearth of information about the enemy, but then made the assertion, without evidence, that either McClellan did not really believe he was outnumbered, or if he did then he should have retreated to the defenses of Washington. Palfrey and Carman overlook the fact that McClellan felt pressured to act, no matter what the odds may or may not have been. In short, the choices were not as simple as Palfrey makes them, and McClellan had far less information about Lee's army than Palfrey did when made this criticism.

prevent delays, to keep the columns moving, to crowd the troops forward, and to bend everything to the encounter. Instead of all this the army moved uncertainly and slowly for lack of inspiration and direction which general headquarters should always supply.[74]

There was one cause of the delay in getting to the front and the want of action when the leading divisions arrived there that must now be noted, and that was the suspension of the order by which Burnside commanded the right wing of the army, composed of the First and Ninth Corps.

It will be remembered that, before McClellan left Washington, it was arranged with Halleck that Burnside and Sumner were to command wings of at least two corps each, and this was done at the suggestion of President Lincoln. The arrangement was observed from the beginning of the campaign and worked well, but the formal orders were not published until September 14th:

SPECIAL ORDERS No. —.
HEADQUARTERS ARMY OF THE POTOMAC,
In the Field, September 14, 1862

Maj. Gen. A. E. Burnside is assigned to the command of the right wing of this army, which will be composed of his own and Hooker's corps.

The Second Corps (Banks'), late Army of Virginia, is placed, until further orders, under the command of Maj. Gen. E. V. Sumner, commanding Second Corps, Army of the Potomac.

By command of Major-General McClellan:

S. WILLIAMS,
Assistant Adjutant-General.[75]

Before the advance was resumed on the morning of the 15th, these orders were suspended by these following orders:

SPECIAL ORDERS No. —.

---

74 Walker, *History of the Second Army Corps in the Army of the Potomac*, p. 612.

75 *OR* 19, pt. 2, p. 290.

HEADQUARTERS ARMY OF THE POTOMAC,
In the Field, September 15, 1862.
The operation of the Special Orders of yesterday's date, assigning General Burnside to the command of the right wing, owing to the necessary separation of the Third [First] Corps, is temporarily suspended. General Hooker will report direct to these headquarters.

II. Brig. Gen. J. K. F. Mansfield is temporarily assigned to the command of Banks' corps.

By command of Major-General McClellan:

S. WILLIAMS,
Assistant Adjutant-General.[76]

It is claimed that the detachment of the First Corps was at Hooker's request; this may be true, it is altogether probable, for Hooker was prone to ask such things, but this was no sufficient reason for such action as thwarted the intention of General Halleck and the administration, that Burnside should have command of the two corps, nor was there any military necessity for the separation. The First and Ninth Corps had acted, practically, as a unit on the march and at South Mountain; they were in their proper positions as the right of the army, and it was easy to continue the advance keeping Burnside's right wing intact, and the same as to Sumner's. But by this order Sumner's and Hooker's corps became entangled on the road to Sharpsburg, in fact the framework of the army became disjointed and its divisions reached the Antietam much later than they should and in no relation to each other for quick co-operation, had such been needed.

Burnside was at McClellan's headquarters when the orders were issued and protested against them, to no avail, as there were influences at work too powerful for him to overcome. Grieved at the turn of affairs, he asked McClellan's permission to go forward to join his corps which had been ordered to move. There are good reasons for believing the motive in detaching Hooker and thus reducing Burnside's command was personal and that it was inspired by Fitz-John Porter.[77]

---

76 *Ibid.*, p. 297.

77 Carman's speculation about the ending of the "wing" structure of the army, fueled by Cox's suspicions of nefarious motivations, have reverberated through most histories of the battle and still pervade the interpretative elements of the battle. Common sense and a lack of evidence are ignored as they searched for a scapegoat and decided McClellan had turned on his old friend.

Of all his corps commanders Fitz-John Porter stood highest in McClellan's estimation. "Take him all in all he (Porter) was probably the best general officer I had under me." [*Own Story*, p. 139.] His partiality for him was common talk. He had been appointed a brigadier-general of volunteers at McClellan's request and was favored by him to the exclusion of others. At the siege of Yorktown, April 1862, he was designated director of the siege, although McClellan had with him the best engineering talent of the army, and he was consulted and his advice taken on every important step, though junior to many others in years, length of service and rank. Naturally, this was offensive to his seniors and discourteous to them and resulted in much bad feeling. That he was the confidential advisor of McClellan was well known in Washington and President Lincoln warned McClellan of the mischief likely to ensue, when, in May, he authorized him to form two "provisional corps" one to be commanded by Porter.

On the 8th of March the President ordered the organization of five army corps and designated the senior division generals to command them; these were McDowell, Sumner, Heintzelman, Keyes and Banks. McClellan made an earnest protest, arguing that it was his intention to postpone the formation of army corps until service in the field had indicated the general officers best fitted to exercise these most important commands. McDowell's and Banks' corps were detached from McClellan's immediate command and he renewed his objections to the formation of the corps of Sumner, Heintzelman and Keyes, and proposed the formation of two provisional corps, the troops to be taken from the corps then organized. Mr. Lincoln yielded to his importunities and in doing so, May 9th, gave him a piece of his mind:

I now think it indispensable for you to know how your struggle against it [the order of March 8, 1862] is viewed in quarters, which we cannot entirely disregard. It is looked upon as merely an effort to pamper one or two pets and to persecute and degrade their

---

After the capture of Frederick, the three-pronged advance to feel out the enemy was no longer necessary. McClellan's suspension of the wing arrangement was more a recognition of the status quo of the location of the corps and their route of advance than a critique of anyone. This entire "feud" between McClellan and Burnside is nicely debunked in Ethan Rafuse, "Poor 'Burn?' The Antietam Conspiracy That Wasn't," *Civil War History*, no. 54 (June 2008), pp. 146-75. It is also interesting to compare McClellan's decision to Lee's handling of his army. Both seemed to decentralize their lines of command when they reached the proximity of their opponent. The mix-up in the delivery of the "Lost Order" stemmed, in part, from Jackson's belief that D. H. Hill was under his command. That Lee sent Hill a copy of the order suggests Lee considered Hill directly under his authority. At Antietam, Lee dispatched orders directly to several division commanders. It appears McClellan desired that same structure, and one needs no Machiavellian plot to explain it.

supposed rivals. I have had no word from Sumner, Heintzelman or Keyes. The commanders of these corps are of course the three highest officers with you, but I am constantly told that you have no consultation or communication with them, that you consult and communicate with nobody but General Fitz-John Porter and perhaps General Franklin. I do not say these complaints are true or just, but at all events it is proper that you should know of their existence. Do the commanders of corps disobey your orders in anything. .... Are you strong enough—are you strong enough even with my help—to set your feet upon the necks of Sumner, Heintzelman and Keyes all at once? This is a practical and very serious question for you. The success of your army and the cause of the country are the same, and of course I only desire the good of the cause.[78]

The warning was lost upon McClellan, who still continued to maintain closer relations to Porter than to any other officer in the army. That an officer who stood in such close relation to his chief as did Porter to McClellan should have much influence over him is very natural and this influence was now used to humble and, if possible, injure Burnside, for an act, that unintentionally, was threatening to injure Porter.

The circumstances are these. When the Army of the Potomac was withdrawn from the Peninsula, both Burnside and Porter were landed at Falmouth, on the Rappahannock, Porter being pushed forward to join Pope, while Burnside remained at Falmouth. Pope had by this time been cut off from communication with Washington, and all that could be heard from him was through Burnside, to whom Porter reported Pope's movements and those of the enemy as far as they could be ascertained. In these dispatches of Porter, running from August 25th to August 30th, there was much matter of indiscrete character, sneers at the strategy of the campaign, a great lack of confidence in its management, and expressions of a desire to get ordered out of Pope's command.[79]

78 Letter, May 9, 1862, from Lincoln to McClellan, although in Stanton's handwriting. The original is in the Stanton Papers, Library of Congress. Basler, *Lincoln*, 5, pp. 208-9, is also printed in *OR* 11, pt. 3, pp. 154-5. The March 8 order is found in *ibid*, 5, p. 18. Carman ignored the fact that corps commanders were not approved by McClellan, and all of whom, except Keyes, voted against the Peninsula operation. Under these circumstances, any army commander would have been dissatisfied.

79 See, particularly, Porter to Burnside, August 27 and 29, 1862, *OR* 12, pt. 3, pp. 700, 733. The president and Gen. Halleck were very anxious for news, so Burnside sent them copies of these dispatches. It was all he had to send, and he did not think they would do Porter any harm, and might do the service some good. *OR* 12, pt. 2 *Supplement*, p. 1,003.

In fact, in the most objectionable dispatch, that of August 27, Porter said: "Most of this dispatch is private . . . make what use of this you choose, so it does good." So, without editing the dispatches, copies of them were forwarded to the President, Halleck, and McClellan.[80]

After the close of the campaign Porter became aware of the transmission of these dispatches in their entirety, indiscrete utterances and all, and that they were to be used against him, in the trial by court-martial then impending. Not unnaturally he was greatly incensed at Burnside, held him responsible for furnishing damaging testimony against him, and joined McClellan, on the 14th, with the determination to "even up" matters with him.[81]

As McClellan was also involved in the charges of disloyalty to Pope and the administration it was easy for him to sympathize with Porter and share his feelings toward Burnside, so, putting aside all remembrances of what Burnside had done for him, in twice refusing the command of the army and insisting that McClellan should be retained, joined hands with Porter, and from that hour became Burnside's enemy. This does not show in the official records of that period but it does show in McClellan's *Own Story*. Porter joined McClellan at Middletown, near noon of the 14th, after that McClellan ceased to send orders to Burnside as wing commander, but sent them direct to Hooker and Reno the two corps commanders. The pursuit of revenge and the effort to make a record against Burnside was renewed next day, when Porter asked for written orders to pass the Ninth Corps and endorsed them with an unnecessary criticism of Burnside's delay in marching.[82]

80  These dispatches are properly cited, except that the first one begins on *OR* 12, pt. 3, p. 699. The citation from *ibid.*, pt. 2, p. 1,003, is Burnside's testimony of December 31, 1862, in Porter's courts-marital hearings. Ambrose Burnside responded to a question asking if Porter seemed disinclined to do his whole duty under Pope's command. Burnside adamantly refuted that idea in his testimony, which suggests he was not feuding, or brooding, over Porter's alleged anger. Porter made it clear that he was not alone in his description of affairs in John Pope's army, and it seems illogical that he'd authorize Burnside to use the dispatches and then be angry when he did so.

81  Carman states this as fact, but he offers no support or evidence for his statement. No evidence of Fitz-John Porter's vindictive attitude can be found in Bruce Tap, *Over Lincoln's Shoulder: The Committee on the Conduct of the War* (Lawrence, KA: University Press of Kansas, 1998), Stephen Sears, *Controversy and Commanders: Dispatches from the Army of the Potomac* (Boston: Houghton Mifflin & Co., 1999), and other sources I have examined. Porter was indiscreet in his criticism of General Pope, but no mention is made of any desire by Porter to retaliate against Burnside.

82  McClellan, *Own Story*, p. 535, n. 51.

McClellan or someone at his headquarters continued the nagging, on the 16th and 17th, and, subsequently, both he and Porter filed incorrect and misleading reports as to Burnside and his command at the battle of the 17th.[83]

Such a spirit shown toward a faithful officer of high rank could have but one effect; Burnside did not openly complain but the facts were known to his brother officers and did not serve to strengthen confidence in McClellan or respect for Fitz-John Porter.

Other reasons have been advanced for the tardiness of the movement on the 15th of September. The Comte de Paris says: "The obstruction of the roads, want of exactitude on the part of some of the commanders and the indifference of others had kept back the rest of the army, except Richardson and Porter, which stretched out in interminable column between Boonsboro and the Antietam."[84] General O. O. Howard writes in the *National Tribune*:

> Eager as McClellan was to engage him [Lee] before the return of Jackson and the other Harper's Ferry detachment, he was forced to postpone his attack at least until morning. Taking into account all the sickness, discouragement, disgust, envies and contentions which followed in the wake of the Second Bull Run and the Harper's Ferry disaster, it will not seem strange that much of our army was strung along the thoroughfare between Washington and South Mountain. Even the reaction from our small successes at the South Mountain passes produced additional weariness, willfulness, slowness, and indifference on the part of some of the officers—and some of them too holding responsible commands. These suggestions will account for strange delays in the marches which were ordered and the comparatively small number which we actually had in position in front of Lee as late as the morning of the 16th September.[85]

83 McClellan's *Own Story* references to Burnside are critical of his actions at Antietam, but also include warm personal regard for him. There is nothing in *Own Story* that suggests this conspiracy of McClellan and Porter against Burnside. Again, Carman suggests a plot against Burnside, but does not offer proof for it. Yet, this theme is still repeated and included in histories of the battle. Rafuse, "Poor Burn: The Antietam Controversy That Wasn't," pp. 146-75, is the first to demonstrate the lack of evidence of this supposed conspiracy.

84 Comte de Paris, *History of the Civil War in America*, 2, p. 333. Among the reasons Carman cited earlier, but now ignored, was the presence of many Confederate guns on the heights east of Sharpsburg and Hooker's observation on the afternoon of September 15 that 30,000 Confederates were visible across Antietam Creek, far outnumbering Richardson's and Sykes' troops. Hooker's report, *OR* 19, pt. 1, p. 217.

85 Oliver O. Howard, "Personal Reminiscences of the War of the Rebellion," *National Tribune*, pt. 24, March 27, 1884.

Palfrey says: "The success of our army was immediately greatly lessened by jealousy, distrust and general want of the *entente cordiale*.[86]

There is evidence that in starting from Washington on the Maryland campaign McClellan and some of his prominent lieutenants would have been satisfied with checking the invasion of Pennsylvania and repelling Lee from Maryland without risking a general engagement. They did not consider the army in proper condition as to morale and organization.[87] Upon this point we quote McClellan:

> The Army of the Potomac was thoroughly exhausted and depleted by its desperate fighting and severe marches in the unhealthy regions of the Chickahominy and afterward, in the second Bull Run campaign; its trains, administration services and supplies were disorganized or lacking in consequence of the rapidity and manner of its removal from the Peninsula as well as from the nature of its operations in the second Bull Run campaign. In the departure from the Peninsula, trains, supplies, cavalry and artillery in many instances had been necessarily left at Fort Monroe and Yorktown for the lack of vessels as the important point was to remove the infantry divisions rapidly to the support General Pope. The divisions of the Army of Virginia were also exhausted and weakened, and their trains were disorganized and their supplies deficient by reason of the movements in which they had been engaged.
>
> Had General Lee remained in front of Washington it would have been the part of wisdom to hold our own army quiet until its pressing wants were fully supplied, its organization was restored, and its ranks were filled with recruits – in brief, until it was prepared for a campaign. But as the enemy maintained the offensive and crossed the Upper Potomac to threaten or invade Pennsylvania, it became necessary to meet him at any cost notwithstanding the condition of the troops, to put a stop to the invasion, save Baltimore and Washington, and throw him back across the Potomac. Nothing but sheer necessity justified the advance of the Army of the Potomac to South Mountain and Antietam in its then condition and it is to the eternal honor of the men who composed it that under such adverse circumstances they gained those victories. . .
> It must then be borne constantly in mind that the purpose of advancing from Washington was simply to meet the necessities of the moment by frustrating Lee's invasion of the Northern States, and, when that was accomplished, to push with the

---

86 Palfrey, *Antietam and Fredericksburg*, p. 59, n. 1. The tone of this note is critical of Burnside's performance, not McClellan's.

87 This "accusation" in fact reiterates McClellan's goals imparted by Halleck and Lincoln; defending the capital and Baltimore, which were impressed upon him when the campaign began. OR 19, pt. 1, pp. 25, 39. On September 15, Lincoln also asked him to "destroy the rebel army, if possible," a less limited goal that justified a limited operational plan considering how little McClellan knew about his opponent's army.

utmost rapidity the work of reorganization and supply so that a new campaign might be promptly inaugurated with the army in condition to prosecute it to a successful termination without intermission."[88]

From McClellan's tardiness in reaching the front and other surrounding circumstances we are led to the conclusion that he had no serious intention of giving Lee battle on the 15th. Indeed there were many camp rumors that McClellan and some of his most trusted lieutenants were well satisfied that Lee had fallen back behind the Antietam and that they would have been still further satisfied had he continued an immediate retreat beyond the Potomac.[89]

McClellan had around him a large circle of officers, who were his partisans against what, in army parlance, was called "the politicians" and some of those were on his staff, who openly characterized the war, as a politicians' war for the abolition of slavery. Some of those before the campaign opened publicly declared that the time had come for McClellan to proclaim himself dictator, and this idea was prevalent when the army began the march from Washington. There was as much discussion in the army about politics as there was at Washington and elsewhere, and it was a shade of political discussion antagonistic to the administration and indulged in unceasingly. Those who visited headquarters at this time were astonished at the more or less disloyal talk and the disloyal influences at work, and of the assurance given McClellan that the people had assumed that the army was so devoted to him that they would as one man enforce any decision he should make as to any part of the war policy.

"It would seem," says General Cox, "that treasonable notions were rife about him to an extent that was never suspected, unless he was made the dupe of pretenders who saw some profit in what might be regarded as a gross form of adulation. He must be condemned for the weakness which made such approaches to him possible . . . to accept as one of the strange elements of the situation a

---

88 Restating the goal from his reports, McClellan alludes to the constant concern for the safety of Washington expressed by Halleck to McClellan throughout the campaign. See Chapter Five. Carman's implied demand for battle more reflects after-the-fact knowledge than the administrative and political climate of the time. See *B&L*, pp. 553-554.

89 Rumors notwithstanding, McClellan's orders for the pursuit and possible attack on September 15 are unambiguous. *Ibid.*, pp. 29, 53. The specific orders to Burnside, Hooker, Franklin, and Sumner are found in *ibid.*, 51 pt. 1, pp. 834-7, and are dated between 8:00 a.m. and 8:45 a.m., September 15. These orders make it clear that Richardson and the cavalry were already moving.

constant stream of treasonable suggestions from professed friends in the army and out of it."[90]

Those of the press hostile to the administration were editorially advising McClellan to insist upon a reconstruction of the cabinet, by the expulsion of the radical element from it. The New York *Herald* (September 11) in discussing the situation and McClellan's relation to it, said:

> The political vultures still hover over Washington...waiting to give him a stab in the back, like stealthy Indians, and then raise their hideous war-whoop against him once more.
>
> Under these circumstances what is the duty of General McClellan? His position is like that of Wellington in the Spanish peninsula, when he was interfered with by the British cabinet; and it is a duty he owes to the country, no less than to himself, to follow the example of that illustrious and patriotic general. When "the Iron Duke" found that the administration were bent on his destruction and the defeat of the army he was leading, he firmly took his stand and insisted that the cabinet should be broken up. His country was in danger, and he was in a position to dictate terms. His remonstrance had the desired effect; the meddling cabinet was overthrown, and thenceforward victory crowned the British arms. Now this is the ground which McClellan ought to take in reference to that portion of the administration at Washington which is responsible for the present condition of things. He ought to insist upon the modification and reconstruction of the Cabinet, in order to have it purged of the radical taint which may again infuse its poison over the whole. Now is the time for him to prove himself not only a great general, but a statesman worthy of the occasion and of the responsibility which he has assumed. The safety of the country is entrusted to him. He is bound to see that no insidious enemy lurks behind about his base of operations. His own security and the security of his army are involved, and the fate of the republic itself is at stake. He is master of the situation. He is the only man in whom the troops and the country have confidence as a general for the chief command of the army in the field. He has a right to demand indemnity for the past and security for the future, and he

90 Carman perhaps exaggerates the situation, but certainly the political strife was evident to all observers at the time. It was no secret that McClellan and many professional soldiers advocated a different strategy for the war, and held the Republicans in low esteem. That was no disloyalty to the country, although subsequent historians have interpreted it as such. While many people in the army may have indeed held the beliefs Cox suggests, no evidence pointing to any disloyalty on McClellan's part has been presented. Indeed, many accounts record that he always rebuffed such notions. Neither has any evidence been presented to show that political considerations outweighed his military conduct. See, for example, McClellan, *Own Story*, pp. 195-6, Rafuse, *McClellan's War*, pp. 377-9. Cox's political affiliations often color his memoirs, and this quotation is an example of it.

ought not to rest satisfied till he is assured by facts, not mere promises, that his plans shall not be interfered with hereafter. The game is now in his hands, and unless he plays his best trump and disposes effectually of the radicals, as he has the power to do, they will soon dispose of him by striking him down in the very crisis of the campaign now opened in Maryland, on which hang the destinies of the American republic and of millions of the human race yet unborn.[91]

On the next day, September 12th, the *Herald* said: "Let President Lincoln keep our abolition disorganizers from intermeddling any more with the plans of General McClellan, and R. E. Lee will soon get his ragged liberating rebel army back to Richmond."[92]

The sentiments expressed in the *Herald* of the 11th were fully shared by those who surrounded McClellan and they were not slow to discuss matters of that kind. A correspondent of the New York *Tribune* writes:

Three days before the battle of Antietam I had quarters one night in a farm house. Judge Key of Cincinnati, whom Chase had gotten appointed Judge Advocate General on McClellan's staff, rode up about dark and told me he felt too ill to sleep in a tent or on the ground. I offered to share my room with him. A headache prevented him from sleeping, and he talked a large part of the night. He told me that a plan to countermarch to Washington and intimidate the President had been seriously discussed the night before [Sept. 13] by members of McClellan's staff, and that his [Key's] opposition to it had, he thought, caused its abandonment. Judge Key was a lawyer of unusual ability and of high social standing in Cincinnati. I did not doubt the entire accuracy of the statement. Indeed, I was not greatly surprised at the time, for I knew that the men McClellan had gathered around him were nearly all copperheads who had no heart in the war.[93]

---

91 The title of the article in the *New York Herald* was "The Important Position of General McClellan—The Attitude He Ought to Assume," September 11, 1862, p. 4.

92 "The Campaign in Maryland—General Lee's Proclamation," *New York Herald*, September 12, 1862, p. 4. For reasons unknown, the word "soon" was omitted in Carman's manuscript.

93 This article is entitled "Unwritten History of the War," p. 5, *New York Tribune*, March 14, 1880. Colonel Key was the brother of Thomas Key, who was cashiered from the army by Lincoln for uttering treasonous talk. The incident was interpreted as a warning to McClellan and to those officers who failed to embrace the Republican agenda for fighting the war. This article implies that Col. Key was aware of his brother's treason, but it was written long after the war to advance a partisan point of view. Either Carman and Cox accepted that point of view or ignored the bias of the article. See Rafuse, *McClellan's War*, pp. 338-42, for this affair and examples of the political situation McClellan faced.

The plan was to expel Stanton from the war office and compel Mr. Lincoln to change his war policy. In taking this course those officers did not consider their action treasonable. They considered the administration entirely wrong and would check its unconstitutional acts. There is good reason to believe that McClellan was ignorant of this design; though listening to much adverse criticism of his civilian superiors. He himself admits that he was urged to put himself in open opposition to the political tendencies of the administration, but he was the last man who would have listened to the use of the army for such a purpose; and the Army of the Potomac could not have been so used. But the fact remains that the Army of the Potomac was officered by that class of men, who, yet true to the National flag, limited their efforts to the strict requirements of duty, solicitous that no disaster should come to the country, and more than willing that the Confederates should get away without battle.

Under all these circumstances, it is easy to understand why, now that the battle of South Mountain had been fought and the army leisurely marched to the Antietam, there was a hesitation to attack. Those in high command, and to some extent McClellan shared their views, thought that the expulsion of Lee from Maryland had been accomplished by the success at South Mountain. The risk of a battle was discussed with some misgivings, and there was a hope that Lee would recross the Potomac without further bloodshed.[94]

When Lee disposed his command on the height east of Sharpsburg, fronting the Antietam, on the morning of the 15th, it was for the purpose of delaying McClellan and forming a junction with McLaws. He had no present intention of giving battle north of the Potomac. But events decided otherwise. Before his dispositions were fairly completed he received this dispatch from Jackson, dated 8 a. m. September 15th:

> Through God's blessing, Harper's Ferry and its garrison are to be surrendered. As Hill's troops have borne the heaviest part in the engagement, he will be left in command until the prisoners and public property shall be disposed of, unless you

---

94 While McClellan never expressed such sentiments, as Carman acknowledged, Carman makes a leap of logic to assign the delay in advancing to Sharpsburg to political rather than logistical reasons. As stated before, the pursuit orders are clear, and his reluctance perhaps had more to do with the reports of Lee's army outnumbering his than it did to any political scheming. Carman, a loyal Republican, may simply be politically sniping at McClellan and the Democrats, which is not altogether surprising since he owed his position at the Agriculture Department to a Republican, President Hayes.

direct otherwise. The other forces can move off this evening so soon as they get their rations. To what point shall they move?[95]

It will be remembered that soon after sending the dispatch to McLaws, at 5 p. m. of the 14th, Lee advised Jackson of the reverse at South Mountain, and ordered him to march to Shepherdstown to cover his crossing into Virginia. When Jackson sent the dispatch just quoted, of 8 a. m., that Harper's Ferry was to be surrendered and asking where he should go, this dispatch of Lee's, ordering his march to Shepherdstown, had not been received, but it came later. Jackson lost no time, and without comment on the dispatch folded and endorsed it: "I will join you at Sharpsburg;"[96] then handed to a courier for swift delivery and by midday it was in Lee's hands at Sharpsburg. It was this message from Jackson that determined Lee to accept battle north of the Potomac and on the banks of the Antietam. He was now certain that Jackson, closely followed by Walker, would be with him in the morning of the next day and had the best of reasons for the belief that McLaws would not be far behind.[97]

Prof. H. A. White, in his life of General Lee, says: "Noonday (September 15) brought him a note from Jackson written at an early hour: 'Through God's blessing Harper's Ferry and its garrison are to be surrendered.' Not until the receipt of this news, with the additional knowledge that 'Stonewall' was making all speed to join him did Lee determine to stand and give battle at Sharpsburg."[98] The "additional

---

95 The idea that Lee initially had no intention of fighting at Sharpsburg, or at least of fighting the battle he did on September 17 until it was forced upon him the day before by Hooker's crossing, has been overlooked by many authors, most of whom castigate Lee for his rashness, aggressive nature, and so forth. As Carman makes clear, the intent was to provide support for McLaws, who Lee ordered the previous night to make his way to Sharpsburg. The dispatch arrived about noon, according to Harsh, *Taken at the Flood*, p. 307, and is examined more thoroughly in Harsh, *Sounding the Shallows*, Chapter 8, Section L.

96 Statement to Carman by Henry Kyd Douglas of Jackson's staff. See also Ropes, *Story of the Civil War*, 2 Vols. (New York: Putnum's Sons, 1898, )2, p. 348.

97 It is debatable whether Lee's decision was to "accept battle," as Carman states it, or simply allow his army to bluff his Union pursuers long enough, (as Lee hoped, early on the 16th) to move by his left up the Hagerstown Pike and resume his campaign. Harsh, *Taken at the Flood*, pp. 306-7, 324. The dispatch from Jackson is in *OR* 19, pt. 1, p. 951. The "statement" from Douglas has not appeared in writing, but he and Carman conversed several times and it may be a verbal comment. Ropes is one of the authors puzzled by Lee's stand, and in the passage cited, which extends to the next page, summarizes the exchange of messages and decisions by Lee.

98 Henry A. White, *Robert E. Lee and the Southern Confederacy* (New York: G.P. Putnam and Sons, 1897), p. 207.

knowledge" that Jackson was making all speed to join Lee was derived from Jackson's subsequent dispatch that he would join Lee at Sharpsburg.

Longstreet says: "A few minutes after our lines were manned information came of the capitulation of Harper's Ferry" and that up to this time Lee had no intention of giving battle at Sharpsburg.

Longstreet opposed a battle at Sharpsburg. He had opposed the movement from Hagerstown back to Turner's Gap, the day before, and suggested the withdrawal of his own force from Hagerstown and D. H. Hill's from South Mountain, and their concentration behind the Antietam, at Sharpsburg, where they could get together in season to make a strong defensive fight and at the same time check McClellan's advance toward Harper's Ferry, in case he thought to relieve Miles by that route. Now that Miles had surrendered Longstreet was opposed to giving battle at Sharpsburg and proposed that the army cross over into Virginia. He gives his reasons:

As long as the armies were linked to Harper's Ferry, the heights in front of Sharpsburg offered a more formidable defensive line, and in view of possible operations from Harper's Ferry, through the river pass, east of South Mountain, formed a beautiful point of strategic diversion. But when it transpired that Harper's Ferry was surrendered and the position was not utilized, that the troops there were to join us by a march on the south side, its charms were changed to perplexities. The threatening attitude towards the enemy's rear vanished, his line of communication was open and free of further care, and his army, relieved of entanglements, was at liberty to cross the Antietam by the upper fords and bridges, and approach from vantage-ground Lee's left. At the same time the Federal left was reasonably secured from aggression by cramped and rugged ground along the Confederate right. Thus the altered circumstances changed all of the features in favor of the Federals.[99]

Again Longstreet writes:

That night (September 15)after we heard of the fall of Harper's Ferry, General Lee ordered Stonewall Jackson to march to Sharpsburg as rapidly as he could come. Then it was that we should have retired from Sharpsburg and gone to the Virginia side of the Potomac. The moral effect of our move into Maryland had been lost by our discomfiture at South Mountain, and it was then evident that we could not hope to

---

99 Longstreet, *From Manassas to Appomattox*, p. 228. In addition to the portion quoted, Carman referred to Longstreet's earlier suggestions, pp. 219-220. Longstreet's memoirs were first published in 1896, and the advantage of hindsight made him appear more prescient than he likely was in 1862.

concentrate in time to do more than make a respectable retreat, whereas retiring before the battle, we could have claimed a very successful campaign."[100]

It is quite true, as Longstreet here argues and as he argued that day with Lee, that, in recrossing the Potomac, Lee would have avoided all the chances of a disaster and would have been observant of recognized principals of war, but, at the same time, he would have lost prestige by retiring from Maryland without trying conclusions with McClellan in a general engagement. He had entered Maryland for the purpose, among others, of relieving Virginia from the ravages of war and Maryland from the despotism of the Union. He had not found that Union despotism was particularly distasteful to Maryland people and could have dismissed this phase of the campaign from his mind without any compunction, but he was averse to carrying back to Virginia the horrors of war that he knew would follow his retreat beyond the Potomac. He knew that if he recrossed into Virginia he would be giving time to McClellan to reorganize and discipline his army for an advance into Virginia, at his convenience, and he considered his wiser policy to be to give McClellan no time to reorganize his army and drill and discipline his new recruits, but force him to a battle before his troops had fully recovered from the disastrous defeat on the plains of Manassas, and he had such a sublime confidence in his men that he doubted not the result.

It is also true that the moral effect of the move into Maryland had been lost by the discomfiture at South Mountain, yet that loss had its compensation in the success at Harper's Ferry and still other successes were possible. Beyond military considerations there were those of a political character to be considered, political causes which had rendered the invasion of Maryland and the North an imperative necessity, and to which we have already referred, at some length, in a previous chapter. To abandon the friends of the South, who were fighting her battles in the North at the ballot box, was not to [be] thought of, nor could the dreams and hopes of foreign intervention be dashed by a return to Virginia without trying the fortune of arms on Maryland soil. All these things Lee had to consider. He was upon the defensive. He had been foiled in strategy and forced from the roads by which he proposed to enter Pennsylvania, back to the banks of the Potomac and within the angle formed by that stream and the Antietam, and compelled to give battle with a river at his back or go back to Virginia with a loss of prestige. It required a resolute commander to accept battle under all the circumstances, and Lee was a resolute commander. His front was covered by the Antietam, a stream presenting many

---

100 *B&L*, p. 666. Again, Longstreet made a case in hindsight that was proven true by events he may not have completely foreseen at the time.

difficulties for an enemy to cross, and behind it he concluded to challenge a contest that must be decisive. If victorious, he could force McClellan out of the Antietam Valley and back to South Mountain, and the fears of the administration would, probably, have carried him back to Washington, and the way would be open to Pennsylvania; if defeated he could recross the Potomac by the Shepherdstown Ford. His army had been elated by many successes, the victory at Harper's Ferry gave it, says Lee "renewed occasion for gratitude" and he believed in its invincibility; he counted much on the supposed demoralization of the Army of the Potomac.[101]

Lee well knew Jackson's views. He knew that this trusted lieutenant had, from the beginning, favored active operations in the enemy's country, and that a return to Virginia, under the circumstances, would be greatly disappointing to him. If he had any reason to doubt Jackson's views, it was dispelled by his dispatch of the morning that he would join him at Sharpsburg. In a letter written to Mrs. Jackson, January 25, 1866, General Lee says: "When he (Jackson) came upon the field [September 16] having preceded his troops, and learned my reasons for offering battle, he emphatically concurred with me. When I determined to withdraw across the Potomac, he also concurred, but said then, in view of all the circumstances, it was better to have fought the battle in Maryland than to have left it without a struggle."[102]

But Lee had a most critical condition to face and his daring was never more fully shown than when he made up his mind to fight at Antietam, and it has been much cited by his admirers as the test of his great generalship and as an expression of the sublime confidence he reposed in his army and of his ability to reunite his detachments before the enemy could strike him. McClellan's large army was already filling the valley of the Antietam; could Jackson march sixteen miles and ford the Potomac before Lee was struck? Walker was twenty miles distant, beyond the Shenandoah; and McLaws and R. H. Anderson were in Pleasant Valley and no way was open to them save by way of Harper's Ferry, or more than twenty-five miles. Was it possible for them to come up before McClellan attacked in overwhelming

---

101  Using a small snippet of a letter from Lee to Davis, September 16, 1862, OR 19, pt. 1, p. 141, Carman accurately summarized the reasons why Lee chose not to follow Longstreet's advice, and why he believed the campaign should continue.

102  This letter was printed in Henderson, *Stonewall Jackson*, 2, p. 583.

force? Lee, knowing McClellan's caution and relying upon the energy of his own lieutenants, assumed in the affirmative.[103]

Having concluded to receive battle on the Antietam Lee replied to Jackson's dispatch by ordering him to join him as quickly as possible. Then, with his field glass, he inspected the wooded height to the northeast, as if to discover whether or not troops were being passed through them. While thus engaged General Stuart came up from the rear, just from Harper's Ferry, his horse covered with foam, and, dismounting, said to General Lee: "We got 11,000 prisoners and all their commissary and quartermaster stores, including wagons and teams." Lee, before making any reply, told the orderly to keep Stuart's horse moving, not to let him cool off too soon, and then turning to Stuart, said: "General, did they have any shoes? These good men are barefoot;" referring to the men of the 6th North Carolina of Hood's Division, drawn up in line about ten paces to his rear.[104]

This was about noon, Stuart soon rode away to the left and Lee continued his examination of the field with a view to the better disposition of his forces. It was seen that the left, near the Dunkard Church, was the weakest point, and most likely to be attacked, and Hood's two brigades, were moved from Cemetery Hill to guard and hold that point. In moving to the position Hood lost a few men from the fire of the guns beyond the Antietam. Colonel Stephen D. Lee's artillery battalion, except Moody's and Eubank's batteries, were ordered to the left, also. The right of the line was extended by the transfer of the brigades of Garnett, Jenkins, Drayton and Kemper from Cemetery Hill across the road leading to the Burnside Bridge.[105]

This bridge, as we have said was assigned to the care of General Toombs. Its surroundings and how he utilized them are described in his official report:

103 Lee never personally asserted that he "had made up his mind to fight at Antietam," as Carman states it. Harsh, *Taken at the Flood*, Chapter Seven, argues that Lee still planned to move by his left to Hagerstown and slip around the Union army without fighting it. Augmenting that suggestion is the fact that Lee made no effort to entrench the bluffs and create breastworks that would enhance the power of his small force. Even if he intended to move and not fight, it does not materially diminish the risks Carman describes, for both options depended upon a quiescent Union force for at least twenty-four hours.

104 Carman erred slightly, for Lee's bandaged hands did not allow him to hold the telescope. See Harsh, *Taken at the Flood*, pp. 72, 88, 368. Samuel M (McDowell) Tate letter to Gould, April 15, 1891, Antietam Collection, Dartmouth College Library, Hanover, NH; Statement of Lt. Col. Samuel McD. Tate, 6th North Carolina.

105 The order to move is mentioned in Hood's report, OR 19, pt. 1, pp. 922-3, and Wofford's report, *ibid.*, p. 927, mentions losses in the 4th Texas Regiment during the move. The movement of Stephen D. Lee's battalion is mentioned in his report, *ibid.*, p. 844, and the shifting of the four brigades from D. R. Jones's Division is mentioned in Col. Walker's report of Jenkins's Brigade, *ibid.*, p. 907.

The Antietam River runs comparatively straight from a point about 100 paces above the bridge to a point about 300 paces below the bridge, and then curves suddenly around a hill to a ford on a neighborhood road. About 600 yards to my right and rear the road from Sharpsburg to Harper's Ferry from the foot of the bridge over the Antietam turns suddenly down the river, and runs nearly upon its margin for about 300 paces; then leaves the river nearly at right angles. Upon examining the position, I found a narrow wood upon the margin of the river just above the bridge (an important and commanding position) occupied by a company of Texans from Brigadier-General Hood's command. I then ordered the Twentieth to take position, with its left near the foot of the bridge, on the Sharpsburg side, extending down the river near its margin, and the Second Georgia on its right, prolonging the line down to the point where the road on the other side from the mountain approached the river. This required a more open order than was desirable, on account of the smallness of the regiments, both together numbering but a little over 400 muskets.[106]

Meanwhile the Union divisions, numbering 50,000, were arriving in the valley of the Antietam presenting to the Confederates, "then shattered by battles and scattered by long and tiresome marches" an awe inspiring spectacle. Lee had to oppose this force D. R. Jones' and Hood's Divisions (8 brigades) and the brigade of Evans, of Longstreet's command; and the division of D. H. Hill (5 brigades), of Jackson's command, 14 brigades in all, say 12,000 men, with the cavalry and reserve artillery, less than 4,000 men, or an aggregate of about 16,000 men. When night came and Lee knew that not a Union skirmisher had approached the Burnside Bridge, not an enemy appeared at the upper bridge and the adjacent fords, he was much relieved—he knew that Jackson and Walker soon would be with him—his only solicitude was for McLaws.

Let us see what has become of McLaws, whom we left in Pleasant Valley.[107]

---

106 Toombs' report, *ibid.*, p. 889.

107 The quoted phrase is from Longstreet, *B&L*, p. 667. Carman's estimate of Lee's forces on September 15 are consistent with his figures for the infantry, but he may have underestimated the cavalry and artillery, which by his own figures should total more than 4,500, even with the absence of Hampton's Brigade. Still, it is likely the force did not exceed 18,000 given the casualties and straggling of the past two days. A figure between 16,000 and 18,000 seems reasonable.

# Chapter 11

# McLaws and Franklin in Pleasant Valley

W hen McLaws lost Crampton's Gap and was cut off from Lee, on the evening of September 14th, he found himself in a critical and perplexing position. After consultation with R. H. Anderson it was decided to bring from Maryland Heights the brigades of Kershaw and Barksdale, except one regiment (13th Mississippi) of Barksdale, and all of the artillery but two rifled guns, and form a line of battle across Pleasant Valley, about 1 1/2 miles below Crampton's Gap, to make head against Franklin's advance down the valley. The line was formed with the remnants of the brigades of Cobb, Mahone and Semmes; Kershaw and Barksdale were marched down from Maryland Heights and Wilcox was brought back from near the mouth of the valley. These commands were disposed in two lines, and artillery, under direction of Major S. P. Hamilton, was placed on swells of ground in the rear and on the left flank, and so formidable was the appearance of the line that it deterred Franklin from attacking it. This line was placed especially under command of R. H. Anderson.[1]

1  McLaws's report is the source for this information, and Carman, as usual, supplied the identity of the regiment left behind by Barksdale. OR 19, pt. 1, pp. 854-5.

Wright and Pryor were kept in position guarding Weverton Pass and Armistead and Featherston that from Harper's Ferry, the Sandy Hook road. Harper's Ferry had not yet been taken and McLaws had to watch and wait the movements of his enemy; to present a front against Franklin, marching down Pleasant Valley; to prevent Miles' escape and attempting an advance, in conjunction with Franklin, on Weverton. He was in constant expectation of an attack at Weverton, because, by doing this, the Union commander would give ocular evidence to Miles at Harper's Ferry, that relief was near.[2]

During the night McLaws received several dispatches from General Lee, advising him to abandon his position, including Maryland Heights, and join him at Keedysville or Sharpsburg. The first dispatch was that of 8 p. m., by which he was ordered to recross the Potomac. This McLaws considered as clearly impractical, as his command was then situated—a regiment and two pieces of artillery on top of the high and precipitous Maryland Heights, two brigades and a battery on top of South Mountain, overlooking Weverton, and the remainder in line of battle against Franklin. He could not have assembled his command before daylight, and it was also impracticable, as it was contemplated, that he should go up the valley, that route Franklin had closed by his entrance into the valley; nor could he go up the river with his trains and artillery. It is true that he might have passed under the precipice at the foot of Maryland Heights by going up the bed of the canal, the water having been let out, but his wagons and artillery could not have gone that way.[3]

Later came Lee's dispatches of 10.30 and 11.15 p. m., the former to Munford, who forwarded it to McLaws; the purport of both being that McLaws should leave Pleasant Valley and Maryland Heights and go by way of the river road past Harper's Ferry or over Elk Ridge to Sharpsburg. McLaws contends, and his contention is a good one, that had he desired to leave the valley, he could not have done so that night, for there was but one way to go with his artillery, wagons filled with nearly 400 wounded men, and trains of supplies, and that way was down the river. To do this his troops must be well in hand, to meet a probable assault from Franklin, who was but a short distance, not two miles, above him. To have attempted a retreat, unless he was prepared to fight, if pursued, would have resulted in a "helter-skelter" movement, and in all probability ended in a complete rout, disgraceful to everyone

---

2  *Ibid.*, p. 855.

3  McLaws's presented his options in this same report, and elaborated on them in a series of newspaper articles for the *Philadelphia Weekly Press* in a serialized article entitled "The Capture of Harpers Ferry," which ran from September 5 to 19, 1888.

concerned in it, and especially to the responsible commander. Franklin might not have attacked, if he saw McLaws compact and ready for it, and such was the case, especially, if he were moving away from Harper's Ferry and Lee, but he may have done so, and, if McLaws went, he would have rapidly advanced to the relief of Harper's Ferry, and at once have crossed the river with his whole force, and assuming the offensive, force Jackson to retire precipitously from the front of Bolivar Heights and cut off Walker. This done McClellan, with his army on one side, and Franklin with the nearly 12,000 reinforcements at Harper's Ferry, could have had the disposal of events in their own hands, as there would have been Franklin with a larger force than Lee could assemble, in Lee's rear, on his line of retreat, and McClellan himself, with a very superior force in his front.

All this McLaws feared would happen if he abandoned his position on the night of the 14th, as Lee twice ordered him, most positively to do, or even if he complied with the order early on the morning of the 15th.[4]

He could not reason to his own satisfaction otherwise than that, while he was saving his own command by retreating, even under orders to do so, a possible disaster might happen to himself and that great disaster might result to the whole army, and that if he remained and boldly faced Franklin, there was a possibility of good results to follow, so he notified Lee that he had a strong position and would defend himself where he was and relied upon Lee's operations to relieve him. "At any rate," he says: "I would wait and see what fortune the morrow would bring me."[5]

The repeated messages sent by McLaws to Lee, during the night of the 14th, never reached Lee, and their non-receipt caused him much concern.[6]

It was after daylight on the morning of the 15th, when McLaws had completed all his arrangements to resist Franklin's advance, and he was both surprised and satisfied to see, as the hours advanced, that Franklin gave no sign of molesting him. Although more concerned how his own command could escape capture, than he

---

4   The dispatches of September 14 mentioned by Carman are Chilton to McLaws, 8:00 p.m. ordering him to abandon the siege, *OR* 51, pt. 2, pp. 618-9; Chilton to Munford 10:15 p.m. ordering him to find a road for McLaws to escape, *ibid.*, 19, pt. 2, p. 609, and Chilton to McLaws, 11:15 p.m. suggesting routes for McLaws to escape, *ibid.*, p. 608. Carman summarized McLaws's reasoning from *Philadelphia Weekly Press,* "The Capture of Harpers Ferry," September 19, 1888, which McLaws used to defend his actions. His report has a similar tone.

5   "Taken from 'The Maryland Campaign," Addresses Delivered before the Confederate Veterans Association, April 19 1895, to which is added the President's Annual Report (Savannah: George N. Nichols, 1896), p. 18.

6   McLaws's report mentioned sending Lt. Tucker as a courier to Lee who met a large Union force and was forced to return. *OR* 19, pt. 1, p. 855.

was whether Miles could be made to surrender, he did all in his power that his force would permit to prevent his escape, as his orders directed him to do, and to this end his guns on Maryland Heights were ordered to continue their plunging fire upon Harper's Ferry and its garrison.

About 10 a. m. it was signaled McLaws from Maryland Heights that the garrison at Harper's Ferry had hoisted a white flag and ceased firing. He at once ordered the troops defending the Weverton Pass and those on Sandy Hooks road to advance skirmishers along the road to the bridge at Harper's Ferry, or until they were fired on, and directed all his trains to be sent to the bridge. He still watched Franklin and kept his line of battle in his front. About this time also, it was reported to him that Franklin was putting batteries in position on South Mountain, near Brownsville Gap, to operate against his artillery on the other side of the valley; this, apparently, gave him little concern.[7]

Early in the day he had sent Lieutenant Thomas S. B. Tucker of his staff, to communicate with Jackson. Tucker returned about 1 p. m. with a message to McLaws that Jackson desired to see him. As Franklin showed no disposition to be aggressive McLaws left the command to R. H. Anderson, with directions to push the trains down the valley and across the river as soon as possible and follow with the infantry when the trains were well over.

At 2 p. m. Anderson began to withdraw down the valley towards Weverton and accomplished the withdrawal deliberately and without molestation; Franklin reports that Smith went in pursuit with a brigade and battery, but could not catch him; Anderson could see no evidence that Smith was in pursuit. Anderson halted at the foot of the valley, about 3 miles from the first position, and formed a second line, still holding Weverton and Maryland Heights, and awaited the passage of the trains over the bridge into Harper's Ferry—the bridge which Miles would not permit to be destroyed when he abandoned Maryland Heights.[8]

When McLaws reported to Jackson, at Harper's Ferry, he gave the situation of affairs in Pleasant Valley and suggested that if he would cross over, or send even a portion of his force they could dispose of Franklin. Jackson did not think it of

---

7  The actual appearance of the white flag occurred earlier in the day, but because McLaws was on Maryland Heights watching the bombardment, he did not receive the flag message until 10:00 a.m. See Gen. John G. Walker's report, OR 19, pt. 1, p. 914, which puts the surrender flag appearance at 9:30 a.m. This report conflicts with the finding of the court of inquiry, which concluded the flag was put up at 7:30 a.m. and firing ceased by 8:30 a.m. *Ibid.*, p. 797.

8  Carman again uses McLaws's report to describe the events that morning, and inserted his criticism of Miles about his failure to destroy the bridge, which was now a salvation to McLaws's command. *Ibid.*, pp. 855-6.

sufficient importance to warrant a non-compliance of his orders to go to Sharpsburg and ordered McLaws to follow him as soon as possible. When asked if he could go round the mountain from where he was Jackson made no reply. "It was well," says McLaws: "I did not try, as McClellan was already ahead of me."[9]

When McLaws returned to his command he found that R. H. Anderson had skillfully withdrawn it and was waiting for the trains to pass over the river. Although some of this had gone over by noon, much of it was prevented from doing so, because the paroled prisoners were being sent over it from Harper's Ferry, thus occupying it to the exclusion of McLaws' wagons and troops. It was now dark, McLaws' command had been in line all day expecting attack and his wagons were full of wounded men. It was not until 2 a.m. of the 16th that the bridge was clear for his crossing, when he moved out of the valley by Sandy Hook, thence up the river road and passed rapidly over, marched through Harper's Ferry and camped at Halltown, about four miles distant. His entire command did not cross over until 11 a.m., no advance or interruption being offered by Franklin. Had he been permitted the use of the bridge during daylight of the 15th and provisions allowed his men, his forces could have been rested and refreshed, and he would have been at Sharpsburg early on the 16th. As it was his men were allowed rest, whilst he went in search of provisions for them, for Jackson's men had already appropriated everything that was captured at Harper's Ferry.[10]

Regarding his operations in Pleasant Valley, McLaws made this report to General Lee's adjutant general:

> The enemy having forced Crampton's Gap, thereby completely cutting off my route up the valley to join the forces with General Lee, as Solomon's Gap, the only road over Elk Ridge, was just in front of the one over the Blue Ridge occupied by the enemy, I had nothing to do but to defend my position. I could not retire under the bluffs along the river, with the enemy pressing my rear and the forces at Harper's Ferry operating in conjunction, unless under a combination of circumstances I could not rely on to happen at the exact time needed; could not pass over the mountain except in a scattered and disorganized condition, nor could have gone through the Weverton Pass into the open country beyond to cross a doubtful ford when the enemy was in force on the other side of the Blue Ridge and coming down in my rear. There was no outlet in

9  McLaws, "The Maryland Campaign," p. 18. Harsh, *Taken at the Flood*, p. 319, suggests that Jackson had already considered this option. McLaws also repeated this conversation with Jackson in "The Capture of Harpers Ferry," *Philadephia Weekly Press*, September 12, 1888, p. 4.

10  McLaws's report is unclear about the times mentioned by Carman, but are more concrete in his article "The Capture of Harpers Ferry," *Philadelphia Weekly Press*, September 12, 1888, p. 4.

any direction for anything but the troops, and that very doubtful. In no contingency could I have saved the trains and artillery. I therefore determined to defend myself in the valley, holding the two heights and the two lower passes in order to force a direct advance down the valley, to prevent co-operation from Harper's Ferry, and at the same time to carry out my orders in relation to the capture of that place. I received several communications from your headquarters in relation to my position, which were obeyed so far as circumstances permitted, and I acted, in departing from them, as I believed the commanding general would have ordered had he known the circumstances. The force in Harper's Ferry was nearly, if not quite, equal to my own, and that above was far superior. No attempt was made to cooperate from Harper's Ferry with the force above, and the force above did not press down upon me, because, I believe, General Lee offered battle at Sharpsburg. The early surrender of Harper's Ferry relieved me from the situation, and my command joined the main army at Sharps-burg on the morning of the 17th.[11]

We return to Franklin. About noon of the 14th McClellan, then at Middletown, advised Franklin of what was transpiring at Turner's Gap; that Miles had abandoned Maryland Heights and occupied Bolivar Heights, and reminded him to keep in view "the necessity of relieving Colonel Miles if possible."[12] Two hours later he dispatched Franklin to mass his troops and carry Crampton's Gap "at any cost" and that if he (McClellan) succeeded in carrying Turner's Gap it would clear the way for him (Franklin) to go through Crampton's Gap, and that he must follow the enemy as rapidly as possible.[13] About the same time he sent from Middletown this dispatch to Colonel Miles:

> The army is being rapidly concentrated here. We are now attacking the pass on the Hagerstown road over the Blue Ridge. A column is about attacking the Burkittsville and Boonsborough Passes. You may count on our making every effort to relieve you. You may rely upon my speedily accomplishing that object. Hold out to the last extremity. If it is possible, reoccupy the Maryland Heights with your whole force. If you can do that, I will certainly be able to relieve you. As the Catoctin Valley is in our possession, you can safely cross the river at Berlin or its vicinity, so far as opposition on this side of the river is concerned. Hold out to the last.

11  McLaws's report, OR 19, pt. 1, p. 856.

12  The actual time of the dispatch was 11:45 a.m. OR 51, pt.1, p. 833. This dispatch also told Franklin that Crampton's Gap was only held by cavalry.

13  The quotation and the other information are contained in the 2:00 p.m. dispatch to Franklin, *ibid.*, 19, pt. 1, p. 46.

Three copies of this were sent by three different messengers on different roads; it is not known that any of them ever reached Miles, but the dispatch is here given to show what McClellan desired Miles to do and what he believed Miles was doing, while he was pushing Franklin to his relief.[14]

At 1 a.m. of the 15th, when he knew that Crampton's Gap had been carried, he ordered Franklin to occupy the road from Rohrersville to Harper's Ferry, placing a sufficient force at Rohrersville to hold that position, should it be attacked by the enemy from the direction of Boonsboro. He was to open communications with Miles at Harper's Ferry by attacking and destroying such of the enemy as should be found in Pleasant Valley. If he succeeded in opening communications with Miles he was directed to withdraw him from Harper's Ferry, with all the guns and public property he could carry, destroy what he could not carry, and attach him to his own command; and then proceed to Boonsboro, which place he (McClellan) intended to attack on the morrow (the 15th), and join the main body of the army at that place; should he find, however, that the enemy had retreated from Boonsboro towards Sharpsburg, he should endeavor to fall upon him and cut off his retreat.[15]

When this order was received by Franklin it was not possible to relieve Miles, we believe that possibility had passed with the setting sun of the 14th, but it was possible to crush McLaws before anyone could come to his relief and it is possible that the sound of an engagement, very early on the 15th, might have been heard by Miles and encouraged him to a more determined resistance. Exclusive of Hancock's Brigade, which was left near Burkittsville, and the 121st New York, which was burying the dead and caring for the wounded, Franklin had in his two divisions 11,000 men, which number had been augmented by the arrival of Couch's Division of over 7,000 men. It is safe to say that he had "present for duty" 18,000 men, as good men as the Army of the Potomac could muster. To oppose them McLaws had not to exceed 10,000 men (6,000 in Franklin's front and 4,000 at hand near Weverton) and many of them had been sadly demoralized the night before. But Franklin did not feel sufficient confidence in the result to make an attack.

He says that as he was crossing the mountain about 7 o'clock on the morning of the 15th he had a good view of McLaws' force below, which seemed to be well posted on hills stretching across the valley, which was about two miles wide. When

14 The direct quotation, and the method of delivery, are found in McClellan's order to Miles, McClellan's report, *ibid.*, p. 45.

15 This information was contained in a dispatch sent to Franklin and is found in McClellan's report, *ibid.*, p. 47. The significance of Rohrersville was that roads running from Harpers Ferry to Boonsboro and Crampton's Gap to Keedysville and Sharpsburg converged there. That was why Munford's Confederate cavalry also were ordered to hold Rohrersville.

he reached General Smith's headquarters an examination was made of the position and both he and Smith came to the conclusion that it would be suicidal to attack it. The whole breadth of the valley was occupied and batteries swept the only approaches to the position. They estimated McLaws' force as quite as large as their own, and in a position which, properly defended, would require a much greater force than they could command to carry."[16]

At 8.50 a.m., apparently before he had made this examination and in response to McClellan's order of 1 a.m., Franklin reported, 3 miles from Rohrersville:

> My command started at daylight this morning and I am waiting to have it closed up here. General Couch arrived about 10 o'clock last night. I have ordered one of his brigades [Howe's] and one battery to Rohrersville or the strongest point in its vicinity. The enemy is drawn up in line of battle about two miles to our front, one brigade in sight. A soon as I am sure that Rohrersville is occupied, I shall move forward to attack the enemy. This may be two hours from now. If Harper's Ferry has fallen—and the cessation of firing makes me fear that it has—it is my opinion that I should be strongly reinforced."[17]

At the hour this dispatch was penned McClellan prepared an order to Franklin to communicate with Burnside at the intersection of the Rohrersville and

---

16 There is much controversy about Franklin's actions on September 14 and 15. Carman assumed the garrison at Harpers Ferry was beyond rescue, a point contested by McLaws in his articles in the *Philadelphia Weekly Press*, although McLaws has the timing of the actual surrender much later than most sources. Franklin omitted much of the activity of September 15 from his report, but in his article "Notes on Crampton's Gap and Antietam," *B&L*, pp. 595-6, he minimized his own strength while citing maximum figures for Lee's Army from the chief clerk of the Adjutant General's office. Also, Franklin's admission that it was 7:00 a.m. before he crossed the mountain to view McLaws's line is damning, as that was more than an hour past sunrise and only one-half hour before the white flag went up at Harpers Ferry. Franklin's biographer, Mark Snell, heavily criticized Franklin's lethargy on September 15. Snell, *From First to Last*, pp. 186-90. In fairness, it should be noted that McLaws's line in Pleasant Valley was very strong. His roughly 6,000 men confronting Franklin (using Carman's figure) would have been deployed on a front of some one and one-half miles between South Mountain and Elk Ridge, with artillery well placed on the flanks. That would create density of about one man per one and one-half feet of line. In double ranks, they would have a solid line with no possibility of flanking. While Franklin was wrong to say he was outnumbered, he was facing a difficult task.

17 This dispatch is in McClellan's report, timed at 8:50 a.m., *OR* 19, pt. 1, p. 47, and reflects Franklin's hesitation on the 15th. Reese, *Sealed With Their Lives*, pp. 175-6, pointed out that a small force of Union soldiers captured Brownsville Gap in McLaws' rear some time that morning, but McLaws simply withdrew his line farther southward, making it even stronger. Again, the opportunity lost by Franklin to at least hold McLaws in Pleasant Valley looms large in the story of the campaign.

Boonsboro roads, and if the intelligence of the retreat of the enemy towards Shepherdstown Ford was confirmed to push on with his whole command (cautiously keeping up communications with Burnside), to Sharpsburg, and endeavor to fall upon the enemy and cut off his retreat, and to use his cavalry with the utmost vigor in following up the pursuit.[18] There was not a word in the dispatch regarding McLaws' force in front and a strict obedience to the instructions contained in it would have been the abandonment of Pleasant Valley to McLaws and permission for him to retire unmolested and at his leisure, which, later, he actually did, with Franklin still in his front.

Franklin asserts that he never received this order. We know that he did not act upon it. But, apparently, he did receive this or a similar order by the hands of Captain O'Keeffe, after he had made an examination of McLaws' position, and this he answered at 11 a. M.:

> I have received your dispatch by Captain O'Keeffe. The enemy is in large force in my front, in two lines of battle stretching across the valley, and a large column of artillery and infantry on the right of the valley looking toward Harper's Ferry. They outnumber me two to one. It will, of course, not answer to pursue the enemy under these circumstances. I shall communicate with Burnside as soon as possible. In the mean time I shall wait here until I learn what is the prospect of re-enforcement. I have not the force to justify an attack on the force I see in front. I have had a very close view of it, and its position is very strong.[19]

It was this dispatch of Franklin's that caused the order to Burnside and Porter, elsewhere noted, to halt at Rohrersville road or march on Rohrersville and join Franklin. McClellan replied to it at 1.30 p. m.:

> Burnside's corps and Sykes' division are moving on Porterstown and Sharpsburg by the road about one mile south of Hagerstown pike, with orders to turn and attack a force of the enemy supposed to be at Centerville. I will instruct them to communicate with you at Rohrersville, and if necessary re-enforce you. It is important to drive in the enemy in your front, but be cautious in doing it until you have some idea of his force. The corps of Sumner, Hooker, and Banks are moving to Boonsborough on the main

---

18 This dispatch is found in OR 51, pt. 1, p. 836.

19 The dispatch from Franklin to McClellan is part of McClellan's report, *ibid.*, 19, pt. 1, p. 47. The only place that Franklin implies not receiving this order is in his *B&L* account, p. 596, in which he wrote that he received no orders from McClellan until the evening of September 16. If Carman knew of a more concrete denial, it has yet to be uncovered.

pike. At least one division has already passed down toward Centerville. I will direct a portion to turn to the left at the first road beyond the mountain (west), so as to be in a position to re-enforce you or to move on Portersville [sic]. Sykes will be at the Boonsborough and Rohrersville road in about one hour and a half, Burnside following close. Thus far our success is complete, but let us follow it up closely, but warily. Attack whenever you see a fair chance of success. Lose no time in communicating with Sykes and Burnside.[20]

After McClellan's arrival at Boonsboro and his troops had occupied Keedysville, thus covering Franklin's rear, he ordered him to withdraw the brigades at Rohrersville to join his main body and to hold his position without attacking McLaws unless presented with a favorable opportunity. He advised of his efforts to concentrate everything during the evening on the enemy at or near Sharpsburg and said that he would be satisfied could he (Franklin) keep the enemy in his front without anything decisive until the Sharpsburg affair was settled, when he would at once move directly to his assistance, and also endeavor to cut off the enemy in his front. How he proposed to cut off McLaws he did not say. He was spared the effort, for even then McLaws had escaped.[21] General W. F. Smith, whose division was Franklin's advance, made a demonstration from his left, late in the afternoon, on Brownsville Gap, with two regiments of infantry and a section of horse artillery. Later the Confederates were detected to be withdrawing but this, very correctly, was not attributed to the demonstration. Smith started in pursuit with a brigade of infantry and a battery, and soon reported to Franklin that McLaws was drawing off through the valley too fast for him.[22]McLaws says that his movement down the valley of but 3 miles was not so rapid as to prevent its being overtaken by Smith "and if a pursuit was made it is strange that none of his commanders, nor any one of

---

20 McClellan's 1:20 p.m. dispatch to Franklin, OR 51, pt. 1, p. 836. McClellan seemed to want Franklin to protect the left flank of the army as he concentrated at Keedysville. Although Carman was critical of McClellan for not leading the pursuit of Lee, this dispatch suggests he was concerned about the overall strategic situation. Keedysville was known as Centreville until 1840, when it received a post office.

21 For the 4:30 p.m. dispatch to Franklin, see *ibid.*, p. 836.

22 Carman drew this information from a dispatch to McClellan, which Franklin wrote at 3:00 p.m., *ibid.*, 19, pt. 1, p. 296. The demonstration at Brownsville Pass was made by the 6th Maine and 4th Vermont regiments. See Gen. Winfield S. Hancock's report, *ibid.*, pp. 405-6.

his staff, nor anyone else reported or mentioned that there had been seen at any time any evidence of any advance."[23]

Before hearing from Smith, who had gone in languid pursuit of McLaws, Franklin had written McClellan that, under his orders of 1:20 p. m., he did not feel justified in putting his whole command in motion to the front (toward Sharpsburg) but should act according to the dictates of his judgment, as circumstances occurred, and that he had sent a squadron of the Rush Lancers to communicate with Burnside, and if they succeeded in getting to him, the information that Burnside might give should determine his action. After preparing this dispatch, but before sending it, he heard from Smith that McLaws was retiring, upon which, he added a postscript to his dispatch that he should start for Sharpsburg at once. Before he was ready to move he received McClellan's dispatch from Boonsboro, of 4.30 p. m., to hold his position until the Sharpsburg affair was settled, and Franklin held his position, with no enemy in front, until the morning of the 17th. It does not appear that at any time during the 15th Franklin got near enough to McLaws for serious skirmishing, but convinced of his overwhelming numbers was well content to observe him at a respectful distance. For nearly two whole days he was kept in position where he was doing no service, when his presence was much needed elsewhere.[24]

There has been much criticism upon the course of both McClellan and Franklin in the conduct of affairs in Pleasant Valley, on the 15th, and the detention of Franklin there, with no enemy in front, on the 16th. Franklin briefly replies to some of this criticism:

> The evidence before the court of inquiry on the surrender of Harper's Ferry shows that the white flag was shown at 7.30 a. m., on the 15th, and the firing ceased about one hour afterward. It is evident, therefore, that a fight between General McLaws' forces and mine could have had no effect upon the surrender of Harper's Ferry. Success on my part would have drawn me farther away from the army and would have brought me in dangerous nearness to Jackson's force, already set free by the surrender. McLaws'

---

23 *Philadelphia Weekly Press*, September 12, 1888. Although it was a weak effort, Hancock does mention pursuing and firing artillery at McLaws' retreating cavalry. *OR* 19, pt. 1, p. 406.

24 Carman continued to use Franklin's 3:00 p.m. dispatch for information about Franklin's lack of vigor, and made his opinion of Franklin's position at Crampton's Gap clear. As will soon be seen, Carman mitigated some of this criticism of Franklin's contributions to the Federal cause.

supports were three and a half miles from him, while my force was seven miles from the main army.[25]

It is all very true that an attack after 8 o'clock on the morning of the 15th would have had no effect upon the situation of affairs at Harper's Ferry, but why was McLaws not attacked very early on the morning of the 15th, as intended by the spirit of all the orders given by McClellan, not for the purpose of relieving Miles but to destroy McLaws? And why was it necessary to suspend effort when it became known that Miles had surrendered? Then it was that a supreme effort should have been made to crush McLaws or keep so close to him that he could not get away, but it was not done, nor an attempt made to do it, unless Smith's feeble efforts are taken seriously.[26]

Mr. John C. Ropes defends Franklin. In his *Story of the War* (Vol. II, p. 347) he says:

> In considering the caution exhibited by Franklin in this affair we must remember that he had been warned to provide against an attack on his right rear by way of Rohrersville, which might be made for the purpose of relieving his pressure on McLaws, and that Couch's Division was accordingly occupying that place, and also, that, for all he knew, Jackson might send a portion of his command across the river to the assistance of McLaws.[27]

Up to noon of the 16th this defense is a good one. McClellan's advance to the Antietam, on the afternoon of the 15th, had rendered the presence of Couch at Rohrersville unnecessary, but there was danger that Jackson might cross from Harper's Ferry, join McLaws and gain McClellan's left and rear, thus interposing between him and Washington, and of this danger McClellan was almost daily cautioned by Halleck, specially on the 16th, who, after he had been informed by McClellan that he had reached the Antietam and that Lee confronted him dispatched: "I think, however, you will find that the whole force of the enemy in

---

25 Franklin, *B&L*, p. 596.

26 Carman's sharp critique is valid only if Franklin knew that McLaws was positively withdrawing. If Harpers Ferry's surrender allowed Jackson and Walker to cross the river into Maryland and, with McLaws, menace McClellan's left flank, then Franklin's position becomes quite important. In short, Carman passed judgment on what he knew in 1904, not on what any Union commander might have known in September 1862.

27 Carman's Note: John Codman Ropes, *The Story of the Civil War*. Ropes added another point to why Franklin's position appears needless at first glance, but made sense to McClellan.

your front has crossed the river. I fear now more than ever that they will recross at Harper's Ferry or below and turn your left, thus cutting you off from Washington. This has appeared to me to be a part of their plan, and hence my anxiety on the subject."[28]

This was not a part of Lee's plan but it suggested itself to some of his subordinates and doubtless was in Lee's thoughts. We have noted McLaws' suggestion to Jackson that he join him in Pleasant Valley and attack Franklin. It is quite probable that Jackson had already thought of this or a similar movement, indeed, some of his staff officers have assured us that he discussed it, and that without further orders from Lee he would have made it, thus carrying out the original intention that he should rejoin his chief by the north side of the Potomac, but, when, under the changed condition of affairs, and the uncertainty of Lee's position and his necessities, he asked for Lee's order where to go and received his instructions to join him at Sharpsburg, he was no longer at liberty to follow his own inclination, and answered McLaws that he did not feel warranted in disregarding Lee's order to go to Sharpsburg. In fact nothing could have justified such a movement by Jackson except Lee's direct order.[29]

It is known that Longstreet was not favorable to joining battle at Sharpsburg, but would have reunited the army beyond the Potomac, and there is a fair inference that he looked favorably upon a movement on McClellan's left and rear. In his From Manassas to Appomattox Longstreet says:

The "lost order" directed the commands of Generals Jackson, McLaws and Walker, after accomplishing the objects for which they had been detached, to join the main body of the army at Boonsboro or Hagerstown. Under the order and the changed condition of affairs, they were expected, in case of early capitulation at Harper's Ferry, to march up the Rohrersville-Boonsboro road against McClellan's left. There were in those columns 26 of Lee's 40 brigades supplied with a fair apportionment of artillery and cavalry. So it seemed to be possible that Jackson would order McLaws and Walker up the Rohrersville road, and move with his own corps through the river pass [at Weverton] east of South Mountain, against McClellan's rear, as the speedier means of

28 Halleck's dispatch is part of McClellan's report, OR 19, pt. 1, p. 41. Halleck's concern adds yet another dimension as to why Franklin was ordered to stay in place at Crampton's Gap.

29 Carman did not identify which of Jackson's staff officers discussed this proposed offensive movement. Since Jed Hotchkiss was on the Antietam Battlefield Board with Carman, he is a possibility, although Henry Kyd Douglas held numerous conversations with Carman and is a more likely candidate. Jackson's most recent biographer, James I. Robertson Jr. discounts the idea suggesting that neither Lee nor Jackson had a firm idea of the location of the Federal army. Robertson, Stonewall Jackson, p. 607, 84n.

relief to General Lee's forces. But prudence would have gone with the bolder move of his entire command east of the mountain against McClellan's rear, with a fair field for strategy and tactics. This move would have disturbed McClellan's plans on the afternoon of the 15th, while there seemed little hope that McClellan would delay his attack until Jackson could join us, marching by the south side. The field, and extreme of condition, were more encouraging of results than was Napoleon's work at Arcola.[30]

McLaws says:

I could not help thinking when looking over the country, that if when Harper's Ferry surrendered, General Jackson had crossed to my side in Pleasant Valley with his divisions and Walker's, the forces of General Lee could have easily joined us, and our army united could have held Harper's Ferry and Maryland Heights as our stronghold for the time, and perhaps have forced McClellan to have attacked us in some strong position of our own choosing, and with more chances for out success and with less wear and tear of our men, and less prospect of great disaster than now seemed imminent. But I supposed that General Lee had weighed all these chances, and whatever seemed to him the best, was the best, nevertheless, I could not but think that it would have been better for us than Sharpsburg, under the circumstances.[31]

It is not difficult to agree with McLaws in this matter. That a movement of Jackson, Walker and McLaws through Weverton and east of South Mountain, promptly followed by Lee's recrossing the Potomac on the night of the 15th, and uniting with them, would have played havoc with McClellan's campaign and led to results which it is idle to speculate upon. (It is evident to us now, and was then evident to Halleck and McClellan, and their reasons for caution were sound, but when, on the morning of the 16th, it was known or should have been known, that McLaws had entirely abandoned Pleasant Valley and crossed over to Harper's Ferry, and that Lee was still on the Antietam and that Jackson was believed to

---

30 Longstreet, Manassas to Appomattox, pp. 232-3. Robertson, *Stonewall Jackson*, pp. 232-3, discounted Longstreet's suggestion of this movement as pure hindsight. Given that Longstreet had been in Hagerstown until the 14th, it is even less likely that he knew of the opportunity for offensive maneuver at the time than it was for Jackson. Also, consider that Lee's order was positive and allowed no interpretation. Arcola refers to a battle in 1796 that Napoleon won by boldly flanking the enemy army.

31 Like Longstreet's previous speculation, this postwar memoir from "The Maryland Campaign," p. 27, reflects more hindsight that contemporary analysis.

have joined him,[32] there seems to have been no reason why Franklin should not have marched for the Antietam at noon of the 16th, ready for action early next day; Couch's Division being left in Pleasant Valley. Franklin remained in Pleasant Valley all day of the 16th; in the evening he received McClellan's order to march next morning and join him before Sharpsburg.[33]

32 Telegram from Captain W. J. Palmer, Hagerstown, to Governor Curtin. Sept. 16, 1862: "I rode to General McClellan's headquarters at Keedysville at 12 o'clock last night, and have just returned, leaving there at noon. The general believes that Harper's Ferry surrendered yesterday morning, and that Jackson reinforced Lee at Sharpsburg last night. Rebels appear encouraged at arrival of their reinforcements." Palmer's telegram is incorporated into a message from Gov. Curtin to President Lincoln sent at 11:00 on September 16. It is found in OR 19, pt. 2, p. 311, and also mentions McClellan's preparations for attack on that day.

33 Carman's criticism that Franklin should have been recalled to Keedysville on the 16th is open to charges of hindsight. The divisions of Walker, McLaws, and Anderson were still unaccounted for, and constituted a potent force that might still threaten the Union left if not protected by Franklin's presence in Pleasant Valley.

# Organization of the Union and Confederate Armies in the Maryland Campaign of September 1862

### Organization of the Army of the Potomac

Maj. General George B. McClellan, U.S. Army, commanding.[1]

*General Headquarters*
Escort
Capt. James B. McIntyre
Independent Company Oneida (New York) Cavalry, Capt. Daniel P. Mann
4th U.S. Cavalry, Company A, Lt. Thomas H. McCormick
4th U.S. Cavalry, Company E, Capt. James B. McIntyre

*Regular Engineer Battalion*
Capt. James C. Duane
Lieutenant Charles E. Cross

---

1  Because Carman created a Table of Organization for the battles of South Mountain and Antietam, there are some significant differences from the table taken from the Adjutant General's Office as found in *OR* 19, pt. 1, pp. 170-180, which covers the entire campaign. Even with this caveat, much of what Carman presented reflects the organization after the fighting at Antietam than before it. Therefore, Appendix 1 presents the forces Carman described in his narrative up to this point in his manuscript.

*Provost Guard*[2]
Maj. William H. Wood

2d U.S. Cavalry, Companies E, F, H, and K, Capt. George A. Gordon
8th U.S. Infantry, Companies A, D, F, and G, Capt. Royal T. Frank
19th U.S. Infantry, Company G, Capt. Edmund L. Smith
19th U.S. Infantry, Company H, Capt. Henry S. Welton

*Headquarters Guard*
Maj. Granville O. Haller
93d New York, Lt. Col. Benjamin C. Butler

*Quartermaster's Guard*
1st U. S. Cavalry, Companies B, C, H, and I, Capt. Marcus A. Reno

### First Army Corps[3]
Maj. Gen. Joseph Hooker

*Escort*
2d New York Cavalry, Companies A, B, I, and K, Capt. John E. Naylor

*First Division*
Brig. Gen. John P. Hatch  (wounded, Sept 14) / Brig. Gen. Abner Doubleday

*First Brigade*
Col. Walter Phelps Jr.
22d New York, Lt. Col. John McKie, Jr.
24th New York, Capt. John D. O'Brian
30th New York, Col. William M. Searing
84th New York (14th Militia), Maj. William H. de Bevoise
2d U. S. Sharpshooters, Col. Henry A. V. Post

*Second Brigade*
(1) Brig. Gen. Abner Doubleday
(2) Col. William P. Wainwright (wounded, Sept. 14)
(3) Lt. Col. J. William Hofmann
7th Indiana, Maj. Ira G. Grover
76th New York, Col. William P. Wainwright / Capt. John W. Young

---

2   The composition of this command is not fully reported on the returns, *OR 19*, pt. 1, p. 170.

3   Carman used the corps numbers from the re-designation effective September 12, 1862. *Ibid.*, p. 157.

95th New York, Maj. Edward Pye
56th Pennsylvania, Lt. Col. J. William Hofmann / Capt. Frederick Williams

*Third Brigade*
Brig. Gen. Marsena R. Patrick
21st New York, Col. William F. Rogers
23d New York, Col. Henry C. Hoffman
35th New York, Col. Newton B Lord
80th New York (20th Militia), Lt. Col. Theodore B. Gates

*Fourth Brigade*
Brig. Gen. John Gibbon
19th Indiana, Col. Solomon Meredith[4]
2d Wisconsin, Col. Lucius Fairchild (wounded, Sept. 14)
6th Wisconsin, Lt. Col. Edward S. Bragg
7th Wisconsin, Capt. John B. Callis

*Artillery*
Capt. J. Albert Monroe
New Hampshire Light, First Battery, Lt. Frederick M. Edgell
1st Rhode Island Light, Battery D, Capt. J. Albert Monroe
1st New York Light, Battery L, Capt. John A. Reynolds
4th United States, Battery B, Capt. Joseph B. Campbell

*Second Division*
Brig. Gen. James B. Ricketts

*First Brigade*
Brig. Gen. Abram Duryee
97th New York, Maj. Charles Northrup, Capt. R. S. Egleston[5]
104th New York, Maj. Lewis C. Skinner
105th New York, Col. Howard Carroll
107th Pennsylvania, Capt. James Mac Thomson

---

4   Carman did not explain Meredith's absence. However, see *OR* 19, pt. 1, p. 251: "Owing to the fall which Colonel Meredith received in the battle of the 28th of August, and the subsequent fatigue and exposure of the marches up to the 16th instant, he was unable to take command on our movement across the Antietam Creek. The command now fell upon Lieutenant-Colonel Bachman."

5   Carman misspelled his name "Eggelston." *Official Register*, 2, p. 593.

*Second Brigade*
Col. William A. Christian
26th New York, Lt. Col. Richard H. Richardson
94th New York, Lt. Col. Calvin Littlefield
88th Pennsylvania, Lt. Col. George W. Gile
90th Pennsylvania, Col. Peter Lyle / Lt. Col. W. A. Leech

*Third Brigade*
Brig. Gen. George L. Hartsuff
12th Massachusetts, Maj. Elisha Burbank
13th Massachusetts, Maj. J. Parker Gould
83d New York (9th Militia), Lt. Col. William Atterbury
11th Pennsylvania, Col. Richard Coulter / Capt. David M. Cook
16th Maine, Col. A. W. Wildes[6]

*Artillery*
1st Pennsylvania Light, Battery F, Capt. Ezra W. Matthews
Pennsylvania Light, Battery C, Capt. James Thompson

*Third Division*
Brig. Gen. George G. Meade

*First Brigade*
Brig. Gen. Truman Seymour
1st Pennsylvania Reserves, Col. R. Biddle Roberts
2d Pennsylvania Reserves, Capt. James N. Byrnes
5th Pennsylvania Reserves, Col. Joseph W. Fisher
6th Pennsylvania Reserves, Col. William Sinclair
13th Pennsylvania Reserves Col. Hugh W. McNeil

*Second Brigade*
Col. Albert L. Magilton
3d Pennsylvania Reserves, Lt. Col. John Clark
4th Pennsylvania Reserves, Maj. John Nyce
7th Pennsylvania Reserves, Col. Henry C. Bolinger (wounded, Sept. 14)
/ Maj. Chauncey A. Lyman
8th Pennsylvania Reserves, Maj. Silas M. Baily

---

6   Carman identified this as the 19th Maine. It was detached on September 13. *Ibid.*, p. 171n.

*Third Brigade*
Col. Thomas F. Gallagher
9th Pennsylvania Reserves, Lt. Col. Robert Anderson
10th Pennsylvania Reserves, Lt. Col. Adoniram J.Warner
11th Pennsylvania Reserves, Lt. Col. Samuel M. Jackson
12th Pennsylvania Reserves, Capt. Richard Gustin

*Artillery*
1st Pennsylvania Light, Battery A, Lt. John G. Simpson
1st Pennsylvania Light, Battery B, Capt. James H. Cooper
5th United States, Battery C, Capt. Dunbar R. Ransom

## Second Army Corps
Maj. Gen. Edwin V. Sumner

*Escort*
6th New York Cavalry, Company D, Capt.. Henry W. Lyon
6th New York Cavalry, Company K, Capt. Riley Johnson

*First Division*
Maj. Gen. Israel B. Richardson

*First Brigade*
Brig. Gen. John C. Caldwell
5th New Hampshire, Col. Edward E. Cross
7th New York, Capt. Charles Brestel
61st & 64 New York, Col. Francis C. Barlow
81st Pennsylvania, Maj. H. Boyd McKeen

*Second Brigade*
Brig. Gen. Thomas F. Meagher
29th Massachusetts, Lt. Col. Joseph H. Barnes
63d New York, Col. John Burke
69th New York Lt. Col. James Kelly
88th New York, Lt. Col. Patrick Kelly

*Third Brigade*
Col. John R. Brooke

*Artillery*
1st New York Light, Battery B, Capt. Rufus D. Pettit
4th U. S., Batteries A and C, Lt. Evan Thomas

*Second Division*
Maj. Gen. John Sedgwick

*Third Division*
Brig. Gen. William B. French

**Fourth Army Corps**
General Erasmus D. Keyes

*First Division*
Maj. Gen. Darius N. Couch

**Fifth Army Corps**
Maj. Gen. Fitz John Porter

*First Division*
Maj. Gen. George W. Morell

*Second Division*
Brig. Gen. George Sykes

*Third Division*[7]
Brig. Gen. Andrew A. Humphreys

**Sixth Army Corps**
Maj. Gen. William B. Franklin

*Escort*
6th Pennsylvania Cavalry, Companies B and G, Capt. Henry P. Muirheid

*First Division*
Maj. Gen. Henry W. Slocum

*First Brigade*
Col. Alfred T. A. Torbert
1st New Jersey, Lt. Col. Mark W. Collet
2d New Jersey, Col. Samuel L. Buck
3d New Jersey, Col. Henry W. Brown
4th New Jersey, Col. William B. Hatch

---

7   The division was marching to join the Army of the Potomac, but was not with it.

*Second Brigade*
Col. Joseph J. Bartlett
5th Maine, Col. Nathaniel J. Jackson
16th New York, Lt. Col. Joel J. Seaver
27th New York, Lt. Col. Alexander D. Adams
96th Pennsylvania, Col. Henry L. Cake
121st New York, Col. Richard Franchot[8]

*Third Brigade*
Brig. Gen. John Newton
18th New York, Lt. Col. George R. Myers
31st New York, Lt. Col. Francis E. Pinto
32d New York, Col. Roderick Matheson (killed, Sept. 14)
/ Maj. George F. Lemon (m/wounded, Sept. 14)
96th Pennsylvania, Col. Gustavus W. Town
121st New York, Col. Richard Franchot

*Artillery*
Capt. Emory Upton
Maryland Light, Battery A, Capt. John W. Wolcott
Massachusetts Light, Battery A, Capt. Josiah Porter
New Jersey Light, Battery A, Capt. William Hexamer
2d United States, Battery D, Lt. Edward B. Williston

*Second Division*
Maj. Gen. William F. Smith

*First Brigade*
Brig. Gen. Winfield S. Hancock
6th Maine, Col. Hiram Burnham
43d New York, Maj. John Wilson
49th Pennsylvania, Lt. Col. William Brisbane
137th Pennsylvania, Col. Henry M. Bossert
5th Wisconsin, Col. Amasa Cobb

*Second Brigade*
Brig. Gen. W. T. H. Brooks
2d Vermont, Maj. James H. Walbridge
3d Vermont, Col. Breed N. Hyde

---

8   Carman listed this regiment in the Third Brigade, and the table in *OR* 19, pt. 1, p. 176, does not list it at all. Frederick H. Dyer, *A Compendium of the War of the Rebellion* (Dayton OH: Morningside Publishers, 1978), p. 1,452, show it assigned to the Second Brigade.

4th Vermont, Lt. Col. Charles B. Stoughton
5th Vermont, Col. Lewis A. Grant
6th Vermont, Maj. Oscar L. Tuttle

*Third Brigade*
Col. William H. Irwin
7th Maine, Maj. Thomas W. Hyde
20th New York, Col. Ernest von Vegesack
33d New York, Lt. Col. Joseph W. Coming
49th New York, Lt. Col. William C. Alberger
77th New York, Capt. Nathan S. Babcock

*Artillery*
Capt. Romeyn B. Ayres
Maryland Light, Battery B, Lt. Theodore J. Vanneman
New York Light, 1st Battery, Capt. Andrew Cowan
5th United States, Battery F, Lt. Leonard Martin

**Ninth Army Corps**
Maj. Gen. A. E. Burnside / Maj. Gen. Jesse L. Reno (killed, Sept. 14)
/ Brig. Gen. Jacob D. Cox

*Escort*
1st Maine Cavalry, Company G, Capt. Zebulon B. Blethen

*First Division*
Brig. Gen. Orlando B. Willcox

*First Brigade*
Col. Benjamin C. Christ
28th Massachusetts, Capt. Andrew P. Caraher
17th Michigan, Col. William H. Withington
79th New York, Lt. Col. David Morrison
50th Pennsylvania, Maj. Edward Overton
8th Michigan,[9] Lt. Col. Frank Graves, Maj. Ralph Ely

---

9   The 8th Michigan transferred out of the First brigade on September 16. *OR* 19, pt. 1, p.
177n.

*Second Brigade*
Col. Thomas Welsh
46th New York, Lt. Col. Joseph Gerhardt
45th Pennsylvania, Lt. Col. John I. Curtin
100th Pennsylvania, Lt. Col. David A. Leckey

*Artillery*
Massachusetts Light, Eighth Battery, Capt. Asa M. Cook
2d United States, Battery E, Lt. Samuel N. Benjamin

*Second Division*
Brig. Gen. Samuel D. Sturgis

*First Brigade*
Brig. Gen. James Nagle[10]
2d Maryland, Lt. Col. J. Eugene Duryee
6th New Hampshire, Col. Simon G. Griffin
9th New Hampshire, Col. Enoch Q. Fellows
48th Pennsylvania, Lt. Col. Joshua K. Sigfried

*Second Brigade*
Brig. Gen. Edward Ferrero
21st Massachusetts, Col. William S. Clark
35th Massachusetts, Col. Edward A. Wild
51st New York, Col. Robert B. Potter
51st Pennsylvania, Col. John F. Hartranft

*Artillery*
Pennsylvania Light, Battery D, Capt. George W. Durell
4th United States, Battery E, Capt. Joseph C. Clark, Jr.

*Third Division*
(1) Brig. Gen. Isaac P. Rodman

*First Brigade*
Col. Harrison S. Fairchild
9th New York, Lt. Col. Edgar A. Kimball
89th New York, Maj Edward Jardine of the 9th New York
103d New York, Maj. Benjamin Ringold

---

10 Nagle received his commission during the campaign (officially September 10); Carman credited him with the higher rank for this table and the tablet on the field. *Official Register*, 3 p. 852.

*Second Brigade*
Col. Edward Harland
8th Connecticut, Lt. Col. Hiram Appelman[11]
11th Connecticut, Col. Henry W. Kingsbury
16th Connecticut, Col. Francis Beach
4th Rhode Island, Col. William H. P. Steere

*Artillery*
5th United States, Battery A, Lt. Charles P. Muhlenberg

*Kanawha Division*
Brig. Gen. Jacob D. Cox / Col. Eliakim P. Scammon

*First Brigade*
Col. Hugh Ewing
12th Ohio, Col. Carr B. White
23d Ohio, Lt. Col. Rutherford B. Hayes (wounded, Sept. 14) / Maj. James M. Comly
30th Ohio, Lt. Col. Theodore Jones
Ohio Light Artillery, First Battery, Capt. James R. McMullin
Gilmore's company West Virginia Cavalry, Lt. James Abraham
Harrison's company West Virginia Cavalry, Lt. Dennis Delaney

*Second Brigade*
Col. George Crook
11th Ohio, Lt. Col. Augustus H, Coleman
28th Ohio, Lt. Col. Gottfried Becker
36th Ohio, Lt. Col. Melvin Clarke
Schambeck's company Chicago Dragoons, Capt. Frederick Schambeck
Kentucky Light Artillery, Simmonds' Battery, Capt. Seth J. Simmonds

*Unattached*
6th New York Cavalry (eight companies), Col. Thomas C. Devin
Ohio Cavalry, Third Independent Company, Lt. Jonas Seamen
3d U. S. Artillery, Batteries L and M, Capt. John Edwards, Jr.
2nd New York Artillery, Battery L,[12] Capt. Jacob Roemer

---

11 Carman misspelled this in his manuscript as "Appleman."

12 Carman incorrectly listed this battery as part of the 3rd New York Artillery, although he correctly identifies it elsewhere in the manuscript.

### Twelfth Army Corps
Brig. Gen. Alpheus S. Williams[13]

*Escort*
1st Michigan Cavalry, Company L., Capt. Melvin Brewer

*First Division*
Brig. Gen. Samuel W. Crawford

*Second Division*
Brig. Gen. George S. Greene

### Cavalry Division[14]
Brig. Gen. Alfred Pleasonton

*First Brigade*
Maj. Charles J. Whiting
5th United States, Capt. Joseph H. McArthur
1st & 6th United States, Capt. William P. Sanders

*Second Brigade*
Col. John F. Farnsworth
8th Illinois, Maj. William H. Medill
3d Indiana, Maj. George H. Chapman
1st Massachusetts, Col. Robert Williams[15]
8th Pennsylvania, Lt. Col. A. E. Griffiths

*Third Brigade*
Col. Richard H. Rush
4th Pennsylvania, Col. James H. Childs
6th Pennsylvania, Lt. Col. C. Ross Smith

---

13 Williams commanded the corps up to September 15, when Brig. Gen. Joseph Mansfield assumed command until the morning of September 17, when he was fatally wounded.

14 The structure of this division with four brigades of cavalry reflects the situation after the battle more than it does September 17, 1862. Several of these regiments did not arrive in time to participate in the battle, and the references to these brigades did not exist in the correspondence at the time of the battle or only fielded a few companies.

15 Carman initially wrote "Capt. Casper Crowninshield," and then crossed it out to insert Williams's name. Letters from Maj. Henry L. Higginson August 28, 1899, NA-AS, and Adjutant C. F. Adams, Gould Papers, and Crowninshield, *First Regiment of Massachusetts Cavalry Volunteers*, p. 72, make it clear that Williams was present and in command. Why the editors of the *OR* got this wrong in unknown.

*Fourth Brigade*
Col. Andrew T. McReynolds
1st New York, Maj. Alonzo W. Adams
12th Pennsylvania, Maj. James A. Congdon

*Artillery*
2d United States, Battery A, Capt. John C. Tidball
2d United States, Batteries B and L, Capt. James M. Robertson
2d United States, Battery M, Lt. Peter C. Hains
3d United States, Batteries C and G, Capt. Horatio G. Gibson

*Unattached*
1st Maine Cavalry, Col. Samuel H. Allen
15th Pennsylvania Cavalry (detachment), Col. William J. Palmer

## Organization of the Army of Northern Virginia

General Robert E. Lee, commanding,

### Longstreet's Command[16]
Maj. Gen. James Longstreet

*McLaws' Division*
Maj. Gen. Lafayette McLaws

*Kershaw's Brigade*
Brig. Gen. J. B. Kershaw
2d South Carolina, Col. John D. Kennedy
3d South Carolina, Col. James D. Nance
7th South Carolina, Col. D. Wyatt Aiken
8th South Carolina, Lt. Col. A. J. Hoole

---

16 Carman's note: "At this date there was no corps organization, the corps organization was adopted in the spring of 1863." Carman adopted a framework of two "commands" for the Southern army. This had led to confusion concerning the structures and commands of these two "wings," as they were also called. The most thoughtful treatment of the organization of the Army of Northern Virginia is in Harsh, *Taken at the Flood*, and for a more detailed discussion, see Harsh, *Sounding the Shallows*, Chapter Two. Like the Army of the Potomac, Carman's table reflects the status quo on September 17 and does not include leaders killed or wounded earlier in the campaign. Even at the time Carman was writing, many Confederate commanders were unknown to the editors of the *Official Records*. Carman did a remarkable job filling in many of the blanks left in the OR. His letters to Southern veterans often inquired about commanders' names. I filled in the few he missed with sources unavailable to him.

*Cobb's Brigade*
Brig. Gen. Howell Cobb / Lt. Col. C. C. Sanders / Lt. Col. William McRae
16th Georgia, Lt. Col. Henry P. Thomas
24th Georgia, Maj. R. E. McMillan
Cobb's (Georgia) Legion, Lt. Col. L. J. Glenn[17]
15th North Carolina, Lt. Col. Wm. McRae

*Semmes' Brigade*
Brig. Gen. Paul J. Semmes
10th Georgia, Maj. Willis C. Holt
Capt. William Johnston
53d Georgia, Lt. Col. Thomas Sloan
15th Virginia, Capt. E. M. Morrison
32d Virginia, Col. E. B. Montague

*Barksdale's Brigade*
Brig. Gen. William Barksdale
13th Mississippi, Lt. Col. Kennon McElroy
17th Mississippi, Lt. Col. John C. Fiser
18th Mississippi, Maj. J. C. Campbell
21st Mississippi, Capt. John Sims

*Artillery of McLaws' Division*
Col. H. C. Cabell
Manly's (North Carolina) battery, Capt. B. C. Manly
Pulaski (Georgia) Artillery, Capt. J. P. N. Read
Richmond (Fayette) Artillery, Capt. M. C. Macon
Richmond Howitzers, (1st company), Capt. E. S. McCarthy
Troup (Georgia) Artillery, Capt. H. H. Carlton

*Anderson's Division*
Maj. Gen. Richard H. Anderson

*Wilcox's Brigade*
Col. Alfred Cumming
8th Alabama, Maj. H.A. Herbert
9th Alabama, Maj. J. H. J. Williams
10th Alabama, Capt. G. C. Wheatley
11th Alabama, Maj. John C. C. Sanders

17 Glenn was a Maj. at the time of the battle. See Krick, *Lee's Colonels*, p. 158.

*Mahone's Brigade*
Lt. Col. William A. Parham
6th Virginia, Capt. John R. Ludlow
12th Virginia, Capt. John R. Llewellyn
16th Virginia, Maj. Francis D. Holladay
41st Virginia, ——

*Featherston's Brigade*
Brig. Gen. Winfield Scott Featherston

*Armistead's Brigade*
Brig. Gen. Lewis A. Armistead

*Pryor's Brigade*
Brig. Gen. Roger A. Pryor

*Wright's Brigade*
Brig. Gen. A. R. Wright

*Jones' Division*
Brig. Gen. David R. Jones

*Toombs' Brigade*
Brig. Gen. Robert Toombs[18]
2d Georgia, Lt. Col. William R. Holmes
15th Georgia, Col. W. T. Millican
17th Georgia, Col. Henry Benning
20th Georgia, Col. J. B. Cumming

*Drayton's Brigade*[19]
Brig. Gen. Thomas F. Drayton
50th Georgia, Lt. Col. F. Kearse
51st Georgia, ——

---

18 Toombs's report, OR 19, pt. 1, pp. 888-893, make it clear he was commanding a temporary division of three of the six brigades in D. R. Jones's Division. In fact, the heading reads "Commanding Division (temporary)," and this report refers to Benning commanding the brigade.

19 Carman also omitted the Phillips (Georgia) Legion from his table, as did the OR editors, but there is no question that this organization was part of this brigade. See Harsh, *Sounding the Shallows*, pp. 34, 55. See also Richard M. Coffman and Kurt Graham, *To Honor These Men: A History of the Phillips Georgia Legion Infantry Battalion* (Macon: Mercer University Press, 2007), pp. 55-56.

15th South Carolina, Col. W. D. DeSaussure
3d South Carolina Battalion, Lt. Col. George S. James (killed, Sept. 14)[20]
Phillips [GA] Legion, Lt. Col. Robert T. Cook

*Garnett's Brigade*
Brig. Gen. R. B. Garnett
8th Virginia, Col. Eppa Hunton
18th Virginia, Maj George C. Cabell
19th Virginia, Col. J. B. Strange (killed, Sept. 14) / Lt. W. N. Wood /
Capt. J. L. Cochran[21]
28th Virginia, Captain Wingfield
56th Virginia, Col. William D. Stuart

*Kemper's Brigade*
Brig. Gen. J. L. Kemper
1st Virginia, Capt. Geo. F. Norton
7th Virginia, Maj. Arthur Herbert
11th Virginia, Maj. Adam Clement
17th Virginia, Col. M. D. Corse
24th Virginia, Col. W. R. Terry

*Jenkins' Brigade*
Col. Joseph Walker
1st South Carolina (Volunteers), Lt. Col. D. Livingston
2d South Carolina Rifles, Lt. Col. Robert A. Thompson
5th South Carolina, Capt. T. C. Beckham
6th South Carolina, Lt. Col. J. M. Steedman
4th South Carolina Battalion, Lt. W. F. Field
Palmetto (South Carolina) Sharpshooters, Capt. A. H. Foster

*Anderson's Brigade*
Col. George T. Anderson
1st Georgia (Regulars), Col. W. J. Magill
7th Georgia, Col. G. H. Carmical[22]
8th Georgia, Col. John F. Towers
9th Georgia, Lt. Col. John C. F. Mounger
11th Georgia, Maj. F. H. Little

---

20 Carman has James listed as a major. He was killed at Fox's Gap. Krick, *Lee's Colonels,* p. 207.

21 The brigade report, *OR* 19, pt. 1, pp. 901-2, makes it is clear that Cochran preceded Wood in command of the regiment.

22 Carman misspelled his name as "Carmichael." Krick, *Lee's Colonels*, p. 79.

*Artillery of Jones' Division*
Wise (VA) Artillery, Capt. J. S. Brown

*Walker's Division*
Brig. Gen. John G. Walker

*Walker's Brigade*
Col. Van H. Manning

*Ransom's Brigade*
Brig. Gen. Robert Ransom Jr.

*Artillery of Walker's Division*
French's (VA) battery, Capt. Thomas B. French[23]
Branch's (VA) Artillery, Captain Branch

*Hood's Division*
Brig. Gen. John B. Hood

*Hood's Brigade*[24]
Col. W. T. Wofford
18th Georgia, Lt. Col. S. Z. Ruff
Hampton (South Carolina) Legion, Lt. Col. M. W. Gary
1st Texas, Lt. Col. P. A. Work
4th Texas, Lt. Col. B. F. Carter
5th Texas, Capt. I.N.M. Turner

*Law's Brigade*
Col. Evander M. Law
4th Alabama, Lt. Col. O.K. McLemore
2d Mississippi, Col. J. M. Stone
11th Mississippi, Col. P. F. Liddell
6th North Carolina, Maj. Robert F. Webb

*Artillery*
Maj. B. W. Frobel
German Artillery (South Carolina), Capt. W. K. Bachman

---

23 Listed on War Department plaque #367 as attached to Manning's brigade, and Branch's battery attached to Ransom's brigade, plaque # 362.

24 Carman routinely referred to this command as Wofford's, but he pasted in the *OR* table for this brigade, and the editors used Hood's name instead.

Palmetto Artillery (South Carolina), Capt. H. R. Garden
Rowan Artillery (North Carolina), Capt. James Reilly

*Evans' Brigade*
Brig. Gen. Nathan G. Evans[25] / Col. P. F. Stevens
17th South Carolina, Col. F. W. McMaster
18th South Carolina, Col. W. H. Wallace
22d South Carolina. Lt. Col. T. C. Watkins (m/wounded, Sept. 14)[26] / Maj. M. Hilton
23d South Carolina. Capt. S. A. Durham[27] / Lt. E. R. White
Holcombe (South Carolina) Legion, Col. P. F. Stevens
Macbeth (South Carolina) Artillery, Capt. R. Boyce

*Artillery*
Washington (Louisiana) Artillery
Col. J. B. Walton

*Lee's Battalion*
Col. S. D. Lee

*Jackson's Command*
Maj. Gen. Thomas J. Jackson

*Ewell's Division*
Brig. Gen. A. R. Lawton

*Lawton's Brigade*
Col. Marcellus Douglass

*Trimble's Brigade*
Col. James A. Walker

*Hays' Brigade*
Brig. Gen. Harry T. Hays

---

25 Although present and on the field, Evans still saw himself as a division commander and designated Stevens to command the brigade. See Harsh, *Sounding the Shallows*, p. 59.

26 Carman listed Watkins as "killed," but he did not die until September 20. Krick, *Lee's Colonels*, p. 388.

27 Durham was wounded on September 14 and probably relinquished command to White. *OR* 19, pt. 1, p. 949.

*Early's Brigade*
Brig. Gen. Jubal A. Early

*Artillery of Ewell's Division*
Maj. A. R. Courtney
Johnson's (Virginia) battery, Capt. John R. Johnson
Louisiana Guard Artillery, Capt. Louis E. D'Aquin
First Maryland Battery, Capt. W. F. Dement
Staunton (Virginia) Artillery, Lt. A. W. Garber

*Hill's Light Division*
Maj. Gen. Ambrose P. Hill

*Branch's Brigade*
Brig. Gen. L. O'B. Branch
7th North Carolina, Col. E. G. Haywood
18th North Carolina, Lieutenant Colonel Thomas J. Purdie
28th North Carolina, Col. James H. Lane
33d North Carolina, Lt. Col. R. F. Hoke
37th North Carolina, Capt. William G. Morris

*Gregg's Brigade*
Brig. Gen. Maxcy Gregg
1st South Carolina (Provisional Army), Col. D. H. Hamilton
1st South Carolina Rifles, Lt. Col. James M. Perrin
12th South Carolina, Col. Dixon Barnes
13th South Carolina, Col. O. E. Edwards
14th South Carolina, Lt. Col. W. D. Simpson

*Archer' s Brigade*
Brig. Gen. J. J. Archer[28] /Col. Peter Turney
19th Georgia, Maj. J. H. Neal
1st Tennessee (Provisional Army), Col. Peter Turney.
7th Tennessee, Maj. S. G. Shepard, Lt. G. A. Howard
14th Tennessee, Col. William McComb
5th Alabama Battalion, Captain Chas. M. Hooper

*Field's Brigade*
Col. John M. Brockenbrough
40th Virginia, Lt. Col. Fleet W. Cox

---

28 Archer was in command at Sharpsburg, but before and after the battle he turned over command to Turney. See Archer's report, *OR* 19, pt. 1, p. 1,001.

47th Virginia, Lt. Col. John W. Lyell
55th Virginia, Maj. Charles N. Lawson
22d Virginia Battalion, Maj. E. Poinsett Tayloe

*Thomas' Brigade*
Col. Edward L. Thomas
14th Georgia, Col. R. W. Folsom
35th Georgia,[29] ——
45th Georgia, Maj. W. L. Grice
49th Georgia, Lt. Col. S. M. Manning

*Pender's Brigade*
Brig. Gen. William D. Pender
16th North Carolina, Lt. Col. William A. Stowe
22d North Carolina, Maj. C. C. Cole.
34th North Carolina, Lt. Col. J. L. McDowell
38th North Carolina,[30] ——

*Artillery of A. P. Hill's Division*
Lt. Col. R. L. Walker
Crenshaw's (Virginia) battery, Capt. W. G. Crenshaw
Fredericksburg (Virginia) Artillery, Capt. Carter Braxton
Pee Dee (South Carolina) Artillery, Capt. D. G. McIntosh
Purcell (Virginia) Artillery, Capt. W. J. Pegram
Letcher (Virginia) Artillery, Capt. Greenlee Davidson

*Jackson's Division*
Brig. Gen. John R. Jones

29 It is likely that Lt. Col. Bolling C. Holt was in command. See John J. Fox III, *Red Clay to Richmond: Trail of the 35th Georgia Infantry Regiment, C.S.A.* (Winchester VA: Angle Valley Press, 2004), pp. 122-3.

30 Lt. Col. Robert F. Armfield was identified by Pender in his report as commanding the regiment at Shepherdstown, where he was wounded. The report also stated that Armfield had re-joined the regiment the day before, and mentions Capt. John Ashford in command of the regiment at Second Manassas, where he was wounded. This makes it unclear who was in command of the regiment at Sharpsburg. See Pender's report, *OR* 19 pt. 1, p. 1,005, and Clark, *North Carolina Regiments*, 3, p. 686-7.

*Winder's Brigade*[31]
Col. A. J. Grigsby

*Jones' Brigade*
Col. Bradley T. Johnson[32] / Capt. John E. Penn
21st Virginia, Capt. A. C. Page
42d Virginia, Capt. R. W. Withers, Capt. D. W. Garrett
48th Virginia, Captain Candler
1st Virginia Battalion, Lt. C. A. Davidson

*Taliaferro's Brigade*
Col. E. T. H. Warren

*Starke's Brigade*
Brig. Gen. William E. Starke

*Artillery*[33]
Maj. L. M. Shumaker
Alleghany (VA), Artillery Capt. John Carpenter[34]
Brockenbrough's (MD) battery, Capt. J. B. Brockenbrough
Danville (VA) Artillery, G. A. Wooding
Lee (VA) Battery, Capt. Charles J. Raine
Rockbridge (VA) Artillery, Capt. W. T. Poague

*Hill's Division*
Maj. Gen. Daniel H. Hill

31 More famously known as the Stonewall Brigade, Carman correctly omitted the 2nd Virginia, which was on provost duty in Martinsburg. Dennis Frye, *2nd Virginia Infantry* (Lynchburg, VA: H.E. Howard, 1984), pp. 43-4.

32 Carman's inclusion of Johnson departs from his habit of listing commanders only on the day of the battle. Johnson was relieved of his command in Frederick and so was no longer with the army when it fought at Sharpsburg. W. W. Goldsborough, *The Maryland Line in the Confederate Army 1861-1865* (Baltimore Guggenheimer, Weil & Co., 1900), p. 71.

33 It is unclear if Capt. William Caskie's Hampden (Virginia) Battery was present in the campaign. Gen. John R. Jones mentioned them in his report, *OR* 19, pt. 1, p. 1008, but Maj. Shumaker's artillery report dated September 22, 1862, *ibid.*, p. 964, lists Caskie but gives no report of equipment. Carman omitted mention of them, probably from veteran's accounts.

34 Carman mistakenly listed Joseph Carpenter, who was killed at Cedar Mountain on August 9, 1862, instead of his brother John, who took command through Sharpsburg, where he was wounded severely in the leg. C. A., Fonerden, *History of Carpenter's Battery of the Stonewall Brigade, 1861-1865* (New Market, VA: Henkel and Company, 1911), pp. 30, 38.

*Ripley's Brigade*
Brig. Gen. Roswell S. Ripley
4th Georgia, Col. George Doles, Maj. Robert Smith
44th Georgia, Captain John C. Key
1st North Carolina, Lt. Col. H.A. Brown
3d North Carolina, Col. William L. De Rosset

*Rodes' Brigade*
Brig. Gen. R. E. Rodes
3d Alabama, Col. C. A. Battle
5th Alabama. Maj. E. L. Hobson
6th Alabama, Col. John B. Gordon
12th Alabama, Col. B. B. Gayle (killed, Sept. 14)
Lt. Col. S. B. Pickens (wounded, Sept. 14) / Capt. Tucker
26th Alabama, Col. E. A. O'Neal (wounded, Sept. 14[35])

*Garland's Brigade*
Brig. Gen. Samuel Garland, Jr (killed, Sept. 14) / Col. D. K. McRae
5th North Carolina, Col. D. K. McRae / Capt. Thomas M. Garrett
12th North Carolina, Capt. S. Snow.
13th North Carolina, Lt. Col. Thomas Ruffin, Jr.
20th North Carolina, Col. Alfred Iverson
23d North Carolina, Col. D. H. Christie[36]

*Anderson's Brigade*
Brig. Gen. George B. Anderson
2d North Carolina, Col. C. C. Tew
4th North Carolina. Col. Bryan Grimes
14th North Carolina, Col. R. T. Bennett
30th North Carolina, Col. F. M. Parker

*Colquitt's Brigade*
Col. A. H. Colquitt
13th Alabama, Col. B. D. Fry[37]
6th Georgia, Lt. Col. J.M. Newton
23d Georgia, Col. W. P. Barclay

35 Carman mistakenly listed O'Neal's wounding as September 17, when it was at South Mountain on September 14. *OR* 19, pt. 1, p. 1,021.

36 Carman elsewhere in the manuscript recognized Lt. Col. Robert D. Johnston as in command on September 17. This is also mentioned in Clark, *North Carolina Regiments*, 2, p. 223.

37 In his manuscript, Carman transposed the first two initials of Birkett D. Fry's name.

27th Georgia, Col. L. B. Smith
28th Georgia, Maj. T. Graybill (wounded, Sept. 14) / Capt. N. J. Garrison

*Artillery of D. H. Hill's Division*
Maj. S. F. Pierson
Hardaway's (AL) Battery, Lt. John W. Tullis
Jeff. Davis (AL) Artillery, Capt. J. W. Bondurant
Jones' (VA) Battery, Capt. William B. Jones
King William (VA) Artillery, Capt. T. H. Carter

*Reserve Artillery*
Brig. Gen. William N. Pendleton

*Cutts' Battalion*
Lt. Col. A. S. Cutts
Blackshears' (GA) Battery, Capt. James A. Blackshear
Irwin (GA) Artillery, Capt. John Lane
Lloyd's (NC) Battery, Capt. W. P. Lloyd
Patterson's (GA) Battery, Capt. Geo. M. Patterson
Ross'(GA) Battery, Capt. H. M. Ross

*Jones' Battalion*
Maj. H. P. Jones

*Brown's Battalion*
Col. J. Thompson Brown

*Nelson's Battalion*
Maj. William Nelson

*Cavalry*
Maj. Gen. James E. B. Stuart

*Hampton's Brigade*[38]
Brig. Gen. Wade Hampton
1st North Carolina, Col. L. S. Baker
2d South Carolina, Col. M. C. Butler

38 Carman omitted the 10th Virginia Cavalry from this brigade, but it did appear on the field late on September 17. Robert Driver, *10th Virginia Cavalry* (Lynchburg VA: H. E. Howard, 1992), pp. 23-4.

Cobb's (Georgia) Legion, Maj. W. G. Deloney[39]
Jeff Davis Legion, Lt. Col. W. T. Martin
10th Virginia, Col. J. Lucius Davis

*Lee's Brigade*
Brig. Gen. Fitz Hugh Lee
1st Virginia, Lt. Col. L. Tiernan Brien
3d Virginia, Lt. Col. John T. Thornton
4th Virginia, Col. Williams C. Wickham
5th Virginia, Col. T. L. Rosser
9th Virginia, Col. W. H. F. Lee[40] (wounded Sept. 15)

*Munford's Brigade*
Col. Thomas T. Munford
2d Virginia, Lt. Col. Richard A. Burke
7th Virginia, Capt. S. B. Myers
12th Virginia, Col. A. W. Harman
17th Virginia Battalion, Maj. Thomas B. Massie[41]

*Horse Artillery*
Capt. John Pelham

Chew's (VA) Battery, Capt. R. P. Chew
Hart's (SC) Battery, Capt. J. F. Hart
Pelham's (VA) Battery, Capt. John Pelham

39 After several instances of listing earlier casualties, Carman inexplicably omitted from Cobb's Legion command Lt. Col. Pierce M. B. Young, who was wounded on September 13.

40 in his manuscript, Carman mistakenly listed W. H. F. Lee as W. H. H. Lee.

41 After not listing the 2nd and 10th Virginia Infantry (because they were in Martinsburg and Shepherdstown), Carman decided to list the 17th Virginia Battalion despite the fact that it never crossed the Potomac River into Maryland. The battalion assisted Jackson at Harpers Ferry. See OR 19 pt. 1, p. 825, and William McDonald and Bushrod Washington, *A History of the Laurel Brigade* (Baltimore: Mrs Kate S McDonald, 1907), pp. 75-7, 87, 94-95.

# Interview with Thomas G. Clemens

*SB: I know you have spent a lot of time working with the Carman manuscript. Let's set up what you are publishing and then dig into the details.*

TC: Sure. I am publishing what is known as The Carman Manuscript on the Maryland Campaign of 1862 in two volumes. Volume 1, which comes out in May 2010, covers all the preliminary matters of interest through the South Mountain fighting, and Volume 2 will cover the rest of the campaign, with the focus of course being the September 17th battle of Antietam.

*SB: What got you interested in Carman and his work, and when did you begin?*

TC: I had been aware of it for many years, but never really paid much attention to it. It was in the mid-1990s when I was assisting Professor Joseph Harsh in teaching his summer "Touring Battlefields" course at George Mason University that we first discussed it. By the way, the course title was a misnomer . . .

*SB: How so?*

TC: We didn't tour—we studied, in depth! It was an unforgettable experience. Joe was working on his Confederate trilogy of the Maryland Campaign and told me he was typing out Carman's manuscript. When I expressed surprise and asked him why he did not pay someone to do it for him, he replied, "I learn so much doing it myself." Now, roughly fifteen years later, I understand what he meant. When I was finishing up my degree there I needed a dissertation topic and Joe suggested I finish his typescript and edit the manuscript. When the committee discovered the typescript was roughly 1,200 pages, they quickly suggested that the first seven chapters would be fine for the dissertation! I graduated in 2002 and for a few years some personal issues took precedence, but began to seriously work on it again in 2004.

*SB: What is so special about the Carman manuscript?*

TC: Carman's work has an immediacy and an intimacy about it that no other work on this (or probably any campaign) possesses. The strength of his work was his connection with the campaign (he fought in it as a Union officer) and with the participants. He wrote to hundreds of them, read firsthand articles in the *National Tribune* and *Battles & Leaders,* and guided them on tours of the field when they returned to visit in the 1890s. The Battlefield Board amassed hundreds, and probably thousands, of letters from veterans of the battle on both sides.

*SB: So Carman both knew things nobody else could know, and learned things few others knew.*

TC: Exactly right. And because of that, his narration is the most thorough and complete ever done. While modern historians can cite memoirs, regimental histories, etc., only Carman could talk to the men who wrote them and then receive their personal replies. There is good reason why his manuscript is recognized as the starting point for all studies of the Maryland Campaign in general, and the battles of South Mountain and Antietam in particular.

*SB: Tell us about those letters. Where are they now?*

TC: Well, they are not in one place. Many are in the National Archives in the Antietam Studies boxes. Others are at the Library of Congress, and a substantial number are in the New York Public Library. Carman's friend and fellow historian John Gould collected hundreds of letters pertaining to the East Woods fighting and Mansfield's death. He and Carman shared many letters too, so I needed to look at all these letters to understand what Carman knew, and how he came to know it. I eventually wound up copying them and sorting them by regiment and brigade so I could examine what Carman was told by these men and then compare it to what he wrote in the manuscript.

*SB: That is a monumental job in and of itself!*

TC: It was tedious and time-consuming, but very enjoyable. The database has well over 2,000 entries so far. More letters turn up now and then in private hands. Some brigades have hundreds of responses, others almost none, which makes me suspect some of these letters have been lost or have unfortunately "migrated" over the years.

*SB: How do your footnotes and annotations enhance Carman's original manuscript?*

TC: What I have endeavored to do with the footnotes is allow the reader to see where Carman got his information, and give them some idea of how reliable the source might be. Although Carman cited some sources, he often copied others word-for-word, without attribution at all.

*SB: So is it fair to say that tracking down his sources was something of an investigative nightmare?*

TC: That's a good way to put it! Luckily, there were substantially fewer books in print back then for him to work from, which narrowed the search a bit. My hope is that the reader can now study the footnotes and judge for themselves whether Carman's descriptions of events and people are accurate and balanced, what influenced his judgment, and so forth.

*SB: Can you provide an example or two?*

TC: Carman seems to take Confederate General John G. Walker's *Battles & Leaders* account at face value, but additional research shows Walker's recollections are hopelessly flawed. I have alerted readers to that fact, and why that is so. Some stories that Carman related in the manuscript have a single letter as their sole source, so the reader needs to be alerted to that fact. That doesn't mean they are not true, but just that the story cannot be confirmed by other sources. Overall, I hope readers find that this enhances Carman's manuscript as a narrative of the campaign, and also as a source for those writing detailed studies of portions of the campaign.

*SB: Carman was not a professional writer or literary master . . .*

TC: (laughing) He was far from it. It is important to keep in mind that Carman was, as I like to phrase it, "a government employee writing a government report." Although occasional bursts of eloquence slip in now and then, his writing style in the manuscript is straightforward and usually mundane. Sometimes it has all the charm of a grocery list! What is compelling to me and others familiar with his work is that Carman wrote to veterans asking specific questions about positions, movements, and bivouac sites, and often got back incredible detailed personal recollections and anecdotes, most of which he ignored. He was just collecting facts, not looking for human interest stories, many of which are buried in the letter collections.

*SB: Tell us about the maps that appear in Volume 1 on South Mountain.*

TC: I am thrilled with the maps! Gene Thorp, cartographer for the *Washington Post* and a certified Maryland Campaign maniac, put a lot of his art into these maps. In fact, I frequently had to restrain him from depicting virtually every regiment or brigade in certain maps. Occasionally he even wanted to display individual cavalry squadrons! I kept telling him that Carman was more general than that, and we needed to go a little more in-depth—but not to that level!

*SB: We were very pleased to see the first round of maps and discover the creative style Gene employed.*

TC: Aren't they something? Gene used miniature figures rather than the usual rectangles and they appealed to me right away. We created maps for every day of the march to Sharpsburg for both armies, which includes, of course, the battles at South Mountain. There was not much to go on sometimes, and Gene did a fabulous job of making things clear, and yet providing sufficient detail.

*SB: What can you tell us about Carman's methods?*

TC: As I alluded earlier, Carman collected a huge amount of material. He and the other board members, Jed Hotchkiss, Henry Heth, J. C. Stearns, George B. Davis, and George W. Davis, collected material from all available sources. They agreed upon what they judged as the most reliable and honest accounts and summarized them, both for the manuscript, and also for the cast iron interpretive plaques that mark the battlefield to this day. Often these summaries are in Carman's papers, and they cite whose letters they relied upon.

*SB: Did Carman exhibit any bias in his work?*

TC: He did, but not, perhaps, the ones you might think. Although a veteran of the battle, he did not degrade the Confederate cause or its leaders. In fact, if anything his admiration of Generals Robert E. Lee and Thomas "Stonewall" Jackson reflects the historiography of his time, the 1890s to early 1900s, when the dominant theme was "both sides were right, both sides were brave" and most differences were buried.

*SB: Any particular lapses in bias come to mind?*

TC: Yes, I would say the way he treated Union General Henry W. Halleck. Carman obviously loathed the man and never missed an opportunity to bash Halleck, to a point where it almost makes the reader sympathetic to "Old Brains." Almost. On the other hand, many Confederates complimented Carman for his help and interest in their memoirs.

*SB: When do you think Volume 2 on Antietam will appear?*

TC: Well, that's a tough question because I am still working on the notes and annotations. My guess is at least a year. There is so much there to unravel, so many letters to read, so much to digest and map out. Typically I work on one chapter at a time, getting it to where I think I have discovered all the proper sources, and then send it to several other experts to make sure I have looked at all the angles. I have to say Steve Stotelmyer and several of the rangers at Antietam have been patient and helpful critics, making this work much better for their input. This all takes time, but I'd rather have it right than fast, and I hope that in the end the wait will be worth it.

*SB: You mentioned earlier something called the Battlefield Board. What exactly was Carman's role on the Battlefield Board?*

TC: The Board was charged with three main tasks. One was to mark any points of interest and prominent roles of Regular troops. This resulted in the creation of the cast iron plaques that still mark the field today. Carman and the board members used the *Official Records*, regimental histories, and the letters from veterans to create the text for these plaques. Many of the drafts for these are in the National Archives. In a way, they are a summary of the battle and campaign. The second task was to create maps of the main features of the terrain and the principle movements of the armies. This resulted in fourteen time-sequenced maps depicting the most detailed tracking of the ebb and flow of the battle that has ever been created. These maps will be featured in Volume 2. The third task was to create a pamphlet to guide Congress in the future development of the field. And, believe it or not, the original 1,800-page manuscript researched and written by Carman is this "pamphlet." Much of it is keyed to the maps as the two were designed to complement one another.

*SB: Did Carman create maps for the rest of the campaign, or just the battle of Antietam?*

TC: He created maps for the routes of both armies from September 4, 1862, through September 14. These are crude, just colored pencil blocks on a large map, and they do not show starting and stopping points for each day. We decided not to use them, and instead created new maps with Gene Thorp that are much more detailed. Carman did, however, mention making maps of South Mountain, but I have not found any so far. Likewise, no Carman maps of Shepherdstown Ford or the subsequent campaign in Virginia have been found.

*SB: Did Carman have anything to do with the monuments on the battlefield?*

TC: He did. Carman helped many veterans organizations visit the battlefield and locate where they fought. When they wanted to erect monuments, he helped them negotiate with private property owners to buy small parcels of land. He attended many of the dedications, too.

*SB: I assume Carman visited the battlefield before it was created in 1890?*

TC: Yes, he was a frequent visitor to Sharpsburg. He served on the Board of the National Cemetery for several years and spent a lot of time on the field. He also got to know some of the people in the community.

*SB: Another book of the edited version of Carman's manuscript appeared in 2008. How does yours differ from that effort?*

TC: They are similar in some aspects. My version has more footnotes and more detailed analysis. To be fair, the previous author acknowledged he was just annotating Carman's study, and so did not go into as much depth as I do. My edition also has a lot of maps—22 of them—and they are quite detailed. The earlier version does not contain maps. Volume 2 on Antietam will have many more maps than Volume 1. I believe it is critical to be able to look at maps while reading about the movements of the armies and the various engagements. I also included a photo gallery with some unusual images that have not circulated widely. I also included various photos of Carman that show him from wartime through his older years. He was a very distinguished looking fellow and deserves to be included in a book based upon his own work.

*SB: Thank you, Tom. What an achievement.*

TC: Thank you. I hope others find it worthwhile.

# Bibliography

## Manuscript Collections

Antietam National Battlefield, Sharpsburg, MD
    Datzman, Richard Carroll. Who Found Lee's Lost Dispatch, Lost Order
        File. Vertical Files: Library, 1973
    Auction Broadside, Earl Roulette Collection

Dartmouth College Library, Hanover NH
    Antietam Collection, from John M. Gould

Library of Congress. Washington, DC
    Ezra Carman Papers. Manuscript Division

New Jersey Historical Society. Newark, NJ.
    Bilkes, Eva. "Biography of Ezra Carman." Manuscript Group Series No.
        MG-1761
    Carman, Ezra. Diary, edited by Eva Bilkes. Document M 1003
    Ezra Carman Papers. Manuscript Group Series No. MG-1761

New York Public Library. New York City, NY
    Ezra Carman Papers. Manuscripts and Archives Division, MSS-473

Southern Historical Collection, Manuscript Division. U. of NC at Chapel Hill
    Francis W. Dawson Papers

University of Virginia, Charlottesville VA
    Venable, Charles. Personal Reminiscences of the Confederate War. Accession #
        2969-a, September 28, 1889

U.S. National Archives and Records Administration (NARA)
    Microfilm: Compiled Service Records. n.p., n.d.
    Record Group 15: Records of the Veterans Administration, Civil War Pension
        Application Files. n.p., n.d.
    Antietam National Battlefield Board. Antietam Studies. RG 94. Records of the
        Adjutant General's Office
    Papers, RG 92. Records of the Office of the Quartermaster General

Virginia State Library, Richmond, Virginia
    Journals and Papers of the Virginia State Convention 1861


## Newspapers

Baltimore *Sun*
Columbus (GA) *Daily Sun*
London *Times*
Hagerstown *Herald of Freedom and Torchlight*
Montgomery *County Sentinel*
*National Tribune* (Washington, DC)
New York *Herald*
New York *Journal of Commerce*
New York *Times*
New York *Tribune*
New York *World*
Philadelphia *Weekly Times*
Richmond *Dispatch*
Richmond *Enquirer*
Richmond *Examiner*

## Maps

Griffith, Dennis. Map of Maryland 1794. copy in Washington County Free Library.

Varle, Charles Map of Frederick and Washington County Maryland 1808. copy in Washington County Free Library.

Taggert, Thomas Map of Washington County. Editor's collection.


## Primary Sources

Allan, William. *The Army of Northern Virginia in 1862*. Boston: Houghton Mifflin and Co., 1995.
——. "Strategy of the Campaign of Sharpsburg or Antietam, September 1862" *Papers of the Military History Society of Massachusetts*. Boston: Griffith-Stillings Press, 1903.
Bartlett, Joseph Jackson. "Crampton's Pass: The Start of the Great Maryland Campaign." *National Tribune* (Washington, DC). 19 December 1889.
Basler, Roy. *The Collected Works of Abraham Lincoln*. 8 vols. New Brunswick, NJ: Rutgers University, 1953.
Beale, George W. "The Cavalry Fight at Boonsboro Graphically Described" *Southern Historical Society Papers*. Richmond VA. #25, 1897.
Beale, Howard K., ed. *Diary of Gideon Welles, Secretary of the Navy Under Lincoln and Johnson*. 3 vols. New York: W. W. Norton and Co., 1960.
Beale, Richard R. L. T. *History of the Ninth Virginia Cavalry, War Between the States*. Richmond: B.F. Johnson Publishing Company, 1899.
Biddle, William F. "Recollections of McClellan" Vol. 9, #5 1895, *United Services Magazine, a Monthly Magazine of Military and Naval Affairs*. New York: R.L. Hamersly
Bigelow, John. *Retrospectives of an Active Life*. 5 vols. New York: Baker & Taylor Co. 1909
Bloss, John H. "The Lost Order." *Kansas Commandery of Military Order of the Loyal Legions of the United States*. Military Essays and Recollections Series. Chicago: A. C. McClurg and Co., 1892.
Borke, Heros von. *Memoirs of The Confederate War for Independence*. Philadelphia: J. B. Lippincott and Co., 1867.
Brown, Edmund Randolf. *The Twenty Seventh Indiana Volunteer Infantry in the War of the Rebellion*. Monticello, VA, 1899.
Brown, George William. *Baltimore and the 19th of April, 1861*. Baltimore: Johns Hopkins University Press, 1887.

Clark, Walter. *Histories of the Several Regiments and Battalions from North Carolina in the Great War, 1861-1865, Written by Members of the Respective Commands.* 5 vols. Goldsboro, NC: Published by the State, 1901. Reprint, Wendall, NC: Broadfoot Publishing Co., 1982.

Committee of the Regimental Association. *History of the Thirty-Fifth Regiment, Massachusetts Volunteers.* Boston: Mills, Knight & Co. 1884.

Cooke, John Esten. *A Life of Robert E. Lee.* New York: D. Appleton and Co., 1871.

——. *Life of Stonewall Jackson.* Richmond: Ayres and Wade, 1863.

Cox, Jacob D. *Military Reminiscences of the Civil War.* New York: Charles Scribner & Sons, 1900.

——. "Forcing Fox's and Turner's Gap." Johnson and Buell, eds. *Battles & Leaders of the Civil War*, 4 vols. New York: Century Magazine, 1884-1887.

Crist, Lynda Lasswell, and Mary Seaton Dix, eds. *The Papers of Jefferson Davis.* 8 vols. Baton Rouge: Louisiana State University Press, 1971–1992.

Croffut, W. A., ed. *Fifty Years in Camp and Field: Diary of Ethan Allen Hitchcock.* New York: Putnam's Sons, 1909.

Crowninshield, Benjamin W. A. *History of the First Massachusetts Cavalry Volunteers.* Boston: Houghton Mifflin & Co. 1891.

Cutts, Allen S. "Cutts battalion at Sharpsburg." *Southern Historical Society Papers.* Richmond VA. Vol. 10, 1882.

Dabney, Robert Lewis. *Life and Campaigns of Lieut. Gen. Thomas J. Jackson.* New York: Blelock and Co., 1866.

Davenport, Alfred. *Camp and Field Life of the Fifth New York Volunteer Infantry, Duryee's Zouaves.* New York: Dick and Fitzgerald, 1879.

Davis, Henry Winter. *Speeches and Addresses Delivered in the Congress of the United States and Other Occasions.* New York: Harper & Brothers, 1867.

Davis, Jefferson. *Rise and Fall of the Confederate Government.* 2 vols. New York: Yoseloff, 1958.

Davis, Reuben. *Recollections of Mississippi.* Cambridge: Houghton Mifflin and Co., 1889.

Dawson, Francis Warrington. *Reminiscences of Confederate Service.* Charleston: News and Courier Book Presses, 1882.

Dennett, Tyler. *Lincoln and the Civil War in the Letters and Diaries of John Hay.* New York: Dodd, Mead and Co., 1939.

Douglas, H. K. *I Rode With Stonewall.* Chapel Hill: University of North Carolina Press, 1940.

——. "Stonewall Jackson's in Maryland." Johnson & Buell, eds., *Battles and Leaders of the Civil War*, 4 vols. New York: Century Magazine, 1884-1887.

Emory, Frederick. "The Baltimore Riots," in Alexander K. McClure, *Annals of the War Written by the Leading Participants North and South*. Philadelphia, PA: Weekly Times, 1878.

Fonerden, C. A. *History of Carpenter's Battery of the Stonewall Brigade 1861-1865*. New Market VA: Henkel and Company, 1911.

Franklin, William B. "Notes on Crampton's Gap and Antietam," Johnson and Buell, eds. *Battles and Leaders of the Civil War*, 4 vols. New York: Century Magazine, 1884-1887.

Goodhart, Briscoe. *History of the Independent Loudoun Virigina Rangers*. Washington, DC: McGill and Wallace Press, 1896.

Grattan, George. "Battle of Boonsboro Gap or South Mountain." *Southern Historical Society Papers*. 52 vols. Richmond 1876-1959.

Greeley, Horace. *The American Conflict: A History of the Great Rebellion in the United States*. 2 vols. Hartford: O.D. Case and Co., 1864-1866.

Hard, Abner. *History of the Eighth Illinois Cavalry Regiment*. Aurora: n.p., 1868.

Hill, Daniel H. "The Battle of South Mountain or Boonsboro'. Fighting for Time at Turner's and Fox's Gap." Johnson and Buell, eds. *Battles and Leaders of the Civil War*, 4 vols. New York: Century Magazine, 1884-1887.

Hood, John Bell. *Advance and Retreat*. New Orleans: The Hood Orphans Memorial Fund, 1880.

Howard, Oliver O. "Personal Reminiscences of the War of the Rebellion." National Tribune Company, Washington D.C., March 1884.

Illinois Adjutant General's Report. Vol. 4. Springfield, IL: Published by the State, 1886.

Johnson, Bradley Tyler. "Memoirs of the First Maryland (Confederate) Regiment." *Southern Historical Society Papers*, Richmond VA. 12 (January-December 1884).

——. "Stonewall Jackson's Intentions at Harpers Ferry." Johnson and Buell, eds. *Battles and Leaders of the Civil War*, 4 vols. New York: Century Magazine, 1884-1887.

Johnston, David E. *Four Years a Soldier*. Princeton, WV: n.p. 1887.

Johnston, Joseph E. *Narrative of Military Operation During the Late War Between the States*. New York: D. Appleton & Co., 1874.

Long, Armistead Lindsay. *Memoirs of Robert E. Lee*. Philadelphia: J. M. Stoddart and Co., 1886.

Longstreet, James. *From Manassas to Appomattox*. Bloomington, IN: Indiana University Press, 1960.

——. "The Invasion of Maryland." Johnson and Buell, eds. *Battles & Leaders of the Civil War*, 4 vols. New York: Century Magazine, 1884-1887.

Luff, William M. "March of the Cavalry From Harper's Ferry September 14th 1862." *Illinois Commandery of Military Order of the Loyal Legion of the United States*. Military Essays and Recollections Series, vol. 2. Chicago: A. C. McClurg and Co., 1894.

McClellan, George B. *McClellan's Own Story*. New York: Charles L. Webster and Co., 1887.

——. Letter to the Secretary of War Transmitting Report on the Organization of the Army of the Potomac and of its Campaigns in Virginia and Maryland. Washington, DC: Government Printing Office, 1864.

——. "From the Peninsula to Antietam." Johnson and Buell, eds. *Battles and Leaders of the Civil War*, 4 vols., New York: Century Magazine, 1884-1887.

McClellan, Henry B. *The Life and Campaigns of Major General J. E. B. Stuart, Commander of the Cavalry of the Army of Northern Virginia*. New Jersey: Blue Gray Press, 1993.

McClure, K. Alexander. *Annals of the War Written by the Leading Participants North and South*. Philadelphia: *Weekly Times*, 1878.

——. *Abraham Lincoln and Men of War Times*. Philadelphia: *Weekly Press*, 1892.

McDonald, William, Bushrod Washington, ed. *A History of the Laurel Brigade, Originally the Ashby's Cavalry of the Army of Northern Virginia and Chew's Battery*. Baltimore: Mrs. Kate S. McDonald, 1907.

McLaws, Lafayette. "The Capture of Harper's Ferry." Philadelphia *Weekly Press*, 5, 12, and 19 September 1888.

——. "The Maryland Campaign" Addresses Delivered before the Confederate Veterans Association, April 19, 1895, to which is added the President's Annual Report. Savannah: George N. Nichols, 1896.

Maryland General Assembly. Maryland Senate Journal. 27 April 1861. Maryland State Archives Web Site. Retrieved January 2002: http://www.mdarchives.state.md.us

——. House and Senate Documents. 1861. Maryland State Archives Web Site.

Retrieved January 2002: http://www.mdarchives.state.md.us

Massachusettes Adjutant General, comp. Massachusetts Soldiers, Sailors and Marines in the Civil War. Norwood, MA: Norwood Press, 1933.

Moore, Frank, ed. *The Rebellion Record: A Diary of American Events, With Documents, Narratives, Illustrative Incidents, Poetry, etc*. New York: G. P. Putnam, 1861-1863; Van Nostrand, 1864-1868.

Myers, Frank. *The Comanches: White's Battalion Virginia Cavalry, C.S.A*. Baltimore: Kelly, Piet and Co., 1871.

Nichols, William H. "The Siege and Capture of Harper's Ferry by the Confederates." Soldiers and Sailor's Historical Society of Rhode Island, 4th Series. Providence: The Providence Press, 1889.

——. "A Cavalry Escape." National Tribune Company, Washington, DC. 12 April 1894.

Nicolay, John G., and John Hay. *Abraham Lincoln: A History.* 10 vols. New York: Century Co., 1890.

*Official Roster of the Soldiers of the State of Ohio in the War of the Rebellion, 1861-1865.* Cincinnati: Ohio Valley Publ. Co., 1886.

Owen, Henry T. "Incidents of the Battle of South Moutain." Philadelphia *Weekly Times,* July 23, 1880.

Owen, William M. *In Camp and Field with the Washington Artillery: A Narrative of Events During the Late War...* Boston,: Ticknor & Co., 1885.

Palfrey, Francis W. *The Antietam and Fredericksburg.* Campaigns of the Civil War series. New York: Scribner and Sons, 1882.

Paris, Louis Phillippe d' Orleans, Comte de. *History of the Civil War in America.* 2 vols. Philadelphia: Porter and Coates, 1876.

Parker, Thomas H. *History of the 51st P.V. and V. V....* Philadelphia: King and Baird Printers, 1869.

Pettingill, Samuel P. *The College Cavaliers.* Chicago: Ft. McAllister and Co. Printers, 1883.

Pickerill, W. N. *History of the Third Indiana Cavalry.* Indianapolis: Aetna Printing Co., 1906.

Pollard, Edward A. *Life of Jefferson Davis, with a Secret History of the Southern Confederacy Gathered Behind the Scenes in Richmond.* Philadelphia: National Publishing Co., 1869.

——. *Lost Cause and Southern History of the War.* New York: E. B. Treat and Co., 1867.

Powell, William H. *The Fifth Army Corps.* New York: G. P. Putnam's Sons, 1896.

Ropes, John C. *The Story of the Civil War.* 2 vols. New York: Putnam's Sons, 1898.

Rowland, Dunbar, Ed. *Jefferson Davis, Constitutionalist: His Letters, Papers and Speeches.* 10 vols. Jackson, MS: Mississippi Department of Archives and History, 1923.

"Secession Ordinance." Confederate Veteran 26, no. 1 (January 1918).

Shreve, William P. *The Story of the Third Army Corps Union.* Boston: privately printed, 1910.

Steiner, Lewis. *Report of Lewis Steiner M.D. Inspector of the Sanitary Commission, containing a Diary Kept During the Rebel Occupation of Frederick, MD.* New York: Anson D. F. Randolf, 1862.

Stephens, Alexander Hamilton. *A Constitutional View of the Late War Between the States: Its Causes, Character, Conduct, and Results Presented in a Series of Colloquies at Liberty Hall.* 2 vols. Philadelphia: National Publishing Co., 1868-1870.

Sterling, Pound (William P. Maxson). *Campfire of the Twenty-Third. Sketches of the Camp Life, Marches, and Battles of the Twenty-Third Regiment, N.Y.V.* New York: Davis Kent Printers, 1863.

Stevenson, James H. *"Boots and Saddles": A History of the First Volunteer Cavalry of the War, Known as the First New York (Lincoln) Cavalry.* Harrisburg PA: Patriot Publishing Co. 1879.

Taliaferro, William. "Jackson's Raid Around Pope." Johnson and Buell, eds.,*Battles and Leaders of the Civil War*, 4 vols. New York: Century Magazine, 1884-1887.

Taylor, Walter H., edited by James I. Robertson, Jr. *Four Years With General Lee.* New York: D. Appleton and Co., 1877.

U.S. Adjutant General's Office. *Official Army Register of the Volunteer Force of the United States Army for the Years 1861-1865.* 8 vols. plus index. Washington, DC: Adjutant General's Office, 1865. Reprint, Gaithersburg MD: Van Sickle Books, 1987.

U.S. Bureau of the Census. *Population of the United States in 1860, Compiled from Original Returns of the Eighth Census.* Washington, DC: Government Printing Office, 1864.

Unknown author, "Unwritten War." *New York Daily Tribune*, March 14, 1889.

U.S. Congress. *Report of the Joint Committee on the Conduct of the War.* 3 vols. Washington, DC: Government Printing Office, 1863.

———. *58th Congess, 2nd Session, 1904, Journal of the House of Representatives of the First Congress of the Confederate States of America, 1861-1865.*

U.S. Navy Department. *The War of the Rebellion: Official Records of the Union and Confederate Navies.* 30 vols. Washington, DC: Government Printing Office, 1894-1927.

U.S. War Department. *The War of the Rebellion: Official Records of the Union and Confederate Armies.* 70 vols. in 128 parts. Washington, DC: Government Printing Office, 1880-1901.

———. *Atlas to Accompany the Official Records of the Union and Confederate Armies.* Washington D.C.: Government Printing Office, 1891-1895

Walker, John G. "Jackson's Capture of Harpers Ferry." Johnson and Buell, eds. Battles and Leaders of the Civil War, 4 vols. New York: Century Magazine, 1884-1887.

Wall, H. C. "Thirteenth Regiment (later the Twenty-Third) of Infantry" in Raleigh (NC) *News and Observer*, April 11, 1897.

Wallis, Severn Teakle. *Report of the Committee of Federal Relations.* Maryland State Archives Web Site. Retrieved January 2002: http://www.mdarchives.state.md.us

Warden, Robert P. *An Account of the Private Life and Public Services of Chase.* Cincinnati: Wilstach, Baldwin and Co., 1874.

Warren, Kittrel J. *History of the Eleventh Georgia Volunteers, Embracing the Muster Rolls together with a Special and Succint Account of the Marshes, Engagements, Casualties etc.* Richmond: Smith Bailey & Co. 1863.

Welles, Gideon. *Lincoln and Seward: Remarks Upon the Memorial Address of Charles F. Adams on the Late Wm. H. Seward.* New York: Sheldon and Co., 1874.

Wild, Frederick. *Memoirs and History of F. W. Alexander's Baltimore Battery of Light Artillery, USV.* Baltimore, MD: Maryland School for Boys, 1912.

Wilson, *Henry Rise of the Slave Power in America*. Boston: Houghton Osgood & Co. 1879.

Wilson, James Grant. "General Halleck, A Memoir," parts 1 and 2. *Journal of the Military Service Institution*, 36 (May 1862): 334-56 (June 1862).

Wise, George. *The History of the 17th Virginia*. Baltimore: Kelly Piet & Company, 1870.

Wood, Joseph H., Elijah S. Watts, and John W. Palmer. *Memorials of Deceased Companions of the Commandery of the State of Illinois, Military Order of the Loyal Legions of the United States*. Military Essays and Recollections Series, vol. 1. Chicago: A. C. McClurg and Co., 1891.

Worsham, John. *One of Jackson's Foot Cavalry*. New York: Neale Publishing Co., 1912.

## Secondary Sources

Adams, Charles Francis, Jr. *Charles Francis Adams, By His Son*. Cambridge, MA: Houghton Mifflin and Co., 1900.

Adams, Ephriam Douglas. *Great Britain and the American Civil War*. New York: Russell and Russell, 1924.

*The American Annual Cyclopedia and Register of Important Events*, 14 vols. New York: D. Appleton, 1862-1875.

Armstrong, Richard L. *Seventh Virginia Cavalry*. Lynchburg, VA: H. E. Howard Publishing Co., 1992.

Ashley, Evelyn. *The Life of Henry John Temple, Viscount Palmerston: 1846-1865, With Selections From his Speeches and Correspondence*. London: R. Bentley and Son, 1876.

Bacarella, Michael. *Lincoln's Foreign Legion: The Thirty-Ninth New York Infantry: The Garibaldi Guard*. Shippensburg, PA: White Mane Publishing Co., 1996.

Bailey, Ronald, and Jay Luvaas. *The Military Legacy of the Civil War*. Topeka: University of Kansas Press, 1988.

Bancroft, Frederick, *Life of William H. Seward*. New York, Harper & Brothers, 1900.

Banks, Louis A. *Immortal Songs of Camp and Field*. Cleveland: Burrows Bros. 1898.

Barnet, James. *Biographical Sketch of William Medill*. Chicago: J. Barnet, Printer, 1864.

*Biographical Cyclopedia of Representative Men of Maryland and the District of Columbia*. Baltimore: National Biographical Publishing Co., 1879.

*Biographical Directory of the U.S. Congress, 1774-Present*. Retrieved February 2002: http://bioguide.congress.gov

Boatner, Mark. *Civil War Dictionary*. New York: David McKay Company, 1959.

Bohannon, Keith. *The Giles, Alleghany and Jackson Artillery*. Lynchburg, VA: H. E. Howard, 1990.

Brugger, Robert J. *Maryland: A Middle Temperament, 1634-1980*. Baltimore: Johns Hopkins University Press, 1988.

Cannistraro, Phillip V., and John J. Reich. *The Western Perspective*. Ft. Worth, TX: Harcourt Brace College Publishers, 1999.

Cannon, Devereaux D., Jr. *The Flags of the Confederacy: An Illustrated History*. Memphis TN: St. Luke's and Broadfoot Publishing, 1988.

Carmichael, Peter. *The Purcell, Crenshaw and Letcher Artillery*. Lynchburg, VA: H.E. Howard, 1990.

Clark, Charles Branch. *Politics in Maryland During the Civil War*. Chestertown, MD: n.p., 1952.

Clarkson, Thomas. *History of the Abolition of the Slave Trade*. On-line collection, Afro-American Collection, University of Michigan. www.umich.edu/~iinet/caas/

Connelly, Thomas. *The Marble Man: Robert E. Lee and his Image in American Society*. Baton Rouge: Louisiana State University Press, 1977.

Conrad, W. P., and Ted Alexander. *When War Passed This Way*. Shippensburg, PA: Beidel Printing House, 1982.

Cozzens, Peter, and Robert Girardi. *Military Memoirs of General John Pope*. Chapel Hill: University of North Carolina Press, 1998.

Crew, R. Thomas, Jr. and Benjamin Trask. *Grimes', Grandy's and Huger's Battery, Virginia Artillery*. Lynchburg, VA: H. E. Howard, 1995.

Coffman, Richard M. and Graham Kurt D. *To Honor These Men: A History of the Phillips Georgia Legion Infantry Battalion*. Macon: Mercer University Press, 2007.

Crute, Joseph. *Confederate Staff Officers*. Powhatan, VA: Derwent Books, 1982.

Cullum, George. *Register of Graduates and Former Cadets, United States Military Academy*. West Point, NY: West Point Alumni Foundation, 1960.

Current, Richard, ed. *Encyclopedia of the Confederacy*. 4 vols. New York: Simon and Schuster, 1993.

Curtis, George Ticknor. *Life of James Buchanan*. New York: Harper and Brothers, 1883.

——. *McClellan's Last Service to the Republic*. New York: D. Appleton and Co., 1886.

Denton, Lawrence M. *A Southern Star for Maryland*. Baltimore: Publishing Concepts, 1995.

Dew, Charles. *Apostles of Disunion: Southern Secession Commissioners and the Causes of the Civil War*. Charlottesville, VA: University Press of Virginia, 2001.

——. "Apostles of Secession." *North and South Magazine*, 4, no. 4 (April 2001).

Donald, David. *Inside Lincoln's Cabinet: The Civil War Diaries of Salmon Chase*. New York: Longmans, Green and Co., 1954.

Driver, Robert J., Jr. *Second Virginia Cavalry*. Lynchburg VA: H. E. Howard, 1995.

_____. *The Staunton Artillery.* Lynchburg VA: H. E. Howard, 1992.

_____. *10th Virginia Cavalry.* Lynchburg VA: H. E. Howard, 1988.

_____. *10th Virginia Infantry.* Lynchburg VA: H. E. Howard 1992.

Dyer, Frederick H. *A Compendium of the War of the Rebellion.* Dayton, OH: Morningside Press, 1978.

Eicher, John H., and David J. Eicher. *Civil War High Commands.* Stanford, CA: Stanford University Press, 2001.

Evans, Clement, ed. *Confederate Military History.* 12 vols. Secaucus, NJ: Blue and Gray Press, 1975.

Every Name File. Retrieved February 2002: http://home.earthlink.net /~ntgreen/html/index2/htm

Evitts, William J. *A Matter of Allegiances: Maryland From 1850-1861.* Baltimore: Johns Hopkins University Press, 1974.

Foner, Eric, and John Garraty, eds. *The Reader's Companion to American History.* Boston: Houghton Mifflin Co., 1991.

Fox, John J. III. *Red Clay to Richmond: Trail of the 35th Georgia Infantry Regiment C.S.A.* Winchester VA: Angle Valley Press, 2004.

Fox, William F. *Regimental Losses in the Civil War.* Dayton OH: Morningside, 1888. Reprint 1985.

_____. *New York at Gettysburg.* Albany: Lyon and Co., 1900.

Frye, Dennis. "Henry Kyd Douglas Challenged by His Peers." *Civil War: The Magazine of the Civil War Society,* 9, no. 5 (September/October 1991).

_____. "Stonewall Attacks: Siege and Capture of Harpers Ferry." *Blue and Gray Magazine,* 5, no. 1 (August-September 1987).

_____. *Twelfth Virginia Cavalry.* Lynchburg, VA: H.E. Howard, 1988.

Gallagher, Gary, ed. *Lee the Soldier.* Lincoln, NE: University of Nebraska Press, 1996.

_____. *The Antietam Campaign: Essays on the 1862 Maryland Campaign.* Chapel Hill, NC: University of North Carolina Press, 1999.

Gary, Keith. *Answering the Call: Organization and Recruitment of the Potomac Home Brigade Maryland Volunteers, Summer and Fall 1861.* Bowie, MD: Heritage Books, 1996.

Graham, Matthew J. *History of the Ninth New York Volunteers, Hawkins Zouaves, Being a History of the Regiment and Veteran Association from 1860 to 1900.* New York: E. P. Cohy & Co. 1900.

Greene, A. Wilson, ed. *Whatever You Resolve To Be: Essays on Stonewall Jackson.* Baltimore: Butternut and Blue Publishing Co., 1992.

Hafendorfer, Kenneth. *Perryville.* Louisville, KY: KH Press, 1991.

Harsh, Joseph L. *Confederate Tide Rising: Robert E. Lee and the Making of Southern Strategy, 1861-1862.* Kent, OH: Kent State University Press, 1998.

———. *Taken at the Flood: Robert E. Lee and Confederate Strategy in the Maryland Campaign of 1862*. Kent, OH: Kent State University Press, 1999.

———. *Sounding the Shallows: A Confederate Companion for the Maryland Campaign of 1862*. Kent, OH: Kent State University Press, 2000.

Hart, A. B. *Salmon P. Chase*. Boston: Houghton Mifflin and Co., 1899.

Hartzler, Dan. *Marylanders in the Confederacy*. Silver Spring, MD: Family Line Publications, 1986.

Harwell, Richard, ed. *The Union Reader*. New York: Longmans, Green and Co., 1958.

Hearns, David C. *The Lincoln Papers: The Story of the Collection, With Selections to July 4, 1861*. 2 vols. Garden City, NY: Doubleday, 1948.

Heitman, Francis B. *Historical Register and Dictionary of the United States Army, 9/29/1789 - 3/2/1903*. 2 vols. Washington, DC: GPO, 1903.

Henderson, G. F. R. *Stonewall Jackson and the American Civil War*. New York: Grossett and Dunlap, 1898.

Hendrickson, Robert. *Sumter: The First Day of the Civil War*. New York: Promontory Press, 1990.

Herbert, Walter H. *Fighting Joe Hooker*. Indianapolis: Bobbs-Merrill Co., 1944.

Hewitt, Janet B., ed. *Roster of Confederate Soldiers*. Wilmington, NC: Broadfoot Publishing Co., 1996.

Hopkins, Donald. *The Little Jeff: The Jeff Davis Legion Cavalry Army of Northern Virginia*. Shippensburg, PA: White Mane Publishing Co. 1999.

Hughes, Robert M. *General Johnston*. New York: M. D. Appleton and Co., 1893.

Hunt, Roger D. *Brevet Brigadier Generals in Blue*. Gaithersburg, MD: Old Soldier Books, 1990.

———. *Colonels in Blue, Union Army Colonels of the Civil War: The New England States, Connecticut, Maine, Massachusetts, New Hampshire, Rhode Island, Vermont*. Atglen PA: Schiffer Military History 2001.

———. *Colonels in Blue, Union Army Colonels of the Civil War: New York*. Atglen PA: Schiffer Military History 2003.

———. *Colonels in Blue, Union Army Colonels of the Civil War: The Mid-Atlantic States, Pennsylvania, New Jersey, Maryland, Delaware and the District of Columbia*. Mechanicsburg PA: Stackpole Books, 2007.

Hyman, Harold, and Benjamin P. Thomas. *Stanton: The Life and Times of Lincoln's Secretary of War*. New York: Knopf, 1962.

Johnson, Curt, and Richard Anderson. *Artillery Hell: The Employment of Artillery at Antietam*. College Station, TX: Texas A&M University Press, 1995.

Jones, Wilbur D., Jr. "Who Lost the Lost Order? Stonewall Jackson, His Courier, and Special Order 191." *Civil War Regiments: A Journal of the American Civil War*, 5, no. 3.

Kegel, James. *North With Lee and Jackson.* Mechanicsburg, PA: Stackpole Books, 1996.

Kelly, William D. *Lincoln and Stanton: A Study of the War Administration of 1861 and 1862, with Special Consideration of Some Recent Statements of Gen'l. George B. McClellan.* New York: G. P. Putnam's Sons, 1885.

Kinsley, Philip. *The Chicago Tribune: Its First Hundred Years.* New York: Alfred Knopf, 1943.

Krick, Robert E. L. *Staff Officers in Gray: A Biographical Register of the Staff Officers in the Army of Northern Virginia.* Chapel Hill: University of North Carolina Press, 2003.

Krick, Robert K. *Lee's Colonels: A Biographical Register of the Field Officers of the Army of Northern Virginia,* 4th ed., rev. Dayton, OH: Morningside Press, 1992.

Large, George, and Joe Swisher. *Battle of Antietam: The Official History of the Battlefield Board.* Shippensburg, PA: Burd Street Press, 1998.

Longford, Elizabeth. *Wellington: Pillar of the State.* Vol. 2. New York: Harper and Row, c. 1969-1972.

Lossing, Benson. *A Pictorial History of the Civil War in America.* 2 vols. Philadelphia: George W. Childs, 1866.

Malone, Dumas, ed. *Dictionary of American Biography.* New York: Charles Scribner's Sons, 1937.

Manarin, Louis H. and Jordan, Weymouth T. *North Carolina Troops 1861-1865: A Roster.* 17 vols. Raleigh NC: State Division of Archives and History, 1973.

Marks, Bayly, and Mark Schatz. *Between North and South: A Maryland Journalist Views the Civil War: Narrative of William Wilkens Glenn 1861-1869.* Cranbury, NJ: Associated University Presses, 1976.

Marvel, William, *Burnside.* Chapel Hill: University of North Carolina Press, 1991.

———. comp. "Sketches of the Contributors." *Military Order of the Loyal Legion of the United States.* 62 vols. Wilmington, NC: Broadfoot, 1991.

Maryland State Archives, Biographical Series. Retrieved February 2002: www.mdarchives.state.md.us

McPherson, Edward. *The Political History of the United States of America, During the Great Rebellion, Including a Classified Summary of the Legislation of the Second Session of the Thirty-Sixth Congress, the Three Sessions of the Thirty-Seventh Congress, the First Session of the Thirty-Eighth Congress, With the Votes Thereon, and the Important Executive, Judicial, and Politico-Military Facts of That Eventful Period; Together With the Organization, Legislation, and General Proceedings of the Rebel Administration; and an Appendix Containing the Principal Political Facts of the Campaign of 1864, a Chapter on the Church and the Rebellion, and the Proceedings of the Second Session of the Thirty-Eighth Congress.* Washington, DC: Philp and Solomons, 1865.

McPherson, James. *Ordeal By Fire: The Civil War and Reconstruction.* New York: McGraw Hill, 1992.

Mescher, Virginia. *Dates of Selected Inventions and Occurrences During the Latter Part of the Eighteenth Century and During Nineteenth Century.* Burke, VA: by the author, 1994.

Murfin, James. *Gleam of Bayonets: The Battle Of Antietam And Robert E. Lee's Maryland Campaign, September 1862.* New York: Thomas Yoseloff, 1965.

*National Cyclopedia of American Biography.* 9 vols. New York: James White and Co., 1892-1899.

New Advent. "Charles Louis Napoleon." Catholic Encyclopedia. Retrieved February 2002: http://www.newadvent.org

*New York Tribune Almanac 1862.* New York: Tribune Publishing Co., 1863.

Noe, Kenneth. *Perryville: This Grand Havoc of Battle.* Lexington: University of Kentucky Press, 2001.

Nolan, Alan. *Lee Considered: General Robert E. Lee and Civil War History.* Chapel Hill: University of North Carolina Press, 1991.

Patterson, Michael Robert. "Allabach, P. H." Arlington National Cemetery Website. Retrieved January 2002: http://www.arlingtoncemetery.com/phallabach

Phisterer, Frederick. *New York in the War of the Rebellion 1861-1865.* 3rd ed. 5 vols. Albany: J. B. Lyons, 1912.

Piatt, Don & Boynton, Henry V. *General George H. Thomas: A Critical Biography.* Cincinnati: Robert Clarke, 1893.

———. *Memories of the Men Who Saved the Union.* New York: Belford, Clark and Company, 1887.

Priest, John M. *Before Antietam: the Battle of South Mountain.* Shippensburg PA: White Mane Publishing Co. 1992.

Rafuse, Ethan S. *McClellan's War: The Failure of Moderation in the Struggle for the Union.* Bloomington: Indiana University Press, 2005.

———. "Former Whigs in Conflict, Winfield Scott, Abraham Lincoln and the Secession Crisis Revisited" *Lincoln Herald*, #103, Spring 2001, p. 8-21

———. "Poor Burn?! The Antietam Conspiracy That Wasn't." *Civil War History*, #54 (June 2008) Kent: Kent State University Press.

Radcliffe, George L. *Governor Thomas H. Hicks of Maryland and the Civil War.* Baltimore, MD: Johns Hopkins Press, 1901.

Foner, Eric and Garraty, John A., eds. *Reader's Companion to American History.* Boston: Houghton Mifflin Co., 1991.

Reilly, O. T. *The Battlefield of Antietam.* Hagerstown, MD: Hagerstown Bookbinding and Printing Co., 1906.

Reese, Tim. *Sealed With Their Lives: Battle of Crampton's Gap, Burkittsville, MD, Sept. 14, 1862.* Baltimore: Butternut and Blue, 1998.

Rhodes, James Ford. *History of theUnited States from the Compromise of 1850.* New York: Harper & Brothers, 1899.

Richardson, James. *Compilation of the Messages and Papers of Presidents 1787-1897.* 20 vols. Washington DC: 1897-1913.

Robertson, James I., Jr. *Stonewall Jackson: The Man, The Soldier The Legend.* New York: Simon and Shuster MacMillan Publishing, 1997.

Robertson, John. *Michigan in the War.* Lansing MI: W.S. George & Co. State Printers and Binders, 1882.

Rowland, Thomas J. *In the Shadow of Grant and Sherman: George B. McClellan and Civil War History.* Kent, OH: Kent State University Press, 1998.

Ruffner, Kevin. *Maryland's Blue and Gray.* Baton Rouge: Louisiana State University Press, 1997.

Sawchuk, Brown and Associates. Albany Heritage: Website of Local Interest. Retrieved February 2002: www.sawchukbrown.com/albany/d1hisb.htm

Scharf, Thomas. *History of Maryland From Earliest Period to Present.* Hatboro, PA: Tradition Press, 1967.

Sears, Stephen, ed. *The Civil War Papers of George McClellan.* New York: Ticknor and Fields, 1989.

——. *Landscape Turned Red: The Battle of Antietam.* New Haven, CT: Ticknor and Fields, 1983.

——. *George B. McClellan: The Young Napoleon.* New York: Ticknor and Fields, 1988.

——. "The Last Word on the Lost Order." *Military History Quarterly*, Special Issue #2: The Civil War, 1995.

——. *Controversy and Commanders: Dispatches From the Army of the Potomac.* Boston: Houghton Mifflin & Co. 1999.

Shannon, Fred Albert. *Organization and Administration of the Union Army 1861-1865.* Gloucester MA: Peter Smith, 1965.

Sheads, Scott, and Daniel Toomey. *Baltimore During the Civil War.* Baltimore, MD: Toomey Press, 1997.

Sherlock, Scott. "The Lost Order and the Press." *Civil War Regiments: A Journal of the American Civil War* (January 2000).

Sifakis, Stewart. *Who Was Who in the Civil War.* New York: Facts on File, 1988.

Smith, G. W. *Confederate War Papers.* New York: Atlantic Publishing Co., 1884.

Snell, Charles W., and Sharon A. Brown. *Antietam National Battlefield and National Cemetery: An Administrative History.* Washington, DC: Dept. of the Interior/National Park Service, 1982.

Snell, Mark A. *From First to Last: The Life of Major General William B. Franklin.* New York: Fordham University Press, 2002.

Steiner, Bernard C. *Life of Henry Winter Davis.* Baltimore, MD: John Murphy Co., 1916.

Stovall, Pleasant A. *Robert Toombs: Statesman, Speaker, Soldier, Sage.* New York: Cassell Publishing Co., 1892.

Swanburg, W. A. *First Blood: The Story of Fort Sumter*. New York: Scribner's, 1957.

Swinton, William. *Twelve Decisive Battles of the War. A History of the Eastern and Western Campaign*. New York: Charles Scribner and Sons, 1882.

Tap, Bruce. *Over Lincoln's Shoulder: The Committee on the Conduct of the War*. Lawrence: University of Press of Kansas, 1998.

"Thayer." The Political Graveyard: A Database of Historic Cemeteries. Retrieved February 2002: http://politicalgraveyard.com/bio/Thayer

Tischler, Allan. *The History of the Harpers Ferry Cavalry Expedition, September 14 and15, 1862*. Winchester, VA: Five Cedars Press, 1993.

Toomey, Daniel Carroll, and Charles Albert Earp. *Marylanders in Blue: Artillery and Cavalry*. Baltimore, MD: Toomey Press, 1999.

Walker, Francis, *History of the Second Corps in the Army of the Potomac*. New York: Charles Scribner's Sons, 1887.

Wallace, Lee A. *Fifth Virginia Infantry*. Lynchburg, VA: H. E. Howard, 1988.

——. *Guide to Virginia Military Organizations*. Richmond: Virginia Civil War Commission, 1964.

Walpole, Spencer. *Life of Lord John Russell*. 2 vols. London: Longmans, Green and Co. 1889.

Waugh, John C. *The Class of 1846: From West Point to Appomattox: Stonewall Jackson, George McClellan, and Their Brothers*. New York: Warner Books, 1994.

Warner, Ezra. *Generals in Blue: Lives of the Union Commanders*. Baton Rouge: Louisiana State University Press, 1964.

Warner, Ezra. *Generals in Gray: Lives of the Confederate Commanders*. Baton Rouge: Louisiana State University Press, 1959.

Weaver, Jeffery. *Branch, Harrington and Staunton Artillery*. Lynchburg, VA: H. E. Howard, 1997.

White, Henry Alexander. *Robert E. Lee and the Southern Confederacy*. New York: G. P. Putnam and Sons, 1897.

Williams, T. Harry. *Lincoln and His Generals*. New York: Alfred A. Knopf, 1952.

Wilmer, Allison L., J. H. Jarrett, and George W. W. Vernon, eds. *History and Roster: Maryland Volunteers, 1861-1865*. Baltimore: Guggenheim and Weil Co., 1898.

Woodbury, Augustus. *Major General Ambrose E. Burnside and the Ninth Corps: A Narrative of Campaigns in North Carolina, Maryland, Virginia, Ohio, Kentucky, Mississippi, and Tennessee During the War for Preservation of the Republic*. Providence RI: Sidney S. Rider & Brother, 1867.

# Index

## About the Author

**Ezra Ayres Carman** was born in Oak Tree, New Jersey, on February 27, 1834, educated at Western Military Academy in Kentucky, and fought with New Jersey organizations through the Civil War. He was appointed to the Antietam National Cemetery Board of Trustees and later to the Antietam Battlefield Board in 1894.

## About the Editor

**Thomas G. Clemens** earned his doctoral degree at George Mason University, where he studied under Maryland Campaign historian Dr. Joseph L. Harsh. Tom has published a wide variety of magazine articles and book reviews, has appeared in several documentaries, and is a licensed tour guide at Antietam National Battlefield. An instructor at Hagerstown Community College, he also helped found and is the current president of Save Historic Antietam Foundation, Inc., a preservation group dedicated to saving historic properties.